Kennedy's Wars

Kennedy's Wars

—

Berlin, Cuba, Laos, and Vietnam

Lawrence Freedman

New York   Oxford
OXFORD UNIVERSITY PRESS
2000

Oxford University Press

Oxford   New York
Athens   Auckland   Bangkok   Bogotá
Buenos Aires   Calcutta   Cape Town   Chennai   Dar es Salaam   Delhi
Florence   Hong Kong   Istanbul   Karachi
Kuala Lumpur   Madrid   Melbourne
Mexico City   Mumbai   Nairobi   Paris   São Paulo   Shanghai
Singapore   Taipei   Tokyo   Toronto   Warsaw

and associated companies in
Berlin   Ibadan

Published by Oxford University Press, Inc.
198 Madison Avenue, New York, New York, 10016

http://www.oup-usa.org

Oxford is a registered trademark of Oxford University Press

Library of Congress Cataloging-in-Publication Data
Freedman, Lawrence.
Kennedy's wars : Berlin, Cuba, Laos, and Vietnam / Lawrence Freedman.
p. cm.   Includes bibliographical references and index.
ISBN 0-19-513453-2
1. Kennedy, John F. (John Fitzgerald), 1917–1963.
2. Kennedy, John F. (John Fitzgerald), 1917–1963—Military leadership.
3. United States—Foreign relations—1961–1963.
4. United States—Military policy.
5. Berlin Wall, Berlin, Germany, 1961–1989.
6. Cuba—History—Invasion, 1961.
7. Cuban Missile Crisis, 1962.
8. Vietnamese Conflict, 1961–1975. I. Title.
E841 .F69 2000   973.922—dc21   99–087898

Printing number: 1 3 5 7 9 8 6 4 2
Printed in the United States of America
on acid-free paper

TO SAM

Contents

Preface: Kennedy's Wars

On 22 November 1963 John Fitzgerald Kennedy, thirty-fifth president of the United States, was shot by an assassin while campaigning in Dallas, Texas. Such a shocking death for a glamorous figure, at the peak of his power, encouraged a "Kennedy industry" that has already generated some one thousand books. The fact that his surviving family enjoyed achievement and adulation while suffering scandal and tragedy helps to explain the enduring fascination with all aspects of the Kennedy legend. The questions left unanswered, the policies still undeveloped, and the tragic sense of promise unfulfilled continue to draw historians to the early 1960s.

The history of his presidency was shaped at first by the rich and loving memoirs of two of his more liberal aides, Theodore Sorensen and Arthur Schlesinger Jr.[1] Later writings challenged the image of a gifted and wise leader, potentially one of the great modern presidents, in two crucial respects. First, his achievements in foreign policy were subject to increasing scrutiny. He was blamed for helping to trigger those crises over Berlin and Cuba that also provided his finest hours, and for allowing the drift into the Vietnam War to gather pace. Kennedy "had his chance" to introduce a more enlightened American foreign policy, according to Thomas Paterson, "and he failed."[2] Second, revelations were made about a private life somewhat at odds with a public image dominated by charm, wit, and intellect. An apparently insatiable sexual appetite and dubious associations sit uneasily with an image of family man and responsible public servant. The issue of whether Kennedy's private flaws impinged on his public duties made the character issue the central question of Kennedy historiography.[3]

The drive to replace history as celebration by history as indictment culminated in Seymour Hersh's *The Dark Side of Camelot*.[4] However, the tendency in the more serious biographies has been to present Kennedy as a complex personality, in office at a difficult time, and with a mixed performance during his short tenure as president.[5] In following this approach, I am more concerned with explanation than judgment. This book does not attempt to be a full biography of Kennedy. It looks only at foreign policy and concentrates on those issues most related to the fundamental issues of war and peace. The cold war was at its height and at times risked becoming extremely hot, yet catastrophe was avoided. Was this through good luck or good management? Kennedy inherited a troublesome commitment to South Vietnam and bequeathed it in an even worse condition to his successor. Does this mean that he would have got into as much of a mess in Vietnam as Lyndon Johnson, or might he have found an acceptable escape route?

Questions such as these are not new, but this does seem to be a good time to look for new answers. The recent growth of the documentary record of the Kennedy years has been quite astonishing, and there is a need to take stock of all the new material. These include the completion of the twenty-five-volume official documentary history of the foreign relations of the United States during the Kennedy years, an edition of transcripts from the Cuban missile crisis, a number of biographies of key players, and some fine works by academics. Furthermore, the opening up of Russian archives has made it possible to check with greater confidence than before Moscow's views on the same set of crises. This is in addition to some well-established earlier works, substantial archive collections, and a rich set of memoirs (few involved with Kennedy seem to have been able to resist setting down their recollections). More keeps coming.

All this makes it much easier for a historian to develop interpretations based on evidence rather than speculation. The corollary of this privileged position is enormous difficulty when it comes to reproducing the partial visions, uncertainties, and fears that the actors experienced as they participated in the unfolding dramas, and in identifying what was not known and could not be grasped at the time. The key actors were often in the dark about the attitudes and behavior of other members of the same government, never mind the calculations of their enemies. The historian can see all sorts of things that were at best then dimly perceived and at worst missed altogether, yet while doing so can miss the connections between quite disparate events that happened to be coincident in time and were obvious to those involved.

In particular, the historian knows what happened next and so is always tempted to point to missed opportunities, recklessness, unnecessary caution, misperceptions, and miscalculations. We now know that Kennedy never got a chance at a second term, that Vietnam turned into a cruel and tragic war, that Castro outlived (at last count) another seven American presidents without renouncing his revolution, that the cold war was not only survived but concluded with communism completely discredited as an economic system as well as a political creed. It is hard to recall that Soviet communism once offered a serious ideological competitor to liberal capitalism and a fearful military threat. It is tempting to suppose that what now appears as blatantly self-serving and ideological language on the Western side was always recognized as such, and barely taken seriously by those who spoke it. The worldviews of the past are easy to caricature, without noting that they were rarely held unconditionally or without irony, and that there were wide variations in belief.

Part of the challenge for the historian in trying to get the measure of the Kennedy presidency is therefore to get back to the assumptions and expectations with which it started. Many of those who now write about Kennedy find it difficult to take the cold war seriously and are unimpressed by the fact that Kennedy took it very seriously indeed. In part this was expedience—he knew that appeasement was the gravest charge that might be leveled against him—but it was also conviction. Communism was something to be both despised and feared.

I have therefore attempted to set the intellectual as well as political context by referring to the concepts and theories circulating at the time around the American foreign policy establishment, as elaborated in important articles and books. Because their actual influence depended on the individuals who carried them into the heart of government, I also spend time on the key figures of the administration. Pen portraits of the striking individuals around Kennedy—the assertive Robert McNamara, the diffident Dean Rusk, the assured McGeorge Bundy, the intense Robert Kennedy—have become almost de rigueur for any study of this period, but the role of such figures as Dean Acheson and Walt Rostow also deserves attention.

It is tempting to re-create the atmosphere of the Kennedy presidency, as some authors have successfully done, by recording the interplay of events, individuals, and decisions on an almost daily basis.[6] Such a method brings home the numerous issues that a political leader faces simultaneously, all competing for time, and the complex interconnections that develop between them. Berlin, Cuba, Laos, and Vietnam were managed at more or less the same time by more or less the same group of people. These interconnections are important and I have tried to explore them, but I have also found it useful to address these crises in their own terms. I have tried to show how they would have appeared to Kennedy at the time, how policy options came to be defined, and how these were phrased in terms of prevalent beliefs about the nature of the underlying conflict, the risks attached to alternative courses of action, and the quality of available information.

The Kennedy that emerges out of this study is more flawed and human than the far-seeing statesman of unusual insight and courageous decision of posthumous flattery. He is also more thoughtful, serious, and consistent than the ambitious playboy of the revisionists, who see him as without principle or long-term strategic vision, skilled only in manipulating the media and thereby his own future image. I have tried to present Kennedy as a product of his time in his attitudes and assumptions, and with a keen sense of the fragility of his political base in his caution and his preoccupation, to the point of obsession, with media depictions of his presidency and policies. I have sought to demonstrate that when it came to the fundamental issues of foreign policy his strategy was dominated by a determination to avoid the nuclear cataclysm that he feared above all else without giving ground in the cold war.

Few American servicemen died in combat during Kennedy's thousand days as commander in chief of the armed forces of the United States. Fortunately his wars largely went no further than contingency plans, fought in prospect, without the trauma, drama, and heartache of real wars. Yet though he did not face this supreme test, Kennedy was in charge during some of the most frightening and dangerous days of the cold war. He gave active consideration to large-scale conventional military operations and thought hard about the danger in all cases of escalation to nuclear exchanges, as if he had been picked by history to decide on whether the Western way of life should be either abandoned or sacrificed. Somehow he had to steer a course between the advance of the free world's ideological foes and a disastrous nuclear confrontation, between "Red" and "dead." His subsequent reputation was built on the claim that he had successfully found such a course.

Even when he accepted the need for fighting, his instinct was to avoid combat roles for American forces. So he authorized the invasion of Cuba by a rebel brigade in April 1961 but refused to allow American forces to be involved directly. Even as he made conspicuous military moves in expectation of imminent conflict, as in Berlin in the summer of 1961 and Cuba in the fall of 1962, he was looking for diplomatic escape routes. He stepped up support for the South Vietnamese government in its fight against a communist insurgency but sought to restrict American forces to an advisory role. From 1961 to 1963 73 American soldiers died in Vietnam, though the number of advisers rose from 685 to 16,732. Only after Kennedy's death did the Americans become fully engaged in Vietnam.

Questions of what might have been still dominate considerations of Kennedy's presidency, and they are addressed in this book. Part of any answer can be found in his legacy. He did preside over a shift in official attitudes toward nuclear weapons. At the same time he passed on the impasse with Castro's Cuba and the deepening involvement in Vietnam to his successor. While there are grounds for supposing that he might have found some modus vivendi with Castro and avoided full-scale combat in Vietnam, in neither case can we be sure. The early 1960s are now recognized as a turning point in the cold war, after which it never seemed quite so dangerous again. In this vital arena, the one that he set as his first priority, Kennedy can be said to have succeeded. He left East-West relations in a far better state, with tension over Berlin replaced by a test ban treaty. In his second priority in the cold war, to find a safe but effective way to take on the communists in the third world, he was far less successful, leaving behind the question of whether, had he lived, he would have compounded or mitigated the errors of his first thousand days.

Dramatis Personae

Acheson, Dean, former secretary of state; adviser to Presidents Kennedy and Johnson

Adenauer, Konrad, chancellor of the Federal Republic of Germany until October 1963

Adzhubei, Aleksei I., editor in chief of *Izvestia* and Khrushchev's son-in-law

Alsop, Joseph, syndicated columnist

Amory, Robert, deputy director for intelligence, Central Intelligence Agency

Anderson, Admiral George W., chief of naval operations 1 August 1961–1 August 1963

Attwood, William, ambassador to Guinea, 29 March 1961–27 May 1963

Ball, George W., undersecretary of state for economic affairs until December 1961; thereafter undersecretary of state

Barnes, C. Tracy, assistant deputy director (plans) for covert action, Central Intelligence Agency

Bissell, Richard M., Jr., deputy director for plans, Central Intelligence Agency, until February 1962

Bohlen, Charles E., special assistant to the secretary of state until September 1962; thereafter ambassador to France

Bolshakov, Georgi N., editor in chief of *USSR* magazine; counselor at the Soviet embassy in the United States from October 1962

Bowles, Chester A., undersecretary of state, January–December 1961; thereafter special representative and adviser on African, Asian, and Latin American affairs

Brezhnev, Leonid I., chairman of the Presidium of the Supreme Soviet of the Union of Soviet Socialist Republics

Bundy, McGeorge, special assistant to the president for national security affairs

Bundy, William P., deputy assistant secretary of defense for international security affairs

Burke, Admiral Arleigh A., chief of naval operations until August 1961

Cabell, General Charles P., deputy director of central intelligence until January 1962

Castro, Fidel, president of Cuba

Castro, Raul, Cuban minister of the armed forces

Chase, Gordon, National Security Council staff member

Chayes, Abram J., legal adviser of the Department of State from February 1961

Chiang Kai-shek, Generalissimo, president of the Republic of China

Cline, Ray, CIA chief of station in Taipei until June 1962; thereafter deputy director for intelligence, Central Intelligence Agency

Colby, William E., Office of the Special Assistant to the Ambassador in Vietnam, Central Intelligence Agency

Cooper, Chester, assistant for policy support and the deputy director for Intelligence, CIA

Cottrell, Sterling J., deputy assistant secretary, Bureau of Inter-American Affairs, and coordinator of Cuban affairs, Department of State, after January 1963

Dean, Arthur H., chairman of the delegation to the eighteen-nation disarmament committee at Geneva until December 1962

Decker, General George H., army chief of staff until 30 September 1962

de Gaulle, Charles, president of France

Dennison, Admiral Robert L., commander in chief, Atlantic

Dillon, C. Douglas, secretary of the treasury

Dobrynin, Anatoly F., chief of the American Countries Division, Soviet Foreign Ministry, until March 1962; thereafter ambassador to the United States

Donovan, James B., lawyer involved in efforts to secure the release of prisoners captured at the Bay of Pigs

Dulles, Allen W., director of Central Intelligence Agency until November 1961

Duong Van Minh, Maj. Gen., "Big Minh," commander of the Army Field Command, Republic of Vietnam Army

Durbrow, Elbridge, ambassador to Vietnam until 3 May 1961

Eisenhower, Dwight D., president of the United States until 20 January 1961

Enthoven, Alain C., deputy comptroller of the Department of Defense

Esterline, J. D., chief of Branch 4, Western Hemisphere Division, Directorate for Plans, Central Intelligence Agency

Felt, Admiral Harry D., commander in chief, Pacific

Finletter, Thomas K., ambassador to the North Atlantic Treaty Organization

Fitzgerald, Desmond, Directorate of Plans, Central Intelligence Agency

Forrestal, Michael V., member, National Security Council staff, from January 1962

Foster, William C., director of the Arms Control and Disarmament Agency

Fulbright, J. William, senator from Arkansas and chairman of the Senate Foreign Relations Committee

Galbraith, John Kenneth, ambassador to India from 18 April 1961

Gilpatric, Roswell L., deputy secretary of defense from January 1961

Goodpaster, General Andrew J., special assistant to the chairman of the Joint Chiefs of Staff

Goodwin, Richard N., assistant special counsel to the president until November 1961; thereafter deputy assistant secretary of state for inter-American affairs

Gray, Major General David W., chief of the Subsidiary Activities Division, Plans and Policy, Joint Staff, Joint Chiefs of Staff

Gromyko, Andrei A., Soviet foreign minister

Guevara Serna, Ernesto (Che), president of the Cuban National Bank

Halberstam, David, correspondent, *New York Times*

Harkins, General Paul, U.S. commander, military assistance command, Vietnam

Harriman, W. Averell, ambassador at large, February–December 1961; assistant secretary of state for Far Eastern affairs until April 1963; thereafter undersecretary of state for political affairs

Harvey, William K., chief of Task Force W, Directorate for Plans, Central Intelligence Agency; project officer for Operation Mongoose

Hawkins, Colonel Jack, chief of paramilitary operations, Branch 4, Western Hemisphere Division, Directorate for Plans, Central Intelligence Agency

Helms, Richard M., chief of operations, Directorate for Plans, Central Intelligence Agency, until February 1962; thereafter deputy director for plans

Hilsman, Roger, Jr., director of the Bureau of Intelligence and Research, Department of State, from February 1961 until 25 April, 1963; thereafter assistant secretary of state for Far Eastern affairs

Hitch, Charles J., assistant secretary of defense (comptroller) from 17 February 1961

Ho Chi Minh, president of the Democratic Republic of Vietnam

Home, Alexander Frederick Douglas (Lord), British secretary of state for foreign affairs until October 1963; prime minister thereafter

Howard, Lisa, correspondent, American Broadcasting Company

Hughes, Thomas L., deputy director, Bureau of Intelligence and Research, Department of State, until 28 April 1963; thereafter director

Johnson, Lyndon B., vice president of the United States until 22 November 1963; thereafter president

Johnson, Robert H., member, National Security Council Staff, until February 1962; member, Policy Planning Council, Department of State, after August 1963

Johnson, U. Alexis, deputy undersecretary of state for political affairs from April 1961

Kattenburg, Paul, director, interdepartmental working group, Vietnam from 4 August 1963

Kaysen, Carl, member, National Security Council staff, June–December 1961; thereafter deputy special assistant to the president for national security affairs

Kennedy, John F., president of the United States until 22 November 1963

Kennedy, Robert F., attorney general of the United States

Kent, Sherman, assistant director and chairman, Board of National Estimates, Office of National Estimates, Central Intelligence Agency

Khrushchev, Nikita S., chairman of the Council of Ministers of the Soviet Union

Kohler, Foy D., assistant secretary of state for European affairs until August 1962; thereafter ambassador to the Soviet Union

Komer, Robert W., member, National Security Council staff

Kozlov, Frol R., secretary of the Central Committee of the Communist Party of the Soviet Union

Kuznetsov, Vasily V., Soviet first deputy foreign minister

Lansdale, Brigadier General Edward G., deputy assistant for special operations to the secretary of defense until May 1961; thereafter assistant for special operations; also chief of operations for Operation Mongoose after November 1961

LeMay, General Curtis E., chief of staff, U.S. Air Force, from 30 June 1961

Lemnitzer, General Lyman L., chairman, Joint Chiefs of Staff, until 30 September 1962; supreme Allied commander, Europe, from 1 November 1962

Lightner, Allen, minister, U.S. Mission, Berlin.

Macmillan, Harold, prime minister of the United Kingdom until October 1963

McCloy, John J., presidential adviser and coordinator for U.S.-Soviet negotiations over Cuba at the United Nations

McCone, John A., director for Central Intelligence from November 1961

McGarr, General Lionel, commander, military assistance advisory group, Vietnam

McGhee, George C., counselor of the Department of State and chairman, Policy Planning Council, 16 February–3 December 1961; undersecretary of state for political affairs, 4 December 1961–27 March 1963; ambassador to Germany from 18 May 1963

McNamara, Robert S., secretary of defense

Maechling, Charles W., Jr., director for internal defense, Office of Politico-Military Affairs, Department of State, from 6 February 1962

Malinovsky, Rodion Ya., marshal of the Soviet Union and minister of defense

Mann, Thomas C., assistant secretary of state for inter-American affairs until April 1961

Mansfield, Mike, senator from Montana and member of the Foreign Relations Committee; majority leader after 3 January 1961

Mao Zedong, chairman of the Central Committee, People's Republic of China

Martin, Edwin M., assistant secretary of state for economic affairs until May 1962; thereafter assistant secretary of state for inter American affairs

Mecklin, John, counsellor for public affairs of Embassy, Vietnam

Mendenhall, Joseph, deputy director of the office of Southeast Asia

Mikoyan, Anastas I., first deputy chairman of the Soviet Council of Ministers

Miro Cardona, José, president of the Cuban Revolutionary Council

Murrow, Edward R., director of the United States Information Agency

Nehru, Jawaharlal (Pandit), prime minister and minister of external affairs and for atomic energy of India

Ngo Dinh Diem, president of the Republic of Vietnam until November 1963

Ngo Dinh Nhu, brother of President Diem and political adviser to the president

Ngo Dinh Nhu, Madame, sister-in-law of President Diem and official hostess for the president

Nitze, Paul H., assistant secretary of defense for international security affairs from January 1961

Nixon, Richard M., vice president of the United States until 20 January 1961

Nolting, Frederick E., Jr., ambassador to Vietnam from 10 May 1961 to August 1963

Norstad, General Lauris C., supreme Allied commander, Europe, until 1 November 1962

O'Donnell, P. Kenneth, special assistant to the president

Ormsby-Gore, Sir David, British ambassador to the United States from October 1961

Owen, Henry, member, Policy Planning Council, Department of State, until 25 November 1962; thereafter vice chairman

Parsons, J. Graham, assistant secretary of state for Far Eastern affairs until 30 March 1961

Phoumi Nosovan, General, Laotian deputy premier and minister of defense

Pushkin, Georgi, Soviet deputy foreign minister and ambassador to the Geneva talks on Laos, 1961–62.

Rostow, Walt W., deputy special assistant to the president for national security affairs until December 1961; thereafter counselor of the Department of State and chairman of the Policy Planning Council

Rowen, Henry S., deputy assistant secretary of defense for international security affairs

Rusk, Dean, secretary of state

Salinger, Pierre, president's press secretary

Sarit Thanarat, Thai prime minister

Scali, John, correspondent, American Broadcasting Company

Schlesinger, Arthur, Jr., special assistant to the president

Seaborg, Glenn T., chairman of the Atomic Energy Commission from March 1961

Sihanouk, Prince Norodom, Cambodian chief of state

Shoup, General David M., commandant of the U.S. Marine Corps

Smith, Bromley, acting executive secretary of the National Security Council until August 1961; thereafter executive secretary

Smith, Major (later Colonel) William Y., assistant to General Maxwell D. Taylor

Sorensen, Theodore C., special counsel to the president

Souphanouvong, Prince, leader of the Pathet Lao; after June 1962, vice premier and minister of economy and plan

Souvanna Phouma, Prince, leader of the neutralist political forces in Laos; after June 1962, prime minister of Laos and minister of defense, veterans affairs, and social action

Stevenson, Adlai E., III, permanent representative to the United Nations

Sullivan, William, UN adviser, bureau of far eastern affairs, Department of State until 28 April 1963; thereafter assistant to undersecretary of state

Suslov, Mikhail A., member of the Supreme Soviet of the Soviet Union and secretary of the Central Committee of the Communist Party of the Soviet Union

Taylor, General Maxwell D., chairman of the Cuba Study Group, April-June 1961, president's military representative from July 1961– 1 October 1962; thereafter chairman, Joint Chiefs of Staff

Thompson, Llewellyn E., Jr., ambassador to the Soviet Union until 27 July 1962; ambassador at large from 3 October 1962

Thompson, Robert G. K., former British permanent secretary of defense in the Malayan Federation, head of the British advisory mission, Vietnam, from September 1961

Trueheart, William C., counselor and deputy chief of mission at the U.S. embassy in Vietnam from 29 October 1961

Tyler, William R., deputy assistant secretary of state for European affairs until August 1962; thereafter assistant secretary

Udall, Stewart, secretary of the interior

Ulbricht, Walter, chairman of the Council of State and of the Socialist Unity Party of the German Democratic Republic

Wheeler, General Earle G., director, Joint Chiefs of Staff, until 24 February 1962; chief of staff, U.S. Army, from 1 October 1962

White, General Thomas D., chief of staff of the air force until June 1961

Wiesner, Jerome B., president's special assistant for science and technology and director of the White House Office of Science and Technology from January 1961

Zorin, Valerian A., deputy Soviet foreign minister and permanent representative to the United Nations

Kennedy's Wars

Introduction

JOHN FITZGERALD KENNEDY was the second of nine children. His father, Joseph Kennedy, was the grandson of an Irish immigrant who had made his fortune by the time he was forty. Well established in Boston and a substantial contributor to Democratic Party funds, he had a succession of appointments under Roosevelt, culminating in his appointment as American ambassador to London in 1937. After the fall of France in the spring of 1940 his open view that a German victory was all but inevitable became deeply unpopular in Britain. After he resigned from the post at the end of that year he devoted himself to the political careers of his sons.

When Joseph junior, who shared his father's isolationist views, died in action in 1944, hopes came to rest upon John, until this point more prepared to be a playboy journalist than a serious politician. John graduated from Harvard in 1940, having spent some time in London before the war. He joined the navy in 1941 and two years later was almost killed when the patrol torpedo (PT) boat he was commanding in the South Pacific was rammed and severed by an enemy destroyer. He still managed to lead his crew to safety. The PT boat provided some long-lasting friendships (including later members of his administration) and served as a formidable symbol of personal courage. After a brief spell as a journalist, during which he covered the opening session of the United Nations, he began his meteoric political rise. He never lost an election. He reached the House of Representatives in 1946, at the age of twenty-nine. Six years later he won election to the Senate, and after another eight years he won the November 1960 presidential election. On 20 January 1961, at the age of forty-three, he was inaugurated as the thirty-fifth president of the United States. An assassin cut him down on 22 November 1963.

KENNEDY'S CHARACTER

While he lived, with the aid of Jacqueline, whom he had married in 1953, Kennedy's life invited adjectives invoking charm, charisma, gaiety, vigor, glamour, and culture. After he died a picture emerged completely at odds with the renaissance man of legend: the happy family man who was a serial adulterer, the energetic man of action who was physically incapacitated, the refined intellectual whose language was coarse and whose favorite reading was spy novels. Over time a more intriguing personality was identified, shaped by a powerful father, a tough war, constant pain, and a fast political advance. His relationship with Jacqueline, who was aware of his philandering, had its tensions but also its ties, and there was no doubting his affection for his two children. His staff was extraordinarily loyal, and remained so after he died. Many of those who watched him with a critical eye during his first faltering months as president felt he was learning quickly on the job. Few support the view that the less admirable aspects of his private life noticeably affected the performance of his public duties.[1]

Kennedy himself appears to have assumed that his public and private lives could be kept in separate compartments. When a particular association threatened political damage, Kennedy was ready to detach himself quickly. Friends, family, and staff aware of his sexual appetites, and engaged in covering them up, did not share his confidence in their essential irrelevance. Regardless, it is a fact that his indiscretions failed to cause him any political damage.

As far as Kennedy himself was concerned, a more vital secret was his near invalidity. Pain was a constant companion as he fought against Addison's disease and chronic back trouble. Kennedy's stoical attitude, though heroic, left him vulnerable to the charge of being unable to cope. To gain relief he took a cocktail of drugs, some from imprudent sources. These might have had long-term effects, but they did not lead to bizarre behavior or eccentric decisions. It would be surprising if his overactive sex life, illness, and treatment had not at times affected his moods and concentration, but none of his key decisions to be examined in this book defy explanation in terms other than those in which they were framed at the time, nor do any become clearer with recourse to conspiracy or perversity.

Two personal issues were relevant. The first was Kennedy's Catholicism, potentially a serious problem in a Protestant country, even though he was not conspicuously religious. He went out of his way while campaigning in 1960 to emphasize that he understood the need for the separation of church and state. To some extent the issue was put to rest when he defeated Hubert Humphrey in the Democratic primary in Protestant West Virgina, but he remained conscious of the ease with which his religion could be used against him.

The most serious issue he faced, at least during his journey to the presidency, concerned not so much his own personality but that of his father. Joe Kennedy's darker side was well known and led to reluctance by many, especially on the liberal wing of the Democratic Party, to associate with his progeny. This dislike extended to the way that Kennedy senior had acquired and used his wealth, and the conduct of his personal life, but at root it was political. Joe was an instinctive isolationist and had been castigated for his readiness to appease Hitler and his defeatist attitude toward Britain's prospects while he was in London. For John, overcoming the character issue was a matter of demonstrating that he was his own man. Particularly troubling was Joe's association with Senator Joseph McCarthy, who did appalling damage to American political life with his cruel and indiscriminate anticommunism but who had a loyal following among Irish-Americans. John Kennedy gained the suspicion of liberals for failing to vote on the Senate's censure of McCarthy in 1954. He had an excuse, in that he was in the hospital at the time, and he had a prepared pro-censure speech, but he was not displeased to have reason to avoid the vote.

KENNEDY'S POLITICS

Kennedy grew up in a highly political household, picking up at an early age arguments about policy, gossip about the nation's leaders, and stories of deal making and electoral gambits. He had been preparing for the presidency since 1956 and had won it having first beaten some seasoned professionals for the Democratic Party nomination and then Richard Nixon, the vice president, in the election. In this he proved himself to be a master tactician. Part of this came naturally to any politician, especially to one who prided himself on his pragmatism. The constant recalculation of power relationships was almost second nature. Broad rules could be applied to any situation: avoid getting boxed into a corner; keep options open for as long as possible; maintain lines of communication to opponents as well as to friends; when the time comes to strike, be prepared to strike hard. As with other highly ambitious politicians, these rules led Kennedy to gravitate naturally toward the center ground and play for time, waiting for the right moment for any decisive move.

Kennedy had, however, pondered the nature of political leadership more than most of his fellow professionals. It was the theme of his two books—*Why England Slept* and *Profiles in Courage*.[2] The first of these, published in 1940 when he was only twenty-three, was a best-selling version of his senior-year thesis at Harvard, which drew on the time spent with his father in London. Its importance lay in its distance from his father's views and its call to arms, but it is interesting also as a treatise on the problems of democratic politicians when confronting a major international crisis. His view was that Munich was not so much a failure of will as the natural consequence of a failure to make proper military provision.[3] The Pulitzer prize–winning *Profiles in Courage*, published in 1956, was an engaging collection of essays on leading American political figures. It was held together by the same question of how a democratic politician can stay elected while doing the right thing. The underlying philosophy was that the expedients necessary to hold on to power could be justified if they create the store of political capital that enables the statesman to act responsibly at times of great exigency.

Kennedy understood that to be acknowledged as a serious statesman he would be obliged at times to take stands that might weaken his domestic political position. He also understood that should his position deteriorate beyond a certain point, his freedom of maneuver would be severely restricted. The margin of victory over Richard Nixon in the November 1960 election had been slight, a mere 118,000 votes, and he had run behind his own party. The Democrats still controlled Congress, but their position had weakened, with twenty-two extra Republicans coming into the House of Representatives. Kennedy's own power base remained the liberal, urban, industrial North, to which he offered more federal expenditure on education and a higher minimum wage. But conservative southern Democrats enjoyed a pivotal position in Congress and represented an obstacle he never quite managed to overcome in his domestic policy. It led him to equivocate initially on long-promised and much-needed civil rights legislation for black Americans. To anxious supporters he promised that his first term in office was laying the foundations for a more courageous second. The fragility of his position was the dominant political fact of his presidency and influenced every move. He worried about the effect of particular courses of action on the national, and in particular congressional, balance of power between Republicans and Democrats as well as on his own standing with the American people. He had to consider the strategies of his likely opponents in the 1964 election: Nelson Rockefeller, a moderate northern Republican demanding a strong defense; Richard Nixon, swift to denounce Kennedy for any signs of appeasement; the ultraconservative Barry Goldwater, moving to the fore after Nixon's 1962 defeat in California, ready to urge belligerence in any crisis.

Kennedy was always asking himself what the political marketplace would bear, how easy it would be to sell particular courses of action to the American people. He was notoriously sensitive to press comment and would go to great lengths to influence the media's coverage of his administration and his policies. His starting point for policy discussion was often a comment on the morning's newspapers, and he went out of his way to cultivate the leading columnists of his time—such as Walter Lippmann, James Reston, and Joe Alsop (a good friend). He charmed his media friends and made them feel true confidants, although he could soon fall out with those he felt had maligned him.[4] His use of television and press conferences in the marketing of policy, and at the same time of himself, set the standards for others to follow.

Kennedy spoke about the need to give a visionary edge to foreign policy and be guided by core principles, yet advisers found him fixated by the short term and impatient with think pieces that did not have an immediate and obvious policy implication. Certainly Kennedy liked his intellectuals to be hard-edged and practical rather than soft and woolly. The cool pragmatist was far more respected than the committed zealot. This fitted in with the temper of the times, with leading figures from the intelligentsia arguing the need to move beyond the ideological battles of the past and to develop a capacity for analytical problem solving.

A sensitivity to popular opinion often provided an invaluable filter through which to assess alternative options, for if a convincing rationale could not be found for popular consumption, that might be because the policy was a bad one. This concern with presentation was also reflected in the importance Kennedy attached to language and ideas. He was looking for a way to manage the twin pressures that all cold-war presidents confronted: avoiding charges of appeasing communism, on one hand, and of a rash rush toward war, on the other. The right phraseology was critical if he was to carry public opinion, and in 1953 Kennedy hired a young academic wordsmith, Theodore Sorensen, who thereafter gave all his speeches and publications a lucid and elegant quality (and was responsible for much of *Profiles in Courage*). Few modern presidents used the English language so well.

Part of his appeal was also his intelligence and the bright people who surrounded him. A memorable phrase in Kennedy's inauguration speech referred to a torch passing to a new generation: The junior officers of the Second World War were taking over from the generals. The ideal candidate for his administration, it was observed, would have a brilliant academic record, impressive war service, athletic achievement, and a glittering professional career. The rhetoric of the administration was activist, confident, and ambitious. With sufficient energy, imagination, intellect, and resources, few human problems were beyond solution. Many commentaries on his administration stress its tough and militant character. Even the Peace Corps director had a sign in his office: Good Guys Don't Win Ball Games. At the time old hands such as Adlai Stevenson bemoaned "the damndest bunch of boy commandos running around." Later, the most boyish commando of all, Robert Kennedy, wondered whether the administration had not paid "a very great price for being more energetic than wise, especially Cuba."[5]

He prided himself on his knowledge of foreign policy and had taken some brave stances as a senator, but there had been no opportunity for Kennedy to demonstrate executive competence, let alone an ability to cope with crises. The youth that made him an attractive candidate also marked him out as an inexperienced statesman, and in the first months of 1961 it was this inexperience that seemed to count most, especially when taking over from Eisenhower, who had been a real war leader. Kennedy was a lowly lieutenant following a supreme commander.

Kennedy's own experience of war, and a brush with death, left him alert to the pain of battle. He had a front-liner's suspicion of headquarters' bombast and a skeptical view of the judgment of senior commanders. He saw courage—defined in his book (following Hemingway) as "grace under pressure"—of all types as admirable, but he realized that the daring and sacrifice that an individual might demonstrate in military service would be inappropriate on behalf of a whole people and way of life. At times he seemed to yearn for forms of conflict in which the intelligence and the bravery of special agents could make all the difference as an alternative to the bleak choices that he might face in the event of total war. It was in part because he recoiled from this prospect, as well as because of his politician's natural caution, that his actions in government were often more tentative and noncommittal than his activist rhetoric implied. His policies often denied the necessity of choice, insisting that it was possible to promise peace and prepare for war at the same time, to talk tough and display compassion, to point to a glittering future while warning of the dangers of impatience. This caution was reinforced as early setbacks, and in particular the Bay of Pigs, underscored how bold initiatives could soon appear as crazy gambles, and how the most assured advice might be little more than special pleading.

Before completing three months in office, Kennedy approved an attempt to overthrow the regime of Fidel Castro by sponsoring a rebel invasion of Cuba at the Bay of Pigs. This turned into a calamitous and humiliating fiasco leaving almost 1,400 men killed or captured, and supporters at home and abroad astonished and disappointed. The first question Kennedy asked himself was "How could I have been so stupid?" and it was appropriate. He had taken at face value assurances that so many men could be landed into Cuba, with sufficient mystery that their endeavor could not be blamed on Washington, with sufficient stealth that they would not be blocked on the shore, with sufficient noise that they might soon spark an uprising in Cuba, and with sufficient flexibility that they could take to the hills and conduct guerrilla operations if need be. The plan was driven by the CIA and barely monitored by military officers on the mistaken assumption that in the end Kennedy would reverse himself and authorize a direct American intervention. The few advisers from outside the inner circle who had an inkling of what was being planned all instinctively saw a disaster in the making, but few anticipated the sheer incompetence of the actual operation and most kept their reservations to themselves. Politically, the episode left Kennedy fearful of appearing weak, yet he was thereafter suspicious of advisers arguing early and vigorous military action without having thought through the consequences.

Kennedy's prescription for leadership in the cold war might well have been taken from a book by the British strategist Basil Liddell Hart, which he reviewed in 1960:

> Keep strong, if possible. In any case, keep cool. Have unlimited patience.
> Never corner an opponent, and always assist him to save his face. Put your-

self in his shoes—so as to see things through his eyes. Avoid self-righteousness like the devil—nothing is so blinding.[6]

Advice such as this put a premium on an ability to read a crisis—the sources of its urgency, the interests of those involved, and the options available to them. It required a readiness to focus hard on primary interests, if necessary letting the secondary go, and developing military options carrying a minimal risk of escalating into a catastrophic war. Forms of activity that signaled resolve without recklessness were required. All this led under Kennedy to what became known as graduated or flexible response, moving forward in crises one step at a time, raising at each stage the pressure on opponents, probing their will, exploring opportunities for a settlement even while preparing to up the ante. It was his method when dealing with awkward clients as much as with dangerous adversaries. It was a method that came naturally to Kennedy the politician, but it was reinforced by his conviction that it was the only way to manage the cold war.

I

THE COLD WAR AND HOW TO FIGHT IT

1

Liberal Anticommunism

COLD WAR LIBERALISM had a distinctive framework of its own. Traditional liberalism, as Arthur Schlesinger Jr. explained at the start of 1949, had been "fundamentally reshaped by the hope of the New Deal, by the exposure of the Soviet Union, and by the deepening of our knowledge of man."[1] Still in his early thirties, Schlesinger was already a Pulitzer prize–winning historian and a Democratic Party activist. A decade later he became resident intellectual in the Kennedy White House and thereafter its most effective and prolific historian.

The quote is taken from his influential book *The Vital Center* and indicates the three key features of cold war liberalism. The first was pride in Roosevelt's New Deal and the war against German Nazism and Japanese militarism. These had demonstrated the capacity of the democratic system to reform itself and mobilize the nation's energies for great endeavors. The second was a belief that communism posed as great a danger to those of a liberal faith as rightist reaction. In the late 1940s this might have seemed an unavoidable stance. It was the centerpiece of Truman's foreign policy. Schlesinger certainly understood that if liberals were quiet on the subject of communism, they would be vulnerable to the obnoxious Red-baiting that so disfigured American political life during the first years of the cold war.

But to believe that liberal anticommunism was no more than an expedient form of self-protection is to misunderstand its character. The step from being a noncommunist to being an anticommunist was not an easy one to take. It required setting aside the wartime alliance with Russia on the grounds that the crumbling of this alliance was Moscow's responsibility. While working in Europe in 1947–48 Schlesinger had seen the more manipulative and vicious features of Soviet practice, including attempts to destabilize the Western democracies. It was against this background that he became one of the founding members of the anti-communist liberal group Americans for Democratic Action (ADA), a direct organizational response to the formation of the Progressive Citizens of America by those who still feared the right more than the left.[2]

The position taken by ADA was mirrored by democrats with more overt socialist sympathies in Western Europe. They soon felt vindicated, as it became apparent that accounts of Stalin's purges, once dismissed as the crude exaggerations of right-wingers, were, in all essentials, correct. For many of those who had been attracted to communism during the Great Depression of the 1930s, this was "the god that failed."[3] Embarrassed by their former innocence, they often became its most forceful antagonists. It was no longer possible to continue to defend the excesses of Josef Stalin's rule as a regrettable response to the demands of harsh times. It was vital to assert that democracy also offered a system with extraordinary strengths, capable of looking after the common man, laying claim to be following the line of history but, critically, without any need to resort to repressive methods. Against the House Committee on Un-American Activities and the supporters of Senator McCarthy, liberals argued that it was precisely the respect for civil rights that made democracy such a formidable foe of communism.

So it was that Schlesinger argued that common cause must be made with all those who believed in a free society, and who recognized that "the totalitarian left and the totalitarian right meet at last on the murky grounds of tyranny and terror." Here he reflected what was becoming a dominant theme among Western intellectuals. The shock of a supposedly civilized country such as Germany perpetrating the Holocaust, the iron grip that Stalin appeared to have over the vast Russian population, soon to be emulated by Mao Zedong in China, led to some gloomy philosophies. The new disciplines of psychology and sociology assessed forms of political extremism as disorders of mass society, a consequence of the yearning of the alienated and disoriented for ideological certainty, institutional order, and the guidance of a supreme leader. In this context the sacred texts of Marxism-Leninism offered a quasi-rationalist route to the same totalitarian destination as the romantic nationalism of the Nazis. The similarities were striking: both "dictatorships of a new and terrible kind, violent, ideologically inspired, endlessly aggressive, and possessed of extraordinary new technological means to dominate their helpless subjects utterly."[4]

This helps explain the third of the factors shaping modern liberalism mentioned by Schlesinger—"deepening of our knowledge of man." The persistence of war and the apparent susceptibility of the masses to demagogues had undermined liberal idealism. Freedom and prosperity could no longer be taken for granted as the natural consequence of the onward march of progress and the triumph of enlightenment. Instead they required a constant defense. While communism claimed to have found the secret of progress, liberals sensed that they had lost it. If liberalism was to prosper, it could not rely on an appeal to reason alone; attention had to be paid to issues of power and interest. Liberal idealism thus gave way to liberal realism.

The great philosopher of liberal realism was the theologian Reinhold Niebuhr. Since the early 1930s he had been grappling with the relationship between individual morality and participation in a wider society. A sentimental approach to international affairs, based on a belief in human perfectibility, was not only wrong, he declared, but dangerous. The problem of war could not simply be wished away or banished through schemes for world government. It was better to acknowledge with honesty the pride of nations and their instinct to self-interest lest democrats find themselves the victims of either their own naïveté or the cynicism of darker forces. Communism was dangerous precisely because it was driven to seek a monopoly of power. The democracies must meet this challenge, although he added that it would be best if they did this without resort to a fanaticism and self-righteousness of their own.[5]

Another key figure much influenced by Niebuhr was Hans Morgenthau, professor of international relations at the University of Chicago. When Morgenthau escaped from the Nazis in the 1930s he brought to the United States the tough-minded traditions of German political theory, but found in Niebuhr a framework to give it an ethical expression. As the founder of the realist school in international relations, Morgenthau sensed the dangers of liberals relying on rationalism and failing to appreciate the irrational passions that can drive human affairs. If democratic statesmen wanted to promote their most cherished values, they still had to acquire power. Without power nothing could be accomplished and everything could be lost.[6] Schlesinger picked up on the message. "The beginnings of maturity in foreign policy lie in the understanding that a nation has certain unalterable interests which no government can abandon." In defending Truman's policy of containment, he observed that while it might be the case that ideas cannot be fought with guns, "it is equally true that you cannot fight guns with ideas alone."[7]

As a theory, realism was not that controversial; it merely reflected the categories in which political leaders thought and acted. The speed with which the cold war followed the Second World War undermined the idealist tradition, which looked to international law and institutions to transcend these struggles. But the realist pursuit of the national interest still required some definition of the national interest, which could be framed in narrow or expansive terms, and views about how this interest might best be promoted, which required an analysis of the forces at work elsewhere in the international system. It could thus be used to justify almost any policy advocated for the cold war. George Kennan, normally credited as the architect of containment, considered himself a realist, but so did the commentator Walter Lippmann, who opposed containment, in the process putting the phrase "cold war" into political circulation.[8] By adopting a realist and anticommunist philosophy, liberals gained entrance to a foreign policy debate that would otherwise have left them behind, but it did not by itself provide policy guidance.

GUARDIANS OF CONTAINMENT

For liberal realists President Truman's containment doctrine, pledging the United States to prevent the further expansion of communism, epitomized the virtues of their approach. The reconstruction of Europe under the generous Marshall Plan, the Berlin airlift, the formation of NATO, and the readiness to fight back against communist aggression in Korea demonstrated the possibility of an internationalist consensus founded on firm principle, generosity to allies, prudent applications of force, and avoidance of provocation. The architect of this achievement was Dean Acheson, a key figure in the Truman administration even before he became secretary of state in 1949. He had been, as his memoirs put it, "present at the creation" of the key institutions of the postwar world.[9] During the 1950s he remained at the fore of Democrat foreign policy making in opposition, acting to guard Truman's legacy so that it could be handed on intact to the next Democratic president.

For this purpose the most important forum was the Foreign Affairs Committee of the Democratic Advisory Council (DAC), which Acheson chaired with Paul Nitze acting as his deputy, just as he had done in the State Department. While liberals, such as Chester Bowles and Kenneth Galbraith, were also on the DAC, at best they could only qualify Acheson's firm views. His stamp was on every relevant publication. The message was consistent. The Soviet threat was not easing on its own accord and could not be mitigated through grand negotiations. It could be assumed that any proposals that interested Moscow would damage the Western alliance. Satisfied with a status quo he had helped to construct, he took particular exception to any radical suggestions for its transformation, notably Kennan's well-publicized ideas on "disengagement" in central Europe.[10]

Acheson's views hardened and darkened over the Eisenhower years. Embarrassed by his apparent role at giving a green light for North Korea to invade the South in 1950 (by placing the latter explicitly outside America's "defense perimeter"), scarred by Republican abuse while in office for the "betrayal" of Yalta and "losing" China, he became steadily more dogmatic and acerbic. This gave an edge to his indictments of Eisenhower as president, tending to exaggerate the degree of discontinuity with Truman, but probably enhancing Acheson's role as a Democratic Party activist. Through the 1950s, as the party's most prominent and consistent spokesman, Acheson sustained a withering critique of the conduct of his successor at the State Department, John Foster Dulles. Acheson found

Dulles's self-righteousness irritating and his insensitivity to alliance concerns and regional nuance indicative of a failure to grasp the essentials of statecraft.

The gravamen of Acheson's approach to international affairs lay in his sense of what great-power status required. A country of the size and wealth of the United States could not avoid an active international role, especially when its economic and political interests in critical parts of the world were threatened by another great power. The integrity of its commitments and the stiffness of its resolve were under constant scrutiny; if it visibly weakened or hesitated, then its whole international position could soon unravel. To avoid this, commitments should not be taken on casually, and once accepted, they should be properly supported. Without adequate military strength great-power diplomacy would become well nigh impossible. Alternative approaches, based on aspirations to world government or helping only the nice regimes, were "messianic globaloney," bound to fail because they neglected the vital factors of power and interest.[11]

His 1958 book, *Power and Diplomacy*, argued that though military power was commonly regarded as morally suspect, it was "fundamental in the relations between states"—far more so than "the most solemn and sweeping pledges made to enforce peace." This was well understood in the Kremlin. Unfortunately, "present trends and common prudence" led to "the hypothesis that, in the absence of a new and vigorous effort on our part, Soviet productive power will approximate that of the United States well before this century is over." There was therefore no escaping the harsh realities of "power politics."[12] It is not surprising to find that one of Acheson's closest intellectual friends was Hans Morgenthau,[13] who described him as "one of the best Secretaries of State the United States had ever had."[14] Together they drew on the principles of power politics to challenge the foreign policy of Eisenhower and Dulles.

2

Beyond Massive Retaliation

AS SECRETARY OF STATE, Dean Acheson had used the sudden end to the U.S. atomic monopoly in August 1949, when the first Soviet test was detected, to initiate a reappraisal of security policy. One outcome was the development of thermonuclear weapons in order to maintain superiority for as long as possible; another, adopted after the start of the Korean War, was a sustained rearmament program to reduce dependence upon this superiority before its inevitable loss. The Eisenhower administration criticized this stance as unnecessarily expensive in its reliance on conventional forces and constraining in its reluctance to exploit America's prime strategic asset. This was summed up by the stalemate in Korea, where self-imposed limitations left the Americans fighting in a framework that played to the communists' advantages. In a famous speech of January 1954 Dulles asserted, "The way to deter aggression is for the free community to be willing and able to respond vigorously at places and with means of its own choosing."[1] America's means of choice appeared to be "massive retaliatory power" (hence the policy's label of "massive retaliation"). To its critics, the obvious flaw lay in the excessive dependence placed on the credibility of U.S. nuclear threats, even as it declined when the Soviet Union acquired its own massive retaliatory power. Prominent among the policy's critics was Acheson, who denounced it as an "Orwellian attempt to persuade the country that it got stronger by getting weaker," charging that it would preclude the United States from making a forceful response to local aggression.[2]

This critique accorded with that developed by disgruntled army and navy officers, who saw their budgets being cut to accommodate the massive expansion of strategic air power as a means of sustaining U.S. nuclear superiority. Particularly influential was General Maxwell Taylor, army chief of staff from 1955 to 1959 after a dazzling career as an airborne general in the Second World War and a commander in Korea. Taylor warned that the cuts in army manpower rendered it incapable of fighting the limited wars that he anticipated for the future. Once retired, he developed his core theme in a celebrated book, *The Uncertain Trumpet*. This had the great advantage of swapping one slogan for another:

> The strategic doctrine which I propose to replace Massive Retaliation is called herein the Strategy of Flexible Response. This name suggests the need for a capability to react across the entire spectrum of possible challenge, for coping with anything from general atomic war to infiltrations and aggressions such as threaten Laos and Berlin in 1959.[3]

Though written with the stylistic flourish of a typical military briefing, this critique of the Eisenhower administration by such a senior army figure was seized upon by the Democrats, including Kennedy. Taylor acquired a reputation as something of an intellectual and an imaginative military reformer. By the end of the 1950s it was generally assumed, including by many Republicans, that excessive dependence upon nuclear threats was unwise and conventional forces had to be rebuilt.

Acheson saw this as vindication of the conclusion he had reached in 1950. In the nuclear age an attempt to fight a total war on the lines of the two world wars was a recipe for disaster. It was necessary therefore to reject the past practice of applying "force complete, absolute, overpowering . . . until the enemy's will to resist and capacity to exist as a nation were broken." Morgenthau demonstrated that Dulles's policy of identifying "force with atomic force" had led to a self-imposed restraint: "The use of atomic force, however narrowly circumscribed by the initial intent, entails the enormous and unbearable risk that it may develop, imperceptibly but ineluctably, into the use of all-out atomic force."[4]

This was the conventional wisdom among academics with an interest in foreign policy, and it helped stimulate a whole new school of strategic analysis, founded on realism. To this school the Korean War was a model of restraint rather than an abject failure. Excessive casualties and frustration were the result of the attempt to transcend the war's natural limits—by seeking to "liberate" North Korea—rather than accept the need to work within them. The threat of total war might well be required to deter the crudest forms of Soviet aggression, but more subtle Soviet methods required more tailored Western responses. The best known work of this school was Henry Kissinger's formidable tome *Nuclear Weapons and Foreign Policy*, on the best-seller lists for fourteen weeks.[5] Kissinger, another refugee from Nazi Germany, stressed the importance of a diplomacy backed by force and bemoaned the American absolutist tendency that assigned war and peace, the military and the diplomatic, to separate compartments. "The key problem for present day strategy," according to Kissinger and most others writing at the time, was "to devise a spectrum of capabilities with which to resist Soviet challenges."[6] The most distinctive and most criticized feature of Kissinger's approach was the inclusion of limited nuclear war in this spectrum. By the end of the decade he had joined the consensus that equated a limited-war philosophy with a buildup of conventional forces.[7]

Even with such a buildup, few strategists were confident that a war in Europe could be kept limited. Here both the vital interests and the mightiest forces of East and West confronted each other so directly that any war appeared likely to burst through all restraints, culminating in a nuclear catastrophe. Containing Soviet power in Europe remained the first priority, but the task was becoming harder. Acheson accused the Eisenhower administration of paying insufficient attention to the growth of Soviet strength, the needs of allies, and the demands of a strong defense. The Russians, ready "to act to the limit of their capacity" in imposing their will on Europe, could only be deterred by "the belief that from the outset of any such attempt American power would be employed in stopping it, and if necessary, would inflict on the Soviet Union injury which the Moscow regime would not wish to suffer."[8]

PREPARING FOR NUCLEAR WAR

America's nuclear guarantee to Europe was supposed to be so unequivocal that the risk of Soviet miscalculation would be minimized. But new technologies were complicating deterrence. It had seemed simple enough: The prospect of nuclear attack was a powerful argument for caution. But clever minds quickly started to think of ingenious ways to reduce this prospect. The RAND Corporation at Santa Monica in California, set up by the air force in the late 1940s, was the prototypical "think tank," the place where smart people could think the unthinkable. The atmosphere at RAND during the 1950s appears to have been genuinely collegial (with a due quota of the rivalries and personality clashes found in the best colleges), so it becomes difficult to disentangle individual responsibility for the stream of theories, methods, and concepts that it generated.[9] The most notorious figure was Herman Kahn, bubbling with ideas, famous for briefings that extended over days. He was the model for the madcap figure satirized in Stanley Kubrick's film *Dr. Strangelove*, a man whose intellectual brilliance was never matched by common sense. Kahn's first major book, *On Thermonuclear War*, was stirring up controversy as Kennedy came to power, largely because of the flip way that Kahn appeared to be prepared to talk about varieties of nuclear war.[10]

Kahn's notoriety and delight in causing outrage, and his developing role as an advocate of civil defence, ran counter to RAND's corporate image, which was one reason why he eventually left. RAND's basic mission of expanding the range of nuclear options tended to be pursued in a more subversive manner, simply by forcing the defense establishment to think through the fearsome uncertainties of the nuclear age. The message lay in the method and the standards set for rigorous analysis. Instead of the intuitive logic of realist historians and philosophers, they applied the methods of the natural sciences and economics, and relished the counterintuitive.[11]

The most celebrated analytical technique was game theory, developed by the mathematicians John von Neumann and Oskar Morgenstern, both with RAND connections.[12] The great value of game theory was that it could suggest how alternative courses of action for one player depended on the courses available to another. Another important influence was systems theory, which encouraged analysis from the perspective of the system as a whole rather than that of an individual actor within the system. From the actor's point of view, for example, it might make sense to arms race, but from the broader perspective this would be damaging to the overall system and so eventually to the actor himself. In RAND this was turned into systems analysis, capable of relating sets of disparate factors to each other, comparing the costs and benefits of every alternative.[13] The cumulative effect of RAND's analytical work was to demonstrate the interdependence of the United States and the Soviet Union, how their fates were bound together by a shared interest in avoiding nuclear war and the ways in which the decision making of one affected that of the other.

Instead of thinking about the superpower confrontation as a zero-sum game—what one gained the other must lose—it was non-zero sum. Strategies could be followed that worked to the benefit—or the detriment—of both. The idea that potential enemies needed to cooperate to prevent their antagonism from getting out of hand was central to much diplomatic activity, but the thought that this might be reinforced by military strategies forged with the interests of the enemy in mind was less familiar. The new strategists provided a theoretical foundation for this thought with immediate and practical applications.

The framework of new thinking about deterrence was developed by Albert Wohlstetter, a mathematician. In a classic study his team used an apparently simple problem—where to deploy strategic bombers—to demonstrate the potential vulnerability of bombers to a surprise Soviet attack.[14] This challenged the comforting assumption that that the parallel development of two nuclear arsenals would produce a naturally stable stalemate. Outlining the theoretical conditions in which one side could achieve a nuclear victory through striking first and pointing to technological developments that might turn this theory into reality, Wohlstetter advocated defensive measures such as putting missiles into protective silos able to withstand nuclear explosions in their vicinity and relying more on the less vulnerable submarine-based missiles. This would produce what he called a "second-strike" capability, the ability to retaliate with great force even after absorbing a surprise first strike.

Employing this framework, the economist Thomas Schelling argued for deliberately choosing weapons that were neither vulnerable to an enemy first strike nor suitable for mounting one. Confidence in invulnerability removed incentives to adopt potentially disastrous postures, such as a readiness to launch on warning of attack (especially as the warning systems were not error-free). The counterintuitive quality of such thinking went further, for the logic of restraint meant that it made more sense to target cities rather than missiles.

> A weapon that can hurt only people, and cannot possibly damage the other side's striking force, is profoundly defensive; it provides its possessor no incentive to strike first. It is the weapon that is designed or deployed to destroy "military" targets—to seek out the enemy's missiles and bombers— that *can* exploit the advantage of striking first and consequently provide a temptation to do so.[15]

On this basis the United States should be reassured rather than frustrated if the Soviet Union went for systems such as missile-carrying nuclear submarines. Air force generals had considered Wohlstetter's worries about protecting their bombers and missiles from Soviet attack irrelevant, as they had every intention of firing first. Schelling's readiness to encourage opponents to keep their most formidable weapons out of harm's way was bizarre, bordering on treasonable.

CONTROL AND ESCALATION

Liberals were uneasy with this way of thinking. The idea of deliberately targeting centers of population was perverse and macabre, while the new strategists seemed too ready to live with nuclear weapons rather than work for their abolition. Since the First World War the instinctive response of liberals to an arms race had been to call for it to be thrown into reverse, creating a virtuous cycle of disarmament. Fewer weapons were assumed to lead logically to more peace. The run-up to the Second World War had somewhat discredited this approach, along with the attempt to build up trust with dictators, but it had been revived by the sheer awfulness of nuclear weapons. Even without a war the weapons seemed to pose a sinister danger. In 1954 Japanese fishermen on board *The Lucky Dragon* received a lethal dose of radiation from an atmospheric test, and the testing program itself became a major area of controversy. A movement for nuclear disarmament gathered momentum, with such figures as Linus Pauling, Bertrand Russell, and Albert Schweitzer to the fore.[16] And almost despite itself, the Eisenhower administration found itself drawn into discussions with Moscow on a nuclear test ban.[17] Though fruitless, the talks were carried out with a degree of seriousness and high-level involvement that set them apart from the normal rhetorical gestures in the direction of disarmament.

The problems faced by those attached to traditional notions of disarmament were evident in *The Liberal Papers*, an influential volume of essays put together by Democratic Party congressmen and academic supporters in 1960, though not published until 1962. The introduction by the sociologists David Riesman and Michael Macoby reflected on the problems of liberals finding a voice in a debate where accusations of appeasement and procommunism were almost automatic and Soviet subversion was found in the most unlikely places (such as the fluoridation of water supplies). They also conveyed their wariness over what had happened to the intellectual insights of the immediate postwar period. Realism of the Niebuhr variety had been turned into the simple opposite of "idealism, reasonableness and morality" and a "suspicious negativism toward any efforts at a *modus vivendi*." Yet hopes for stabilizing the arms race depended on the Soviet side being as realistic as the American. True realists now, they suggested, would recognize that the "arms race cannot go on without something going amiss just because of the nature of man . . . one psychotic commander could set off a catalytic war." Because of this, they were skeptical of the "polished rationality of the game-theory sort," though it was preferable to the blustering of generals.[18]

Though the nuclear danger appeared as the outstanding problem of the age, the authors of *The Liberal Papers* offered no easy solutions. They could point to the long-term unreliability of deterrence, and they could encourage the idea that disarmament measures need not threaten security and could be planned on a practical basis, but the arsenals seemed too large and complex, and the distrust between the superpowers too deep, for there to be much prospect of progress.[19] At the same time, coping with the nuclear danger for the indefinite future also seemed a dismal prospect, and some claimed that statistically it just could not be done. Something was bound to go wrong.

Theorists of stable deterrence were more confident. Rather than worry about arduous treaty negotiations, they believed the desired results could be achieved if both sides configured their forces prudently. They shifted attention from the size of arsenals to their quality. "Arms control" became the vogue term to stress the distinction between this approach and old-fashioned disarmament.[20] Its intellectual underpinnings were firmly in place by 1960, when proposals were presented to a major conference, attended by many figures who would soon be connected with the Kennedy administration.[21] Whereas disarmament was about solving the problem of war by eliminating the means by which it could be conducted, arms control looked instead to the ways in which armed forces were structured and whether they allowed politicians to control the military instrument.

But was it truly realistic to expect the superpower confrontation to retain an inner stability even as it lurched from one crisis to another? An offhand comment by Dulles during an interview—"If you are scared to go to the brink, you are lost"—conveyed an attitude that could lead to disaster, pointing to a disturbing contradiction at the heart of the new strategic analysis. So long as decisions on war and peace could be governed by rational calculations, then measures could be taken to reinforce caution. It might, however, require no more than matters being allowed to follow the traditional military route, with both sides targeting each other's weapons, for a terrible and tragic hazard to emerge. Anxiety about what the other might be up to could turn the prudent into the reckless. Schelling called this "the reciprocal fear of surprise attack."

> A modest temptation on each side to sneak in a first blow—a temptation too small by itself to motivate an attack—might become compounded through a process of interacting expectations, with additional motive for attack being produced by successive cycles of "He thinks we think he thinks we think . . . he thinks we think he'll attack; so he thinks we shall; so he will; so we must."

His image was of a gradual loss of control until war became total and all-encompassing. During the early stages of this process this prospect might be exploited to induce in the enemy "an overpowering incentive to lay off." But fear itself might move situations out of control: "People may vaguely feel they perceive that the situation is inherently explosive, and respond by exploding."[22] The word to describe this type of danger was *escalation*. Moving staircases served as a natural source of metaphor, an upward movement that could not be stopped. Once committed, one had to move upward (or downward), however much the original decision to step on the escalator might be later resented or regretted. This was the basic problem in limited-war theory. It could not be assumed that once war began, limited political objectives would guarantee a limited war, the objectives with which belligerents start wars rarely stay fixed. Each side would be forced to choose its methods with reference to those adopted by the other side.

First used in its contemporary context in Britain in 1959, *escalation* soon appeared in the mainstream American literature. Henry Kissinger, as always with a keen sense for strategic fashions, used it in 1960 to refer to "the addition of increments of power until limited war insensibly merges into all-out war" and presented it as a problem with theories of limited nuclear war, such as his own of a few years earlier (which was being reassessed in this essay).[23] Escalation was not so much a strategy as something to be avoided.

Gradually escalation started to be thought of as a strategy itself. Central to Herman Kahn's approach was his conviction that control was possible in all types of conflict, even nuclear, and so escalation was a dragon to be slain: not so much a phenomenon operating independently of human action but a possible product of inadequate intellectual and physical preparation.[24] He introduced the idea that escalation might be a deliberate act, albeit misguided. The noun acquired a verb when he referred to "people who wish to escalate a little themselves, but somehow feel that the other side would not be willing to go one step further."[25] Escalation was being transformed from a description of a process to be avoided to one that might be tamed and possibly manipulated. This was to become a central issue during the Kennedy years, as the possibility of eventually prevailing by upping the ante had to be weighed against the potentially dire consequences of a loss of control.

SPUTNIK 1

The new strategists had an attentive audience in the late 1950s. Although there had been a theoretical vulnerability to nuclear attack since the start of the decade, the full extent of the potential danger had not fully imposed itself on the national consciousness. The trouble spots of Europe and Asia were oceans away, and America still set the pace in the development of weapon technology. Then in the summer of 1957 the Soviet Union completed the first successful test of an intercontinental ballistic missile (ICBM), to be followed that October by a far more dramatic and politically significant achievement that caught the popular imagination. The first artificial earth satellite—*Sputnik 1*—was sent into orbit.

The shock to the American system was profound. Suddenly it could no longer be assumed that the United States was without rival in its technological capacity. There was a revival of the old fears about slack, decadent, complacent democracies allowing themselves to be caught by ruthless totalitarian states, which could mobilize all social resources in pursuit of their fixed goal. The specter was raised of a "nuclear Pearl Harbor." The call went out to galvanize America for action, and the revitalization of America's scientific base was presented as essential to national security.

In this frenzied atmosphere President Eisenhower's calm and slightly detached image became a liability. Five days after *Sputnik* he was embarrassed by the report of a high-level defense panel, the contents of which soon leaked, warning of the dangers of the United States falling behind and becoming vulnerable to a first strike.[26] The pot was stirred further by the U.S. Air Force. Sure of its own nuclear strategy, it assumed that the Soviet Union must be following the same course but was further ahead in its preparations. So while Democrats echoed the army in chastising Eisenhower for failing to make provision for limited wars, they also picked up air force alarmism about Soviet strategic advances that put the United States in physical danger and jeopardized the credibility of its international commitments.[27] Eisenhower, on the defensive, refused to be panicked, suspecting that the services were scare-mongering to get the defense budget raised. He could not talk about the CIA's U-2 flights over Soviet territory, which were steadily giving him greater confidence that his caution was justified, although only on the negative grounds that no evidence was found of missile deployment. Nonetheless, for the rest of his term in office he had to cope with the accusation that he was allowing a "missile gap" to develop.[28]

3

The Third World Alternative

THE DEBATE ON HOW TO CONDUCT the nuclear arms race was at root a debate about foreign policy. Whether or not either side had something approximating to a first-strike capability mattered only if it was felt that the dynamics of international affairs were pushing the superpowers inexorably to the brink of war or that alliance commitments depended on a readiness to take the highest risks. Although the ideas of limited war and arms control allowed members of the liberal wing of the Democratic Party to appear responsible realists rather than naive idealists, they tended to doubt that the Soviet Union was really contemplating total war, and they suspected that by showing greater flexibility the West could move toward some sort of accommodation with the East. More seriously, they believed that the preoccupation with European geopolitics, the cold war, and the arms race meant that the big story of the contemporary era, the struggles in the third world for political independence and economic development, was being missed. To the fore in arguing for the need to pay attention to the exciting possibilities opening up in the third world were Adlai Stevenson and his good friend Chester Bowles, who had been ambassador to India from 1951 to 1953. During the Eisenhower years Bowles had made the needs of the developing countries his special project.

The starting point for this approach was the belief that the American experience had a special appeal to countries breaking free from colonial shackles. It had fought its own war of independence and then refrained (strictly speaking) from acquiring colonies of its own. The vitality of its economic and political system offered a further source of potential inspiration. This meant that the United States was well placed to bond with the nationalist regimes of the third world and help guide them into representative democracy and successful industrialization. By using its economic clout to encourage those who were prepared to follow American guidance, the third worlders could point to real gains in terms of access to raw materials, markets for American goods and services, and a strong foundation from which to fend off communist advances. In the truest sense this would be enlightened self-interest. Bowles believed that as the numbers of independent states grew and their levels of development progressed, they would change the character of international politics: "The Cold War conflict is paralleled by a growing partnership between the United States and the peoples of Asia, Africa and Latin America. It is this evolving world which helps shape the United Nations and which, increasingly, may be shaped by it."[1]

By and large realists were unconvinced by this line of argument. This was not so much because of the unreality of its premise, that political leaders in the underdeveloped world might have a natural affinity with a wealthy status-quo power, but because they simply considered over-developed Europe to be more important. The European empires were attempting to sustain their international positions in the face of anti-imperialist demands. Acheson, for example, took the view that alliance cohesion required sympathy for the predicaments of Britain, France, Holland, and Belgium as they coped with this challenge.

In his skepticism about the third world, he was joined by other realists with whom, in other respects, he strongly disagreed, including Lippmann and Kennan. The lawyer George Ball, for example, who was close to Stevenson and well informed about third world issues, was unconvinced. When Ball drafted a report on foreign policy issues to be submitted in Stevenson's name to the president-elect in December 1960, Stevenson commended it but felt obliged to note that there was insufficient focus on third world issues. Ball was a committed Europhile. His doubts about intervention in third world affairs eventually became the basis of his opposition to Lyndon Johnson's policies in Vietnam. When he commented later on the "young movers and shakers" of the Kennedy administration, he contrasted their "surfeit of theories regarding the economic development of the Third World" with their "lack of settled views on the structure of relations among the Western industrialized democracies."[2]

WALT ROSTOW

For Ball the chief source of mischief was less the rather woolly views of Stevenson and Bowles than those of the militant development theorists, such as Walt Rostow. Rostow was spokesman for those who believed that the third world provided the new arena in which to fight the cold war. He later reciprocated Ball's disdain and also noted how the Eurocentric orientation of Acheson reflected a "different world" from the one that the Kennedy team had to deal with in 1961. Now American foreign policy had to be as tuned in to Latin America, Asia, Africa, and the Middle East as it was to Europe.[3] Rostow was as hostile to communism as he had once been sympathetic, convinced that the American way of life was exportable to the benefit of all. His book *Stages of Economic Growth* was subtitled *A Non-Communist Manifesto* and conveyed confidence in capitalism as a motor to growth for underdeveloped countries if only these countries could avoid subversion by communism.[4] The extra ingredient he brought to the policy debate was his conviction that policies for the third world must include a vigorous counterinsurgency program, earning him the later White House nickname "Chet Bowles with Machine Guns."

During the Second World War he had chosen targets for the strategic bombing campaign and remained a firm believer in the effectiveness of air power. As a result of studies of communism in East Asia undertaken at the Massachusetts Institute of Technology in 1953–55, he had identified a "soft war" under way, which would determine the fate of territories emerging out of colonialism. Combining subversion with guerrilla warfare, it required neither "masses of troops nor modern equipment." In such wars the communist "enemy" was "a professional and we are amateurs."[5]

Communist guerrillas had the benefit of a compelling social theory to inspire and direct them. The West must root its own ideological claims for political freedom and capitalism in a profound analysis of the great changes that were affecting so many societies as the result of decolonization and the embrace of modernization. Thus Rostow's own work on the problems of underdevelopment had helped him develop a framework within which the cold war could be understood as it manifested itself in "societies in transition from traditional to modern forms of organization," a time of "inherent vulnerability to guerrilla warfare."

Rostow was, for a brief time, the first director of the Center for International Studies (CENIS) at the Massachusetts Institute of Technology, which was established with the unpublicized help of the CIA. He worked closely with a group of development theorists who had become convinced that the underdeveloped world offered an unparalleled opportunity for social science to prove its worth by helping new states join the modern, advanced industrialized world on the side of the West.[6] If these emerging societies were to escape from the mire of poverty and dependency, then it was vital to understand the linkages between the structures of rural society and the impact of urbanization, traditional patterns of belief and imported Western value systems, subsistence economies and global markets, established sources of authority and the innovative role of political elites.

These theories offered guidance to officials charged with dispersing development aid and diplomats trying to make sense of confusing local politics as well as military advisers coping with insurgencies. They had to address such troubling phenomena as the apparent requirement to uproot well-established social systems in the name of modernization and the prominent role of the military in this process. As Lucien Pye asserted, "the heart of the problem of nation-building is the question of how the diffusion of world culture can be facilitated while its disruptive consequences are minimized."[7] This was a grand project, and it stimulated a heady mixture of genuine insight and convenient myth, enlightenment and rationalization. It reflected the academic climate in its optimism about the ability of social theory to attain the level of "science," in the enthusiasm of the intellectuals for a chance to demonstrate their value to the world of policy, and in the willingness of their audience to believe them.

Modernization, they explained, was vital but traumatic. The processes of social change were disruptive and unruly, even if the end result was to the greater good. The successful management of this change was in the hands of the local elites. They carried the responsibility for refining but also embodying a national identity. As they had to be prepared to take tough measures, somehow they had to find the symbols, as well as the performance levels, that could endow their actions with sufficient legitimacy. Facing them would be the inertia, apathy, and sullen resentments of those who saw their old way of life being dislocated and damaged beyond repair. This provided the communists with their opportunity, for they could play on the fears and anger of the deracinated and the disaffected.

Walt Rostow was a conduit for the introduction of these ideas into the policy arena. His main contribution to public debate during the last years of the Eisenhower administration was in stark contrast to Acheson's. Whereas the latter's book had been short, pithy, and opinionated, Rostow's *The United States in the World Arena* was long, meandering, almost encyclopedic in its range; while its subtitle called it an "essay," it was divided up into six "books." It was, however, as opinionated as Acheson's Rostow listed three challenges to American military and foreign policy. The third of these was uncontroversial, reflecting the consensus of the time: the "military, economic, diplomatic, and intellectual success of Soviet society and . . . its ability to maintain itself as an ongoing system." The first two, however, were less recognized and were to dog policy making in the coming years. One was the need to "contemplate the role of force as a measured instrument of foreign policy." This required building on the lesson of the Korean War—"that Americans might have to die for limited objectives of a political or strategic nature and not simply in a once-and-for-all moral crusade." The other turned on what Rostow saw as the tension between the American commitment to the democratic process and the requirements of underdeveloped areas. Attempts "to apply in the transitional areas the moral and institutional canons of American democratic practice yielded a series of frustrations and failures." The United States had been forced to face the fact that societies with which alliance is needed in the national interest may stand at stages in their own history which do not offer as a realistic possibility the immediate creation of democratic regimes on the Western model; and . . . that allies whose policies are built simply on the concept of a shared enemy and who are inefficient in moving toward the constructive objectives of their societies become weak allies.[8]

4

Policies and People

KENNEDY WAS SYMPATHETIC to the idea that the United States should embrace and support the new and largely nationalist leaders of the third world, and in this way divert them from any communist tendencies, even at the risk of offending the old colonial powers who were also America's closest allies. This had been one of the most distinctive features of his preelection foreign policy pronouncements, and was reflected in an unusual (for an American senator) interest in African affairs. At the same time he was impatient with the inflexible posturing surrounding the cold war in Europe as well as alarmed by its implications.

Kennedy had taken on board the idea that nationalism was the most potent political force of the era. As the Europeans could not expect to hold on to their colonies, or even their residual influence through support of white regimes in Africa, it would be unwise if the United States appeared to support any attempt to do so. In July 1957, in one of his first contributions to a Senate foreign policy debate, Kennedy supported the Algerian efforts to gain independence from France, leading to a rebuke from Acheson. Kennedy was not even hostile to the idea of neutrality for third world countries that wanted to keep clear of the cold war, although he suspected that some of the new leaders who proclaimed neutrality were communists in all but name. The thrust of policy would be not to line everybody up behind an American banner but rather to ensure that they kept firmly away from a Soviet banner. He warned in 1958 against the "illusion" that in Latin America "every anti-American voice is the voice of Moscow" and said that most citizens shared "our dedication to an anti-Communist crusade to save what we call free enterprise."[1] If the United States failed to embrace the new nationalism, then the Soviet Union surely would. Support of "national liberation struggles" had appeared as the new priority in Soviet strategy. Yet there was no reason why it could not be turned against communism. As he told a European newspaper in 1960:

> The desire to be free—of all foreign tutelage—the desire for self-determination is the most powerful force in the modern world. It has destroyed old empires, created new nations and redrawn the maps of Asia, the Middle East and Africa. America must be on the side of the right of man to govern himself because that is one of our historical principles, because the final victory of nationalism is inevitable and because nationalism is the force which disposes of sufficient power and determination to threaten the integrity of the communist empire itself.[2]

The arrival of the nuclear age also challenged traditional patterns of thought and added to the need to avoid following slavishly a Eurocentric cold war agenda. He was always wary of overreliance upon nuclear deterrence, and so responded immediately to Dulles's speech about massive retaliation, questioning the policy's relevance in areas where a communist advance rested "not upon military invasion but upon local insurrection and political deterioration."[3] That was why he attached such importance to developing tailored responses to "Sputnik diplomacy, limited brushfire wars, indirect non-overt aggression, intimidation and subversion, internal revolution." Against these threats nuclear weapons were useless, for each individual incident was too small to justify massive retaliation.[4]

Following this line of argument allowed Kennedy to champion military capabilities across the whole spectrum, and this provided him with a usefully prodefense reputation. In addition, while concerned about the dangers of overreliance on nuclear threats, he could also see the dangers of conceding nuclear superiority to the Soviet Union. In 1958 he picked up on the issue of a looming missile gap, having been alerted to it by Joe Alsop, whose columns carried detailed accounts of the gloomier intelligence estimates of surging Soviet missile production. Alsop was already a family friend but only began to take Kennedy seriously as a presidential aspirant in 1958. He encouraged him to warn against the balance of power shifting against the United States and then rewarded him with plaudits in his columns when he did so.[5] The disturbing picture of the developing balance of power presented to Kennedy in CIA briefings as a member of the Foreign Relations Committee reinforced this position. His argument for greater military preparedness was never solely one of seeking victory in war should diplomacy fail. Based on his analysis of appeasement in the 1930s, he believed that military strength was the only basis for a constructive diplomacy and thus the avoidance of war. He liked to quote Churchill on this, as on other issues: "[W]e arm to parley."[6] His instinct was always to parley rather than to fight. The consequences of any war, even with every determination to respect limits, were incalculable. Escalation could happen despite the beliefs of the belligerents that they knew what they were doing and had everything under control. This fear of even a skirmish getting out of hand stemmed, according to one of his biographers, from a course on the origins of World War I at Harvard, later reinforced by a reading of Barbara Tuchman's *Guns of August*. "A favorite Kennedy word was 'miscalculation.' "[7]

To guard against this, he believed statesmanship required viewing the world from the adversary's perspective and not just dealing with him as an implacable, single-minded foe with whom no common ground could be shared and with whom communication and cooperation were impossible. As a politician, he understood all too well the pressures that would oblige a president to take a tough stance at times of crisis, and he assumed that his opponent would face similar pressures, adding to the dangers inherent in any unfolding crisis. His Soviet opposite number, however, could not have been more different. Nikita Khrushchev was an old-style communist of peasant stock who had learned the art of survival during the Stalin years. He faced few institutional checks and balances on his behavior, even as it became more erratic and impetuous. Kennedy was initially caught off guard by Khrushchev's more tempestuous political style and continued to assume that the Soviet leader was tougher and in a stronger position than was in fact the case.

FROM CANDIDATE TO PRESIDENT

During the 1960 campaign Kennedy's attacks on the Eisenhower administration followed orthodox lines. As it had suited Eisenhower to present himself as being rather dull and unimaginative, there were plenty of opportunities to emphasize a contrasting style full of vigor and vision. In language common to all politicians in opposition, Kennedy called for strong leadership, coherent long-term strategies, policies that anticipated rather than reacted, and an end to confusion, uncertainty, and vacillation. To convey the idea that under his leadership the United States could ride the tide of change rather than be swept along by it, he adopted the metaphor of the New Frontier, famously evoked when accepting the Democratic Party nomination in July 1960. "The frontier of the 1960s, a frontier of unknown opportunities and paths, a frontier of unfulfilled hopes and threats . . . beyond that frontier are uncharted areas of science and space, unsolved problems of peace and war."

Candidate Kennedy dealt with contrasting stances on foreign policy by denying that there was a choice to be made. He sought to reconcile the extremes. Hard-liners would note his assertions that the United States was losing ground to the Soviet Union as a result of unnecessary budgetary restrictions. Until this strength could be rebuilt, substantive negotiations with Moscow were doomed to failure. He spoke of how the "Soviet program for world domination . . . skillfully blends the weapons of military might, political subversion, economic penetration and ideological conquest." Specific proposals started with the need for an "invulnerable . . . nuclear retaliatory power second to none" and then moved on to an ability "to intervene effectively and swiftly in any limited war any-where in the world" through improvements in conventional capabilities. Yet liberals were encouraged by support for measures of arms control, including a nuclear test ban; promises for more imaginative openings and assistance to Latin America, the Middle East, Asia, and Africa; and his readiness to reconsider the inflexible attitude toward "Red China." Even on Europe he indicated an interest in a "solution to the problem of Berlin."[8]

These themes were followed through in the inauguration speech of 20 January 1961. By deciding to concentrate on foreign policy, to the chagrin of those who looked for a clear domestic agenda and early commitment to civil rights, he asserted his own priorities and set the criteria against which he expected his presidency to be judged. From the start he was seeking to find his own distinctive tone, which reached out to the rest of the world without betraying any sign of softness. He told Sorensen that he "wanted neither the customary cold war rhetoric about the Communist menace nor any weasel words that Khrushchev might misinterpret."[9]

The speech's early paragraphs established the revolutionary credentials of the United States and, in a famous passage, proclaimed that the United States would "pay any price, bear any burden, meet any hardship, support any friend, oppose any foe, to ensure the survival and the success of lib-erty." He briefly "pledged the loyalty of faithful friends" to "those old allies whose cultural and spiritual origins we share," encouraging them to stay united. He then moved on to "those new states whom we welcome to the ranks of the free," to which Kennedy gave his word "that one form of colonial control shall not have passed away merely to be replaced by a far more iron tyranny." He also pledged the best efforts of his country to help "those people in the huts and villages of half the globe struggling to break the bonds of mass misery." After a nod in the direction of Latin America and the United Nations, he offered cooperation as well as res-olution "to those nations who would make themselves our adversary," saying, "Let us never negotiate out of fear, but let us never fear to ne-gotiate." One of the most memorable of inaugural addresses, it gave the abiding impression of a self-confident activism.

THE BALANCE OF APPOINTMENTS

There was a mismatch between Kennedy's foreign policy team and the message of the inaugural address. Reconciling the idealist and realist traditions with the Democratic Party required not only a balance of rhet-oric but also a balance of appointment in the construction of the admin-istration. The strength of the more idealist third world perspective was always going to depend on the role of Adlai Stevenson, the effective leader of the Democratic Party for much of the 1950s and its nominee in the 1952 and 1956 presidential elections.

Still much admired in the party, Stevenson's self-deprecating wit had been an asset at a time when victory was probably beyond any Democrat. Now, however, he had the image of a loser. With Chester Bowles he shared a political style that was explicitly idealistic, visionary, and crusading, in sharp contrast to Kennedy's preference for the skeptical and analytical. The flow of words that emanated from Stevenson and Bowles had a soft center, short on detail, exasperating those who tried to pin them down. Even Stevenson's advisers found him indecisive. Kennedy had his own reason to be disenchanted with Stevenson, who had held back an endorsement during 1960 in the forlorn hope that he might get a last-minute draft as the party's nominee. Nonetheless, the affection in which Stevenson was held meant that some role had to be found for him, and he was offered the job of ambassador to the United Nations. He took it, though feeling this was less than he deserved—he would have preferred the State Department.

In the absence of a third Stevenson campaign for the presidency Bowles had attached himself to Kennedy in 1959, one of the first influential liberals to do so. This earned him the latter's gratitude and for a while the title of foreign policy adviser. He became undersecretary of state. Kennedy hoped that Bowles's undoubted energy might shake up the State Department, but organizational reform was not really his forte, although an ability to spot young talent was. Other, more radical figures such as John Kenneth Galbraith and George Kennan also found themselves in significant but not quite central positions—as ambassadors to India and Yugoslavia, respectively. In the White House Arthur Schlesinger Jr. spent much of his time keeping lines open to liberals and soothing their bruised egos.

Meanwhile Acheson was able to exert a substantial influence on appointments. He had opted for John Kennedy only a month before the nomination, but then helped to convince his old boss and now close friend, former president Harry Truman, to back the young man. With his network of international contacts, formidable intellect, and intense commitment to the policy framework of containment, Acheson was not a man Kennedy could ignore, in spite of his controversial character. He was deeply resented by the liberal wing of the party and by numerous victims of his arrogant disdain for those whose style, wit, and opinions did not match his own. Stevenson was a special target for Acheson's scorn ("a third-rate mind which he can't make up.")[10]

Kennedy remarked on Acheson's "intimidating seniority" and judged him to have far too many opponents and be too much of a maverick to be allowed back into his old office at the State Department.[11] This in itself was not a serious disappointment to Acheson. He was, after all, already in his late sixties. By way of compensation he made the most of an opportunity to advise on appointments. With Robert Lovett, another scion of the old foreign policy establishment, he suggested Dean Rusk for secretary of state. As assistant secretary of state for Far Eastern affairs under Truman, Rusk had been appreciated for demonstrating the appropriate combination of firmness and restraint, as well as great loyalty and a sure touch, during the Korean War. Yet since then, as president of the Rockefeller Foundation, Rusk had been out of the limelight and was suspected of being something of a lightweight. The logic of Kennedy's determination to be a foreign policy president meant that he was expecting to take the lead himself on most of the major issues. This was coupled with suspicion of the State Department's innate conservatism. The prospect of a weak secretary of state did not bother him.

Acheson would dearly have loved to have Paul Nitze in this position. Nitze had been one of his closest lieutenants as head of the Policy Planning Staff, and then as vice chairman of the foreign policy committee of the Democratic Advisory Council. Unfortunately Kennedy did not take to him. Nitze was given the job of assistant secretary for international security affairs in the Pentagon—the "little State Department," as it was known. There his deputy was to be William Bundy, Acheson's son-in-law, who had become something of a cause celebre while working at the CIA as the focal point for the agency's resistance to an attack by McCarthy. He was the brother of national security adviser McGeorge Bundy, who had once edited a collection of Acheson's speeches.[12]

Robert McNamara's appointment as secretary of defense came not at Acheson's recommendation but at Lovett's. In foreign policy terms McNamara was something of an unknown quantity. He lacked any prior association with either Kennedy or, except for his wartime experience, the substantive issues of defense policy. Initially it was assumed that his main impact would be to improve the management of the Pentagon, considered to be unruly, wasteful, and in dire need of a firm hand. It was notorious both for the amount of money it consumed and the intensive rivalry between the three services as they jockeyed for roles and resources. McNamara had worked at the Ford Motor Company since the war and had only just been appointed president when the call came from Washington. Soon McNamara was making his presence felt throughout the whole range of national security policy. In part this was because of the sheer force of his personality and the clarity of his thinking; in part it was also because of the quality of the people he recruited to the Pentagon and his readiness to back their initiatives.

The people who mattered most to Kennedy in the development of foreign policy were those closest to him, working in the White House. McGeorge Bundy came from Harvard to bring formidable intellectual powers to his job as the president's assistant for national security affairs. A precocious talent who was born into the foreign policy establishment and appointed dean of arts and humanities at Harvard when only thirty-four, Bundy's guiding principle was a belief in intellectual excellence.[13] His mind was quick and agile, incisive in argument, even when defending what turned out to be tentative conclusions. For his deputy he accepted his old friend (going back to prewar Yale) and Cambridge associate, Walt Rostow. Rostow had become—erroneously—fixed in Kennedy's mind as the source of the compelling idea of the New Frontier.[14] Already with a reputation for volubility and eccentricity, Rostow enjoyed at the NSC "all the flexibility of a tenured member of the faculty." Within the Kennedy administration his twin enthusiasms for air power and guerrilla warfare were treated almost as an amusing affectation.[15] Yet while his personality may have led to a certain condescension, his ideas and prescriptions were still taken seriously.[16] He was soon bending Kennedy's ear over how to handle the problems of the third world and indulging his passion for counterinsurgency operations.

The moderate realists, who would become steadily more influential through the administration, initially only squeezed into more marginal positions. Kennedy had to be persuaded to make Averell Harriman, whom he considered unfashionably old, an ambassador at large, and then only on condition that he purchase a hearing aid. As wartime ambassador to the Soviet Union, Harriman had been one of the first to warn of Stalin's determination to dominate his neighborhood. His reputation now, after a well-publicized interview of Khrushchev for *Life* magazine, was of being a little too close to the Russians. He tended to mock the more avid cold warriors.[17] Harriman, for whom life seemed to have meaning only if he could get close to power, was happy to take on any job so long as he got a chance to prove his worth. Eventually Kennedy came to appreciate Harriman's substantial political and diplomatic talents, and he rose to take over Far Eastern affairs before becoming in 1963 undersecretary for political affairs. In the same way extensive lobbying was needed before George Ball was made undersecretary of state for economic affairs.

Before the end of the first year, after he had found out the hard way about the respective strengths and weaknesses of his aides, Kennedy inflicted a major shake-up on his foreign policy team, known as the "Thanksgiving Day Massacre." Bowles was the main casualty. His popularity among liberals had been sufficient to save him in the summer, when demotion was first mooted. But his poor relations with Rusk (who found it difficult to work with a deputy imposed upon him), lack of administrative competence, and diffuse contributions to policy debates led Kennedy to push him to one side, making him an ambassador at large. Ball took over the number two slot. Ball was the exception who broke the rule: a close friend of Acheson from the early 1930s, but someone who considered Acheson too much of a cold warrior; a trusted adviser to Stevenson who was constantly exasperated by Stevenson's inability to make his mind up, inattention to detail, and infatuation with the third world.

Kennedy could claim to be bringing to government individuals who could contribute to the national good because of their unique talents rather than their political commitments. After the sloth of the Eisenhower years, the country could now move forward into the New Frontier. His appointments were young—the average age of the most senior group was under fifty. There were more professors than businessmen, and a number of lawyers. Many were neophytes, without much experience in foreign policy or a grasp of its nuances.

Looking at the new cabinet, House Speaker Sam Rayburn acknowledged the quality, but observed to Vice President Lyndon Johnson that "they may be every bit as intelligent as you say, but I'd feel a whole lot better about them if just one of them had run for sheriff once."[18] Criticism of intellectuals detached from the rough-and-tumble of political life and the concerns of ordinary people is a familiar response from the professionals. Those who have learned the hard way about the limits to good intentions, the need to make deals, and the necessity of keeping in touch with public opinion naturally have low expectations of those who are disdainful of such activities and seem to prefer instead to rely on analytical prowess laced with sweet reason. Kennedy himself was a consummate politician who knew all about deal making, compromises, and treating vested interests with great respect, and he saw it as his job to ensure that those aspects of power were never neglected. The overall composition of his government betrayed a careful political hand, with respect for America's regional and religious differences (though not women and blacks), and lines kept open to Republicans.

Furthermore, Kennedy ensured himself savvy and intimate political advice by appointing as attorney general his brother and former campaign manager, Robert Kennedy. Age thirty-five and never having practiced law, Bobby was intense and combative, fiercely protective of the president. After the letdown of the Bay of Pigs he gradually became much more involved in foreign affairs. To start with, at least, Robert's interest in policy was less than his interest in securing loyalty to his brother. For this reason he was cordially disliked by many in the executive branch who objected to being lectured and admonished by a young man whose position was based on no qualifications other than family ties. John understood that the terrierlike instincts of his brother could alarm and irritate his senior advisers and he counseled them against taking it too seriously. Robert served as a foil and a sounding board, an occasional conduit for awkward and sensitive observations, and the purveyor of confidential communications, including to the Kremlin.

More irritated by Robert than most was Vice President Lyndon Johnson. Their relationship had never been close and had been strained further by the last-minute dealing surrounding the nomination for the vice presidency. Johnson, whose political experience and mastery of Congress was unequaled, felt marginalized in the Kennedy White House and intimidated by the East Coast intellectuals surrounding the president. Kennedy himself had not been known as a diligent legislator during his years in Congress, putting his greatest effort into developing his national reputation. His administration might have been more successful, especially in domestic policy, if Johnson had been better integrated into the inner circle.

Two holdovers from the Eisenhower administration—J. Edgar Hoover at the FBI and Allen Dulles at the CIA—kept conservatives reassured. For similar reasons Kennedy did not attempt to purge the Joint Chiefs of Staff. After the Bay of Pigs he was left disenchanted with his military advisers and brought General Maxwell Taylor into the White House until he could make him chairman of the Joint Chiefs, replacing General Lyman Lemnitzer. In 1963 Admiral David McDonald, a politically adept officer, was selected to replace Admiral George Anderson as chief of naval operations, while General Earle Wheeler, Taylor's own recommendation and a loyal staff officer, was brought in as army chief of staff. Only the popular and belligerent Curtis LeMay as air force chief of staff—in a state of constant irritation with his colleagues, and cross with Taylor for challenging his views on the primacy of air power—was beyond Kennedy's reach (although he did have his second term restricted to one year).

STRUCTURES

Kennedy wanted a national security staff to suit his temperament as Eisenhower's staff had suited his. He was as inclined to the model of an academic faculty as his predecessor had inclined to a military staff. The case for an academic-type model, based on a comparison of the Roosevelt administration with Eisenhower's, had been made by Richard Neustadt in a book, *Presidential Power*, read by both Kennedy and Bundy.[19] This model offered influence on merit, while the military model required a clear line of command. Kennedy saw hierarchy as an obstacle, a means of filtering out the unorthodox and the awkward while giving undue prominence to the bureaucratic interests of the key agencies.

Kennedy wanted a system that extended the range of his options and did not box him in when the moment came to choose. He disliked organizational charts, elaborate committee structures, and large formal gatherings, preferring small, intense groups. So Bundy operated as a Harvard dean. Brilliant people were to be brought to Washington and given their head, with access to the president when appropriate. Junior officials had sudden calls from the president and could take part in high-level brainstorming.

An informal structure allowed a range of views to get a full airing, but there were costs. Policy making does not always lend itself to intellectual competition. This less orderly structure produced few clear and properly considered recommendations. Hard questions of interests and priorities were addressed, and options assessed, without adequate evidence or time for deliberation. There were soon complaints that the ad hoc approach made for inadequate record keeping and poor circulation of information, with nobody quite clear on whether the president knew all he needed to know or exactly what he had decided.

Even Bundy soon got frustrated with this disorderly way of doing business. He complained to Kennedy that they rarely met for supposedly regular meetings and when they did he was as often as not treated to a tirade against press leaks. Sudden surges of NSC meetings were followed by prolonged fallow periods. Papers were demanded and never read. Topics of utmost fascination one moment were forgotten the next.[20] Bundy knew better than to expect the president to change his habits, but he understood that the system would work only with a stronger and more cohesive NSC staff able to act quite explicitly as the president's agents in their dealings with the rest of the government.

As we shall see, one result of this policy-making structure was that issues tended to be defined by enthusiasts only then to be moderated by Kennedy as he began to appreciate their implications. He was thus content to let Walt Rostow lead in the design of policies to defeat communism in underdeveloped areas while Dean Acheson led on the continuing containment of communism in Europe. In both cases this resulted in policies with an alarming logic, which the president himself never quite embraced but took time to work out how to resist.

II

BERLIN AND NUCLEAR STRATEGY

5

The New Strategy

ROBERT MCNAMARA ENTERED THE PENTAGON as something of a whirlwind, firing off detailed questions in all directions. His capacity to digest information, zoom in on discrepancies, compute costs, and assess alternatives astonished and alarmed subordinates. The military appeared as amateurs in his presence, fumbling for answers to questions that had never been asked before, expected to explain their programs without recourse to the normal slogans or a sense of what the political marketplace would bear. He was the best briefed, the most articulate, and the most decisive. Whatever deep and intense emotions welled up inside as he confronted his awesome responsibilities, they did not show. He intended to cope through the disciplined application of reason and a readiness to accept a leadership role. It was not long before this extraordinary figure—an "IBM on legs"—became the most remarked upon and praised of Kennedy's appointments.[1] The force of his personality and his activism, in contrast to Dean Rusk's self-effacing restraint, allowed McNamara, almost by default, to extend his influence well beyond the Pentagon.

For his staff he looked to like-minded people. The recruitment drive started with Charles Hitch, director of the Economics Division at the RAND Corporation. McNamara read his *The Economics of Defense in the Nuclear Age* and detected immediately a kindred spirit, with the same analytical, quantitative approach to management.[2] Hitch was appointed Pentagon comptroller. Hitch in turn recruited from RAND an intense young analyst, Alain Enthoven, as his deputy. Enthoven was familiar with all the current ideas about strategic forces and was a keen exponent of RAND's analytical techniques. Joined by other RAND alumni, they began to enrage the military as they dismissed cherished beliefs and expensive programs with an analytical flourish. "Their initial position," recalled one of their victims, "was that military people were border-line literate at best and communicated by animal noises."

That these smart young whiz kids, claiming to understand national security better than battle-hardened professionals, were quite exasperating was one of the few things upon which the various chiefs of staff could agree. General Thomas White, after his retirement as air force chief of staff, referred scathingly to "pipe-smoking, tree-full-of-owls type of so-called professional 'defense intellectuals' who have been brought into this nation's capital." The air force, which had established RAND in the 1940s, became so irate with its products in government that in September 1961 they issued a directive prohibiting RAND from contracting with other government agencies without air force approval. This was quashed with support from McNamara's office.[3]

Yet the broad outlines of the strategy they were promoting were not controversial. They could be discerned in the deluge of task force reports, think tank analyses, official briefings, and individual submissions circulating around Washington in late 1960 and early 1961. One of Kennedy's campaign themes had been the need for a stronger defense. On the assumption that the Russians were racing ahead in missile production, the Americans had to accelerate their own even as they also pushed extra dollars into nonnuclear forces.

CHOOSING TARGETS

Despite the surge in missile production, military policy was to be geared more to limited wars than nuclear exchanges. Nuclear forces would be designed more to survive a Soviet first strike than to inflict one upon the enemy, and so submarine-based forces were a high priority, but there was also a premium to be placed on maintaining central control at all times.[4] The first proposals stressed the importance of deterring a deliberate attack through an "ability to strike back *after* a direct Soviet attack designed to destroy our retaliatory forces"; this required reduced vulnerability of individual systems, and also action to avoid war coming about "in an irrational or premeditated fashion." The list of ways such a tragedy—judged "perhaps more likely" than a deliberate attack—might come about provides an insight into the administration's most grievous fears. The causes might be the "mistaken triggering of alert forces, by miscalculation by one side of the opponent's intentions, by irrational or pathological actions by individuals, by spread and escalation of local wars, or by nuclear attack by a minor power." These concerns were essentially prudential and defensive in nature. More controversially, and tentatively, the Pentagon was also looking for ways to influence the conduct and outcome of a nuclear war, so as to exercise some control over its impact. This theme reflected the RAND influence.[5]

This touched on the fundamental tension at the heart of the new strategy. In order to deter war it was necessary to threaten utter devastation, requiring the targeting of cities, yet should war start there would be every incentive to impose restraints and limit damage, suggesting a higher priority for military targets. Even as they recoiled at the prospect of nuclear war the analysts were drawn to its mastery as the supreme intellectual challenge. The obvious way to avoid a headlong rush to utter destruction appeared to lie in counterforce, that is, attacks on only military targets, leaving enough forces in reserve to attack more civilian targets if need be. William Kaufman was the expert on this topic, and he gave a briefing to McNamara early in his tenure at the Pentagon.[6]

McNamara was impressed and for the moment prepared to accept the logic of counterforce as the least bad way to fight a nuclear war. Furthermore, having just been briefed on the Strategic Air Command's plan for nuclear war—the Single Integrated Operations Plan (SIOP)—he was horrified by the enormous violence it contemplated. Two thousand five hundred targets were to be hit, resulting in up to 350 million deaths. Targets were to be attacked many times over with thermonuclear weapons just to be sure that they had been destroyed. Any communist country was to be hit whatever the character of the conflict that prompted the first American strike. Fallout would drift into neutral and friendly countries.[7] McNamara sensed the problem with counterforce, as did Kaufman. It offered flexibility but no surefire way to bring a war to a successful conclusion, and so contained potential for the dreaded escalation. Just as serious, it provided no answer to the question of sufficiency. Rather, it was a recipe for an arms race, for as one side proliferated targets the other would have to add extra weapons to hit them.

The full implications of this for the new strategy, therefore, depended on the state of the military balance. The Kennedy team had come to power assuming that the United States would be catching up with the Soviet Union. Little thought had been given to the policy implications of actually being ahead, other than that few political points were going to be lost by ending up with a nuclear surplus. The missile gap thesis, pushed by Kennedy as hard as anyone in 1960, had provided the main rhetorical justification for an expanded defense effort. After the Soviet Union's technical breakthroughs of 1957 it was assumed that the ICBM testing program was complete and that deployment in numbers would surely follow. That a gap existed was part of the conventional wisdom. Maxwell Taylor, a previous defender of the army line that the gap was a put-up job by the air force, stated in 1959, "Reluctantly, I have concluded that there is indeed such a gap."[8] In fact the first-generation Soviet ICBM was cumbersome and unwieldy, unsuitable for large-scale production and deployment. As successive U-2 aerial surveillance flights over Soviet territory failed to find any missile bases, those who suspected that this was because there were none or very few grew in confidence. The air force continued to insist that the missiles must be there and that the problem lay in the limited coverage of the U-2s or the Soviet capacity for camouflage and deception. Unfortunately the U-2 flight over Plesetsk, which was suspected of being the first operational site and so able to clarify the precise configuration of Soviet deployments, was shot down by Soviet air defenses in May 1960. The analysts were left in the dark: pictures from the first Discoverer satellites, of August and December 1960, were suggestive but not conclusive. The debate was not yet over.[9]

The missile gap did not suddenly come to an end at the start of the new administration, although Robert McNamara managed to give that impression. On entering office he gave the air force intelligence chief the opportunity to persuade him that the sanguine view expressed by the CIA (which still assumed a gap of sorts) was wrong. Together they reviewed the old photographs, and McNamara concluded that the CIA was right. In his first meeting with the Pentagon press corps, failing to grasp the ways of journalism, he observed that he had looked into the matter and that, though the information was tentative, the United States was in neither an inferior position nor a superior one.[10] When this came out as a disavowal of claims made during the campaign the administration moved quickly to insist that the only reason why there would be no gap in the future was that it was moving so quickly to remedy matters.

However disingenuous this might have been, there was certainly no reason for Kennedy to suppose that the strategic balance was particularly favorable. That this was so was only suspected in June and confirmed in September. Until then the best judgment was that matters were not as bad as they might have been or as the air force claimed. The estimate in use in January 1961 was that by the middle of the year the Russians would have 50–150 ICBMs, while the United States would have 36 ICBMs. By mid-1963 the numbers were to be 200–400 ICBMs to 340, respectively.[11] This may have vindicated Eisenhower but hardly justified complacency. Certainly Kennedy assumed for the first months of his presidency that there was little he could do about the retaliatory capability of the Soviet Union.

NATO

Something had to be done about NATO's assumption that because it could not afford to match the conventional strength of the Warsaw Pact, it had no choice but to deter war by threatening to "go nuclear." Without a useable superiority, the new administration judged such threats extraordinarily rash. This was not even a matter of interagency debate. The State Department was explicit in its input into the new defense budget: nonnuclear forces had to be built up, including those of allies, to avoid a rush to nuclear use. The Pentagon agreed. The White House could see no real opposition to this drive for extra flexibility.[12] It all seemed self-evident until the moment came when the allies had to be persuaded.

In Europe, American motives were suspect. The demand for flexibility and additional nonnuclear forces was seen as a means of uncoupling

American nuclear forces from the defense of Europe, thereby weakening its deterrent effect. This was in addition to the extra demands that would be placed on them to find the extra resources to increase conventional forces. Most countries did not share the administration's sense of urgency or of the inadequacy of existing procedures and provisions.[13] To counter the presumption that the Americans were preparing to renege on their commitment to use nuclear weapons on behalf of allies, Kennedy found himself accentuating the nuclear guarantee rather than playing it down. When he spoke to France's President de Gaulle in early June he stuck to the standard formula: If the Soviet Union looked as though it could over-run Europe, "US must strike first with nuclear weapons." An attack on Europe "would be physically and automatically an attack on us."[14]

NATO plans did not assume that as soon as war began, all-out nuclear exchanges would immediately follow. General Lauris Norstad, supreme allied commander, Europe (SACEUR), had been arguing the need to raise the nuclear threshold to enforce a "pause" that would give diplomacy a chance. The danger lay, as Norstad tried to explain to Dean Acheson, in pushing the case for extra general-purpose forces too hard. Acheson disagreed. He was ostensibly in charge of a study group charged by Kennedy with setting the outlines for a new NATO strategy, but there was little he needed to study.[15] All he required was time to set out his thoughts and circulate them around the bureaucracy. The report, "A Review of North Atlantic Problems for the Future," was submitted in March and approved on 21 April as National Security Action Memorandum 40. The importance of the Atlantic alliance was reasserted and Europe was encouraged to get closer together to provide a more coherent partner for the United States. Military priorities should be shifted away from preparations for general war and toward the more likely contingencies that would not require or deserve a nuclear response.

Nuclear forces should be a lower priority for the allies as well as the United States. Britain was an established member of the nuclear club and France had just joined; there was concern that they could complicate American planning for the most extreme contingencies and so should be subject to American veto and control. Acheson was quite prepared to push the British out of the nuclear business and frustrate French attempts to get properly into it. This in turn should prevent the Germans from even thinking about becoming a nuclear power. Such considerations raised rather than lowered the importance of the nuclear guarantee to the allies, but the allies also had to realize that it was incredible to expect early recourse to nuclear weapons, which is why they also had a stake in stronger conventional forces that would enable NATO to prove its determination.

Unfortunately Acheson, the champion of NATO, had paid little heed to the change in relations between the United States and Western Europe since the Truman administration. Then the allies, fearful that the cold war was about to turn hot, were grateful to both Truman and Acheson for their readiness to take responsibility for European security. In 1950 North Korean aggression was seen either as a distraction from or as a dry run for something similar in Europe. Perilous times called for a major rearmament effort. By 1961 they had no desire to return to those fraught days. Stalin was long dead, the "years of maximum peril" had come and gone, and Eisenhower had taught them how a long haul could justify less painful levels of military expenditure. They had adjusted to massive retaliation and refused to be bothered about disparities in conventional forces so long as the risks of nuclear war continued to impress themselves on Moscow. In January 1961 the NATO Council cut the number of active divisions allocated to the central front. According to this view, the key to deterrence and alliance was that the Americans tied their fate and their nuclear arsenal closely to that of Europe. Anything that might break this link was a threat to both.

To the Americans a line of reasoning that presented a strengthening of conventional forces as undermining deterrence and signaling a reduced commitment to European security was bizarre. Christian Herter, Eisenhower's last secretary of state, had already made the point that Americans would be loath to use nuclear weapons first, even in the course of a major European war. It seemed to be self-evident that regular recourse to threats to initiate a nuclear catastrophe did not constitute a sensible strategy. When Acheson began to evangelize along these lines in Europe he was greeted with considerable suspicion. Soon alliance officials were debating what they found most irritating: the brash Pentagon whiz kids, with minimal political judgment, speaking in a mysterious, quasi-scientific language of matters they were too young to understand, or the imperious Acheson accusing them of flaccidity and parsimony in the face of a dire threat. Their irritation became mingled with alarm as the allies attempted to get the measure of yet another developing crisis over Berlin.

6

To Vienna and Back

IN EARLY JUNE 1961 Kennedy met Khrushchev for a brief summit in Vienna. Expected to set the scene for improved relations, it ended with talk of war. The previous attempt at summit diplomacy, in Paris in May 1960, had also ended in acrimony when Khrushchev walked out because of Eisenhower's refusal to apologize for the U-2 incident.[1] For those who believed that the large issues of the cold war could only be resolved through high-level diplomacy, this was a frustrating time.

After Paris Khrushchev publicly decided to wait for a new administration before any more initiatives. He assumed that this stance helped Kennedy defeat Nixon. Then, as a gesture of goodwill, after the inauguration he released two U.S. airmen whose RB-47 reconnaissance plane had been shot down in the summer of 1960 after straying into Soviet airspace. In return, one of Kennedy's first decisions was to lift a ban on the import of Soviet crabmeat. The point of all of this, as far as Khrushchev was concerned, was to create a climate in which the issue of Berlin, and Germany more generally, could be dealt with once and for all. Kennedy, however, saw the Berlin issue as treacherous and wanted instead to work on agreements to reduce the dangers of nuclear war.

TEST BAN AND BACK CHANNELS

Kennedy was ready to address the nuclear issue through agreements on disarmament and arms control. Unfortunately, the most dynamic area of military technology—long-range missiles—was not obviously susceptible to control. From everything that Khrushchev had said in recent years, including boasts about missiles coming off the production line like sausages, there was no reason to suppose that he was looking for anything other than a huge arsenal. The Americans were in turn stepping up missile production. More promising, and where discussions had been active and focused, was the question of nuclear testing. There were, as we shall see, a number of reasons for the failure of the Vienna summit. Other than differences in temperament and tactics, one critical factor was that the two leaders were working on different agendas.

Kennedy was convinced of the hazards of radioactive fallout resulting from atmospheric tests and worried by the possibility of more countries entering the nuclear club.[2] He had decided not to resume nuclear testing but to stick with the moratorium on future tests, agreed to by Moscow in the fall of 1958; he would continue with the negotiations in Geneva and attempt to ban the tests altogether. Unconvinced that a test ban would jeopardize U.S. nuclear security, so long as the Russians were placed under similar restraint, he was aware that the crunch issue was whether a treaty would be verifiable. Under Eisenhower this issue had almost closed down negotiations. The military and the Atomic Energy Commission, backed by anti-ban scientists, produced nonnegotiable positions and scare stories, such as the idea that the Soviet Union might be able to dig a hole large enough to muffle the seismic signals of an exploding nuclear weapon. To prevent cheating, the U.S. position was that at least twenty annual on-site inspections were required to check on any suspicious seismic events on Soviet territory. The most Moscow was prepared to offer was three.

The argument against a resumption of testing was simple: Internationally it would be judged as a blow to peace, and so a public relations disaster.[3] Kennedy accepted this, with the proviso that he could not sustain a posture of no testing and no treaty indefinitely. Furthermore, he was advised that a test ban was the best means of improving relations with the Soviet Union and that this was also Moscow's view.[4] To get a breakthrough in negotiations, Kennedy therefore began to explore possible compromises, such as reducing the minimum number of inspections.[5]

Unfortunately the Soviet delegation to the talks showed no interest in moving matters forward. Content to present itself as the champion of disarmament, Moscow was unwilling to offer serious concessions to obtain an agreement, especially if this involved opening up any aspect of the Soviet security apparatus to prying Western eyes. As this became apparent the Joint Chiefs, backed by McNamara, pressed for an early resumption of underground nuclear tests. Kennedy demurred. If a resumption of tests was unavoidable, he preferred to wait until an international event—he mentioned Berlin—justified it. He hoped to generate international pro-disarmament pressure against Moscow and achieve a consensus on the proposition that the risk of the diffusion of nuclear power to a range of countries justified a push for a treaty.[6]

With official channels unable to generate a breakthrough, Kennedy decided to try an unofficial channel. Two foreign policy bureaucracies locked into interminable exchanges of long-established positions offended his activist tendencies. When dealing with such a centralized system as the Soviet Union, whose diplomats were grandmasters in the art of repeating the official line until it was altered from above, nothing could be changed except by the man at the top. He therefore looked for intermediaries who could put him in direct contact with Khrushchev. The Soviet ambassador to Washington, Mikhail "Smiling Mike" Menshikov, was generally considered second-rate. More promising was Aleksei Adzhubei, editor of *Izvestia* and Khrushchev's son-in-law. Kennedy granted him a number of interviews. Khrushchev appreciated the favors granted his family, and an uncut transcript of a November 1961 interview was published in the Russian newspaper. This allowed Kennedy to talk directly to some of his pet themes and demonstrate sympathy for Soviet concerns. But this could never be a secret channel and no deals could be arranged. In addition, Ambassador Llewellyn Thompson advised that Adzhubei was anti-American and a ruthless careerist: Adzhubei worried that an image as an "American boy" might affect his political ambitions.[7]

For deal making, Kennedy eventually opted for a curious channel, through his brother Robert, to Georgi Bolshakov, a friend of Adzhubei, who worked for Soviet military intelligence in Washington under the cover of the TASS news agency. The first meeting, arranged by a mutual acquaintance, took place on 9 May 1961, and they stayed in regular contact for the next eighteen months. Both appeared to have enjoyed the other's company and trusted the integrity of the mode of communication. The association was based, however, on a misapprehension. Robert incorrectly assumed Bolshakov to be "Khrushchev's representative" searching for a direct route to the president.[8] In fact the connection was viewed with suspicion by Bolshakov's superiors.[9] So while Robert had the confidence of his brother, Bolshakov was in no position to explore innovative approaches to tricky problems. He could do little more than pass on important messages. With not even Kennedy's closest aides, such as Bundy and Sorensen, initially aware of the existence of this back channel, there were no independent checks on the reliability of the messages received or the wisdom of those transmitted.

The first meeting came after the Bay of Pigs and intimations from Foreign Minister Andrei Gromyko that Moscow might still be interested in a summit. Robert told Bolshakov that, despite the debacle, the Soviet leadership should not underestimate the new president. If necessary, he could be tough, but he wanted to follow a more progressive foreign policy and hoped for a summit that focused on a test ban. To move the stalled Geneva negotiations along he was prepared to accept a minimum of ten inspections, so long as it appeared as a Soviet proposal.

For Khrushchev the most important piece of news to emerge from this unexpected report from Bolshakov was that Kennedy remained interested in a summit. There was a quick move to confirm the meeting, but Khrushchev did not back this with any positive gestures. The Kennedys might be able to circumvent their bureaucracy, but Bolshakov was the creature of his, and so his replies had been officially crafted to reflect the current line: moderately positive about Laos, tough on Berlin, and unyielding on a test ban. He repeated the Soviet line that any oversight body for a test ban should be run by a troika, representing in equal measure the Western and Soviet blocs and the third world.

Already wondering whether to compromise on this question, Kennedy got his brother to meet with Bolshakov again on 21 May. Robert once more stressed the importance of improving US-Soviet relations and now offered another concession: The president would accept a troika so long as the Soviet Union would give up a right of veto. That is, the United States would not mind who was on the controlling body so long as it could not be stopped from conducting inspections wherever required. He even indicated that he understood Russian concerns about German revanchism, although he did not suggest that the essential position on Berlin was changed.[10]

Meanwhile Khrushchev had also decided on the advantages of informal channels of communication, but he trusted his message to his preferred intermediary, Ambassador Thompson, rather than Bolshakov. On 23 May he took Thompson aside during an ice skating revue in an attempt to make sure that the administration understood his summit agenda. Khrushchev warned that without an agreement on Berlin by that fall, they would take unilateral action later in the year. The message was clear: A breakthrough in disarmament negotiations was impossible until the problem of Berlin was resolved.[11]

The tone alarmed Kennedy. Back went Robert to find out from Bolshakov what it all meant and tell him that the president, having tried to be conciliatory only to be rebuffed, was now losing patience. He would be obliged to take a tougher line than intended when he spoke to Congress in a couple of days. Nonetheless, he was still looking for a constructive summit.[12] On May 25 Kennedy announced further measures to improve conventional forces and an expanded fallout shelter program, as well as setting as a national objective the placing of a man on the moon by the end of the decade. The latter was a last-minute decision and not the result of any conviction as to the value of space exploration. Rather, Kennedy saw the way that Khrushchev had used April's first successful manned space flight by Yuri Gagarin to bolster national prestige, and decided that he had better follow suit. He was being drawn into competition with Moscow rather than cooperation.

TO THE SUMMIT

In late May, as he sat at the family compound at Hyannis Port, his forty-fourth birthday celebration marred by increasing back pain, Kennedy immersed himself in the mass of briefing materials provided for the upcoming summit, complete with detailed position papers on key issues and psychological profiles of Khrushchev. The composite picture of Khrushchev to emerge was of a crude peasant with opinions on everything, a mischievous charmer one moment and a loud bully the next, a student of power with a tendency to gamble and push his luck, a committed Marxist who was always prepared to bargain. In short, the Soviet leader was quite unpredictable and often deliberately so.[13]

Khrushchev had decided on a hard line. His grasp of American politics was simplistic. He tended to see it as a struggle between aggressive militarists and sober realists. The basic objective of Soviet policy had to be to keep the first group out of power. The second group was distinguished by respect for Soviet strength and so could, with the right combination of bullying and blandishments, be persuaded to adopt reasonable policies. Kennedy fell into this second group, but his administration was divided and he was surrounded by hard-liners. The use of a back channel indicated to Khrushchev just how hemmed in the president was by his own government. Crucially, Khrushchev viewed this as a symptom of weakness. He assessed Kennedy as young, inexperienced, and apparently inept, a man who took the line of least resistance, yielding most to whoever put him under the greatest pressure. This explained why he had embarked on the Cuban adventure and had failed to see it through. Against the advice of his America watchers, Khrushchev decided that he could get the breakthroughs over Berlin he so badly needed by applying pressure himself. Rather than offer inducements on a test ban, which he saw largely as a device to freeze in place forever the American lead in nuclear technology, Khrushchev concluded that Kennedy needed to be shown that the road to détente began in Berlin.[14]

Kennedy had no inkling that this was Khrushchev's strategy for the summit. His own strategy was to get over to his Soviet counterpart his toughness if pressed and reasonableness if compromise was in the air, relying on his ability to charm and impress in intimate conversation. He remained convinced that areas of common interest tended to be obscured by normal diplomatic intercourse. This was also the hope of his advisers. They harbored no illusions about the nature of the Soviet state but did believe that the post-Stalin leadership was rational and anxious to get relations onto a stable footing. After the negativism of the Dulles years they believed that a summit was an opportunity to demonstrate that both powers were ready to move beyond antagonism.

Of Khrushchev's own distinctive agenda there had been warning enough, especially in his conversation with Thompson. Nonetheless, the State Department briefing materials for Vienna pictured a Soviet leader seeking respect for Soviet power but also real agreements. Kennan promised that Khrushchev would be cautious: "Whatever pressures he may be planning to exert on US in Berlin in coming period, they are not likely to be ones which, in his opinion, would present us with an overt and clear challenge" that could result in a military confrontation. Even Thompson, who had experienced Khrushchev's belligerence, still felt that "he seemed to be groping for some way out of impasse." The ambassador still believed that Khrushchev wanted a pleasant meeting, had something to offer on Laos, and probably wanted to talk about disarmament. On Berlin he judged that Khrushchev had neither a firm policy nor a timetable. He might wish to "put off crisis" until he had consolidated his position at the forthcoming Communist Party congress. The only risk, on this analysis, was that if the West sounded too warlike, then he would have to respond. Thompson, like Kennedy, believed that patience and nonprovocation suited the West.[15]

From the moment the meetings between the two leaders began in Vienna it was apparent that for Khrushchev the summit was not so much a means of rising above the cold war but of fighting it. The first exchanges between the two, on 3 June, turned into a rather futile ideological debate, exactly the sort that Kennedy had been warned to avoid. This allowed a shameless and bellicose Khrushchev to score points off Kennedy, who made a vain attempt to inject notes of reasonableness.

Kennedy introduced one of his favorite themes—the danger of escalation of war through "miscalculation." But Khrushchev, who had been educated in a different school, was not going to accept that he might ever miscalculate. That itself would constitute a sign of weakness and unreliability. Kennedy later recounted that at this point Khrushchev went "berserk."

> He started yelling "Miscalculation! Miscalculation! Miscalculation! All I ever hear from your people and your news correspondents and your friends in Europe and every-place else is that damned word, miscalculation! You ought to take that word and bury it in cold storage and never use it again! I'm sick of it!"

Kennedy made a mental note never to use the term again.[16] The idea of a direct Washington–Moscow hotline to avoid mistakes had been mooted before the summit; Kennedy did not find the moment propitious to raise it.[17]

Some progress was made on Laos, but none on a test ban, which was "struck a serious blow."[18] Khrushchev focused on Berlin, ranting about "this thorn, this ulcer," from which the United States wished to unleash war. Kennedy acknowledged the abnormality of the situation but yielded little.[19] He also got Khrushchev to reveal his limited ambitions via the Russian leader's insistence that he wanted nothing more than a "formalization of the situation resulting from the war." This included recognition of the Polish and Czech borders as well as acceptance of East German sovereignty.

After the encounter Kennedy professed himself shocked by the readiness of Khrushchev to bring the political struggle so forcefully into a personal encounter, and fearful that this revealed a readiness to pursue a radical agenda with scant regard for the risks. Yet had he not lacked confidence in his own position, Kennedy might have recognized that Khrushchev's bluster also betrayed weakness. Contrary to the Russian's boasts of the late 1950s, the military balance was moving against the Soviet Union, and it was the communist position that was crumbling in Berlin. As it was, Kennedy was most struck by Khrushchev's willingness to up the ante. According to a Russian source, Khrushchev urged Kennedy, in a remark that disappeared from both the Russian and American transcripts, to "let the war be better now, before the emergence of new, even more terrible means of warfare."[20] He certainly insisted that it was up to the United States "to choose peace or war." Kennedy warned that it would be "a cold winter." In practice the temperature was already rising fast.

7

The Berlin Anomaly

KENNEDY FELT THAT HE HAD BEEN AMBUSHED by Khrushchev on Berlin at the summit, though that was the result of American wishful thinking as much as Soviet tactics. Khrushchev had given clear notice of his priority before the start of the administration and he had done so again before the summit. Why, then, did the Americans believe that the problems of Berlin and a divided Germany could be taken slowly?

The curious situation in Berlin was the result of the agreement reached by the wartime allies on the occupation of Germany. The capital was, like the rest of the country, divided into four sectors pending a long-term settlement. The American, British, and French sectors had coalesced into West Germany and West Berlin. Because of their rights as occupying powers, the allies retained privileges in all Berlin. The West was wedded to the principle of an undivided Berlin with open access, as it was to the principle of an undivided Germany. The East feared the reunification of Germany under capitalism; the West feared the reunification of Berlin under communism.

On paper Kennedy had the most radical agenda, as the United States supported West German demands for an end to the postwar division of its country. In practice Khrushchev had the most urgent agenda, because the open city of Berlin, in the middle of East Germany, was threatening the viability of a communist state. Disaffected citizens could simply walk from one sector to the other to escape the communist world, and Berlin was also a convenient place from which to spy upon and subvert the GDR. In addition, the Soviet leader's own incessant demands had turned Berlin into a test case for his diplomacy. His campaign to hand the city over to East German rule, launched in 1958 at a time when everyone agreed that the "correlation of forces" was moving in a Soviet direction, had foundered on the West's refusal to budge and his own unwillingness to push the crisis to the point of war.

Khrushchev wanted a four-power agreement, involving a proper peace treaty with the two Germanys that recognized their distinctive characters, plus an agreement that would turn Berlin into a "free city." This would give the East legitimacy and stability, and create conditions for the gradual incorporation of Berlin into the communist system. To get this, or at least to move diplomacy in the right direction, he threatened unilateral action: a peace treaty between the Soviet Union and the German Democratic Republic (GDR). The problem for Washington was not a peace treaty in itself but any provisions within it that undermined allied rights in Berlin; also problematic was the fact that responsibility for honoring those rights would be passed over to the East German government. This would have the dual effect of putting into the driver's seat a regime that was determined to cut off West Berlin from the Federal Republic of Germany (FRG), and it would oblige the West to recognize this regime if they wished to negotiate on the matter. Khrushchev's dilemma was that he knew that this could trigger a wider war. He gambled that he could extract sufficient concessions because of the greater Western fear of war. His device to bring the crisis to a head was an ultimatum. He had set one down in November 1958 and then lifted it. At the Vienna summit he issued a new ultimatum: either progress in negotiations or a separate peace treaty by the end of the year.

Khrushchev went on the offensive for profoundly defensive reasons. To make progress he needed to be convincing about the strength and determination of the Soviet bloc, yet he needed progress because of East Germany's weakness.[1] A compromise with the West that did not address this weakness would not suffice, and a separate peace treaty setting in motion the annexation of West Berlin risked war. The East Germans, who perhaps did not appreciate just how much Khrushchev had been bluffing in his boasts about Soviet missile production, were ready to go the distance and expected Khrushchev to do the same. They had, however, developed the alternative fallback option of a barrier along the sector border within Berlin.

Unfortunately for the communists, the greater the sense of crisis they generated in order to put pressure on the West, the more they added to the weakness of the GDR. Though they did not want to acknowledge that people might want to escape from a socialist paradise, far too many trained and educated people were leaving. The population of the GDR had fallen by two million since 1949. This was having an unsettling effect on those who were thinking of going and on those who preferred to stay, thereby creating a risk within East Germany of riots and even insurrection. Food shortages in 1960 following enforced collectivization had added to the urge to leave. The prospect that the bolt-hole would be closed encouraged potential emigrants to leave at the first opportunity. In February 1961 13,576 East Germans escaped via this route, almost a 40 percent increase over February 1960. In March the number reached 16,098.[2]

KENNEDY'S APPROACH

The logical solution to the Berlin crisis, one that eventually came about, was to reinforce the division of the city to match that of Germany as a whole. But this was not an outcome that the responsible allied powers— Britain, France, and the United States—could readily embrace, let alone propose, so long as the federal German government in Bonn insisted on the principle of reunification. It was hard to argue for people being forced to live within a closed, communist state. Chancellor Konrad Adenauer, of the Federal Republic of Germany, was not actually in a great hurry to unify his country. His core objective was to get Germany, rehabilitated as a "normal" country, and his chosen method was close cooperation with the West. In Germany this was criticized for accentuating the differences with the GDR and so pulling the country further apart. The alternative was a private, neutralist deal with the GDR to bring Germany together and end its uncomfortable status as the likely battleground for a third world war. In his struggle against this approach Adenauer had insisted that the extra strength Germany gained from its ties with the West was an essential prerequisite to reunification. This required the allies to keep faith with this objective even though everyone understood it could not be realized in the short-term. To have it disavowed by the allies in the name of a wider rapprochement with Moscow would leave Adenauer politically exposed and, he would insist, reinforce the neutralists. To keep Germany tied to its new moorings with the West therefore required that the allies pay homage to the myth of reunification, disavow attempts to single out Germany for special treatment (for example, by denying it access forever to nuclear weapons), and promise not to negotiate behind its back. Adenauer was dogged constantly by anxiety that he was about to be let down, and bombarded his allies with demands for reassurance, which by and large they gave him, although with increasing irritation that he never seemed to believe them.

President Charles de Gaulle of France gave the most sympathetic ear to Adenauer's concerns, because he saw in Adenauer's worries an opportunity to reduce Anglo-Saxon influence over the Continent's affairs. He took the view that nobody wanted to go to war over Berlin, including the Russians, and therefore the most prudent and productive course was to persevere with established positions and take a firm stand against all provocations. Prime Minister Harold Macmillan of Britain, by contrast, worried that regular Soviet assertiveness would at some point force a showdown. He was haunted by the possibility of a third world war breaking out over the fate of a country that had recently been a bitter enemy. For some time, and to Adenauer's increasing exasperation, Britain had searched for some formula that would remove this irritant from an otherwise stable Europe.[3]

Kennedy was inclined to the British view. It was for this reason that of all the crises he might face, Kennedy feared one in Berlin most. This was the American commitment most likely to lead to nuclear war. American troops had fought and died to get to Germany. American airmen had helped the city survive Stalin's siege of 1948–49. The city had acquired a special significance as a capitalist oasis in a communist desert. It was also indefensible by conventional military means, with only a small garrison in the city and reinforcement vulnerable to communist interference, leaving military options ranging from the ineffectual to the unpalatable. The management of this problem would have an impact on every aspect of the Atlantic alliance, from the relations with individual allies to long-term NATO strategy. It was not surprising that Kennedy wanted to postpone a full-blown crisis over Berlin until he was ready to deal with it.

As a senator, he had declared Adenauer, born in 1876, to be a "shadow of the past" and his policy "too rigid and unyielding." He instinctively spoke of responsibilities to West Berlin rather than to Berlin as a whole, and considered reunification a long-term goal "not in the cards for many years." Dwelling on this issue, he suggested, made it difficult to develop a dialogue with Moscow. These were the sort of views Adenauer feared most; a 1960 headline indicated that the German government would prefer a Nixon victory.[4]

As president, Kennedy was prepared for a courteous working relationship with Adenauer but did not want to become ensnared by Berlin. The line in January was that the new administration wanted time to look at policy toward Germany and Berlin with fresh eyes. Alternative approaches were to be explored. Meanwhile a reference to Berlin was removed from the final draft of Kennedy's first State of the Union address. In March, when explaining to Willy Brandt, the mayor of West Berlin, why his administration had said so little on the subject, Kennedy observed that "it was better . . . to leave the launching of any challenges to Khrushchev." That same month, in Berlin, Averell Harriman reported that Washington did not consider itself bound by any previous negotiations with Moscow over Berlin. From now on all discussions "would begin from the start." This removed from the table the few concessions that Eisenhower had been prepared to make, but in opening up new areas for discussion it could also presage a softer line. Bowles gave the latter possibility support a few days later by stressing that the United States wished to make it clear to Moscow "that we are prepared at all times to negotiate any issue or difference that arises between us."[5]

ACHESON'S APPROACH

Yet despite the diplomatic possibilities all this implied, Kennedy had already made a decision that was to ensure that policy on Berlin became harder rather than softer. When he asked Dean Acheson to think about alliance policy in general he also requested that Acheson address the specific problem of Berlin. This was a fateful decision, for when the crisis rushed in on the president over the summer, Acheson had set the agenda as to how the administration debate ought to develop. Options on the most sensitive and dangerous issue of the cold war were taken down and presented to the president from an accessible and well-maintained shelf.

Acheson believed a Soviet challenge was imminent and that when it came a robust and unequivocal stand was essential. He saw no need for a reappraisal of Berlin policy except to find ways to toughen it up. When, in November 1958, Khrushchev had put down his first, six-month ultimatum on Berlin, Acheson interpreted this in the gravest terms and began to demand preparations for war. The deadline was a clever device, he warned, designed to allow those who could not countenance war over Berlin to develop a case for compromise. To counter such views Acheson argued that it was President Eisenhower's duty to convince Moscow that the United States was "genuinely determined to keep traffic to Berlin open, at whatever risk, rather than abandon the people and permit the whole Western position to crumble." To this end he urged a conspicuous and effective military buildup.[6]

Eisenhower had disagreed. Relying on the Soviet leader's fear of a thermonuclear conflict to keep him cautious, he offered Khrushchev no concessions and procrastinated. This worked. Khrushchev dropped his ultimatum, and for a while, infused with the "spirit of Camp David," East–West relations even began to improve.

Acheson drew no lessons from this episode. He was not given to second thoughts, nor was he the sort of elder statesman who offered a judicious assessment of alternative approaches. He knew from experience that policy reviews could perform an important didactic function, educating the bureaucracy as much as refining options. His influence within the bureaucracy was already strong, touching senior figures who were close to him, including Rusk and Bundy, as well as the two key desk officers. Paul Nitze acquired responsibility for Berlin in the Pentagon, while another acolyte, Foy Kohler, was assistant secretary of state for European affairs.

Why did Kennedy put a known hard-liner into such a crucial position when he personally was in favor of flexibility and negotiations? It may be that he wanted to know what the hard line looked like before making up his own mind.[7] He was also probably still somewhat in awe of Acheson, whose knowledge and experience were undoubted, and he admired the clarity of his views, often in preference to the vaguer fare that came from liberals. Giving Acheson this role was itself a signal of Kennedy's readiness to take a tough stance, but it was also a policy choice in itself, as it allowed Acheson to set the terms of a vital debate and even qualified him at times to speak for the administration.

At the start of April 1961 Harold Macmillan made his first visit to Washington to meet the new, and to his eye rather young, president. Macmillan had never concealed his enthusiasm for high-level dialogue with Moscow, exactly the sort of approach to which Acheson was adamantly opposed. Prior to the meeting Bundy pronounced Acheson's first memorandum on the minimal possibilities for a settlement "first-rate" and urged the president to "press hard for British firmness at this moment of truth."[8] Acheson was asked to brief the prime minister on why he considered confrontation more likely than compromise. At first the British were relieved that Acheson did not consider the issue of whether it was an East German or a Russian who stamped a pass at a border control deserving of a military response and that he thought a nuclear response would be reckless even if the interference was serious. But British unease soon set in over Acheson's ideas on an appropriate response to a major challenge. This was to prepare for a "test of will" on the ground, requiring the dispatch of a division through to Berlin, with one division in reserve.[9]

Macmillan, along with Lord Home, his foreign secretary, was appalled by Acheson's uncompromising manner and "bloodcurdling" discussion of military options. Their alarm was shared by others present, including Averell Harriman and Adlai Stevenson, as they watched Acheson recycle his old thoughts. Nonetheless, Kennedy did not contradict him during the meeting nor repudiate his views thereafter. Instead he was effectively left in charge of Berlin policy.[10]

Soon after this encounter Acheson was sent off to calm down Adenauer. The German chancellor was becoming progressively restless about trends in American policy, including the readiness to negotiate with Moscow on every topic. He feared that the move to a strategy of flexible response would allow the Warsaw Pact to treat German territory as an exploratory battlefield. Deterrence required that Moscow be left in no doubt that an attack on any part of Germany would trigger a nuclear war. Adenauer was also sensitive to the legacy of the Second World War, only fifteen years past. The Eichmann trial in Israel, where the former top Nazi was being tried for his war crimes, and the interest generated by William Shirer's *The Rise and Fall of the Third Reich* in the United States left Germans unsure as to whether they could ever be accepted as good allies by their old enemies. Americans found it difficult to put out of their minds the damage that Germany had done and the menace it might once again become.

When the two men met on 9 April, Acheson could provide little reassurance on flexible response because this was the direction in which he too was trying to push American policy. He was more successful in convincing the chancellor that the new president was not about to sell out German interests. Acheson's own involvement proved a welcome factor, Adenauer confiding in his old colleague that "you have lifted a stone from my heart."[11] A few days later Adenauer visited Washington to meet Kennedy. He took care to question neither the policy of attempting to develop new channels of communication between Washington and Moscow nor the current preference for a low-key stance on Berlin. He just wanted to know what would happen if a Soviet challenge did materialize and whether his country could become more directly involved in the contingency planning rather than wait to hear the results of American, British, and French deliberations. He did not get full answers.

Then came the Bay of Pigs. The international reaction was scathing. Acheson described how in Europe it reflected "the sort of unbelieving attitude that somebody might have as he watched a gifted amateur practicing with a boomerang and suddenly knocking himself cold. They were amazed that so inexperienced a person should play with so lethal a weapon."[12] This was exactly the sort of move—gambling on the basis of insufficient strength and then abandoning the operation before it was complete—that made Acheson despair. He was not at all surprised when Kennedy was given a hard time at Vienna.

CRISIS MODE

Khrushchev's stance at Vienna added to the credibility of Acheson's position, as he alone had warned that Khrushchev was itching for a confrontation. The president had been left shocked by Khrushchev's belligerence and worried that his stance had not been robust enough. An air of crisis began to envelop Washington. Soviet and East German propaganda added to this, anticipating enthusiastically the end of the "occupation regime" in the West. At Vienna the Russians had handed over an aide-mémoire that demanded a settlement in "no more than six months." Its publication on 10 June underlined the extent of Khrushchev's commitment.[13]

There was a sudden shift in gear. Having neglected the issue for the first months of his presidency, now Kennedy "thought about little else," saturating himself in all the details of policy on Berlin, from military contingency plans to diplomatic initiatives.[14] This revealed an admirable sense of responsibility but was not necessarily wise. Having spent insufficient time on the problem before Vienna, he could not suddenly grasp the full ramifications of this long diplomatic saga. His loss of confidence in the State Department did not help. After reinforcing his hope that a showdown could be deferred and leading him to expect a much more conciliatory Khrushchev, it now did not noticeably change gear at all. The Foreign Service officers who had been dealing with this problem for years and had seen ultimata come and go saw little wrong with a policy based on reiterating past positions. Moreover, these positions had been worked out with allies who would soon take umbrage at unilateral shifts in policy.

Rusk later recalled trying with his staff to impress upon their White House counterparts "the importance of diplomacy, the rules of protocol, the process of negotiation, the role of the United Nations and international law, but it was rough go." The secretary of state had been involved with the problem since 1945. His view was that the best course was a firm resolve to outtalk the Russians rather than outfight them. To Kennedy, this sort of dogged diplomacy seemed inappropriate when the issue had acquired such a sense of drama and urgency. It was not that he expected that Khrushchev would sign the treaty come what may; before the summit he had agreed in Paris with de Gaulle about the Soviet leader's tendency to bluff. His concern was largely that he would not be able to call the bluff without strengthening the Western position, and this in turn required swinging the American people behind a tough stance.[15] His political task was to convey the seriousness of the situation (hence his gloomy comments to journalists) and to ensure that the stakes were defined in an appealing way, as the defense of freedom in the West rather than arcane aspects of four-power agreements.

The president's exasperation with the State Department made itself felt in the affair of the response to the Soviet aide-mémoire. He expected the Berlin task force to produce a quick reply, but for some reason it failed to materialize until mid-July. One reason was that the White House kept losing the draft response. Another was that the draft itself was essentially and unavoidably a rehash of established positions, negotiated with three allied countries that had distinctive and in some respects opposing views. The White House wanted something less dry, so Sorensen provided an alternative draft. The diplomats found this wholly inappropriate, full of "flowery language that read like an inaugural address." They pressed to get the "exciting adverbs and purple prose toned down," adding to the delay. Even then it could only be used as a covering note.[16]

The episode was indicative of the extent to which the management of foreign policy was slipping away from the State Department to the White House. Rusk lacked a strong political profile. His officials were distracted by a president determined to act as his own desk officer and who was clearly impatient with the tortuous requirements of negotiations among allies. McNamara, with his strong personality, was active in foreign policy formation, thereby furnishing it with a more pronounced military aspect than it had under Eisenhower. As Kennedy came to rely more upon his immediate advisers, the role of the National Security Council staff shifted from coordinators of policy to advocates.

8

A Contest of Resolve

IN MID-JUNE Acheson set out his views to the interdepartmental group on Berlin contingency planning, preliminary to the release of his final report at the end of the month.[1] His starting point was that the exercise was for real—"Khrushchev meant what he said"—and that this involved "deeply the prestige of the United States and perhaps its very survival." As there was no evident political solution available, the issue was one of "US will," and America had to be prepared to act "regardless of the opinions of our allies." When on 14 June Lord Home expressed concern that Acheson's proposed measures would all appear rather warlike, Acheson replied that was precisely the point.[2]

Defining the issue as a contest of resolve directed American efforts at the opponent's will. Acheson's analysis was that Khrushchev was under more pressure than before to act, yet with less reason to fear the consequences. He diagnosed two problems. First, contingency planning assumed that an attempt to block access to Berlin would result first in a symbolic probe and then in an attempt to send a battalion up the autobahn; blocking the move would lead to nuclear use. The flaw in this plan was that the seriousness of Western intent would become apparent only after the critical Soviet decisions had been taken. In effect it was a plan for preemptive war with nothing being done first to increase credibility. Second, Khrushchev did not believe that he would be opposed with nuclear weapons.

To remedy the situation Acheson wanted an urgent boost for American credibility. If the United States was not prepared for nuclear use, then it had better not pretend that it was. The alternatives were to rely on "more luck than could be expected by any stretch of the imagination, or to withdraw from Berlin." The worst course of all would be to start and then back down. His preference was to raise the military profile of the

United States "over a period of time beginning around the first of July and timed as an increasingly somber course." Spreading out the measures would increase their effect while "excluding panic." He wanted a call-up of reserves, intensive training, extra troops and strategic aircraft moved to Europe, increases in defense budgets, and a resumption of nuclear testing. Further down the line there would be "proclamations of limited and unlimited national emergencies, supporting resolutions in the Congress, and substantial increases in the military budget. There should be movement of troops to Europe and a general alert of SAC." If this did not do the trick, the next steps would be "a garrison airlift for Berlin" and continued presentation of ground traffic at the checkpoints. Following this there could be "a military movement indicating the eventual use of tactical nuclear weapons and then strategic nuclear weapons."

The risk of these measures was that they would scare not only the Russians but also allies. When British anxiety was pointed out, Acheson observed, "If our allies had serious inhibitions against action, we had better find out. We should proceed not by asking them if they would be afraid if we said 'boo!' We should, instead, say 'boo!' and see how far they jump." Only if "the Germans buckled" would it be necessary to hold back. At least then the United States would "not have led the way to surrender."

Acheson's report was passed to Kennedy on 28 June. In the opening passage he observed that it was "not too much to say that the whole position of the United States is in the balance." The theme was then set. Negotiations were pointless unless the United States was prepared to demonstrate to Khrushchev that it was prepared to do whatever was necessary to stop him changing the status of Berlin unilaterally, and this required restoring the credibility of nuclear deterrence. This in turn required attention to the detail of preparations for a dispute over access rights. These preparations should be neither concealed nor dramatized. They should be offered to allies as a reflection of American leadership rather than as matters for consultation. Acheson took seriously the end of 1961 as a deadline for Khrushchev and assumed that little would happen before the West German elections on 17 September. By the time that a Soviet-GDR peace treaty had been concluded and before the control of access to Berlin was handed over to the GDR, he wanted Western preparations to have been completed. Following a preliminary discussion of the issues at a National Security Council meeting, the deadline set for getting military preparations in order was 15 October.[3]

ALTERNATIVES

Having told the American people about his somber meeting at Vienna, Kennedy initially made little attempt to lead public opinion on Berlin. Nixon was soon attacking him for having "talked big and backed down when the chips were down" at Vienna. This had come after Kennedy had been ready to commit American prestige at the Bay of Pigs, only to fail "at the critical moment to commit our power."[4] At a press conference on 28 June Kennedy's comments were largely Achesonian, accusing Russia of manufacturing the crisis, favoring German reunification, and indicating that a military buildup was on the way. He did, however, give a hint of possible negotiating flexibility. Polls were showing little support for soft-line policies. One in New York in early July indicated that almost 85 percent supported "standing firm," while only 3.5 percent would make concessions. Over 54 percent were prepared to go to war over Berlin, with barely 20 percent opposed.[5]

The opposition to Acheson's position was led from neither the State Department nor the Pentagon but the White House. After a meeting on 5 July with his contact at the Soviet embassy, Georgi Kornienko, Arthur Schlesinger became convinced that Moscow wanted to avoid a collision with the West over Berlin and sought a negotiated outcome. Kornienko suggested that the Americans should come up with their own ideas if they did not find Russia's proposed guarantees on maintaining the established way of life of the citizens of Berlin in a new free city satisfactory. Whether or not this was a serious diplomatic opening, the effect on Schlesinger was to help him crystallize his own misgivings about Acheson's approach.[6] It led to a memo to Kennedy.

Schlesinger drew on the lessons of the Bay of Pigs. These were, he suggested, "excessive concentration on military and operational problems and the wholly inadequate consideration of political issues," plus a tendency to define the issue as "Are you chicken or not?" He warned against allowing the debate to be polarized between a hard, tough stance and one that was "soft, idealistic, mushy, etc." The risk was that Washington, anticipating a blockade of West Berlin, would prepare hard responses only to find that these appeared "rigid and warlike" when confronted with Soviet proposals apparently offering guarantees to West Berlin.[7] Kennedy appeared grateful for an alternative line to follow and encouraged Schlesinger to develop his ideas further. This he did with the aid of Abram Chayes, legal adviser in the State Department, and Henry Kissinger, acting as a consultant to the White House on Berlin.

Chayes took his cue from a comment Kennedy had made to him: "If the issue is talking to the East Germans or having a war, we are obviously going to talk to the East Germans."[8] Kissinger, frustrated that he had not been offered a job with the administration, saw an opportunity to prove his worth. Though the president tended to dismiss him as ponderous and long-winded, Kissinger had recognized expertise on Berlin. He was also a known conservative, and so his conviction that a "refusal to negotiate" should not become "a test of firmness" was significant.[9]

Working furiously on 7 July, they produced a memo in a few hours. They sought to identify available political moves, their relationship to military action, the objectives for which nuclear war might be risked, the responses available for eventualities other than an interruption of military access to West Berlin, and how to gain the support of allies. They challenged the idea that Berlin was essentially a test of wills that had nothing in particular to do with the city itself and criticized the focus on a single contingency—the blockade of Berlin—rather than the "whole spectrum of harassments" available to the communists, though, like Acheson, they failed to mention the absolute division of Berlin as one contingency.[10] There was backing elsewhere from liberals. Bowles chipped in with a memo of his own to Rusk. Harriman, who had worked with Acheson on his report, made known his own concern about its belligerent tone.[11]

Kennedy seized the chance to change course. Rusk was asked: "Are there useful political settlements, which might not be ordinarily feasible but which might conceivably be acceptable to our allies and to the Soviets if a Berlin crisis dramatized the need for drastic measures to render the Berlin and German situation less explosive?"[12] Acheson was also asked to try his hand at "a political program" for Berlin. By arguing so strongly that the negotiations were futile, he had prompted a reaction among those who could see no point in ruling them out.

The policy framework Acheson had established was modified but not overturned. His basic assumption on negotiations was correct. The status quo suited the West and frustrated the East, and there was no halfway position that could satisfy them both. The areas where the West could offer concessions were essentially trivial. He was also correct in his assumption that Khrushchev would be deterred from taking drastic action against Berlin by the perils of war. He was, however, incorrect in his estimate of the harm that a negotiating effort might cause and the positive benefits of being seen to make the effort.[13] He also overestimated Khrushchev's readiness to take risks. Deterrence was easier than Acheson dared assume, while the search for a negotiated settlement was more barren than many of its advocates supposed.

CHOICES

Acheson made his stand on a declaration of a national emergency rather than on whether there should be a negotiating track. Such a declaration, he believed, had worked to great effect when the Korean War had begun. It now became another test of the seriousness of the American intent, the alternative to "doing it with mirrors." He was not alone in believing this necessary. At a meeting of the Interdepartmental Coordinating Group on 12 July Maxwell Taylor, now the president's military adviser, expressed the view that it was "illogical to wait until we were challenged to start our buildup. It appeared preferable to start the buildup in the expectation of the likelihood of a challenge." For this a prerequisite was an early declaration of a national emergency. The point was also made forcefully by Nitze, who reported that the Pentagon was thinking of such a declaration on 1 August, with reserve divisions being called up two weeks later and then a continued increase in military provisions. This was to get things ready for the anticipated trigger of the real crisis—the signature of a GDR-USSR peace treaty. Once the declaration had been made, future actions could be hard or soft, fast or slow, depending upon developments.

Yet, as Bundy cautioned, the declaration would be a "quantum jump." There could be no "limited" national emergency. Bundy suggested that the group think about what could be done with a later target date and no early declaration. At the NSC meeting on 13 July Rusk warned that a declaration would have "a dangerous sound of mobilization," and reminded Acheson of his earlier proposals that the first steps in any buildup should be low key.[14] He did not take the hint. This had become the litmus test of the president's readiness "to support a full program of decisive action," a means of ensuring that the gravity of the situation was fully understood.

The issue had arisen only out of a presumption that it was a legal requirement for calling up the reserves. Now McNamara, with the support of the Joint Chiefs, indicated that no declaration would be necessary before 1 September.[15] The option was killed when the NSC met on 19 July. Bundy advertised the meeting to the president as "probably the most important . . . that we have had." McNamara's intervention was critical. He saw no need for a declaration because he did not want a large reserve force on hand without a mission. Acheson still wanted something "more energetic and definite," but Kennedy kept the discussion going until it became clear that McNamara's timetable would permit a sufficiently rapid deployment in the event of a deepening crisis.

> The essential point was that the present preparations would rapidly create a force in being, in the continental U.S., of six Army and two Marine divisions. In the event of a rapidly developing crisis, appropriate numbers of these divisions could be deployed to Europe and reserve divisions called up to take their place, so that up to six divisions and supporting units could be promptly deployed as needed.

Now that policy was decided, it was agreed that allies should be informed and a nationwide address prepared for 25 July.[16]

Aware that his test would not be met, Acheson allowed his disenchantment with the mismanagement of foreign policy to show. Kennedy, who felt that those involved in the process should grumble only in private, became irritated. Moreover, Acheson's latest task for the president, a consideration of the political dimensions to the crisis, did not engage his convictions. This second report was lukewarm, lacking the cutting edge and clear sense of direction of the original report.[17] Acheson's star began to wane. He had played down negotiations and focused on the use of conspicuous military steps to deter Khrushchev from an attempt to change the status quo. Kennedy wanted steps sufficient to demonstrate resolve, but he did not want to push the crisis beyond a "point of no return." His readiness to offer negotiations was in part based on a politician's belief that there was always a deal to be done if two sides were willing to find one, but also on a politician's recognition that even if no deal was available, it was usually best to leave that call to the other side.

POLICY ANNOUNCED

The position on Berlin was announced in a broadcast speech of 25 July.[18] Kennedy warned, "We cannot and will not permit the communists to drive us out of Berlin, either gradually or by force." To prepare for any eventuality he would seek a higher defense budget, call up some reserves, procure new weapons, and enlarge the civil defense program. These military measures, however, were to be combined with diplomatic efforts. He derided the Soviet approach as claiming that "what's mine is mine and what's yours is negotiable" but promised to seek a peaceful solution, asserting a readiness "to consider any arrangement or treaty in Germany consistent with the maintenance of peace and freedom, and with the legitimate security interests of all nations." In closing he also repeated his familiar concern: "In the thermonuclear age, any misjudgment on either side about the intentions of the other could rain more devastation in several hours than has been wrought in all the wars of human history."

Given the battle that had gone into avoiding a declaration of national emergency and inserting a reference to negotiations, the liberals assumed that this would be seen as an essentially moderate speech. But it was moderate only in comparison to an extreme Acheson line. Outside the inner circle a mention of negotiations hardly appeared as a great concession, while a declaration of a national emergency had not been expected. The impression was more hard-line and militarist (especially with the alarming inclusion of a reference to civil defense). So to the dismay of liberals the military firmness was picked up on but not the offer of negotiations.[19] Politically that did not seem to have done Kennedy any harm. A thousand telegrams reached the White House by the morning, running twenty to one in favor. The Gallup Poll still showed 85 percent of Americans ready to risk war to keep U.S. troops in Berlin. Congress gave an overwhelming vote to new defense expenditures.[20]

Those who watched the nuances more than the headlines, including the Germans, noted at once the careful specification of West Berlin as the vital interest rather than the quadripartite agreement of 1945.[21] Few assumed that the speech would resolve anything. In early August Rusk met with the foreign ministers of Britain (in favor of talks for some time), France (opposed to any talks), and West Germany (not sure what it wanted). They could not agree on either the timing or the substance of an offer to Moscow. Rusk anticipated "weeks and months of confusion, tension and danger."[22]

9

The Wall

EVENTS HAD NOT TURNED OUT as Khrushchev had intended. Kennedy had not retreated after Vienna and the crisis atmosphere was just making the position in Berlin even worse. A fortune was going into keeping the East German economy afloat. This was welcome to those who worked in the West and used their high wages to buy subsidized goods in the East, but it was doing little to stem the flow of people out of the country. In July, thirty thousand moved across to the refugee camps in West Berlin, the largest monthly number since 1953. Though the East German authorities were using a variety of desperate measures to oblige people to stay put, Berlin remained a relatively open city. After Vienna, on most days around a thousand Easterners stayed behind in the West to register as refugees.

The East German leader Walter Ulbricht may have been deliberately aggravating the crisis to force Khrushchev's hand. His rhetoric tended to undermine Soviet claims that the West Berliners would barely notice a change under the "free city" proposal and encouraged East Berliners to leave. Of particular interest was a press conference of 15 June, which the Western press was encouraged to attend. When asked whether "the state boundary" would be "erected at the Brandenburg Gate," he replied:

> I understand by your question that there are men in West Germany who wish that we [would] mobilize the construction workers of the GDR in order to build a wall. I don't know of any such intention. The construction workers of our country are principally occupied with home building and their strength is completely consumed by this task. Nobody has the intention of building a wall.[1]

The result was a boost in the outflow of refugees, although most commentators took the denial at face value. The closure of the inner Berlin border was not yet policy, but Ulbricht was getting desperate. By early

July he was warning the Kremlin that "if the present situation of open borders remains, collapse is inevitable." The situation could get out of control, and by the end of the month he was publicly demanding that "all means" be used to stem the flow.

Meanwhile reports coming to Moscow from Washington indicated that the United States was developing new military options in anticipation of a Berlin crisis.[2] To preempt this Khrushchev announced on 8 July a halt to planned cutbacks of the armed forces and a one-third increase in the military budget. In ruble terms this was almost precisely the same as the $3.4 billion increase in defense spending announced by Kennedy on 25 May. It was against this backdrop that Khrushchev read Kennedy's broadcast of 25 July. John McCloy, Kennedy's disarmament negotiator, was visiting at the time and was soon treated to a harangue about this being a virtual declaration of war. Moscow stood ready to respond to all provocations. Khrushchev may well have been genuinely worried. Given his concept of the eternal struggle at the heart of the American government between militarists and moderates, he may have concluded that dangerous forces were starting to get the upper hand. Perhaps the lightweight Kennedy was not in control and was unable to back down even if he wanted to.

At the same time Kennedy's stress on the defense of West Berlin rather than allied rights in Berlin as a whole had given him an option to calm the crisis down. Until this point his planners, along with the East Germans, were gearing themselves for a separate peace treaty and control over the movement of people in and out of Berlin. Khrushchev reverted abruptly to Ulbricht's proposal for a wall. This was a fallback position. Ulbricht's first preference had been to close the air corridors, the means by which refugees were taken to their new homes in the West, but Khrushchev would allow him only a wall, provided that it could be done quickly, keeping the East German population under control and without provoking the West. It was to go "not one millimeter further" than the border. The construction process, starting with barbed wire before more permanent concrete, would allow time to assess the Western reaction. As Ulbricht's plans were well developed, he was able to get the process under way at once.[3] Just after midnight on 13 August, with Soviet forces on alert and ringed around Berlin, the East German police stopped the subways before they could travel into West Berlin and then created a physical barrier along the boundary with the West using obstacles and barbed wire. Over the next few days this barrier was strengthened. Construction of the actual wall itself did not begin until 19 August.

WESTERN SURPRISE

The West had been caught by surprise. Their best spy, Colonel Oleg Penkovsky, of the Soviet General Staff's Chief Intelligence Directorate, reported that plans were still in progress to sign a peace treaty later in the year. When he did receive a hint about the wall it was too late to contact his handlers.[4] Neither the CIA nor the State Department anticipated it. There was a precedent in 1952 for a temporary closing of borders, but Berlin seemed such a vibrant city, with much cross-border activity. Its population was known to be tempestuous. Its very physical structure, with its tall apartment blocks, requiring numerous doors and windows to be sealed, argued against attempts to cut a swath through the city. Of all the options available to the communists it seemed to carry the highest risk, for it was dependent, in the first instance, on Western restraint. Those looking would have found evidence of Ulbricht's plan, but nobody was really looking.[5] Some observers, such as Thompson, had spoken of "closing" the eastern sector boundary, but this conveyed little of the physical aspects of such an act.

The severity of the crisis facing the GDR was understood. In early July the U.S. embassy in Bonn reported how the crisis was generating growing unease among the East's population. Though the "Soviet Zone regime's current attempt to hold popular concern will probably succeed for the time being," should the tension continue to increase then the "refugee flow may increase to actual flood." An explosive response to the mean conditions of life was always in the cards, although ordinary East Germans were well aware that the possibilities of revolt and material Western support were limited.

The West's focus was on the worst case, not a wall but some sort of insurrection. The United States had failed to respond in 1953, and if it stood on the sidelines again, this "would mean end of our prestige and influence in Germany." CIA analyses indicated that there was little likelihood of an uprising—but this would increase if possibilities of "escape to the West are drastically reduced." The United States would not like to see Berlin divided, noted John Ausland of the State Department, "particularly since this might only fan the flames in East Germany." It should protest any action taken to end the refugee flow, though "so long . . . as these measures do not involve the division of Berlin and access to West Berlin from the Federal Republic is not interfered with, the US should take no countermeasures."[6]

The advice from Washington to the American embassy in Bonn was that nothing should be done to exacerbate the situation. The first version of the cable had mentioned measures to be taken in the event of an open rebellion, from statements of sympathy to a meeting of the "Big Four." Even these had been removed to avoid prior commitment. The embassy agreed with the diagnosis. The key question was whether the danger of unrest might lead Khrushchev to "hold back rather than to precipitate showdown." As the uncertain state of the popular mood appeared to be a major factor in Moscow's decisions, it was suggested that the Russians

might be reminded that so far the West had been restrained in not encouraging refugees—but this could change.[7]

By 7 August the Bonn embassy was warning that the refugee problem
was becoming so acute that this might prompt restrictive measures and
so precipitate a crisis. When Rusk replied on 12 August, the image in his
mind was still not the wall to come but the 1953 uprisings. A repetition
would be "highly unfortunate," particularly if based "on expectation of
Western military assistance." Even when the issue of popular disaffection
in the East was addressed, the question of how the refugee flow might be
restricted was less of an issue than how to respond in the event of a
political explosion within East Germany. Asking for what should be done
in the most difficult of contingencies was perfectly responsible, but
it distracted attention from one of the relatively easy—though bad
enough—contingencies.

Another factor was the prior existence of a mental wall. More substantial border controls were never thought to be problematic for the East
German authorities. According to Rostow, Kennedy told him at the start
of August that the situation was "unbearable" for Khrushchev. "The entire East bloc is in danger. He has to do something to stop this. Perhaps
a wall. And there's not a damn thing I can do about it."[8] Almost casually,
Kennedy tended to write off East Berlin, paying little attention to allied
rights there. The communists were in control and nobody was suggesting
a direct challenge. Though he had obligations to the whole city, it was
already divided in Kennedy's mind. He was not alone in this neglect. It
was shared by most of the other political leaders of the time. Their options for helping people on the eastern side of the Iron Curtain were few,
and most seemed to involve a heightened risk of great-power war. Senators Mansfield and Fulbright, both influential Democrats, mused aloud
over the possibility of closing the sector boundary as August began,
thereby encouraging Ulbricht in his conviction that he would get away
with such an act. "I don't understand why the East Germans don't close
their border," remarked Fulbright, to German fury.[9] The failure of policy
was not so much acquiescence in the denial of freedom to the East, painful
though that was, but in not grasping the implications for the morale of
the West. The distinction between East and West did not seem as sharp
to the people of Berlin as it did to everyone else.

POST-WALL

In retrospect the construction of the wall transformed the cold war. From
this point on it is possible to trace the start of the European détente,
based upon a shift in West Germany's foreign policy to a tolerance of
the territorial status quo and a readiness to open up lines of communication to the East. This culminated almost exactly a decade later in the

four-power agreement on Berlin, which consolidated the status quo and established procedures to solve any disputes by peaceful means. At the time, it was not at all obvious that this was a turning point.

On 14 August 1961 the initial inclination was to see the barrier as a brutal reinforcement of the current position. The communist crime of physically preventing the free movement of people was hardly a first offense, and the West had no better instruments for dealing with the closing of this last gap than they had for dealing with the rest of the Iron Curtain. The Republicans had dabbled in 1952 with the idea of "rolling back" the Curtain, but the response of Eisenhower to the uprisings in East Germany, Poland, and Hungary had confirmed a reluctance in practice to get into the liberation business. Given the false impressions conveyed to the "captive nations" and the subsequent disillusion, care was now taken as a matter of course not to encourage insurrections. This was not a courageous policy, but it was undoubtedly prudent, and few seriously argued for an alternative.

Prudence ruled again. Information out of Berlin was also poor, so it took twelve hours before it registered that this was to be a total sealing of the inner sector borders. No high-level routines, whether business or leisure, were broken in response to the news. No recommendations came from Berlin to mount any operations to sustain Berlin as an open city. According to Nitze, discussions of this option in the Pentagon came to an abrupt end when news came in that two East German divisions and three Soviet ones had been moved to the Berlin area. As this had been done surreptitiously rather than openly, which would have been for purposes of deterrence, a trap was suspected. If the West moved to break down the barriers, the communists would have a pretext to occupy all of Berlin. Nobody was prepared to cope with the military or psychological consequences of such a step. There would have been mobs on the street on the Western side as well as in the Eastern portion, and the situation could have got out of control.[10]

The response of senior Washington figures was remarkably relaxed. Bundy reported the consensus taking in both Joe Alsop and George Kennan: The communists had always had the power to take such an action, and it was bound to happen sooner or later if they were unable to control movements out of West Berlin. All things considered, "it is as well to have it happen early, as *their* doing and *their* responsibility." Kennedy saw a valuable propaganda opportunity. Rusk also judged that the Berlin crisis itself might ease now that the border was effectively closed.[11] The decision was to demonstrate that war was not imminent. Kennedy went sailing as a mild statement was issued in his name. He said nothing more in public for a week. Rusk went to a ball game. Khrushchev was given no reason to worry that he had triggered a crisis by his drastic action.

Kennedy's stance was less the result of complacency, an assumption that the wall would lead to an easing of tension, than of anxiety. On 14 August he sent a quick note to McNamara on the pressure he would face to adopt a harder military posture, and on the need to spend any money offered by Congress and push ahead with a civil defense program.[12] He also, as we shall discuss later, intensified efforts to get negotiations under way. Meanwhile public opinion was content with the president's handling of the crisis. There was little criticism from either Republicans or the leading columnists.

The Soviet action combined with the business-as-usual response from the allies, beyond expressions of protest, unsettled West Berliners. Even Chancellor Adenauer kept his distance, wary about acting apart from the allies and preoccupied with the forthcoming elections. He was convinced that Khrushchev's whole strategy was geared to getting him out of office.[13] The view that not much could be done did not accord with the feelings of fury and helplessness in Berlin itself. This was more than just a question of people feeling jittery. The GDR clearly hoped that the West Berliners would feel even more isolated than before. It was always an effort to keep the city fully populated, involving special favors and subsidies. If life started to appear too stressful or dangerous, then people might start to flow to West Germany proper, undermining the effort to preserve the status quo.

The mayor of West Berlin, Willy Brandt, complained to Kennedy about the weak, defensive, passive response to the outrage of the wall. He warned that after this "first act" a "second act" would surely follow. Then "Berlin would be like a ghetto, which has not only lost its function as a refuge of freedom and symbol of hope for reunification but which would also be severed from the free part of Germany. Instead of flight to Berlin, we might then experience flight from Berlin." He wanted a political initiative, some strengthening of the Berlin garrison, and other forms of reassurance.[14] The terms of the letter infuriated the president, but the sentiments it expressed were difficult to dismiss.

The tension had already been reflected in an alarmist construction on events provided by Allen Lightner, the head of the State Department mission in Berlin. What might have been anticipated as a result of a USSR-GDR peace treaty, he observed, had now been achieved unilaterally. If Moscow believed that it had got away with a fait accompli, then the Russians might become more ambitious:

> Having taken such a big slice of salami and successfully digested it, with no hindrance, they may be expected to snatch further pieces greedily. . . .
>
> If our view as to proper interpretation is correct, it means we have now entered phase of actual practical confrontation with Sovs on Berlin, that we have moved out of a phase of confrontation, by words and threats and into phase of deeds. If so, it is highly doubtful whether it can possibly suffice to reply to deeds with words of protestation.

In this situation it was essential to respond vigorously. The equivalent of a slap on the wrist would not be enough. "To have a deterrent effect, countermeasures must not be calculated to fit the violation, but must to a certain extent overshoot the mark."[15]

10

Tests and Tension

A GENERAL UNEASE SOON DEVELOPED. The Berlin issue was apparently no closer to resolution. Nothing really had changed for West Berlin, except that its isolation was more complete. Khrushchev gave no grounds for assuming that the wall had resolved anything other than the immediate problem of mass defection. He was not about to admit that it was an alternative to a separate peace treaty.[1] So by the time the Berlin Steering Group met on 17 August, the mood was far less relaxed and much more alive to the danger, as McNamara put it, that "this Bloc action might portend a speed-up of Khrushchev's schedule." The conclusion: "[O]ur own military preparations should be hastened accordingly." Though there was some disagreement with his diagnosis, there was none with his prescription. Kennedy was now coming around to the view that "the Communists in East Berlin might become 'dizzy with success' and act rashly."[2]

Kennedy wrote back to Brandt explaining that there were "no steps available to us which can force a significant material change in this present situation." Put bluntly, the United States could not "go to war on this point."

> I myself have decided that the best immediate response is a significant reinforcement of the Western garrisons. The importance of this reinforcement is symbolic—but not symbolic only. We know that the Soviet Union continues to emphasize its demand for the removal of Allied protection from West Berlin. We believe that even a modest reinforcement will underline our rejection of this concept.[3]

In order to raise morale, this letter was to be delivered personally by Vice President Johnson. As important, he was to be accompanied to Berlin by General Lucien Clay, the hero of the 1948 siege. This was the idea of conservative columnist Marguerite Higgins (an advocate of urging the administration to support a revolt in East Germany). Higgins, having been one of the administration's main critics over inaction, publicized the trip and later proclaimed it a success.[4]

Timed to coincide with the arrival of the dignitaries on 18 August was a convoy of 1,600 American troops who had traveled down the autobahn. Kennedy worried that this was a high-risk move and demanded to be kept in touch at each stage of the journey. The Soviet authorities used pro-cedural formalities to delay the convoy but did not prevent it arriving in Berlin to great popular acclaim. Moscow did not ignore these gestures, and soon came the first concrete indication that the crisis might indeed be moving to a new and more dangerous phase. On 23 August came a note from Moscow accusing the Western powers of allowing the air cor-ridors to be used for transferring back and forth the worst types—"re-vanchists, extremists, subverters, spies and saboteurs of all kinds." This, it was claimed, was in direct violation of the 1946 Air Agreement. The ground had been set for a direct challenge to Western air access, although there was no reason to suppose that Moscow intended to act immediately. The Western powers responded quickly, warning of the "the most serious consequences" that any action would entail.[5]

Further confirmation of tough times ahead came at the end of August. As the crisis deepened in the summer the moratorium on nuclear testing had become increasingly fragile. Khrushchev had told John McCloy at the end of July that he was under pressure to resume testing "because many inventions and discoveries had accumulated." On the same day Mc-Namara made a strong push to get preparations under way for the re-sumption of American tests, arguing that the Geneva negotiations were hopelessly stalled. Kennedy was still hoping that something could be sal-vaged from Geneva and decided to send Arthur Dean, the U.S. ambas-sador to the talks, back for another push.[6] To no avail: Intelligence chan-nels alerted Washington to an imminent TASS announcement that nuclear testing was to be resumed, with the prospect of one test well above 50 megatons. When the announcement came on the evening of 30 August a condemnatory White House statement was ready for immediate release. The first test was on 1 September.

Kennedy's reaction was, according to Sorensen, "unprintable"; another source prints it as "Fucked again."[7] The announcement led, Robert re-corded, to "the most gloomy meeting at the White House . . . since early in the Berlin crisis." The two brothers conferred beforehand about Soviet intentions. Robert's view was that "they do not want war but they will carry us to the brink." After the meeting his brother asked him what he thought. He said he wanted "to get off." "Get off what?" asked John. "Get off the planet," replied Robert.[8]

There was an argument for using American restraint to put the Soviet Union on the defensive in "the court of world opinion," so that the test became, as Stevenson put it, "not a blow but a bonanza." Kennedy's first response was a joint message with Prime Minister Macmillan to Khrushchev calling for negotiations leading to a test ban. Three additional Soviet tests in quick succession left him with little choice but to order the resumption of American tests. "We have to show both our friends and our own people," he explained to Macmillan, "that we are ready to meet our own needs in the face of these new Soviet acts." "They had spit in our eye three times," he told Stevenson. "We couldn't possibly sit back and do nothing." Nor did he have high expectations for third world opinion after a lame response to the Berlin Wall: "I don't hear of any windows being broken because of the Soviet decision." With no tests planned beforehand, American scientists had to improvise a program.[9] To highlight the difference with the Soviet Union, the tests were to be underground rather than in the atmosphere.

An intelligence estimate concluded that Khrushchev's intention was "to raise the level of fear and anxiety in the world in general, and to create a powerful impression of the strength and ruthlessness with which the Soviets intend to pursue their objectives."[10] His actual motives may have reflected Soviet weaknesses rather than strengths. After his bragging in the 1950s, which had encouraged the missile gap clamor in the United States, he was disappointed in the actual progress of ICBM deployment. At the June summit Kennedy acquiesced in the notion that the two sides were, to all extents and purposes, equal in their strength, without having given much thought to the matter. Khrushchev had prized this statement, for his bargaining position depended upon the Americans continuing to take his military capability seriously. He needed to boost his position but dared not make too many claims about missile numbers; at least he could shock Western countries by the sheer size of Soviet bombs and unnerve individual nations by drawing their attention to their vulnerability to just a few weapons. This started with a warning to the British in late July about how they could be obliterated with just six hydrogen bombs.[11]

Those confident in the West's position believed that they had seen through this braggadocio, but a more general response was still to take Khrushchev at his word. For example, from General Maxwell Taylor:

> Recent events provide pretty clear evidence that Khrushchev intends using military force, or the threat thereof, to gain his ends in Berlin. He has raised his ante by progressively isolating West Berlin, by retaining in service several hundred thousand men due for discharge, and by reverting to atomic testing.
>
> Thus far our own defense efforts have been deliberately kept in a low key and at a comparatively normal tempo. I have a strong feeling that the moment has come to shift into a higher gear.[12]

Acheson also had chosen to interpret events in the worst possible light. It looked as though the Soviet Union had accelerated its schedule as a result of the refugee problem. The United States must accelerate in response. He wrote a grumpy letter to Truman with some familiar themes: an imminent "humiliating defeat over Berlin," vacillation in policy, allies in retreat ("I hope I am wrong, but do not think that there is the remotest chance that I am").[13]

END OF THE MISSILE GAP

Yet around this time it became apparent that, so far as the arms race was concerned, the United States was doing fine. Starting in the summer of 1961 the United States flew a number of successful missions of the Corona satellite, which provided details on a number of Soviet sites. In addition there were now materials from Penkovsky documenting Russian difficulties with their ICBM program as well as submarines stuck at port, a lack of bombers on alert, and gaps in early warning coverage. Because this material jarred so much with prior expectations, and Penkovsky's own reliability was still uncertain, it did not have an immediate impact on estimates.[14] The extent of the US comparative advantage dawned on American officials over the summer. The June National Intelligence Estimate (NIE), providing the official view for the height of the Berlin crisis, remained in cautious mode. Although almost as soon as it was completed analysts suspected it was over pessimistic, it was not until the start of September that the president was informed that earlier estimates of 50 to 100 operational Soviet missiles were "probably too high."[15] It was the September 1961 NIE that decisively brought down the estimated number of operational Russian ICBMs from between 140 and 200 to between 10 and 25 (still an exaggeration). Important was that the force level would "not increase markedly during the months immediately ahead." It described the problems the Kremlin had with its first-generation ICBMs, too cumbersome to be deployed in any number.[16]

Should Khrushchev, in the throes of using nuclear intimidation to weaken Western resolve on Berlin, be told that the Americans knew just how boastful his claims had been? The Soviet leader had habitually inflated his country's relative strength. Some deflation might be in order. On the other hand, there was a risk that the uncomfortable news would appear threatening and lead to a surge of Soviet activity in an effort to catch up, while also revealing to Moscow the quality of American intelligence. Unofficially the news soon leaked. Joe Alsop, the leading promoter of the "missile gap" thesis, reported on the drastic reduction of the figures at the end of September.[17] On 11 October Kennedy was asked at a news conference whether the United States had done enough to convince the "leaders of the Soviet Union that we are determined to meet force with force in Berlin." He replied by recounting all that had been achieved on the American side since the start of the year: 14 percent more on the defense budget, increases in nuclear delivery vehicles and their alert status; more nonnuclear forces, including two extra divisions. He said nothing, however, about the Soviet side.

Even this claim goaded Khrushchev. A week later, when speaking at the Twenty-second Party Congress, he went out of his way to deny American strength.

> We believe today that the forces of socialism, all the forces that stand for peace, are today more powerful than the aggressive imperialist forces. But even if one agreed with the President of the United States that our forces are equal—he said this quite recently—it would plainly be unwise to threaten war.

His theme was that the aggressive Western nations ("imperialist Americans" in league with "revanchist and militarist Germans" and so on) had required the socialist bloc to step up its own military efforts. The response he announced, however, was hardly modest: The current nuclear test series was to end that month with a 50-megaton bomb.[18] This was, as one of the scientists involved later acknowledged, more about intimidation than military need. It could have been boosted to 100 megatons and then "would have generated a gigantic, fiery tornado, engulfing an area larger than . . . the state of Maryland."[19] No rocket could actually carry such a weapon. This was a time when the most the Soviet strategic rocket forces could accomplish was one launch against four "hostage cities"—New York, Washington, Chicago, and Los Angeles.[20]

Before the test, Washington had taken the propaganda war a step further. On 21 October Deputy Secretary of Defense Roswell Gilpatric, in a deliberately dry presentation, enumerated American nuclear strength— six hundred strategic bombers, six Polaris submarines, dozens of intercontinental ballistic missiles—and then continued:

> The destructive power which the United States could bring to bear even after a Soviet surprise attack upon our forces would be as great as—perhaps greater than—the total undamaged forces which the enemy can threaten to launch against the United States in a first strike. In short, we have a second strike capability which is at least as extensive as what the Soviets can deliver by striking first.

To ensure that the message got back to Moscow there were briefings for NATO allies, complete with pictures, that were almost certain to be picked up by the KGB.[21]

The party congress had already been a difficult one for Khrushchev, as he had denounced domestic critics and argued publicly with the Chinese, who had walked out. Now the United States was challenging his central strategic claim. When details reached the congress, the planned speech of Defense Minister Marshal Rodion Malinovsky was brought forward to 23 October. Malinovsky repeated Kennedy's description of the American buildup and then mentioned Gilpatric's speech: "What is there to say to this latest threat, to this petty speech? Only one thing: The threat does not frighten us! (*stormy applause*)."

While American warheads were only 5 megatons, Russian warheads had yields ranging from "20 to 30 to 100 megatons" and could be delivered anywhere. The American "madmen" had better recalculate.[22]

Kennedy's main recalculation, given Khrushchev's reliance on his testing program, was that he could no longer delay authorizing preparations for U.S. atmospheric tests. A National Security Council (NSC) committee urged their resumption by the start of April 1962. Kennedy agreed, but only if reductions could be made in the number of tests, the duration of the series, and the amount of radioactive fallout generated, and he still reserved judgment on the final decision to test.[23] The disappointment this caused among the liberals in the White House was reflected in a powerful memo from Schlesinger. If it was the case, as was continually asserted, that the United States was "ahead" in the technology, then it was hard to explain why the United States would suddenly become weak if it desisted from further tests. As a clincher, Schlesinger added a Gallup Poll: American opinion was evenly divided on the matter, but there had been a real swing against resumption compared with the commanding majority four months earlier (during the height of the Berlin crisis). Bundy urged the president to reconsider, although every other senior figure in the administration wanted the testing. The NSC staff now provided the only opposition. In January Carl Kaysen produced a paper demonstrating the virtues of proposing a ban only on atmospheric tests, which would both sustain the nuclear standoff and put the onus back on Moscow. John McNaughton in the Pentagon was already coming to a similar conclusion.[24] The new ideas neither stopped the resumption of testing nor led to immediate modifications of Western proposals for a comprehensive test ban, but they planted the seeds of a thought.

Another issue for reappraisal was the size of the American missile force. The developing missile gap in reverse had been sufficiently striking for Kaysen to raise the question as to whether the United States was now aiming too high, with numbers having been based on an exaggerated NIE. Was there a risk that this might influence adversely a future Soviet buildup? He continued to argue from this point that the proposed missile force was too high, although with limited effect.[25] Enthoven's analysis also supported the view that the relatively small number of large cities in the Soviet Union meant that adding extra nuclear weapons soon reached a point of diminishing marginal returns. In the end—at a meeting in November—ICBM numbers were set at 1,200 (they were cut in 1963 to 1,000). This was half the number the air force was seeking, though about 50 percent higher than McNamara and Kennedy thought really justified, but the minimum sustainable politically.[26] The fact that this decision was accompanied by public assertions of American nuclear superiority—from Kennedy at a press conference on 8 November ("[W]e . . . would not trade places with anyone in the world") and then McNamara in a magazine interview ("[W]e have nuclear power several times that of the Soviet Union")—indicates that Kennedy was not expecting to be criticized for excess.[27] He acknowledged this in early 1962, blaming the congressional demand for more weapons. "I don't think such sentiments can be rationally defended, but there it is."[28]

NEGOTIATIONS

Through the furore over testing and the trade of claims of military superiority, diplomatic efforts were under way to calm the situation down. Since the 25 July speech the argument within the administration had been between the White House's readiness to search for a fast track to a settlement against the State Department's insistence that the only appropriate route was through the slow track of intra-alliance discussions.

Bundy complained just before the Berlin Wall went up that "new ideas will not come out of the 4-power rut," and took the view immediately afterward that it was vital to move ahead with an initiative on negotiations. This was because the episode revealed "dangerous and explosive weakness" in the GDR. On this, he told the president, there was "unanimity in your immediate staff," although Rusk's professionals were more cautious, because of their commitment to four-power planning. Kennedy directed Rusk to pull together some ideas on negotiations. In fact, the day the barriers went up Rusk took one extraordinary initiative—to write to Kennan, ambassador in Yugoslavia, suggesting that he might explore informally with his Soviet counterparts whether there was any new way forward. Kennan made some progress, concluding that the core German demands would be a peace treaty combined with a formula recognizing the existence of two Germanys.[29]

A week later Kennedy wrote to Rusk insisting that the United States take a stronger lead on negotiations, to the point where allies might be told that vetoes were unacceptable. He wanted a policy that was fresh, stressing the freedom and protection of West Berliners rather than occupation rights, providing that strong guarantees could be designed. Proposals should be serious, with as little distance as possible between the initial presentation and the fallback position.[30] White House thoughts turned naturally toward accepting the European status quo, including the GDR as the government of East Germany and the Oder-Neisse Line as the boundary between Germany and Poland. Unification might come about only after discussion between the two German governments and some consideration of mutual security guarantees.[31] At the core of this position was the reluctance to run risks to preserve the demand for a reunified Germany; the de facto existence of two German states was to be accepted.

Another important issue was the question of German nuclear weapons. It has been argued that this was the dominant issue for both Kennedy and Khrushchev at this time.[32] A core objective of Soviet foreign policy was undoubtedly to prevent Germany from returning to the path of aggression, with or without nuclear weapons. To achieve this it looked for ways to tie Germany down with special provisions and render it as militarily impotent as possible. Moscow had failed with regard to conventional forces. NATO had agreed to West German rearmament in 1954, though at the same time Bonn agreed not to produce its own nuclear weapons. The view of the Kennedy administration was that the Soviet concern was understandable but overblown. The problem, as with so many issues at the time touching on German security, was not whether the Federal Republic had serious nuclear ambitions but whether it would accept any extraordinary restrictions of its freedom of maneuver. Every time the Kennedy administration appeared to agree to special measures to be applied to Germany alone, Adenauer got upset. The more this issue was pushed to the fore, the greater the risk of a self-fulfilling prophecy. If the Germans refused a reasonable request to confirm a nonnuclear status, the Russians became more suspicious; if the Americans appeared to side with the Russians, the Germans would come to assume that they could not rely on their allies but must look to their own security needs.

As the Federal Republic was dependent upon the United States for its security, Kennedy had a reasonable expectation that in the end Adenauer would come into line, albeit making the most terrible fuss. The Americans had the backing of the British, who had long been urging the Americans to follow the negotiating route, although even London was taken aback at just how far Kennedy appeared ready to go. For West Germany there was, however, still another possibility, which was to reduce dependence on the United States by creating a stronger European bloc, based on the Franco-German axis that was now the driving force behind the European Common Market. President de Gaulle was establishing himself as a distinctive political force in Western politics, with his own arguments with Washington over the development of an independent nuclear capability and the domineering American role in NATO. He spotted German anxiety as providing an opportunity to undercut the American position. Adenauer now had a way to disagree with Kennedy without being left totally isolated. Together the two old men questioned Kennedy's search for concessions when the communist bloc was acting in such a menacing fashion.

On 4 September Kennedy replied to the latest expression of German concerns. Given the extra military measures he had approved, there was no reason to doubt American resolution; Khrushchev should be clear that a readiness to talk was not a sign of weakness. "At the same time," he explained, "both public opinion in democratic countries and the sheer logic of a thermonuclear war demand that we exhaust every effort to find a peaceful solution consistent with the preservation of a vital interest." Only then could the American people be asked to prepare themselves for war.[33]

That same day Kennan met with his Soviet counterpart in Belgrade, and although the message from Khrushchev did not seem to be saying anything strikingly different, there was a clear interest in establishing a bilateral channel of communication.[34] At the same time a message was received directly from Khrushchev via the columnist Cyrus L. Sulzberger, which again conveyed an interest in informal contacts. The Soviet leader seemed to have the view that while Kennedy himself was amenable to compromise, with no desire to fight for Berlin, he was being "contaminated" by Rusk, who was, in the eyes of Khrushchev, an "agent" of Rockefeller.[35]

If Rusk was annoying Khrushchev, it was because he understood that despite Kennedy's search for a true settlement of the issue, there was probably not going to be one. Even before the deadline had been lifted, he and British Foreign Secretary Lord Home had decided that they "could talk just as long and just as repetitively as Gromyko." Rusk saw this as his own contribution to taking some steam out of the crisis. Those who still believed in the possibility of a settlement on his own side found this behavior as frustrating as did Khrushchev. Bundy complained of an excessively tactical approach, stuck on the status quo. For this it was not so much Rockefeller who was to blame as the allies, who limited what could be achieved in a multilateral setting. So long as Rusk was working with the allies he would be tied to the established Western peace plan, including the nonnegotiable notion of reunification.[36]

The Germans objected to any hint of a softening in the American stance. A few days after his position had been weakened in federal elections, Adenauer was once again complaining, this time over the implications of a 22 September remark by General Clay that the German government would have to accept the reality of two German states. Kennedy found this constant nagging increasingly irritating. Rather than bind him closer to his ally, it led him to look for ways to break free from this constraint.[37] For this purpose he needed an effective back-door channel, and one was at last developing between Washington and Moscow.

The origins were in Khrushchev's concern that he was pushing Kennedy too hard and that this might lead to a hard-line speech to the UN General Assembly at the end of September. He instructed his spokesman, Mikhail Kharmalov, in town with Gromyko for the UN session, to visit his opposite number, Pierre Salinger, Kennedy's press secretary. The message was that Khrushchev was interested in another summit to discuss

American views on Berlin. Apparently the deadline on a peace treaty was being lifted so long as Kennedy did not set down any new ultimatums of his own. Salinger responded positively.

As it happened, there was no need for Kennedy to change his UN speech. He reaffirmed his commitment to West Berlin's freedom and the allied presence but noted the possibility of a peaceful agreement that recognized "the historic and legitimate interests of others in assuring European security." He also spoke of a "nuclear sword of Damocles, hanging by the slenderest of threads, capable of being cut at any moment by accident or miscalculation or by madness," and concluded by challenging Moscow to a "peace race" rather than an "arms race."[38]

Soon Bolshakov, who had accompanied Kharmalov, was back in touch. In a furtive meeting with Salinger he handed him a letter from Khrushchev to Kennedy. This was the start of the so-called pen pal correspondence.[39] The letter was dated 29 September. It set out at some length thoughts on a summit and peaceful coexistence (using the metaphor of Noah's ark, where both the "clean" and the "unclean" found sanctuary). He described current dangers in terms that would strike a responsive chord with Kennedy.

> Evidently both one side and the other are compelled to undertake their actions under the pressure of the various factors and conditions which exist and which—unless we exert a restraining influence—will propel the development of events in a direction in which you and I, and the more so the peoples of all countries, would not like them to be propelled. It would be most of all unwise from the standpoint of peace to enter into such a vicious circle when some would be responding with counter-measures to the measures of others, and vice versa. The whole world could bog down in such measures and counter-measures.

He reiterated the Soviet case on Germany and dismissed the concerns generated by his policy of turning Berlin into a "free city."

> It is in the Western countries that they create all sorts of fears and allege that the socialist States intend well-nigh to swallow up West Berlin. You may believe my word, the word of the Soviet Government that neither we nor our allies need West Berlin.

His offer, not new, was to end the occupation regime while still safeguarding rights, and he urged that discussions continue through any or all of the various channels now established: the formal channel between Gromyko and Rusk, or the informal one involving Kennan in Belgrade. Perhaps Ambassador Thompson could move things forward in Moscow.[40]

After some unsatisfactory discussions with Gromyko, Kennedy wrote back to Khrushchev. Kennedy's letter of 16 October confirmed that he valued the correspondence, declared his intention to keep it private, expressed the hope that it could be kept free from cold war polemics, and emphasized the special responsibilities of the two men in the thermonuclear age. He picked up on Khrushchev's warning of "bitter measures and countermeasures" leading to a war neither wanted. He did not commit himself to any position and acknowledged the limits to dialogue. Khrushchev would not agree to German reunification, while he could not legalize the abnormal division of Germany. Nonetheless, he believed that "an accommodation of our interests is possible." At one level Ambassador Thompson could continue with "exploratory talks" between the two countries, while at another those involving the allies proceeded at their own pace. A summit would have to wait "until a preliminary understanding can be reached through quieter channels on positive decisions which might appropriately be formalized at such a meeting."[41]

The letter had an immediate effect. The next day, speaking to the party congress, in the midst of some tough language, including the announcement of the 50-megaton test, Khrushchev slipped in an important concession. From the talks that foreign ministers had been having, he observed "a certain understanding of the German problem" and a readiness to seek a settlement—in which case, without withdrawing the objective of getting the "status of West Berlin . . . normalized," the Soviet Union "shall not . . . absolutely insist on signing the peace treaty [with East Germany] before December 31, 1961."[42]

Any positive signs noted by Khrushchev were in tone rather than substance. There was a basis for a tacit understanding on the German problem, as nobody believed that the old Germany could be put together again in the foreseeable future, and few of Germany's neighbors, East or West, actually relished this prospect. Kennedy might have judged the risks of adopting this position formally, including a consequent upsurge in German nationalism, to be bearable. But having accepted its division, Kennedy had no flexibility on the status of Berlin. Communist promises to protect the West Berliners' way of life were considered risible. Without the visible support of the allies, morale would plummet and the city would decline. None of the various back channels could get around this problem. Without a real change in Berlin's status, Khrushchev's campaign could not claim success.

CHECKPOINT CONFRONTATION

As assessments of the balance of power were being traded at one level and private correspondence at a higher one, a minor crisis erupted in the middle of Berlin. On 19 September General Clay had reappeared in Berlin, now as a special adviser to Kennedy, but clearly expecting to call the shots. He was a tough hard-liner, popular with the Berliners as one committed to their cause. His relations with all the other American generals in Europe with responsibility for Berlin, from Norstad down, were poor, and those with the State Department were no better. Clay did admire Acheson, and Kennedy may have wanted to use him in the same way, to demonstrate the participation of all shades of opinion, but like all his personal appointments that cut across formal bureaucratic and military lines of command, it sowed confusion and complicated policy making.

Clay also had a different attitude to risk taking than Kennedy. He outlined his theory to Rusk:

> Harassments not in direct conflict with our basic rights do not worry me although I think they should be checked as they occur to the extent possible without show of force. To show force when we do not intend to use it is one thing we must avoid. However, I cannot accept the escalation theory that any reaction on our part leads to further actions and possible war. The complete acceptance of this policy would lead to the continuing erosion of an already eroded position.[43]

On his return to Berlin Clay decided to prepare for a big confrontation by ordering the U.S. military commandant, General Watson, to get his engineers to build a replica section of the wall in a secluded part of West Berlin in order to experiment on various ways to break it down. When the Commander in Chief (CINC) Europe, General Bruce Clarke, heard of this, he demanded that the experiment be stopped and the replica dismantled, but not before it had been photographed by Soviet intelligence. The news reached Moscow on 20 October.[44] It was in this context that the communists viewed Clay's moves. Washington was ignorant of this episode.

Clay wanted to probe the limits of communist tolerance, just as Ulbricht wanted to do with the West. Khrushchev was blustering to obscure what was in effect a retreat, but the East German leader was still bent on eroding the Western position in Berlin. This was a gradual campaign, independent of Soviet direction, and the target of its next stage was the rights of allied civilian personnel to move in and out of East Berlin.

On 22 October the State Department's Allen Lightner was stopped going to the opera in East Berlin with his wife. He refused to show identification. To assert his rights, Lightner returned, this time accompanied by military police, and went into East Berlin. Ulbricht then issued a decree stating that allied civilians would have to identify themselves. Though the British and French had already allowed their officials to show passports to East German guards, the Americans continued as before, with an armed patrol. On 25 October, as the latest American probe was following its customary procedure, Clay asked General Watson to place U.S. tanks on alert near the sector boundary at Checkpoint Charlie. This appeared in Moscow as potential confirmation of Clay's intentions to move against the wall. Coupled with Gilpatric's speech, this all began to look sinister in Moscow. Had easing the deadline emboldened Kennedy?

Civilians showing identification was not an issue upon which many others than Clay wanted to make a stand, yet he was allowed to continue. On 27 October American tanks once again drew up to back a patrol, but this time Marshal Ivan Konev, like Clay taken out of retirement to add weight to the Soviet military command, decided to respond by pushing his own tanks up to face the Americans. The East Germans announced that the checkpoint would be closed until the American tanks were removed. Clay responded by moving some tanks directly onto the demarcation line, to be followed by Soviet tanks moving to a hundred yards from the Americans. So on 28 October at Checkpoint Charlie, the new flash point of the cold war, American and Russian tanks pointed their guns at each other.

Kennedy rang Clay to compliment him on his nerve. The general responded that he had not lost his but he was worried about those in Washington. "I don't know about those of my associates," replied the president, "but mine are all right."[45] This was highly unlikely. This was the sort of situation Kennedy dreaded: a contrived incident over a secondary issue that could lead to a tank battle in the middle of Berlin with who knew what consequences to follow. It is likely that Clay was told that an opportunity to withdraw would soon come. The previous day Robert had got in touch with Bolshakov to pass on the message to Khrushchev that American tanks would withdraw if Soviet tanks did so, and that it would be possible for the two leaders to have a productive exchange of opinions.[46] Soon Russian tanks were pulled back a bit, and American tanks followed suit. The communists did not, however, back down on their demand for identification.

Clay's view was that the Soviet Union was not going to let the East Germans lead them to war barely fifteen years after the last one, and so he was looking for ways to limit the ability of the East Germans to operate unilaterally. The issue of who was in charge in Berlin was a sensitive one for the Russians, and in this incident they attempted to hide their role by obscuring unit markings on tanks and dressing the crews in overalls rather than uniforms. Reporters still noted that officers directing the tanks were wearing Soviet uniforms. In this way the exercise proved a point and may have sown distrust between the East Germans and the Russians. For their part the Russians may have felt that they had thwarted an American escalation of the crisis. Both leaders had noted the utility of "back-door diplomacy."

The episode was an "exercise in military theatricality."[47] Ausland reports that American officials in Berlin believed that the conflict would have been contained but notes that "Kennedy and Khrushchev proceeded thereafter with even more caution regarding Berlin."[48] A lasting legacy of the dramatic images of confrontation left over from this episode was that Checkpoint Charlie became the starting point for war-gamers, novelists, and documentary makers when they were trying to work out how to start a third world war.

11

Flexible Response

BERLIN OBLIGED KENNEDY to address the fundamental questions of war and peace in the nuclear age. He was torn between the need to appear unyielding in the defense of America's interests and his real fear of sudden lurches into crisis and then war.

The peculiar vulnerability of Berlin set an extremely demanding strategic challenge. Deep in East Germany, surrounded by Soviet and East German divisions, was not a good place to pick a fight. The West would soon face the famous choice between holocaust or humiliation, suicide or surrender. Existing contingency planning, based on National Security Council Report 5803 of February 1958, suggested that the United States would be prepared to go to general nuclear war after using only limited force to open access to Berlin.[1] This, as McNamara observed to Kennedy, was not consistent with the new thinking that stressed a much more substantial conventional phase before recourse to nuclear weapons.[2]

The more force that could be brought to bear on the immediate problem, the less the pressure to expand the fight sideways or upward. In early thinking McNamara wanted to get sufficient forces in play to stand up to available East German divisions. The Soviet Union needed to understand that they could not leave the East Germans to do it by themselves in the hope that they would not be implicated. "I do not believe," McNamara observed, "that a great power such as the United States should select a course of action which could lead to defeat by a Soviet puppet regime." One possibility was to exploit West Germany's growing military potential. This was a sensitive issue. German rearmament had been viewed with misgivings throughout Europe, including in Germany itself. While the Americans may not have appreciated how much this prospect, including access to nuclear weapons, had colored Soviet thinking, they could see the problems of giving it an even greater prominence. In addition, strictly speaking, Berlin was not part of the Federal Republic. Another possibility mooted by McNamara was an "uprising in East Germany and other satellite countries," which might be reinforced by U.S. special forces.[3] It was hard to take this option seriously given the painful history of how the West had watched the suppression of uprisings in the past.

The military believed that nuclear options had to be part of Berlin planning and that it was vital for deterrence and the cohesion of the alliance that this be generally understood. This, in the end, was Acheson's line as well; the only restraint on Khrushchev, Acheson felt, was his fear of nuclear war, but the credibility of nuclear deterrence depended on the ability to fight a non-nuclear war. By the time that the Berlin crisis came to a head in August the main conclusion was that nuclear weapons would not be relied on at the start of any military engagements. The particular measures announced on 25 July by the president were largely designed to strengthen general conventional capabilities in Europe, but it would take until 1962 before these would have effect, and they did not specify any type of action as an initial response to an early, hostile Soviet/East German move against Berlin.

On 9 August, with the East Germans putting the final touches to their construction plans for Berlin, the secretary of state met with American ambassadors to European countries to brief them on Berlin policy. When he discussed contingency planning, he observed that

> the degree of escalation we might expect would vary with our assumption as to the likelihood or unlikelihood of nuclear warfare. The Secretary pointed out that to plan on going from a minor, small-scale military probe directly to all-out nuclear war is a satisfactory policy only if one is sure of never actually reaching that point. We were trying to create a situation where we could gain time through economic and other measures before any shooting actually started. The US no longer anticipated a situation in which interruption of our access rights would be immediately followed by "the big bang" of nuclear warfare, and all the Ambassadors could assure their clients that the United States was not disposed to be rash in this matter.[4]

Inasmuch as the allies had to be reassured that the United States would not be rash, the Soviet Union had to be persuaded that it just might be.

POODLE BLANKET

One difficulty was that the debate on how to respond to a crisis over Berlin became bound up with a debate on NATO strategy. From the start of 1961 the administration had been seeking to improve NATO's nonnuclear options. This involved setting long-term goals for force improvements and then nagging the allies into meeting them. The very nature of the exercise meant that it tended to get caught up in long, quasi-theoretical debates within the alliance, and that allowed plenty of opportunities for procrastination. Berlin, however, was a more urgent problem. Washington wanted the extra nonnuclear options as soon as possible. Rather than push forward in the same direction in two different settings at two different paces, it made sense to concentrate on Berlin on the grounds that any short-term success in this context would have a long-term payoff in the reorienting of NATO strategy. For this reason Rusk suggested to McNamara in July that they concentrate entirely on "the additional military measures we expect of our allies as part of the Berlin program." Within days McNamara was communicating this view to the allies. This was followed up both in the president's broadcast, with its stress on conventional forces, and the NATO Council on 8 August.[5]

On 8 August the United States had called for thirty-two active fully manned, combat-ready divisions on NATO's central region backed up by eight reserve divisions. The United States already had five divisions and was intending to send an extra one. By late August McNamara felt that he had got more of a response in terms of extra forces than many had anticipated but not enough to satisfy him. Moreover, he was still meeting resistance in terms of getting the allies to plan for large-scale nonnuclear naval, air, and ground actions. He believed that it was only as they confronted in the starkest terms the implications of alternative courses for national survival that they would see the value of as many productive steps as possible before the last resort of nuclear action. "If they look the problem in the eye, I believe they will come to the conclusions we have reached."[6]

Concentrating on Berlin did not necessarily help the American campaign, because of the inadequacy of the conventional options compared to wider European scenarios. The first attempts to relate Berlin contingencies to available capabilities in a systematic fashion produced a matrix so large and complicated that it was known within the Pentagon as "Horse Blanket." This was then reduced to Pony Blanket, which concentrated on the most likely and important contingencies and most available responses, until it was reduced after a White House meeting on 10 October to "Poodle Blanket."

This pointed to a "preferred sequence" involving four phases of graduated response. Each phase corresponded to a development in a Berlin crisis. The first was interference with access; then came actual blockage of access, which would require countermeasures, followed, if these failed, by an attempt to restore access by nonnuclear means. During these first three phases there would be movement involving pressure through diplomatic channels, economic embargoes, maritime harassment, and UN action, followed by or in combination with NATO mobilization and then conventional military measures, such as sending armed convoy probes down the autobahn. If the battle group was stopped, the next step was an airlift and possibly a blockade, using any time gained for further military preparations. These initial steps would also make it easier to justify later military moves. If all this failed, the fourth phase would involve the escalating use of nuclear weapons. This was approved as National Security Action Memorandum (NSAM) 109 on 23 October.[7] Phase four was the least discussed of all these phases, though attitudes toward the first three were conditional on what one supposed this might contain.

The relevance of the military planning to actual events was unclear. Already the Americans had been caught out by a Soviet move—the construction of the wall—that had not been predicted. It was by no means inevitable that the next challenge would represent an unequivocal threat to the integrity of West Berlin. For example, at the end of August Kennedy identified a set of situations that bothered him precisely because of their ambiguity: interference with civil air traffic, conflicts between West Berliners and the East German police, and an East German revolt.[8] Nor was even the first response to a communist siege easy to identify. Another airlift could be attempted but would be vulnerable to Soviet air defenses. Naval measures up to and including a full blockade would have a negligible effect upon the Soviet Union and only a temporary effect on East Germany, while the allies worried that a blockade would still constitute an act of war.

The main impetus to planning for conventional options was less their inherent feasibility and credibility than McNamara's conviction that the military "didn't have any plan to use nuclear weapons that I would want to implement."[9] This view had been developing since he discovered that the Single Integrated Operations Plan (SIOP) required nuclear weapons to rain down on every conceivable target. McNamara was bothered by more than a lack of flexibility. He was coming to believe that there were no circumstances in which it would make sense to initiate nuclear war. The view that notions of nuclear victory were fanciful and dangerous, so that the most responsible policy was to stress the horrors of nuclear exchanges and rely on mutual deterrence, was well on its way to becoming official doctrine by the time of Kennedy's assassination. In 1961, however, with tensions high and nonnuclear options underdeveloped, he was obliged to promise that the United States was prepared to go the distance. At times it seemed almost as if the allies were trying to trap the Americans in their nuclear commitments and were not prepared to allow any flexibility unless they could be sure that those commitments remained intact.

A further factor was that among those working for Kennedy and McNamara the challenge of 1961 appeared to be to explore alternative ways of fighting nuclear war in such a way as to reduce its horrors. There were three aspects of particular significance to this problem. The first concerned the possibility of effective civil defense. The second, associated with strategist Tom Schelling, involved moving into a nuclear war gradually. The third, investigated by Paul Nitze in the Pentagon and Carl Kaysen of the NSC staff, implied a decisive move into nuclear war by means of a first strike designed to deny the enemy the possibility of retaliation.

CIVIL DEFENSE

In his first year in office, as he tried to come to terms with the prospect of a nuclear war, Kennedy believed that he had to explore all possible ways of sparing the American people the worst effects of such a catastrophe. A debate on civil defense had been simmering during the 1950s, with enthusiasts arguing that a responsible government that saw even a remote possibility of a future nuclear war should take steps to save lives. Governor Nelson Rockefeller, a leading Republican, had instigated a major fallout shelter program in New York and was urging Kennedy to make this nationwide. The problem was that a national program could provide serious protection only against radioactive fallout, there was no protection against the blast, heat, and fire of nuclear explosions in the neighborhood.

Kennedy could trace back his own interest in civil defense to the news of the first Soviet test in 1949.[10] In office he was at first noncommittal, largely because of the cost. When, in late March, he asked Carl Kaysen of the NSC staff to address the issue, he posed the question in terms of whether there was anything worth doing that could save lives, was nonprovocative, did not suggest that the United States was preparing a first strike, and was not too costly.[11] He decided to step up the national effort, without turning civil defense into a major commitment, as a way of bringing home to the American people the seriousness of the situation they now confronted. Plans were developed for public fallout shelters, with storage of food, medicines, and water, and advice was given on private shelters. This policy was announced on 25 May.

It may be an indication of the impact of the Vienna summit upon Kennedy that he raised the civil defense issue in the first NSC meeting after his encounter with Khrushchev.[12] He was now inclined to the view that in a dangerous world some sort of protection made sense and that it was prudent to start preparations.[13] Over the coming year available space would be surveyed, followed by construction spread over four years to create 54 million shelter spaces in existing buildings. To achieve between 5 million and 6 million spaces by January 1962 would require a large effort. Kaysen and science adviser Jerome Wiesner had misgivings. They did not see Berlin in itself as providing a new rationale for this program. Not only might that be provocative, it might also offer a false hope of what could be achieved. The difference that 5 million shelter spaces would make was not between zero and 5 million lives lost but between 35 million and 40 million—a "point sobering to contemplate."[14] Nonetheless, in his Berlin broadcast of 25 July, Kennedy emphasized the steps "every citizen . . . can take without delay to protect his family in case of attack."

Many families began to prepare for survival, stockpiling the necessities of life and buying firearms to protect themselves. The administration at first encouraged magazine articles with advice on family protection and shelter construction, but the program soon got caught out by the basic unreality of the proposition that straightforward measures were available to survive a nuclear war. If such measures really made a difference, then questions of access raised fundamental issues. Should only the rich be saved? If it could not really make a difference, then pretending that it could might encourage demands for reckless international action. Kennedy had not anticipated the macabre debates to which it led, the selfishness and inequality it exposed, and the general apathy shown by the majority of the population, who quickly concluded that in the event of nuclear war there was no real defense.[15] Analysis a year later was showing that a shelter program could save 30 million lives—but only in the context of an attack that still claimed around 140 million. Not surprisingly, the necessary legislation in Congress made little progress and Kennedy's requests for funds dropped sharply.[16] In public and private Kennedy dwelled far more on the lives that would be lost in a nuclear war than on those that might be saved.

FIRST STRIKES

Even on the more optimistic assumptions, a comprehensive civil defense program was never going to allow Kennedy to act without fear of a nuclear catastrophe. If he wanted to remove the nuclear threat to the United States, then that had to be done at the source, which would require a preemptive strike against the Soviet nuclear arsenal. If there was some Soviet retaliation following such an attack, fallout shelters might help reduce its impact. Kennedy understood this relationship between offensive and defensive measures. At an NSC meeting on 20 July he raised the question of preemption (apparently getting the message that this option would become easier as the United States built up its missile force) and then asked about the time necessary to stay in shelters following an attack (about two weeks).[17] He directed that no one in attendance should disclose even the subject of the meeting.

This whole question of preemption was the most sensitive of issues. A week later, when asked by the Joint Chiefs when he might contemplate using nuclear weapons, Kennedy replied that "he felt that the critical point is to be able to use nuclear weapons at a crucial moment before they use them." As he recognized, this begged questions about the ability of the Americans to make such a decision "without letting the enemy know that we are about to do it."[18] It also depended on the quality of the Soviet second-strike capability.

In his first weeks in office he asked the Joint Chiefs, "If we decided to make the first strike, could we eliminate the Soviet strike-back?" The reply was unequivocal:

The Joint Chiefs answered no, the USSR could strike back and especially in the missile age it is becoming more and more difficult to actually know where the targets are—that is, the Soviet Union capabilities—and we couldn't possibly get them all. Their estimate was that under any circumstances the Soviet Union could strike back hard.[19]

This, however, was in the context of an assumed missile gap. By early September 1961 new intelligence demonstrated that the Soviet missile force was negligible. It required no great insight to realize that a fresh analysis might produce quite different results. As the situation over Berlin remained tense, Kaysen thought it prudent to see whether new strategic possibilities really had opened up. Working with Kaufman, he had long been bothered by the indiscriminate destruction that would follow the implementation of the SIOP and had been pressing for some time to increase its flexibility. SIOP-62, for example had 1,077 targets or "designated ground zeroes" (DGZs), reflecting a belief that winning a general nuclear war meant coming out relatively better than the enemy, regardless of the magnitude of losses, and employing tactics that made some Soviet retaliation inevitable. It seemed inappropriate to Berlin contingencies. One problem was that the alert and launch procedures could soon aggravate a crisis in the event of a false alarm or a Soviet strategic feint.

He posed the problem of identifying the most effective SIOP causing the minimum damage. After a discussion of the issue with McNamara approval was given for a study undertaken with Nitze and Strategic Air Command (SAC). The objective was to find ways to get at Soviet long-range nuclear offensive capabilities in a way that would also limit damage to all concerned. This meant that it would employ small numbers, low-altitude penetration, and the use of weapons with a yield of no more than 1 megaton. Excellent intelligence on Soviet capabilities was assumed, as was the continuation of a major civil defense program in the United States. The core threat of eighty-eight DGZs included air bases, twenty-six staging bases for refueling, and ICBM sites. Some forty-two of these targets were co-located, to be attacked by twenty-one bombers in the first wave. Staging bases could be attacked in a second wave. Nitze's group identified three vital airfields for Soviet heavy bombers and their three forward staging bases in the Far North, where surviving bombers would need to be refueled for an attack on the United States and where a surprise attack might with luck find them at a lower state of readiness. An attack against these could be executed by two or three Polaris submarines, backed by a small number of heavy bombers. This might result in Soviet casualties of less than one million and perhaps not much more than five hundred thousand. Another advantage of these smaller-scale attacks was that they would be easier to recall at the last minute without having already triggered a major Soviet alert.

Not long after this analysis was completed, but before Kennedy had been told of its conclusions, the president visited SAC on 13 September 1961 to be briefed on the SIOP. Here he was told of 1,530 missiles and bombers on full alert, with another 1,737 available, all together capable of accounting for almost four thousand targets. Yet in spite of the size of this force, SAC could not promise relief from a Soviet second strike.[20] The plans made no provision for an American bolt from the blue: A first strike would be launched only on evidence of Soviet preparations for something similar. By this time the strike would be more difficult precisely because of these preparations. Even if conducted under the best circumstances, the United States would be hit by some portion of Soviet strike forces. There could not even be confidence that all of the weak Soviet submarine force off the East Coast could be found before some missiles had been launched. Lemnitzer, taking the briefing, stressed that the risks would be even greater if only a part of the plan was executed. In his briefing Lemnitzer argued against an attempt to introduce greater flexibility on the grounds that it would be pointless: The Soviet authorities would have difficulty distinguishing between an all-out attack and one notionally confined to military capabilities because of the large number of targets still to be attacked, their proximity to cities, and the consequences of fallout. He promised that the United States would prevail, but this seems mostly on the basis that the large numbers of Sino-Soviet targets in the plan would actually be destroyed rather than by reference to any political goals. Kennedy was deeply unimpressed. His best option appeared to be to inflict massive destruction on the enemy with the expectation that it would be followed by massive destruction on the United States and its allies. "And we call ourselves the human race," he observed to Rusk as they left. All of this underscored just how little control he had over this vast and devastating arsenal.[21]

A week later he learned more about why there was little confidence in the decisiveness of a first strike. The problem, explained General Power of Strategic Air Command, was a lack of confident intelligence on all Soviet ICBM sites. Here the air force had been hoist with its own petard. By claiming that there were numbers of Soviet missiles that had not yet been detected, they added to the risks of a first strike. Indeed, Power raised his concern about the imminent danger of a Soviet surprise attack.[22] The argument was that satellites could not provide the same quality of photography as U-2s. The argument was of sufficient importance for Kennedy to receive proposals to resume U-2 flights over the Soviet Union, with all the risks of a diplomatic storm if another aircraft was shot down, especially after the president had said publicly, if not definitively, that the flights would not be resumed.[23] In the end the State Department's and CIA's objections to new flights won, but that the issue was raised was in itself an indication that Kennedy could not be wholly confident in the intelligence supporting any attempt at preemption. It was not only a question of numbers of Soviet missiles; Kennedy was also curious about their reaction times in the face of an American attack. If the Soviet missiles were caught cold, with crews on routine standby, they would need from one to three hours to respond, but on alert this could be reduced to below thirty minutes, and at full readiness to between five and ten minutes.[24]

After his SIOP briefing Kennedy received from Taylor a copy of Kaysen's analysis with a recommendation that an alternative to SIOP-62 be developed, focused solely on the Soviet Union, based on a minimum warning and minimum size, and directed against the targets most vital for Soviet retaliation.[25] McNamara was already in the process of developing force options to attack this sort of target, holding the ability to attack urban-industrial targets in reserve, but only as a second-strike option. He argued against a "full first strike capability" on the grounds that it would be expensive, almost certainly infeasible (as it could not deal with Soviet submarines), and provocative. However, this judgment was not based on the Kaysen/Nitze analysis, but instead drew on the SIOP-62 assumptions and so a requirement for much larger American forces. Nor did it address the problem of how Moscow might distinguish, in terms of provocation, a counterforce capability designed for a second strike as against one designed for a first strike.[26]

The effect of Kaysen's exercise was also cautionary. Some were appalled at the idea being discussed at all, and Kaysen himself was nervous that it might be taken up too enthusiastically by military planners. In fact, LeMay's reaction was to be cross that White House staffers were meddling in SAC business. Much depended on the validity of the assumptions, from Soviet detection capabilities to American skill. As Kaufman later noted, the realization that a 90 percent chance of success still left a 10 percent chance that "it would all go haywire" was sobering. Another basic problem was that there would have remained a massive retaliatory capability versus West European targets.[27] At a time when the American position was unexpectedly strong, Kennedy was given little confidence that he could get away with the greatest strategic gamble of all.

DEMONSTRATIVE NUCLEAR USE

An alternative approach argued for basing strategy on the unique features of these weapons, that is, their terrible destructiveness, rather than attempting to fit them into an orthodox military framework. Thomas Schelling argued in an essay, "On the Problems of NATO's Nuclear Strategy," that "a main consequence of limited war, and the main reason for engaging in it, is to *raise the risks of general war.*" The proposition that deterrence might be restored, even once a war had begun, through the threat of further escalation impressed Acheson, who had read this essay when preparing his first report for Kennedy.[28] Schelling's views reached the president in the form of a paper on nuclear strategy in the context of the Berlin crisis. This was in Kennedy's reading material on the weekend of

21 July as he prepared for his forthcoming television address. Even when it came to the first use of nuclear weapons, Schelling argued, the objective should be a heightening of the risk to the enemy and not a futile bid to win a decisive victory. "We should plan for a war of nerve, of demonstration and of bargaining, not of tactical target destruction." This study apparently made a "deep impression" on Kennedy.

The paper had been influenced by Schelling's own conversations with Bundy, who then sought to use it to encourage Kennedy to get the Pentagon to address the "hideous jump between conventional warfare and a single massive all-out blast."[29] This may have been because of the fancy ways that Schelling could think of using nuclear weapons to make a political point or his emphasis on control at every point. It may also have been because his analysis reinforced the sense that military preparations and operations had to be thought of in conjunction with political measures, including negotiation with the Soviet Union, and not as separate activities.

Out of a conversation between Schelling and Rostow in July came a significant exercise. Rostow had participated in some crisis games while at MIT, designed to simulate the confused and stressful conditions decision makers might face and the questions they would have to address. This led to a series of games on Berlin organized in September by Schelling with Alan Ferguson to impress on the participants the "bargaining aspect of a military crisis."[30]

The games forced senior policy makers, both military and civilian, to work out responses to various contingencies. The conclusions, which had an impact on both official thought and Schelling's future theorizing, emphasized the pressure of events. It was far harder to communicate efficiently than was often assumed, as the enemy saw only the actions and not the intent behind them, and there would be far less time for diplomacy to operate than hoped. Yet it also became extraordinarily difficult to trigger a large-scale conventional war, never mind nuclear use. According to Ferguson, "our inability to get a fight started" was the "single most striking result." This message was so important that in 1962 another game was run with selected alliance participation at Camp David (to give it a White House cachet). It reached exactly the same conclusion.[31] The games also highlighted a problem with Berlin: "[W]hoever it is who has to initiate the action that neither side wants is the side that is deterred. In a fragile situation, good strategy involves leaving the overt act up to the other side."[32]

The game therefore gave little support to the idea that any nuclear use, even for signaling purposes, provided realistic options for NATO in the event that the Berlin crisis worsened. Reporting back to Kennedy, Kaysen highlighted the difficulty of using "military power flexibly and effectively for tactical purposes in the conduct of the day to day political struggle with the Soviet Union." Even if the United States government could steel itself to a bold move, it would be held back by a fear of alliance noncooperation.[33] If nuclear weapons were to be used, then a first symbolic use might just be a missed opportunity. Nitze thought this a "mug's game," while William Kaufman worried that if nuclear weapons were to be used, "you should be very serious about them, and not blow one up over a test base."[34]

The president addressed the problem of nuclear strategy at a meeting on 10 October at the White House. Three levels of nuclear activity were discussed: selective use to demonstrate the will to use nuclear weapons, à la Schelling; limited tactical employment to gain some significant tactical advantage; and general nuclear war. Kennedy found it difficult to believe that the first stages could be undertaken without inevitably reaching the third. McNamara explained that it was nonetheless important to try, given the gravity of general nuclear war. Nitze then came in with his proposal: If the first two stages would increase the probability of Moscow coming in with a strategic strike, then should not the United States consider taking the nuclear initiative? He argued that with a first strike "we could in some real sense be victorious in the series of nuclear exchanges, while we might well lose if we allowed the Soviets to strike first in the strategic battle." McNamara questioned the assumption that either side could feel confident in its ability to win by striking first, so that they both had an interest in avoiding such an exchange. Rusk added that the first side to use nuclear weapons would carry a grave responsibility. Nothing was resolved.[35]

Nitze continued to place a first-strike capability at the heart of strategy. This was evident in the "rationale paper" drafted by Admiral John Lee and his staff, based on Poodle Blanket, and eventually endorsed by Kennedy. The most important aspects of this paper had to do with the first three phases of Berlin planning, but it touched on phase four, general nuclear war. The strategy depended on developing conventional operations to "such levels of intensity that the imminence of general nuclear war would ultimately be obvious, unmistakable, and impossible to sidestep." If the enemy failed to reconsider its position and general war resulted, in the best case the United States might be able to limit damage to levels "that would not imperil national survival." The unfortunate allies could expect "to suffer grave and wide-spread destruction." The logic pointed to a first strike as not necessarily decisive but exerting a "very great weight in the course and results of the war." As a "matter of action policy," therefore, NATO would "make every effort to strike first when the situation demands general nuclear war." This could not be broadcast beforehand, however, so when it came to "declaratory policy," references to "pre-emption would have serious damaging effects." They would be destabilizing and also lead the enemy to take precautions that would reduce the strike's effectiveness.[36]

According to Nitze, this paper was so sensitive that ministers of allied countries were allowed to read it but not retain a copy. The controversy, however, rested not so much with discussion of first strikes as with the proposals for larger conventional probes toward West Berlin than the allies thought necessary, and the evolution of a clear demarcation line between conventional and nuclear operations.[37] The first-strike discussion was largely irrelevant in that if it could not be used in declaratory policy, it would be of little value in deterrence. For the allies there might have been a theoretical benefit in making it easier for the Americans to take nuclear risks if they believed that they might escape relatively unscathed. On no calculations, however, could Europe escape total devastation.

A DEBATE ON ESCALATION

The administration's push to reduce dependence on nuclear threats by increasing nonnuclear options had met great resistance from the NATO allies. In this their champion was an American, the supreme allied commander, Europe (SACEUR), General Lauris Norstad. Like all SACEURs, he had twin loyalties. He was the top American general in Europe and as such took orders from the Pentagon. He was also the top general in NATO and as such had to develop his plans in consultation with the allies. Under Eisenhower he had managed these twin loyalties successfully and enjoyed considerable prestige in Europe. However, this was based on plans devised under massive retaliation, emphasizing the early use of nuclear weapons.

Under the new administration he was torn. He was being pushed by Washington to develop nonnuclear options that were of little interest to the allies. He would have been an unusual commander not to see merit in extra forces. But because of the presumption of Warsaw Pact conventional superiority, he had come to share the allies' rather fatalistic approach to nonnuclear options. He was quite happy to take the extra 40,000 U.S. troops from the reserves raised in July (announced on 9 September) and was hoping for some strengthening of allied forces, but beyond that he did not see the value of extra numbers. In late August Kennedy had wondered whether the United States should not send a full six extra divisions to Europe (thereby increasing effective fighting strength by over a third) rather than leave some of the extra troops to be called up as reserves in the United States. McNamara was wary of this himself, as it would be expensive and let the allies off the hook, as well as leaving the United States less capable of coping with non-European contingencies. Norstad believed that he would have his work cut out absorbing even one division, and that the Soviet response could always negate a Western buildup. This was a crucial aspect of the debate: McNamara considered that there was an effective practical maximum of fifty-five

Soviet divisions, while Norstad put the ceiling at almost twice this level. McNamara believed that with extra forces the forward line might be held for a month; Norstad believed the actual amount of time was much less.[38]

Whether or not the Warsaw Pact forces could trump each new conventional move by NATO, the risks were obviously greater in a battle over Berlin, far away from NATO's front line, than elsewhere in Europe. The only option of any real interest in the Berlin case was one in which the United States took on the GDR but not the Soviet Union. The Joint Chiefs made clear their view that this scenario was based on an invalid hypothesis: that East German forces would fight without their Soviet allies, especially in circumstances where they might lose. If the hypothesis was accepted, however, then the calculation was quite straightforward. Active GDR forces of six divisions and 225 aircraft could be defeated by seven NATO divisions plus four air wings. Should Soviet forces join in, then something like fifty divisions would be required. It would take a year of committed allied mobilization to begin to be in a position to meet such a challenge.[39] Hence the virtue of planned early nuclear use as reinforcing deterrence. This was the general European view, and it was also Norstad's. This was a logic quite alien to McNamara. He saw little point in committing the United States to the terrible because of an inability to improve on the merely bad. It stood to reason that it was better to have more options than fewer, that nonnuclear options were better than nuclear ones, and that more forces equaled more options.

The argument intensified through 1961 as Washington paid more attention to the military issues. For example, just after the barriers went up in Berlin Norstad was told by Washington that he had to develop detailed plans "on a unilateral U.S. basis as a matter of urgency" to employ much larger nonnuclear forces than hitherto envisaged to reopen access to Berlin.[40] Norstad took the view that the measures announced by Kennedy in July were sufficient. Goaded by Khrushchev's apparent belligerence, Kennedy was prepared to go further.

The debate was joined in early October when Norstad came to Washington for consultations. Norstad had been worried for some time about the impact of Acheson's ideas on the allies. McNamara was not only formalizing these ideas but also expressing them in such a brilliant manner that it was hard for Norstad to argue back. He had taken comfort, however, in the fact that Acheson had lost some of his influence and the president told him privately that he agreed with his views.[41]

Norstad's critique of the Pentagon's thinking was in part directed at the theory of flexible response and in part at its practicality.[42] His theoretical concern was that the administration was exaggerating the ability of one side to control the pace and development of a battle. He warned in a letter on 16 September to McNamara against overestimating NATO's ability "to enforce a gradual, controlled development of the battle and . . . the extent to which we can dictate the Soviet response." He later observed that "escalation is apt to be explosive" and warned against assuming a "serial progression in which we move easily and by prepared steps from one stage to another of a development within our control." The probable efficiency of attempts to signal precisely to Moscow through the application of armed force was exaggerated. There could be no confidence in a particular Soviet response. It was "more difficult to convey discriminate intent in war than in peace, the 'fog' or 'noise level' being much higher." The worst possible contingencies might therefore arrive sooner than was supposed, and that had to be reflected in plans.[43] On a more practical level, he warned of the need to have a strategy acceptable to allies, and that it would be unwise to allow debate about actions in extreme circumstances to produce the divisions that might allow those circumstances to arise.

Though phrased in the often bloodless language of military strategy, the debate had a sharp personal aspect. Tall, urbane, and confident, Norstad appeared to many in Washington to consider himself not so much a senior American officer but, as supreme allied commander, almost the head of another country. His manner as well as his analysis challenged the White House's concept of central control under all circumstances. Maxwell Taylor saw in Norstad not only another candidate for most charismatic general but also a direct challenge to his own views on flexible response. So while McNamara was still trying to build on points of agreement with Norstad, Taylor was to the fore in urging Kennedy to lay down the law. Bundy took Taylor's point but was worried about a rift developing with this "very able and devoted officer . . . just about indispensable to NATO."[44] Kennedy wrote to Norstad reminding him of his "unusual responsibility in expounding the United States position and convincing our allies of its soundness."[45]

Kennedy was not yet sure of his own position, however. In a letter of 8 October to Clay asking for his views, he outlined his predicament:

> The central question is whether we should treat a blockade of ground access as requiring prompt resort to force on the scene, with possible rapid escalation toward general war, or whether we should proceed by stages, allowing the Soviets to understand the consequences and risks of their action.

The former course allowed for no misunderstanding of the gravity of the situation and prevented the "hardening of a new status quo." With the latter, the allies might not support such steps. If the Soviet Union chose to respond with conventional forces, then the choice between "defeat and escalation" would soon be faced. Kennedy added.

> It is central to our policy that we shall have to use nuclear weapons in the end, if all else fails, in order to save Berlin, and it is fundamental that the Russians should understand this fact. I think they are beginning to do so. But the specific course of military contingency planning remains open.[46]

Writing to Norstad, Kennedy emphasised that at "this juncture I place as much significance on developing our capacity and readiness to fight with significant non-nuclear forces as on measures designed primarily to make our nuclear deterrent more credible." To this he appended NSAM 109.[47]

Norstad had already made known his dissatisfaction with NSAM 109 and urged that no action be taken until he could visit the president on 7 November. At the meeting Norstad defended his position. Would the Germans accept NSAM 109? wondered Kennedy. Not a chance, responded Norstad. A gradual approach would allow the Soviet Union to seize German territory in a quick thrust and then declare a cease-fire. (This was known in the argot of the time as "the Hamburg Grab.") He described NSAM 109 as being "replete with clichés and jargon which were probably clear to people in Washington" but not to him. It was "poorly drafted, ambiguous and contradictory." It was fine to plan *for* a graduated sequence of steps, he said, "but we cannot plan *on* them."

When asked by the president what he would do if access down the autobahn to Berlin was blocked, Norstad suggested a military probe that would clarify the severity of the situation and the nature of the political stakes. That would be the time for intense diplomatic activity, possibly at the highest level.[48] Norstad gave no impression that he had better ideas than anyone else as to what would happen next. He was relying, with the Europeans, on the prospect that a swift escalation from a relatively modest step to general war would concentrate minds and move the parties to a quick resolution of a crisis. This meant that there was no need for a major military effort in the first instance, and no point in preparing for a massive conventional battle thereafter.

He promised Kennedy a paper that would be consistent with U.S. policy while at the same time acceptable to the allies. Crucially, though, he could not accept the idea of an extended phase of conventional operations.

> We cannot afford to exchange ground meter by meter with the Soviets. There is no way that satellite territory can be equated with that of NATO countries we are charged with defending. . . . The use of armed forces, even in limited quantity, risks the danger of explosive expansion to higher levels of conflict, including to the highest level. The risk is accepted, and therefore we stand ready to use all forces and weapons available, including nuclear weapons, if necessary, to protect the territory and people of the NATO nations and to defend our other vital interests.[49]

Kennedy turned to Rusk and McNamara, requesting a joint response. This came back on 1 December, urging Kennedy to insist on graduated response.

> It may not be possible to carry out Phase III [major conventional engagements] so as to face the Soviets with a progressively intensifying situation

and to give them time enough, stage by stage, to reconsider, but to the degree that it is possible, this is what we must do.

The administration was by now getting exasperated with the supreme commander. The president sent the McNamara-Rusk paper to Norstad with a brief covering letter saying that this was enclosed for "his guidance" and that Rusk and McNamara would talk to him about it in Paris. This meeting went badly. After he was asked to whom he had an obligation, thereby challenging his loyalty, the supreme commander tried to mask his anger in an explanation of "what NATO meant" and how he fitted in. "And I said, 'Well gentlemen, I think this ends the meeting.' Whereupon I walked out and slammed the door."[50] After this he knew that his days as SACEUR were numbered.

Yet Norstad had been providing an accurate account of alliance views. The allies could not be ordered into submission. McNamara's attempts in December to persuade them to adopt flexible response resulted in NATO's first nonconsensual communiqué. Norstad, now with little to lose, continued to give Washington scant support. In April, for example, he told an audience in Paris (including Enthoven) that NATO would need sixty-five divisions before it could dispense with tactical nuclear weapons.

MCNAMARA'S CHALLENGE

In arguing that a conventional buildup was neither necessary nor affordable, the Europeans had pointed to assessments of the conventional balance that NATO had fewer than 20 divisions on its central front while the Soviet Union supposedly had 22 divisions in East Germany alone, with substantial reinforcements close by in Russia. The gap suggested that any attempt to raise NATO's conventional capabilities was pointless.[51] McNamara began to challenge this assessment. His analysts had asked some hard questions. If a million American troops supported 16 combat divisions, how come that twice that number of Soviet troops supported 175 divisions? Either the Americans were terribly inefficient, or else Soviet divisions were a fraction the size of NATO divisions. In reality, the analysts argued, NATO and the Warsaw Pact had approximately equal numbers of troops on the ground. "In other words, Soviet forces appeared to represent a threat sufficiently modest to permit an extended conventional allied defense if NATO's deficiencies in weapons, modernization, and munitions were corrected." The United States had already expanded from 11 divisions to 16 and had stockpiled equipment in Europe for 2 further divisions. The problem was "not one of ability but of will," and McNamara now set a goal of 30 divisions for NATO, pointing his finger at Germany and France.[52]

Aware of the political purpose behind the new analysis, the military and the allies were inclined to dismiss it as wishful thinking. But McNamara was now utterly convinced of the possibility as well as the necessity of reducing dependence on nuclear weapons. He later recalled how, following upon a recommendation from "a senior allied officer" (probably Norstad) to consider the use of nuclear weapons under certain circumstances, Lord Louis Mountbatten, then the British chief of defense staff, had asked to meet him. "He said that under no circumstances, even with the great superiority in nuclear weapons that NATO had at that time . . . should we consider the use of nuclear weapons. I agreed with him. I subsequently recommended such a policy to President Kennedy."[53] There was no mistaking McNamara's drift. Yet he was unable to abandon the nuclear pledges that had been made by successive American presidents, including his own. All the developing tensions in this position came together duirng a landmark speech delivered on 5 May 1962 to the NATO Council meeting in Athens.[54]

There he reaffirmed Kennedy's commitment to use nuclear weapons in response to Soviet use and in the event of the alliance being overwhelmed by a Soviet conventional attack, but he did not hold out much hope of a nuclear response improving matters. He cited the Berlin crisis as exemplary: "In such a crisis the provocation, while severe, does not immediately require or justify our most violent reaction." Nonetheless, if the crisis escalated, the two sides' nuclear postures would become increasingly alert and engaged, reducing the chances of a satisfactory outcome.

> In short, faced with the most likely contingencies, NATO not the Soviets, would have to make the momentous decision to use nuclear weapons, and we would have to do so in the knowledge that the consequences might be catastrophic for all of us.

Further, he offered little hope that tactical nuclear weapons could turn the tide of war. Limited use for demonstrative purposes "might bring Soviet aggression to a halt without substantial retaliation, and without escalation." This was a "next-to-last option" not to be dismissed but neither to be relied upon.

> As we understand the dynamics of nuclear warfare, we believe that a local nuclear engagement would do grave damage to Europe, be militarily ineffective, and would probably expand very rapidly into general nuclear war.[55]

If McNamara's presentation had been confined to his misgivings about the nuclear bias in NATO strategy, then the thrust of American strategy would have been clear. Unfortunately the waters had been muddied right at the start of his speech by its most dramatic announcement. The U.S. government had

> come to the conclusion that to the extent feasible basic military strategy in a possible general nuclear war should be approached in much the same way that more conventional military operations have been regarded in the past.

That is to say, our principal military objectives, in the event of a nuclear war stemming from a major attack on the Alliance, should be the destruction of the enemy's military forces while attempting to preserve the fabric as well as the integrity of allied society.

McNamara was clear that he saw no possibility of a successful first strike, "destroying enemy forces while preserving our own societies." His point was only that the outcomes would be less terrible if both sides refrained from attacking cities: "The more discriminating the attacks the less the damage." McNamara had never been taken by the thought that Soviet inferiority created, for them, an acute sense of vulnerability. However small the Soviet nuclear force, it was sufficiently devastating for the United States to be deterred.

McNamara wanted to maintain a modicum of control once nuclear hostilities had started. He could not rule out nuclear war, so he sought to hold to the possibility that even at this most cataclysmic of times, something might be done to prevent events from moving to their most disastrous conclusion, even if the stopping point was disastrous enough. It was essentially the argument, popularized by Herman Kahn, that serious options were available for responsible (or "sober," as Kahn would put it) policy makers well into a nuclear war. It was better for the United States to lose (to use the numbers of the Athens speech) twenty-five million people than to lose seventy-five million.

It was hard, however, to get too enthusiastic about this prospect. Either way the numbers were awful and beyond imagination. More seriously, McNamara's presentation implied what he did not really believe: that nuclear war could be fought in a rational way, as an extension of a conventional battle. In the context of the actual trends in the strategic balance, rather than those that had been anticipated by RAND analysts in the late 1950s, McNamara's strategy appeared to be perilously close to a blueprint for a first strike. If it was at all possible to target Soviet missile forces accurately, it made more sense to attack them before they could be launched. This is, after all, what Nitze's rationale paper had suggested. That was why the Americans were going to great lengths at the time to protect their most precious military assets from a Soviet strike.

Moscow's suspicions had already been aroused by an article in the *Saturday Evening Post* in March 1962, in which Stewart Alsop described Kennedy's belief that "Khrushchev must not be certain that, where its vital interests are threatened, the United States will never strike first . . . in some circumstances we might have to take the initiative."[56] The article was intended to reassure the allies that Kennedy still adhered to NATO doctrine; the Russians interpreted it in a much more ominous light, ordering a special military alert.[57] Malinovsky alleged that Kennedy was prepared to initiate a preventative nuclear war against the Soviet bloc. McNamara himself was never quite able to disavow this interpretation.

After discovering for himself during a trip to Germany what he had been told often enough, that there was intense suspicion that the Kennedy administration was unwilling to fight for Berlin, he insisted on 28 September 1962 that the allies were ready to use nuclear weapons to defend Berlin.[58]

AFTER ATHENS

The response to the Athens speech was less than fulsome. The allies had not enjoyed the lecture. One difficulty was that it had come at the end of the meeting, with no notes allowed; this precluded any significant discussion, and the full implications were not appreciated at once.[59] Afterward the allies agreed to do no more than place the question of the role of conventional forces under "continuous examination." McNamara's decision to repeat the speech in June at the University of Michigan at Ann Arbor on an unclassified basis added to the irritation, especially as in one passage he directly attacked the case for independent British and French nuclear forces. The alliance sense of grievance was further aggravated when, without consultation, it was announced that General Norstad, seen as the champion of the allies in Washington, was leaving his post. In July McNamara told Norstad to his face what he had been saying to journalists and even to allies. "I am sorry that your health problems are going to force you to retire."[60] It was futile for Norstad to protest that he felt fine. The new SACEUR was to be Lyman Lemnitzer, who would be retiring as chairman of the Joint Chiefs of Staff to make way for Taylor, and was presumed to be an aficionado of flexible response. The allies were finding it difficult to "catch breath."[61]

As serious for McNamara was that his no-cities doctrine had been seized upon by the air force as a means of promoting new programs, including the expensive B-70 bomber. McNamara's resistance to this aircraft had generated a ferocious bureaucratic and congressional battle. Furthermore, to the extent that it was believed by Europeans to add credibility to the nuclear deterrent, it provided them with an excuse for not exerting themselves in the development of conventional options. Having delivered the speech, McNamara barely mentioned the doctrine again. At the end of the year he explained to NATO that

> it now appears that general nuclear war is likely to be even more devastating than appeared probable when I spoke to you at Athens, however much we might try further to strengthen our offensive capabilities.[62]

These arguments left Berlin planning confused with a marked lack of alliance consensus. When Kennedy met with officials in July 1962

> the apparent impression conveyed . . . by the extensive discussion was that months would be required before any substantial operative plans came into

existence, that not very much had been accomplished with our Allies—especially at NATO level since last year, and that a great deal of time seemed to have been expended on planning for unlikely contingencies.[63]

This meeting left the president, and not only the president, perplexed.[64] A full briefing was arranged for him on the state of the plans.

There McNamara reiterated his concerns about the allies' stance: exaggeration of Soviet strength, underestimation of the effects of tactical nuclear use, and the search for an excuse not to build up conventional forces. Kennedy wondered whether there was much difference between the U.S. and allied positions on tactical nuclear use. He was worried that the argument was "theoretical ... and no one ever gives in on these." Europeans who might argue for early nuclear use in plans were unlikely to be so enthusiastic in the event. Kennedy could see contingencies, such as a mass attack against Europe, where there might be little choice but to go nuclear. Unfortunately, rationales for conventional force levels turned on this theoretical argument (and McNamara spoke of the allies' "errors in judgment"). The allies saw little point in spending on unnecessary forces when they thought war was unlikely and they had, as one of Kennedy's advisors put it, "a lingering attachment to the old philosophy that if you simply threaten to use nuclear weapons, then the Soviets will be deterred from any military action."[65] Nothing was settled: the argument persisted.[66] Given the state of contingency planning through this period, it is just as well that there never was a serious attempt to block allied access to Berlin and that old-fashioned deterrence continued to work.

Kennedy was coming to appreciate that nuclear deterrence might be more persuasive in practice than in theory. He would not abandon flexible response so long as it was advocated with such conviction by his senior aides. As a philosophy that argued for keeping the widest range of options open for the longest possible time it conformed to his approach to all political problems. But as a politician he could see the difficulties. The allies were unimpressed and if they were not going to spend more on conventional forces he saw little point in finding extra foreign exchange to deploy more American troops abroad. The danger of nuclear exchanges appeared to reside in the first hostile encounter and would not necessarily be eased by more nonnuclear options. The value of the extra forces was largely that they strengthened the West's bargaining position.

12

Berlin to Cuba

KENNEDY'S APPROACH TO BERLIN and the wider issues of European security was straightforward. He followed the twin tracks of rearmament and negotiation. He wanted a settlement with Moscow and assumed that the quality of the bargain to be struck would be improved the stronger the Western military position. This made it harder to understand the position of France and Germany, who were as unwilling to raise their defense effort as they were to enter into serious negotiations with the Soviet Union. Their view was that the situation in Europe was far more stable than Kennedy allowed, the risk of war was small, and so no extraordinary military or political measures were necessary. Kennedy assumed that they were simply content to shape the political agenda on the assumption that the United States would bail them out in the event of trouble. His views on the close relationship between military muscle and political gain in fact had more in common with those of Khrushchev.

NEGOTIATIONS

From the autumn of 1961 to the spring of 1962 talks between the United States and the USSR continued at various levels in an effort to find a way out of the Berlin impasse. During this time there was no reason to suppose that intensive negotiations and heightened tensions were exclusive. They could feed off each other.

This became evident with an American proposal for an International Access Authority (composed of Warsaw Pact, NATO, and neutral representatives) to replace troops monitoring the movement of goods and people in and out of Berlin. Kennedy released this idea on 25 November 1961 in an interview with Adzhubei.[1] When the GDR described the idea as humiliating and colonialist Kennedy might have dropped the idea, yet he persisted by adding air flights to the scheme. The proposal touched a sensitive nerve. This was the only form of transport with which the East could not interfere except by direct military action, and it had already proved critical during the 1948–49 siege. Instead of finding Kennedy's new proposal a sign of good faith, Khrushchev saw it in exactly the opposite terms: a mischievous attempt to push things in the wrong direction.[2] Accordingly he instructed Soviet air controllers in the four-power Berlin Air Safety Center to assert the right for Soviet military aircraft to fly under 7,000 feet in the corridor used by traffic between Frankfurt and Berlin. They could already fly over 10,000 feet. The United States responded by keeping civilian aircraft flying within the 7,000–10,000 band while their military aircraft also flew below 7,000 feet. The same exercise then followed with other corridors. During the next stage some MiG fighters began to harass allied planes. There was pressure, notably from Clay, for a more aggressive stance, but Kennedy backed Norstad's more moderate strategy.[3] A negotiating proposal made in good faith thus sparked a full-scale crisis. The three Western powers held the Soviet Union responsible for any consequences of their dangerous actions. Soviet pilots buzzed civil aircraft, though without actually ever quite stopping them from operating.

Even against this unpromising backdrop, Kennedy was prepared to explore a deal with Moscow, and even at the cost of a deterioration in relations with Germany. Kennedy was activist, but he took as his starting point the fixed nature of cold war divisions, and this left him on the diplomatic defensive, looking for ways to persuade Khrushchev to back off. Adenauer preferred a more passive stance. So long as it was safe to assume that Khrushchev did not intend to back his diplomatic offensive with a military offensive, then there was no need to offer more than symbolic concessions, especially as all the concessions on offer came at his country's expense. The chancellor therefore saw in the president's stance a disregard for his country's long-term aspirations, excessive solicitude for Soviet worries about German nationalism and militarism, and indifference to a carefully cultivated myth that the route to reunification was through association with Western strength.

Precisely because there were so few real concessions that could be made on the allied position on Berlin itself, Kennedy was forced to look to the wider issues of European security. Some proposals, such as a NATO–Warsaw Pact nonaggression pact, posed few problems largely because they had so little substance. Language might be found to acknowledge the existence of two Germanys and the eastern border with Poland. More controversial was the issue of fixing West Germany's nonnuclear status. To Kennedy this appeared as an area where some agreement ought to be possible, so long as Western reassurances on this matter could be traded for Soviet reassurances on Berlin.

In October 1961 this seemed to attract some Russian interest, and in his November 1961 interview with Adzhubei, Kennedy stated quite bluntly that he was "extremely reluctant to see West Germany acquire a nuclear capacity of its own." Adenauer refused to have anything to do with any suggestion that the status quo could be frozen in any way. He would not preclude Germany seeking access to nuclear arms, though he still denied any such intention.[4] Having identified a way forward, Kennedy found German intransigence even more exasperating. Rusk was quite content to talk endlessly with Gromyko, on the assumption that there was little real progress that could be made, but it suited both sides to give the appearance of negotiating rather than gear up for a confrontation. Confidential discussions conducted through Ambassador Thompson and Gromyko also turned into formal exchanges of established positions. Kennedy wanted progress, but he could not get it through the established framework, where Rusk was bound by agreed alliance positions.

To get a more direct exploration of the possibilities for a wider settlement, a modus vivendi with the Soviet bloc was proposed. The key elements of this could be developed in written proposals, but it would be backed up by more informal indications to Moscow that the United States was looking for an agreement that would last. So long as there was reciprocity the Americans would take seriously Soviet concerns. In the first weeks of 1962 the Robert Kennedy–Bolshakov channel was used for some substantial exchanges to identify the various issues that needed to be addressed, and open up the possibility of another Kennedy-Khrushchev summit if progress could be made.[5] This was followed up by Kennedy with a private letter to Khrushchev on 15 February, expressing his disappointment at the lack of diplomatic progress and negative political consequences of Soviet activities along the air corridors. He warned that not only were there dangers in upsetting a comparatively tranquil situation in Germany, but "the prospects for alleviating the other concerns which you have expressed and which I fully understand—a future excess of German nationalism and the proliferation of nuclear weapons, for example—are certain to be increased rather than diminished by each new increase in tension and pressure." More pressures would only "increase the pressure within France and the Federal Republic of Germany to build a greater military force, to secure an independent nuclear capacity and to adopt a more rigid attitude on any accommodation." He therefore wanted the Thompson-Gromyko talks to be allowed to focus on concrete issues. If it was possible to "find some modus vivendi in regard to Berlin or a more solid long-range agreement," Kennedy suggested,

> this will open up the possibility of agreements on many other questions . . . including the question of German frontiers, respect for the sovereignty of the GDR, prohibition of nuclear weapons for both parts of Germany, and the conclusion of a pact of non-aggression between NATO and the Warsaw powers.

When Khrushchev replied, on 10 March, he reiterated his position that West Berlin was being used as a "NATO beachhead and military base against us inside the GDR." The latest document handed by Thompson to Gromyko on 6 March was too vague, he complained, adding that "one way or another we will sign a German peace treaty." Nonetheless, he had been sufficiently encouraged to offer some responses to the American ideas. He would not agree to an international body controlling access to Berlin but could imagine one acting as arbiter if difficulties arose when implementing agreements on access. This still depended on Western troops leaving Berlin and consolidation of the existing German borders. No mention was made of the German nuclear issue, and as on 2 March Kennedy had announced the resumption of nuclear testing, he did not provide much basis for optimism in that area either.

On 12 March Rusk met with Gromyko to outline the new American approach, and ten days later the Soviet foreign minister was handed an American paper setting out the principles on which a modus vivendi might be reached. The essential concept was to stabilize on the basis of the status quo: those aspects that Bonn disliked in exchange for those aspects that Moscow disliked, plus initiatives on nonaggression pacts, test bans, and nuclear proliferation.[6] Moscow now recognized Kennedy's seriousness. The initiative was sufficient for it to call off the harassment of aircraft along the air corridor at the end of March. The difficulty for Khrushchev was that while it was evident that Kennedy was sincere in wanting a peaceful settlement, this was not the settlement he wanted. He was not that bothered about the wider issues but wanted something concrete on Berlin. His diplomats began to probe American intentions to see if there was more that could be extracted. The Americans were cautious. For the moment they could give general assurances, for example, on future German access to nuclear weapons, but they were aware that this was not a good time to try to tie Bonn down too firmly.

The caution was advisable because Adenauer was by now close to exploding. His government had been informed in general terms of American intentions on the modus vivendi but had actually received the principles paper after Moscow, although the foreign ministry had seen the first draft. It was widely assumed that Adenauer was to blame when it was leaked to the German press.[7] In the middle of the month Adenauer sent a short, sharp note to Kennedy urging him to interrupt the negotiations.[8] He objected to proposals on the International Access Authority, although this had been assumed to cause more problems for East Germany, and to the singling out of Germany on the nuclear issue. Kennedy was once again irritated at being castigated in the German press for weakness despite the fact that he had taken the risk of standing firm against Khrushchev and had substantially increased American defense spending to do so, with minimal backup from his allies. He found it even more irritating for the French to be held up as heroes in Germany when they were now actively stirring the pot, questioning the whole American role in European affairs, but were never ready to support vigorous action and had barely two divisions in Germany.

As the arguments within the alliance were so public, the Russians could not but be aware that Kennedy was already taking substantial political risks to get a treaty. The disagreement, as ever, was about the West's position in Berlin. This was where the dispute had begun, and however important all the other matters were for Khrushchev, this was where it had to end. If he had to accept the special status of West Berlin, then years of demands and threats would have been to no avail and exposed as bluster and tantrums.[9] After Rusk reiterated on 26 April that the allied garrisons in Berlin were not negotiable, *Pravda* suggested that there was no point in negotiating. Dobrynin and Rusk held another meeting on 30 May but matters could be taken no further. A week later Khrushchev complained about provocations from "Fascist elements in West Berlin." Tensions began to rise again.[10]

By early June Kennedy had effectively closed down the pen pal correspondence on Berlin. In a generally warm letter to Khrushchev he observed that "matters relating to Berlin are currently being discussed in careful detail by Secretary Rusk and Ambassador Dobrynin, and I think it may be best to leave the discussion in their capable hands at this time." Khrushchev came back at the start of July with a proposal to deal with "the main outstanding question—that of withdrawal of the occupation troops of the U.S., Great Britain and France from West Berlin and of abolition there of the occupation status." This was to replace them with UN troops as an interim measure. Kennedy's reply was swift and brusque, pointing to Moscow's "consistent failure, even in the very formulation of the problem, to take any real account of what we have made clear are the vital interests of the United States and its Allies."[11] He still, however, urged the Soviet leader to look at the American paper of 22 March as "an acceptable way out of the present impasse."

CRISIS AGAIN

There is no reason to suppose that Khrushchev wanted a crisis at this time. In February he had dismissed yet another plea from Ulbricht to move forward on the peace treaty. The Soviet leader's reluctance stemmed not so much from a fear of war, which he did not expect, as from the prospect of an economic boycott. The economic consequences of another Berlin crisis had become an increasingly important aspect of Khrushchev's thinking.[12] Most Warsaw Pact states retained substantial economic ties with the West, in particular with West Germany, and resented these being put at risk when the prospects for getting further concessions on Berlin without a fight were so low. As economic growth in the socialist bloc was starting to falter, the need to subsidize the GDR put a strain on socialist solidarity. The East German regime was turning into something of an albatross, not viable on its own and seeking salvation through policies that would inevitably lead to more crises with the West. One reason for the construction of the wall was that it would help stabilize the GDR's economy. It would be hard to take any further initiatives until this had been further strengthened. This in turn, as Khrushchev pointedly noted, could require closer economic ties between East Germany and West Germany.

He might not want a crisis, but supposing that the Americans were planning an initiative of their own, instead of Khrushchev being the one demanding concessions, the boot could soon be on the other foot. Whether he considered himself to be on the offensive or on the defensive, however, Khrushchev's tactics were the same—assertions of Soviet strength and repetition of demands. It was because of this that Gilpatric's October disclosure of the strength of America's military position had rattled him. The Soviet ICBM program was still in trouble, while the American program was acquiring an awesome momentum. While the Soviet leader was prepared to accept that Kennedy did not want war, the American president was now in charge of rampant rearmament. Perhaps the militarists had taken him over? For someone who paid attention to the detail of the military balance, this was disturbing. He could see that Kennedy had a genuine interest in a deal over Berlin but was constrained by opinion in Washington as well as in Germany. Meanwhile his own bargaining cards were limited in the face of American assertions of strategic superiority. He could test nuclear weapons—another series began in August 1962—but so could Kennedy. He could deny Kennedy things he wanted, such as test bans, but that hardly helped his international standing. He could also continue harassment of allied movements in and out of Berlin, but that was largely symbolic. He was also aware through his spies of the contingency planning under Live Oak, a special planning group for Berlin, established by Norstad in 1959.[13] If he took his intelligence seriously, there was no need to worry about any early escalation, but nuclear war was still clearly part of Western thinking.

A number of developments contributed to his anxiety about trends in Washington. In June Bolshakov reported a discussion with Robert Kennedy suggesting that, left to themselves, the Joint Chiefs of Staff would "probe the forces of the Soviet Union." The attorney general added that his brother was much more cautious and firmly in control.[14] While Khrushchev did not want Kennedy to believe that the pressure was off, neither did he want to see the president lose control to the hard-liners.[15]

For his part Kennedy was still worried that Khrushchev would be inclined to take directly what he could not acquire through negotiation. In the pen pal correspondence he had dismissed Khrushchev's claims that the United States was relying on military strength to sustain an unreasonable bargaining position, but he could not help noting the extent to which perceptions of the military balance apparently mattered to Moscow. In June 1962 McNamara produced a summary of the military balance for Kennedy. Khrushchev had reversed some planned cuts in Soviet general purpose forces and pushed ahead with missile production in response to increases in American forces. "But, on balance, we believe there is no question that the relative imbalance has been in our favor and the Soviet leadership knows it." Moscow had come to recognize that "the West cannot be persuaded to accept their inflated strategic claims" so that "their real accomplishments in strategic weapons cannot be so readily translated into concessions by the West as they had earlier imagined." If this was the case, then Khrushchev would probably pursue his objectives in Berlin through negotiations rather than unilateral action.[16]

One reason why the two sides could not be sure of keeping control of the situation was the tensions within Berlin itself, with anger over the wall and the vicious attitudes shown by the East German police to any would-be refugees caught trying to escape. The allies became almost as anxious as the communists as abuse was hurled and shots were exchanged across the no-man's-land. Sometimes explosions were set off against the wall. The first anniversary of the wall's construction, on 13 August, was particularly tense. It passed, but a few days later Peter Fechter, an East German, was shot by border guards and then bled to death at the foot of the wall because nobody prepared to take the risk to help him. The response was a riot directed against the East German guards. Stones were thrown at Soviet troops on a bus returning from the Soviet war memorial, in the British sector. Now the Soviet troops began to move through West Berlin in armored personnel carriers. At the same time the Russians announced the abolition of their commandant's post in East Berlin, thereby obliging the allied commandants to deal with the East German authorities. While none of this directly affected allied rights, as Kennedy kept on pointing out to his officials, it was doing morale and reputation no good for the allies to appear passive. Yet Kennedy himself worried about the offense that could be given by denying access to the Soviet war memorial.[17] Eventually the Russians went back to buses.

In late August, reflecting on these incidents, Bundy concluded that the Berlin crisis "has warmed up a lot in recent weeks and looks as if it is getting worse." One way or another the Kremlin wanted Western occupation forces out of Berlin. He commented on how the "constant increase in Soviet noises" had not been matched by "any correspondingly angry statement" on the American side. This he put down to "the President's own temper" and the fact that "the Soviets have been crying wolf since 1958." It was important to get across to Moscow that this calm did not reflect a lack of determination. Kennedy had been reluctant to make any sort of stand on East Berlin, describing it to Senator Mansfield as "the remnants of our role in a section of the city which has been under effective Soviet control for a decade and a half."[18] But he and his officials had stressed the importance of West Berlin ad nauseam in countless diplomatic encounters. Kennedy had taken the negotiating route as far as it could go, accepting in the process some bitter arguments with allies, and had received nothing in return for his troubles. There was no deal left to explore. He approached the coming months with a degree of resignation. If the Russians wanted a crisis, he had no option but to take on the challenge directly. In doing so he could take some comfort in America's commanding, although probably temporary, nuclear superiority.

Moscow now faced a quandary. Kennedy's refusal to budge on Berlin was a great disappointment, especially in the light of his evident willingness to offer concessions elsewhere. There was no reason to suppose this position was about to change. In late July, anxious about trends in Washington and having received Kennedy's latest missive, Khrushchev asked Ambassador Thompson to raise privately with the president "whether it would be better for him if Berlin question was brought to a head before or after Congressional elections" in early November, as if the two could orchestrate a crisis to occur at a mutually convenient time. Khrushchev claimed that he was in no hurry. Thompson's assumption was that Khrushchev intended to bring Berlin before the UN General Assembly but was still reluctant to push it to real risk of war.[19] His sense that matters might improve by the winter but not before was confirmed by Sorensen, who explained to Dobrynin on 23 August that Kennedy "could not possibly lay himself open to Republican charges of appeasement in his response to any buildup in Berlin pressures between now and November 6." This reassurance, with a sting, came back on 6 September. The president should know that "nothing would be undertaken before the congressional elections to complicate the international situation or aggravate tensions between the United States and the Soviet Union."[20]

The implication was that the storm would break after the elections. As Dobrynin passed the message to Sorensen, Secretary of the Interior Stuart Udall was called in to meet Khrushchev while on a visit to the Soviet Union. In his way of exploiting any senior American at hand, Khrushchev unburdened himself. Kennedy could be a great president, Udall was informed, if he solved the Berlin problem. After the elections, with a more supportive Congress, Kennedy would have his chance. If, on the other hand,

> any lunatics in your country want war, Western Europe will hold them back. Except for Adenauer and DeGaulle—those two have some unusual ideas of their own. But they will get wise in a hurry. War in this day and age means no Paris and no France, all in the space of an hour. It's been a long time since you could spank us like a little boy—now we can swat your ass.[21]

On 11 September the Russians pronounced the Berlin talks a failure, although without ruling out a resumption of negotiations. By late September the United States was moving toward a view that whatever

Khrushchev had planned for after the elections was probably linked to the UN General Assembly—that he intended to use the occasion to meet directly with Kennedy and possibly to develop UN sentiment as an instrument of pressure.[22] Some Germans were expecting some sort of action, including even the sudden signature of a peace treaty, although Americans assumed that Khrushchev understood that unilateral action would be provocative.[23] A letter to Kennedy from Khrushchev, after making conciliatory noises on a test ban, acknowledged "worsening" of relations but saw a remedy in doing away with the "abnormal situation" in Berlin through a peace treaty with the East and the removal of Western forces. Nothing would be done until after the elections (a time when "common sense" loses out to "absurd" statements), but he had to speak out on Berlin because Kennedy's incendiary remarks on Cuba had aggravated the situation. So while Berlin was the priority, the link had been made to Cuba. Kennedy might also have pondered why Cuba and "thermonuclear" weapons twice appeared in the same sentence.[24]

III

CUBA

13

Removing Castro

THE CUBAN REVOLUTION of late 1958, when Fidel Castro marched into Havana and overthrew the old dictator Fulgencio Batista, was a curiosity. Castro's allegiances at the time were by no means clear; his later claim to long-standing Marxist-Leninist sympathies was retrospective. He had come to power as the only available leader of a broadly based coalition, having received some support from liberal opinion in the United States. However, this support dispersed as Castro clashed with U.S. economic interests and showed no interest in elections. It was feared that Cuba would trigger similar uprisings throughout the Americas and so extend Soviet influence. As Latin America was the United States' natural sphere of influence, any communist foothold appeared as an affront. When the foothold was Cuba, so close to the coast of Florida, and personalized by such a charismatic and bombastic figure as Fidel, the affront was all the greater.

Senator Kennedy had acknowledged the sense of injustice that had led so many Cubans to turn against Batista and the extent to which the United States had treated the country as a colony, apparently more "interested in the money we took out of Cuba than . . . in seeing Cuba raise its standard of living for its people."[1] The Eisenhower administration had hardly made it easy for Castro to come to terms with the United States, supposing he had been inclined to do so. Its drive to deflect the regime from communism only served to confirm it on this course. An early readiness to admit that there were injustices to be rectified might have served as a basis for some sort of accommodation with revolutionary Cuba. However, as Castro's policy became more stridently anti-American a series of tit-for-tat moves led to a complete breakdown in relations, and a sympathetic approach became an impossible position for any ambitious politician to hold.

President Kennedy was told as he arrived in power that Cuba was to all extents and purposes "a communist-controlled state," developing ever closer links with the Soviet Union. He was warned in the gravest terms about the implications of this for hemispheric stability. Kennedy's view was that to limit the influence of the Cuban model the United States must both address the political conditions that provided socialism with its appeal and cut Castro down to size. On 13 March 1961 he launched the Alliance for Progress, "a vast co-operative effort," with measures to promote economic development, education, and welfare throughout the Americas to be backed by the United States with resources of sufficient "scope and magnitude." The ideological message was clear: The American continent was to be transformed into "a vast crucible of revolutionary ideas and efforts—a tribute to the power of the creative energies of free men and women—an example to all the world that liberty and progress walk hand in hand."[2] If hemispheric stability required a combination of carrots and sticks, the carrots would come from the Alliance for Progress. The anti-Castro stick arrived in a ready-packaged form from the Central Intelligence Agency.

BISSELL'S PLAN

The CIA had a plan to deal with Castro and a New Frontiersman to sell it. Richard Bissell had the familiar Groton and Yale background of the policy-making elite. As a young economics professor at Yale, he had taught both Walt Rostow and McGeorge Bundy, although he had been an isolationist to Bundy's fervent interventionism. He had gained notice as a formidable administrator in charge of shipping during the war and then as a key figure in the implementation of the Marshall Plan. In 1952 he joined the Ford Foundation but remained close to the CIA as a consultant. His ideas developed in line with those who assumed that the accepted wisdom on the cold war was rapidly becoming dated, that the most threatening contingency was not "an overt invasion of Western Europe or Japan but a Communist-led internal revolution in the weaker states of Asia, Africa and Latin America." He encouraged Ford to support MIT's Center for International Studies (CENIS) in which there was a pronounced CIA influence. In February 1954 he joined the CIA as a special assistant to the director, Allen Dulles. His first major project was the procurement and then early employment of the U-2 reconnaissance aircraft.

As a result of the U-2's extraordinary success, Bissell became the CIA's director for plans in 1959. His background in covert operations was patchy, but he had the director's confidence and the conviction of one whose big projects had always been successful. Among those successes was the most successful CIA operation in Latin America during the 1950s, with apparent implications for Cuba. In 1954 the leftist regime of Jacob

Arbenz in Guatemala had been toppled without serious resistance when an exile force had been inserted into the country by the agency, and this encouraged the thought that Castro might also be so shocked by the prospect of taking on the United States that his regime would simply collapse.[3] The rosy glow surrounding this memory had obscured both the many chaotic elements of that enterprise and the critical factor of an army group in Guatemala poised to act against Arbenz when the Americans provided the pretext. There was no such group in Cuba. For Bissell a striking feature of this case was that the Guatemala operation had been planned on the basis that there should be no overt American involvement, yet when it came to the crunch and the rebels appeared on the verge of defeat, President Eisenhower agreed to provide supporting air power.[4] Bissell had accompanied Dulles to the critical meeting when the president had acceded to this request.[5]

Guatemala, and an earlier operation against Iran, had sealed the CIA's reputation as a source of quick fixes to awkward foreign policy problems. Thereafter both the agency itself and the wider policy-making community became inclined to overestimate its covert-action capabilities. Less well known was a more recent failure in Indonesia where, in the spring of 1958, a CIA-backed rebellion against President Sukarno had collapsed.

By 1961 Bissell appeared as an impressive salesman for the CIA, with extraordinary energy and intellect. A liberal anticommunist at the cutting edge of attempts to find a way to deal with the new Soviet threat in the third world, a popular figure on the Washington social circuit, and friendly with Rostow, Bundy, and Alsop, he was a natural member of Kennedy's New Frontier. He epitomized the CIA's can-do, decisive attitude, which Kennedy was soon contrasting favorably with the vagueness that seemed to engulf the State Department. Though senior figures at State were wary of clandestine operations and distrusted the judgment of those who promoted them, they too were impressed by Bissell. If Kennedy had not earmarked him as an eventual director of the CIA, Bissell might have gone to the State Department.[6] With Allen Dulles having been quickly reappointed as director, the agency's position within the new administration was generally strong, well placed to promote a plan to topple Castro.

The decision to overthrow Castro's regime had been taken by the Eisenhower administration in January 1960, and by March of that year the CIA had developed a program of action. This included assembling and training in the United States a paramilitary force capable of covert operations. The cadres would be deployed in Cuba "to organize, train and lead resistance forces recruited there both before and after the establishment of one or more active centers of resistance." By this time the original supporters of Batista who had fled to the United States had been joined by others, many of whom had been previously neutral or sympathetic to Castro but were now hostile. About four hundred were to be organized to overthrow Castro through the methods he had used against Batista, that is, by sustaining a broadly based political grouping through guerrilla warfare. This required highly trained fighters who could link up with the various anti-Castro groups already springing up throughout Cuba. On 18 August 1960, when the Eisenhower administration approved a progress report and funds, it was specified that "no United States military personnel were to be used in combat units."[7]

This approach came to be questioned for two reasons. First, Castro's forces were becoming both better armed (with the help of deliveries of weapons from Czechoslovakia) and capable of an effective counterinsurgency campaign. Second, early experience with guerrilla operations tended to the farcical. Attempts at infiltration failed, airdrops were too late, and communications were poor.[8] Bissell lost confidence in this scheme and increasingly took the view that Castro's grip on the country was being established so firmly that it could be released only by a severe shock.

So an awareness of the difficulty of fomenting an uprising in Cuba did not lead to plans being scaled down. Instead, Bissell became more ambitious and increasingly enamored of the idea of supplementing the guerrilla operations with the landing of a small infantry group backed by a tactical air force. The consequence of this shift was fateful, for it left uncertain the relationship between the landing itself and the subsequent course of the insurgency, and raised the requirements for the operation in terms of numbers and training as well as American support.

By the end of the year the idea of a landing had superseded that of guerrilla operations, and minimal guerrilla training was being given. Attempts were made to weld the disparate Cuban groups opposed to Castro into a coherent whole despite the resentments this began to generate. Unsavory elements left over from the old regime were included. The enterprise was an open secret, discussed throughout Latin America, encouraging Castro to refine his own contingency plans.[9]

The new strategy was formally presented to Eisenhower on 8 December 1960. The concept now consisted of the infiltration of 60 to 80 men as guerrillas, preliminary air strikes launched from Nicaragua against military targets, and then an amphibious landing on the Cuban coast by 600 to 750 well-equipped men. Air strikes as well as supply flights would continue after the landing. The objective would be to seize and hold a limited area in Cuba. As it became a powerful and visible presence, the landing force would attract and inspire dissident elements. With the uprising and probable chaos in Havana, the United States would be able to recognize a provisional government and send in a pacification force. The idea of supporting an amphibious operation involving Cuban rebels run by the CIA left the Pentagon deeply unimpressed, but Eisenhower appeared enthusiastic. He had taken an increasing interest in the operation, was reviewing plans regularly, gave the planners every reason to believe that they should be more bold, not less. At the start of January 1961, after Castro had called the American embassy, not inaccurately, a "nest of spies" and demanded reductions in its staff, Washington broke diplomatic relations. Eisenhower hardened his attitude, recommending "helping to mobilize a stronger invasion force so that a failure in the first effort would not wipe out the whole project." When he saw Kennedy the day before the inauguration he reported that he had sought to help the anti-Castro forces being trained in Guatemala "to the utmost" and urged "that this effort be continued and accelerated."[10]

PERSUADING KENNEDY

So Kennedy took over an advanced plan that had momentum behind it and was backed by his predecessor. It was reaching a climax while senior figures in the administration were still new to their jobs and the decision-making process had yet to settle down. The few responsible officials who drove the project forward exuded enthusiasm and confidence. To the fore was Bissell, well organized and persuasive, with the appropriate blend of analysis and advocacy and a salesman's sense of the telling phrase. Though Bundy was aware of Bissell's reluctance to look at all sides of a question, he too was taken in. He later observed "It was the stupidity of freshmen on our part, and the stupidity on their part of being wrapped in their own illusions."[11] Vital information was kept for verbal briefings, while what was written down was largely conceptual. This left, as Rusk later explained, a series of impressions: that "1200 highly trained men would get ashore and run into some militia units and beat the hell out of them," that there would be "no fighting on beach as virtually empty," and that "the ability of this force to pass to guerrilla activities presented no difficulty."[12] Skeptics within the agency kept clear, while the military pulled its punches at critical meetings.[13] Among those in the know, dissents were few and not very voluble. The doubters were halfhearted and busied themselves with other tasks, with few props to fall back on other than such vague and intangible concepts as the moral position of the United States and world opinion.[14]

Politically, Kennedy saw trouble. He was aware of his vulnerability to accusations of timidity and betrayal, not least from Eisenhower himself, if he had refused to follow through on the daring Republican plan. Dulles was not above playing on such fears. As Kennedy was being pressed on Cuba he was also considering, with great reluctance, a major military intervention in Laos, and there was no doubt that the popular priority lay firmly in the Caribbean. More awkward still was that he was widely seen as a supporter of the Cuban exiles. During the election campaign he had wrong-footed Nixon by supporting "fighters for freedom" in Cuba. At the time Nixon was furious, for as vice president, he knew what was being planned, but in public he felt obliged to address the issue in terms of uncharacteristic moderation. Later he blamed the CIA for having briefed Kennedy, and Kennedy for having let the secret out.[15]

It is certainly true that Allen Dulles briefed Kennedy in July 1960. Anti-Castro activities may have been mentioned, but at that time the program had not advanced much beyond propaganda and political action.[16] Regardless, it would have been surprising if Kennedy had not picked up some news from people associated with a project never famed for dedication to operational secrecy.[17] He may have raised the issue in October 1960 because he feared (as did Castro) that Eisenhower was going to secure Nixon's victory by launching a preelection attack, or just in order to dent the Republican claim to foreign policy strength by pointing to its most evident failure. Either way Kennedy had publicly committed himself to an activist stance. Once president and briefed by Dulles and Bissell, he was more surprised by the scale of the plan than by its existence.

The CIA warned that delay could be fatal to the operation.[18] He was told that the exile army was fully trained and raring to go, though in fact morale was low. The imminent rainy season would bring training to a halt. The sense of "now or never" was encouraged by the publicity attracted by the training camps in Guatemala. The president of Guatemala, under pressure to close the camps, had pressed for the Cubans to be removed by the end of April. At this point the exiles would have to be either brought to the United States, where possibly they would cause Kennedy trouble, or else sent to Cuba—where they wanted to go—and cause Castro trouble. The CIA stressed this "disposal" problem, and it appears to have forced Kennedy's hand. He later acknowledged his concern that expatriate Cubans would soon be complaining "that the United States would not support their activities."[19]

Yet numbers at the camp grew despite this "disposal" problem. In November 1960 there were 475 air and ground trainees. Following the decision to move toward a more straightforward amphibious operation, there had been substantial recruitment. By the end of January 1961 the force had grown to 644. It then more than doubled, reaching the full strength of 1,390 by early April.[20] At the same time, Castro was being strengthened by an influx of Soviet arms, including the makings of a decent air force. By April 1961 Cuba had received 125 tanks, 167,000 rifles, and 7,250 machine guns, plus considerable antiaircraft and antitank support. None of the MiG fighters promised had yet been sent, but Dulles was worried that they would arrive soon. Castro's position was becoming more entrenched all the time. The chance to dislodge Castro might be passing. In another six months his overthrow would become "militarily infeasible."[21]

14

A Deniable Plan

AT THE END OF THE EISENHOWER ADMINISTRATION the Pentagon set down requirements for an *overt* invasion of Cuba able to secure a "lodgement" undertaken by volunteers, properly trained and supported by the United States. It would need a minimum force of five thousand plus air cover, and would take seven months to train to minimum standards. A force substantial enough for the task "would require a sustained source of supply in such quantity and by such means, that it would obviously be beyond the capabilities of Cuban exiles and beyond the U.S. capability to provide covertly."[1] On this basis General David Gray of the Joint Chiefs of Staff, the main point of contact between the Joint Chiefs and the CIA on this project, concluded that the only action with a certain outcome was a unilateral invasion by the United States.

With Tracy Barnes of the CIA, Bissell's right-hand man on the project, Gray considered a graduated scale of operations. Each step would require more effort and commitment from the United States. CIA planning was satisfactory if an internal uprising was under way and needed to be supported, or else if it was to be stimulated by a small invasion force or even a sustained guerrilla campaign. Problems arose with a volunteer army operating with U.S. support. Gray argued that the planning needed to take in all possible steps, "including the final step of overt U.S. military action."

It was assumed that such overt action would stem from the recognition of a provisional government, which would then call for support. The current plan was that this would be the Frente Revolucionario Democrático (FRD). Gray expressed his concern that the FRD force might be landed "without having first decided upon and prepared the supporting U.S. effort." It would be too late to try to do this once the force was on its way. Barnes told him that "all of us agreed thoroughly with him and we were all equally anxious to obtain firm plans and decisions that would permit the use of such forces as the situation may require."[2]

This establishes two critical and connected features of operational thinking as the new administration entered power. First, the objective was not simply to stimulate a general uprising, but to provide a base on Cuban soil for a provisional government. Second, once established, that government would ask for overt U.S. support. The final interagency review before Kennedy's inauguration assumed that the air attacks and covert landing embodied in the plan "would not be triggered unless the U.S. government were prepared to do everything else needed overtly or covertly in the light of the existing evaluation in order to guarantee success."[3] This was the concept confirmed by Allen Dulles on 22 January when he first briefed Dean Rusk, Robert McNamara, and Robert Kennedy (who were together in a meeting on substance for the first time). The idea was to hold "a beachhead long enough for us to recognize a provisional government and aid that government openly." Unfortunately, as Lemnitzer noted when meeting with the president and the other chiefs of staff on 25 January, instead of a recognized alternative Cuban leader and political force there was only a multitude of splinter groups. The president himself then commented that "Castro has been able to develop a great and striking personality throughout Latin America and this gives him a great advantage."

A CIA memo the next day described how a landing site would contain an airstrip and permit access by sea so that the force could be supplied. There was a reasonable chance that this event "would set in motion forces that would cause the downfall of the regime," and a greater than even likelihood that it "would elicit wide-spread rebellious activities and great disorganization." Even if this did not lead to the downfall of the regime, it would "produce a set of affairs describable as continuing civil war." Under these conditions, assuming that the provisional government was recognized by the United States, "there would appear to be a basis for an overt, open U.S. initiative, to institute a military occupation of the island by a composite OAS (Organization of American States) force to put a stop to the civil war."

At this point the military and political assumptions underpinning the plan were questioned. The chiefs' preference was for a traditional military operation. The current plan did not contain enough on how to follow up success or how to take direct action if facing failure. In particular there was concern that the proposed force was too small to achieve a worthwhile objective. McNamara agreed with them that the CIA had to be told that their plan was "not considered to be a good one." Meanwhile the State Department was also getting anxious. At the end of the 22 January meeting Rusk had commented on the enormous political implications of putting U.S. forces ashore in Cuba: "We should consider everything short of this, including rough stuff, before doing so."[4]

Kennedy now set the planning on a new course. His instincts were all to reduce the operation's profile. There was to be no overt U.S. participation. According to Sorensen, his sense of escalation played a part here. Once there was an open commitment, then anything less than Castro's overthrow could not have been tolerated. Sorensen quotes him: "Obviously, if you are going to have United States air cover, you might as well have a complete United States commitment, which would have meant a full-fledged invasion by the United States."[5] If that was the likely end point, there was no reason to start with a Cuban brigade.

But if this was to be a Cuban operation, then Kennedy wanted to return to the previous idea of a guerrilla force rather than "a strike force landing," although this would involve "a greater number of teams and a much longer approach to the problem."[6] Given the direction of the military arguments toward an American invasion of Cuba, he asked the Pentagon only to provide a full evaluation of the CIA plan and not a plan of their own. Kennedy understood one part of the bureaucratic game but not the other. An explicitly overt plan would have been a military responsibility. So for the CIA to keep responsibility the proposed operation had to be described as "covert." That did not mean that it would necessarily be so.

CONCERNS

At this point the Pentagon could have delivered a fatal blow but failed to do so. To get the full benefit of its evaluation when it came in at the start of February required some reading between the lines—not so easy for a civilian leadership not yet used to military formulations. The conditions were stringent. The air plan would be successful if surprise was achieved and so long as estimates of Cuban air defenses were correct. The amphibious landing would be successful if lightly opposed but inadequate against "moderate, determined resistance." Without a popular uprising or substantial follow-up forces, Castro's forces would eventually reduce the beachhead. "The operation as presently envisaged would not necessarily require overt U.S. intervention." That "favorable assessment," however, depended crucially on the political aspects of the operation working as well as the military ones.

Especially important was a credible and coherent leadership able to attract widespread political support. Instead of being inserted into Cuba simply to ask for U.S. support, it now had to be prepared, if all else failed, to get into the mountains and join existing guerrilla bands. Otherwise a demand for U.S. action could soon arise. If a provisional government had been supported and it then looked as though it was failing or being surrounded and destroyed, "U.S. overt support would have to be given to uphold U.S. prestige regardless of the international consequences." Bissell does not appear to have read the full report, only the executive summary in which the punch was pulled: "Despite the shortcomings pointed out in the assessment, the Joint Chiefs consider that timely execution of this plan has a fair chance of ultimate success." Civilians did not always appreciate that "fair" meant no more than a 30 percent chance of a favorable result.[7]

The retiring assistant secretary of state for inter-American affairs, Thomas Mann, produced a potentially devastating critique of the CIA's plan in the middle of February. As he judged a popular uprising to be unlikely, the Americans would be left with three unattractive alternatives: abandoning the group to its fate, "which would cost us dearly in prestige and respect"; getting them into the mountains, which would pose prolonged logistical problems; or overt U.S. intervention. As the attack would be in violation of international law, rather than weaken Castro's position it might strengthen it, earning him sympathy and support. In conveying to Kennedy this paper plus Bissell's position, Bundy acknowledged that the president leaned toward Mann's view. For his part he suspected that the gloomier parts of both papers were right. Diplomatic and public opinion were not ready for an invasion, but Castro's internal strength continued to grow. The conclusion Bundy drew was that it would make sense to build up a government in exile while holding back on Bissell's plan for a number of months. Unfortunately, an outfit that was neither communist nor pro-Batista would inevitably be a contrived affair. The rivalries among the different groups and personalities continued to undermine the political side of the anti-Castro campaign. After the fiasco one of the CIA officials observed that "one of the greatest problems in developing the force was the difficulty in getting the Cubans to sublimate their petty differences for the common good."[8]

The more overt the U.S. involvement, the higher the potential political costs. It was one thing to help patriotic Cubans but quite another to invade a small neighboring country in an obvious breach of international law and at a time when memories of Russia's crushing of the Hungarian rebellion of 1956 were still fresh. Khrushchev might have viewed an American invasion of Cuba with the same respect for the other superpower's sphere of influence that Eisenhower had shown to him over Hungary, with much political noise but little practical action. For Moscow, Cuba was the wrong place to lock horns with the United States. But, what if Khrushchev responded where he knew he could make trouble—Berlin? Kennedy was not yet ready to confront the full implications of that crisis, which at this time was still brewing. In a press conference on 5 April he publicly discounted the idea of a blockade of Cuba because it would give Khrushchev an excuse to mount a counterblockade of Berlin.[9]

The potential damage to U.S. prestige was the basis of objections from presidential adviser Arthur Schlesinger, who sustained a constant barrage of memos, and from Senator William Fulbright, who was on the Senate Foreign Relations Committee. It was one of the committee's staffers who had alerted Fulbright to the planning, itself an indication of how poor a secret this was, and who persuaded the senator to make his doubts known to the president.[10] The potential political costs appeared too high in relation to the limited nature of the Cuban "threat," though Schlesinger specifically discounted any risk of the affair turning into a major superpower confrontation.[11] This political dimension was also the basis of Dean Rusk's misgivings. At the start of April he warned of how difficult it would be to keep the operation covert and of the likely uproar in the Organization of American States and the United Nations.[12]

DENIABILITY AND VIABILITY

Though Rusk later lamented that he never expressed his doubts "explicitly in our planning sessions," at no point during the preinvasion period was Kennedy ever allowed to suppose that the political risks were not high. Nor did he discount them. That was why he demanded that the operation be shaped by the dictates of deniability above all else. No weapons, facilities or personnel were to be employed that could serve, if captured, of proof of U.S. sponsorship. Bissell went along with these demands, never suggesting that there was any tension between "deniability" and "viability" or anything fundamentally implausible in an effort to pretend that the United States was innocent of an invasion force of the size now contemplated. As the CIA's inspector general observed, the project had in effect ceased to be covert the previous November. The preparations for an invasion had received regular press coverage. "Plausible denial was a pathetic illusion."[13]

The plan Bissell recommended to the president on 11 March took the following form:

> The assault in force was to consist of an amphibious/airborne assault with concurrent (but no prior) tactical air support, to seize a beachhead contiguous to terrain suitable for guerrilla operations. The provisional government would land as soon as the beachhead had been secured. If initial military operations were successful and, especially, if there were evidence of spreading disaffection against the Castro regime, the provisional government could be recognized and a legal basis provided for U.S. logistic support.[14]

The operation had to be on a serious scale both to cope with the Cuban militia and then, it was hoped, lower its morale and encourage defections. Bissell assumed effective air strikes before the actual landing and tactical air cover thereafter. The proposed landing site was the town of Trinidad. This had a number of advantages. It was a good distance from Castro's known troop locations, it might even have permitted reversion to guerrilla operations in the Escambray Mountains if all else failed, and the local population had already shown itself sympathetic to anti-Castro guerrillas.[15] The Joint Chiefs' support for the operation had been based on the presumption that Trinidad would be chosen.

The president, however, objected. He had been pressing for a month for the guerrilla operations to be the focus rather than the fallback, asking in February if the force could be "landed gradually and quietly and make its first major military effort from the mountains—then taking shape as a Cuban force within Cuba, not as an invasion force sent by the Yankees." Compared with this, the Trinidad plan seemed too "spectacular." Instead he directed the agency to come back with something more quiet, without the appearance of a World War II–type amphibious assault. He wanted to avoid a conspicuous operation at the start or demands for overt U.S. military involvement at the end. Thereafter he consistently pushed for a reduced American involvement. On 15 March he averred that it would be better to have "uprisings all along the island" than "to concentrate and strike." On 4 April he suggested that the optimum size of the units being infiltrated would be 200–250 men. Two days later he reiterated his belief that the operation must appears as one emerging from within Cuba but supported from without, so that for the United States denial of association would appear quite plausible even in the face of the inevitable accusations.[16]

The answer given was as constant as the question. This form of infiltration was impractical, largely because small units tended to get caught and give the game away. A 17 February CIA paper concluded that "the least costly and most efficient way to infiltrate the force into a terrain suitable for protracted and powerful guerrilla operations would be by a single landing of the whole force." The objective was still to establish "a powerful guerrilla force," although apparently one able to operate on a sufficient scale to have a profound "psychological effect." As Dulles later acknowledged, "a mere quiet landing reduced the chance of bringing about a revolt or defections to the landing places." It needed to be noisy, indeed quite shocking, so that the Cuban people would know what was under way.[17]

To placate the president the CIA made a promise. If all went badly, the anti-Castro forces would be able to escape and then set up guerrilla operations.[18] Bundy explained the enthusiasm for invasion from "Defense and CIA" on the basis that "[a]t the worst, they think the invaders would get into the mountains, and at best they think they might get a full-fledged civil war in which we could then back the anti-Castro forces openly."[19] This promise was unrealistic from the start. The leaders of the anti-Castro forces saw the exercise largely as an invasion. They had originally been keen enough on guerrilla operations, and some of the earlier recruits had been trained accordingly. Then they had been persuaded of the "advantages of massed firepower" and encouraged to believe that "the shock action against Castro's forces in meeting this firepower would cause the militia to break and run, and spark mass defections." So no more training for guerrilla operations took place, apparently on the grounds that contemplation of failure would have lowered morale and caused anger. The brigade was told that in the event of failure they were to disperse for evacuation by boat. (When failure came this is what the remnants of the brigade did, only to be rounded up by Castro's forces.)[20]

If amphibious operations were so easy, the marine corps commandant observed, then his men were wasting their time training so hard in regular divisions.[21] A successful landing on a hostile shore, one of the most difficult of all military operations, requires surprise and air superiority. The landing force must establish itself quickly and then sustain itself in the face of enemy attempts to dislodge it.[22] Yet the Cuban air force was discounted by the CIA in the plans, described as "entirely disorganized" with "for the most part obsolete and inoperative" aircraft and "almost non-existent" combat efficiency.[23] This small force was to be depleted as much as possible through air raids, but if it could not be destroyed on the ground, then the CIA's original plans, framed during the Eisenhower administration, assumed that the United States would intervene with naval aircraft.[24]

As Kennedy had insisted that there must be no overt U.S. support, the rebels needed their own air support. This was to be in the form of B-26 aircraft of World War II vintage, flown by American contract pilots.[25] The State Department had opposed the case for preliminary air strikes on D-1 (the day before the landing) because of their "spectacular" nature. Not until early April was a compromise reached: It was decided to link air strikes on D-2 with a diversionary action planned for that day, and to give the impression of Cuban pilots defecting from the Cuban air force. It was felt that it would all look too coincidental if the air strikes and the landing were at the same time, though it is not apparent why it was supposed that two days would make any difference. The Joint Chiefs, by contrast, felt that these strikes would be ineffective and would alarm Castro's force prematurely. They would have concentrated a big strike at the time of the landings to take out the Cuban air force and cause general chaos and mayhem.[26]

The limited range of the B-26 meant they would be able to operate over the beachhead for only an hour. All this put a higher premium on surprise. According to the March military evaluation, without surprise "it is most likely that the air mission will fail," and with it the whole operation. This had already been put at risk by the publicity attracted by the preparations in Guatemala and Nicaragua. The odds were put at 84 percent against surprise being achieved.[27]

THE NEW PLAN

After the 11 March meeting McGeorge Bundy drafted NSAM 31, stating the president's expectation that he would "authorize US support for an appropriate number of patriotic Cubans to return to their homeland," but also that the "best plan" had "not yet been presented."[28] Anxious to get the operation under way in any form, the CIA team worked intensively over a couple of days and came up with three alternative options. The preference now was for the Bay of Pigs (Bahía de Cochinos) site, known as Zapata. Its advantages were described as follows:

> The area selected is at the head of a well protected deep water estuary on the south coast of Cuba. It is almost surrounded by swamps impenetrable to infantry in any numbers and entirely impenetrable to vehicles, except along two narrow and easily defended approaches. Although strategically isolated by these terrain features, the area is near the center of the island and the presence of an opposition force there will soon become known to the entire population of Cuba and constitute a serious threat to the regime. The beachhead area contains one and possibly two air strips adequate to handle B-26's. There are several good landing beaches. It is of interest that this area has been the scene of resistance activities and of outright guerrilla warfare for over a hundred years.[29]

The speed with which the new site had been chosen meant that there was little time for detailed evaluation. Gray later acknowledged that because they were racing against the clock, with the rainy season approaching, Castro's forces being strengthened, Guatemala wanting the rebels out, some rebels threatening to desert, and newsmen sniffing around the whole operation, he "did not even have time to war-game the plan." Unfortunately, the length of the available runway (to which tactical air operations were to be attributed) was overestimated, just as the strength of Cuban forces in the vicinity was underestimated. Most seriously, the new site also effectively removed the possibility of escaping to the hills. The Escambray Mountains were eighty miles of impassable swamp away.[30] Bissell later recalled a "lighthearted" assumption that the swamps might support guerrilla operations. He also admitted that he had failed to warn the president that the fallback plan had to be quite different now. Kennedy assumed that the guerrilla option had been left intact by the switch to Zapata.[31] The briefing paper gave him no reason to suppose otherwise.

It is hard to know what was more extraordinary, the president's belief that a plan could be changed in such a material fashion so rapidly or the CIA's readiness to acquiesce. When the CIA returned so quickly with the new scheme, the Kennedy team, with its own can-do ethos, was impressed rather than incredulous. Bundy told Kennedy that the CIA had "done a remarkable job of reframing the landing so as to make it unspectacular and quiet, and plausibly Cuban in its essentials." The "one major problem is the air battle . . . the only really noisy enterprise that remains." He concluded: "I have been a skeptic about Bissell's operation, but now I think we are on the edge of a good answer."[32]

The Joint Chiefs signaled "acceptance" of Zapata as the best alternative to Trinidad on 15 March without making it clear that they still preferred Trinidad, so that even McNamara, who did not miss much, missed this.[33] They appear to have spent twenty minutes on the matter. After the president was briefed again that day, further modifications were made that pushed the landing into the night. The airdrops would be at first light, while the unloading of ships would stop before daylight to allow for withdrawal. This was presented to Kennedy the next day, and he declared himself to be more satisfied. So it was that the possibility of committed rebels taking to the hills to practice guerrilla warfare, an idea to which the president was romantically attached, was sacrificed in a desperate attempt to design an amphibious landing, complete with tanks and supporting aircraft, that could past the test of deniability. The result was a project of "a dangerously marginal character," with not enough troops, not enough air support, and too much dependence on local volunteers in Cuba who had yet to be mobilized.[34]

AFTER THE LANDING

This left the question of exactly what was supposed to happen after the beachhead even vaguer than before. The original plan was that the call would go out for U.S. intervention. That was no longer allowed. By themselves, the group could not expect to engage and defeat the Cuban armed forces. So everything depended on the quality and impact of the political response from within Cuba. The CIA had estimated that from 2,500 to 3,000 persons, supported by 20,000 sympathizers, were engaged in resistance activities, and that up to 25 percent of the population might support a well-organized, well-armed force. This was the basis upon which the Joint Chiefs offered their support. Afterward their chairman, General Lemnitzer, recollected, "Dick Bissell, evaluating this for the President, indicating that there was sabotage, bombings, and there were also various groups . . . asking or begging for arms."[35]

This conjures up an image of disaffected civilians swarming to the beachhead for supplies. Certainly the reserve supplies were sufficient for up to 30,000 spontaneous recruits. There were fifteen million leaflets calling for an uprising awaiting delivery from an air base in Nicaragua. Yet Dulles later claimed that it was never intended to win through a "spontaneous uprising of the unarmed population of Cuba." For any successful uprising, the bridgehead would have to be seized and then consolidated; the mere fact of a landing would not be enough. According to Bissell, if this could be done, with more diversionary landings taking place and radio transmissions from the beachhead sowing confusion, after at least a week "internal resistance might begin to materialize, probably more in the form of guerrilla action than of an uprising." The CIA received no assurances that assistance would come to the rebels from "identified, known, controlled, trained, and organized guerrillas." In fact, as the CIA's own investigation later observed, the invasion was a consequence of the lack of organized internal resistance. Somehow it was now intended to generate that resistance "by providing the focus and acting as a catalyst."[36]

Castro was perfectly well aware of what had happened to Arbenz in Guatemala in 1954 (his close comrade Che Guevara had been there) and had taken precautions against a coup. He was building up a substantial army, with a militia that U.S. intelligence estimates put at 200,000 men in addition to a 32,000-man-strong Revolutionary Army. Further, a Special National Intelligence Estimate of December 1960 had foreseen no development "likely to bring about a critical shift of popular opinion away from Castro." Any disaffection would be "offset by the growing effectiveness of the state's instrumentalities of control."[37] This was not shown to the incoming Kennedy team, though a similar assessment appears to have been made on 10 March 1961.[38] Nor was the Directorate of Intelligence in the CIA consulted on the assumptions informing the project by the Directorate of Plans, although Bissell assumed that they must have known what was going on. Kennedy's generally informal approach to government added to the problems of coordination.

The CIA had started the year assuming that a provisional government could be pitched onto Cuba and defended long enough to call Washington for an overt intervention. Having been told by Kennedy that there was to be no U.S. involvement, they did not abandon the plan but claimed that any successful landing would have remarkable political effects, that any American role would be deniable, and that a regular military operation being conducted by an irregular force could readily turn into protracted guerrilla warfare. The best explanation for the failure to challenge the president's insistence on noninvolvement of U.S. forces is that the CIA did not actually take it very seriously. When the moment of truth arrived, Kennedy, like Eisenhower, would authorize overt action to prevent the ignominy of failure. "It never occurred to Bissell," Bundy later observed, "that if push came to shove, Kennedy wouldn't put in his stack."[39] As Dulles later acknowledged in a draft of an article that was never published, "We felt that when the chips were down—when the crisis arose in reality, any request required for success would be authorized rather than permit the enterprise to fail."[40]

15

An Undeniable Fiasco

ON 1 APRIL the code name for the operation was changed from "Cross-patch" to "Bumpy Road." Whether or not intentional, the new name was appropriate. As D day approached, presidential input into the planning process was largely driven by Kennedy's misconceived preoccupation with deniability. Bissell agreed with all of the president's demands to trim the operation without ever warning of the consequences for its integrity. This exasperated his staff, who saw all the dangers. All modifications requested were immediately delivered. Faced with such responsiveness, the administration could not be churlish. Having been led to believe that his criteria had been honored, Kennedy prepared to authorize a relatively quiet and deniable operation, with no requirement for an overt American involvement, leading at best to an uprising and at least sustained guerrilla activity.

Such assumptions were not warranted by the circumstances and were not shared by the CIA, the military, or the Cuban brigade. The National Security Council meeting on 4 April found Kennedy in a resolute mood. Perhaps fortified by a meeting with his father, he was ready for the fight. His "earthy expression" conveyed his attitude to those who recoiled from the prospect.[1] He took the sense of the meeting to be favorable, with only Fulbright, present in an unofficial capacity, arguing against—the only one, as Kennedy admitted after the meeting, who could say "I told you so." Others suppressed their misgivings, reassured by the CIA's claims that in Cuba small insurrections often triumphed over the established order and that this was probably the last chance to take action against Castro without a direct American intervention. Robert Kennedy reminded doubters that now that the president's mind was made up, their duty was to open their mouths only in support.

As the day of the landing grew nearer, the leaks from Guatemala became more numerous and the deniability problem grew proportionately.

Pleas were made to editors to remove stories. In one case the president asked the *New York Times* to kill another story by Tad Szulc that described the preparations being made by a Cuban exile force for an invasion. The story was published, but not as a front page scoop—enough to alert interested parties but not enough to create a political sensation.[2] As leaks refused to be fully plugged, Kennedy became even more desperate to distance the American military from the operation. He told his aides on 12 April

> The minute I land one marine, we're in this thing up to our necks. I can't get the United States into a war and then lose it, no matter what it takes. I'm not going to risk an American Hungary. And that's what it could be, a fucking slaughter. *Is that understood Gentlemen?*[3]

Later that day he turned this into a public commitment, stating in a press conference that "there will not be, under any conditions, an intervention in Cuba by United States armed forces." This position, Kennedy reported, was "understood and shared by the anti-Castro exiles from Cuba in this country." Their acquiescence was exaggerated. When informed of the president's restriction, the Cuban leaders were troubled but still wanted to go ahead.[4]

The effort to reduce the U.S. role continued right up to the end. On 13 April Lemnitzer explained to the commander in chief, Atlantic (Dennison):

> Original concept for U.S. naval support of Bumpy Road was to ensure that when once embarked this operation must not fail. This concept modified by later plan which provides that cancellation possible until landing phase actually starts. This concept further modified by provision in rules of engagement that if intervention by U.S. military element is required and actually takes place while CEF en route to transport area then operation must abort.[5]

Aware of this, the Cuban exile leadership had accepted the need for their ships to take greater risks in preference to abandoning the operation.[6] Very likely the Cubans, along with the CIA, assumed that an operation planned on this basis would have the limits removed at the last moment in response to the exigencies of the situation. American pilots were recruited on this assumption.[7] The CIA expected valor to get the better of discretion during the course of the operation.

THE OPERATION

One of the last-minute changes came when Kennedy told Bissell to keep the number of aircraft involved to the minimum. It was agreed that there would be two air strikes against the Cuban air bases. The first took place using eight B-26s launched from Nicaragua on Friday, 14 April. The aircraft arrived in the early hours of Saturday morning and struck to only marginal effect. Apparently Kennedy received a sufficiently optimistic assessment of the results of this strike, which, combined with a report from the marine colonel with the brigade exuding confidence in their motivation and capability, convinced him to give final approval for the whole operation.[8]

Although the planes flew a path designed to give an impression of a defection from Cuban airfields, this fooled few, especially when one of the planes had to make an emergency landing in Key West. Specialists soon spotted the difference between Cuban and American B-26s. Matters were not helped by the lack of the diversionary attack scheduled for that night. It apparently failed to take place because of second thoughts by the leader of the group. At the United Nations, a furious Adlai Stevenson found himself trying to deny the undeniable. He had been poorly briefed and opened his defense of the American position actually believing the cover story. The timing could not have been worse, with a UN General Assembly debate on Cuba a couple of days away.[9] Washington soon heard of his fury.

On Sunday, 16 April, General Cabell, Dulles's deputy, in charge of the agency while the director was out of town (itself part of the cover), made a fateful intervention. Cabell was not *au fait* with the details of the operation, and on being told that a second raid was about to be launched, he thought that he had better check with Rusk. This raid had entered the plan at a late stage, and neither the State Department nor the White House had fully taken it on board. With the cover blown, little chance of a second air attack being attributed to defectors, and Stevenson irate, Rusk soon concluded that yet another raid would put the United States in an untenable position internationally. He recommended to Bundy that no further strike should be authorized until the planes could fly (or appear to fly) from the airstrip that was supposed to be available on the beachhead. He assumed that another air strike was not vital at this time and that the supply ships would unload under cover of darkness.[10]

At 9:30 P.M. on 16 April Bundy phoned Cabell to inform him that there should be no more air strikes unless actually launched from the beachhead. Any further discussion should be with Rusk. Bissell and Cabell immediately went to Rusk to persuade him to get the strike reinstated. They warned of the risks to the shipping supporting the operation and the brigade itself. Rusk relented but only so far as more strikes in the immediate beachhead area, where a continuous cover of two B-26s was laid on. He was not only concerned about Stevenson's delicate situation; from his own wartime military experience he could not see how a couple of air strikes could make sufficient difference. They even discussed calling off the landing, but Bissell said it was now too late.[11]

Rusk rang the president and explained the CIA's objections while sustaining his own recommendation. Kennedy accepted Rusk's advice. When the two officials were offered the opportunity to telephone the president directly, they declined. Kennedy later claimed that if the case had been argued properly to him, he would have approved the strike.[12] The Joint Chiefs were not informed of the cancellation and so were unable to comment.[13]

Forty sorties had originally been planned. Only eight were eventually allowed, and these had already taken place, with only modest results. It is unclear whether further raids would have achieved much more. It has been claimed that Castro had concentrated his remaining aircraft in one field, and as sixteen CIA aircraft were supposed to target this field, it is not inconceivable that the Cuban air force could have been effectively disabled. However, it has also been suggested that after the first raid Castro dispersed his aircraft and once the invasion began moved antiaircraft guns into the area, thereby inhibiting air support operations. It is unlikely that this cancellation was a decisive, fatal blow, though the contrary view was soon propounded as the main explanation for the fiasco.[14]

The CIA must now have suspected that more overt U.S. involvement would soon be necessary to rescue the operation. Cabell arranged with Admiral Arleigh Burke, chief of naval operations, to alert the fleet to a possible requirement for air cover and early warning destroyers. At 4:30 A.M. on 17 April Cabell woke up Rusk with an urgent plea that aircraft from the carrier *Essex* be used. Rusk reminded him of the president's explicit statement that no U.S. forces would be involved. This time Cabell was put through to Kennedy, who, after he had spoken again to Rusk, refused the request.[15]

Despite these early setbacks the operation went ahead. Early on the morning of 17 April the brigade of 1,400 men landed. The advance party had already lost tactical surprise. The landing craft floundered through unanticipated coral reefs and in the face of unexpected fire from the shore. Ships carrying men, equipment, and stores came under repeated aerial attack. One battalion was effectively lost when its ship, the *Houston*, grounded sixty yards from shore and several miles away from their comrades. The other battalion landed without adequate supplies and could not withstand a sustained onslaught by some 20,000 Cuban soldiers. It fought bravely and inflicted severe casualties, but apart from one small airdrop it received no extra supplies. It was obliged to surrender by the end of the third day.

A ten-day supply of ammunition along with communications equipment and vital food and medical supplies was on the freighter *Rio Escondido*, which was sunk offshore by the Cuban air force, along with the *Houston*. The loss of the *Rio* deprived the brigade of signaling equipment, which meant that communications with Washington thereafter were minimal. At this point two other supply ships ran away from the scene and could not be regrouped in time to get back under cover of darkness. The crews were prepared to try again only with a U.S. Navy destroyer escort and jet cover. The convoy commander requested the CIA in Washington to seek help, but the CIA did not appreciate the severity of the situation and called off the convoy.

The morning of 18 April was grim. The situation in Cuba was "not good," Bundy told Kennedy; "the Cuban armed forces are stronger, the popular response is weaker, and our tactical position is feebler than we had hoped." He warned of imminent pleas for more help "in rapid crescendo, because we are up against a formidable enemy, who is reacting with military know-how and vigor." The issue was whether to reopen the possibility of further intervention or to accept the high probability that our people, at best, will go into the mountains in defeat." "In my own judgment," concluded Bundy, "the right course now is to eliminate the Castro air force, by neutrally-painted US planes if necessary, and then let the battle go its way."[16]

America's allies were troubled while its opponents were in the full flow of vituperation. Khrushchev denounced the invasion as "fraught with danger to world peace" and urged the United States to act to stop the "conflagration" from spreading. A so-called small war, he warned, "can produce a chain reaction in all parts of the world." Kennedy may well have picked on that statement and Khrushchev's next line about rendering the Cuban people and their government "all necessary assistance in beating back the armed attack" as more of an explicit warning than was intended. That evening a message from the president went back to Moscow, explaining the events in Cuba as part of a continuing struggle by Cubans for freedom, confirming that the United States would not intervene militarily, although it would act "to protect this hemisphere against external aggression." He added, "I trust this does not mean that the Soviet government, using the situation in Cuba as a pretext, is planning to inflame other areas of the world." He told Eisenhower after the affair that he had not provided air cover to the rebels because he feared that Moscow "would be very apt to cause trouble over Berlin."[17]

Yet when, as expected, the CIA and the Joint Chiefs asked Kennedy to reverse his public pledge and openly introduce air and naval power to back the brigade on the beach, Kennedy was initially inclined to agree. His first response to the bad news was "that he'd rather be called an aggressor than a bum." A clear and credible proposal might have been approved. None was forthcoming. Late that morning Admiral Burke arrived at the cabinet room in the White House to find a "real big mess." Alert to a likely request to salvage a botched operation, he had already positioned two battalions of marines on ships cruising close to Cuba.[18] But nobody offered a concrete plan and, other than an occasional comment of "Balls," he felt he himself had little to offer initially. Nevertheless, he at least gave the impression of knowing what he was doing. Because of this, and because most of the possible options involved the navy, Kennedy decided to work directly with him, in effect bypassing Lemnitzer.[19]

That evening, as the principals emerged from the annual congressional reception, (Kennedy still in white tie and tails), Rostow and Bissell returned to the White House with more desperate news and pressure from the CIA team for direct action to rescue the operation. Bundy told Schlesinger that he "would not be able to accept Dick's estimate of the situation."[20] This did not stop Bissell from arguing for direct American air support to save the invasion. In this he was supported by Burke, who had spent the afternoon trying to find out was going on and identify options. He had asked Admiral Dennison whether the "anti-Castro forces can go into bush as guerrillas, any possibility that can still break through, can they be rescued by unmarked US amphibious boats?" He had considered how unmarked U.S. aircraft might be used to protect rebel forces.[21] Two unmarked navy planes were prepared for possible combat use.[22] He now proposed using them to engage Cuban aircraft in combat, knock out the T-33s, and so free the brigade's B-26s to attack Castro's tanks.

Having wavered, Kennedy realized that the proposed course of action was tantamount to digging a deeper hole for himself. He reiterated his insistence that U.S. forces would not be committed to combat. When he told Burke that he did not "want the United States involved in this," the admiral responded, "Hell, Mr. President, but we *are* involved." Burke pushed him:

"Can I not send in an air strike?"

"No."

"Can we send a few planes?"

"No, because they could be identified as United States."

"Can we paint out their numbers or any of this?"

"No."

"Can we get something in there?"

"No."

". . . [I]f you'll let me have two destroyers, we'll give gunfire support and we can hold that beachhead with two ships forever."

"No."

"One destroyer, Mr President?"

"No."[23]

Kennedy was eventually persuaded to try a compromise. At three in the morning he authorized a limited operation for hours later, in the hope that at least it might be possible to evacuate the brigade from the beachhead. Six unmarked jets from the *Essex* were to fly over the Bay of Pigs for an hour to cover a B-26 airdrop already planned for six-thirty. They were not to engage any Cuban targets on the ground or go looking for a fight. Rusk warned this meant a deeper commitment, a risk of appearing "in the light of being a liar"; the president raised his hand above his nose and said, "We're already in it up to here." Unlike Rusk, he was not quite ready to let the operation just die. Having been impressed with Burke, he was inclined to follow his advice, although as ever he was still looking for the minimalist option when the only real possibilities were maximalist in nature. The night found the president in tears.[24]

The next morning the news remained unremittingly gloomy. Dennison had reported back that there was no move to any sort of guerrilla activity and that the idea of evacuation was "fantastically unrealistic" unless he was allowed to put a substantial American force ashore. Notwithstanding this, Burke told him to go ahead, keeping the involvement to as low a level as possible. "Goodness knows this operation is as difficult as possible and we are trying to do all we can without much info and without having been in on all initial stages. I am too irked and tired."[25] The planned air operation had not taken place; the two air forces had got their time zones mixed, so the B-26s (some with U.S. instructors having taken over from their frightened Cuban pupils) arrived an hour earlier than their American escorts and were soon downed or gone.

The exiles began to surrender. The few who did attempt to flee inland to initiate guerrilla operations were soon captured. In the end 1,189 were taken prisoner, while 140 were killed. The chances of a general uprising had been effectively removed at the start of the invasion. As soon as Castro realized what was going on he ordered as many as a hundred thousand potential dissidents to be rounded up by his security forces. Nobody had bothered to inform the leaders of these groups that an invasion was imminent, and so they had been unable to give support.

Allen Dulles later acknowledged ruefully that Kennedy had been only "half sold" on the plan. The "doubting Thomases" in his entourage had been powerful enough "to dull the attack but not enough to bring about its cancellation."[26] The political flaws in the plan were known, and Kennedy did not misunderstand their gravity. He had decided that the political costs of not acting would be higher and that the potential gains of success would be substantial. He had gambled and lost. Faced with impending failure, he had to raise the stakes or quit. He dithered for a while, but in the end there was no serious attempt to rescue the operation by exceeding the original limitations. If this instinctive presidential position had been better understood, then the CIA might have held back. Past experience suggested to the CIA and the military that these commitments were never fixed and that the pressure of events would oblige the president to bring American power to bear. For his part the president knew of no reason why his orders should be discounted. "The military *assumed* the President would order American intervention. The President *assumed* they knew he would refuse to escalate the miniature war."[27]

He took the blame—"victory," he observed, "has a hundred fathers and defeat is an orphan."[28] This was the point at which Maxwell Taylor entered the government. He was asked to chair the Cuba Study Group, intended to learn lessons from the failure at the Bay of Pigs. The other members of the group were hardly detached critics: Burke, Dulles, and Robert Kennedy. Their report, delivered on 13 June, concluded: "A paramilitary operation of the magnitude of Zapata should not be prepared or conducted in such a way that all U.S. support of it and connection with it could be plausibly denied."[29]

This weakness in the decision making reflected the problems of an administration that had not yet sorted out its lines of responsibility. Kennedy was still learning whom he could trust, how to take advice, and how to balance different types of risk, including the extent to which he should worry about domestic critics when making foreign policy. The Bay of Pigs thus had a lasting effect, altering the entire approach of the president to crisis management. The careers of Dulles and Bissell were soon concluded. At the Pentagon, McNamara became reluctant to take military opinions at face value without checking the data upon which they were based. The American public, however, rallied around their president. His approval rating jumped ten points, to 83 percent. "The worse you do," Kennedy ruefully quipped, "the better they like you."[30]

16

Still Castro

THE POLITICAL DAMAGE was more evident abroad than at home, where there was seen to be nothing intrinsically wrong in having a go at Castro. Kennedy realized that his main error was in authorizing the operation in the first place, but the episode left him most vulnerable to the charge of irresolution in crisis. That argued as much for his standing firm in future crises as seeking compromises.

The affair did nothing to force a reappraisal of attitudes toward Castro or the search for an effective means of conducting the cold war in the third world. Kennedy's conclusion was that the fight against communism had to be based on a proper understanding of the methods of this "monolithic and ruthless conspiracy." It relied, he explained in a speech on 27 April, "primarily on covert means for expanding its sphere of influence—on infiltration instead of invasion, on subversion instead of elections, on intimidation instead of free choice, on guerrillas by night instead of armies by day." The Bay of Pigs provided a lesson from which his government intended to profit in preparing for this struggle.[1] When he asked Taylor to conduct his postmortem he urged the panel to "take a close look at all our practices and programs in the areas of military and paramilitary, guerrilla and anti-guerrilla activities which fall short of outright war."[2] Taylor's recommendations, delivered in June, led eventually to the establishment of a Special Group Counterinsurgency, which, as military representative of the president, he chaired.

It is often suggested that for the Kennedys it was almost a matter of family pride to "get even" with Castro for the humiliation he had inflicted upon them. This may have been truer for Robert than John. The president was more bothered by the extent to which the Cuban issue was now forced to the fore in American domestic politics. If nothing was done about Castro, not only would the Cuban leader be able to fan the flames of revolution throughout Latin America, but he also would stand as a living indictment of the president's great foreign policy failure. Castro had used the Bay of Pigs to declare his regime to be fully communist and to crack down on all dissent. The simple truth was Cuba was slipping away from the United States.

CASTRO: OVERTHROW OR CONTAINMENT?

On 19 April 1961, as the debacle reached its painful conclusion, Robert wrote a memo to his brother, reassuring him that he had done the right thing. They dared not revert back to the previous policy of wishful thinking. He continued to pose the problem in terms of a communist base—arms had been sent to Cuba "not only to keep Castro in power but to provide the necessary tools for Communist agitators in other South American and Central American countries to overthrow their governments." For this reason "[o]ur long-range foreign policy objectives in Cuba are tied to survival far more than what is happening in Laos or the Congo or any other place in the world." His conclusion: "If we don't want Russia to set up missile bases in Cuba, we had better decide now what we are willing to do to stop it."

Less clear from this memo was what was to be done. This lacuna was to dog Robert's personal campaign for the next eighteen months. His brother had just ruled out an invasion. That implied living with Castro but containing his subversion. That required convincing other nations in the region to take the threat seriously. This would be difficult. Perhaps, Robert surmised, a fake attack on the U.S. base at Guantánamo might get some action from the Organization of American States (OAS) to prevent arms getting into Cuba.[3] It was an idea that would recur, including at the start of the missile crisis, as the attorney general floundered around for a way to bypass the obstacles to decisive action set by domestic and international law and by the need for regional consensus.[4]

The next day Robert shared his feelings with others, including Chester Bowles, whose card was being marked for making sure his own opposition to the invasion was known.[5] Bowles recorded a cabinet meeting with the president looking shattered and "everyone . . . jumping on everyone else." Robert appeared the "most angry." His "tough, savage comments" continued in a postmeeting discussion with the president, vice president, and McNamara, and most appeared directed against the State Department. This led to a row with Bowles, who was unimpressed by the "almost frantic reaction for an action program which people could grab onto." Bowles's anxiety was not eased when the subject came up at an NSC meeting at which Robert again took the lead, "slamming into anyone who suggested that we go slowly and try to move calmly and not repeat previous mistakes."[6]

After one of Robert's tirades, demanding action to show the Russians that the Americans were not paper tigers, Rostow went up to him to encourage him to calm down. There would be "plenty of occasions to show we are serious." Rostow went so far as to hint to the president that his brother was going over the top. "As I said to the Attorney General the other day," he reported tactfully, "when you are in a fight and knocked off your feet, the most dangerous thing to do is to come out swinging wildly." He also warned, again in contrast to Robert, against letting Cuba dominate U.S. foreign policy. In doing so he posed some awkward questions. Was Cuba a problem as a local communist state or as a base for aggressive activities? If the United States was not going to invade the island, did it matter if Castro acquired defensive arms? Evidence of "a communist military base threatening to the U.S. itself" could be taken "virtually as a cause of war," but, he added, "we should bear in mind what the placing of missiles in Turkey looks like in the USSR."[7] Rostow did not want the Caribbean to distract attention from Southeast Asia.

The tension between overthrow and containment of Castro was left unresolved as the bureaucracy was sent back to the drawing board. None of a long list of actions for consideration bridged the gap between capability and aspiration. The Joint Chiefs were instructed to prepare "a plan for the overthrow of the Castro government by the application of U.S. military force."[8] There were to be studies of working with Latin American countries on internal security and counterguerrilla activities, a Caribbean Security Agency to which any nation attacked could appeal for help, better intelligence gathering on what Castro was up to in the United States and Soviet assistance to Cuba, a "freedom brigade" in the U.S. Army of Cubans who would be prepared to engage in guerrilla campaigns or stay behind after a U.S. invasion, and so on.[9]

By late April the State Department had produced a paper for the NSC setting out the choice, without deciding, between a quick move against Castro or his long-term isolation and containment. The officials struggled to find language that reflected the fury of their political masters while discouraging them from precipitate action. Though the Cuban situation was "intolerable," it was "not so bad that ill-considered, poorly-timed action would not make it infinitely worse." Examples of "infinitely worse" would be turning the OAS against the United States or starting a world war. The paper focused on removing the Castro threat, but none who read it could have expected the early elimination of his regime.[10]

As the atmosphere in the NSC began to calm down, a consensus began to emerge. There was a remote possibility of Cuba being turned into a strategic offensive base, but any weapons going to Cuba were unlikely to pose much of a threat to the United States. The problem elsewhere in Latin America was not so much the direct export of revolution as imitative action by enthusiastic followers of Castro's example. As there was no sure way of overthrowing Castro other than by direct intervention, his isolation was the best option. Kennedy backed neither the navy's interest in a blockade nor the air force's ideas for bombing the Cubans into submission. Strong advocacy for some action was now coming from another quarter, his brother Robert. Until mid-June the attorney general had been occupied with the postmortem on Zapata. Rather than diminishing appetites for another go at Castro, Taylor's group recommended "a positive course of action against Castro without delay." There could be no "long-term living" with the Cuban leader as "a neighbor."[11]

ASSASSINATION

If Castro was to be removed and an American invasion was ruled out, then the options left were continuing economic warfare, which reflected pique as much as strategy but might encourage the Cuban leadership to seek some sort of accommodation, and covert operations. The CIA, battered by its recent failure, was an organization in shock, developing new ideas only in the most desultory fashion. Castro's position had been strengthened significantly by recent events, while factional disputes among the anti-Castro groups were as intense as ever. At most Castro would be harassed, his regime weakened rather than overthrown.[12]

There was one other option—the ultimate "quick fix" of assassination. There is clear evidence that senior policy makers asked themselves what difference Castro's murder might make. However, they never got answers suggesting that it would solve very much, even if the ethical and legal issues raised by the question could be squared. It would probably make matters worse. Discussions at this time, and indeed during the whole of the Kennedy period, are replete with comments by senior policy makers of the need to "get rid" of, "remove," or even "eliminate" Castro. Those responsible tend to insist that this language referred to any action designed to force a change in regime, although one might add that under most of the more dramatic scenarios, such as a military coup, Castro might well have been killed. CIA veterans also suggest that they would never use clear language when discussing assassination but had euphemisms all of their own. There is no reason to suppose that the CIA expected direct political accountability in these matters. Over the Eisenhower years the agency had become accustomed to the idea that their political masters might appreciate the results of extreme action so long as they were not directly implicated. There is no evidence that Kennedy ordered the assassination of Castro (or anyone else). All one can say is that the obsession with Castro, and Robert's constant goading of the CIA, created a climate in which CIA officials might have been forgiven for believing that the higher authorities would not be unhappy with the Cuban leader's demise. The CIA's own report stressed the extent to which "responsible Agency officers felt themselves under the Kennedy administration's severe pressures to do something about Castro and his regime."

However, it also states categorically, contrary to allegations, that Robert Kennedy did not approve an assassination plot.[13]

Castro had plenty of enemies who would be happy to see him dead other than the government of the United States. In 1975 he informed Senator George McGovern of twenty-four alleged attempts to assassinate him from 1960 to 1965. None of these appears to have been either instigated or supported by the CIA.[14] Nonetheless, assassination plots against Castro were considered by the CIA, many bizarre, such as the famous toxic cigars. During the Kennedy period three got to the point of delivery of a murder weapon to a possible assassin.

The plotting began under Eisenhower. In August 1960 the CIA made contact with Robert Maheu, a former FBI agent, and told him that $150,000 was available for Castro's assassination. At his advice contact was made with the Mafia through John Rosselli, who brought in leading mobsters, including Sam Giancana. It was assumed that they would have their own reasons to see a return to the lucrative, seedy world of prerevolution Havana—and some residual contacts who might be prepared to undertake some dirty work. The idea was to use a Cuban to poison Castro at a favorite restaurant. For this purpose poison pills were sent to Cuba. The plot appears to have been bound up in Bissell's mind with the Bay of Pigs, although it was not part of the formal planning, and if he had hoped that Castro would be dead by the start of the landing at the Bay of Pigs, he was disappointed. After the failed invasion the scheme was abandoned.[15]

Neither Bissell nor Dulles informed members of the incoming administration of this plot. However, according to the later CIA postmortem, in the first weeks of the Kennedy administration, Bissell asked William Harvey to establish an "Executive Action Capability" as a standby capability for assassinations, having twice been urged to do so by the White House. There were conversations between Bissell and Bundy at this time, although who was urging whom is now difficult to tell. As this program had no particular target in mind, Bundy later explained, he did not pay much attention. The program, called ZR/RIFLE, was described as being concerned with the overthrow of foreign leaders, including the "last resort" of assassinations. The capability appeared to be one agent with some Congo experience, who was released after deciding that he wanted no part in such a venture. There is no evidence that this program had any relevance for future operations other than the person of Harvey, who later moved on to a leading role on Cuba.[16]

In the fall of 1961, with the Castro issue still unresolved, the possibility of assassination was on Kennedy's mind. On 5 October, in NSAM 100, Bundy wrote to Rusk asking for a plan for a particular Cuban contingency. The contingency, conveyed orally, was that "Castro would in some way or other be removed from the Cuban scene." It seems reasonably clear that Kennedy had asked for the plan. That State was required to answer indicates that this was not a request for direct action.[17] The basic conclusion of the paper was that in the absence of Fidel, his brother Raul would take over, a reign of terror would ensue, and a successor regime would establish itself, thereby crushing "any hope of effective U.S. intervention short of a massive assault." The United States would be blamed for the death, and this would be generally believed throughout Latin America. The occasion might provide the pretext for an invasion, but that would need a civil war and calls from within Cuba for help.[18] The Board of National Estimates addressed the same question and reached more or less the same conclusions. Castro's loss "by assassination or natural causes, would certainly have an unsettling effect, but would probably not prove fatal" to the regime. He might even be more useful to a communist regime as a martyr.[19]

On 9 November Richard Goodwin of the White House staff brought the journalist Tad Szulc to see the president. Szulc was considered knowledgeable about Cuba and thought willing to help the administration's anti-Castro activity in some capacity. During their conversation, which also included the possibility of establishing some sort of dialogue with Castro, Kennedy indicated that he was being pressured—Szulc thought he said from within the intelligence community—to murder Castro, and asked for Szulc's opinion. The journalist's pragmatic response was that this would not achieve much, a view that conformed to the analyses Kennedy had just received. He added that he thought that it would be morally wrong, and Kennedy agreed. Later the president told Goodwin that "we can't get into that kind of thing, or we would all be targets." A few days later he explicitly stated: "We cannot as a free nation, compete with our adversaries in tactics of terror, assassination, false promises, counterfeit mobs and crises."[20]

As the fate of the Kennedy brothers was to demonstrate, politicians in open, Western societies are more vulnerable than well-protected maximum leaders. Dictators tend to be more vulnerable to palace coups than to hit men sent from afar.

17

Mongoose

WHILE BALKING AT ASSASSINATION, Kennedy had by this time accepted the need for a more aggressive program against Castro's regime. His brother had proposed a dedicated "command operation" designed to trigger a revolt within the island. This reflected the White House staff's view that, contrary to the CIA's preference for operations established outside of Cuba using groups under direct CIA control, more independent anti-Castro forces would be more effective. "My idea," noted Robert, "is to stir things up on island with espionage, sabotage, general disorder, run & operated by Cubans themselves with every group but Batistaites & Communists."[1]

Robert had already begun to keep an eye on the CIA, having resisted as inappropriate John's first thought, that he should replace Allen Dulles as CIA director. Instead the job went to John McCone, a hawkish Republican, but with known administrative competence. At the start of November Goodwin, knowingly pushing at an open door, urged that the attorney general be put in charge of a focused campaign to replace the CIA's disorganized efforts. This might not overthrow Castro, but "at least we will emerge with a stronger underground, better propaganda and a far clearer idea of the dimensions of the problem." On 30 November the president signed a memorandum that added two powerful figures—Douglas Dillon and Robert Kennedy—to the interagency Special Group, chaired by Taylor, and turned it into the Special Group-Augmented (SGA). Its purpose was to oversee Operation Mongoose, a covert action program intended to overthrow Castro's regime.[2] It is of note that Robert Kennedy developed close personal relationships with each of the leading players on this group. He was so enamored of Taylor that he named one of his many children after him. He went to church with McCone, and their families became close. He was also friends with General Krulak, the army's man on the group. The intensity of his commitment to the individuals on this task may have reflected his commitment to the task. He had picked up his brother's fascination with this murky world of men of action, bent rules, and shortcuts. He even had the Green Berets give a demonstration of their art at the family compound at Hyannis Port.[3]

THE UGLY AMERICAN

To stress the independence of his operation from the CIA, Robert turned to Edward Lansdale, an air force brigadier general who had achieved fame through a work of fiction. In the Philippines during the early 1950s Edward Lansdale had advised Ramón Magsaysay in his successful campaign against the Hukbalahaps, considered exemplary because of a combination of social action and political reform with sensitive military operations. Lansdale had then worked closely, and effectively, with South Vietnam's prime minister, Ngo Dinh Diem, during the early years of the latter's rule. He had been loaned by the air force to the CIA as head of the Saigon military mission. During this period he tried his hand at most types of operations in the general area of psychological warfare and counterinsurgency, from black propaganda against communists and minor acts of sabotage against North Vietnam to training paramilitaries in South Vietnam.[4] He was pulled out of Saigon at the end of 1956, but over the next few years he continued to play a role in developing counterinsurgency policy and achieved, for a supposedly covert figure, some notoriety.

The British author Graham Greene denied that he had modeled the earnest but naive Alden Pyle—in *The Quiet American*—on anyone in particular. However, the portrait of this American operator in Vietnam who was "sincere in his way" but as "incapable of imagining pain or danger to himself as he was incapable of conceiving the pain he might cause others" seemed to fit Lansdale.[5] In 1958 Lansdale was even more obvious, and more flattered, as the model for Colonel Edwin Hillendale in the book *The Ugly American*, who was shown to be engaged in heroic efforts in turning the tide against communist guerrillas in South Vietnam and the Philippines. This book was a publishing phenomenon. It spent seventy-two weeks on the best-seller lists, was regularly referred to in debates over the course of American foreign policy, and was tellingly endorsed by Senator Kennedy.[6] Its impact reflected the perplexed public response to the evidence of widespread anti-Americanism in the third world. The two authors, a university professor (Eugene Burdick) and a military officer who had been serving with U.S. Pacific forces (Captain William Lederer), had intended to write a nonfictional account of the various mistakes made by Americans when attempting to influence events in Southeast Asia. Instead they dramatized their message by rewriting it as fiction.

The message of the book was that the Americans failed overseas be-

cause they were not as well prepared or trained as their Soviet counterparts, lacked a grasp of the language and cultures of the societies in which
they operated, and lived in "golden ghettos" away from the local population. Although in many ways a cold war tract, it understood nonalignment and the need for political sensitivity. Hillendale claims in the book,
"Every person and every nation has a key which will open their hearts.
If you use the right key, you can maneuver any person or any nation any
way you want."[7] The link with the fictional Hillendale worked on occasion to Lansdale's advantage, but on balance it worked against him, creating a mystique to which he could never do justice. Schlesinger describes
Lansdale as combining "confident ideological naiveté and a disregard of
consequences with genuine affection for alien lands and a certain political
realism."[8]

The Pentagon found Lansdale a nuisance and may have been happy
to get him away from the Vietnam issues on which he wanted to work.
Robert Kennedy knew him only by reputation (his notes referred to the
"ugly American"). Lansdale reluctantly accepted his new commission and
soon came to a view of the problem in which the most appropriate core
of a campaign would be anti-Batista Cubans now opposed to Castro, in
accord with White House preconceptions. His plan, presented on 18 January 1962, was to build a movement within Cuba to the point where it
could mount an insurrection—if possible by October 1962, conveniently
just before the November congressional elections. It left open the question of "the use of open U.S. force to aid the Cuban people in winning
their liberty."[9]

The next day Robert Kennedy exhorted a group from the CIA and
Pentagon to meet the plan's targets. This was the government's top priority, and "all else is secondary—no time, money, effort, or manpower
to be spared." He reported the president's words: "[T]he final chapter on
Cuba has not been written."[10] Hundreds of CIA operatives and millions
of dollars were assigned to the program.

The plan, however, was detached from reality. There was real evidence
in Cuba of middle-class disillusion over the move to socialism and the
abandoned promise to hold free elections, plus fear of the police and
discomfort as a result of economic hardships. None of this gave reason
to suppose that the country was on the verge of an insurrection. Castro
still enjoyed strong popular support. All intelligence estimates pointed to
the deep setback to American objectives resulting from the Bay of Pigs
invasion, which had been used by Castro to move against opponents and
strengthen his regime.

Even if Cuba had been close to an uprising, Lansdale had no serious
notion of how to trigger one. His overblown reputation was as a counterinsurgency specialist. He had never organized an insurgency. The CIA
was intensely suspicious. Always irritated when outsiders took over their
functions, they were fearful of an amateur whose enthusiasm was matched

only by his imagination and who was making promises that could never be delivered. At a meeting with John McCone, the new director, senior CIA figures aired a number of misgivings. It was "not easy to start a mass political movement in a police state"; "no authoritarian regime has been overthrown in the 20th Century by popular uprising from within without some kind of support—war or otherwise"; Lansdale was "often inclined to commit the Agency to a task it cannot fulfill." McCone complained to the attorney general that Lansdale's plan was "extreme" and unwarranted in its criticism of the CIA's estimate, doubting that the resistance groups could become self-sustaining. If they did and there was an uprising, then there was a basic problem. As McCone observed, a popular uprising would be brutally suppressed in the manner of Hungary. The United States would have to either provide overt assistance or allow the failure of an opportunity to unseat Castro. Roger Hilsman, of the State Department's Bureau of Intelligence and Research, described the "Lansdale approach" as "fragmentary to say the least" and wondered whether "an even worse fiasco than the Bay of Pigs was on the way."[11]

In assigning William Harvey to be the CIA's senior operative to work on Mongoose, one wonders if Bissell had decided, in his parting shot before retirement, to give Kennedy and Lansdale the agent they deserved. Harvey had gained fame in the agency for the "Berlin tunnel" of 1955, which had successfully intercepted communist communications for a number of months. Since early 1961 he had been in charge of the ZR/RIFLE program, which covered an assassination capability; Bissell now suggested he might apply it to Cuba. Squat and fond of a liquid lunch, he was far removed from the James Bond figure the president had been hoping to meet.[12] Not unusually for this milieu, his ways had become intensely secretive and paranoid and he disliked sharing control with anyone. He clashed regularly with Lansdale.[13] Harvey wanted to be running agents from Miami, mounting sabotage attacks when possible, and picking up intelligence. He showed scant interest in building up an armed resistance within Cuba but could argue plausibly that if that was what was wanted, then he needed better intelligence on what was going on inside Cuba.

Cutting Cuba's economic ties with the rest of the world, as well as the United States itself, was by far the most important means available to put pressure on the regime, especially given the prerevolution dependence of Cuba on American trade. The inevitable consequence of this policy was to increase dependence upon the Soviet bloc countries, which became major importers of Cuban sugar, as well as to lead to arguments with other countries, including Britain and Canada, who saw no basis for exceptional economic sanctions.

The Mongoose concept was that any acts of sabotage should be linked to economic warfare. Their effect was to prompt increased Cuban security, thereby interfering with intelligence collection. It also attracted attention, raising issues of deniability. Covert activity that was effectual would soon become overt. The Bay of Pigs had made it far more difficult to credibly deny CIA activity, even when the agency was not responsible. This meant that planned operations with excessively "high noise levels" worried the president and led him to withhold approval.[14] Officials became exasperated with an administration that willed the ends but not the means. Particularly exasperating was the attorney general. More than time and intelligence, he invested emotion in Mongoose, hectoring, demanding more action, yet always dissatisfied with what was on offer. Halpern, of Harvey's staff, recalls Robert's response to a rare successful act of sabotage, widely reported in the media: "I thought you did things secretly. How come it's all over the papers?" It was as if attacks could be executed without anybody knowing except Castro and the resistance. Harvey and Robert soon held each other in deep contempt.[15]

By early April Harvey had become extremely frustrated with Mongoose and its lack of progress. The Board of National Estimate pronounced in March that the "forces available to the regime to suppress insurrection or repel invasion have been and are being greatly improved" and the "active resistance . . . is limited, uncoordinated, unsupported, and desperate." Evidence of a split between Castro and old-style communists led Harvey to ask the board to reconsider its views. The conclusion was as before: Castro was still in charge and could cope with all likely threats to his regime. Harvey followed this with his own assessment of the Mongoose plan. As it could not result in its declared aim of overthrowing the regime, he made a pitch for loosening the restraints, making "maximum use of CIA and military resources" to stir up a revolt or a provocation against U.S. lives and property, either of which would serve to justify a full military intervention. Otherwise he doubted that Mongoose was worth the effort.[16]

The pitch fell on deaf ears. In early March the president had allowed planning to continue on the assumption that decisive military action might be needed, but he had "expressed skepticism that in so far as can be now foreseen circumstances will arise that would justify and make desirable the use of American forces for overt military action." At the end of that month Bundy told Jose Miro Cordona, head of the Cuban government-in-exile, that the U.S. considered "open war against Cuba" inadvisable. Kennedy gave him the same message when they met on 10 April, refusing to promise to back a revolt with U.S. troops. The priority, therefore, was to collect intelligence and not for the moment engage in covert operations of a sort that could trigger an uprising. Despite growing restlessness in the exile community, Harvey's entreaties, and some sympathy from McCone, the SGA decided to go for some more substantial and possibly noisier actions but not a revision of the guidelines.[17]

It appears that in his frustration Harvey decided to have another go at assassination. Bissell's successor as deputy director for plans, Richard

Helms, had noted how few "assets" the CIA had in Cuba and so was "willing to try almost anything." The two decided to explore the reactivation of the Mafia connection but not to tell McCone.[18] The day before writing his gloomy memo, Harvey had met with Rosselli in New York. Maheu and Giancana were now to be excluded. A week after the SGA meeting Harvey picked up four more poison pills and proceeded to Miami, where he handed them to Rosselli, already in touch with his Cuban contacts, who promised to use them to assassinate the Castro brothers plus Guevara. Some guns and other equipment were also requested and provided.[19] Nothing happened as a result.

The choice of the Mafia as accomplices promised the maximum possible discomfiture for an administration, and an attorney general, determined to step up the drive against organized crime. The FBI was soon aware of the CIA-Mafia connections. As early as May 1961 Robert Kennedy had been alerted to Giancana's involvement in some unspecified CIA operation. Even more disturbing was the discovery the next year that Judith Campbell, one of John's mistresses since 1960 (following an introduction by the singer Frank Sinatra), had also enjoyed a liaison with Giancana. This was one of the few occasions when the president's extramarital affairs risked serious embarrassment. On 22 March 1962 J. Edgar Hoover, the director of the FBI, reported to the president on what was known about the affair. The association with Campbell (and Sinatra) was abruptly concluded.

As Giancana was one of his prime targets in the campaign against organized crime, we can presume that Robert was distressed by his brother's choice of companion. However, it was the CIA link, not the presidential one, that posed the main obstacle to Giancana's trial. In another bizarre twist, in 1960 the CIA had agreed to a request from the mobster to put a wiretap on the comedian Dan Rowan (whom he suspected of stealing his girlfriend). The wiretap was discovered by the FBI, but when a prosecution was being prepared the CIA intervened to get it dropped for reasons of national security. In May 1962 Hoover informed the attorney general, who asked for a briefing. The memorandum given to Kennedy described an assassination operation that had concluded in May 1961, noted that the offer of payment had been withdrawn, and said that the CIA's involvement was known only within the agency.[20] Kennedy was deeply unimpressed, telling Lawrence Houston, the CIA's general counsel, "I trust that if you ever try to do business with organized crime agents—with gangsters—you will let me know."[21] In fact he was not told of continuing contact.

The assassination issue then subsided until it was raised by McNamara at a meeting of the SGA in August, only to be quickly dismissed as out of bounds. Yet following this meeting Lansdale circulated a memorandum mentioning a need to prepare contingency plans for, inter alia, the "liquidation of leaders." John McCone, who had taken strong exception to the idea of assassination, insisted, with McNamara's agreement, that the reference should be excised.[22] Harvey had also complained that these things should not be put in writing. Nonetheless Lansdale did talk with Harvey after the meeting and then the CIA man agreed to see what he could do. It may have been as a result of this that he met up again with Rosselli in September to find out what had happened to the material he had handed over in April. It became clear that this operation was not going anywhere and had to be discontinued.[23]

WHEN TO INTERVENE

Covert operations had the attraction of any conspiracy: the thrill of creating an illusion, masterminding events that are attributed to other causes, gaining the benefits of interference in the internal affairs of another country without the costs. In practice the illusion worked in the other direction. The CIA was the victim of its own mythology, the first explanation for all political mysteries. American denials were no longer taken seriously. Furthermore, the most successful covert operations tended to be those that reinforced tendencies already in evidence in the political system of the target. Those tendencies were evident in Cuba but were simply not strong enough to threaten Castro. Militants did not have the confidence that they could prevail on their own and, after the Bay of Pigs, had no confidence in vague promises of American support. They were not disposed to take risks unless they could bank on direct, overt American intervention.

Kennedy never ruled out an invasion. An insurrection might occur without American prompting or Castro might attack the Guantánamo base, so he directed the Joint Chiefs to keep their contingency plans for an invasion or a total blockade up to date. Their preparedness was underlined by exercises in the Caribbean in April and May 1962, which involved landing marines on an island. These inevitably attracted the attention of Cuba and the Soviet Union, and helped to convince Khrushchev that he might have to take dramatic steps to protect Cuba. Given the signals being sent by the United States at this time, Khrushchev's inference that the United States might yet mount an invasion was not unreasonable, even though Kennedy remained extremely wary of any such step.

By the summer of 1962 there was still no confidence that the Cuban regime could be overthrown without substantial outside support. Robert expressed his disappointment to McCone. Intelligence had been gained through Mongoose, "but the program had not advanced to the point we had hoped." A debate began over familiar ground: overthrow or containment? If overthrow, with or without direct U.S. military action? The CIA and Pentagon inclined toward using some provocation to overthrow Castro by U.S. force. The State Department's view was that the "gap between the present CIA estimate of what it can accomplish and what we feel should be the minimum condition in Cuba where we might consider using U.S. military force" was sufficiently great for the issue to remain moot.[24]

By the middle of August the SGA had decided to concentrate on the "further containment, undermining and discrediting of the target regime while isolating it from other Hemispheric nations" rather than its over-throw. Priority was to be given to intelligence collection. Taylor explained the problem to the president: "[F]rom what we know we perceive no likelihood of an overthrow of the government by internal means and with-out the direct use of US military force." The best that could be done would be to add to the difficulties of the regime and increase the visibility of its failures.[25] As the group met again early in October Robert was grumbling at the lack of progress. McCone reminded him that the project was largely focused on intelligence gathering and that no sabotage had been authorized, and that when proposals were made those higher up were hesitant about any action that might be attributed to the United States. A "sharp exchange" followed, the upshot of which was that Ken-nedy was demanding more dynamic action, with less concern about noise. Lansdale was to come forward with new proposals.[26]

With Taylor now chairing the Joint Chiefs of Staff, Robert took over the chair of the SGA. On 16 October, the scheduled time for Lansdale's projected uprising, Robert Kennedy was still complaining. There had been "no acts of sabotage and even the one which had been attempted had failed twice."[27] He was more angry that usual that day. News had just come in that Soviet medium-range ballistic missiles had arrived in Cuba. Soon there was a full-blown crisis that could in part be blamed on Mongoose and the thinking that lay behind it, and all sabotage operations were halted.

18

Searching for Missiles

FROM AUGUST 1962 the policy debate on Cuba had acquired a new focus and become altogether more serious. For over a month the question of Castro's overthrow had been displaced by perplexity on the meaning of substantial deliveries of men and equipment from the Soviet Union. These threatened to aggravate what was already a difficult issue for an administration just months away from important midterm elections.

At the start of 1962 opinion polls suggested that of all foreign policy issues, Cuba was the only one where the administration got a negative rating (of 62 percent). By September the mood had hardened. Of those with an opinion about Cuba, over 70 percent wanted action of some sort, and though few wanted war, many were prepared for tough action, including proposals to "starve them out."[1] Raids by rebel groups against targets in Cuba were praised by the press and set as an example for the U.S. government to emulate (though the government had to deny any actual support for the groups). Liberal as much as conservative columnists were encouraging an anti-Castro uprising.

The administration policy was caught by the logic of deniability. It was hoping that the economic squeeze on Cuba, plus covert operations, might produce an uprising, but if one failed to materialize, then at least some officials recognized that the logical course would be to reach an accommodation with Castro. Thus McGeorge Bundy, skeptical about covert action, asserted to John McCone that policy toward Cuba had to be resolved. Bundy thought the choices were either direct military action, which he considered "intolerable," or learning "to live with Castro, and his Cuba," and adjust policies accordingly.[2] The polls indicated just how difficult this would be. The suspicion that Cuba was being turned into a Soviet base was not going to make it any easier.

KHRUSHCHEV'S PLAN

By early 1962 Moscow had come to the view that while Kennedy was not likely to authorize an invasion of Cuba, he was impatient with the situation. In the interview he gave to Khrushchev's son-in-law Adzhubei on 30 January 1962, the president had perhaps implied more than he intended. Asked why the United States was so unfriendly to Cuba, he explained that the country had no experience of an unfriendly country so close to its borders: "The President pointed out that the USSR would have the same reaction if a hostile group arose in the vicinity of its borders. In this connection, the President referred to the Soviet reaction to the Hungarian uprising."[3] The Russians had, of course, invaded Hungary.

The KGB reported, quite accurately, on the CIA's preoccupation with intelligence gathering and sabotage and suspected, again accurately, that the Americans were banking on the economic pressure on Cuba to spark some sort of uprising. This did not point to anything specific, but Khrushchev was now anxious on Cuba's behalf. That a full invasion could not be ruled out was underscored by American-Caribbean military exercises of April 1962, which involved two ostentatious amphibious landings. In addition, he was worried that the Soviet position in Cuba had been undermined by internecine fighting, which had led to the dismissal from the government of Anibal Escalante, a leading communist, following a power play that backfired. So far the Soviet Union had only responded positively to Castro's post–Bay of Pigs requests for assistance. Perhaps they should do more?

The first decision, taken in April, was to meet Cuban demands for air defenses. On 12 April the Soviet Presidium approved delivery of 180 SA-2 missiles to Cuba, plus a battery of cruise missiles intended for coastal defense, prudent precautions against an invasion. In May Khrushchev began to develop the thought that he might usefully send nuclear weapons as well. He had the safety of Cuba in mind, but this was now bound up with the international position of the Soviet Union and the rather irritating state of the strategic balance.[4] At the time the Russians had twenty ICBMs, feeble compared with the burgeoning American arsenal. The United States had—on 25 April—just started an atmospheric nuclear testing program in the Pacific. An additional Soviet force in Cuba would be a great leap forward in closing the gap, and there were plenty of spare medium-range missiles. Putting missiles into Cuba would add significantly to the Soviet threat to the United States while complicating any American first-strike plans. The Strategic Rocket Forces, assigned responsibility for the deployment in Cuba, had little knowledge of the Caribbean but a keen sense of the strategic balance.

Khrushchev was warned by his Cuban specialists that Castro would be loath to accept the missiles—he had publicly rejected the idea of Cuba becoming a military base for another state in January. The Soviet leader believed it unthinkable that fraternal assistance of such quality could be rejected. The plan was presented to the Defense Council in Moscow on 21 May and approved on 24 May. Castro then reluctantly agreed on the basis that he was doing a good turn for the socialist camp by helping shift the global balance of power. The Russians insisted that they were doing the Cubans a good turn by bolstering their defense. Castro was reassured that he could rely on Soviet global strength to deter an American attack if the missiles were discovered and a crisis developed. He did not, at the time, appreciate just how weak the Soviet strategic position actually was.[5]

The plan was to deploy forty land-based ballistic missile launchers and sixty missiles in five missile regiments. This was to be accompanied by a full-sized group of Soviet forces, more than 45,000 strong, with four motorized rifle regiments (and more than 250 armored fighting vehicles), a wing of the latest Soviet fighter aircraft (the MiG-21), about eighty nuclear-capable cruise missiles for coastal defense, and a regiment of forty-two Il-28 aircraft. A submarine base with an initial deployment of eleven submarines, of which seven would have carried submarine-launched ballistic missiles (SLBMs), was also planned. The medium-range missile—known in the West as the SS-4—had a 1,000-mile range, a megaton warhead, and some mobility, in that they could be moved to new sites if necessary. The 2,000-mile-range SS-5 intermediate-range ballistic missiles (IRBMs) required a more permanent construction if they were to be launched. The idea was to get them in before the November congressional elections but announce them afterward. Having been advised by the military that deception could be achieved, secrecy was the key to Khrushchev's plan.[6] In the light of the minimal measures taken to conceal the deliveries, he should not have been so confident.

AMERICAN SUSPICIONS

At the start of July American intelligence picked up the news that Raul Castro had arrived in Moscow for unknown discussions. While the CIA did not believe that the Soviet Union had sent to Cuba any guided missiles or nuclear weapons, it was "possible that some surface-to-air missiles [SAMs] are to be delivered, but none are believed to have arrived thus far." The estimate at the end of July commented on the Soviet commitment to the Castro regime but expressed doubt that the Cubans would be provided with the capability "to undertake major independent military operations overseas" or that "the Bloc will station in Cuba combat units of any description."[7]

Soon it became apparent that something exceptional was going on. At the end of August a U-2 aircraft over Cuba spotted the SA-2 air defense missiles. This not only put the U-2s themselves at risk in further flights but also implied that there was something worth defending. To McCone the most likely answer was nuclear missiles.[8] He took the line that the

Soviet Union would not let Cuba fail, and he anticipated the insertion of conventional military aid plus ballistic missiles into the island, justified by reference to U.S. missile bases in Turkey and Italy.[9] He was alone. His own estimators concurred with senior policy makers that Khrushchev would not be so bold. They acknowledged that Cuba "could be used as a military base from which to threaten the US" but saw little point to this, noting that the provocation would carry risks. Little could be added to "the weight of attack which the Soviets could direct against the US." At most the objective would probably be "to deter an anticipated US military intervention against Castro."[10]

There may have been no supposition that nuclear missiles were being taken to Cuba, but that did not mean that the possibility was ignored. It was first considered in a meeting in Dean Rusk's office on 21 August. In this one meeting most of the issues that would be obsessing policy makers two months later were raised. Would the appropriate response be "blockades of Soviet and bloc shipping into Cuba or alternatively a total blockade of Cuba"? Might it be better to take direct action against missile sites in Cuba? What would be the Soviet response—a blockade of Berlin or retaliation against U.S. missile sites in Italy and Turkey? This was bound up with continued discussions of the prospects for Mongoose and whether this might lead to overt intervention.

McCone gave a very doubtful response to the likely benefits of "possible aggressive action in the fields of intelligence, sabotage and guerrilla warfare," as proposed by McNamara, while Bundy warned of the need for only covert actions at this time, as overt actions would have serious international consequences. This was in response to Robert Kennedy's revival of a favored scheme to provoke "action against Guantanamo which would permit us to retaliate, or involving a third country in some way."[11]

Two days later, in a meeting with the president, it was agreed that an analysis was needed on the danger posed to the United States by, and the effect on Latin America of, Soviet missile installations. The president raised the question of what might be done against missile sites in Cuba: "Could we take them out by air or would a ground offensive be necessary or alternatively could they be destroyed by a substantial guerrilla effort"? The question was not answered.[12] Again more study was need. Intriguingly, given later events, the consequent National Security Action Memorandum (NSAM 181) started with the only firm instruction given on 23 August: The Pentagon was asked to find a way of getting Jupiter missiles out of Turkey. The other actions were to encourage allies to realize the importance of sustaining the economic squeeze on Cuba, step up Project Mongoose, analyze the "probable military, political and psychological impact" of offensive missiles arriving in Cuba, and examine the value of a U.S. statement saying that such a move would be intolerable. A study was also required on potential action: "What would be the pros and cons, for example, of pinpoint attack, general counter-force attack, and outright invasion?" Kennedy knew he could not tolerate Soviet nuclear missiles in Cuba, should McCone's warnings turn out to be correct, but for the moment he was looking to deterrence rather than preventative action.

While these meetings were going on, the CIA was collating the most recent intelligence. Even if Cuba was not being turned into an offensive military base, there was no doubt that this was military aid on an extensive scale. An "unusually large number of Soviet ships" were reported to be delivering military cargoes, with "military construction under way at several locations" and "unconfirmed reports" that Soviet bloc personnel might now total as many as five thousand. The best guess was that the basic objective was to establish an air defense system. Commenting on this for Bundy, Schlesinger observed the "striking change in Soviet policy" but still assumed that any military construction would be defensive in function—"a launching pad directed against the U.S. would be too blatant a provocation." The State Department concurred that the buildup was a largely defensive move, reflecting concerns about the threat to Cuba.[13]

In the White House the policy issue was whether a statement should be made drawing a line that Moscow must not pass. Bundy suggested a position to Kennedy. First the new activities should be described as evidence of a "Cuban sell-out to the Soviets" but not of a new threat to the United States. Second, "the grounds on which aggressive action or offensive capability would call us into action" should be clarified. While he was not too bothered if, as expected, the main Soviet interest was in air defenses, a Soviet missile base would be a matter of "elemental national security." Missiles could attack American population centers with short warning time. On "military grounds alone, the establishment of such a capability would be unacceptable." There would also be a profound political and psychological effect.[14]

The Soviet ambassador, Anatoly Dobrynin, was warned of the concern; he replied that Khrushchev had told him that nothing would be done to unsettle America's internal politics before the election.[15] On 4 September Salinger issued on Kennedy's behalf a warning that the "gravest issues would arise" if the Soviet Union sent a "significant offensive capability" to Cuba.[16] A week later the president stated bluntly

> If at any time the Communist build-up in Cuba were to endanger or interfere with our security in any way, . . . or if Cuba should ever attempt to export its aggressive purposes by force . . . or become an offensive military base of significant capacity for the Soviet Union, then this country will do whatever must be done to protect its own security and that of its allies.[17]

Robert told Bolshakov that if Khrushchev wanted improved relations, he had to understand the effect of such developments on the president's position. The reply came on 6 October: Only "exclusively defensive weapons" were being supplied. No action would be taken until after the elections. Later Bolshakov rang to inform Robert that "under no circumstances" would surface-to-surface missiles be sent to Cuba.[18]

The American warnings created a quandary for Khrushchev. The missiles were now en route. Kennedy would eventually discover that his warnings had been ignored. It has been argued that, having decided it was too late to change course, Khrushchev instead upped the ante. The actual response was more equivocal. Now more aware of the risks of premature disclosure, he certainly sought to expedite the dispatch of weaponry to Cuba. He also decided to augment the tactical nuclear forces. In addition to eighty nuclear-armed cruise missiles with 12-kiloton warheads, which had been part of the original plan, Khrushchev decided to add six Luna rocket launchers (known in the West as FROGs) with two 2-kiloton warheads each, along with six 12-kiloton nuclear bombs for the Il-28s already en route, and possibly six nuclear depth charges. Later in September, perhaps to avoid more overt provocation, he decided not to send seven missile-launching submarines and six warships, as had been planned.[19]

There had been virtually no analysis of the actual role tactical nuclear weapons could usefully play in an unfolding conflict, or of the risks of escalation. It is probable that Khrushchev believed that they might be necessary in the event of an attempted amphibious landing by the Americans, perhaps before the missiles were operational, but that the wider naval deployments carried a risk of a substantial naval battle and even of general war. Sending the tactical systems made no sense in terms of a show of strength. There is no indication that Khrushchev ever intended to disclose their existence. Their purpose was to prepare for a confrontation, though he also made sure that these weapons could be used only with Moscow's permission.[20] Initially Khrushchev wanted to send the missiles by plane, but the Defense Ministry persuaded him that a ship would be more prudent. They arrived at the end of September, to be followed by the first shipments of nuclear warheads on 4 October. Work on the SS-4 sites was accelerated.

THE ESTIMATES

On 19 September the Office of National Estimates published its considered view on the Soviet buildup in Cuba, concluding

> We believe that the USSR values its position in Cuba primarily for the political advantages to be derived from it, and consequently that the main purpose of the present military buildup in Cuba is to strengthen the Communist regime there against what the Cubans and the Soviets conceive to be a danger that the US may attempt by one means or another to overthrow it. The Soviets evidently hope to deter any such attempt by enhancing

Castro's defensive capabilities and by threatening Soviet military retaliation. At the same time, they evidently recognize that the development of an offensive military base in Cuba might provoke US military intervention and thus defeat their present purpose.

It saw the possibility of weapons of a more "offensive" character being introduced, such as light bombers, submarines, and short-range missiles, depending on whether they thought that their introduction would provoke a U.S. military reaction. As far as the most dangerous contingency was concerned, however, the estimate was sanguine:

> The USSR could derive considerable military advantage from the establishment of Soviet medium and intermediate range ballistic missiles in Cuba, or from the establishment of a Soviet submarine base there. As between these two, the establishment of a submarine base would be the more likely. Either development, however, would be incompatible with Soviet practice to date and with Soviet policy as we presently estimate it. It would indicate a far greater willingness to increase the level of risk in US-Soviet relations than the USSR has displayed thus far, and consequently would have important policy implications with respect to other areas and other problems in East-West relations.[21]

The analysts thus discounted the possibility of Moscow making an imprudent departure from past practice. Khrushchev, they judged, would not be so foolish as to send missiles to Cuba when the risks had just been underscored publicly by the president. Events were to prove that this was indeed a foolish move, but foolish moves are made and intelligence analysts are rarely able to spot them in advance.[22] McCone, the CIA director, who might have insisted on a different view, was then on his honeymoon in France. All he could do was cable back regular expressions of his concern, but this was concern based on a hunch, not facts. At the time there was no hard evidence of missile deployment.

In retrospect something might have been gleaned by looking closely at some of the ships en route to Cuba, with exceptionally large hatches and space for heavy loads yet apparently riding high in the water. Reconnaissance satellites were now on reasonably regular duty over Russia but not over Cuba, and diversion would have taken time. U-2 imagery was not a straightforward option. U-2 flights on 29 August and 5 September were hampered by unusually poor weather. In addition, because of some awkward incidents with U-2 flights over Russia and China (the latter involving the loss of an aircraft), Rusk was reluctant to risk yet more incidents over Cuba. The need to avoid flying right over the SAMs meant that the U-2s took pictures at a slant, limiting the coverage. Robert Kennedy was unimpressed by the caution: "What's the matter, Dean, no guts?"[23] The restricted flights of 17, 26, and 29 September did little more than undermine a variety of reports from observers in Cuba.

During the second half of September reports started to come in from observers that seemed to describe Soviet SS-4 medium-range ballistic missiles (MRBMs). Out of thousands of reports, many of which claimed missile sightings, all but about eight might have given the analysts pause for thought.[24] A report disseminated on 18 September from an agent recruited under Mongoose warned that an area was being cleared of people and livestock. A report received on 21 September was of a sighting on 12 September of a convoy of twenty objects sixty-five to seventy feet long that resembled missiles on trailers. Six days later another report came in of the same convoy. Given that the SS-4s had not yet arrived, the sightings almost certainly were actually of SAM trailers. Nonetheless, because of their size, these were considered to be of sufficient interest to justify a close look at the San Cristóbal area in Pinar del Río Province. On 1 October McNamara and the Joint Chiefs were briefed on the fact that fifteen SA-2 SAM sites had been confirmed, that there was some peculiar activity in Pinar del Río Province, including the evacuation of Cubans and an influx of Soviet personnel, as well as a report of a sighting of SS-4 missiles.[25]

Anxiety levels were increasing—"everyone's antennae were already quivering."[26] This briefing appears to have spurred McNamara to discuss contingency plans further with the Joint Chiefs of Staff, so it does not seem to be wholly the case that the American government was caught completely by surprise in the middle of the month. There were then essentially two plans: an air strike on Cuba to eliminate the missiles and an invasion preceded by an air strike.[27] The commander in chief of the Atlantic Fleet was also told to prepare a blockade—though this was to prevent missiles being replaced once destroyed rather than as an alternative to their destruction. Given the potential urgency, if the reports of missile sites did turn out to be valid, the military were told to have their plans completed by 20 October.[28] Yet the suspicions within the Pentagon were not so firm as to be shared among the rest of the bureaucracy. McNamara told Taylor on 15 October that the president wanted "no military action within the next three months, but he can't be sure as he does not control events."[29]

On 2 October McNamara sent around a memo providing more guidance for military planning. In the event of Soviet weapons systems being discovered, the threat they posed would have to be removed, but so would the Castro regime. So long as this regime was in place such threats to U.S. national security might recur. This latter task was the more difficult, so that was the one to plan for.[30] Over the following two weeks forces were readied to implement either of the contingency plans in short order should it be deemed necessary. This included some prepositioning of units.[31] An amphibious exercise was due to start on 15 October and scheduled to last for two weeks, in which twenty thousand naval personnel and four thousand marines were to overthrow the imaginary tyrant

"Ortsac."[32] It was presumed that a missile base would prompt the most drastic and decisive action.

Despite the worrying information and the preparation of contingency plans, the administration still publicly denied that Cuba was being turned into an offensive missile base. This was the result of the need to counter escalating claims from Senator Kenneth Keating about the more menacing aspects of the Soviet buildup, which had culminated with an allegation on 10 October that six IRBM sites were being constructed. As this was wrong in the detail but right in the essentials, it remains unclear as to whether this was based on an inspired guess or a garbled leak. Either way it had the effect of requiring administration spokesmen to state firmly, on the basis of the best estimates at the time, that he was wrong.[33] So it was that Bundy asserted on television on 14 October: "I *know* there is no evidence, and I think there is no present likelihood that the Cubans and the Cuban government and the Soviet government would in combination attempt to install a major offensive capability."

The intelligence community was no longer so sure. On 4 and 9 October the interagency Committee on Overhead Reconnaissance agreed to U-2 flights over San Cristóbal as soon as weather permitted. There was then a further delay, because McNamara insisted that in case a U-2 was shot down in a repeat of the 1960 incident, it was better that it be flown by a uniformed air force officer than by a civilian CIA pilot.[34] Eventually, on 14 October, the first MRBM site was photographed. The next day the National Photographic Intelligence Center confirmed that three sites were being developed in the San Cristóbal area. Two further U-2 missions showed another site plus an IRBM site at Guanjay, and crates for Il-28 Beagle medium-range bombers at San Julián airfield.[35] That evening the CIA's Ray Cline reported to McGeorge Bundy, who decided that nothing could be done about the matter until the morning. The president was tired after a day's campaigning. On the morning of 16 October Kennedy was told of the discovery. The president took it personally: "He can't do that to me!" was his first reaction.[36]

19

The Options Debated

ON 16 OCTOBER the evidence was incontrovertible. The Soviet Union was attempting to insert missiles covertly into Cuba. Over the next thirteen days Kennedy took the advice of a group that met regularly—almost continually—for the duration of the crisis. This group has come to be known as ExComm (for Executive Committee of the National Security Council) although it was not formally designated as such until a week into the crisis. Though membership fluctuated, the key members were McNamara, Gilpatric, and Nitze from the Pentagon; Taylor, now chairing the Joint Chiefs of Staff; Rusk, George Ball, Edwin Martin (assistant for Latin American affairs), and, briefly, Charles Bohlen, about to become ambassador to Paris, from the State Department; Bundy and Sorensen from the White House, with Llewellyn Thompson, recently returned from the U.S. embassy in Moscow, acting as advisor on Soviet affairs; and McCone from the CIA. In addition to those with formal responsibility, others joined the group because of their special status or knowledge: Douglas Dillon, secretary of the treasury; Dean Acheson; and, of particular importance, Robert Kennedy. Stevenson also contributed. Taylor provided a link with his military colleagues, who on one occasion had their own meeting with the president.[1]

It was, as participants observed at the time and later, an odd way to manage a crisis. Conversations were freewheeling and conducted without obvious respect for hierarchy. Dean Acheson and Dean Rusk, with their traditional notions of the responsible workings of a government, were appalled. Correctly or not, they assumed that ExComm was a device for marginalizing the State Department and keeping Robert Kennedy in charge when his brother was not able to preside himself. Always prepared to ask hard and searching questions himself, Robert, intensely suspicious on his brother's behalf, could easily turn a difference of opinion into a question of loyalty. Rusk, already irritated by the attorney general's forays into foreign affairs, barely contributed in seminar mode, preferring to keep his opinions for direct delivery to the president. Acheson made unflattering comparisons with the Truman method, which required leadership rather than incessant group discussions to forge a consensus.

When the transcripts of some key meetings were first released they were commented upon for revealing an unstructured, undisciplined discussion, without any clear sense of agenda, and with important topics dropped as quickly as they were raised. The criticism is unjust: The transcripts reveal people searching for a way out of a dreadful quandary, displaying raw emotion as much as steely rationality, occasionally rambling, sometimes reflective, rarely systematic. Looking through them now, the reader cannot doubt their seriousness.[2] However chaotic the process of policy formation, there is no question that ExComm did shift opinions and help the president ensure that all points of view were exposed and a consensus forged around his preferred option. It did not, however, provide the setting for many of the key decisions.

THE ISSUE

The first meeting of the president and his advisers on 16 October began with an intelligence briefing, followed by Dean Rusk's opening view that it was imperative to establish "a chain of events that will eliminate this base." There was no dissent. A clear political objective was set from the beginning. The central topic of conversation during this and the subsequent days was how to achieve this objective.

Why was it so important to eliminate this base? Up to this point the line within the intelligence community was that the Soviet buildup in Cuba reflected a desire to protect the communist regime from an American attempt to overthrow it. But if the idea was to defend Cuba, why send offensive weapons? The answer to this question lay in the structure of the debate that had developed over the previous few months within the administration over the observed Soviet military buildup. The standard distinction, made throughout, was between defensive and offensive weapons. It was natural for policy makers to think that with offensive missiles came a more offensive purpose.

This distinction, essentially between those weapons that protect territory from attack and those that can attack another's territory, tends to mislead, in that a preponderance of defending or attacking weapons in an arsenal says little about political objectives. Aggressive countries that have seized territory need to hold it "defensively" against counterattack while those rushing to the aid of a beleaguered ally may need the mobility and reach associated with offensive systems. Countries unsure of the ability to resist a ground offensive may hope to deter attack by threatening the enemy homeland with missile strikes. This was a theme of deterrence theory as it developed around the introduction of long-range missiles into the arsenals of both superpowers. On this basis it was not outlandish for the Cubans and Russians to claim, as they did, that the Cuban missiles could have a defensive purpose.

All this was appreciated from the start by CIA analysts. On 16 October they presented the missiles as testimony to a "determination to deter any active US intervention" as well as shifting "the world balance of power" in "the Bloc's" favor, perhaps in the hope that it would encourage the West to be more accommodating on Berlin. McCone, however, with his hunch having been proved right, invariably stressed a more "offensive" construction, and this view appears to have been soon transmitted to the Board of National Estimates. In the estimates produced for 19 and 20 October, the defense of Cuba barely appears as a motive, and catching up to the United States in strategic capacity appears as secondary. Primary emphasis was placed on demonstrating a shift in the balance of power so far in favor of the Soviet Union "that the US can no longer prevent the advance of Soviet offensive power even into its own hemisphere."[3]

Even if that was the Soviet objective, need it worry the United States? For McNamara, who tended toward absolutist views on these matters, the core strategic fact was the existing Soviet ability to inflict terrible damage on the United States; extra missiles did not alter the fundamentals. His view was stated authoritatively during the afternoon of 16 October, and he never deviated from it.[4] The Joint Chiefs and McCone did not agree. They were sure of the military difference, noting the immediate threat posed to critical American installations and the fact that raw numbers still mattered, especially when the "military balance" was being viewed (as it was in the Kremlin) from a position of inferiority.

At the time the strategic balance was estimated to be about 172 American to 75 Soviet ICBMs. In practice the Soviet inventory was a third of this number, and it is interesting to speculate on whether a more accurate assessment would have affected the American debate.[5] Those who assumed that the missiles would not by themselves change the fundamentals of the strategic balance were less perturbed, at least in military terms, about them becoming a fixture and more anxious about initiating a war that might then be fought on uncomfortably equal terms.

Those who assumed that Khrushchev's motives did lie in rectifying a strategic imbalance presumed that he wanted to do this in order to prepare the ground for new political offensives over Berlin or Southeast Asia. The first NIE considered it unlikely that the Soviet motive was "primarily in order to use them in bargaining for US concessions elsewhere." The second, however, put as an immediate consequence of U.S. acquiescence in missile deployment that "the Soviets would probably estimate lower risks in pressing the US hard in other confrontations, particularly Berlin."[6] As Berlin was still so much on the minds of Kennedy and his senior colleagues, this struck a responsive chord. On the other hand, if Khrushchev was already well endowed with strategic assets, then he did not need to wait for new missiles; he was already suitably positioned to respond to any setbacks in the Caribbean with initiatives that could wrong-foot the United States in Europe. From both perspectives this was therefore a global game.

The crisis came at a time when Moscow had apparently been preparing Washington for a new Soviet offensive on Berlin after the November elections. The intriguing possibility has been raised that this was a deliberate ploy, designed by Khrushchev to distract American attention from what was going on with Cuba. Anastas Mikoyan, Khrushchev's deputy, later stated this explicitly to Castro. This may have been to placate, by assuring him that Cuba was really the highest priority. Gromyko's report after meeting with Kennedy on 18 October indicates satisfaction that "the anti-Cuban campaign" was subsiding as the Berlin question became sharper. This might confirm that what really mattered to Khrushchev all along was Cuba and not the global balance, yet the tone of Gromyko's remarks was that further deterrence was not needed to keep Kennedy off Cuba. As likely everything, including future measures on Berlin, depended on the Cuban gamble succeeding and had to be subordinate to this aim. When the crisis broke Khrushchev certainly showed no inclination to add a high-risk situation in Europe to the one developing in the Caribbean.[7] Bundy later observed that the fears of retaliation resulted from "taking too much counsel of our own long anxieties and too little note of demonstrated Soviet patience."[8] That may be so, but the high salience given to Berlin by Khrushchev beforehand paid off now. Berlin preyed on Kennedy's mind throughout the crisis, acting as a significant constraint. Even before the crisis he had remarked to Willy Brandt, "If it were not for Berlin we could feel free to take action in Cuba."[9] He explained to the Joint Chiefs of Staff on 19 October that the United States was damned whatever was done. An attack on Cuba would be an excuse for an attack on Berlin by the Russians (for which the allies would blame "the trigger-happy Americans") while inaction could also result in the Soviet Union feeling it was better able to take action on Berlin. "Our problem," he told them, "is not merely Cuba but it is also Berlin. And when we recognize the importance of Berlin to Europe, and recognize the importance of our allies to us, that's what has made this thing be a dilemma."[10]

This challenge related to another aspect of Kennedy's difficulty, one of which he was acutely aware. Over the previous six weeks the evidence of the nonnuclear Soviet buildup had caused him acute political problems, with Republicans claiming this confirmed that under the Democrats the United States had become a soft touch for communism. Turning Cuba into an offensive military base for a non-American power went against the spirit of the Monroe Doctrine, which for over a hundred years had been used (mostly ineffectually) to insist that European great powers should not meddle in the Americas.

There were plenty of columnists who made the case for restraint, but during September the headlines had been made by the critics. Only the fracas at the University of Mississippi, where James Meredith was attempting to register as the first black student, competed with Cuba for media space. At the start of October, Louis Harris, the president's pollster, wrote to him that tensions were still high on foreign policy. "Majorities ranging from 70–80 percent are with you on Berlin," Harris reported, but on Cuba "the balance is still 38–62 percent negative." The *Washington Post* reported on 18 October that 344 editors and 208 members of Congress considered Cuba to be the primary campaign issue.[11] When McCone met with the president on 11 October to show him some pictures of Soviet medium-range bombers, Kennedy's main concern was that these not get in the press and ignite a crisis prior to the election. He added, "We'll have to do something drastic about Cuba."

"Last month," Kennedy told ExComm, referring to his September statement when he had said that missiles must not come to Cuba, "I should have said that we don't care." That was with hindsight. If he had tried such a calm approach and argued for passivity he would, like Eisenhower with the "missile gap" in 1957, have been denounced for complacency. Instead he had sought to head off this pressure by warning against turning Cuba into an offensive missile base. Now that public effort had aggravated the problem. What he had demanded must not happen was now happening. An unequivocal commitment to the American people would be exposed as a bluff unless it could be enforced. If Khrushchev had declared the entry of the missiles in advance (as Castro suggested), then politically Kennedy would have been faced with a much trickier problem.[12] He would have understood the problems of justifying tough action internationally but he would have had even greater problems explaining acquiescence domestically. The presumption that the Americans would act to stop an overt buildup probably influenced Khrushchev's decision. The effect of the deception, however, was to intensify Kennedy's sense of grievance. Even Bolshakov, who had been kept in the dark, had told Robert that there was no intention to put missiles in Cuba.[13]

Anger at Soviet duplicity was reinforced by Foreign Minister Gromyko's performance when he met with the president at the White House on 18 October. The president got no response when he read transcripts of his press conferences warning of the consequences of offensive missiles going into Cuba.[14] Perhaps Kennedy should have brought matters to a head immediately by revealing what he knew. He did not do so because he was still sorting out his own policy and did not want the initiative to pass back to Moscow.[15] Yet he did communicate the reasons for his concern and the basis for the eventual deal. Gromyko, who knew all about the missiles, sent a full report back to Moscow referring to Kennedy's complaints about "intensified armament supplies" to Cuba, but also to five separate occasions when the president pledged that there would be no invasion either by refugees or U.S. forces. If Khrushchev "addressed me on this issue," Kennedy promised, he would be given "corresponding assurances." Gromyko's brief overall assessment, however, complacently described the "overall situation" as "completely satisfactory," and claimed that plans for intervention against Cuba had been abandoned because "American ruling circles are amazed by the Soviet Union's courage in assisting Cuba."[16]

INVASION

The discovery of offensive missiles in Cuba provided precisely the pretext that the United States would need to launch an invasion of Cuba. The opportunity was passed by. Whatever the views of his military colleagues, Maxwell Taylor hoped to avoid an invasion—an option "we should look at very closely before we get our feet in that deep mud in Cuba."[17] He could envisage a long commitment, tying down conventional forces in the face of a guerrilla campaign.[18] ExComm spent very little time discussing this option, though its members appreciated that it was implied as soon as serious military action began. It might become a dire necessity, but with the emphasis on dire. By 21 October the planning had come to focus on men being put ashore seven days after air strikes, with as many as 25,000 arriving on the first day, building up to 90,000 over the following week. The preparations were put in train and many units moved to Florida, eventually involving 100,000 army and 40,000 marine combat troops, but hard analysis of the reception occupation troops might have received was lacking. Plans involved 579 tactical aircraft and 183 ships, including 8 aircraft carriers. They assumed an estimated 18,500 American casualties in ten days of combat.[19]

The intelligence on the number of Soviet troops available to fight was inaccurate. Instead of facing only indigenous Cuban troops, American forces would have found themselves confronting Soviet combat units. There were estimated to be just 8,000 Soviet military personnel in Cuba until 22 October, when this was revised upward to 10,000. Two days later the estimates jumped up to 22,000. Soviet sources later claimed that the actual number was twice as high: 41,902 as against 45,000 planned.[20]

An accurate American appreciation of the size of the Soviet combat force, given the political rumblings in the United States and Kennedy's 4 September warning (which referred to "any organized combat force"), could have precipitated a serious crisis.[21] The U.S. intelligence community had noted the air defense missiles (twenty-four sites with 144 SA-2 missiles), as well as MiG-21 aircraft and over forty Il-28 aircraft, most of which were still in crates at the start of the crisis. They were aware of the Luna missiles and that they were nuclear capable, but they had not discovered the warheads. American casualties could therefore have been much higher, although it was still probable that the Soviet troops would have been overwhelmed by American forces and that the Lunas would have been caught by air strikes. Subsequent occupation would also have been troublesome. This would have required a diversion of resources from the Asian and European theaters at a time when Kennedy assumed that Berlin would be put under siege, and it would have sparked an international outcry. Just after the crisis, reviewing contingency plans for an invasion, Kennedy wrote to McNamara:

> Considering the size of the problem, the equipment that is involved on the other side, the Nationalists' fervor which may be encouraged, it seems to me that we should end up bogged down.
>   I think that we should keep continually in mind the British in the Boer War, the Russians in the last war with the Finnish and our own experience with the North Koreans.[22]

As with Berlin, it took a real crisis to bring home the full meaning of strategic moves discussed almost casually in military war games, think-tank seminars, and any number of Washington meetings.

AIR STRIKES: FIRST THOUGHTS

The same process occurred with air strikes, the main military option to be discussed. A variety of versions were discussed, from one euphemistically described as "surgical," directed at the offending missiles and nothing else, and others with extended targets, from the air defense network to air bases. Kennedy initially inclined toward an air strike, although even then he was struggling to identify the most limited option available.

When the deliberations began just before noon on 16 October, the practicalities of an air strike soon came to the fore. During the day all the major issues relating to an air strike were aired, though the discussion was less than systematic. At issue was not whether an air strike should take place but when, how, and against what. How important was it to strike before the missiles became operational? Could the strike be limited to missile bases, or would it also be necessary to attack the SAM sites, airfields, and possible nuclear storage sites? Would an air strike achieve what was asked of it? Dare the United States risk the loss of surprise by warning that an attack was imminent? Should air strikes be followed by an invasion? What would be the Soviet response?

Of these the question of effectiveness was, surprisingly, one of the least explored. When the president asked about the extent of the "take-out," Taylor cautioned him that it would "never be 100 percent . . . we hope to take out a vast majority in the first strike." Taylor anticipated that any discovery of a target would prompt continuous air attack for a number of days. He also warned against targeting the missile bases alone while neglecting the surface-to-air missiles lest these intercept the incoming aircraft.[23] This followed a tentative query from Bundy as to whether the strike could be limited "in surgical terms to the thing that is the cause of action," suggesting that this would have a substantial political advantage.[24] Rusk and McNamara both accepted that a strike would have to be comprehensive, covering airfields and possible nuclear storage sites. The more targets added, the more substantial the operation and the greater the number of civilian casualties likely.

In his first remarks McNamara insisted that any air strike must be undertaken before the missiles became operational. When Rusk queried this on the grounds that the Soviet Union knew that any nuclear weapons launched against the United States, from whatever source, would mean "general nuclear war," McNamara cautioned that there could be no confidence in the quality of Soviet control over the warheads. McNamara also raised the question of whether to "precede the military action with political action," answering in the affirmative and apparently envisaging direct contact with Khrushchev. By contrast, Dillon suggested that the best way to avoid a Russian reaction was a quick strike "with a statement at the time saying this is all there is to it." Once the issue was in the open, he maintained, Khrushchev would be obliged to threaten retaliation to any U.S. action.

Summing up toward the end of the midday discussions, the president was reconciled to the likelihood of an air strike at least against the missiles.

> We're certainly going to do number one; we're going to take out these missiles. . . . The questions will be whether, which, what I describe as number two, which would be a general air strike. That we're not ready to say, but we should be in preparation for it. The third is the general invasion. At least we're going to do number one.[25]

What is important about this statement is not so much that he was prepared to authorize an air strike but that he was looking for a minimalist version. There had been no clear recommendation to limit the attack in this way; if anything, the weight of argument had been against this, especially from the military.

Late that afternoon the Joint Chiefs of Staff met to consider a series of questions posed by McNamara.[26] They rejected all limited strikes as being "unsound," risking a loss of surprise, and inviting retaliatory attacks on the United States and the Guantánamo base. No strike could proceed without taking out the air defenses. They also looked to striking "tanks and all other significant military targets." But this assumed greater ambition: "Objectives—eliminate threat to US and liberate Cuba." They were also convinced that the threat from the missiles was such that they should be attacked even after they became operational. To the question posed by McNamara, "What Soviet reaction may be anticipated?" the answer was "Soviet reaction unknown."[27]

Just as the Joint Chiefs' meeting was ending, ExComm began another session. It took a long time to move beyond the problems that had pre-occupied the group earlier. The State Department had done some work on the possibility of direct messages to Castro, with the idea that the Cuban leader might be convinced that he was becoming the victim of Moscow's policies.[28] The president soon moved the discussion back to the military options and a limited air strike. McNamara warned that even a limited air strike would involve "several hundred sorties" (there was not the intelligence at that time to be more precise). The judgment of the Joint Chiefs, reported Taylor, was that such a strike would be a mistake. They argued for two or three days to get full intelligence and then, if the "target system . . . really threatens the United States, then take it right out with one hard crack."[29]

Kennedy resisted this conclusion, reluctant to "abandon just knocking out these missile bases." This was a much more "defensible, explicable, politically or satisfactory-in-every way action than the general strike which takes us . . . into the city of Havana." Once again McGeorge Bundy provided the only support for going solely for the missiles: "The punishment fits the crime in political terms . . . we are doing only what we *warned* repeatedly and publicly we would *have* to do. We are *not* generalizing the attack."[30] The advantages of a "surgical" strike were that it was in some way proportionate, and that it avoided expanding the crisis into one deciding the whole future of Cuba.

Kennedy also inclined toward a prior public statement. Taylor was worried that any warning would mean that the missiles could be pulled "in under trees and forest and disappear almost at once." McNamara added that the missiles could be readied "between the time we, in effect, *say* we're going to come in and the time we *do* come in," and argued against an announcement if a strike was chosen.[31] This was where the diplomats began to feel uneasy. Almost as the meeting ended George Ball brought in the comparison with Pearl Harbor and expressed his fear as to where things were leading: "You go in there with a surprise attack. You put out all the missiles. This isn't the *end*. This is the beginning, I think."[32] Robert Kennedy had already been struck by the same analogy, passing his famous note to Sorensen: "I know how Tojo felt when he was planning Pearl Harbor."[33]

AIR STRIKES: SECOND THOUGHTS

By the next day four distinct levels of air strikes had been identified: (1) against known MRBM installations; (2) plus airfields; (3) plus SAM sites and coastal missile sites; (4) plus other significant sites. The most limited air strike conceivable involved a "50 sortie, 1 swoop air strike limited to the missile complex, followed by open surveillance and announcement that future missile sites would be similarly struck." The stronger action would aim to "eliminate all Cuban air power or other retaliatory capacity" and would involve up to two hundred sorties per day. These options combined in a number of permutations, in part depending on whether they would come with or without warning. A trade began to emerge between military and political moderation. A small strike might be manageable without warning, but warning mandated a big strike. The risk of not attacking the SAM sites was reduced so long as there was no opportunity for them to be readied for action.[34] Kennedy had not attended the meeting, but McCone's view, after briefing him, was that the president was "inclined to act promptly if at all, without warning, targeting on MRBM's and possibly airfields."[35]

At the time this was Rusk's position. His colleagues in the State Department had more qualms about surprise attacks and no diplomatic initiatives. They had heard talk of swift and decisive action limiting political damage before and were unconvinced. It was an "illusion" that would probably lead to full war, judged Charles Bohlen, about to leave for Paris. He wrote in haste to Rusk to urge that diplomatic channels be fully "tested out" prior to military action, if only to establish a case for the action.[36] George Ball was becoming concerned about the irreversibility of any air strike, as well as the large number of Russian casualties that would result from a full strike, and the consequent risk of a violent Soviet reaction.[37] In a note on 17 October he stressed the importance of a moral line, given the stance adopted by the United States on Pearl Harbor, Hungary, and Suez. "It is my strongly held view," he now observed, "that we cannot launch a surprise attack against Cuba without destroying our moral position and alienating our friends and allies."

Robert Kennedy, crucially, was now of this opinion. During the previous day's discussion he had been in a transitional mode. One part of him was still in Mongoose, searching for ways to get at Castro and even at one point musing about the possibility of fabricating an incident to provide a pretext for intervention. His few interventions had a hard-nosed ring to them, though he never obviously argued for one course of action. By the day's end, sensing his brother's line, he grasped the set of political concerns that he held on to for the rest of the crisis. By the second day he saw how the European allies, having been "under the gun" for years, would now take the position that this reaction to a few missiles in America's backyard was "hysterical."[38] The president was aware of the same risk: The allies thought the United States "fixated . . . slightly demented on this subject."[39] When Ball spoke of "carrying the mark of Cain on your brow for the rest of your life," Robert again backed him up. The Americans had resisted a Russian first strike. "Now, in the interest of time, we do that to a small country. I think it's a hell of a burden to carry."[40]

Even civilian hawks such as Dillon and McCone were clearly uncomfortable with the idea of launching a surprise attack. On 18 October

Robert Lovett, another prominent and generally hard-line figure in the foreign policy establishment, told the president that an air strike that resulted in great bloodshed would be deemed excessive when the insertion of missiles into Cuba was not a self-evidently aggressive act, "a sledge-hammer . . . to kill a fly."[41]

Also working against an air strike was evidence of the difficulty of keeping it limited. More intelligence came in on the Soviet offensive capability that would have to be destroyed. The discussion had started, on the Tuesday, with three possible missile sites. By Thursday, 18 October, the previous day's U-2 imagery indicated a possible five sites, two of which might take the longer-range SS-5. Some sixteen of the shorter-range SS-4 were deemed operational and could be launched eighteen hours after a decision was made to do so. The SS-5s, by contrast, would take longer, possibly until December. There was no hard evidence that nuclear warheads had arrived.[42]

The Joint Chiefs continued to oppose restricted strikes. In part this was because they were more politically ambitious. On 17 October they wrote to McNamara still proposing a comprehensive strike combined with a naval blockade, although the actual elimination of the Castro regime was now only an option (requiring an invasion) rather than a prime objective. Having failed to consider possible Soviet reactions the previous day, they now addressed this problem at some length and concluded that they would be manageable.[43] Robert records his brother's skepticism: "They, no more than we, can let these things go by without doing something. They can't, after all their statements, permit us to take out their missiles, kill a lot of Russians, and then do nothing. If they don't take action in Cuba, they certainly will in Berlin."[44]

For the U.S. Air Force, dominated by a strategic bombing philosophy, a limited strike appeared as an unnatural act. No merit was seen in doing less than possible, and certainly not less than necessary. If there was a risk of failure, then the response was to add to, not subtract from, the scale and intensity of the strikes. In a transparent reference to Chief of Air Staff Curtis LeMay, Robert Kennedy later recalled "the many times that I had heard the military take positions which, if wrong, had the advantage that no one would be around at the end to know." LeMay's own immediate comment on possibly the same exchange was somewhat more coarse. He had just returned from Europe and was infuriated that he had not been consulted about the developing crisis. His conversation with Robert Kennedy was cut short after the latter had been informed that B-52s could only use nuclear weapons. LeMay, angry at being denied the opportunity to brief the White House, observed, "What a Dumb Shit!"

The Joint Chiefs never deviated in their advocacy of a comprehensive military strike. Moreover, their assessments of the number of aircraft required tended to grow, as they not only found new targets but also identified new tasks. Taylor at one point warned his colleagues, "You are defeating yourselves with your own cleverness, Gentlemen."[45] This was exasperating enough to the doves, anxious about the military's insensitivity to the dynamics of the crisis. If anything, it was even more so to civilian supporters of an air strike, who found themselves being asked to subscribe to something far more substantial than necessary.[46] This was particularly galling for Dean Acheson, one of the most forceful proponents of a surprise limited air strike aimed at taking out missiles. He observed later that when developing plans the military became so anxious to remove all possibilities of doubt that "the proposals are apt to be at least as dangerous as the original danger."[47]

On 18 October Sorensen reported that the tide was running against a limited strike, and the next day that this was "no longer recommended even by those who first proposed it because of the dangers presented by a surviving and substantial air capability. This build-up should be hit as a whole complex or not at all." Yet Kennedy remained unconvinced. He never accepted the arguments for a comprehensive air strike. When the full NSC met on 20 October he "directed that air strike plans include only missiles and missile sites."[48]

20

Blockade

THE ALTERNATIVE TO AN AIR STRIKE took time to crystallize. Early on the afternoon of 16 October, in a way that suggested prior preparation, Mc-Namara had raised the idea of a blockade. A previous mention had been as a supplement rather than an alternative to an air strike, to prevent missiles arriving after the original set had been destroyed. It was on this basis that Maxwell Taylor had stated it as a requirement in his initial presentation, along with the reinforcement of the American base at Guantánamo.

Now McNamara raised it as part of a search for a course of action between the military and the purely political. This course, he thought, could take the form of a "declaration of open surveillance; a statement that we would immediately impose a blockade against *offensive* weapons entering Cuba in the future."[1] This was the policy eventually adopted. Yet initially its potential was not recognized. It was not until toward the end of the meeting that McNamara was able to give it another push. He was also careful not to oversell it, stressing that it was not a perfect solution. "Now this alternative doesn't seem to be a very acceptable one, but wait until you work on the others."

The next day, Wednesday, 17 October, the potential role of the blockade began to be clarified, but McNamara's idea of a focus on preventing the insertion of further offensive missiles into Cuba appeared to have been forgotten. Early on in the discussions the blockade was considered a "more extreme action than a limited air strike." Vice President Johnson had termed blockade an "act of war" in a speech as recently as 6 October in the context of fears over future Soviet action with regard to Berlin. This reinforced the association between a blockade against Cuba and a likely Soviet reciprocal action against Berlin.[2] Blockades required declarations of war. Stopping, seizing, and searching a Russian ship on the high seas might have grave consequences and seemed replete with danger.[3]

The sort of blockade considered in connection with Cuba before the crisis would have been the traditional sort, designed to interrupt all incoming shipping, to produce a "slow strangulation" and thereby—perhaps—bring down Castro's regime. Sorensen in his analysis of the options on 17 October still had in mind "a total naval blockade," much more than an intermediate option.[4]

The idea of a more focused operation had come up during the late August deliberations on the possibility of Soviet missiles in Cuba. One of Robert Kennedy's staff at the Department of Justice had developed the concept of what he called a "visit and search" blockade, which could be justified in international law as a proportionate response to the development of an offensive missile base. He revised this option when the crisis broke.[5] By the afternoon of 17 October this partial blockade was gaining advocates, led by Llewellyn Thompson.

McNamara could still see virtue in a limited blockade, with a contraband list confined to offensive weapons. It would be possible to move on to petroleum products later and, if necessary, to an air strike or even an invasion. "Nothing would be lost," he observed, "by starting at the bottom of the scale."[6] This course still carried risks, including a blockade against Berlin or the possibility that enforcement could lead to Soviet ships or submarines being sunk and consequent retaliation. Nonetheless, the advantage of appearing tough but restrained at the same time had appeal.

The merits were set out in an internal State Department paper, stressing the formidable advantages in terms of a graduated response:

> ascending political steps, at each stage of which Khrushchev and Castro could find an "out" if they desired and by maximum consultation reduce strain on our alliances and permits the action to be undertaken with the maximum possibility of such allied support as can be obtained. It also avoids the necessity of major military action directed against Cuban soil and could accomplish our objectives with minimum casualties on both sides.[7]

Unlike with an air strike, it was thought possible to mobilize political support for this action. The Soviet Union would obviously veto any move in the UN Security Council and delay an attempt to take the issue to the General Assembly. The State Department Latin Americanists were confident, however, that they could get the two-thirds majority (fourteen votes) required by the Rio Pact Organ of Consultation. Foreign ministers had already indicated concern over the Soviet buildup and would respond strongly to evidence of the introduction of nuclear missiles into the Caribbean. Edwin Martin, assistant secretary of state for inter-American affairs, told the president that with twenty-four hours' notice they could get the votes.[8]

The decisive shift toward the blockade came on 18 October. That morning, at eleven o'clock, Kennedy met with ExComm. Two issues were addressed. First, did a blockade require a declaration of war? After receiving a range of replies, he suggested that a declaration might not be necessary unless the blockade was geared to an invasion. Others demurred. A blockade was illegal, an act of aggression. But Ball and Thompson contended that this concern was overdone: Moscow would appreciate the difference between a blockade coming with a declaration of war and one coming without.[9] The second issue, addressed less clearly, was whether the blockade was to be total or just directed against missiles. Much of the discussion still assumed a total blockade, putting a stranglehold on the Cuban economy and possibly, some hoped, bringing down Castro.[10]

McCone viewed a limited blockade in the same light that he viewed a limited air strike. With both, "the main objective of taking Cuba away from Castro had been lost and we have been overly consumed with the missile problem." Disposing of the missile sites would not necessarily rid the Western Hemisphere of Castro's communism. This critical dichotomy took the debate beyond tactics and into basic political objectives. An air strike could not be limited and so tended toward an invasion of Cuba and Castro's overthrow; a limited blockade encouraged a focus on the missiles. McCone saw the focus narrowing further, with a "differentiation in the minds of some in the policy of blockading offensive weapons as contrasted to blockading all weapons."[11]

McCone also noted that during the meeting of ExComm on the morning of 18 October, just before lunch, "McNamara seemed to be reconsidering his prior position of advocating military action," and that this was linked to his concern over Soviet retaliation. Over lunch the secretary of defense and his deputy concluded in favor of a blockade after spending two hours in their own war-gaming, imagining moves and countermoves between the United States and the Soviet Union. Now McNamara was set in his convictions that a blockade was the best course.[12] His substantial political weight was shifting well away from an air strike. There would be no point in any strike other than a comprehensive one, but this could lead inexorably to an invasion, possibly as the Americans felt obliged to support a consequent uprising in Cuba.

At the president's request, that afternoon his advisers split into two groups—one to examine the blockade, possibly followed by further action, and the other a strike of substantial proportions, with or without notice. The critics of a blockade now got a chance to develop their case. While the Americans waited to see if it was working, the missiles would become operational. Acheson thought this the "glaring weakness" in the blockade approach; as he later put it, once "this occurred Cuba would become a combination of porcupine and cobra."[13]

Taylor cautioned that Khrushchev might not need to break the blockade but could simply carry on building up the weapons in Cuba. Rather than an air strike that could eliminate the problem expeditiously, the United States might then find itself with a much larger problem that could be solved only through invasion, with all that entailed. Paradoxically, from his perspective, the blockade was more likely to "develop into a choice between invading Cuba and backing down than was the seemingly more violent alternative of the air attack." This argument might have carried more weight had his military colleagues identified any point where the movement from a comprehensive air strike to an invasion could be broken.

TENTATIVE DECISIONS

Late on the evening of 18 October, having already had his meeting with Gromyko, Kennedy listened to his advisers until after midnight. Some basic decisions began to be taken.

> The Soviet Union was to be held accountable for the missiles; Cuba was seen as a pawn, a useful piece of geography for the Soviets. It was recognized that the U.S. must act but that we have "too much self-respect to respond by an act of aggression," as one participant put it. . . .
>
> A blockade won wide approval on the ground that it permitted better control of events and the exercise of subsequent options. The President made a tentative decision to impose a blockade and announce it Monday night.[14]

The idea was, as Kennedy put it, that "we should begin by blockading Soviets against the shipment of additional offensive capacity, [and] that we could tighten the blockade as the situation requires." There would be no declaration of war—"it would be a limited blockade for a limited purpose." Despite this apparent decision, Robert Kennedy indicates that the president was still not fully convinced of this course and wanted further thought.[15]

McCone was sufficiently convinced of the trend of the debate to tell the United States Intelligence Board (USIB) the next morning (Friday, 19 October) that the most probable course of action would be "a limited blockade designed to prevent the importation into Cuba of additional arms." This course did not preclude very severe Soviet reactions, and it carried the disadvantages of being protracted and encouraging attention on the United States' own complex of foreign bases while not reversing the Soviet buildup. Against this had to be put the costs of direct military action:

> the impact of current and future world opinion, the spectacle of a powerful nation attacking by surprise a weak and insignificant neighbor, engagement by the United States in a "surprise attack" thus giving license to others to

do the same, the undefendable position we would be in with our allies, and finally, the price to us of extreme actions of which the Soviets appear capable of executing.[16]

On Friday morning the president met with the Joint Chiefs, who were still arguing for a surprise attack on comprehensive targets, leading to complete blockade and invasion. They assumed that the crisis would lead to a war anyway, in which case the Americans should fight it on the best possible terms. LeMay told the president that a blockade would allow the missiles to be concealed, would not get Berlin off the hook (because "they've got us *on the run*"), and would lead "right into war. This is almost as bad as the appeasement at Munich." The last statement was followed by a pause. Later he told the president, "You're in a pretty bad fix." After Kennedy left, General Shoup congratulated LeMay on "pulling the rug out from under him." The key word, according to Shoup, was *escalation*.

> Somebody's got to keep them from doing the goddam thing piecemeal. That's our problem. Go in there and friggin' around with the missiles. You're screwed. Go in there and friggin' around with the lift. You're screwed. You're screwed, screwed, screwed. Some goddam thing, some way, that they either do the son of a bitch and do it right, and quit friggin' around.[17]

Gilptaric described Kennedy afterward as "just choleric. He was just beside himself, as close as he ever got."[18]

The president, however, still judged it politically unwise to dismiss the Joint Chiefs' case until it had been fully explored. As he left to do some previously scheduled election campaigning, he asked his advisers to return to the options.[19] As most participants had now made up their minds, this appears to have made for a bad-tempered day.

Bundy was one of the few still equivocating. Having unsuccessfully explored the diplomatic route and uneasy with the blockade, he now led the counterattack:

> A blockade would not remove the missiles. Its effects were uncertain and in any case would be slow to be felt. Something more would be needed to get the missiles out of Cuba. This would be made more difficult by the prior publicity of a blockade and the consequent pressures from the United Nations for a negotiated settlement. An air strike would be quick and would take out the bases in a clean surgical operation. He favored decisive action with its advantages of surprise and confronting the world with a *fait accompli*.[20]

Acheson followed with a restatement of his support for this action, arguing for a showdown with Khrushchev. This was not just another instance of Soviet missiles aimed at the United States, for these "were in the hands of a madman whose actions would be perfectly irresponsible," and so the "usual restraints" need not apply. Dillon and McCone both favored a quick air strike. Taylor then attacked the notion that a blockade merely postponed an air strike. Rather, he said, it would be a decision "to abandon the possibility of an air strike." He urged a strike within a few days, before the first missiles became operational.

After this onslaught, the antistrike forces regathered. Robert Kennedy expressed himself strongly:

> [I]t would be very, very difficult indeed for the President if the decision were to be an air strike with all the memory of Pearl Harbor and with all the implications this would have for us in whatever world there would be afterward. For 175 years we had not been that sort of country. A sneak attack was not in our tradition. Thousands of Cubans would be killed without warning, and a lot of Russians too.

The attorney general wanted the United States to show determination to get the missiles out of Cuba, but in such a way that allowed Moscow some room to pull back. Rusk backed this up. Any action should be followed by "a pause in which the great powers could step back from the brink." They needed time to "work out a solution rather than be drawn inexorably from one action to another and escalate into general nuclear war."[21]

With the issues restated, the group split into two to produce the best cases for the air strike option and the blockade. The air strike option was weakened by the departure of Acheson. He had become convinced the blockade would be chosen and had given up on the exercise, although he would later return when asked. He was as grumpy and frustrated as ever, offering vivid descriptions of the president as "a cow with seven stomachs, constantly ruminating and incapable of culminating in a digested decision" and of his brother with "so many hands on his backside he looked like a tarantula." Without Acheson there was no powerful advocate for an attack directed solely at the missiles, and so the air strike group found themselves justifying a comprehensive strike, politically the hardest case to defend.[22] Sorensen provided a draft speech for a blockade announcement that became the basis of the eventual consensus. Bundy later recalled, "No such speech could be written for the air strike."[23]

Rusk had come to see the blockade's advantage in providing a feasible "theory of the case," an argument that could demonstrate the legality of any action taken and so build international political support. He considered those such as Acheson, who dismissed legal concerns, as mistaken. The 1956 Suez crisis, and for that matter the Bay of Pigs, had illustrated the problems democratic states faced when they were perceived to be acting illegally. For this reason, once the crisis went public, he wanted to use the Organization of American States to declare the missiles a threat to peace, and so provide a basis for whatever action had to be taken.[24] To avoid connotations of belligerency in the word *blockade*, the substitute *quarantine* was proposed, having been suggested, despite his impatience with international law, by Acheson.[25] Kennedy finally opted for *quarantine* because that allowed for *blockade* to be something more serious, to be implemented later if need be.[26]

It was hard to gauge the practical impact of the quarantine. Intelligence estimates on its likely effect were of only marginal value. The first, released on 19 October,[27] had been slightly off beam because it considered only a total blockade designed to undermine Castro's position, which was unlikely to succeed.[28] The next day, better informed by McCone, a more refined estimate observed that no blockade could guarantee that individual aircraft and submarines would not get through with critical military items, including nuclear warheads, or actually "deprive the Soviets of the use of missiles already in Cuba for a nuclear strike on the U.S."[29] Because it could not guarantee a solution of the problem, the quarantine was scheduled to last less than a week, allowing for intensive political activity, before it would be time for the air strike, with possible invasion and occupation soon after.[30] On 20 October the navy began to plan for a limited blockade, as opposed to the total blockade for which they were already prepared. The position papers were completed and provided to the White House on the same day.[31]

RETALIATION

The debate had proceeded on the basis of uncertainty over likely Soviet and Cuban responses and with a keener sense of what sort of action could be best justified to domestic and allied opinion. The most recent Soviet statement, on 11 September 1962, had warned that an aggressor against Cuba could not expect to stay "free from punishment." If an attack was made, "this will be the beginning of the unleashing of war."[32] This was standard fare. By and large the input from the intelligence community was reassuring rather than alarming; if anything, it argued against blockade. The 19 October estimate acknowledged that direct military action against Cuba would put great pressure on the Soviet Union "to respond in ways which, if they could not save Cuba, would inflict an offsetting injury to U.S. interests."[33] It was possible that the Soviet Union might "again miscalculate and respond in ways which, through a series of actions and reactions, could escalate to general war." Yet with no actual treaty obligations to Cuba and no acknowledgment of the missile bases, a surprise strike might offer a

> pretext for treating U.S. military action against Cuba as an affair which does not directly involve them, and thereby avoiding the risks of a strong response. We do not believe that the USSR would attack the U.S., either from Soviet bases or with its missiles in Cuba, even if the latter were operational and not put out of action before they were ready for firing.

But if Moscow could not resort to general war and could not hope to prevail locally, then it "would almost certainly consider retaliatory actions outside Cuba." Berlin seemed the obvious location. "They might react here with major harassments, interruptions of access or even a blockade, with or without the signing of a separate peace treaty."

Whatever course of retaliation was taken, however, nothing would be done that would risk general war. In an appendix the analysts expressed their belief that "the Soviets are less likely to retaliate with military force outside of Cuba in response to a speedy and effective all-out invasion than to other forms of U.S. military action." Because of this, "a rapid occupation of Cuba would be more likely to make the Soviets pause in opening new theaters of conflict than limited action or action which drags out."

This estimate failed to address the question of reaction outside the Soviet bloc to the spectacle of the United States launching substantial attacks against a small neighbor, which was the main reason for this option to fall out of favor. On the other hand, while playing down the dangers of general war, it did encourage the tendency, when wondering how things might escalate, to assume tit-for-tat responses: a blockade would bring renewed pressure on Berlin; an air strike against the missile bases in Cuba could be countered by a similar strike against the Jupiter bases in Turkey.

Most hawks doubted a severe Soviet response. Only Acheson anticipated a showdown with Khrushchev (as he had over Berlin). It was to be expected that the Soviets "will react some place," but the risk had to be accepted.[34] An attack on Cuban missiles might be followed by a Soviet attack on U.S. missiles in Turkey. The United States would then be obliged to knock out a missile base in the Soviet Union. At that point, it was necessary to hope that "cooler heads will prevail, and they'll stop and talk."

One aspect of the situation stood out: The Soviet Union was at a severe tactical disadvantage in the Caribbean, where the United States enjoyed air and sea dominance. For this reason it would probably look closer to home for countermeasures, where they would have their own options for air strikes, blockades, or even invasions. Kennedy himself never seemed to doubt that the almost inevitable response to most actions by the United States was some form of equivalent pressure on Berlin. If anything, he saw Cuba as an extension of the Berlin crisis, with a move against the city an almost inevitable consequence of virtually any action he took. This was a major constraint. He would be blamed by allies for precipitating a huge crisis in Europe because the United States had suddenly found missiles in their neighborhood, a circumstance with which West Europeans and Russians alike were already familiar. At one point Bundy became so worried about a Soviet reprisal against Berlin for which the United States would be blamed that he argued for waiting on Cuba until the inevitable crunch came in Berlin. This was a minority view; others argued that allies were more likely to be unnerved and the Soviet Union emboldened if the United States did nothing over Cuba.[35] Even more out on a limb on this matter was Robert Kennedy who, in successive NSC meetings, proposed handing over nuclear weapons and missiles to West Germans, even putting them in Berlin, in order to make a point to the Russians. As neither nuclear weapons nor missiles had ever been brought into Berlin, one advantage of a quarantine restricted to offensive weapons was to remove a basis for retaliatory action. Even then it was feared the Russians might use the precedent as an excuse to review land or air traffic into Berlin.[36]

The president kept in touch with the Berlin situation as the crisis reached its climax. On the morning of 22 October he received a briefing on the planned response to any Soviet attempt to hinder the movement of food and supplies to West Berlin.[37] One of the decisions taken the next day was to set up a special subcommittee, chaired by Paul Nitze, to look into the possible repercussions of the crisis on Berlin.[38] The intelligence community's assessment of the impact of a blockade on Berlin was that stocks were sufficient to last for at least six months. The critical factor was psychological. A failure by the United States to respond would mean that Berliners would lose all hope, while even an airlift would only sustain morale for some time unless the United States showed itself ready to break the blockade. They would be "suspicious of any indication from either side that the Cuban crisis might produce an accommodation at their expense."[39]

DECISIONS

At 2:30 P.M. on 20 October the National Security Council met with all the key participants present. Although Taylor and Bundy spoke for the air strike, the two senior cabinet members, Rusk and McNamara, gave a clear recommendation for the blockade. Gilpatric put the case succinctly: "Essentially, Mr President, this is a choice between limited action and unlimited action; and most of us here think that it's better to start with limited action."[40]

Taylor was still pressing on the risk that more missiles would become operational the longer the United States waited. He did not accept that nuclear weapons would be used against the United States even if it used nuclear weapons against Cuba. Robert Kennedy came in supporting the blockade, although with a readiness to move to air strikes soon after if there was no positive response to American demands. The president, observing that the air strike plan as presented was "not surgical," saw the naval quarantine as the only "course of action compatible with our principles. There was only a small risk that this action would 'pull the lanyard'; at the same time it was a substantial initiative which permitted the subsequent exercise of other options."[41]

At last the basic objectives and methods of policy could be clarified. The first priority was the removal of the missiles; the bombers were less of a problem. The "Castro problem" also had to be kept separate from the "missile problem." A first step had been agreed upon, which looked moderate in comparison with the alternatives. Rusk told the president that the quarantine was not "an inconsequential action" and "would produce a crisis of the gravest importance."[42] The group did not look ahead with optimism:

> If after several days there was a continuation of missile site construction an airstrike might be necessary against a minimum number of targets to eliminate the main nuclear threat. It was held unlikely that the Soviets would retaliate, especially since the Strategic Air Command would be in a full alert condition. If surviving Cuban missiles after an airstrike were used against the U.S., it might be necessary to invade Cuba, but not to use nuclear weapons against Cuba. However it might be necessary to make a compensatory attack against the USSR.[43]

The planners now had a set of clear guidelines, and they could begin to prepare the military and diplomatic moves necessary to accompany the president's speech, scheduled now for Monday, 22 October.

One issue had been left undecided with the quarantine. Including petroleum, oil, and lubricants (POL) would punish and threaten Castro. It could also be readily enforced because of the ease with which tankers could be recognized. The main problem was that this would mean shifting the objective toward the regime itself rather than the missiles and would remove a later option for escalation pressure.[44] Again, the advantage of a limited blockade was that it could enforce limited objectives; expanding the blockade would mean expanding objectives. Still resisting any graduated approach, the Joint Chiefs wanted to include POL. Rusk wanted to exclude it to sustain the distinction between an objective geared to eliminating strategic missiles and one geared to overthrowing Castro. Kennedy leaned toward Rusk's position. For the moment the policy was to confine the conflict to the two superpowers.[45]

While the blockade was narrowed down, the air strike still expanded. That morning the president, with his brother in attendance, met with McNamara, Taylor, and General Walter C. Sweeny Jr., commander in chief of the Tactical Air Command. Kennedy felt that he ought to hear the full military case by the responsible commander before deciding firmly against the air strike as the first step.[46] McNamara reported the latest intelligence picture. There was now equipment in Cuba for approximately forty MRBM or IRBM launchers. The location of the sites for thirty-six of these launchers was known, and of these thirty-two appeared to have sufficient equipment on them to be included in any air strike directed against Cuba's missile capability. As many as forty-eight missiles could be available, although only thirty had been located. General Sweeny's plan involved 100 sorties to knock out five SAM sites and three MiG airfields, approximately 250 sorties to attack missile launchers at eight or nine known sites, and, to ensure the destruction of the MiG and Il-28 aircraft, a further 150 sorties, making for 500 in total.

While Sweeny expressed his confidence that an air strike would be "successful," it was not clear whether his criteria of success were rigorous enough. If everything went well, not all the known missiles would be destroyed, and the known missiles might be no more than 60 percent of the total on the island. Taylor stated, "The best we can offer you is to destroy 90 percent of the known missiles." Furthermore, the initial air strikes might not have a permanent effect and so would have to be followed up on subsequent days, and this in turn "would inevitably lead to an invasion." Kennedy was now convinced that the air strike was not a serious option. The blockade might not actually remove the missiles— but then neither necessarily would the air strike.[47]

According to CIA representatives, the eight to twelve missiles believed to be operational could be got ready for firing within two and a half to four hours and could then maintain this capability indefinitely. This would include a countdown requiring twenty to forty minutes. The first wave of attacking U.S. aircraft would give ten minutes of warning; the second wave, forty minutes; and the third wave, something proportionately greater. The implication was clear: Anything missed in the first strike would have a chance to fire before it was attacked again. By now the president was ready at last to acknowledge that there was no limited air option. Taylor, almost for form's sake, requested a comprehensive strike the next day with surprise. His request was refused.[48]

21

Military Steps

THE PRESIDENT'S SPEECH announcing the discovery of the missiles was due to be broadcast on the evening of 22 October 1962. It was crafted with great care. Many audiences had to be addressed simultaneously, requiring a blend of restraint and resolve, a sense of risk and reassurance, so that the public would get behind the government, the Latin Americans would be supportive, the allies would remain calm, the Russians would be despondent but not fearful, and the Cubans would start looking for a way out.

Kennedy informed the American people that sites for Soviet missile bases had been discovered in Cuba and that the U.S. government found this unacceptable and was taking a number of steps to get them removed. First, there was to be a "strict quarantine of all offensive military equipment under shipment to Cuba," which could be "extended, if needed, to other types of cargo and carriers." The necessities of life would not be denied. Second, he had directed continued close surveillance of Cuba and had ordered "the Armed Forces to prepare for any eventualities." Third, the president declared that any nuclear missile launched from Cuba against any nation in the Western Hemisphere would be taken to be equivalent to a Soviet attack on the United States and would prompt a "full retaliatory response upon the Soviet Union." Fourth, dependents of U.S. personnel at the Guantánamo base were to be evacuated and additional military units placed on standby. Fifth and sixth, support was to be sought at the OAS and the UN. Seventh, he called upon Khrushchev to eliminate this threat and to work with the United States for "stable relations," so helping to "move the world back from the abyss of destruction." Further Soviet threats, including any made "in response to our actions this week," would be met "with determination." In this context he particularly singled out the possibility of a "hostile move" against "the brave people of West Berlin." He warned his fellow citizens that it could not be foreseen "precisely what course it will take or what costs or casualties will be incurred." He warned of "months of sacrifice and self-discipline."[1] The warnings were clear: The quarantine might only be a first step of many in a crisis that could take months to resolve.[2]

The drama was accentuated by the administration's success in achieving political surprise. Kennedy had not wanted a public debate until he was sure of the facts and his own position. To maintain secrecy, senior officials had used subterfuge to hide their movements. The press secretary, Pierre Salinger, was kept in the dark until 20 October lest he inadvertently let something slip. That day Kennedy needed to get back from campaigning in Chicago to take the final decisions, and dictated a press release to Salinger: "I've got a bad cold; 99.2 degrees temperature. The doctor says I have to go back to Washington for medical care." Flying back with Kennedy, Salinger observed the lack of a cold and was told, "The minute you get back in Washington you're going to find what it is. And when you do, grab your balls."[3] Inevitably a number of reporters began to put the story together, and Kennedy had to intercede with publishers to keep it quiet for the sake of national security.[4] Now, after the presidential announcement, the press briefing was the largest Salinger had ever conducted. He was able to add to the drama by taking aside reporters who were supposed to follow the president to the Virginia caves in the event of war, telling them that they must stay close to the White House.[5]

The most worrying initial reaction for the president had come from the congressional leadership just before the broadcast. This warned that a policy appearing tough outside the United States might still appear weak within. The strong and immediate response of these men, led by Senator Russell but even including Senator Fulbright, in favor of air strikes rather than blockade, indicated just how far the internal discussions had moved since the president first heard the news six days earlier.[6] During the course of a stormy meeting Kennedy read them a supportive letter from British prime minister Harold Macmillan, confirming his reading of European reactions.

> While you know how deeply I sympathize with all your difficulty and how much we will do to help in every way, it would only be right to tell you that there are two aspects which give me concern. Many of us in Europe have lived so long in close proximity to the enemy's nuclear weapons of the most devastating kind that we have got accustomed to it. So European opinion would need attention. The second, which is more worrying, is that if Khrushchev comes to a conference he will of course try to trade his Cuban position against his ambitions in Berlin and elsewhere. This we must avoid at all costs, as it will endanger the unity of the Alliance.[7]

Acheson, meanwhile, had been explaining the policy to General de Gaulle. Demonstrating his professionalism as a diplomat, he did not share with the French president his own forebodings, but agreed that it was unlikely that the Russians would attempt to force the blockade or that they would retaliate against Berlin and Turkey. When asked what would happen if neither the blockade was challenged nor the missiles removed, Acheson (who had not been given an official answer) demonstrated his grasp of Kennedy's likely preference by suggesting, "We will immediately tighten this blockade and the next thing we would do is to stop tankers—and this will bring Cuba to a standstill in no time at all." De Gaulle expressed his solidarity in the event of war but was confident that there would be none.[8]

The lack of hard intelligence on why the Soviet Union had now taken such a provocative step had left assessments of likely responses speculative. Soviet threats tended to be lurid but imprecise. In a letter to Khrushchev the president expressed his fears of escalation, using this in the process to exert pressure. He stated that he assumed that the Soviet leader understood the American will and determination and would not therefore "deliberately plunge the world into war in which it was crystal clear no country could win and which could only result in catastrophic consequences to the whole world, including the aggressor."[9] Kennedy wanted to keep the Soviet leader calm. Recalling that in Vienna Khrushchev had objected to the word *miscalculate* when it was translated into Russian, Kennedy ensured that the word was taken out of the draft of his 22 October broadcast.[10]

The initial Soviet response to the broadcast provided few clues. It had the appearance of a holding action. Only defensive weapons were going into Cuba. Moscow was willing to negotiate all matters, but the main dispute was between the United States and Cuba. The statement railed against the blockade but gave no indication as to whether it was to be run or whether any other military steps might be taken, just a standard promise to "mete out an appropriate rebuff to an aggressor." It also stated that "as never before, statesmen must show calm and prudence, and must not countenance the rattling of weapons," adding that the United States was "taking on itself a heavy responsibility for the fate of the world and recklessly playing with fire."[11]

Khrushchev, as was his wont, found a convenient American, in this case businessman William Knox, and admitted the existence of the missiles but warned that his submarines would retaliate if Soviet ships were sunk as a result of the blockade. Learning little from Georgi Bolshakov (whose value was now diminished by his unwitting part in Soviet duplicity), Robert Kennedy decided to talk directly to the Soviet ambassador, Anatoly Dobrynin. They met at 9:30 that evening. Kennedy was told that the instructions for ships approaching Cuba were to carry on. He left worried.[12]

IMPLEMENTING THE QUARANTINE

The details of the quarantine were not worked out until 23 October and it was not to become effective until 10:00 the next day. The stress was on minimum force. The rule was to disable, not sink. After being briefed on the plans, David Ormsby-Gore, the British ambassador, suggested that Khrushchev could be given more time by drawing the quarantine line closer to Cuba (from a radius of eight hundred miles to five hundred miles). Over navy protests that this might give the vessels air support, Kennedy agreed, though there never was in fact a fixed line, as the tactics of interception had to be kept flexible.[13] The Russians were not formally informed of the general location of the quarantine line until three days later.

If the quarantine was going to be tested, the Americans were anxious that they stop appropriate ships. McNamara observed: "It would be an unfortunate incident if we hailed a ship that refused to stop; we then disable it and found it didn't have offensive weapons on it. That would be the poor way to start."[14] Later on 23 October he identified the *Kimovsk* as probably loaded with offensive weapons and likely to be approached at around 11:30 A.M. or 12:00 the next day.[15] This encounter would take place out of range of any MiG-19 or MiG-21 aircraft flying from Cuba, but there was anxiety about escorting Soviet submarines, and so a destroyer with an antisubmarine capability was designated to conduct the intercept.

That Wednesday morning the CIA reported "16 dry cargo ships and 6 tanker ships" en route to Cuba, of which three "had hatches suitable for missile handling."[16] McNamara received this information from the U.S. Navy at 9:00 that morning, then went on to a press conference to inform reporters that the blockade was about to be tested. Two Soviet ships—the *Gagarin* and the *Kimovsk*—were approaching the line with a submarine between them. The U.S. carrier *Essex* was ordered to move in for the interception. Helicopters would signal the submarine by sonar to surface and identify itself. If it refused, small explosive depth charges were to be used to force it to the surface.

ExComm began to meet at 10:00 as the quarantine officially came into effect. The crucial first engagement was expected by noon, and McNamara described in detail the means by which a Soviet submarine could be attacked—an opening step that did not fit in with Kennedy's graduated response and which drew, for him, a straight line into a Berlin crisis.[17] The president wondered whether this had to be the first exchange, but McNamara insisted that there was no alternative because of the danger to American ships if the submarine was left alone. So all that could be done was wait. In a memorable passage Robert Kennedy described the moment:

I think these few minutes were the time of greatest concern for the President. Was the world on the brink of a holocaust? Was it our error? A mistake? Was there something further that should have been done? Or not done? His hand went up to his face and covered his mouth. He opened and closed his fist. His face seemed drawn, his eyes pained, almost gray.

His own thought was that "we were on the edge of a precipice with no way off."[18]

Yet at 10:25 McCone had already received information from the Office of Naval Intelligence that six ships in Cuban waters had either stopped or reversed course. Kennedy's gray moment had occurred while the CIA director was out of the room checking the report. Fifteen minutes later he returned to confirm that these ships had turned back. Sixteen of the Soviet ships approaching the quarantine line had changed course or stopped dead in the water. So as to give the *Gagarin* and *Kimovsk* time to turn, the president ordered the *Essex* not to intervene, though this may have come too late for there not to have been one attempted intercept.[19] This occasioned Dean Rusk's famous line: "We're eyeball to eyeball and I think the other fellow just blinked."[20]

It appears that orders had gone out from Moscow by midday (EST) on 23 October to change course.[21] The ship *Poltava*, which had carried the first set of warheads to Cuba and was now returning with a second set of twenty, turned back before reaching the quarantine line, along with other ships capable of carrying offensive weapons, including Il-28 bombers. In addition to worries about incidents at sea, Khrushchev had not wanted this equipment to fall into American hands.[22] This critical point in favor of the blockade had not even occurred to U.S. policy makers when considering the option. Now it gradually dawned on them, as Rusk put it, that when it came to allowing the Americans "to capture, and seize, and analyze, and examine their missiles and their warheads and things," the Russians were "going to be sensitive as a boil." The Soviet secrets contained in these ships were not of great interest to ExComm (at least that is what McNamara had said on the first day of deliberations), but as Bundy later acknowledged, this "made it harder for us to understand how much they were valued by their owners."[23]

This initial success, and relief, did not lead to complacency. Talking to Ball that night, Kennedy commented on the "impression" that the "Russians are giving way," adding that it was "not quite accurate."[24] Nonetheless, this tense moment having passed, he became reluctant to provoke an incident, resisting, for example, a suggestion from Nitze that one of the big ships carrying missiles should be pursued and boarded before it had a chance to rendezvous with escorting submarines. The president, at Ball's suggestion, decided that any ships approaching the quarantine line were to be followed and watched carefully but no action should be taken unless specifically instructed.

By the morning of 25 October the CIA could report that fourteen Soviet ships had turned back. Five tankers were still progressing plus three dry cargo ships, of which one, the *Belovodsk*, might have military equipment on board.[25] The key question now was what to do about the Soviet tankers. McNamara reported to ExComm that one tanker, the *Bucharest*, had been intercepted that morning and had claimed that it was carrying petroleum to Cuba. There was a recommendation that it should be boarded, as should the next tanker coming into view, the *Groznyy*, which was "carrying a deck load which might be missile field tanks." This potential interception was already controversial after McNamara and the chief of naval operations, Admiral George Anderson, had clashed over the navy's plan to stop this ship using, if necessary, a shot into the rudder. McNamara wanted Anderson to understand that the objective was to send a message to Khrushchev rather than humiliate him, lest Khrushchev "react in a nuclear spasm."[26]

The decision was taken not to challenge the *Bucharest*, because its cargo had been ascertained, but to prepare to board the *Groznyy*. There was a growing feeling that with no problematic ships moving toward the line, the implementation of the quarantine was becoming a "little flat," sending mixed signals because only the wrong sort of boat could be challenged. The feeling was correct. Khrushchev had wanted to get at least one ship through the cordon and the *Bucharest* fitted the bill. He was pleased to get it through and saw this as evidence of an equivocal American attitude to enforcement.[27] Kennedy preferred that the first ship to be boarded should be from the third world or the Soviet bloc but not the Soviet Union.[28] This led to another argument with the navy, which was keen to intercept a Soviet ship as soon as possible.[29] Then along came an East German passenger ship. The problem here was that any action against the ship—shooting or ramming—could put at risk some fifteen hundred passengers. It would seem strange to harm people on an East German ship after letting a Soviet ship go through, especially if, as was probable, no missiles were found. The president decided not to stop the East German ship. The ideal was a non-Soviet cargo ship. It took until Friday morning before one was available. The Lebanese-registered but Russian-operated *Marcula* had been loaded in Riga. It was boarded, inspected, and allowed to proceed.

On the morning of 27 October a U.S. destroyer pulled alongside the Soviet tanker, the *Groznyy*, carrying a cargo of ammonia. As previous tankers had been allowed through, there was no reason for Moscow to assume that this one would be stopped. The U.S. Navy, however, took a different view. It issued a warning and prepared to fire a shot. On this, the most tense day of the crisis, McNamara wanted no shots fired, and this led to yet another argument with Admiral Anderson, who was getting increasingly exasperated with the secretary's micromanagement of his military operation. As the *Groznyy* had been warned, the navy's failure to

CIA Estimates of Soviet Missile Capability in Cuba

Date	MRBM (Soviet R-12; NATO SS-4)	IRBM (Soviet R-14; NATO SS-5)
Soviet Plan	3 regiments; 24 launchers; 36 missiles.	2 regiments; 16 launchers; 24 missiles.
16 Oct	Possibly 4 launchers; 3 possible sites.	
17 Oct	8 launchers; 4 missiles; 2 confirmed sites; another possible.	
	At least 16 and possibly 32 missiles operational in next week or so.	
18 Oct	One regiment; 8 launchers; 16 missiles; 2 sites.	
19 Oct	One regiment; 8 launchers; 16 missiles; 2 sites.	8 launchers; 2 sites.
		Probably SS-5. Operational within 6 weeks.
20 Oct	2 regiments; 16 launchers; 32 missiles; 4 sites.	1 regiment; 8 launchers; 16 missiles; 2 sites.
	Must now be considered partially operational.	4 launchers operational within 6 weeks, rest in 8 to 10 weeks.
	Can be fired in 8 hours after decision to launch.	Can be fired in 5 hours.
21 Oct	*Identified:* 13 launchers; 23 missiles; 4 sites; 2 other possible sites.	*Identified:* 8 launchers; no missiles.
	One site may have operational readiness. Other will have this in 2 days. Rest by 1 November.	Early stage of construction.
22 Oct	23 launchers; 33 missiles; 6 sites.	12 launchers; 0 missiles; 3 sites.
	16 launchers ready, rest within week.	Ready December.
23 Oct	No change.	No change.
24 Oct	No change.	No change.
25 Oct	No change.	No change.
26 Oct	No change.	Poss. 4th site.
27 Oct	5 of 6 sites operational; 6th tomorrow. 24 missiles could be launched 6 to 8 hours after decision. 33 missiles observed.	No IRBMs observed.
28 Oct	All 24 launchers operational. Operational readiness being improved all the time.	No change.

stop it would undermine the credibility of the quarantine. This was one of the issues playing on McNamara's mind in ExComm that day, for he raised it a number of times.

Again, in ExComm, the doves won. At Robert Kennedy's suggestion it was agreed that the *Groznyy* be allowed to cross the line but no further ships thereafter. In the event, the destroyers now circling the *Groznyy* cleared their loaded guns by firing their shells into the sea, but sufficiently close to alarm the tanker's captain, who, after communicating with Moscow, reversed course and stayed clear of the quarantine line for a few days until the crisis was over and he was allowed to proceed.[30]

THE NEXT STEP

While both sides did their best to avoid a confrontation at sea, the intelligence reports were of feverish work in Cuba at the missile sites, some of which would soon reach a state of readiness. The question of how to keep up the pressure on Moscow had to be faced. When ExComm met on 25 October, the president acknowledged that because of the continuing work on the missiles sites "we must back up very soon the firmness we have displayed up to now."[31] He was anxious lest the talks about to start at the United Nations drag on and inhibit further action. There was no shift in objectives. The "basic structural purpose of this whole enterprise" remained, as Bundy put it, getting the missiles out. "If we can get bring Castro down in the process, dandy."[32]

In search of the next step, McNamara explained that all moves thus far had been "taken with a view to applying force gradually" in such a way as to be "meaningful to the Russians" without forcing escalation.[33] Now he proposed low-level surveillance of Cuba. This was a gamble. He was relying on an assessment that Cuban nationals had been told not to fire on U.S. aircraft and that Cuban MiGs would not take off from airfields. Rather belatedly, the SAM sites were being camouflaged, and this reduced their readiness. There was, he judged, "very little risk of incident." On the positive side, these flights would improve intelligence while establishing a pattern of operation consistent with attack, thereby confirming "that we are not only interested in stopping the flow of offensive weapons to Cuba but also . . . removal of the weapons that are there." To get extra security, he wanted it to be announced that the F8U aircraft that would carry out this task would be unarmed.[34] This was authorized at 10:40 A.M. and flights began that day, without any problems. That night, however, Castro denounced the reconnaissance flights and warned that they would not be tolerated.

Another possible step, toward which both McNamara and Kennedy were leaning, was to add petroleum, oil, and lubricants to the embargo list. This was the consensus view, the exception being Rusk, who saw in this step an escalation of objectives, as it would focus attention back onto Castro.[35] Estimates as to its effectiveness ranged from that of Rostow (in charge of the committee on forward plans), who saw the Cuban economy vulnerable to a cutoff of fuel, to the Pentagon's calculation that it would take up to six months before a stoppage would have a serious effect. The basic advantage of this step was political, a means of adding pressure without moving to drastic military action, still giving Moscow a chance to negotiate.[36] But even as George Ball sought to gain agreement that an oil embargo would be the next step, judging the moment in relation to progress at the UN, the hawks were arguing once again for more direct measures.[37]

If the missiles were the problem, argued Dillon, who was emerging as the main proponent of an air strike, then any confrontation should be over them rather than at sea.[38] He ticked off the advantages: the president's pledge to see the elimination of the offensive missiles would be implemented directly while demonstrating general U.S. resolve; it would have greater legitimacy, because the maintenance of the bases defied a clear resolution from the OAS and the majority view in the Security Council; a series of confrontations carried a higher risk of further escalation than one sharp action in "an area non-vital to the Soviets"; an extended crisis could lead to an erosion of support in Latin America and the promotion of unacceptable solutions. An air strike "could force Khrushchev to react strongly and could result in some type of war," but only if he was ready for war on other grounds. Notably, Dillon's group had returned to the idea of a limited air strike, solely against offensive weapons, though if it was not successful, then follow-up attacks, up to an invasion, might still prove necessary.

The pressure for an air strike was linked to two factors. First, the progress the Russians were making on the ground in Cuba. Though there was still no sign of nuclear warheads and IRBMs, the MRBM sites were being finished and the missiles made operational. By 27 October this had been achieved in five of the six MRBM sites where warhead storage sites had been identified, with the sixth reaching this status the next day. At this point the "capability would exist to launch 24 1100 n.m. missiles within six to eight hours of a decision to launch."[39] Second, civilian scrutiny of the air force analysis revealed that the requirements for an air strike had been overstated. For example, though the missiles were classified as being mobile, thereby raising the number of required sorties, they were really no more mobile than small houses. When McCone met with the president on the afternoon of 26 October he pointed to the "higher probability of immobilizing these missiles, all of them in the strike, than I think our thinking has tended in the last few days."[40]

Yet Kennedy kept on coming back to the likelihood of some missiles firing during the course of an American attack of any sort. Nor would he have been encouraged by McCone's own sober warning about the hazards of land invasion, even with command of the air.[41] Though the hawks were getting stronger as the crisis wore on, and this in itself must have been a factor in the president's thinking, he was still searching for something not too drastic.[42]

1   Inauguration Speech, January 20, 1961. *Courtesy John F. Kennedy Library.*

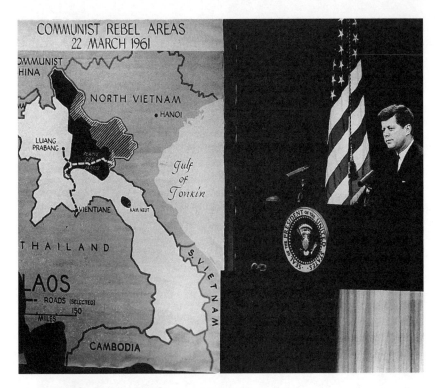

2　Kennedy's news conference on Laos, March 23, 1961.
Courtesy John F. Kennedy Library.

3   A warm greeting between Kennedy and Khrushchev at the start of the Vienna summit in June 1961. *Courtesy John F. Kennedy Library.*

4   By the conclusion of the summit, the atmosphere was noticeably less warm. *Courtesy John F. Kennedy Library (Tretick, LOOK).*

5   Meeting in Hyannis Port in November 1961 with Khrushchev's son-in-law
Adzhubei. To Kennedy's left is U.S. interpreter Alex Akalovsky and then Georgi
Bolshakov. *Courtesy John F. Kennedy Library.*

6   MRBM Launch Site 1: San Cristobal, Cuba, October 23, 1962.
Courtesy John F. Kennedy Library.

7   Kennedy with Soviet Foreign Minister Gromyko and Ambassador Dobrynin
after meeting on October 18, 1962. *Courtesy John F. Kennedy Library.*

8   Meeting of the ExCom on October 29: the President is in front of the flag. From his right around the table the participants are Dean Rusk, George Ball, John McCone, Alexis Johnson, Llewelyn Thompson, Robert Kennedy, Lyndon Johnson, Douglas Dillon, McGeorge Bundy, Theodore Sorenson, Kenneth O'Donnell, Paul Nitze, Maxwell Taylor, Roswell Gilpatric, and Robert McNamara. *Courtesy John F. Kennedy Library*.

9   On the evening of October 29, with the most intense period of the missile crisis over, Kennedy works with Dean Rusk and Robert McNamara on a response to Khrushchev's latest communication, with press secretary Pierre Salinger waiting in the background. *Courtesy John F. Kennedy Library*.

10   A Cuban veteran of the Bay of Pigs listens to the President's speech at the Orange Bowl in Miami on December 29, 1962. *Courtesy John F. Kennedy Library.*

11   John and Robert Kennedy talk outside the Oval Office, March 1963.
Courtesy John F. Kennedy Library.

12   The President examines a crossbow, among other counter-insurgency
weapons, with his military aide, General Clifton, in April 1963.
Courtesy John F. Kennedy Library.

13   The President being introduced before his speech to the American University, June 10, 1963. *Courtesy John F. Kennedy Library.*

14. Large numbers of Berliners listen to the President address them in June 1963. *Courtesy John F. Kennedy Library.*

15 Kennedy meets with McNamara and General Maxwell Taylor on October 2, 1963, after their trip to Vietnam. *Courtesy John F. Kennedy Library.*

16 The President signs the Test Ban Treaty. *Courtesy John F. Kennedy Library.*

22

Political Steps

THE MAIN THRUST of initial diplomatic activity had been to line up support among America's allies, and in particular among the Organization of American States. At a meeting of the Council of the OAS held on the morning of 23 October, ambassadors were asked for authority for the United States to use its armed forces, and in particular to impose the quarantine. With Rusk arguing that this "abrupt and secret alteration of the balance of power" threatened the countries of all those present, eighteen voted in favor of a resolution that called for the prompt removal from Cuba of "all missiles and other weapons with an offensive capability," and Mexico abstained. Bolivia and Uruguay abstained on the specific recommendation to take "all measures, individually and collectively, including the use of armed force." This OAS resolution served Kennedy as his source of authority when proclaiming the quarantine the next day.[1]

NEGOTIATIONS

The OAS, however, was not the forum for resolving the crisis. That honor was more likely to fall to the United Nations. In response to Khrushchev's letter of 23 October, Kennedy had written back immediately suggesting that while the matter was being discussed in the Security Council, "we both show prudence and do nothing to allow events to make the situation more difficult to control than it already is." A truculent reply from Khrushchev, denouncing the quarantine and insisting that Soviet captains could not obey the orders of American naval forces, failed to reinforce the more positive picture emerging at sea as Soviet ships backed away.[2] Khrushchev appeared to be angling for a summit, but the general American view was that this would be at best a distraction and at worst a trap.[3]

A possible negotiation had been raised by UN Secretary-General U Thant on the morning of 24 October. He had proposed that for a period of two to three weeks the Soviet Union should suspend arms shipments and the Americans the quarantine. This was unacceptable to Washington: The proposal contained no verification provision, and it allowed the Russians time to complete the sites and generate international pressure against the American position.[4] Ambassador Stevenson was concerned that outright rejection would be seen to be closing the door too firmly. He refused to pass on the negative response drafted in Washington, which offered only to discuss the matter, until it had been reconsidered. Though frustrated with Stevenson ("kicking like a steer"), Ball passed on to Kennedy the desire for something more positive. Kennedy saw the virtue in giving "them enough of an out to stop their shipments without looking like they completely crawled down." The two therefore decided that a stand-off for a couple of days rather than weeks might be acceptable and help avoid a dangerous clash. Ball went back to Stevenson and persuaded him to take to U Thant the idea of a shorter breathing space.[5] This he did. On the afternoon of 25 October U Thant asked Khrushchev to keep his ships "away from the interception zone for a limited time only, in order to permit discussions of the modalities of a possible agreement," and Kennedy "to do everything possible to avoid direct confrontation with Soviet ships in the next few days."[6] Kennedy agreed at once. Khrushchev accepted later that day.

Rusk gave congressional leaders a "best judgment" that Russians were "scratching their brains very hard at the present time, deciding just exactly how they want to play it, what they want to do about it."[7] The comforting evidence of Soviet caution in the face of the quarantine led the professional analysts to start to question whether the dangers of Soviet recklessness had been exaggerated. Hilsman, of the Bureau of Intelligence and Research (INR), who had previously thought that Moscow would welcome an incident at sea to keep the pressure on the United States at the UN, now on 25 October inferred that Moscow wanted to make sure that the United States was seen as the aggressor in any incident.[8] He took Moscow's agreement to U Thant's proposal as evidence that it was losing confidence in its original plan for the missile base and was now hoping that if the weapons could be kept in Cuba for some time, this would "tend to establish its legitimacy and maximize its value as a bargaining counter." Any decision on countermeasures probably rested on the manner in which the quarantine was implemented. Meanwhile it would soon be coming up with "compromise" proposals.[9]

A similar line was developed by Walt Rostow, reporting the assessment of his group charged with future planning. The Soviet objective was to retain the bases while dissuading the Americans from taking more drastic action and drawing them into prolonged negotiations. Because of the adverse political reaction that would follow an attack on a "manifestly peaceful vessel," Rostow still assumed that Moscow had an interest in a quarantine incident. While they would seek concessions to get rid of missiles, their greatest fear was of a U.S. attack: "If . . . they believed that U.S. military action was all but imminent and unavoidable, they might make a last-minute offer to dismantle the bases in return for some Western concession which, while not offsetting their loss, offered some prospect of saving face."[10]

THE JUPITERS

In the afternoon of 25 October Stevenson was scheduled to make a substantial speech in the UN setting out the American position. At the last minute Kennedy became anxious lest too strong a statement gave the Russians a pretext to give a negative response to U Thant. Stevenson, however, hated being micromanaged through officials. He was prepared to push on regardless until he was asked to take a call from the president while his officials hurriedly cut the speech by two-thirds. After this abbreviated speech news came that the Russians had accepted U Thant's proposal. Then the Soviet ambassador, Valerian Zorin, insisted again that there was no evidence of offensive missiles in Cuba. In a dramatic—and televised—encounter Stevenson demanded to know whether the missiles existed: "I am prepared to wait for my answer until hell freezes over." He then embarrassed Zorin further by using reconnaissance photos to prove his point. The use of these images was in itself an important departure from past practice but was deemed necessary because of the widespread suspicion that the Americans were making up the missile story to justify later military action.[11]

Fortified by this success, the next day Stevenson pushed to extend his room for maneuver by anticipating some of the issues that would arise in any negotiations in the UN, which he expected to conduct.[12] Could the quarantine be relaxed if no more Soviet ships were coming, even without confirmation that the Soviet missiles had been removed? What sort of inspection regime was required to ensure that the missiles were being dismantled? There was also the tricky issue of what the Americans might offer in return. What would be the attitude if, as he predicted, the Russians asked for a "new guarantee of the territorial integrity of Cuba" and for the dismantling of U.S. strategic missiles in Turkey?[13]

On the first possible concession the answer was simple. The United States was, as Dean Rusk pointed out, committed under the UN Charter and Rio Treaty not to invade Cuba. It was not an option that the United States could publicly claim for itself, whatever the private hopes of those supporting covert operations. There were some early indications from the UN that a deal along these lines might be possible.[14] Kennedy had accepted from the start of the crisis that Castro was a secondary issue.

The second proposal was trickier. It had been agreed in 1959 that fifteen Jupiter missiles were to be handed over to Turkey, with their warheads controlled under a dual-key arrangement.[15] Ironically, they became operational and were formally handed over to the Turkish foreign minister on 22 October 1962. It had been agreed early on in the Kennedy administration that they were doing more harm than good and should be removed, but the Turks attached considerable importance to their presence. They had told Rusk in May 1961 that immediate withdrawal of the missiles would be embarrassing, because parliamentary approval had just been secured, and that it would be best if the United States could wait until Polaris submarines began to operate in the Mediterranean in the spring of 1963. The State Department had not pushed the matter, despite prompts from Kennedy, who was now cross that such dispensable systems were causing so much bother.

The potential link between the Cuban bases and the U.S. bases on the periphery of the Soviet Union had been noted prior to the crisis erupting and was raised again at the start of the crisis. On 17 October Stevenson wrote to Kennedy that "the means adopted have such incalculable consequences that I feel you should have made it clear that the existence of nuclear bases anywhere is negotiable before we start anything."[16] Bundy followed this up by raising the possibility of a message to Khrushchev offering a quid pro quo on bases. "If they scrub them, then we do expect to dismantle our Turkish base." This view was supported by Ball and McNamara and also by Kennedy, who agreed that "at the appropriate time we would have to acknowledge that we were willing to take strategic missiles out of Turkey and Italy if this issue was raised by the Russians." He was ready to begin preparatory work on this issue.[17]

So from the start there was something of a consensus behind the view that the United States might need to consider a trade as part of an eventual outcome, but for the moment an offer would contradict the impression of resolution the administration was seeking to generate. There was also discomfort with the notion of equivalence. Turkey was not a trouble spot, many more missiles were going into Cuba, and the Jupiters had not been delivered under a cloak of secrecy (although the move had hardly been well advertised and the details of the Turkish deployment had not been made public).

"From a purely military point of view," a preliminary review of the issue concluded, "some bases could be abandoned without serious consequences to the national defense." The missiles were unhardened first-strike weapons, approaching obsolescence and easily replaced with missile-bearing submarines patrolling the Mediterranean. The problem was their symbolic role as part of the U.S. nuclear guarantee to Europe. Their removal because of a Caribbean problem would be taken as evidence of a declining concern for European security.[18]

The idea of a trade was sufficiently obvious for it soon to be discussed in political and diplomatic circles. Without making any specific proposal,

Soviet statements alluded to missiles in American bases close to their borders. On 24 October George Ball had lunch with Walter Lippmann, who notified him of his intention to advocate a trade. He had already discussed the Jupiters in his column the previous day, although largely to note that they were providing Moscow with a hostage rather than Washington with an asset. Ball did not attempt to dissuade him.[19] That morning Ball had already notified the ambassadors to Turkey and NATO of the possibility of a trade and asked them to assess possible reactions. He was told they would be negative.[20]

The next day Lippmann's article appeared proposing this "face-saving agreement." He compared the missiles in Cuba with those in Turkey: The two bases were on a frontier and neither was of much military value. "Both could be dismantled without altering the world balance of power."[21] He was not contradicted by any public statement from the White House. The same day the *New York Times* confirmed that there was at least "unofficial interest" in the trade among U.S. policy makers.[22] On 26 October Macmillan offered privately to Kennedy that Britain could propose dismantling Thor missiles in England (which were scheduled to leave anyway) as a quid pro quo. Kennedy responded cautiously, but the exchange may have convinced him that faced with the choice of war or a trade of some missiles in Europe, the allies would take the trade.[23]

The most challenging critique of this line of thinking came from Raymond Garthoff, deputy undersecretary for politico-military affairs in the State Department. He was the first to argue that not only did the United States have the upper hand over Khrushchev but that Khrushchev knew it. The only danger was that Washington might miscalculate and underestimate its own strength.

> I am increasingly disturbed over indications that in all of our planning for the development of the Cuban crisis we have to our peril neglected one particular contingency: that the Soviets would react mildly and with great caution. A week ago we were concerned about strangulation of West Berlin, missile firings and exchanges of cities within the U.S. and USSR, and other drastic and dangerous possibilities. Now the danger that looms large is not the exchange of cities, but the exchange of bases—at the extreme, the unhinging of our whole overseas base and alliance structure. It would be a remarkable thing if the Soviets were able to make substantial gains in achieving their main objective of weakening the alliances militarily and politically simply by exhibiting caution and indecision in the face of our initial stand.[24]

23

The Denouement

JOHN KENNEDY SPENT MUCH OF THE CRISIS trying to determine the effect of a particular course of action on Moscow.[1] To do this he put himself in Khrushchev's shoes, supposing that the Soviet leader was cast in the same mold, responding to the same stimuli and facing the same sort of pressures from his own hard-liners. He never felt closer to Khrushchev than when he imagined him having to cope with a Curtis LeMay of his own. He understood the difficulty in backing down from public commitments. The internal debates prior to 22 October also encouraged this sense of symmetry, as if there was a natural inclination to search at all times for an equivalent response so as not to back down but also not up the ante. A missile strike against Cuba gets one against Turkey; a blockade of Cuba gets a blockade of Berlin.

Robert Kennedy describes a discussion meeting between the two brothers and two advisers in the middle of the crisis:

> Neither side wanted war over Cuba, we agreed, but it was possible that either side could take a step that—for reasons of "security" or "pride" or "face"—would require a response by the other side, which in turn, for the same reasons of security, pride, or face, would bring about a counter-response and eventually an escalation into armed conflict. . . . We were not going to misjudge or miscalculate, or challenge the other side needlessly, or precipitously push our adversaries into a course of action that was not intended or anticipated.[2]

Kennedy was looking for a diplomatic outcome that was consistent with his stated objectives yet was one he would accept if he were Khrushchev.

KHRUSHCHEV RESPONDS

A hint of a possible compromise came from an unexpected source on 26 October. Aleksandr Fomin, the chief KGB man in Washington, requested lunch with John Scali, State Department correspondent for ABC. Fomin, who, as it happened, was speaking for nobody but himself, intimated that the Soviet Union might withdraw the missiles if the United States pledged not to invade Cuba. Scali immediately contacted Hilsman, who in turn circulated this information to ExComm members. Rusk told Scali to return to Fomin and say that the proposition offered "real possibilities" but that time was of the essence. This he did that evening.[3]

By the time Scali was back in touch with Fomin, a more authoritative version of what was apparently the same proposal came in a letter from Khrushchev:

> [W]e, for our part, will declare that our ships bound for Cuba are not carrying any armaments. You will declare that the United States will not invade Cuba with its troops and will not support any other forces which might intend to invade Cuba. Then the necessity for the presence of our military specialists in Cuba will be obviated.[4]

The initial reaction was that this was too good to be true. Khrushchev had accepted U Thant's formula, planted by Stevenson, promising to keep his ships out of the quarantine area while the United States refrained from intercepting them, agreed that withdrawal of his missiles was a prerequisite for a settlement, and refrained from raising extraneous matters, such as the Jupiters in Turkey and Italy. Could it be, Hilsman wondered, that a "massive and rapid Cuban military build-up" had really been ordered only for it to be bargained away for a U.S. promise not to invade? Perhaps the offer to negotiate was not actually aimed at agreement but buying time, holding on to this increment of extra power until the Soviet Union was ready for some new action over Berlin.[5]

The mystery then deepened as a second message, much more formal in tone, was broadcast by Moscow. It demanded the removal of the missiles in Turkey.

> We agree to remove those weapons from Cuba which you regard as offensive weapons. We agree to do this and to state this commitment in the United Nations. Your representatives will make a statement to the effect that the United States, on its part, bearing in mind the anxiety and concern of the Soviet state, will evacuate its analogous weapons from Turkey.[6]

TROLLOPE AND TRADES

What had happened? Kennedy's most recent letter to Khrushchev (on 25 October) had done no more than repeat his complaint and had made no new offers, but he had indicated that it had been necessary to restrain colleagues urging stronger action. This reference plus the lack of any movement on Kennedy's part had unnerved the Soviet leader. Perhaps he could not keep the missiles in Cuba unless he was ready for war. It was at this point that Khrushchev formulated the the first letter, for which he got approval on 26 October.[7] By the morning of 27 October (eight hours ahead of U.S. time) he was feeling slightly more confident. Dire warnings from Cuba of an imminent American strike had not materialized, the quarantine was not being vigorously enforced, and Khrushchev could now suppose that Kennedy was in control of his military and there was more time for bargaining. He found it telling that the Jupiter trade had been intruded into the discussion by the well-connected—indeed semiofficial—Lippmann. Instead of a deal that he might present as a draw, he saw an opportunity to notch this up to a win on points.[8]

The sudden introduction of the Jupiter issue was entirely mischievous in its effects. It led to complete confusion in Washington over what the Soviet Union was up to. A whole day was spent sorting the matter out and effectively reaching the conclusion that could have been achieved through an immediate response to the first letter; during this time the situation deteriorated, and both sides became alarmed that they might be moving over the precipice. That day's ExComm discussions are recalled by the participants as being among the most difficult and tense of the crisis. This comes through in both the records of the meetings and the transcripts, during which the participants sound fatigued and nervous.

In Washington, the natural response to the second message was to assume that it was all part of a Soviet attempt to string the United States along. It appeared to confirm Hilsman's view that Moscow was attempting to keep the missiles in place for as long as possible while generating pressure against the United States to ease the quarantine. In terms of the proposal itself, Hilsman noted that many in Europe would welcome any step that averted war, but it could also be seen as a possible first step toward U.S. withdrawal from Europe and would cause numerous problems in relations with Turkey. Garthoff saw the new message as a symptom of weakness, reflecting Khrushchev's inability to secure a favorable international response and his unwillingness to "resort to direct military confrontation or reprisal." He also noted that the new statement evaded any commitment to military action in the event of an air strike—the only contingencies mentioned were a direct invasion of Cuba or an attack on the Soviet Union or any of its allies. He therefore urged a robust stance: "The Soviets can probably still be compelled to withdraw the missile bases if they see the only alternative will be the destruction of them. However, even that outcome would almost certainly not provoke even limited Soviet military escalation."

ExComm met at 10:00 on 27 October, expecting to discuss Khrushchev's letter of the previous evening. Soon they were embroiled in a discussion of the new proposal.[9] Just as the specialists were wary of any compromise over the missiles in Turkey, so were Kennedy's senior officials. Bundy said the proposal was unacceptable. Rusk argued that Khrushchev should be told that these missiles had nothing to do with Cuba.

McNamara noted that only the nuclear warheads were under U.S. control—the missiles belonged to Turkey. Llewellyn Thompson, the senior Sovietologist, criticized the assumed automaticity of a Soviet response to a strong American line.

Kennedy appeared uneasy from the start. He had already instructed Gilpatric to set in motion work to draft a "scenario" for early removal of the Jupiters.[10] George Ball explained the problem of handling the Turks on this matter, a point confirmed by an immediate press statement from the Turkish government explaining that the proposed trade was unacceptable. Because Khrushchev had made his offer in public, the possible ploy of requesting the Turks to ask for the removal of the Jupiters was no longer available. All that could be done was to point out to Turkey the perils that might be faced should the crisis become more dangerous.

All this Kennedy understood, but his political instincts also told him that many outside observers would find a comparison between the two sets of missiles perfectly fair. He saw no long-term role for the missiles in Turkey, and if preserving them led to an uncompromising American stance, this could yield a propaganda advantage to Moscow. The real choice might be between invading Cuba and trading the missiles. He wanted to contact the Turks and explain the situation to the North Atlantic Council (which was to meet the next day). Kennedy felt that the objections from NATO stemmed in part from a lack of appreciation of the seriousness of the situation, and in particular that the alternative was not just a continuation of the quarantine but much more drastic action, made more likely if diplomacy got bogged down by this question. After American strikes led to the seizure of Berlin or retaliation against Turkey, the allies would say, "By God we should have taken it." The Russians also might not realize that a "cheap turndown by them" would put "*us* in the position of then having to do something." So a lack of a positive response now on the Turkey question could mean that "we'll have to invade or make a massive strike on Cuba which may lose *Berlin*. That's what concerns me."

That afternoon Kennedy heard from General Norstad at NATO, warning of the awkward questions that would arise if Turkey and Cuba were treated in an analogous fashion and of the impact on the long-term position of the United States. Later at 5:00, he met with General Lemnitzer, about to succeed Norstad, who gave him the same message. Throughout the day his advisers challenged Kennedy's presumption that Khrushchev would resist a deal without an explicit trade on the missiles in Turkey, and they pointed to other options, such as expanding the blockade, before air strikes had to be contemplated.

Instead of acceding, they suggested, why not reply to the first letter and ignore the second? This became known as the "Trollope ploy" after the Victorian novelist's description of young ladies mistaking a squeeze of the hand for a proposal of marriage. A letter from Kennedy to Khrushchev could ignore the missile trade and accept the no-invasion pledge. Eventually Thompson persuaded him. Kennedy, gloomy, noting that his Soviet counterpart had made a public offer from which it would be harder to back down, concluded that "we're going to have to take our weapons out of Turkey." He looked to Thompson for confirmation but was contradicted: "I don't agree, Mr. President, I think there's still a chance that we can get this line going." Kennedy appeared surprised: "He'll back down?" Thompson continued, "Well, because he's already got this other proposal which he put forward. . . . The important thing for Khrushchev, it seems to me, is to be able to say 'I saved Cuba, I stopped an invasion.' "

Even having been persuaded to ignore the second letter, Kennedy remained skeptical as to whether the ploy would work. He wanted to see the Soviet response before agreeing to anything.

THE U-2 LOSS

This discussion took place against the backdrop of what appeared to be a deteriorating situation. The day before, Castro had informed the local Soviet commanders that his troops would fire on low-level reconnaissance aircraft. As McNamara had intended, Castro saw these flights as preparing the way for a later attack and so threatening morale. He was less bothered by the high-altitude U-2s, out of range of his own air defenses, but he urged the Soviet generals to switch on their radars to get them in their sights. Once the Cubans began firing at low-level American aircraft, the Russians may have decided to join in.[11] A U-2 was shot down at about 10:00 A.M. on 27 October. It did not take long for this news to reach the White House. The demeanor of American policy makers was not helped when further news came through that yet another U-2 had strayed over Russian territory and was being chased by Soviet fighters. This was exactly the sort of unintended escalatory process Kennedy feared, with the risk that mistakes and minor incidents at sensitive moments could have large consequences. "There's always some son-of-a-bitch who doesn't get the word" was his rueful observation on hearing of the stray U-2.[12] These events undermined the assumption that there was no need to panic. Perhaps in the background was the recently published novel *Fail-Safe*, with its depiction of capital cities being destroyed as a consequence of tragic failures in technical systems.[13]

The immediate question was how to respond to the shooting down of the U-2 over Cuba. The possibility that this might happen had been anticipated on 23 October. If this was the "result of hostile action, the recommendation will be for immediate retaliation upon the most likely surface-to-air site involved in this action."[14] Given this presumption, any restraint had to be decided upon at once. The U.S. Air Force's preparations for a strike were interrupted when the White House called LeMay and told him to hold back until the president ordered him to proceed.

The air force chief, thwarted again, never expected the order to come.[15] Yet when the matter was discussed in ExComm, it was supposed that the order would have to be given at some point, to demonstrate a readiness to protect American crews and to make possible further surveillance.[16] Without further surveillance the intelligence upon which the air strike and invasion options depended would increasingly become dated, so larger-scale operations might have to be brought forward.

This was the starting point for a grim soliloquy from McNamara, from this point an increasingly anxious voice in the proceedings. If surveillance aircraft were fired upon, the United States would have to respond. As a result, there would be losses of aircraft and "we'll be shooting up Cuba quite a bit." This was not a position that could be sustained for very long. "So we must be prepared to attack Cuba—quickly." This led to the second proposition.

> When we attack Cuba we're going to have to attack with an all-out attack, and that means 500 sorties at a minimum the first day, and it means sorties every day thereafter, and I personally believe that this is almost certain to lead to an invasion, I won't say certain to, but *almost* certain to lead to an invasion.[17]

The third proposition depended on the presumption of a tit-for-tat reprisal from Khrushchev: "[I]f we do this, and leave those missiles in Turkey the Soviet Union *may*, and I think probably will, attack the Turkish missiles." This led inexorably to the fourth and final proposition:

> *[I]f* the Soviet Union attacks the Turkish missiles, we *must* respond. We *cannot* allow a Soviet attack on the—on the Jupiter missiles in Turkey without a military response by NATO . . . Now the minimum military response by NATO to a Soviet attack on the Turkish Jupiter missiles would be a response with conventional weapons by NATO forces in Turkey, that is to say Turkish and U.S. aircraft, against Soviet warships and/or naval bases in the Black Sea area. Now that to me is the absolute minimum, and I would say that it is *damned dangerous* to—to have had a Soviet attack on Turkey and a NATO response on the Soviet Union.[18]

It may be that McNamara's objective was to make a stark case for defusing the crisis by trading missiles. If so, Ball took the cue. Noting that "we're talking about a course of action which involves military action with enormous casualties and a great—a great risk of escalation," he urged that the United States agree to the missile trade. The Jupiters were obsolete, and replacement with Polaris patrols could be presented as a strengthening of the NATO position. McCone agreed but wanted to combine this with an ultimatum relating to further attacks on surveillance aircraft.[19]

The group even began to draft letters offering the trade when Thompson once again pulled everyone up by wondering whether there was any need for such a step and suggesting that a show of U.S. resolution, such as stopping a ship or taking out a SAM site, could have the desired effect. While this discussion had been going on the president had been out of the room. When he returned it was Thompson who briefed him on the state of the debate, and he used the opportunity to insert his own, anti-trade gloss: "They've upped the price, and they've upped the action. And I think that we have to bring them back by upping our action and by getting them back to this other thing without any mention of Turkey." Kennedy agreed but still mused about going to war over Turkish missiles, saying, "If that's part of the record I don't see how we'll have a very good war."

As for the U-2, he appeared ready, with McNamara, to authorize a reprisal raid if more missiles were used against surveillance missions. Without further attacks he preferred to stay his hand, at least until he had seen the response from the Soviet Union on the diplomatic front. It was not clear whether the downing of the U-2 was a one-time incident or part of a general pattern. Here he was helped by Taylor, who explained that there was no urgency in attacking the air defenses, because extra U-2 flights were not necessary for the moment. Having just received some new photography of the SAM batteries, they were not yet ready to go back with an armed reconnaissance mission.

These extra-hard, imminent decisions led to everything appearing more urgent, including the question of whether the Turks could be persuaded to relent in time to work out a trade on missile bases. All this appears to have convinced Kennedy that he must bring the matter to a head. The steps he then took to do so are discussed below. Most of the group, however, did not know of these steps, and even those that did could not be sure of their success. This uncertainty was evident in the final meeting, which took place at 9:00 that evening.[20] This began with McNamara proposing calling up air reserves and preparing to mobilize private shipping for an invasion. However, despite the somber mood, there was already signs of a search for means of delaying the crunch.

RESOLUTION

Kennedy's letter to Khrushchev had now been drafted. "The first thing that needs to be done," it stated, "is for work to cease on all offensive missile bases in Cuba and for all weapons systems in Cuba capable of offensive use to be rendered inoperable." The Americans would lift the quarantine and "give assurances against an invasion of Cuba." Kennedy avoided mentioning the Jupiter issue either way. He removed from the draft a sentence refuting the connection between missiles in Cuba and NATO bases, though he did allow for a vague reference to a more general arrangement regarding "other weapons," as mentioned in the second letter.[21]

Given all that had happened during the course of his administration, a curious omission from the first State Department draft was a demand that Castro not take any aggressive actions against the United States or other Latin American states. When Edwin Martin queried Rusk over its omission the secretary assumed it must have got lost in the constant redrafting. Alexis Johnson explained the omission as a result of Kennedy trying to combine a hard, explicit draft from Johnson and Ball with a softer draft dictated to him by Stevenson over the phone. As a result, explicit qualifications to the invasion pledge were lost, possibly to get a settlement more quickly.[22]

The letter was sent directly to Moscow and released to the press. To ensure that the message got back clearly and expeditiously to Moscow, Robert Kennedy's back channel with Dobrynin was employed. Rusk suggested that the opportunity and Robert's status in the administration be used to convey the mood of the ExComm discussions. It could only help if Moscow was made to understand that matters were coming to a head. Rusk also proposed that Kennedy could promise, but strictly off the record, that the missiles in Turkey would eventually be removed, and this was apparently accepted as sensible without much discussion.[23]

Rusk recalled, twenty-five years later, that to preserve options he suggested privately to Kennedy that he be allowed to contact Andrew Cordier, then president of Columbia University but a former UN official, to dictate to him a statement that could be passed to U Thant and that would ask for the Jupiters to be removed in exchange for the Soviet missiles. This would have made the trade easier to sell to NATO. Rusk suggests that with U.S. armed forces ready to move into Cuba by Tuesday, this ploy probably would have been used on Monday if there had been no diplomatic breakthrough by then. Some skepticism has been expressed about Rusk's recollection, but the method of getting the UN to ask for an awkward concession had already been used, and the evidence that Cordier and Rusk had already been in communication supports this view.[24]

As Kennedy was now putting the ball back into the Soviet court, there was no need for any further deliberation at ExComm. The allies were to be informed of the current, alarming state of play, but there was no longer pressure to nudge NATO toward a trade when the Council met the next day.[25] The ambassador to Turkey was alerted to the possibility that a trade might become advisable and told that it would then help if the idea came from Turkey or NATO more generally. The British were asked to hold back on any public offer about Thor missiles.

Robert Kennedy invited Anatoly Dobrynin to his office that evening. There were three aspects to his message. The first and most important underlined the urgency of the situation, though he took care to deny that he was issuing an ultimatum. No formal deadline was set by which time noncompliance would result in definite action. There was no need, as the two sides were not that far apart and an ultimatum would have merely raised the temperature. What Dobrynin needed to understand was that time was running out. Without a quick response from Khrushchev the situation would become the more dangerous. He told Dobrynin that "if Cubans were shooting at our planes, then we were going to shoot back." The missile bases "had to go and they had to go right away." A commitment was needed by the next day. If they were not removed, "we would remove them." If his country then took retaliatory action, "he should understand that before this was over, while there might be dead Americans there would also be dead Russians."

Second, Kennedy repeated the gravamen of the president's letter to Khrushchev. If the Soviets removed the weapons and (here he reinserted the lost condition) conducted no more subversive activities in Latin America, the United States would "agree to keep the peace in the Caribbean and not permit an invasion from American soil." Third, he explained that while NATO would not formally and publicly take out the Jupiter missiles from Turkey under duress, Moscow could be assured that they would be out within four or five months.[26]

Dobrynin conveyed the message as intended. He reported not an ultimatum from Kennedy but a sequence of events getting out of control— "a chain reaction . . . that will be hard to stop"—which made no attempt to deny the probability of a Soviet response "somewhere in Europe" and even referred to U.S. generals "itching for a fight." He reported the core deal on offer and the promise to get the missiles out of Turkey.[27]

Early on 28 October (while still late evening in Washington) Khrushchev was reassessing the situation. His starting point was that he was in no position to fight a war with the United States, which enjoyed local and global military superiority, except possibly in central Europe. "Cuba was 11,000 kilometres from the Soviet Union. Our sea and air communications were so precarious that an attack against the United States was unthinkable."[28] The evidence from Cuba was that people were getting agitated and even trigger-happy. He had not authorized the downing of the U-2, yet this was now bound to alarm the Americans and perhaps lead to a response. Further, at 1:00 in the morning a message from Castro was read to him by his ambassador in Cuba, who had just taken dictation from the Cuban leader. Khrushchev took it, not unreasonably, as advocating a preemptive war. Castro had presumed that the logical consequence of his orders to shoot at low-flying American aircraft would be to trigger full combat within a couple of days. Aware of the possibility of escalation to nuclear war, he urged Khrushchev not to "allow the circumstances in which the imperialists could launch the first nuclear strike." The phrase lent itself to an alarmist interpretation, especially given Khrushchev's already anxious state of mind. Soviet intelligence was also reporting that "an invasion would probably be unavoidable unless we came to an agreement with the President quickly."[29]

Then came the official response from Kennedy, accepting a deal on Cuba but saying nothing about Jupiter missiles. He told a quickly convened meeting of the Presidium that he was inclined to accept the offer, especially now that the U-2 incident had evidently raised the tension. "In order to save the world, we must retreat." What happened thereafter changed the urgency with which his reply was delivered but not its content. First, as with ExComm the previous day, another message arrived. This was a call from Gromyko's office with the telegram from Dobrynin. The basic message taken from this was that Kennedy did not want a war but the situation could soon get out of control. Dobrynin's report of generals "itching for a fight" was turned by the Soviet leader into the prospect of a president unsure "that the American military will not overthrow him and seize power."[30] He later wrote to Kennedy that "my role was simpler than yours because there were no people around me who wanted to unleash war."[31] The issue was not wholly fantastical. Two Washington journalists, Fletcher Knebel and Charles Bailey, had published that spring *Seven Days in May*, describing how a military coup might occur in Washington, and Kennedy had not dismissed the idea completely, although the circumstances would have to be far more extreme than he could envisage.[32]

Dobrynin had said that to head all of this off, Kennedy wanted a reply within twenty-four hours. To add to the drama, an army general intervened with a message saying that Kennedy would speak at 5:00 P.M. Moscow time (10:00 A.M. in Washington). "Everyone agreed that Kennedy intended to declare war, to launch an air attack." While the Washington embassy was sent an urgent message to verify this inaccurate piece of news, the Presidium decided to take no chances and drafted a quick message back to Kennedy, broadcasting it on the radio so that it would be heard in Washington before the president spoke. A telegram was also sent to Castro to warn him of what was happening.[33] From Moscow came the message:

> In order to eliminate as rapidly as possible the conflict which endangers the cause of peace . . . the Soviet Government, in addition to earlier instructions on the discontinuation of further work on weapons construction sites, has given a new order to dismantle the arms which you described as offensive, and to crate and return them to the Soviet Union.[34]

Gromyko had already sent an urgent message to Dobrynin to contact Robert with the same message. By the time they met the news had been broadcast. Robert told him it was "a great relief . . . today I will be able to see my kids, for I have been entirely absent from home."[35] His brother heard the message, like most Americans, by listening to the morning radio.

24

A Crisis Managed

KENNEDY HAD ACHIEVED his core political objective of removing the missiles. By avoiding making Castro the issue, it was easier to agree to a deal that required a promise not to invade Cuba. If the overthrow of Castro had been the issue, he would have found it more difficult to back down. It was this, as much as the more often quoted lesson of allowing Khrushchev to "save face," that made the final deal possible. Moscow was never in any doubt about what was required; the only question was what could they extract from Washington in return. If the crisis had been concluded in less of a panic, then the actual deal might have served as the foundation for a more general reassessment of American relations with Cuba.

The tenuous link between the missiles in Turkey and Cuba had been an enormous distraction, giving both countries an anxious day, which could have had grave consequences if an immediate reprisal to the loss of the U-2 had been authorized. The undertaking to Khrushchev on the removal of the missiles was important as an earnest of Kennedy's goodwill, but as it was not part of the public record, it was irrelevant to the political fallout, domestic and international, of the crisis. Indeed, the assumption was that Moscow had been successfully rebuffed.

By the time of the Cuban crisis, according to one of the architects of flexibe response, "top levels of our government had been permeated by the notion of a program of mounting pressures. It was natural that we started with a quarantine and then move on, gradually." Yet in practice, this strategy of mounting pressures to convince the adversary to back down was followed only for a while and was coming under severe strain as the crisis closed. Events did nothing to discredit the choice of quarantine, which had been started off at a sufficiently modest level for it to be extended further if need be. But with the pace of construction at the missile sites being stepped up, sooner rather than later the president would have faced either the embarrassment of the successful installation of a Soviet missile base or else air strikes and even an invasion. By Friday, 26 October, he had concluded that the quarantine by itself would not remove the missiles—he put the options as either invading Cuba or trading, and put like that, there was little doubting the president's preference.[1] However as the looming choice compelled Kennedy to seek a compromise, he was fortunate that it had the same effect on Khrushchev. The settlement came out of a fear of an imminent violent clash.

By this time the frayed nerves of the participants were apparent to all involved. Their fears that the crisis was moving into a new and dangerous stage were palpable. On the evening of 27 October, as the balance in the internal U.S. debate shifted toward the more drastic options, McNamara considered an invasion "almost inevitable" and wondered whether he would ever see another Saturday.[2] Part of the problem was sheer fatigue; on 27 October Hilsman delivered the news of the accidental entry by a U-2 into Soviet airspace and then almost collapsed, not having slept for thirty hours. Kennedy sent him home to bed.[3] Dobrynin describes Robert Kennedy at their meeting that same day as looking exhausted.[4]

On the Soviet side Khrushchev's Friday message indicated signs of panic, as he provided some graphic images of the consequences of a failure to solve the crisis:

> If people do not show wisdom, then in the final analysis warning: they will come to a clash, like blind moles, and then reciprocal extermination will begin. . . . [W]e and you ought not to pull on the ends of the rope in which you have tied the knot of war, because the more the two of us pull, the tighter that knot will be tied. And a moment may come when that knot will be tied so tight that even he who tied it will not have the strength to untie it, and then it will be necessary to cut it, and what that would mean is not for me to explain to you, because you yourself understand perfectly of what terrible forces our countries dispose.[5]

When the end of the crisis came on 28 October the initial assumption was that this was prompted by the fear of war.[6] Kennedy observed to Khrushchev: "Developments were approaching a point where events could have become unmanageable."[7] His convictions on this were reinforced by the reactions of LeMay and Anderson on Sunday morning. The former, railing against "the greatest defeat in our history," wanted to attack in any case, the latter felt betrayed. The Joint Chiefs had interpreted Khrushchev's statement as "efforts to delay direct action by the United States while preparing the ground for diplomatic blackmail." They still wanted an air strike followed soon after by an invasion. Kennedy was shocked.[8] He commented that the "first advice" he would give his successor was "to watch the generals" and not to think that "just because they were military men their opinions on military matters were worth a damn."[9]

This did not mean that he wanted a contrary reputation for being conciliatory. The first impressions—assiduously nurtured—stressed the president's cool nerve during an extraordinarily dangerous situation.[10] The most notorious "instant history" was written for the *Saturday Evening Post* by two of Kennedy's journalist friends, Charles Bartlett and Stewart Alsop. It disparaged Stevenson's role with the comment "Adlai wanted a Munich"—a remark Kennedy had not removed when sent a draft.[11] Stevenson defended himself vigorously, putting Kennedy on the spot. Was he to defend the liberals' favorite or a version of events he had helped to manufacture? As might be expected, he avoided repudiating the article while giving tepid support to the ambassador. The article also gave prominence to the idea of crisis management as a contest between hawks and doves.[12] Kennedy's instincts during the crisis had been dovish, but he did not want too dovish a public image.

LOOSE ENDS

The crisis took time to wind down. The speed with which events had moved meant that the agreement—no invasion for no offensive base— was half-baked. The Russians had made firm promises to remove offensive weapons without clarifying what this included or what the Americans were really offering in return. No better agreement was ever reached, because Castro would not permit the Russians to accept a core American condition of inspections on Cuban territory. Tedious negotiations took place at the UN to formalize the understandings reached at the end of October. They involved Stevenson and McCloy on the American side and Vasily Kuznetsov on the Soviet side, with Anastas Mikoyan camped in Havana trying to coax the Cubans along. They ended on 7 January 1963 with a bland paragraph, having gone through numerous drafts of more detailed statements.[13]

The Americans were able to push the Russians to remove the Il-28 aircraft, claiming they were offensive weapons. Khrushchev had hoped he could avoid removing these along with the missiles, and this argument continued into November with Khrushchev aware that American invasion preparations had not yet stopped. Kennedy himself considered the aircraft a secondary issue but knew that his Washington critics considered this something of a test.

In discussions through the Robert Kennedy–Bolshakov back channel (the last time it was used) the idea of allowing Khrushchev to remove the aircraft quietly by a given date, as the United States had privately agreed to do with the Turkish missiles, appeared as a sensible compromise. Castro, however, was getting increasingly restless with the situation and at one point instructed his own air defenses to prepare to fire at American surveillance aircraft. Khrushchev appeared to be playing for time, but with a presidential press conference looming and no firm agreement on outstanding issues, Kennedy deployed what was becoming a familiar tactic. He combined a major concession—an end to demands for on-site inspection—with an ultimatum. Again it worked. Castro had not wanted to be blamed for yet another crisis and was relieved that at least he did not have to endure American inspectors. He gave his blessing to the removal of the aircraft. The Kremlin had already decided that they would be removed. On 20 November Kennedy was able to announce that the crisis was properly over. The Il-28s would leave within thirty days. The quarantine would now end. On-site inspection had not been agreed to but, he reassured his audience, American surveillance aircraft could do the job. He did not add that out of deference to Castro's ire there would be no low-level flights for the time being.[14]

Khrushchev attempted without success to pin the Americans down on the Turkey trade. On 28 October he wrote to Kennedy confirming his understanding of the arrangement and the need for secrecy but adding that it had been an important factor in his decision to bring the crisis to a close.[15] Dobrynin handed it to Robert Kennedy the next day. The attorney general took the letter back to his house. It appears to have brought home to him the arrangement's potential for political embarrassment. All those on the American side who were present when it was agreed to make the promise had pledged themselves to secrecy. While the meeting had been under way Rusk had rung to ensure that Dobrynin was made to understand that the prospect of the missiles being removed from Turkey was to be treated as information and not a public pledge.[16] Robert had impressed on Dobrynin the importance of secrecy ("so the correspondents don't find out") on Sunday.[17] Only now did he write up his report on Saturday's meeting, stressing his comments on the impossibility of a formal quid pro quo and adding a single sentence on the promise to take out missiles in Turkey before penciling it out. He returned Khrushchev's letter to Dobrynin saying that the understanding stood and the two could keep in touch on its implementation, but the matter was simply too delicate to be written down.

He told Dobrynin frankly that one reason for this was that the sudden appearance of any record "could cause irreparable damage to my political career in the future."[18] Ironically it was Robert who later decided to reveal the arrangement in furtherance of his political career, in his account of the crisis that was published posthumously in 1969.[19] This revelation led to some indignation. Not only Robert's but also John's career had been assisted by the firm denial of any deal involving Turkey. Bundy later acknowledged, "We . . . encouraged the conclusion that it had been enough to stand firm on that Saturday."[20] The president had been portrayed as exercising steely resolve, thwarting a last-minute attempt to undermine the Atlantic alliance. The thanks of the Turkish government were received for the refusal to do a deal, as Rusk reassured Ormsby-Gore that "there had been no 'cozy deals' in connection with the change in the Soviet position."[21]

The issue needs to be kept in perspective. It was not necessary to clinch the overall deal and played no part in Khrushchev's decision to respond positively to Kennedy's letter, which was largely influenced by the fear of matters getting out of hand. Khrushchev himself later described the pledge as symbolic because of the obsolescence of the weapons.[22] Moreover, the promise could not have been made in public because it would then have been necessary to put it through the NATO Council. The idea of European interests being traded in this way could have caused a rumpus. Khrushchev would certainly have understood this, and he made no attempt to press the matter. Castro was already livid because of the original proposal, convinced that his country had been put at risk as a bargaining chip to remove a marginal threat to the Soviet Union.[23] The Americans had their own reasons to get rid of the Jupiters and had been trying to do so before the crisis. The only concession was that they would now override any Turkish objections, using arguments other than a deal with Moscow.

Kennedy appears to have set matters in motion on Monday morning by telling Rusk to contact McNamara, who then told John McNaughton to get a group working on the missiles' removal by 1 April. State Department officials complained about an unnecessary rush. On 14 December McNamara explained to his Turkish opposite number that while the United States had firmly refused to discuss the formal trade, they had been worried that if the United States struck sites in Cuba, the Soviet Union would almost certainly respond by attacking the Jupiter sites in Turkey. Therefore for Turkey's sake the missiles should be "promptly removed." Any direct link with Turkey was obscured by parallel moves with Italy. By 23 April 1963 the missiles had been dismantled. Kennedy wrote to Khrushchev with this news to reassure him that he had not been a victim of American duplicity.[24]

Far more troublesome for Khrushchev were the difficulties he faced over turning the no-invasion promise, Kennedy's most important concession, into a formal nonaggression pledge. Kennedy had allowed the promise to come over during the end game of the crisis as being unconditional, which is not quite what he intended. He recognized the pitfalls in stressing conditions in public, including the damage that Khrushchev might do in return if he revealed his understanding of the Turkish trade. Nonetheless he was not going to be pinned down by Khrushchev and lose any more freedom of maneuver.

In his first letter of 26 October Khrushchev had asked for "assurances ... that the U.S. would not participate itself in an attack on Cuba and would restrain others from actions of this sort." The next letter hardened this into a demand for a pledge to "respect the inviolability of Cuba's borders and its sovereignty . . . not to interfere in Cuba's internal affairs, not to invade Cuba or make its territory available as a bridgehead for such an invasion."[25] In his reply, Kennedy had only promised to "give assurances against an invasion of Cuba" conditional upon the removal of the weapons from Cuba under "appropriate United Nations observation and supervision." As he pointed out later, he had been careful to refer only to an invasion and did "not exclude use of the threat of force."[26]

Robert argued against conceding Khrushchev anything at all, saving even an informal assurance as a bargaining chip for later. Kennedy disagreed: "We do not want to convey to him that we are going back on what he considers to be our bargain."[27] The day after announcing the formal end to the crisis, on 20 November, he wrote to Khrushchev that "there need be no fear of any invasion of Cuba while matters take their present favorable course." Khrushchev chose to interpret the letter as saying that he had confirmed his commitment not to invade Cuba.[28] The conciliatory tone continued when Kennedy met with Mikoyan at the end of November. Then he explained that he had no interest in Cuba's internal developments, just in its "use as a springboard for subversion." The first deputy chairman of the Council of Ministers complained that Kennedy was going back on his unconditional pledge, and he challenged the right of the United States to judge the actions of other governments in this way. Kennedy repeated that it was not the policy of his government to invade Cuba, but if the Soviet Union wanted a binding document, then it would have to come with the necessary guarantees and references to American obligations under the Rio Treaty. The alternative was a simple statement that the United States did not intend to invade Cuba, which he had already given in his press conference of 20 November.[29]

In his next letter to Khrushchev Kennedy returned to the issue:

> We have never wanted to be driven by the acts of others into war with Cuba. The other side of the coin, however, is that we do need to have adequate assurances that all offensive weapons are removed from Cuba and are not reintroduced, and that Cuba itself commits no aggressive acts against any of the nations of the Western Hemisphere. As I understand you, you feel confident that Cuba will not in fact engage in such aggressive acts, and of course I already have your own assurance about the offensive weapons.[30]

Khrushchev tried to improve on this through the UN talks, but the Americans stuck to the position that the assurance was dependent upon both the permanent removal of the offensive weapons and appropriate Cuban conduct. This was a matter of great potential difficulty for Khrushchev. The no-invasion pledge was the only thing he had rescued from the crisis, and he was using it as an example of shining statesmanship in the

Sino-Soviet exchanges. Any hedging on Kennedy's part offered the Chinese extra ammunition. It also made Soviet credibility a hostage to Cuban good behavior at a time when that could not be guaranteed.

This issue was linked with the final piece of uncompleted business, the continued presence of Soviet forces on the island. Kennedy had assumed that all troops were leaving, though Soviet wording had always been vague on this score. In Khrushchev's letter of 26 October he had indicated that without offensive weapons "the necessity for the presence of [Soviet] military specialists in Cuba would disappear." In the November negotiations Kennedy had pressed this point, but he could not claim that the removal of Soviet forces was obligatory. He could only ask "whether a real normalization of the Cuba problem can be envisaged while there remains in Cuba large numbers of Soviet military technicians and major weapons systems and communications complexes under Soviet control."[31] This issue appeared less important than others, but gradually it dawned on the administration that a residual Soviet presence posed a political problem even if its military significance was marginal. It was another indication that October's triumph had been less than complete. After Kennedy referred in a January press conference to between 16,000 and 17,000 Soviet troops, there was concern that this might generate demands for action domestically. For this reason he was anxious not to make too much of the Soviet presence. He was also unclear why these troops had been kept on: perhaps to train Cubans to use conventional equipment, or provide Castro with a guarantee against an American invasion, or keep Castro himself under control.

On 21 February there appeared to be a breakthrough on this issue when Dobrynin came to see Thompson to tell him that the Soviet Union intended to withdraw several thousand military personnel who had been guarding the now removed weapons and also some other military specialists involved in training. By mid-March it could be confirmed that troops were withdrawing, but it was unclear how many and what sort of capability would remain. A month later the evidence was that some 4,000 personnel had withdrawn, but the remaining units appeared to be moving into permanent installations in four encampments of about battalion size with new equipment to support them. By this time it had been accepted that there was little that could be done for the moment, however irritating it might be that troops remained. The United States had used a figure of 21,000–22,000 Soviet troops at the height of the crisis, suggesting 17,000 were still left. We can only speculate on Washington's reaction if it had been known that the actual number was double this. Whether or not a more fulsome nonaggression pledge by Kennedy would have done the trick was never explored. Kennedy was explicit that it was better that Russian troops stay than he give a formal pledge, even though the troops provided an argument against invading.[32]

25

Aftermath

THE "CASTRO PROBLEM" had been played down for the duration of the crisis in order to focus on the "missile problem." As the missiles began to leave, the Castro problem was highlighted once more. By the time of the crisis over 150,000 Cubans had entered the United States as refugees. Out of this ferociously anti-Castro community came demands for action, and militants determined to act themselves. Meanwhile conservative critics, including members of the Joint Chiefs, saw Castro's survival as evidence of a severe failure of nerve on Kennedy's part. With Senator Keating claiming that U.S. intelligence was being hoodwinked once again, talk of missiles being stored in caves, and agents' reports insisting that Soviet weapons were here, there, and everywhere, there was a frenzy of demands for further action.

Invasion was not really the issue. At the end of February only 20 percent of Americans supported this, down from 24 percent just before the crisis. Nevertheless, almost 60 percent still considered Cuba to be a threat to world peace. By the end of March the president's approval rating had dropped from 76 percent to 66 percent, and the situation in Cuba was mentioned as one of the primary reasons for this. Influencing these poll ratings, which showed a two-to-one margin for a full blockade against Cuba, was the continuing presence of Russian forces in Cuba rather than the menace of Castro.[1]

Kennedy had no intention of invading Cuba, but the "ultimate objective" of the United States with respect to Cuba remained "the overthrow of the Castro regime and its replacement by one sharing the aims of the Free World." In December 1962 Kennedy even pledged his determination to see Cuba rid of Castro to forty thousand cheering Cuban exiles gathered in Miami's Orange Bowl. Foreign policy advisers warned against appearing to be preparing another invasion, yet Robert's advice was that

John could not be seen as turning his back on these people once again. The options of tightening the economic screws or of covert operations appeared attractive less as means to the stated end than as a way of heading off pressure for military action.[2]

Khrushchev's reluctance to move all troops out of Cuba, understandable in terms of his need to reassure Castro that he still cared for the island's defense, was having the effect of freezing the Cuba issue in superpower politics. Khrushchev presented the no-invasion pledge to his doubting comrades as his great achievement. If he had seen some of the more confidential internal memoranda circulating within the U.S. government, he might have been forgiven an anxiety attack. These documents betrayed scant evidence of any change either in American objectives toward Cuba or in the methods the Americans were prepared to contemplate to achieve them. Kennedy felt free to take action short of invasion and to "preserve our right to invade Cuba in the event of civil war, if there were guerrilla activities in other Latin American countries or if offensive weapons were re-introduced into Cuba."[3]

Did this mean that Kennedy intended to renege on his pledge? He had never intended to invade Cuba without a pretext, and then, having been handed the perfect pretext, he had shied away. Even as the preparations for invasion progressed, Kennedy shrank from its implications and kept the focus on the offensive missile base rather than an objectionable regime. In this he assumed that this focus also reflected Khrushchev's priorities, that the defense of Cuba was a secondary Soviet motive. The fact that in the end Kennedy did not really think that he was making a big concession on the basis of a no-invasion pledge indicates just how low-grade an option this was.

Mongoose had pointed to a different sort of scenario, a Cuban civil war, in which the United States would come under pressure to intervene. The issue of whether it would had been was left unresolved. In the aftermath of the missile crisis there was some thought that this scenario might materialize. The strains experienced by Cuba might cause it to erupt in some way; Rusk apparently observed that he did not expect Castro to last another couple of months. In February there were reports of a planned uprising, though an INR assessment noted that resistance groups appeared even less coordinated and capable of instigating revolt than before. Military leaders appeared satisfied with Castro. There was some concern that reports of uprisings were part of a trap to get resistance groups into a position where they might expose themselves. Kennedy discussed the continuing refinement of invasion plans by the Joint Chiefs and "expressed particular interest in the possibility of getting some troops quickly into Cuba in the event of a general uprising." Yet he was offered little hope of a speedy response; only the airborne troops could arrive with little delay, and it would take a week before the first marines could land.[4]

Mongoose itself had ended in a shambles midway through the missile crisis, as lines of command got confused. At the start of the crisis Robert Kennedy had demanded more action, and this had led William Harvey to decide to send commando teams by submarine to Cuba. Lansdale had not been informed, and the attorney general was appalled by the idea. The project was suspended on 26 October, and at the end of the month ExComm canceled all "sabotage or militant operations during negotiations with the Soviets."[5] Harvey did not help his cause by telling Robert that the crisis was his fault. At the start of 1963 Bundy observed that "there is well nigh universal agreement that Mongoose is at a dead end." The office was to be disbanded and covert operations handled in the normal way through the Special Group. Bundy added: "The covert aspects of our Cuba enterprise are not the most important ones, at present."[6]

While the experience of October had persuaded Kennedy that an invasion of Cuba was a bad idea, it had left him pondering the island's vulnerability and whether this provided any leverage over Khrushchev. During the crisis Kennedy was impressed by the fact that nothing remarkable happened in Berlin. A blockade against one did not lead automatically to a blockade against another. While he still never doubted that drastic action against Cuba would bring reprisals against Berlin, he now saw a reverse linkage at work. Just as Berlin was being held hostage by Khrushchev, Kennedy was also holding Cuba hostage. He explained this view of the linkage to Macmillan: "He has Cuba in his hands, but he doesn't have Berlin. If he takes Berlin, then we will take Cuba."

Suddenly both these territories had become interchangeable pieces in a superpower game. This idea lingered after the crisis. "The time will probably come," he told the NSC on 22 January, "when we have to act again on Cuba. Cuba might be our response in some future situation—the same way the Russians have used Berlin. We may decide that Cuba might be a more satisfactory response than a nuclear response." (Despite complaints from Strategic Air Command, Cuba was not included as a "bloc satellite" in plans for nuclear war.) Later, in April, when he was becoming exasperated again about the failure of the Russians to live up to their obligations in Laos, he mused about the possibility of upping the ante on Cuba, observing that "we could hardly continue to carry out a mild policy in Cuba at the time the Communists are carrying out an aggressive policy in Laos." His idea for making this point, however, did not extend beyond approving more U-2 flights.[7]

Yet these different conflicts had their own dynamics, and it was always unlikely that moves in one could be coordinated successfully with moves on another. This had been Khrushchev's own experience over Cuba when he found it prudent to leave Berlin alone. It therefore seems that Kennedy was maintaining his military options for no better reason than his preference for never closing any options off, just in case circumstances changed.

ENDS AND MEANS

The presence of Soviet troops ensured that the island remained part of the cold war. To the Cuban exiles Castro was the issue, but to the American public and the government it was the link to Moscow, symbolized by the presence of troops. As the policy reviews began in earnest in January the objective was stated as containing and isolating Cuba and also encouraging "any developments within Cuba that offer the possibility of divorcing the Cuban Government from its support of Sino-Soviet Communist purposes or replacing the Government with a regime which would accomplish this purpose." New measures proposed would prohibit shipping in any way tainted with Cuba from access to U.S. ports, extend the trade embargo throughout Latin America, and nurture dissident groups. This was too tame for the Pentagon, which put as the highest priority the overthrow of the "Castro/Communist regime" with all open military support short of outright invasion.[8] There was a self-defeating logic to this. As the experience of four years of dealing with Castro might have warned, the main effect of economic and diplomatic measures, and even covert operations, was to increase Castro's dependence upon the Soviet Union.

Gordon Chase of the NSC staff pointed out that, having isolated Cuba "from the free world," the United States might at some point focus more on the "real crux of the matter"—"to isolate Cuba from the Soviet bloc."[9] The idea of weaning Castro away from his Soviet alliance was not preposterous. By the end of the crisis, evident strains had developed between Moscow and its vulnerable, long-distance ally. But any moves in this direction were fraught with political danger because of hostility in the United States to Castro. His own demands after the crisis, put to Washington via Moscow, were that the United States end the embargo, subversive activities, violation of airspace, and "piratical" attacks, and also withdraw from Guantánamo.[10] This was a difficult time for America to extend the hand of friendship. The conditions for a more generous and sympathetic approach to Cuba were so unripe that any moves in this direction had to be kept tentative and secret.

Moreover, Castro, although more careful in his rhetoric, had not given up on fomenting further revolutions in the hemisphere. Kennedy remained anxious that another Cuba could suddenly appear elsewhere in Latin America, and he took it for granted that politically and strategically events in his own neighborhood were as important as those across the Atlantic or Pacific Oceans, if not more important. An intelligence estimate just after the missile crisis provided no evidence that Castro's efforts to replicate his revolution elsewhere had produced significant results. His influence was more symbolic than material, relevant because Latin America was already unstable for reasons of its own—"the product of fundamental inequities and historic circumstances" rather than "the creation of Castro and the Soviets."

The Alliance for Progress represented one means of addressing this problem, as did Kennedy's own readiness to visit Latin America and meet with its leaders, to a degree quite unique among American presidents. But the Alliance was slow to get off the ground. The problems it addressed were deep-rooted; implementation was hampered on the U.S. side by bureaucratic inertia and poor understanding of the societies to be rescued by this means. In Latin America it was obstructed by local power structures, anxious to protect privileges. Any political movement that seemed bent on challenging these structures could soon appear dangerously radical. Kennedy was overly conscious of Castro's own route to power, and so he determined to deny others claiming to be non-Marxist democrats the same route. Thus while pressing the British to hold back on independence for British Guiana to prevent the radical Cheddi Jagan sweeping to power, he pointed out that once was enough to be taken in by a communist who first posed as a reformer.[11] The administration worried about any government that failed to be robust enough in its opposition to Castro or was overzealous in reform, even when democratic and in such important countries as Argentina and Brazil. This right to interfere in the affairs of Latin American states was passed from one president to another, but the cold war and the Cuban example provided a rationale for sticking with some unsavory regimes while rejecting those with honorable intentions.[12]

For Kennedy the model regime was that of Venezuela's Romulo Betancourt. Betancourt had been elected president in 1959 as a liberal anticommunist. As a firm supporter of the Alliance for Progress, he was the Latin American leader to whom Kennedy felt closest and was the first to get a presidential visit, in December 1961. He was also the leader the administration considered most vulnerable to Cuban subversion. This was not only because he represented a popular alternative to Castroism but also because Venezuela itself was accessible from Cuba, with a long Caribbean coastline, weak armed forces, a radical student population infuriated by Betancourt's moderation, and oil wealth that would make it an attractive ally. In 1962 the Venezuelan Communist Party decided to support an armed insurrection. Relations with Castro were vituperative. As a member of the Security Council during the missile crisis, Venezuela had been a vocal supporter of the United States.

Betancourt was scheduled to visit Washington in February 1963. Just before he left, a band of guerrillas seized a Venezuelan cargo ship, apparently with the intention of taking it to Cuba. The Venezuelan navy was incapable of recapturing it and asked the U.S. navy to do this for them, but by the time a formal request was made, the ship had taken refuge in Brazil. When in Washington Betancourt and Kennedy issued a joint communiqué that referred to the need to resist "the all-out campaign of the international communists, aided especially by their Cuban allies, to overthrow the constitutional government." With elections planned for December in Venezuela, the Americans were convinced that they needed to help Betancourt "defeat the continued efforts of Castro to oust him."[13]

The presumption that Castro was backing guerrillas in Venezuela led Robert Kennedy to conclude that there was a need to revive anti-Castro activity. Yet when Cuba was discussed at the NSC on 13 March he was left frustrated. The pressure was easing on the president to do something, as the "demands for military action" had decreased "substantially"; in truth, fewer people were training in Cuba to be sent out into Latin America to stir up trouble. Rusk was worried about creating false hopes among the Cuban exiles (who were still split among themselves) and did not want to take action that might have an adverse affect on attempts to get Soviet troops out of Cuba.[14]

This caution was always calculated to irritate the attorney general, who the next day sent his brother a "testy memorandum urging new efforts to counter Cuban-trained operatives in Latin America." He picked up particularly on a remark by McCone to the effect that if Castro fell, it was more likely to be to a military coup than a civilian uprising. Robert wondered whether a coup was really likely and, if it was, what more could be done to bring it about. Once again he worried about missing a big opportunity. "I would not like it said a year from now that we could have had this internal breakup in Cuba but we just did not set the stage for it." Schlesinger suggests that the president was unpersuaded. John did not reply to Robert's memo, leading the younger brother to wonder whether there was "merit" in it.[15]

The reason for the president's reticence was less indifference than that the issue had moved on. On 18 March a Cuban refugee group, Alpha 66, mounted attacks on a Soviet ship and Soviet installations in Cuba. The State Department immediately issued a statement deploring "hit-and-run attacks on Cuba by splinter refugee groups." Kennedy stated publicly that the United States did not support the groups and that he did not think that they were operating from the United States. A week later there was a second raid. Unlike previous raids, it caused serious damage to a Soviet vessel.[16] These raids were now complicating relations with Moscow at a delicate time. It was barely credible for the Americans to insist that they had nothing to do with the raiders and so were unable to restrain them. On the other hand, if they did impose restraint, then the accusation domestically would be one of holding back brave Cuban patriots.

There is no evidence that these groups were actually directed by the CIA, though the agency might have encouraged them, even to the point of helping them locate arms. As the groups grew in number and diversity and as weapons became easier to come by, the CIA found whatever control it had slipping away. These militants were not disposed to specialize in anything excessively dangerous; attacks against Soviet ships appeared to be an easy and dramatic option. Kennedy, who could see how these activities might have to be curtailed, complained about the lack of good intelligence.[17] The ignorance was confined to the FBI. McCone acknowledged that the groups were well known in Florida and Puerto Rico. Their plans were discussed openly; they used U.S. suppliers and moved in and out of the United States, but generally staged their operations from the Bahamas.

The raids prompted heavy Soviet protests and promised to cause the administration considerable embarrassment. Concerned, Rusk wrote directly to Kennedy,[18] leading to him to assemble ExComm for what was its last meeting.[19] Only McCone argued against clamping down on "brave men fighting for freedom of their country." The consensus view was that the raids would not hurt Castro but would result in the Russians further building up Cuban capacity. It could generate a larger crisis as the Cubans and Russians moved outside territorial waters to do something about it (there had already been one incident on 28 March when a U.S. private ship was shot at by two Cuban MiG aircraft) and complicate U.S. surveillance. To pretend that the raids had nothing to with the United States was simply unbelievable; the administration was bound to be blamed no matter what it said.

The president's starting point was that the exile groups were attacking the wrong targets in the wrong way. He saw the difficulty in enforcing restraint and so queried whether they could be encouraged to direct their energies against Cuban rather than Russian targets, "with the result that the raids would draw less press attention and arouse less acrimony in Moscow." He observed sarcastically that, in contrast to real guerrilla activity within Cuba, "these in-and-out raids were probably exciting and rather pleasant for those who engage in them. They were in danger for less than an hour." His brother, the most activist in the administration when it came to going after Castro, accepted that "we would look ridiculous if the raids continue and we say we cannot control or prevent them." As attorney general, he described measures, including the use of the courts, to cut off supplies to the exiles and stop the raids. Along with McNamara, he believed that the coast guard and the navy between them should be able to cope. Others were not so sure, but McCone let it be known that "[t]he CIA has means of informing the raiding groups that they should stop attacks on Soviet shipping or attacks on all shipping."

Kennedy wondered why these groups could not carry out their assignments in Cuba under the guidance of the CIA. The answer was that they knew they would be caught if put ashore. Even with extensive planning it was difficult to insert controlled agents. For the moment, therefore, as the attorney general noted, the decision was "to proceed & work up plan to prevent attacks from continuing."[20] As a first step, a planned air raid about which there was some intelligence was to be stopped, if necessary by making a public statement.[21] On 31 March British and Bahamian police, working on a tip from the United States, intercepted a boat with sixteen exiles and one American. Kennedy wrote to Khrushchev promising to deal with the raiders. The official line was that responsibility for foreign policy could not be handed to such groups, but soon Kennedy faced criticism for "protecting" Castro and the Soviet Union.[22]

A few days later CIA proposals for covert operations began to be discussed. These were largely propagandistic (such as releasing balloons carrying leaflets or distributing cartoons carrying sabotage techniques) but also included attacks on Cuban shipping. These would be designed to cause damage to machinery but not sinkings, although there was some discussion of limpet mines. Another controversial issue was the possible distribution of leaflets inciting attacks on Soviet personnel.

The new head of the covert program, Desmond Fitzgerald, understood that Kennedy wanted a certain amount of "noise" of this type. His job, in which he generally succeeded, was to restore Kennedy's confidence in the CIA. The mood among more senior policy makers, however, remained highly skeptical, especially in the light of Mongoose. Resources had been squandered and lives had been lost to no obvious effect. What was the right level of activity? If nothing was done, Castro would strengthen his control and his opponents would be demoralized, yet the wrong sort of activity could have the same effect. Kennedy did not want the fire of internal opposition to be quenched, but neither did he want it to burn out of control, especially if that would prompt immediate demands for an invasion. The fire had to be dazzling enough to serve as a beacon for anticommunists in Cuba and throughout Latin America but not so impressive that it could not credibly be presented as the work of anti-Castro rebels. He wanted at least the impression that any sabotage attacks were originating from within Cuba, but this required organization, which took time to develop, and direction, which was hard to sustain. Richard Helms observed that once the rebel groups were let go, "you can never be really sure what they will do." They might attack the wrong type of targets at the wrong time—but the CIA would still be assumed to be responsible. Further, McCone had little regard for the effectiveness of Cuban agents and presumed that they would talk if captured.[23]

Work on assassination attempts resumed. When Harvey left he apparently terminated his Mafia connections. Fitzgerald, more fascinated by technical wizardry, considered a variety of ruses to connect explosives or toxic substances to Castro's person. All of these schemes were obviously flawed and none was taken very far. Helms knew what was going on, but it is almost certain that McCone did not, and if he had, he would have disapproved. The only actual effort of this period was initiated by Rolanda Cubela Secandes, a CIA contact in the Cuban leadership who had been reporting since early 1961 on the internal workings of the regime. His usefulness was such that he had been encouraged to stay in place rather than defect. In the fall of 1963 he expressed interest in a coup, and possibly assassination in the process. He wanted evidence of proper support from the United States and so, against the rules, Fitzgerald went to meet him, offering himself as the personal representative of Robert Kennedy, although the attorney general was not informed of this. The Cuban asked for a high-powered rifle to set off the coup. As such a weapon would have unavoidably implicated the United States, he was given a cache of arms and a ballpoint pen rigged with a hypodermic needle (which left him unimpressed). This was being handed over on the day Kennedy was killed.[24]

FIRST CONTACTS

With the covert program so halfhearted, one option was to cut losses and reach some sort of accommodation with Castro. Official contact between the two governments was not wholly absent. There had been one encounter in Uruguay between Richard Goodwin and Che Guevara in August 1961 during which Che had left little doubt that the regime intended to continue with a socialist revolution but was nonetheless interested in some sort of modus vivendi. Goodwin argued for keeping up pressure on Cuba, even while attempting to find some way of continuing the "below ground dialogue" to encourage a severance of all ties with the Soviet Union and democratic elections in Cuba. There is some indication that the president was interested in this; the CIA was asked to find a way of conducting the dialogue, but little happened. The policy was to deny the regime any legitimacy.[25] Nonetheless, Goodwin persisted with the view that a "moderate and face-saving" approach to Castro might split him off from the true communists.[26]

A dialogue did begin on the subject of the 1,189 members of the rebel brigade taken prisoner by Cuban forces at the Bay of Pigs. The fate of these men touched Kennedy's conscience. Aware of this, Castro had almost immediately offered after the fiasco, possibly as a diplomatic bait, to release the prisoners in exchange for five hundred bulldozers. This effort ended after the Vienna summit with recriminations all around. In March 1962 the prisoners were brought to trial, and it was feared that they would be shot. Robert Kennedy, on his own initiative, tried to put together a food-for-prisoners deal.[27] In April the effort bore some fruit when sixty of the weakest men were released by Castro in the expectation of a down payment—which then proved difficult to organize, as the idea of paying ransom to Castro was anathema.

The president then asked James Donovan, former general counsel to the Office of Strategic Services (OSS) and an experienced negotiator, to take over the discussions. He contacted Castro, but efforts to close a deal then got caught up with the anxieties over Soviet arms shipments. It did not seem an opportune moment to hand over millions of dollars to Cuba. After the missile crisis ended, the negotiations were reinstated and Donovan made sufficient progress for a proposal to be developed that offered $53 million in pharmaceuticals and food in return for the remaining prisoners. With the Cuban exile groups themselves desperate to extract their people, it was possible to obtain the ransom from private donations and help from drug companies. The men were home for Christmas.

Bundy, the senior official most interested in a rapprochement, saw in this contact an opportunity. He mentioned to Kennedy an invitation for Donovan to return to Cuba in connection with a proposal "to intensify our investigation of ways and means of communicating with possibly dissident members of the Castro regime, perhaps including even Fidel himself." Donovan returned to Cuba now seeking to get Americans out of Cuban prisons, even though a number were CIA agents. Castro agreed to release them after a short "rehabilitation period." In the course of their discussions Donovan told Castro directly that his problems lay in his dependence upon Moscow, and got a grunt in reply. A more positive indication came from Dr. René Vallejo, Castro's physician and friend, who had acted as interpreter. Vallejo was more idealist than communist, and he was anxious to be on friendlier terms with the United States, having done his medical training in Boston and served with the U.S. Army. He broached the possibility of reestablishing diplomatic relations.

Castro asked Donovan to return, inadvertently establishing a line of communication with a man close to the CIA. Kennedy was intrigued and apparently ready to compromise.[28] He agreed that Donovan should not raise policy issues prior to getting prisoners released, in case Castro recognized that he had some leverage. However, when it was also suggested that Donovan might identify two conditions to Castro—ending ties to the "Sino-Soviet bloc" and noninterference in regional affairs— Kennedy's response was to play down the first condition, on the grounds that it would be difficult for Castro to fulfill. In addition, he wanted Donovan briefed on possible "flies to dangle in front of Castro."[29]

Donovan returned in April and spent some time with Castro, with whom he had now established a rapport sufficient for him to challenge stereotypes of an unwashed and psychotic brigand. Donovan found Castro unsure about the Soviet Union and ready to consider mending fences. He raised the question of how diplomatic relations might be revived, and received the standard reply: "[L]ike porcupines make love—very carefully." Donovan explained that at the very least Castro must not meddle in the affairs of other countries. Vallejo suggested that Castro wanted to move in this direction but was held back by others in the leadership.

Donovan returned to Washington on 10 April with the good news that the Americans would be released on 22 April, so long as Red Cross deliveries came to Cuba. When the CIA debriefed him, he reported Vallejo's opinion that Castro feared chaos if procommunists rebelled but was determined that Cuba would never become a Soviet satellite. He also conveyed Castro's claim that his influence in Latin America was a result of the Cuban example rather than the export of subversion. Not only was Robert interested in the possibility of doing "business with that fellow," but McCone was also enthusiastic.[30] The normally hawkish director of central intelligence observed that Castro's talk with Donovan had been "mild in nature, conciliatory and reasonably frank." The encounter with Vallejo was of greater significance. He raised the possibility of

> working on Castro with the objective of disenchanting him with his Soviet relations causing him to break relations with Khrushchev, to effect the removal of Soviet troops from Cuba, reorient his policies with respect to Latin America, and establish in Cuba government satisfactory to the rest of the Hemisphere.

McCone was not even sure whether this might be a better way to solve the Cuban problem than continued pressure to get Khrushchev to remove his troops and then cause Castro's downfall. Typically, Kennedy saw no need to choose; both tracks could be developed for the moment and even followed simultaneously. Donovan was to return to Cuba on 22 April to oversee the release of the prisoners and keep open line of communication. While this was going on a proposed sabotage operation was postponed.

Bundy took the opportunity to push for a policy shift. A paper circulated on 21 April for the Standing Group (the successor to ExComm) kept the established policy framework but considered new directions. One—forcing "a non-communist solution in Cuba by all necessary means"—required "a willingness to use military force to invade Cuba," while another—"major but limited ends"—required a blockade. In neither case was there a large role for covert operations. The third option—some form of accommodation—grew in attraction by comparison with the other two. It would have political and economic advantages.

The State Department poured cold water on the idea. Edward Martin thought it unlikely that Castro could be persuaded to defect from the Soviet bloc or that Congress would allow the sort of economic package that would encourage him to do so. This was the Standing Group's consensus position, although they allowed that the Donovan contact could continue as a separate track. McCone, however, was now cooling rapidly, as intelligence sources reported that Castro and Khrushchev were patching up their differences. Castro may have toned down his "inflammatory appeals for violent revolutions," but he was still promoting insurgencies, notably in Venezuela.[31]

The Donovan initiative had not yet entirely run out of steam. At Donovan's suggestion, Castro granted an extensive interview to Lisa Howard of ABC. She concluded that he was interested in a rapprochement, largely for economic reasons, and saw restrictions on exile raids as a positive sign.

His government, however, was split on the matter, with his brother Raul (whose communist sympathies were deeply embedded) and Che Guevara opposed. For reasons, the CIA supposed, of Latin pride, any initiative would have to come from Kennedy. When ABC, worried that transmission of an interview generally hostile to the United States would appear unpatriotic, sent Edwin Martin a transcript a week in advance, he objected that it would strengthen opponents of U.S. policy (" 'peace' groups, 'liberal' thinkers, Commies, fellow travelers, and opportunistic political opponents") and encourage others in Latin America to relax their guard.[32]

McCone let it be known that rapprochement was a remote possibility, not deserving of any active steps, and was to be discussed only in the most exclusive circles. His main aim was to draw Cuba out of the Soviet bloc, and this seemed less likely than ever, as at the end of the month Castro had suddenly surfaced in Moscow, where he made himself welcome for a month. McCone later observed that he was sure that Khrushchev had inspired this visit to "forestall any effort by the U.S. to negotiate with Castro."[33]

Khrushchev had anticipated the danger. The immediate postcrisis relations had been poor, as the Soviet leader saw Castro less as a romantic revolutionary and more as a dangerous ally, combustible and unpredictable. The Cubans felt they had been used by Khrushchev to no good purpose, taking unnecessary risks for the socialist cause, girding themselves to die for this cause, and then watching the Russians meekly take their missiles home again. Yet after initially expressing his irritation with Castro for not appreciating the full risks of war, Khrushchev realized that he had better adopt a more conciliatory approach. He had made a substantial investment, and he needed Castro's cooperation to bring the crisis to closure. This was the reason for Mikoyan's trip to Havana in November. In January Khrushchev sent a long letter to Castro that went some way toward mollifying the Cuban leader. During his month-long visit to Moscow Castro was given as earnests of Soviet friendship "vodka, bear hugs, a visit to the super-secret silo of intercontinental ballistic missiles, and more billions of rubles from Soviet state coffers."[34] The framework for a peace initiative had now been transformed. Castro might still have reason to reach a modus vivendi with the United States. Khrushchev was becoming an enthusiast for peaceful coexistence all around. But internally Castro was more committed than ever to a socialist path. Another disastrous sugar crop had made him even more dependent on Soviet aid. Furthermore, although Khrushchev had been warned by Harriman that the existence of Soviet troops in Cuba was giving the president "a great deal of difficulty keeping the country quiet on Cuba," he was only prepared to offer (in a letter to Kennedy) further troop withdrawals according to the "pace at which the atmosphere in the region of the Caribbean Sea will be normalized."[35]

A State Department paper in June acknowledged that Castro's new-found commitment to peaceful coexistence allowed in principle for "normal" relations with the United States. Having denied engaging in subversive activities, the United States would have no problem renouncing them. If the United States ended its harassment of Cuba, thereby supporting its economic recovery, then Castro might end military links with the Soviet Union and regional subversion, and compensate for seized properties. The State Department presumed that Castro needed a deal more than the United States did, and went on to explain why it should not be pursued. Any agreement would be with one man, who might not last and whose word could not be trusted; by definition, covert subversion could not be monitored; Castro's survival would set a precedent in the Americas and encourage other communists; if Latin American countries became complacent, they would become more vulnerable to a takeover, prompting capital flight and the crumbling of the Alliance for Progress; with Castro strengthened, his elimination would be more difficult; and regardless, Congress would never approve the economic legislation required and the exiles in the United States could become riotous.[36] Not a lot of support here for an American initiative.

26

Back to Square One

AS THE STANDING GROUP DECIDED against a diplomatic initiative on 23 April, its members were still short of alternatives. Unless something was done, Castro's position would only improve, and so McNamara argued for going back to the old Pentagon policy of "creating such a situation of dissidence within Cuba as to allow the U.S. to use force in support of anti-Castro forces without leading to retaliation by the USSR on the West." The attorney general moved things along by proposing three studies: how the United States might respond to specific contingencies, including the death of Castro or the shooting down of a U-2; how to overthrow Castro in eighteen months; and how "to cause as much trouble as we can for Communist Cuba during the next eighteen months."[1]

The studies gave little cause for optimism. If a U-2 was shot down, the provocation might justify decisive action against Cuba, but only if the provocation was internationally recognized and continued after the United States escalated up the familiar path of diplomatic protest, quarantine, and suppression of air defenses. A coup or revolt would not necessarily either require an immediate American response or provide a suitable opportunity for one. A more general uprising was simply judged unlikely. If Castro died (for whatever reason), the odds were that "his brother Raul or some other figure would, with Soviet backing and help, take over control." Anti-Moscow Cuban nationalists would "require extensive U.S. help in order to win, and probably U.S. military intervention."[2]

At the end of May, Bundy drew the conclusion that there were no sure ways of overthrowing Castro; none of the contingencies could be controlled by the United States, and all involved a serious risk of confrontation with the Soviet Union. In the absence of anything better, discussion wandered back to covert operations and sabotage. The CIA was still developing its plans. McCone thought they might help subvert Castro and would "at least create a very high noise level." Robert Kennedy believed that it was still necessary to do something against Castro even if he could not be brought down. Bundy acknowledged that the United States could still "give an impression of busyness in Cuba."[3]

Matters had almost reached the point where "noise" of some sort was to be welcomed rather than avoided. Whether or not it made much difference to the Cuban situation, at least it would show those demanding action that something was being done. Deniability had become a hopeless proposition anyway. A host of groups was plotting openly against Cuba, and CIA support was assumed and discussed in the press. In April McCone had insisted future operations could not be authorized unless the political consequences of the unavoidable hubbub were accepted.[4] Robert worried that the open press discussion could lead to a Soviet over-reaction and, in late May, reassured a Soviet intelligence officer that no intervention was being planned.[5] The June NIE observed that with the passage of time, and in the light of Castro's charismatic appeal, there was no reason to suppose that "internal political opposition or economic difficulties will cause the regime to collapse." So the objective became less Castro's overthrow than the prevention of the further consolidation of his position. The available means were the same: the familiar combination of intelligence collection, sabotage, and general agitation. Anti-Castro groups would be allowed to undertake autonomous hit-and-run actions, so long as they were mounted from outside the United States. There was a palpable lack of enthusiasm, even in the CIA, for a noisy operation that promised little and which might harm improved relations with Moscow.[6]

The noise began without action. One example of a spate of press reports was "Backstage with Bobby" from the *Miami Herald* of 14 July, which described the attorney general's conversations with groups planning raids from Central America. Rather than try to sustain secrecy, a hopeless task where the Cubans were concerned, Robert appeared to think it more sensible to float extra rumors, "so that in the welter of press reports no one would know the true facts."[7] Soon the exile groups did get into their stride. Robert later claimed that more was done with "espionage and sabotage in August, September, October." With Fitzgerald, activities were "better organized and were having quite an effect." He cited with pride the "ten or twenty tons of sugar cane that were being burned every week through internal uprisings." But he also indicated that there was always reluctance to give final approval to projects.[8] Nonetheless, the number of approvals rose.[9] By mid-September the Cuban government had reported seven raids, most involving light planes, and was charging the United States with preparing aggression. The public position of the U.S. government remained cautious; it observed that "indiscriminate attacks" did not "actually represent a real blow at Cuba or advance the cause."[10]

On 10 September Dobrynin came to see Thompson with a confidential message for the president from Khrushchev. The Soviet leader, he reported, having believed that the relation between the two countries had taken a turn for the better, was surprised that the signing of the test ban treaty had been followed by unknown planes shelling industrial establishments in Cuba and saboteurs landing on the coast. As these actions could be undertaken only from the United States, Khrushchev now hoped that Kennedy would take action to "stop the piratic attacks." He added that the Soviet Union "would certainly fulfill its commitments if aggression were unleashed against Cuba."

The president's reaction was to stop exile raids emanating from outside the United States as well as from inside. He was only ever really impressed by activities within Cuba. Gordon Chase, an NSC staff member, warned of the problem of winding down all those who had become wound up over Cuba—the exiles themselves plus their supporters in the United States and Latin America. The reply to Khrushchev, sent via Dobrynin, promised that every effort was being made to prevent raids mounted from U.S. territory but that activities elsewhere in the hemisphere could not be controlled. Going on the offensive, Kennedy cited Cuban activities such as guerrillas entering Peru, the provision of funding to communists in Ecuador, and exhortations to terrorism in Venezuela. The argument continued when he met with Gromyko in October. Kennedy observed that "[i]n any event, he did not see any benefit to the U.S. from harassment. This would not unseat Castro and served no useful purpose."[11]

DEALING WITH CASTRO

Rusk was unenthusiastic about covert operations, concerned about the noise level, and interested in the possibility of an accommodation with Castro. Bundy was also interested, although he did not expect a deal until things got much rougher for Castro.[12] In early June the CIA could point to a number of indications that a more conciliatory policy toward the United States was being considered in Havana.[13] McCone himself still considered a rapprochement "out of the question" and even dangerous to contemplate. Notwithstanding a loss of enthusiasm, the consensus view was still to support efforts to probe Castro's mind, perhaps through another visit by Donovan.[14]

An opportunity to start probing arose in September. William Attwood, the American ambassador to Guinea, was spending some time with the U.S. delegation to the UN while he recovered from a bout of polio. In 1959, while editor of *Look* magazine, he had interviewed Castro and had retained an interest in Cuba. Also he had seen in Guinea how a left-wing leader, in this case Sekou Touré, could be eased away from an alignment with Moscow. In late August he met Guinea's ambassador to Havana, who told him Castro was looking to escape from his satellite status. He read Lisa Howard's account of her April conversation with Castro, spoke with her, and then decided to raise the issue with Averell Harriman.[15] This led to a memo arguing for "a discreet inquiry into the possibility of neutralizing Cuba on our terms." In one of the first serious critiques to penetrate into the NSC, he argued that the effects of current policy were negative, aggravating Castro's anti-Americanism and putting the United States in the position of a bully. There was no reason to suppose that the regime was about to fail, and the United States did not intend to overthrow it by force. He had reason to believe that Castro, though not necessarily the communists in his entourage, would like to reduce his dependence upon Moscow and establish some official contact with the United States. He therefore proposed finding an opportunity to discuss this with Cuban diplomats during the coming UN General Assembly session, with an agenda based on neutralization and nonalignment, involving the evacuation of all Soviet-bloc personnel.[16]

Harriman, long dubious about current policy (he had once suggested that the best way to undermine communist leaders was to make them look ridiculous), was instinctively in favor of this. So was Adlai Stevenson, who quickly obtained the president's permission for Attwood to make a discreet contact with Cuba's UN ambassador Carlos Lechuga Hevia. This took place at Lisa Howard's apartment on 23 September. The ambassador reacted positively to the possibility of a further exchange of views. At Harriman's prudent suggestion, a meeting for Attwood was arranged with Robert Kennedy, who also agreed that the contact would be useful, although he was apprehensive about leaks. He thought it unwise for Attwood to go to Havana if invited. The UN would be a better forum. This point was made to Lechuga when they met again on 27 September.

On 7 October Stevenson set out conditions for improving relations: cease being an agent of the Soviet policy, no external subversion, restore constitutional rights. Other contacts suggested that Havana was ready to talk but that Castro was being watched carefully by a resolutely procommunist group. In reporting back to Bundy's office, Attwood observed that while the door was "ajar," he was not optimistic because of Castro's own limited room for maneuver.[17] Certainly all Lechuga could offer for the moment was an informal and occasional chat. Lisa Howard had already concluded that Lechuga would find it difficult to get to Castro via the Foreign Ministry and so she had got in touch with René Vallejo, Donovan's old contact. He replied that Castro was interested but could not leave the country. He would, however, be prepared to send a plane to Mexico to pick up Attwood to fly him to a Cuban meeting.

To get the White House involved, Attwood arranged for a French journalist, Jean Daniel, to visit Kennedy prior to visiting Havana.[18] The president accepted that his country deserved blame for its policies of the Batista era, and he was sympathetic to the ideals that had inspired the Cuban revolution. But Castro had betrayed these ideals by becoming "a

Soviet agent in Latin America." Asked whether "American liberalism and socialist collectivism" could be compatible, Kennedy pointed to good relations with Yugoslavia and Guinea. He told Daniel that "continuation of the blockade depends on the continuation of subversive activities."

When Attwood's mission was discussed by the Special Group on 5 November, others were less sure than Bundy of its advisability.[19] The State Department's Latin American Bureau appeared much more skeptical than the president, adding renunciation of Marxism-Leninism, restoration of capitalism, and compensation for past expropriations to the conditions.[20] When on 12 November Kennedy met with his advisers, they were given no reason to suppose that Castro's grip was being seriously weakened. Rusk observed that the "hit-and-run sabotage tactics" were "unproductive, complicating our relations with the Soviets and also with our friends." McNamara was more positive, though he counseled a "careful watch."[21] That same day Chase produced a rebuttal of the State Department's position, pointing to the political and economic difficulties faced by Castro and the need to make sure he understood that he had an option of rapprochement. If the initiative looked like it was getting anywhere, it might at least sow confusion in the communist ranks. The real challenge would be to convince American public opinion that the government was not being taken for a ride should the dialogue progress.[22]

Possibly on this basis, Bundy spoke with Kennedy about the mission and then encouraged Attwood to take it forward. All that was authorized, however, was a visit by Vallejo to the United States so that Attwood could receive any messages from Castro. It had to be clarified that "we are not supplicants in this matter." Attwood passed this message directly to Vallejo on 18 November, and it was agreed that Lechuga would be in touch in order to discuss an agenda for a later meeting with Castro. Bundy told Attwood that once an agenda was received from the Cubans, the president wanted to see him to discuss the next steps. On Castro's own account, an agenda was soon under preparation.[23]

That same day Kennedy addressed the Cuban issue in a speech in Miami: "Every nation is free to shape its own economic institutions in accordance with its own national needs." The only thing that divided Cuba from the United States was that it was being used by "a small band of conspirators . . . in an effort dictated by external powers to subvert the other American republics. This, and this alone, divides us. As long as this is true, nothing is possible. Without it, everything is possible." According to Schlesinger, the speech was written by Richard Goodwin and reviewed by a White House group, including himself, to help Attwood; he denies that it was designed to send a green light to an anti-Castro coup. However, later Bundy told Lyndon Johnson that the speech was "designed to encourage anti-Castro elements within Cuba to revolt . . . and to indicate that we would not permit another Cuba in the Hemisphere."[24]

Nonetheless, two days later Castro suddenly spoke with Daniel, who had spent three weeks trying to make contact and was about to leave Havana. Castro appeared to think that Kennedy was sincere and a realist, someone who might just learn to coexist with socialists.

> Personally, I consider him responsible for everything, but I will say this: he has come to understand many things over the past few months; and then too, in the last analysis, I'm convinced that anyone else would be worse. . . . You can tell him that I'm willing to declare Goldwater my friend if that will guarantee Kennedy's re-election.[25]

The implication of this is that Castro was playing a longer game. He certainly had not yet given up on his ambitions for the rest of Latin America, with Venezuela his current target. He had been tutored by Khrushchev into supposing that the best time to do business with Kennedy would be after the 1964 election. The opportunity never came. Two days later Kennedy was cut down in Dallas.

The initial reaction on the NSC following Kennedy's assassination was to persevere with the mission out of curiosity, and on the basis that it should do no harm. Word came from Lechuga that Castro had authorized talks with Attwood at the UN. On 2 December the two men met with Lechuga, wanting to know whether in the new circumstances Attwood still could talk. There was already hesitation because President Johnson's views had yet to be canvassed, and there was also concern that Attwood was too much of a "true-believer" to convey a stiff enough message. Though Attwood was told that Castro had approved detailed talks and an agenda, he could only respond by reporting that a policy review was under way.[26]

The initiative petered out. A short note Attwood prepared for Stevenson on the initiative reached President Johnson, who asked Bill Moyers, his special assistant, to find out what had been going on. Moyers spoke to Bromley Smith, executive secretary to the NSC, who reviewed the initiative and recommended that this was not the time to develop this contact, though it could be reactivated at a later date. He appears to have been influenced by a recently signed Cuban-Soviet trade agreement.[27]

There was another issue: Kennedy's alleged assassin, Lee Harvey Oswald, had "been heralded as a pro-Castro type."[28] This was potentially extremely serious, for if Castro could be shown to be in any way behind the murder, then the pressure would be on for retaliation and not rapprochement. For those involved in the murkier side of Kennedy's campaign against Castro, Oswald's Cuban connection and then his own assassination by a man with known Mafia connection was unnerving. The Cuban leader himself appeared shocked by the news, although he had warned that "United States leaders should think that if they are aiding in terrorist plans to eliminate Cuban leaders, they themselves will not be safe."[29] Whether Kennedy was killed by a lone assassin or as a result of the complex plots involving the mob and Cuban exiles that are explored by conspiracy theorists, one way or another he was probably the victim of the Cuban issue in American politics.

Though the new president was anxious to avoid any drastic action, his instincts were more hawkish than his predecessor's. He asked Bundy "how we planned to dispose of Castro" and spoke of the need to "evolve more aggressive policies." A couple of days later he reported to Senator Fulbright that the Cubans were "shipping arms all over the damned hemisphere" and wanted ideas as to how "to pinch their nuts more than we're doing."[30] Efforts to disrupt the December elections in Venezuela had not helped Castro's reputation. Earlier in the year Kennedy had asked McCone if the CIA had any evidence of the direct link between Castro and the insurrectionists in Venezuela that he was sure must exist. At the end of November Venezuela claimed to have found a cache of Cuban arms on a beach, including rifles, machine guns, and ammunition. Because the export of Cuban arms was unusual, CIA analysts were surprised by the find. There were suspicions, never proved, that some of their agents had planted the arms.[31]

In December the new president's reaction to a brief on the contacts was described as "somewhere between lukewarm and cool." Johnson did not want to appear "soft" on Cuba in an election year. Attwood was told to put his initiative on ice for the moment.[32] In February Castro sent a direct message to Johnson via Lisa Howard. The essence of the message was similar to that he had intended to communicate to Kennedy: He preferred a Democratic to a Republican president and would help even if this meant tolerating hostile words or actions against Cuba and no diplomatic movement until after November. He wished it to be known that he was confident in the strength of the Cuban revolution; nonetheless, the president should know that he wanted to sit down and "negotiate our differences." In the right atmosphere all "areas of contention" could be settled. The "hostility between Cuba and the United States is both unnatural and unnecessary—and it can be eliminated." There appears to have been no response.[33] Howard nonetheless continued as a back channel between Castro and the Johnson administration, but the Americans continued to see few advantages in a rapprochement.[34]

Was the Attwood overture just another casualty of the transition from Kennedy to Johnson, another what-might-have-been of history? The Attwood mission was taken seriously by Kennedy, and those in the know considered this to be an initiative of potential importance. Gordon Chase, who had been following the mission for Bundy, observed immediately after the assassination that "President Kennedy could have accommodated with Castro and gotten away with it with a minimum of domestic heat."[35] Yet there is no evidence that the gap between the two men would have been easy to bridge. For both, an abrupt change of course would have been hard to explain at home and then validate in practice. The best that could probably have been arranged would have been a steady easing of tension, with Kennedy decreasing covert efforts and allowing some relaxation of the economic embargo, while Castro demonstrated that he was behaving responsibly in the region as he began to shift the domestic balance of power away from the harder-line communists. Anything more would probably have been for the second term.

IV

ALLIANCES AND DETENTE

27

The Sino-Soviet Split

THE MISSILE CRISIS strengthened Kennedy personally. His approval ratings in opinion polls, below 60 percent prior to the crisis, now shot up to 76 percent. The November elections had given the Democrats a net gain of four seats in the Senate and a net loss of four seats in the House. They had been helped by Cuba but hindered by Kennedy's firmer commitment to civil rights. America's international position also appeared stronger. Kennedy soon saw the crisis as a possible turning point, the conclusion of a period in the cold war that had begun with *Sputnik 1* in late 1957, when Khrushchev boasted that the world's correlation of forces was moving in communism's direction. Five years later, the contradictions within the Western camp, the military technology of the Soviet Union, and the opportunities in the underdeveloped world had all turned into disappointments for Khrushchev. Kennedy wondered whether the "glow" had gone out of the "bubble . . . the concept of communism as an almost inevitable development in history."[1] During 1963 he certainly found Khrushchev more accommodating, but this was not solely because of Cuba. The Kremlin's postcrisis appraisal of its strategic choices became bound up with the developing Sino-Soviet dispute. Indeed, the missile crisis's greatest geopolitical significance may lie in its aggravation of the fracture in the communist alliance.

For both the United States and the Soviet Union the rise of the People's Republic of China (PRC) as a great power in its own right represented the most important strategic development of the early 1960s. China was a difficult enough issue for Kennedy because of the presumed responsibility of Democrats and a tepid diplomacy for its "loss" to communism in 1949 and the residual commitment to the rump Nationalist state that had been set up in Taiwan as the Republic of China (ROC) under the leadership of Generalissimo Chiang Kai-shek. Beijing had provided support and inspiration for communists in East Asia through the 1950s, and an army in Korea, turning the region into the most turbulent and bloody of the cold war. Once it had its own nuclear weapons, there seemed to Kennedy to be no limit to the mischief it might cause.

THE CHINA CARD

During the 1950s there had been a vague hope that when China, a country for whom the United States had long had a soft spot, finally came to its senses the two could join together against Russia. Instead the Chinese sniped at both superpowers from the sidelines, devastated their own economy and society with a "Great Leap Forward," and encouraged militancy everywhere. Kennedy stayed with the position taken in 1950, that the government in Beijing was illegitimate. Because the Communist victory in the Chinese civil war had not been absolute—sufficient Nationalists having managed to escape to Taiwan—the United States had neither recognized the new government nor agreed that it should displace the Nationalists as one of the five permanent members of the United Nations. As Chiang Kai-shek had powerful allies in Congress and the U.S. media, reversing this policy became something the cognoscenti knew to be sensible but never seemed quite worth the effort. Kennedy as a senator had criticized "rigidity" in policy, but that was a word he used to avoid being too specific on what he might do instead. When Rusk asked if he wanted to change U.S.-China policy, Kennedy ruled it out. It was not a good issue on which to do battle, obliging Rusk to play "the Village idiot" when probed by his staff on the question.[2] Kennedy saw no point in attempting recognition so long as China maintained a belligerent posture.

As he entered office the critical issue was the tenability of America's policy of keeping communist China out of the United Nations. There was a danger of losing a critical vote, and this argued for at least hinting that the United States was considering a change. By bowing to the inevitable, it might be possible to extract concessions from Beijing. Kennedy was doubtful. There were no intimations from Beijing of any interest in improved relations, and he could not ignore President Eisenhower's caution that he "would feel it necessary to return to political life if the Chinese communists were admitted to the United Nations."[3] The administration attempted to find a formula that appeared to go some way toward the communist position but would ultimately be rejected by Beijing—for example, by including demands for fundamental political change. This was tricky, as the Nationalists, including their many friends in the United States, were alert to any backsliding on the recognition issue and would probably object to any apparent softening of the American position, however tactical the reason. On the other hand, if there was not some tactical adjustment, the risk was that not only would the communists get into the

UN but the Nationalists would be forced out. Neither the PRC nor the ROC was likely to accept what was in effect a "two Chinas" policy. They were in complete agreement that the country's division was artificial and that it should be reunified; they disagreed only over who should be in charge. This made it difficult to work out a solution involving two separate delegations at the UN, however sensible this seemed to everyone else.

In discussions during October 1961 it emerged that there was a divergence between Adlai Stevenson's basic approach, which was to accept that communist China would join the UN during 1962 and gain as much political credit as possible for its facilitation, and the rest of the administration, which preferred to stick with the old policy of exclusion, even if this meant using its Security Council veto. To avoid too blatant support for the Nationalists, Kennedy decided to reassure Chiang Kai-shek privately that the United States would use its veto if necessary. This must not be disclosed because of the damage that would be done to the American, and ultimately the Nationalist, position at the UN. So sensitive was this matter that the assurance was passed through the CIA's man in Taipei, Ray Cline.[4] This shift infuriated Stevenson, as he realized that any compromise had been precluded.

A channel of communication did exist with China through the two countries' ambassadors in Warsaw. There some exploratory talks took place in the summer of 1961 in which the Chinese (who at this time were in a desperate economic state) seemed to indicate an interest in better relations. The Americans were prepared to move tentatively forward, starting with an exchange of journalists and food aid, but they foundered on the question of Taiwan, which the United States was unwilling to abandon.[5] From the end of 1961 Harriman reshaped the Department of State's Far Eastern Affairs Bureau, which had been cowed by McCarthyism, and collected a more innovative group of officials around him, all of whom favored greater flexibility. There were, however, limits on what could be achieved. China had declared itself an implacable foe of American imperialism and, increasingly, of just about everyone else. Any rapprochement would have had to be on Beijing's terms, as it saw no reason to modify its behavior or its demands to make itself more acceptable to any foreigners. The most that Harriman's team could explore (without success) was using food aid to improve relations.

They had more influence in ensuring that the administration took care in its dealings with the autocratic and unpredictable Chiang Kai-shek. This was particularly important in 1962, as the aging generalissimo appeared to be preparing his last offensive to regain the mainland. The challenge was a serious one, and the way in which Kennedy managed it indicated that this may have been the most important area where the president applied to good effect the lessons learned so painfully at the Bay of Pigs.

RESTRAINING THE GENERALISSIMO

At the start of 1962, China faced an acute economic crisis, with serious food shortages, and isolation from the Soviet Union. If Chiang wanted to reverse the result of the civil war, somehow an uprising had to be provoked on the mainland. For those who had been through the Cuban debates, the options were familiar: an amphibious landing to seize a bridgehead, in this case with the risk of Soviet support for China and counteraction by China elsewhere in Asia, or else small probing actions to see if there was much response. This was more feasible, but it was unlikely to have much effect, and the backlash of failure could undermine the Nationalists. While all this argued for keeping Chiang on a tight leash, on the other hand the administration did not want a public row with the Nationalists on this issue and be accused of missing a chance to liberate millions from the communist yoke.

Chiang appeared bent on a substantial action, dismissing small-scale probes as limited in their effects. Using the Bundy-Cline channel, the Nationalists were to be reminded that it had been accepted in 1954 that any "use of force will be a matter of joint agreement," told that the United States did not agree with their assessment of the situation on the mainland, and urged to listen to Harriman as the president's trusted representative. Harriman's instructions from Kennedy suggested that he might "draw, if you wish, on the Cuban misadventure as proof of the dangers of bad intelligence, and of decisions based more on hope than reality."

> You should of course make it clear that we would like nothing better than the downfall of the mainland regime, and we are fully aware of the advantages such a change would bring in the whole world situation. But it is one thing to desire a result and quite another to make sound judgment on proposed measures to bring that result about.[6]

The American estimate was that despite widespread public dissatisfaction and demoralization in Communist China "the regime's control apparatus is still intact and effective" and able to cope with any internal challenges. Nationalist special forces were likely to be destroyed in short order, while more substantial military operations were unlikely to prosper.[7] Nonetheless, Chiang appeared to be determined on some expedition in the fall, and the embassy was concerned that blanket opposition to all proposals from the Republic of China could "create serious risk of unilateral desperate lunge to take advantage of conjunction of circumstances which Chiang almost certainly regards as unique and most unlikely to recur." Rather than reject Chiang's plan outright, therefore, the Americans decided to engage him in a prolonged discussion of its merits.

Rusk described the plan to Kennedy at the end of March as nonsense, as was the idea (also familiar from Cuba) "that we could keep it covert." There was no disagreement. To avoid a row with the Nationalists, which would animate the China lobby at home, the administration temporized, knowingly risking being drawn into a creeping commitment "in the familiar pattern of the covert operations in Indonesia and Cuba." Cline was given a document to read from but not to hand to Chiang. The ultimate objective was shared, this promised, but unfortunately there was no hard evidence "to support the feasibility of activities on the scale recently discussed with Governor Harriman." More studies were therefore needed. The most favored operations were seaborne raids on the coast, but consideration could be given to a single airdrop involving a maximum of two hundred men. The United States could help with this by preparing two C-123 aircraft in the United States and training Chinese crews. This would take six months, after which the planes would be made available provided that it was agreed that an operation is "feasible and timely." The planning should be quiet, with no published articles in the media advocating a return to the mainland.

Chiang accepted what was on offer but asked for more transport aircraft plus landing ships and bombers. The inclination was to compromise on bringing the number of C-123s up to five. More requests came, and the Americans suspected that they were being drawn into preparations for an invasion of mainland China. Kennedy could see a dilemma. He did not want Chiang "to be able to say that just as they were prepared to go to the mainland, the United States flunked out." Instead he preferred to point to hard intelligence that demonstrated that a landing "was doomed to failure" or at least that the Taiwanese had refused to cooperate on obtaining the necessary intelligence.[8]

McCone was sent to discuss the intelligence with the generalissimo in June. He was told that the present time was one for which the Nationalists had been preparing for thirteen years. Chiang had "a military machine capable of exploiting the deterioration of Communist control on the Mainland." A large enough operation would gain popular support and "succeed in establishing control of an area which by further efforts on a larger scale would expand over all of South China and would ultimately topple the Communist regime." Though he had been persuaded by the United States to postpone these attempts for six months, much to the frustration of his followers, he could not delay beyond this time. McCone warned of the consequences of failure—of Nationalist forces, whether delivered by an airdrop or amphibious operation, encountering large, well-equipped communist forces who could destroy them and then slaughter any civilians who joined the insurgency. He therefore stressed the importance of high-quality intelligence before any troops were committed to combat. Chiang agreed on the need for more intelligence but took the view that the only reliable guide would come once "a sizeable military operation had been launched, an area secured, and the people together with their local leaders given reason to hope for relief from oppression." He was not expecting American combat units to join in this endeavor, but he did expect logistical support. On his return, Kennedy asked McCone what Chiang would do if "told flatly that the United States would not support him in any military operation against the Mainland." The answer was that he might just "go it alone."[9]

By now public speculation about Chiang's intentions had produced a quite different sort of crisis. Reports were coming in of Chinese troop movements, probably simply to defend against a Nationalist attack, but possibly also to create a new crisis over the offshore islands as a diversion. Although this latter possibility was unlikely, if the Communists did decide on such an adventure then the pressure would grow on the United States not only to defend these islands but also to join in any Nationalist coun- terattack. Even if they did nothing, their existence could be used by Chiang to take provocative action. Soon the CIA was reporting that seven Chinese army divisions, with possibly five more on the way, had moved into position across the strait from Taiwan, representing "the largest such movement since the Korean War." One way or another the Americans could find themselves caught in a new round of the Chinese civil war. An immediate message was sent to Taipei urging caution and that no pretext be given to the communists.

Anxiety set in that a major communist attack was imminent and had to be deterred, with the prospect of wider hostilities if that failed. After McCone had delivered the bad news on communist preparations to the president, McNamara "charged in with all guns blazing," arguing that the intelligence community had grossly exaggerated the danger. Putting down both the CIA and the military, he pointed out that with 300 motorized junks and 1,300 sailing vessels, each taking 50 men, the most the com- munists could manage was 100,000 men without heavy equipment. Before taking any rash action, the secretary of defense argued, it was necessary to obtain better intelligence using U-2s.[10] With the press starting to build the issue up, Kennedy moved swiftly, instructing Pierre Salinger to use McNamara's realistic assessment of the situation to calm down the speculation.

Kennedy looked for ways to restrain both sides. Harriman got per- mission to call in Dobrynin to ask him what he knew of the Chinese moves and, in case these were in response to rumors of Nationalist prep- arations for a mainland invasion, to explain that "the U.S. had no inten- tion of supporting such a move under existing circumstances." At the same time the British would be asked to pass a message to the Chinese communists drawing their attention to the fact that the offshore islands could be seized only with a major operation and that this could well draw in American forces. If asked, the British would say that they understood that the United States would not support a Nationalist attack of the main- land. Both steps were soon taken. In a press conference on 27 June Kennedy referred to the troop movements and declared, "Our basic position has always been that we are opposed to the use of force in this area." Movements and increased readiness of U.S. forces accompanied these statements. Kennedy stated that in the event of "aggressive action" by the Chinese against the offshore islands, the United States would "take the action necessary to assure the defense of Formosa and the Pescadores." By 5 July the intelligence community was reporting that there had been no more movements of Chinese forces.[11] It seemed that the Chinese fear of a Nationalist attack had diminished. If they had actually been planning their own attack, then the element of surprise had been lost as the risks of a clash with the Americans grew.

The Americans now took a firmer line with the Nationalists. Having put pressure on the Communists to show restraint, they would look foolish if Chiang attempted a major military operation. This did not stop the generalissimo from continuing to press his case. In April 1963 Kennedy found it necessary to warn against "ill-considered actions that would not work, would end only in disaster for you and might precipitate a situation that neither of us want." The evidence that the mainland was ripe for liberation was still absent. As late as September that year an emissary brought a letter from Chiang arguing for guerrilla airdrops and commando raids, which would "ignite an explosion on the Chinese mainland." Kennedy was told that there had been twenty-eight landings over the past year and that these should be stepped up to cause the communists even greater disruption. The president replied that the United States did "not wish to become involved in military operations where our role would inevitably become known and which would end in failure," and he referred repeatedly to "one bad experience in Cuba where operations had been based more on hope than on a realistic appraisal of the situation." When he asked about the success of the past year's landings, he was told that there had been a casualty rate of 85 percent, but these could be justified by the degree of mobilization they demanded of the communists to defeat them. Kennedy was unimpressed, he drew the lesson that the mainland regime was still in control and had suffered only marginal disruption. He returned to the need for better intelligence operations as an essential preliminary to more action.[12]

THE SINO-SOVIET DISPUTE

Kennedy was somewhat more successful in controlling his Chinese client than was Khrushchev. So long as Stalin had been alive, the Chinese leader Mao Zedong may have bristled at the condescension shown him in Moscow, but he acknowledged Russian primacy in the international communist movement. Mao judged Khrushchev's anti-Stalin campaign unwise, but his main objection to the new Soviet leadership lay in its failure to use its much-trumpeted technological and military strength to support

China's own aspirations. Khrushchev had refused to back any attempts to take the initiative against the Nationalists on Taiwan and had taken steps to impede the development of China's own nuclear capability by withdrawing technical support. The very idea of peaceful coexistence with capitalism, combined with the mismanagement of the crises of the early 1960s, had led Mao to conclude that Khrushchev had forfeited any claim to leadership of the international communist movement.

The first open splits had taken place in the fall of 1960, but both sides tried to prevent a definitive breach. In 1961 and 1962 the arguments rumbled on, largely on the basis of Khrushchev's declared support of measures to stop nuclear proliferation; Chinese leaders took this, not surprisingly, to be an attempt to prevent them from gaining access to nuclear weapons. The Chinese argued that the Soviet Union could not look after all aspects of defense for all socialist countries, and so China needed its own capabilities. Then they could deal directly with such problems as the unification of China and the border dispute with India. This made the Russians nervous. They did not want to risk global war in support of Chinese revanchism, and they hoped for cordial relations with both sides of the Sino-Indian dispute. Mao was furious that China was not supported simply as a matter of class solidarity.[13]

In October 1962 the Sino-Indian dispute flared up at the same time as Cuba. During the worst days of the missile crisis, as the Chinese were providing vocal backing to Moscow, the Russians briefly switched from their previous evenhandedness and gave effusive support to China's claim against India (thereby enraging the Indians). This was a critical moment in the communist alliance. If Khrushchev's Cuban gamble had paid off, then imperialism would indeed have been revealed as a "paper tiger." Mao, who does not appear to have taken the risk of the crisis ending in a nuclear war seriously or believed nuclear war was necessarily catastrophic, could then expect militancy all around. Khrushchev's backing down validated and intensified China's anti-Soviet stance.

The news that the Cuban missiles were to be withdrawn unleashed a barrage of anti-Soviet (and pro-Cuban) propaganda from Beijing, pushing the Sino-Indian conflict to the sidelines. Sino-Soviet relations hit a new low, with Mao ostentatiously refusing to meet the Soviet ambassador. In retaliation Moscow reverted to its old line on the Sino-Indian dispute, but it was too late to repair the damage to its relations with India or to have any effect on the development of a conflict that was already effectively over. After these stormy few months Moscow sought to defuse the row by proposing, on 21 February 1963, ideological consultations. Beijing accepted the offer but suggested no interest in a compromise. On 14 June it published its position on the key ideological issues, still shrill and uncompromising, just as the Soviet Communist Party was engaged in its own ideological discussions. At the start of July the consultations began in Moscow, with the Chinese side led by Deng Xiaoping; representing Russia was Mikhail Suslov, an old Stalinist whose sympathies with Chinese complaints were overridden by loyalty to his leader of the moment. The two delegations spent a couple of weeks "trading insults backed up by texts from the classics of Marxism-Leninism."[14]

Until 1963 American policy makers spoke of the "Sino-Soviet bloc" as if its monolithic quality could be taken for granted. They were well aware of the dispute, however, and talked of it often in private. Kennedy had ordered a major study on the subject upon taking office.[15] Early in 1961 the CIA claimed that "covert reporting on the dispute has been excellent, an intelligence breakthrough of sorts." The agency was certain that the dispute was "genuine, serious and bitter," but the immediate effect was to make both countries harder to deal with. Having failed to coerce the Chinese in 1960, the Russians now had to compromise, and this pulled them toward a more militant stance.[16] The administration suspected that if it had to choose partners, it would go for Russia. In part this was because of the "Russians are more like us" type of argument, but it was also because under Khrushchev there had been some effort to reach an accommodation with the West. Liberals distrusted China not only because of its attempt to put a break on détente but also because of China's quarrel with India. Bowles, a former ambassador to New Delhi, saw India as an important model of a democratic, secular, multinational third world country and admired Prime Minister Nehru. In July 1961 he even urged Kennedy to explore ways to involve Russia in the containment of China.[17]

There was not quite enough in the dispute in 1961 upon which to base policy. Few were prepared to accept the conservative claim that it was in effect a hoax, desired to lull the free world into a false sense of security, but many suspected that the apparent cracks in the monolith amounted to little more than differences of opinion. Dean Rusk referred publicly in the summer of 1961 to the "alleged split between Peiping and Moscow."[18] An August 1961 intelligence estimate was equivocal. It was unlikely that the two could resolve their differences, yet an open rupture appeared equally unlikely. The prospect was for "erratic" relations, cooperative at some times, competitive at others.[19]

At the start of 1962 a paper from the Policy Planning Staff focused the minds of senior officials. It reported that in the communist world there was now "no single line of command, no prime source of authority, no common program of action, no ideological uniformity." As officials began to discuss the paper, James Thomson recalled,

> [t]he impact on the minds around the table . . . was dramatic and you could hear the ice of 12 years begin to snap and crackle as an intellectual thaw set in. . . . One after another State's operators and planners toyed with the

new world possibilities that non-monolithic communism might offer to
U.S. policies.

The problem, as Rostow put it, was that no one knew what to do about
it.[20] The State Department appeared almost tongue-tied when discussing
it with the press. The issue, and its implications for American policy,
continued to be debated inconclusively. Soviet specialists in particular
were dubious about a spring 1962 intelligence estimate arguing that Sino-
Soviet relations had reached a critical phase. The only safe conclusion
appeared to be that of Bohlen. Something important was going on, but
reliable information was sparse and so "we certainly should not predicate
any policy on the fact of the Chinese-Soviet dispute." They assumed that
when it came to the crunch, the two states would think and act alike, and
that view gained support from statements from both Moscow and
Beijing.[21]

As the evidence of a decisive break in the communist world became
inescapable in early 1963, concern grew that while China might be more
isolated, it was also less inhibited. It was developing its own nuclear weapons and calling for universal and permanent revolution. Kennedy observed in an August 1963 press conference that China had "weak countries around it, 700 million people, a Stalinist internal regime, nuclear
power, and a government determined on war as a means of bringing about
its ultimate success." An opinion poll in March, looking ahead to 1970,
found that more Americans considered China the greater threat to world
peace than Russia (47 percent to 34 percent).[22]

In the Kennedy administration arose a strong sense that the future of
the Sino-Soviet alliance might turn on American policy toward Moscow.
A hard line might push them closer together. A softer line, however,
might tear them asunder. This, in effect, had been a result of the missile
crisis. By the end of 1962 the split became an increasingly powerful theme
in intelligence reports. The communist "myth of monolithic unity" had
been shattered. The Cuban crisis had made the Chinese ever more suspicious of Soviet-American negotiations. The CIA argued that this was a
net plus for the West, especially if it sought to isolate China. Whether it
could be turned into improved relations with Moscow depended on how
the Soviet Union resolved the tension between its desire for a more normal relationship with the West as an equal in world councils, solicitous
of the dangers of nuclear war, and its offer of itself as the leader of a
revolutionary movement with universal aspirations.

Not all agreed that Sino-Soviet relations were taking a dramatic and
significant turn. John McCone, director of central intelligence, not for
the first time disagreed with his own analysts. In late February he introduced a note of caution, wondering why CIA reporting appeared to assume that there could be no reconciliation and that the controversy was
moving to new levels, when he found the contrary view in the public

media. It was in Khrushchev's interest to settle with Mao. The Chinese were "hard-pressed technologically and economically," and so it made sense for them to make up, "even at the cost of setting aside some of their basic ideological positions." The analysts, however, stuck to their guns. They saw little prospect of anything other than "a superficial and temporary truce." Beijing was determined to break Moscow's hold on the international communist movement. Given the intensity of Chinese polemics and the extreme nature of their terms, Moscow could not restrain itself indefinitely.[23]

Kennedy saw the Sino-Soviet split as largely an argument about means rather than ends: He assumed both were determined to see the triumph of communism. It offered an opportunity to isolate China, but China as an independent, militant actor was an unappealing prospect. A decade earlier it had given the United States a bloody nose in Korea. What might it do with its own nuclear weapons? He had been advised in 1961 that China could have a nuclear weapon by 1962 and a small arsenal by 1965; at the start of 1962 he had directed the NSC to confront the "special unsolved problem" of a China with nuclear weapons and its effect "on our dispositions in Southeast Asia." Before the Vienna summit he had confided in a journalist that he wanted to make progress in the Geneva talks out of an "intense desire to do everything possible to assure that Communist China won't have a bomb."[24] He was tempted at the summit to explore the possibility of a common front against China with Khrushchev, but the Soviet leader would not bite. Nineteen sixty-one had not been a good year for détente, and the Soviet resumption of atmospheric tests led to the collapse of the trilateral test ban talks and the resumption of American atmospheric tests. With intelligence estimates suggesting that China's first test could come as early as 1963, Kennedy grew increasingly worried. This led to an increasing interest in the role of a test ban in reducing this prospect. The effect it might have in constraining China would turn an initiative of marginal value in relation to the Soviet Union into something that "could be worth very much indeed." The treaty had thus become "more important to the world situation than it had been a year or two ago." In February he observed that "the whole reason for having a test ban is related to the Chinese situation. Otherwise, it wouldn't be worth the disruption and fighting with Congress, etc."[25]

Glenn Seaborg, chairman of the Atomic Energy Commission, wondered at the time why the president put so much stress on this matter. It was already certain that the Chinese would reject any treaty. Either Kennedy had some lingering belief that the Sino-Soviet relationship would survive a treaty and China would feel obliged to abide by its provisions, or else he assumed that Beijing would respond to world opinion. Both were unlikely. The United States was having the same problem with France, which was making rejection of a test ban a point of principle. His advisers may not have bothered to disabuse him of the notion that a test

ban might curtail China if it confirmed his support of a policy they favored. Yet presenting limits on China as a treaty's main attraction could
work against it. Kennedy told David Ormsby-Gore that the worst thing
that could happen to a treaty (and possibly—with Woodrow Wilson's fate
in mind—his own career) would be a Chinese test.[26]

28

Toward a Test Ban

AFTER THE MISSILE CRISIS, the first intelligence assessment of the Soviet reaction anticipated "a period of reconsolidation masked by verbal activity and propagandistic initiatives."[1] Having been worsted in the crisis, Moscow would conclude that its bargaining position in any negotiations had been weakened, and so it would play for time. Yet as the crisis closed, the two leaders had spoken publicly and privately of their desire to move forward on a more constructive agenda. At the end of November, Kennedy met in Washington with Khrushchev's confidant, Anastas Mikoyan, who recently had been in Cuba trying to calm Castro down. The president took the opportunity to confirm his disdain for the U.S. bases in Turkey. He returned to his old theme, which he considered to have been reinforced by the Cuban episode: the need to avoid misjudgment. This time Mikoyan was more sympathetic.[2]

As State Department and NSC officials explored the possibility of turning the missile crisis into a force for good, the two obvious areas for progress were Berlin and disarmament, neither of which had seen much progress in 1962. On close examination there was not much that could or should be done on Berlin. The West remained comfortable with the status quo, even if it could not endorse it in treaty form, and it was unlikely that Moscow would trigger another crisis after its recent experience. By the end of November there was some evidence in both Soviet and GDR statements of a diminished interest in a peace treaty. Gromyko proposed new talks on Berlin that seemed to be less loaded than previous proposals, but then, following the latest twists in Moscow's China policy, relations hardened again. At the same time the signing of a Franco-German defense treaty made Kennedy worried that if he pushed too hard on negotiations with Moscow, Adenauer would be encouraged to follow de Gaulle's independent line. There seemed to be little point in risking further alliance strains when there was no evidence that the Russians really had anything new or interesting to offer.[3] After checking with the Germans the Americans agreed to tentative, exploratory bilateral talks, but the initial Soviet proposal was no more than a rehash of one made before the missile crisis. For their part the Americans were sticking with the 22 March 1962 principles paper as the best they could offer.

In practice there was no longer a strong reason to push for a settlement. The status quo now appeared stable, with neither side able to secure unilateral changes. A treaty might preclude future crises, but it would also involve formal compromises of principle that would cause Kennedy problems with the West Germans and Khrushchev difficulties with the East Germans. Speaking to Harriman in April, Khrushchev suggested that "the socialist countries" had "gained more in Berlin from the wall than they would have gained from a peace treaty," which probably would have prohibited such a construction. "Berlin is no longer a source of any trouble," he asserted. By August Kennedy had reached a similar conclusion.[4]

VERIFICATION

Arms control appeared a much more promising avenue for progress. Khrushchev had referred in his correspondence with Kennedy at the end of the crisis to the importance of disarmament, while Kennedy had urged progress on nuclear proliferation and a test ban. It is important not to understate Kennedy's commitment to preventing the further diffusion of nuclear weapons. Concern about the implications of a German nuclear force was part of this, but it was not the starting point for his policy. He was concerned about the French *"force de frappe"* not only because it might provide Germany with a pretext to move in the same direction, but because it gave Paris an independent capacity to turn a conventional battle in Europe into a general nuclear war. He feared a Chinese nuclear force because of the effect on the American position in Asia. While in the light of the political support enjoyed by Israel in the United States, especially from his own party, Kennedy may have held back from putting pressure on Israel over its apparent attempts to develop a nuclear capability, he still accepted in March 1963 that the American position would no longer be credible if it turned a blind eye to the Israeli program.[5] Nonetheless it was understood in both Washington and Moscow that a general arms control package made it much easier to address the German nuclear issue, as it meant that Bonn was being asked to accede to a universal policy rather than one designed with Germany alone in mind.

With regard to the test ban, not only had the Cuban crisis itself demonstrated the dangers of an unfettered arms race, but also experts judged the results of the latest American atmospheric test series, which concluded in early November, to have been of marginal strategic importance.[6] New weapons were being developed, such as antiballistic missiles, but it was by no means clear that they would change the fundamentals of the strategic balance or warranted further testing. The stumbling block to a comprehensive test ban remained verification. When it came to on-site inspections the Soviet position remained unequivocal: None was acceptable. In the awkward postcrisis discussions over the verification of the removal of Soviet missiles and aircraft from Cuba, no concessions were made on inspections. It was, of course, possible for both sides to end tests without a formal treaty, but the experience with the previous moratorium had set Kennedy against any informal arrangement. There were proposals to solve the problem via so-called black boxes—unmanned stations to be placed on Soviet territory to help detect seismic events. However, this would not remove entirely the need for on-site inspections. The need to confirm that the unmanned stations were working as well as investigate mysterious events would still require random inspections.[7] The Americans had indicated that they would need between twelve and twenty inspections a year; perhaps this number could be slightly reduced.

There then followed a muddle. In the hope that the missile crisis had had a cathartic effect, the arms controllers in the administration made strong overtures to their Soviet counterparts. The U.S. ambassador to the Geneva disarmament talks, Arthur Dean, spoke at the end of October to Soviet Deputy Foreign Minister Kuznetsov about the possibility for reaching an agreement on inspections. He mentioned the possibility of a "small number" of inspections. A week later he was slightly more specific, talking of between eight and ten, of which only two might be in areas where there was normally no seismic activity (thereby exceeding his instructions). At the same time the president's special assistant for science and technology, Jerome Wiesner, was apparently trying to set up a bargain by which Khrushchev would propose three or four inspections, Kennedy would come back with seven or eight, and an agreement would be struck somewhere in the middle.

Wiesner's ploy was ambitious, if only because Kennedy himself did not believe that he could go so low, given the opposition he anticipated in the Senate. More serious was that Khrushchev interpreted these soundings as a definite offer, following his proposal for three black boxes. He was convinced that Dean had proposed three or four inspections. Dean unfortunately had a reputation for being vague—he had caused trouble the previous July with a public statement that implied that there would be no need for detection systems on Soviet territory—so there is no reason to doubt that the Soviet understanding of his new position was honest, if in error.[8] Dean resigned "for personal reasons" at the end of the year. When Kennedy received Khrushchev's letter at the end of December he was delighted by its positive tone and movement from an apparently rigid position. Yet he was also puzzled by the reference to this perceived shift

in American policy. In his reply on 28 December he sought to clarify
Dean's statement and explained that he would need eight to ten
inspections.[9]

Khrushchev was furious. He later complained to American visitors that
he had made an important gesture, only to see the Americans then up
the ante immediately. He had probably worked hard on his own military
to get this far. With the Chinese insisting that deals with imperialism
could never advance the cause of socialism, this apparent American double
cross could not have come at a more awkward time. He was also still
uncertain about a détente with the United States. During the first months
of 1963 he was still hoping to to smooth over relations with China. With
this in mind he set in motion a repressive, ideological clampdown in
Russia and adopted dilatory tactics on Berlin as well as the test ban.

DETENTE ON HOLD

The Americans realized that relations were cooling again. The theme
music of compromise was toned down. Ambassador Foy Kohler reported
back to Washington that the Soviet leader had lost his bounce and vi-
vacity.[10] The strong economic growth, which had help support the regime, was no longer so evident as problems in the agricultural sector
multiplied. In 1961 Khrushchev had described the United States as a
"worn out runner," to be overtaken by the Soviet Union in 1970.[11] This
now looked like another of his barren boasts. The Cuban ploy having
failed, the Soviet Union still needed to repair its position, working to
bridge the reverse missile gap by investing in military strength, even at
the expense of hard-pressed Soviet consumers, whose hopes for greater
prosperity were now being scaled down. Meanwhile Khrushchev lacked
the strength to pursue either a more conciliatory policy or a more aggressive one. The intelligence community concluded in March that the
cold war was at least temporarily on hold.

So for the moment, as Kennedy observed in a letter to Harold Macmillan on 21 March, it seemed that the Sino-Soviet dispute had made it
less likely that Khrushchev would be able to offer concessions. If, as he
surmised, Khrushchev did not care that much for a test ban, then the
Chinese factor would probably dominate. This is why he did not agree
with the prime minister's proposal for a summit to sort out the inspections
issue.[12] He was prepared to explore just how far they could reduce the
number of inspections, or whether they might present them in a more
acceptable way to Khrushchev, but the politics of the situation looked to
be against them.

Meanwhile, opposition to a test ban at home was gathering pace. On
21 February the five senior Democrats on the Senate Armed Services
Committee privately said that they would be unable to support a treaty
based on the current American position. Kennedy knew that as things

stood, he was unlikely to achieve the two-thirds majority in the Senate necessary to secure treaty ratification.[13] In congressional hearings the inspection issue dominated. In the administration the Joint Chiefs and McCone argued that a treaty would impede improvements in U.S. nuclear capability without any true guarantees on Soviet behavior.[14] The political debate was now turning on speculative and hypothetical analyses of how the Soviet Union might be able to beat any system of verification rather than on broader geopolitical considerations.

The only pressure Kennedy was receiving in the opposite direction was from Britain. Harold Macmillan had long been convinced that détente of some sort with Moscow was vital and that there was nothing worth fighting for on the current East-West agenda. Nuclear testing had proved to be a divisive issue at home, and he saw political advantages in presenting himself as a man of peace. He shared Kennedy's concerns about the Chinese nuclear program but, with his mind constantly wandering back to the two wars he had experienced, the idea that the logical outcome of nuclear proliferation might be a German bomb appalled him more. Ambassador David Ormsby-Gore was convinced that Kennedy would welcome a further push from London, and so he persuaded Macmillan to persevere.

Macmillan had a penchant for statesmanlike visions that on close inspection often turned out to be vacuous, but occasionally he struck the right note.[15] His letter to Kennedy was sent on 3 April, arguing that the Sino-Soviet question might play out in many ways but that only a direct approach to Khrushchev could clarify matters. He considered it unwise to get too bogged down in technical issues for the moment; it was more advisable to start with an appeal to Khrushchev's better nature, if only to get discussions going. He appended a draft of a message that the two leaders might consider sending to Khrushchev.[16]

As this was arriving on his desk, Kennedy received a report from his brother apparently confirming that relations had taken a turn for the worse. Dobrynin had handed Robert Kennedy a paper containing some talking points that the attorney general assumed to be a form of communication from Khrushchev to the president. The tone was truculent with regard to sorting out remaining problems over Cuba and offered nothing more on a test ban. The basic theme was this: "The United States had better learn that that the Soviet Union was as strong as the United States and did not enjoy being treated as a second class power." The attorney general returned it to Dobrynin on the grounds that it was "insulting and rude."[17]

The incident appears to have had a sobering effect on the president. He saw opportunities for building on his Cuban success slipping away. Accordingly, a few days later he reopened the pen pal correspondence, writing to Khrushchev to express his concern that Moscow appeared to think that the United States was walking away from a previous position on test ban inspections, reiterating his determination to avoid the spread of nuclear weapons (Russia was convinced that this was implied by proposals for NATO's multilateral force), and asking Khrushchev to exert more influence in Laos. He suggested that he send a personal representative to Moscow to improve relations between the two countries, an idea that Thompson had raised with an enthusiastic Dobrynin a few days after the latter's awkward meeting with Robert Kennedy.[18]

This was followed by a redrafted version of the joint letter proposed by Macmillan on disarmament. It played down the prime minister's suggestions for a summit—an idea he always favored, as it allowed him to appear as a big player on the world stage, but which the president viewed with misgivings, especially after his Vienna experience. The letter recalled the progress made, urged extra effort as a "duty to humanity," and noted that the number of inspections required was now down from twenty to seven, leaving only a small gap to be made up by Khrushchev.[19] When the joint letter was presented to the Soviet leader on 24 April he took a very cool view, reaffirming his position that a nuclear test ban had no great significance and that Germany was the "key to everything."[20]

It was going to take more than letters to thaw relations. Kennedy appears to have decided on another tack following firsthand reports on Khrushchev's mood. Norman Cousins, the editor of the *Saturday Review* and a well-known disarmament activist, visited Khrushchev in late December on a mission for the Vatican. He learned of the Kremlin's belief that Kennedy had hoodwinked them over the inspection issue. Kennedy asked him to find out more about Khrushchev's views during his next visit to Moscow and disabuse the Soviet leader of the notion that the United States was negotiating in anything less than good faith. Cousins met again with Khrushchev on 12 April and reported back to Kennedy ten days later. Kennedy could empathize with the picture Cousins supplied. "He would like to prevent a nuclear war but is under severe pressure from the hard-line crowd. . . . I've got similar problems." Why not, Cousins suggested, get around this with a "breathtaking new approach toward the Russian people, calling for an end to the cold war and a fresh start in American-Russian relations"?[21]

Soon after, Averell Harriman, recently promoted to undersecretary for political affairs in the State Department, also met Khrushchev. Harriman's main purpose in the meeting was to try to hold together his—and the administration's—main negotiating achievement thus far, the agreement on the neutralization of Laos, but he took the opportunity to hold broad-ranging discussions. The Soviet leader proposed a combination of test ban and German settlement; Harriman responded that they could be discussed separately.[22] Still there were no breakthroughs, but Khrushchev was warming to the idea that Kennedy was sincere in his efforts to move relations between the two countries to a more productive level and that he was being opposed by much more hawkish elements in his efforts to do so. Khrushchev's reply to Kennedy's first letter drafted around this time was generally conciliatory in tone, stressing his concern about West Germany acquiring nuclear weapons, but with helpful words on Laos and an expressed readiness to meet with the president's personal representative. Yet this was still not much to show for all the diplomatic activity. Khrushchev's formal reply to the Kennedy-Macmillan joint letter on the test ban was grumpy and offered nothing, although it did not close the door either.[23] The position seemed to be evenly balanced.

THE AMERICAN UNIVERSITY SPEECH

Kennedy decided to make one last push for an agreement. He told a press conference on 22 May that a failure to reach an agreement would allow the nuclear genie to escape: "We are, therefore, going to push very hard in May and June and July, in every forum, to see if we can get an agreement." Once again he used a British draft as the basis for a new letter to Khrushchev, refuting Soviet claims while proposing that the two allies send emissaries to Moscow to negotiate directly. Khrushchev accepted, but he did not budge on the inspection issue.[24] His letter arrived as Kennedy prepared to make his boldest public statement yet on the need for détente and a test ban.

In late May he took Cousins's advice to test the domestic and international political waters by means of a major speech setting out his hopes for an improved superpower relationship. The occasion was a scheduled commencement address at the American University on 10 June. In preparation it became known as the "peace speech" and was protected from those who distrusted such sentiments by being drafted entirely within the White House, largely by Sorensen.[25] Rusk, McNamara, and Taylor saw only a final draft. In this sense it was probably the most authentic statement of Kennedy's views on the nuclear arms race. He insisted to Sorensen that there was no need for any balancing material, "the usual threats of destruction, boasts of nuclear stockpiles and lectures on Soviet treachery."[26] Having proved himself in the missile crisis, he could now reach out to Khrushchev to get a test ban but also prepare the ground for what might prove to be a bruising battle in Congress when it came to getting any treaty ratified.

"World peace, like community peace," he told his audience, "does not require that each man love his neighbor—it requires only that they live together in mutual tolerance, submitting their disputes to a just and peaceful settlement. And history teaches us that enmities between individuals, as between nations, do not last forever." Attitudes toward the Soviet Union should be reexamined, so as "not to see a desperate and distorted view of the other side." The arms race should be reversed, the "massive sums of money" devoted to weapons would be better spent "combating ignorance, poverty, and disease." Otherwise

"[w]e are both caught up in a vicious and dangerous cycle in which suspicion on one side breeds suspicion on the other, and new weapons be-
get counterweapons."

Against this dismal prospect he asserted a basic principle: "We all
breathe the same air. We all cherish our children's future. And we are all
mortal." He explained how American policies were designed to reduce
the risk of catastrophe:

> America's weapons are nonprovocative, carefully controlled, designed to
> deter, and capable of selective use. Our military forces are committed to
> peace and disciplined in self-restraint. Our diplomats are instructed to avoid
> unnecessary irritants and purely rhetorical hostility.

More specifically he urged a treaty to outlaw nuclear tests and promised,
in the most important substantive point, not to resume atmospheric nuclear tests.[27]

The speech hardly electrified the American people. It received barely
a mention in the press, and the White House mailbag failed to bulge. It
represented a rhetorical change of gear in the administration, but there
were conflicting signs around for those who wanted them. That same day
Congress passed the biggest defense budget ever. Furthermore, while this
may now be one of the three best-remembered speeches of the presidency, the first being the inaugural address, the last of the trio came only
two weeks later. This was a powerful statement of ideological commitment and received far more headlines. Only in retrospect does the "peace
speech" stand out; it had the desired effect on its intended audience and
was followed by a test ban treaty.

In the final week of June Kennedy visited Europe. This gave him the
chance to consult with and reassure allies. The highlight was a visit to
West Berlin. This had been viewed with some apprehension by his entourage. Relations with the German government had been poor; he might
best be remembered by Berliners for his tardy response to the construction of the wall in August 1961 and his readiness to negotiate with Moscow on the matter. Their morale was not high, and the local economy
was weak. An unfriendly welcome would play badly back home.[28] There
was no need to worry. Berliners could understand the symbolic significance of the American president's coming to their city to proclaim their
freedom, and they turned out in their thousands to welcome him. He
stood with his back to the Berlin Wall, describing it as the defining difference between the communist and free worlds. Those who did not understand this, who believed that communism was a wave of the future or
a means to economic progress—"Let them come to Berlin!" Whatever
the imperfections of democracy, "we have never had to keep a wall up to
keep our people in, to prevent them leaving us." With a single sentence

he tied his own prestige to the beleaguered city. Recalling how two thousand years earlier the "proudest boast was *Civis Romanus Sum,*" now "in the world of freedom the proudest boast is *Ich bin ein Berliner.*"[29]

Two years earlier this speech would have been deemed deeply provocative in Moscow, and even now Kennedy's advisers worried that he had let himself get carried away and undone some of the good of the American University speech. With Khrushchev's ambitions curtailed, however, the Soviet leader was prepared to dismiss the Berlin speech as routine rhetoric. Meanwhile he commended the American University speech. He later told Harriman that this was "the best statement made by any President since Roosevelt." So unusually in international affairs, communications worked well. The various audiences heard largely what they were supposed to hear (and wanted to hear) and were not distracted by utterances elsewhere.

Kennedy's new tone was welcome to Khrushchev because the Russian's own circumstances had changed, enabling him to respond positively. His domestic position had suddenly been eased in April by the stroke and subsequent incapacity of his deputy Frol Kozlov, who had a more hardline disposition. More important, however, was the apparent futility of efforts to keep China on side. As one participant in the Sino-Soviet discussions later observed:

> As it developed, the conflict with China had positive influences on the policy of Khrushchev, who had been slipping back to Stalinism only too often since 1962. The debate with the Chinese leaders provided the anti-Stalinists with the opportunity, while defending our policies, to speak out on many political and ideological subjects that had lately become taboo.[30]

At the end of March the Soviet Communist Party had sent an appeal to the Chinese party for an end to needless controversy. As Khrushchev read Kennedy's request to the American people to think more positively about the Soviet Union, he received on 14 June the Chinese reply. The gist of this letter, contained in twenty-five points, was that the Soviet party had become hopelessly reformist and deserved to be replaced in its leadership role by the truly revolutionary Chinese party. The Chinese were putting themselves beyond the pale. While at the start of the year there had been an effort to maintain a semblance of comradely relations by responding with restraint to Chinese charges, as the polemics moved up a notch restraint seemed pointless. If the only policy that would satisfy the Chinese was recklessness, then Khrushchev might as well continue to promote peaceful coexistence.

29

The Test Ban Treaty

BY JUNE IT WAS POSSIBLE to look forward to high-level negotiations in Moscow in July, but there was no reason to suppose that the basic obstacles would be overcome. Khrushchev seemed entrenched in his position, while the treaty opponents in the United States had the numbers. At the same time he was negotiating with Moscow, the president also had to negotiate with the Joint Chiefs. They had the right to give their views directly to Congress, and there was no reason to suppose that they would hesitate if they dissented from the administration line. In addition, as early as May calculations in the Senate had predicted that a comprehensive treaty would be ten votes short of the two-thirds majority required. They had also, however, indicated that a limited treaty, which allowed underground tests to continue, had much better prospects.

The idea for a limited ban developed out of the internal American debate over atmospheric testing. The keenest disarmers wanted a comprehensive ban, but the unease caused by atmospheric tests encouraged first the White House staff and then the State Department to take up the idea of a limited ban. The American position was discussed in the summer of 1962. It was clear from analysis undertaken at the Pentagon that a partial ban would have less value in terms of American security than a comprehensive ban. A full prohibition would make it much harder for the Soviet Union to catch up with the United States in nuclear weapons development. As for stopping the spread of nuclear weapons, it might only delay a new power's development process by a few years, though even a comprehensive ban would be a necessary but not sufficient condition in efforts to hold back this process. A comprehensive ban would be better, but the verification issue showed no signs of being solved. Some neutrals, particularly Sweden, alleged that the Americans were exaggerating the problem. If the Americans made a concession by reducing the number of inspections, it would only create problems with the Senate while failing to bring the Russians along, as they still insisted on zero. Therefore a partial ban would be much easier politically, though less advantageous strategically.[1]

At a meeting on 1 August 1962 Ambassador Dean warned that once an atmospheric ban was agreed upon, then the United States would come under enormous pressure to accept a moratorium on underground tests. Kennedy was unimpressed with this argument. He did not see any pressure that would oblige him to agree to an uninspected moratorium.[2] The advantage was that a partial ban would not require such a stringent inspection regime, which the Russians always considered to be tantamount to espionage. It would also address the area of greatest public concern, the poisoning of the atmosphere by radioactive fallout released by atmospheric tests. So by early August 1962 the American position allowed for the limited option. The Russians, however, dismissed the idea as an attempt to legalize underground tests, which the Americans were far better placed to employ. During September Khrushchev appeared to view it more favorably, although only in conjunction with a moratorium on underground tests.

During May 1963 the British and American governments began to focus on this option again, and when Llewellyn Thompson raised it with Dobrynin the interest was notable. On 2 July Khrushchev expressed his "readiness to conclude an agreement on cessation of nuclear tests in the atmosphere, in outer space and under water." Spirits rose. At last a serious arms control deal was in the cards.

On 15 July Harriman arrived in Moscow to conduct the negotiations. The decision to send a known dove, who had been largely kept out of Soviet matters up to this point, generated as much nervousness in Washington as it did encouragement in Moscow. The veteran statesman felt that he had the ideal instructions—"to get an agreement and come home."[3] Moscow would be a good place to negotiate a quick deal (he announced on arrival he wanted it done in two weeks) because decisions could be extracted from the Soviet leadership quickly. He was accompanied by Lord Hailsham, a senior member of the Conservative cabinet but a complete amateur when it came to disarmament matters, who was following instructions from Macmillan to come back with a treaty of some sort almost irrespective of content.

It did not take long in Moscow to discover that Khrushchev had no intention of moving on the inspections issue, so matters turned almost immediately to consideration of the next best option, a partial test ban. Khrushchev angled to get this linked to a nonaggression pact between the two alliances. Harriman pointed out this would take time and consultations, whereas a partial test ban could be wrapped up during the course of the current talks. For his part Khrushchev balked at the American proposal for a nonproliferation treaty. As the two sides pushed forward to a discussion of actual treaty language—the aspirations proclaimed in the preamble, who could adhere, on what terms might states withdraw—Harriman was in his element, doing what he thought he did best, extracting an agreement from tough partners. Hailsham worried that Harriman was being too tough, but by the time his concerns reached Kennedy via Ormsby-Gore the deal was done.[4]

In the run-up to the summit there were proposals to Harriman to explore with the Russians ways of removing China's nuclear capability. One of his briefing books mentioned the possibility of separate or joint use of military forces against China. It has been argued that Kennedy was pushing hard in this direction, but the evidence for this is flimsy.[5] There is evidence that there were some low-level discussions within the administration of a preemptive attack, not necessarily with the Russians, but there was no serious consideration of such a move. In January Bundy reported to McCone the president's concern about the extent to which a Chinese nuclear capability could upset world politics, and he "intimated that we might consider a policy of indicating now that further effort by the Chinese Communists in the nuclear field would be unacceptable to us and that we should prepare to take some form of action unless they agreed to desist from further efforts in this field." Much of their subsequent discussion, however, appears to have been about the limits to intelligence and the need to find out more.[6] There had not been an analysis of China's advanced weapons program since April 1962. Satellite photography indicated a more ambitious program than hitherto realized, but it was still unclear how well it was doing. A new estimate that was not published until late July 1963 concluded (accurately as it turned out) that China's first nuclear test would happen between the spring and the fall of 1964, although an earlier test could not be ruled out. Unless the Chinese government became "intoxicated by its own propaganda," the estimate did not envisage this capability causing a major change in China's attitude toward its neighbors (which was already militant enough).[7]

There was therefore no internal push on Kennedy to go for a preemptive attack. The best evidence that he might nonetheless have been thinking along these lines comes with his persistent pressure on Harriman to raise the issue of China with Khrushchev while in Moscow for the test ban negotiations, and his instructions, drafted in his own hand, to Harriman on 15 July:

> I remain convinced that Chinese problem is more serious than Khrushchev's comments suggest, and believe you should press question in private meeting with him. I agree that large stockpiles are characteristic of U.S. and USSR only, but consider that relatively small forces in hands of people like CHICOMS could be very dangerous to us all. Furthermore believe even limited test ban can and should be means of preventing diffusion. You should try to elicit Khrushchev's view of means of limiting or preventing Chinese nuclear development and his willingness either to take Soviet action or to accept U.S. action aimed in this direction.

Even Seaborg wondered whether this was intended to explore the possibility of a joint preemptive strike.[8]

The difficulty lies in the interpretation of the all-purpose word *action*. In all probability Kennedy himself had no idea what this meant. He was under no internal pressure to take drastic measures against China, which was decades away from turning even a "primitive capability" into "a meaningful deterrent of the U.S."[9] That July Harriman was told to obtain information, not consent. His political antennae would have been twitching if either leader had suggested an attack on China, and Kennedy would probably have been surprised to find himself in a conspiracy. It was more likely, as Harriman had told the president before he went, that Khrushchev would not want to discuss the Chinese problem with him. In the event, when Harriman did get the chance to talk to Khrushchev alone about China, the Soviet leader was not forthcoming.[10] Things had not yet come to such a pass that he was prepared to start plotting with the old enemy against his erstwhile allies, especially when the Chinese at that very moment were denouncing him in another part of town for exactly this sort of collusion.

There is some evidence that Khrushchev hoped that a prohibition on atmospheric testing would put a major obstacle in front of a Chinese nuclear program, but it was not the threat of Chinese nuclear weapons that worried Khrushchev as much as the risk that Chinese militancy might drag everyone into war.[11] He believed that the Chinese repeatedly refused to recognize the real dangers of the courses they advocated. His strategy in the dispute was to highlight this recklessness so as to encourage other communist parties to adhere to the Moscow line, and here the test ban had an advantage. It would force the Chinese to be even more explicit in their irresponsibility. He had little hope now that he could stop a Chinese bomb, any more than the United States seemed able to stop a French one (and in a way this symmetry let both Kennedy and Khrushchev off the hook in concluding a treaty). The goal was, as Mrs. Gromyko put it to Harriman in an unguarded dinner table comment, to be able to call China to account when the eventual test took place.[12]

At the same time Khrushchev had to take care to avoid the appearance of singling out the Chinese. This led to a potentially serious disagreement with the Americans over the conditions under which parties might withdraw from the treaty. The Americans wanted to be able to test if China tested, and specified any "nuclear explosion . . . in the prohibited environments" as reason enough to withdraw.[13] Kennedy judged the Soviet alternative, of "extraordinary circumstances" jeopardizing supreme interests, as being too vague. Eventually compromise was reached on a reference to "extraordinary events related to the contents of this treaty." On 26 July the terms of the treaty were agreed upon.

Although Kennedy maintained a generalized anxiety about the impact of a more militant China on international affairs, as more thought was given to its nuclear capability this started to seem a less threatening development. An interdepartmental analysis discussed at a State Department meeting in October, for example, concluded that this "would heighten already existing issues rather than pose wholly new problems." With a limited capability it would still be deterred from any nuclear use by the threat of a much larger American retaliation. The paper explicitly ruled out a "pre-emptive counter-force strike," and indeed the conclusion was strengthened to make that more explicit, but it also noted that "soft, vulnerable delivery means" must make the Chinese aware of the danger of a U.S. counterforce attack. NSC staff member Robert Komer reported to Bundy that the question of how to "strangle the baby in the cradle" had been discussed, but the thrust of the paper was that there was no great incentive to try.[14]

RATIFICATION

The test ban negotiations brought the Sino-Soviet debate to a dead end. On 12 July, after Khrushchev expressed his view that only madmen would wish to destroy capitalism by means of nuclear war, a Chinese delegation arrived to discuss ideology with their Soviet comrades. They left as the treaty was agreed to. Deng Xiaoping, leading the Chinese delegation, criticized Khrushchev for his two errors of the missile crisis: shipping the missiles to Cuba in the first place (adventurism) and then showing confusion in the face of nuclear blackmail from the United States (capitulation).[15] In vain did the Soviet delegation contend that the outcome was perfectly good from a socialist perspective. Their insistence that nuclear weapons demanded new thinking about international relations and that a better world could not be created via nuclear war similarly fell on deaf Chinese ears. Bundy summarized a CIA report for Kennedy: "[T]he disintegration of the Sino-Soviet alliance was largely our accomplishment."[16]

This was not the line the president took when presenting the issue to the American people. When the treaty was signed he went on television "in a spirit of hope." He described how a nuclear war "lasting less than sixty minutes, with weapons now in existence, could wipe out more than 300 million Americans, Europeans, and Russians, as well as untold numbers elsewhere." He then cited Khrushchev as warning the Chinese that "the survivors would envy the dead." Against this dark background, the treaty was "a shaft of light." The choice of a Chinese proverb to describe moves toward peace was probably no accident: "A journey of a thousand miles must begin with a single step."[17]

His problem was convincing not the American people of the treaty's worth but sixty-six senators. He sent a bipartisan group of senators with Rusk to Moscow for the signing ceremony and then began an intensive campaign to gain support. When the treaty went to the Senate on 8 August he was still uncertain as to whether he had the votes.[18] For the ratification debate there were plenty of authoritative voices warning of the peril of such a step, often alleging that a good agreement with Moscow was a contradiction in terms. Anything Khrushchev could agree to was bound to be against American interests. Others complained that the president now adhered to misguided theories of unilateral disarmament. A more specific objection was that the treaty would prevent the United States from testing an effective antiballistic missile. Behind these criticisms were many senior military figures as well as scientists such as the mischievous and irrepressible Edward Teller, the so-called father of the hydrogen bomb.

All of this gave the Joint Chiefs of Staff unusual bargaining power with Kennedy. Their endorsement would be crucial if there was to be any hope of ratification. He worked hard to maneuver them into supporting the treaty before they could be led by congressional interrogation into airing their doubts.[19] As the negotiations were under way he spoke to the chiefs individually, finding that LeMay was steadfastly opposed while Shoup was positive and Taylor ready to see the political benefits.[20] On 13 August the State Department team, including Rusk and Harriman, met with the Joint Chiefs. They stressed that the treaty did not inhibit America's ability to use nuclear weapons. Rusk also said that "there would not be much life left in the treaty" if the Chinese began an extensive testing program (although the treaty did survive this event). In an argument that appears to have been persuasive, Rusk explained the advantages in terms of aggravating the Sino-Soviet split and encouraging a positive development in U.S.-Soviet relations, on the assumption that Khrushchev was anxious to cut military expenditure. The Joint Chiefs were not ready to say that in military terms the treaty was a plus for national security, but they were prepared to argue that it made sense politically.[21] They also got four crucial safeguards: the ability to conduct an aggressive underground testing program, the maintenance of modern nuclear laboratories, facilities for atmospheric tests should they become necessary again, and improved abilities to detect any violations. Their support was crucial. Attempts to add wrecking amendments (including one from Goldwater to link ratification with withdrawal of Soviet troops from Cuba) failed. The Republican minority leader, Everett Dirksen, put ratification beyond doubt. Having gained assurance that neither underground testing nor nuclear use was affected by the treaty, he gave the treaty his blessing with some old-fashioned oratory. Picking up on Kennedy's Chinese proverb, he announced, "I should not like to have written on my tombstone, 'He knew what happened at Hiroshima, but he did not take a first step.' "

The treaty was ratified, 80 to 19. Kennedy found that the public warmed to this theme, even in conservative locales such as Salt Lake City. He was becoming increasingly vulnerable as white voters deserted him in the South, and the peace issue was one he could see working for him in 1964, especially if the Republicans nominated Goldwater.[22]

30

Measured Response

CUBA PROVIDED KENNEDY with the opportunity to reduce the risk of total war by reducing tensions with the Soviet Union. At the same time the successful management of the crisis encouraged the view that somehow a breakthrough had been made in the manipulation of force and its relation to diplomacy. McNamara was cited as saying that, after Cuba, "[t]here is no longer any such thing as strategy, only crisis management."[1] During the crisis the administration had tended to ignore the views of the military, which had appeared beside the point because they failed to address the agenda the president had clearly set. A limited action had succeeded as the military clamored for stiffer, more dangerous, and more reckless measures. This led to a new concept of measured response that presupposed the use of proportionate force for purposes of coercive diplomacy rather than a decisive battle. The tendency was already apparent in both defense policy and strategic analysis; more military options made it possible to establish greater control over the course and outcome of a crisis and war itself.

This fed into the debate that was already well under way on flexible response in Europe. The initial reaction to Cuba in Europe was relief that it had not led to something much worse and that the pressure might now be off to raise force levels in Europe. They had to be reminded that Cuba had been a crisis in which the United States had "virtually all military chips" and that there was no reason to suppose that Khrushchev would have backed down so quickly if it had been over Berlin. The administration wanted the Europeans to recognize that the lesson learned was the need for flexible response.[2] But Cuba had highlighted another tension in the alliance. While its management had impressed Europeans and strengthened Kennedy's position as the leader of the alliance, it had also revealed their dependence upon the United States. A war started over a small island in the Caribbean could quickly have become a European conflagration.

TROUBLESOME ALLIES

Kennedy viewed NATO in the same way he viewed the State Department, and at times one appeared as an extension of the other. From both bodies were to be heard concerns and anxieties that, while valid in themselves, often seemed to be no more than excuses for inertia. Both expected conspicuous and often laborious forms of consultation and deliberation. Both tended to leak liberally to the press when they were not getting their way. Neither was to be trusted with major initiatives, and this meant consultations about the implementation rather than the structure of policy. Kennedy's instinct therefore was to work with allies he found congenial rather than those who enjoyed some procedural priority. Naturally Anglophile, he made regular contact with Macmillan, whose political instincts were often exaggerated versions of his own. His dealings with Adenauer rarely moved beyond the courteous, while he found de Gaulle impressive as a person but with grandiose expectations for his country that could only be achieved, if at all, at the expense of wider Western interests. At a time when Europe was led by old men, Kennedy's youth was in itself a form of challenge, as was his rapport with the public.

The first post-Cuba crisis was with the British, the closest and most loyal of allies, whose suspicions that the Americans wanted them to get out of the nuclear business were confirmed when McNamara abruptly canceled the Skybolt air-launched missile. This was to be purchased by Britain to sustain its strategic bomber force over the 1960s. With regard to State Department and Pentagon opinion, British suspicions were largely correct, so Macmillan went directly to Kennedy, as one politician to another, to remedy the situation.[3] The result was that the British were allowed to purchase Polaris instead, thus putting their nuclear force on a surer long-term footing. The timing was unfortunate because it meant that the British were given conspicuous special treatment at a delicate time, and while Kennedy himself might have been prepared to extend something similar to de Gaulle as a way of keeping him on the American side, the State Department was even less enthusiastic and stressed a condition to the French that had been neutralized in practice by the British, that is, that the priority was to create an integrated multilateral force, subject to a U.S. veto.[4]

The handling of this issue confirmed de Gaulle in the position to which he was already inclined. His goal was to reestablish his country as a great and independent power and to strike a blow against American hegemony. In challenging the need for NATO he made the case for a reduced European role for the United States. This was founded on France's successes in nuclear testing, which is why he was not about to agree to a test ban, and certainly not from its modest conventional military strength. Because he was largely out to change perceptions, his favored targets were symbols and institutional structures. His most serious move was to veto Britain's application to join the European Common Market, which had been strongly backed by Kennedy. This was taken as a portent of an attempt to lock America out of Europe.

As soon as Macmillan was rejected, Adenauer was embraced. At one level the Franco-German Treaty of February 1963 was a marvelous achievement, bringing together two countries whose traditional enmity had caused three wars over a hundred years. At another level it seemed to depend on antagonism toward the United States. The message was that somehow France was more committed to German security than the United States was. Kennedy was furious with Adenauer after all the risks he had taken on Germany's behalf, and he was exasperated with de Gaulle, who "relies on our power to protect him while he launches his policies based solely on the self-interest of France."[5] What if the next step was some special arrangement between Paris and Moscow? The Germans would tag along, and NATO would break up. The idea that the United States was now competing with France for the affections of Germany appalled those, such as Acheson, who had sought to construct a postwar Europe under American leadership.[6]

In practice, few Europeans were likely to follow where de Gaulle led. Adenauer's enthusiasm was by no means universally shared in Bonn. Gaullist doctrine was naturally selfish. Close scrutiny of French defense policy gave no indication of a readiness to take great risks on Germany's behalf. If anything, de Gaulle hoped that he might get some subsidy for France's nuclear force, and he did not seem too bothered if the next step was for Germany to acquire one of its own, as that would reduce France's security responsibilities. To lose the protection of a superpower for such uncertain benefits was a gamble too far, and the Americans mounted a sustained campaign to clarify to West German politicians the choice their country faced. If the Americans were not welcome, then they might go home, and Germany would be left divided and vulnerable. The politicians understood. The treaty with France became couched in pro-NATO language, and soon Adenauer himself was on the way out, suddenly a liability in Germany's most crucial relationship, which he had done so much to forge.[7] U.S.-German relations were shored up by Kennedy's triumphal visit in the summer. De Gaulle was left isolated, with the special relationship with Germany, at least in the defense field, stillborn.

Whatever Germany's actual nuclear aspirations, Adenauer's main objection to past superpower proposals was that they included exceptional measures directed solely against Germany. There was far less reason to complain about test bans and nuclear proliferation treaties as general measures that happened to impinge on Germany among others. As these happened to be designed with Germany in mind, they continued to cause irritation in Bonn, but little could be done lest it be suggested that Germany was seeking a special exemption.

Germany's interest was in not a national nuclear force on French lines but rather access to a shared nuclear force over which it could exercise some control. It had explored in some detail an arrangement with Italy and France in the 1950s (ironically brought to an end by de Gaulle in 1958).[8] As an alternative NATO option, Norstad had proposed that three hundred medium-range ballistic missiles be based in Europe, effectively turning NATO into a fourth nuclear power. To Kennedy's people this seemed like a very bad idea. The missiles would be vulnerable and subject to attrition. They could see the alliance being drawn into a premature nuclear battle as Washington lost control. During 1961 the administration was cool on the idea without going so far as to reject it. The next year it began to push the alternative of a sea-based missile force. As this force was to be operated by crews drawn from the NATO countries, it was described as the "Multilateral Force" or MLF. Unlike Norstad's scheme, it would be firmly under an American veto. It took considerable arm twisting by McNamara before the Joint Chiefs of Staff were prepared to say that the scheme had any military utility.[9] Its political utility depended on it satisfying German yearnings for some sort of access to nuclear decision making, and on it serving as a pretext for getting Britain and France to abandon their independent deterrents. It was both a complicated and unconvincing way of achieving either objective.

Without spending much time on the matter, Kennedy allowed his officials to market this scheme. Some in the State Department showed unnatural enthusiasm that was never matched in Europe, except among some Germans who appreciated the sentiment. The marketing effort, combined with considerations of the composition of the force, its cost, and control arrangements, was not only controversial but also took up an inordinate amount of time. By the summer of 1963 Bundy was wishing that he and Rusk had spent longer damping down the enthusiasm of the passionate believers who had been pushing the proposal. He persuaded Kennedy to urge study of the proposal but remove any sense of deadline.[10] Kennedy accepted that the MLF issue hindered rather than helped the transatlantic debate and began to play it down, but it would have been too much of a reverse to repudiate the MLF, which lingered on until it was finally killed off under Lyndon Johnson.

NATO DOCTRINE

Kennedy's real disappointment with the Europeans was their unwillingness to contribute more to their own conventional defense. The extra expenditure he had deemed necessary to create additional military options short of all-out nuclear war, which caused some pressure on his country's balance-of-payments position, had not been followed by the Europeans.

They continued to suggest that the American motive was largely to get out of nuclear commitments. Since the previous fall Kennedy had been irritated with the refusal by Germany, and in particular France, to increase spending on conventional forces. At a meeting in August 1962 it had been suggested to him that the West German desire for a forward strategy—that is, one that held Warsaw Pact forces close to the inner German border—would lead them to put pressure on France for extra forces. Those aware of the Adenauer–de Gaulle relationship were less sure. From the American perspective, it was going to be difficult to explain to Congress why more effort should be put into the conventional defense of Europe when this excited no response from the allies. "We're not going to be up for six divisions," observed Kennedy, "while the Germans don't do what they should do, and the French do *nothing.*"[11]

The European refusal to spend more on conventional forces left the United States with supplies to fight a war for ninety days, while the allies would be exhausted after three. Kennedy complained to Adenauer at the end of November that Germany was not doing its share in meetings its NATO commitments.[12] At the December NATO meeting Rusk and McNamara went on the attack, complaining about conventional force deficiencies to give the impression that American patience was running out. Kennedy's was. In late December, when discussing the defense budget, Kennedy said that troops in Europe would have to be "thinned out" unless the Europeans did more to improve their readiness. McNamara promised to submit a plan for the withdrawal of 50,000 to 70,000 men (out of 257,000).[13] "If the Europeans are getting ready to throw us out," Kennedy observed, "we want to be in a position to march out." In vain did his staff point to the incompatibility of cuts with flexible response, as he contemplated Americans fighting alone for Europe. When the Joint Chiefs demurred, he argued that "as far as he could see right now, Europe was probably about eighth on our list of dangers."[14]

Though disinclined to put resources into European defense without some reciprocation, Kennedy nonetheless remained true to the strategic thinking that had led him to push for extra conventional options in the first place. This thinking was reinforced by the study of the lessons of Cuba. A group headed by Walt Rostow charged with drawing those lessons noted that neither U.S. nuclear superiority nor local conventional capability had acted as sufficient deterrent. Moscow had responded to an American

> program of ascending political pressures against a background of military preparations with the aim not of conquest but of restoration of our vital interests intact. Our determination to proceed so far as was necessary through a chain of expanding non-nuclear action and eventually nuclear action was clearly visible throughout, because our preparations for these actions were realistically in train.

After stressing the close interaction between the political and the military in a crisis such as this, they argued the need for continuous and intense central control.

> To apply graduated menacing pressure with the least risk of uncontrollability clearly required one firm hand on the valve wheel.[15]

This served as the basis for a longer paper passed on to Undersecretary of State George Ball on 15 November in which it was argued that once the United States decided on the blockade, Moscow had been faced with an impossible local military problem, added to which "they could not be certain how far a local conflict would escalate." Though the risk of nuclear war had therefore influenced Soviet conduct, they still suggested that this risk had been exaggerated by the United States in public statements.[16] Drawing on this work in an address to NATO parliamentarians, Ball offered as a lesson the "wisdom—indeed the necessity—of the measured response." He noted how Kennedy had eschewed a sudden air strike or an invasion, despite their decisiveness, and instead opted for the more limited response of a quarantine. This avoided excessive violence and gained for the president time "to consult with our allies about the future steps we should take, time also to seek a political solution. Lastly, it enabled him to keep—and he still keeps—an option for further pressure if the situation should require it."

The "doctrine of measured choice," with both economic and military implications, could now be added to the growing arsenal that provided for the free world the widest spectrum of response to military and political threats. He explained the importance for NATO:

> [W]e must increase the spectrum of our military choices on the continent of Europe. If we do so—always preserving intact the ultimate nuclear deterrent—we increase our ability to achieve the purposes of the alliance at the smallest risk of nuclear annihilation.[17]

Cuba was made to support an established position taken in the vigorous debate over NATO strategy and the Kennedy administration's determination to push through its strategic reforms against the resistance of its allies. In McNamara's mind, Cuba and the larger strategic challenge of Berlin were still linked—he assumed that Khrushchev's objective had been to develop a "trump card" for the next round of negotiations.[18] On 11 November 1962, after pointing out how Cuba had reinforced lessons of strength and resolve, he added a third lesson, that of restraint. "We must constrain ourselves to employ the least amount of force that is effective to determine the immediate issues between our adversaries and ourselves."[19] William Kaufman summed up the administration's philosophy: "Multiple options" could make force "more nearly the servant than the master of American objectives." It would not only strengthen deterrence but also, if it failed, offer "the hope that force can still be used in a controlled and deliberate way. In an era of transition and danger, it is doubtful that any alternative defense strategy can offer much more than that."[20]

Evidence that the experience had reinforced the basic mind-set within the administration came over the coming months. McNamara's antinuclear inclinations were becoming formalized, to the point where the Pentagon soon effectively dropped the no-cities doctrine of the previous summer and began to argue that it was pointless to think of gradations of nuclear war. The road to the official adoption of the doctrine of "assured destruction" had begun. The idea that nuclear operations could be seen as an extension of the conventional was disavowed. The concept of the "firebreak" made its first official appearance in December 1962.

John McNaughton, a senior Pentagon official with special responsibilities for arms control, noted "a tendency for every confrontation to spiral upward in violence." He spoke of the mutual desire of the United States and USSR to avoid "the eruption, escalation or prolongation of nuclear war by accident or miscalculation," and of the value of "building firebreaks against escalation of conflict." In February 1963 Alain Enthoven, deputy assistant secretary of defense (systems analysis), described a policy objective of enabling the president to be able to choose from among a range of options when faced with a threat to security

> so that he can apply force adequate to accomplish the objectives at hand without causing any unnecessary damage or loss of life, and while holding to a minimum the risk of escalation to a more destructive level of conflict.

One way of achieving this was to acknowledge and work within the "firebreak" that divides nonnuclear war from nuclear war: "a recognizable qualitative distinction that both combatants can recognize and agree upon, if they want to agree upon one." It would be prudent to agree—for no other obvious "firebreak" could be identified "all the way up the destructive spectrum to large scale thermonuclear war."

Cuba, he argued, had shown that "non-nuclear forces were the cutting edge of our military power."[21] Privately more radical conclusions were being drawn. Bundy told his staff in February that there was "no logic" in nuclear policy, that the calculations that had the United States claiming victory with thirty million deaths to Russia's one hundred million dead were unrealistic: "[T]he President is certainly not going to win the next election on this issue."[22] At the end of July McNamara informed Kennedy that counterforce was to be abandoned as a goal for force planning purposes, and with it the no-cities doctrine of the previous summer. This led Bundy to comment on the short shelf life of these doctrines—in this case "about a year."[23]

Although the Joint Chiefs continued to push for a first-strike capability, it was a military briefing to the National Security Council on the projected outcomes of general nuclear war in the coming years that confirmed that neither side could expect to emerge without extensive damage and high casualties, no matter which side initiated the war. Kennedy received confirmation that "we are in a period of nuclear stalemate." In June he had been told at Omaha that with a first strike and substantial expenditure on defenses, casualties could be kept down to twelve million. Now he was told that they would be a minimum of thirty million. The general responsible for the report argued that it showed the need for means of catching "more of the Soviet missiles before they are launched" and destroying more of them "in the air over the U.S." McNamara countered that there was "no way of launching a no-alert attack against the USSR which was acceptable." Kennedy took away the key conclusion that "preemption was not possible for us."[24] McNamara's staff had now come up with a new criterion by which to judge the adequacy of U.S. strategic forces. This was "assured destruction"—the ability to destroy, even after absorbing a surprise Soviet attack, the Soviet government and military controls, plus a large percentage of their population and economy (e.g., 30 percent of their population, 50 percent of their industrial capacity, and 150 of their cities). A meeting with Bundy's staff to discuss this shift with McNamara was scheduled for 22 November 1963, and was canceled because of the president's assassination.[25]

The basic theme of graduated response was taken up by independent strategic analysts. Many had never doubted the strength of the American position during the Cuban crisis. Schelling wrote enthusiastically that Cuba should be construed as an instance of a new species of limited war, described as a "competition in risk-taking, a military-diplomatic maneuver with or without a military engagement but with the outcome determined by manipulation of risk than by an actual contest of force."[26] The proposition that it demonstrated the possibilities of control rather than escalation was picked up by Albert and Roberta Wohlstetter writing as the crisis concluded. Unlike with Berlin, there was no need to "stress the probabilities of nuclear escalation." It was better to explore "the possibility of control in the *non-nuclear* spectrum."[27] It was at this time that Herman Kahn introduced the "escalation ladder," an oxymoron that captured the tension between automaticity and control, inadvertence and deliberation, and supported his view of conflicts as bargaining processes in which one side might counter the pressure of the other with a stronger pressure of its own.[28]

Of the leading strategists, only Bernard Brodie was conspicuously increasingly dubious about the administration's policy of developing nonnuclear options for NATO. Though an early advocate of limited-war thinking, he had little enthusiasm for the formal, abstract, systematic theorizing that began at RAND and moved into the Pentagon under McNamara. His critique was similar to the one Norstad had pressed unsuccessfully on McNamara in late 1961. He argued that the arrival of strategic stability reduced the general risk of escalation, even as a result of tactical nuclear use. Against the run of opinion in the strategic studies community, and certainly the Kennedy administration, he considered limited nuclear use far more practical than he, among others, had assumed it to be in the 1950s. During the missile crisis, he thought, too many senior people had allowed themselves to get into a panic about the likely sequence of events. His particular target was the idea of the "firebreak" separating nonnuclear from nuclear war. This underestimated the significance of the most important strategic move—the original aggression that causes war—and of the intensity of a nonnuclear war at the level allowed should there be strict adherence to the firebreak.[29] The early use of a few nuclear weapons was less likely to push things out of control than intensive and prolonged nonnuclear warfare.

The Cuban crisis therefore reinforced a tendency that was already apparent in both defense policy and strategic analysis: to insist that by creating more military options it would be possible to establish more control over the course and outcome of a crisis, even involving general war with the Soviet Union. Indeed, it was the prospect of general war with the Soviet Union that had encouraged attention to the possibilities of identifying and sticking with levels of armed force well below the nuclear threshold. Yet in Europe Kennedy was no longer convinced that stability required extra military exertions. Interest in flexible nuclear responses had evaporated in the face of their essential implausibility. Flexible conventional responses appeared expensive and lacked contributions from allies. So although developed for European contingencies, the doctrine of flexible response was becoming more relevant to areas of high conflict. Vietnam offered the first major opportunity following Cuba to discover whether or not strategies based on concepts of graduated response or coercive diplomacy could be applied in circumstances quite different from those of a superpower confrontation.[30]

V

VIETNAM

31

Counterinsurgency

WHERE KENNEDY REALLY WANTED flexible response was not at the nuclear or conventional levels, but with counterinsurgency. He disliked and feared nuclear weapons and sought measures that would prevent them from being used. By contrast, he found special forces and counterinsurgency fascinating and was convinced that they represented the future way of war. He was also convinced that Khrushchev took the same view. The clinching evidence was found in a short section of a long speech given on 6 January 1961, two weeks before Kennedy's inauguration. Khrushchev was well aware of the horrors of traditional warfare and the dangers of a nuclear holocaust. But as for "wars of liberation or popular uprisings," the attitude of Marxists was "most favorable." The Soviet leader described how the anticolonial uprisings had developed to include guerrilla warfare against American imperialism, and spoke enthusiastically about the new front that had opened up in Latin America as a result of the Cuban revolution. The new occupants of the White House read Khrushchev's speech carefully, perhaps too carefully. It confirmed Kennedy's commitment to a dual policy of support for programs of modernization and determined resistance to insurgency. One of the first questions he is reported to have asked was "What are we doing about guerrilla warfare?"[1]

Here, unlike nuclear deterrence, he could not look to a body of strategic theory and distinguished specialists for answers. On offer to the president as America's greatest expert on third world conflicts was General Edward Lansdale. While Walt Rostow thought himself "probably more focused" on the problem of guerrilla warfare than "most of Kennedy's advisers before he came to the presidency," he judged that Lansdale "knew more about guerrilla warfare on the Asian scene than any other American."[2] Before he was given the chance to organize Cuban policy, Lansdale had been offered a platform within the administration to expound on his true interest: stopping communist subversion in South Vietnam.

Lansdale took his philosophy from his communist foes. The key to success lay in the support of the people. Without them there could be "no political base for supporting the fight." Counterinsurgents had to convince people that they could improve their lives—through social action as much as physical protection. This required a responsive, noncorrupt government and professional behavior at all times by the armed forces.[3] At the heart of all of this lay a belief that people in the most desperate societies could still be inspired by a cause. The case for American liberal capitalism had to be made real and vital to people lest they be tempted instead by the communist cause. Brute force was not enough for societies in disrepair. This was the message of *The Ugly American*, and Kennedy was already a convert.

At his first meeting of the National Security Council on 1 February 1961, Kennedy received a Limited War Task Force report that dealt, inter alia, with guerrilla warfare. He was not impressed; the Pentagon was asked to place additional emphasis on counterinsurgency. By contrast, he was extremely impressed by a report by Lansdale on Vietnam handed to him by Rostow, full of proposals for guerrilla warfare. Thereafter Rostow took it upon himself to feed the president's appetite for information and ideas on this topic, and reported on the ability of the American army to cope with this form of warfare. There were fewer than a thousand special forces at the Special Warfare School at Fort Bragg, being trained largely for operations behind enemy lines during a regular war; Kennedy wanted the school to reorganize itself to train for guerrilla warfare in underdeveloped countries.

In May McNamara was instructed to divert $100 million from his budget to encourage a reorientation of forces for "paramilitary and sublimited or conventional wars." They would be given the special skills of the guerrilla fighter, including foreign language fluency. Kennedy encouraged all around him to read Mao and Che Guevara, the theorist of the Cuban revolution; took a personal interest in training manuals and equipment; and, against the army's distaste for privileged units, authorized the special forces to wear a distinctive green beret. Sorensen notes how Kennedy "personally supervised the selection of new equipment—the replacement of heavy, noisy combat boots with sneakers, for example, and when the sneakers proved vulnerable to bamboo spikes, their reinforcement with flexible, steel inner soles."[4] To spread the word Kennedy personally instigated a number of publications, including an excerpt from Lansdale's report in the *Saturday Evening Post*.[5]

By the start of 1962 the effects of this drive were felt through the government but also in the world of policy-oriented academics.[6] Student capacity at Fort Bragg doubled from 527 to 1,212. In June 1961 a new six-week National Interdepartmental Seminar opened for senior figures, which was often audited by top members of the administration, including Robert Kennedy. The course heard from Lansdale, Rostow, and Hilsman, and also the theorists of underdevelopment from MIT's Center for International Studies. The course's lectures examined "the forces unleashed by the development process which complicate the attainment of U.S. objectives by generating disruptive influences, dissidence and targets of exploitable Communist opportunity." At the end of the first course, the members met with the president, who told them it was necessary for everyone to "concentrate their energy on what is going to be one of the great factors in the struggle of the Sixties."[7]

NSAM 124 of January 1962 established a new interagency group, chaired by Maxwell Taylor, to coordinate the "subterranean war": the task of the Special Group (Counterinsurgency) was ensuring "the use of U.S. resources with maximum effectiveness in preventing and resisting subversive insurgency in friendly countries."[8] It was the augmented version of this that oversaw Mongoose. With NSAM 182 this new group offered a comprehensive doctrine—"United States Overseas Internal Defense Policy"—which remained in force for the rest of the decade. The document sustained the focus on the "stresses and strains of the development process" and the problems that could result from weak governmental institutions, poor communications with the countryside, armed forces "estranged from the people," and the ability of the communists to exploit all of this.

> Many years of experience with the techniques of subversion and insurgency have provided the communists with a comprehensive, tested doctrine for conquest from within. Our task is to fashion on an urgent basis an effective plan of action to combat this critical communist threat.

To meet this threat it was necessary to develop an integrated concept of operations to build up "situations of strength within the local society," through addressing "the root causes of disaffection and dissidence, to expose and counter communist efforts, and to cope with increased levels of violence." Somehow the United States, in its training programs for military and the police, had to create such political sensitivity to the demands of nation building that these bodies would become "advocates of democracy and agents for carrying forward the development process." In all of this it was recommended that the use of U.S. forces should be "as limited as the achievements of its objectives permit and only ancillary to the indigenous effort." Otherwise it might "expose the U.S. unnecessarily to the charges of intervention and colonialism." Yet at the same time a "clear demonstration of U.S. willingness to help may be an important factor in strengthening morale and local will to resist."[9]

The seeds of later problems could be discerned. For a start, this doctrine was being imposed on the U.S. military rather than being developed from within its ranks. The top players in the administration, and most particularly the president himself, set the tone, and few with careers to look after dissented. Whatever its intrinsic merits, its external provenance generated suspicion. Military organizations may be adept at picking up the new language of political discourse with which to rationalize their activities, but they also tend to cling to their traditional and familiar patterns of behavior. The military believed that the threat still came from classical cross-border aggression involving substantial armies, and that if forces were developed for these contingencies, they could probably cope quite well with guerrilla campaigns. They did not believe that the reverse was true. In Korea a local army had been trained for internal security duties only to be faced by a massive armored invasion. It did not want to make the same mistake again.[10]

Korea had also led to a distrust of limited interventions. Hilsman refers to the influence of what he calls the "Never Again Club" on the Joint Chiefs, contending that the United States should never again restrict itself when fighting a ground war and should be ready to strike at the sources of enemy power, even if that meant using nuclear weapons. They did not necessarily expect to use nuclear weapons but wanted it understood that military logic and not diplomatic sentiment had to be in command. If they were ordered into limited wars, the record should show that they had warned of dire consequences.[11] The Joint Chiefs' antipathetic attitude toward civilian ideas on the use of armed force intensified during the first months of the Kennedy administration, as the military leaders felt that their advice was either rejected or misunderstood. A new low was reached after the Bay of Pigs debacle in April. Schlesinger concludes that the Joint Chiefs' tactic after this was to be able to show that "whatever the President did, he acted against their advice."[12]

Though civilians also dreaded "the thought of getting bogged down in a niggling, harassing quagmire of a war in the jungles," they saw a need to reshape the military instrument to fit in with political circumstances rather than wait for the circumstances to warrant the use of the inflexible instrument available. They looked to develop what Hilsman called "appropriately tailored responses—with just enough force to deter aggression but not so much as to cause the Communists to believe that we had ulterior designs of our own."[13] In a memo to the president on 10 March Rostow noted that force kept separate from diplomacy meant that diplomacy was not reinforced when it should be and more force was used than would otherwise have been necessary.[14]

A key difficulty with the application of this theory lay in the supposed relationship between local conditions and communist design. American geopolitical thinking of the period had come to assume that Moscow had identified a series of linked pressure points where the "free world" was especially vulnerable. In Southeast Asia, for example, it was taken for granted that the fates of the various noncommunist countries were interrelated: If one fell to a communist insurgency, then the others would surely follow. This came to be known as the domino theory. The strictures in NSAM 124 against tendencies to intervention and colonialism could soon be forgotten once a country's tawdry security problems were represented as a function of the latest stage in the cold war.

Charles Maechling, who chaired the drafting committee for NSAM 182, later described the document as being "somewhat simplistic" in assuming a monolithic form of communist threat, defined in terms of "wars of national liberation." The doctrine failed to discriminate between target governments, nor did it concern itself "with the domestic origins and root causes of internal turmoil." Revolutionary movements were treated as if they were "a clearly articulated military force instead of the apex of a pyramid deeply embedded in society."[15] Shafer notes how the doctrine made heroic assumptions about the nature of the development process, and in particular the extent to which popular support for insurgency must have been "coerced or misled discontent about remediable local inequalities," thereby failing to appreciate that governments and people "might have insuperable differences."[16]

This difficulty stemmed directly from Rostow's definition of the problem. A regime facing indigenous revolutionaries ought to be able to cope by taking no more than sensible advice and some material support from the United States. The only circumstances in which a substantial American counterinsurgency effort would make sense would be those where the insurgency was supported from outside and the regime's resources were inevitably overwhelmed. It therefore suited unstable regimes with self-inflicted problems to present their difficulties as the product of external aggression, directed from Moscow, rather than a response to corruption, authoritarianism, and poverty.

Paul Kattenburg, a State Department official actively involved in Vietnam during the Kennedy years, observed that the very description of opponents as "insurgents" rather than revolutionaries or rebels was disingenuous. It denied the possibility that they might be champions of a popular movement. Rostow's imagery supported the idea of alien intruders suddenly coming upon "peaceful rice-growing villages which they would terrorize mercilessly" after "long forced marches from secure rear bases equipped by China and Russia." It was hard to accept that the opponents were often local and popular, and that their victims were associated with repression.[17]

Lansdale understood the "hearts and minds" problem, which he believed could be addressed through enlightened civic action, and that the Americans could not undertake this on their own. If the local government protected the privileges of the elite and failed to reach out to the people, then its position would deteriorate irrespective of the quality of its counter-insurgency operations. Alexis Johnson, also of the State Department and active in interagency discussions on counterinsurgency and

Vietnam, observed that ameliorating the "worst causes of discontent" and redressing "the most flagrant inequities" would require positive action, and in some cases radical reform, by the local government. He then added, "Yet the measures we advocate may strike at the very foundations of those aspects of a country's social structure and domestic economy on which rest the basis of a government's control." This was almost an aside in an article designed to convey to the Foreign Service bureaucracy the importance and excitement of the new challenge. Rather lamely, Johnson suggested that this particular problem would test the diplomat's power of persuasion. Its full significance was not followed through; nor was it recognized in the literature of the time as a crucial disability.[18]

32

Laos

THESE ISSUES, present in the Cuba case, proved decisive in Indochina. They were first met in Laos. The crisis over this small country now tends to be forgotten because it was eventually subsumed into the larger Vietnam problem and did not result in any direct American military commitments, but until the last few months of his life it took up more of Kennedy's time than Vietnam and served as a test bed for the development of relevant military doctrines, local political deals, and superpower diplomacy.

Laos was small, poor, landlocked, and remote. The population, which could only be estimated, was some two million. It was hardly of great strategic importance in itself, except that it had long borders with China, North Vietnam, and South Vietnam, and so provided a route through which communists might travel to noncommunist areas. It had been forged along with Vietnam and Cambodia out of the former French Indochina. In 1954 an international conference was organized in Geneva, chaired by Britain and the Soviet Union, that led to the division of Vietnam into North and South, while Laos and Cambodia were guaranteed their independence and neutrality. An International Control Commission in Laos (ICC), with members from India, Canada, and Poland, was created to police the agreements. Violations were to be reported to the two cochairmen.

Plans were outlined in each case for internal political settlements. These were poorly defined and proved impossible to implement. There was no basis for integrating communist and anticommunist forces. The domestic politics of Laos reflected traditional and dynastic lines that cut across the simple ideological framework the major powers tried to impose. Within this framework, the issue was whether Laos joined either the communist or the anticommunist blocs, or else sustained a real neutrality but with either a procommunist or prowestern tilt.

Under the leadership of Prince Souvanna Phouma, the prime minister, a coalition took shape and the various armies were integrated. The communists, however, were the strongest and most disciplined group in the coalition. Fearing that they were exercising excessive influence, the Eisenhower administration encouraged anticommunist elements to vote Souvanna Phouma out of office. Beginning in July 1958 the government had become progressively neutralist with a pro-Western tilt. It was challenged by the communist Pathet Lao, who were backed by North Vietnam. This led not quite to civil war but instead to a form of partition. The government forces, especially with American assistance, could contain the Pathet Lao but not defeat them completely. North Vietnam was content to have local control in areas important for infiltration into South Vietnam, even if the communists could not control the central government.

The neutralist government fell victim not to a leftist insurgency but to a rightist coup when a right-wing general, Phoumi Nosavan, assisted by the CIA, took control of the government at the end of 1959. Then, after yet another coup in August 1960, Souvanna Phouma was called back to office. When his attempt to form a government with Phoumi failed, his willingness to start dealing with the Pathet Lao, led by his half-brother, Prince Souphannouvong, alarmed the Americans. Souvanna indicated his readiness to distance himself from the Pathet Lao, but Phoumi was now out for complete power. Despite American misgivings, he gathered the army and took the capital, Vientiane. In December 1960 his regime was recognized by Western governments. Souvanna, still recognized by the Soviet Union, China, and India as the legal ruler, fled, joined forces with the communist Pathet Lao, and called in an airlift of Soviet military supplies. Fortified by these weapons, the new alliance of communists and neutralists made important gains against Phoumi's Royal Laotian Army.

Thus as the Kennedy administration arrived in power, neutralism appeared a lost cause with a civil war taking hold. Eisenhower wanted Kennedy to continue to back Phoumi, even though his position appeared weak. The general was likely to request the South-East Asian Treaty Organization (SEATO) to come to his aid. The September 1954 treaty, which brought together the United States, Britain, France, Australia, and New Zealand with Thailand, Pakistan, and the Philippines, had been forged as a Western response to the Geneva accords. It was designed to provide guarantees against external aggression, including (as the result of a protocol) to South Vietnam, Cambodia, and Laos. Thus Article IV involved each party recognizing that "aggression by means of an armed attack in the treaty area would endanger its own peace and safety, and agrees that it will act to meet the common danger in accordance with its own constitutional processes."

North Vietnam was backing the Pathet Lao. North Vietnamese "aggression" had been precisely what the Eisenhower administration had in mind when promoting SEATO. So it was that, at least for the moment, Laos was presented as the place at which communist expansion in the region must be stopped. Eisenhower gave Kennedy reason to believe that he expected and would back intervention, even though he had not taken matters so far himself.[1] As in these circumstances America would probably be alone, without serious British or French support, Kennedy felt, with some justice, that his distinguished predecessor had bequeathed him a terrible mess.[2]

RETURN TO NEUTRALITY

When Kennedy's own team began to formulate policy immediately after the inauguration, they reaffirmed a determination to back the government, but in a significant departure from the previous administration, they also decided to explore a serious neutralist option.[3] Initially it was hoped that a neutral government in which neither Souvanna nor the Pathet Lao would participate could be created. There were two major difficulties, however. First, Britain, as cochairman of the Geneva conference, believed it had to work with Moscow, and the Russians were not about to exclude the Pathet Lao. Second and perhaps most important, as Kennedy's task force noted in January, within Laos the "only real determination appears to reside in the Pathet Lao."[4]

Even a neutralist option therefore depended on finding some way of checking the communists so that any political solutions would be ideologically balanced. This apparently required boosting the rightist forces in the government through practical military and economic assistance. If the position on the ground could be prevented from deteriorating too quickly, time might be found for careful consideration of the more drastic remedies of direct intervention, a negotiated settlement, or some carefully crafted combination of the two.

At the start of the year the Pathet Lao had taken the Plain of Jars, in the center of the country. If Phoumi could retake it, his cause would be immeasurably stronger. There were reasons to hope for a battlefield success. Despite the claims that the Soviet airlift had made all the difference, American assistance to Phoumi had been on an even larger scale. A Special National Intelligence Estimate, unfortunately based on low-grade information, supported the notion that Phoumi's forces could win against a rather limited Pathet Lao army—and within three weeks. Unfortunately, Phoumi was a less than inspirational military leader and his troops proved no match for the Pathet Lao. Battle generally was a rather halfhearted matter in Laos. Rusk later recalled a report of how the two opposing sides once left a battlefield to attend a water festival. From New Delhi, Ambassador Kenneth Galbraith observed that in military terms, "the entire Laos nation is clearly inferior to a battalion of conscientious objectors from World War I." This rather engaging feature of Buddhist society discredited Laos as a candidate for backbone-stiffening American intervention. Intelligence reports told the president that Laotian soldiers believed that tanks could be stopped with sharpened sticks tipped with phallic symbols, and most believed the world to be flat. "They're charming, indolent, enchanting people," explained Ambassador Winthrop Brown, "but they're just not very vigorous."[5]

By 6 March, Phoumi's forces were in retreat in the face of a communist counteroffensive. After three weeks the communists were even stronger than before. If this was the best that the anticommunists could do, as Kennedy acknowledged, the wisest course was to cut American losses and get a neutralist government in as soon as possible. A negotiated outcome that would provide a genuine guarantee of Laotian neutrality had much to commend it. The Russians appeared ready to accept it. But if the fighting stopped now, Phoumi's earlier losses would be confirmed; if the fighting continued without American backing, the losses would probably accumulate. If Phoumi's negotiating position could not be strengthened through his own efforts, then the only alternative was to prepare to redress the balance through American action, or at least hope that the threat of American involvement might encourage the communists to negotiate seriously.[6] The conspicuous movement of forces backed up by some determined rhetoric might bluff the communists (and at this point Kennedy's resolve had yet to be tested over either Berlin or Cuba). Accordingly, the Laos Task Force came up with a plan to strengthen the American contribution to the war, opening with military advisers and moving upward to massive force.[7]

Kennedy was prepared to go along with the bluff, though he was still uncertain as to what to do if the bluff was called. Meanwhile the situation continued to deteriorate. The Pathet Lao took more land, and diplomatic efforts faltered. In response the United States began to up the ante. On Okinawa 2,600 marines prepared for intervention, along with 1,400 on three aircraft carriers moving toward the South China Sea. Another 150 moved to near the Thai border with Laos. This was backed up by an active press campaign. Up to this point the press had taken scant interest in Laos. Of the leading columnists, only Alsop was interested in the problem (he had even written to Kennedy prior to his inauguration urging him to attend to this issue), and only the *New York Times* had a correspondent in Vientiane. Elsewhere Laos stories were relegated to inside pages. The broad thrust of media commentary was antineutralist, reflecting the old State Department line. Beginning on 15 March the administration decided to give the issue a high profile, including informal leaks and backgrounders, with Rostow active in ensuring that Moscow was blamed for the trouble. The media began to take the issue seriously.[8]

The culmination of this campaign was a press conference on 23 March. The president drew attention to Vietnamese support for the Pathet Lao. "If these attacks do not stop," he warned, "those who support a truly neutral Laos will have to consider their response." A link between Phoumi's fate and American prestige had already been forged in Kennedy's mind. He found himself in what was to be the familiar predicament of his presidency: torn between dismay over being "humiliated" by a communist victory and alarm at the prospect of getting dragged into an unwinnable war.

For a while it appeared that the predicament might be avoided and the bluff might work by virtue of the new stress on neutralism. The Soviet Union seemed ready to cooperate (if only because it saw the fate of Southeast Asia being determined elsewhere, in Vietnam) with a British and American call for an international conference. However, on 4 April Moscow undercut this effort by demanding that this conference begin without waiting for a cease-fire, thus suggesting that the communists expected a steady improvement of their position during its course. As Rostow reported to the president after the Laos Task Force met on 13 April, the "general appreciation" was that the communists wished to see the situation crumble "politically and militarily."[9]

THE DEVELOPMENT OF A MILITARY OPTION

The available American military options had been under study well before Kennedy took office, but without great progress. At the start of the year General Lemnitzer had described to President Eisenhower a plan in which American forces held the two main cities, leaving the countryside to the Laotians. However, the main concern then was with the Soviet airlift. Eisenhower pondered the possibility of medium-sized bombers "pitting the airfield" at the Plain of Jars, which was being used by Russian aircraft, but after being told by Lemnitzer that this could be done with B-26 bombers, he observed that such attacks worked best against fuel supplies and the Soviet airlift had not yet reached that stage. In the light of later debates, Eisenhower's most significant statement was that he held to "the conviction that if we ever resort to force, the thing to do is to clear the problem up completely. We should not allow a running sore like the British had in Egypt or the U.S. had in Korea."[10]

His administration thought of asking the government of Laos to invoke SEATO in response to the Soviet airlift. Washington would then respond, even if the other allies did not. In the discussions between the foreign policy teams of the outgoing and incoming administrations, including Eisenhower and Kennedy, the larger question was one of possible escalation. The trend of opinion appeared to be that the communists' local advantages would allow them to cope with a stepped-up effort on behalf of Phoumi, and that the Russians and Chinese would prefer not to become directly involved. The greatest risks associated with Laos were therefore of a large-scale war in Southeast Asia rather than an all-out superpower war. McNamara later recalled his impression that Eisenhower was "deeply uncertain about the proper course of action" and unable to explain how the Chinese could be kept out of Laos.[11]

The risk of a large-scale war confined to Southeast Asia was alarming enough for the new president. The first interagency analysis prepared for Kennedy noted that Laos was a logistical nightmare—a terrain of mountains and jungles, without sea access, railroads, adequate roads, or airstrips. The Pathet Lao, fortified by the North Vietnamese, would have all the advantages of local knowledge and guerrilla warfare. The judgment was that the introduction of U.S. troops is "not available as a threat if a lower order escalation fails."

One "lower order escalation" would be to introduce Thai troops, a measure that could be trumped readily by more North Vietnamese forces. Alternatively, U.S. fighter aircraft could be used to interdict communist supply lines. But again, on a tit-for-tat basis, this could be trumped by Russian or Chinese aircraft, which would have the advantage of far better targets, given that the government controlled the large cities, road junctions, and supply centers while the communists were using the mountains and jungles. The group failed to identify a sensible escalatory option, even though they advised that the United States should demonstrate its "determination to back the RLG both now and in the indefinite future. It must be made clear that we do not intend to permit the bloc to take Laos."[12]

The Special National Intelligence Estimate, approved on 21 February, provided estimates of the likely Communist reactions to alternative courses of action. In the face of overt military action by the United States confined to air power, the Communists (still assumed to be tied together in a Sino-Soviet bloc)

> would probably move to negotiate, calculating that they could both get a settlement and that would protect Communist assets in Laos and at the same time reap considerable political benefit. It is possible that they might commit Bloc air or ground forces, but would in any event build up their readiness posture in the general area and issue strong threats against the U.S. and participating allies to cease their air operations.

With U.S. ground forces committed, a more "intense" reaction could be expected:

> In particular the chances are about even that the USSR would at the same time sponsor DRV [Democratic Republic of Vietnam] intervention in Laos, and it might even acquiesce in Chinese Communist intervention.[13]

In response to a request from Kennedy on 3 March, the Joint Chiefs produced a plan to seize the Plain of Jars. This required the Royal Laotian Army to mount a two-pronged attack, following air strikes and culminating in an airborne assault. This was completely beyond their capabilities and could only be mounted, if at all, with U.S. assistance. In questioning the plan the president asked about the possibility of Soviet escalation, which Lemnitzer thought unlikely. However, he noted the extra troops that the North Vietnamese could put into battle.[14] While inserting American troops into the plains presented few problems, Lemnitzer was worried about how to extract them if things went wrong. Kennedy finally killed the idea by asking about the impact of an enemy attack before sufficient men had been inserted to defend the airfield. The communists, it was pointed out, could bring in twice as many men per day as the Americans could land.[15]

Rostow and the State Department were trying to develop ideas for interventions designed more for political than military effect. In mid-March State had proposed that U.S. and SEATO troops enter Laos "merely to hold certain key centers for diplomatic bargaining purposes, not to conquer the country. They would shoot only if shot at."[16] On 20 March at an informal meeting with Kennedy it was proposed to move a small number of troops into the Mekong Valley to deter the Pathet Lao and act as a bargaining counter at an international conference. The military was unimpressed with such ideas. Warning of a large-scale response from North Vietnam and even eventual war with China, they put the only prudent level of force at around 60,000 troops plus air cover.[17]

By the end of March it was apparent that negotiations would start with Moscow over the status of Laos. Britain agreed with the Soviet preference for a continuation of Souvanna Phouma as the only available neutral leader, and this option now had advocates in the U.S. administration.[18] Meanwhile, Averell Harriman, as Kennedy's roving ambassador, met Souvanna in New Delhi in March and was convinced that the neutralist option was worth pursuing. This view had already been put with some force by Ambassador Brown, and it was also backed by Senator Mansfield. He explained to Kennedy that while he might be criticized for not making more of a fight in Laos, the public understood that the problem was an inheritance from Eisenhower and that the costs of prolonged involvement could be much worse.[19] The case was strong: A government based on Souvanna would have substantial local and international support. The alternative seemed a civil war and an aggravation of U.S.-Soviet tensions. Despite the requirement for a public reversal of course and the accompanying accusations of giving in to Soviet threats from the conservative press, Kennedy moved to this position.

AFTER ZAPATA

This was the point matters had reached by mid-April, when the focus switched to the Bay of Pigs. While still reeling from the Cuban debacle, Kennedy was once again pressed by his advisers to consider intervention in Laos. As he had just desisted from such intervention in Cuba, it would have been odd if Kennedy had suddenly decided to take an even greater military gamble thousands of miles away where the stakes were less clear. Indeed, the general view is that the Cuban experience tilted the Laos decision. Sorensen reports that this time around the president "was far more skeptical of the experts, their reputations, their recommendations, their promises, premises and facts." He quotes Kennedy: "Thank God the Bay of Pigs happened when it did. Otherwise we'd be in Laos by now—and that would be a hundred times worse."[20]

Kennedy's confidence in military advice was an undoubted casualty of Operation Zapata. He was now less ready to sign up for bold schemes that promised to solve intractable problems at a stroke. It would be unwise, however, to overstate the importance of Cuba. Kennedy was well aware of the intractability of the Laos problem before April, and he had good reason to doubt the military advice he received on that crisis on its own terms. In Laos a compromise solution was available, albeit one that was deeply flawed.

Kennedy knew that a reputation for excessive prudence might be used against him by his political opponents, both international and domestic. Consequently, as the news from Cuba sent the White House into a deep gloom, the president made no effort to cut his losses in Laos. Rather, on 20 April, he approved a recommendation that the special forces in Laos be turned into an overt Military Assistance Advisory Group (MAAG), in full uniform. This signal might actually have had the desired effect, as Moscow, sensing that a beleaguered Kennedy might be tempted into something rash in Laos, agreed to the need for a cease-fire.[21]

While this opened up the possibility of a diplomatic solution, it made the immediate situation much more complicated. As events moved toward a cessation of fighting and then an international conference, the Pathet Lao intensified its military efforts to maximize its bargaining strength before the fighting had to stop. Soon Phoumi's forces were in disarray and Washington received a desperate plea for external intervention. On 26 April Ambassador Brown warned that the Pathet Lao had an open route to the Laotian capital and could be stopped only by air strikes followed up by U.S. or SEATO troops.

In Washington, the president's advisers agreed that "a large-scale involvement in Laos" would be "unjustified, even if the loss of Laos must be accepted." It was not certain that an intervention would provoke a confrontation with the Chinese, but "on balance it seemed wise to avoid a test if possible." It was Kennedy who was most convinced that ruling out intervention would remove the only card left to play in pressing for a cease-fire. "Accordingly," recorded Bundy, "the President explicitly refused to decide against intervention at this time."[22]

The next morning the NSC briefly discussed Laos, and then the president called in congressional leaders. Bowles described the meeting in a telegram to Rusk:

Admiral Burke briefed them on military situation, strongly and repeatedly throughout meeting, expressing view that unless U.S. prepared intervene militarily in Laos, all Southeast Asia will be lost. However, also pointed out extreme difficulty military operations in Laos and, if battle started there, must be prepared for tough, long and hard war which may well involve war with ChiComs.

The president made it clear that no decisions had been taken. The message from Congress was clear:

> [T]here was complete unanimity and strong view among all that, even recognizing possible consequences to our position in remainder Southeast Asia, we should not introduce U.S. forces into Laos.

This was not a blanket prohibition; "there would probably be support for introduction U.S. forces into Thailand and South Viet-Nam." It was the evidence that the Laotian forces did not have their heart in the battle that made congressional support less likely.

Rusk picked this up: "If Laos shows no interest, U.S. arms cannot import freedom into indifferent country." The rest of SEATO might also be indifferent. So any armed force should be "limited in its general mission," and the president must be aware of the possibility of "renewed fighting in Korea, bombing on bases in Okinawa and Japan, air and possibly other forms of attack on off-shore islands and Formosa."[23] Yet that evening the Joint Chiefs sent out a worldwide "general advisory" warning that the situation had "become exceedingly grave." Commands were readied, marines were put into position, and available naval units moved toward Southeast Asia, while the commander in chief, Pacific (CINCPAC), was told to prepare to deal with Chinese intervention and the possible need to take the fighting, by means of air strikes, into North Vietnam and China.[24]

A meeting in Washington the next morning revealed the gap that had developed between the military and the civilians. The president did not need the Bay of Pigs in order to wonder about the quality of the military advice he was receiving. Rostow later described this as the "worst White House meeting he attended in the entire Kennedy administration."[25] Confusion resulted from the immediate question of what to do about Laos becoming caught up with the longer-term question of where, if at all, the United States should make a stand in Southeast Asia against spreading Chinese influence. The fatalistic presumption, articulated by the strongly anti-Chinese Bowles, was that "we were going to have to fight the Chinese anyway in 2, 3, 5 or 10 years and it was just a question of where, when and how." In anticipation of an eventual Chinese nuclear capability, the natural answer was sooner rather than later, as Curtis LeMay was quick to point out.

At some point China might have to be confronted, but it was not evident that Laos was the appropriate place to make a stand. In military terms Vietnam seemed to make more sense, but the loss of Laos was going to make defending Vietnam harder. The North Vietnamese would be better able to reinforce their cadres in the South. America's reputation might suffer if an ally was allowed to collapse without a fight, especially as in his news conference of 23 March Kennedy had asserted publicly his determination to resist a communist advance in Laos.

Admiral Burke, deputizing for Lemnitzer as chairman of the Joint Chiefs of Staff, argued that "each time you give ground it is harder to stand next time." If, having lost Laos, the stand was to be taken in Vietnam and Thailand, then the United States "would have to throw enough in to win—the works." However, as the military described its approach it was hard to see how less than the "works" was going to be needed in Laos. Army chief of staff General George H. Decker took it to be axiomatic that "we cannot win a conventional war in Southeast Asia; if we go in, we should go in to win, and that means bombing Hanoi, China and maybe even using nuclear weapons." This alarming prospect was introduced almost casually, without any sort of coherent plan. Decker wanted to move troops into Thailand and South Vietnam to see if that led to an immediate cease-fire. LeMay believed that the enemy could be slowed and then weakened by air strikes using B-26 aircraft against Pathet Lao supplies. McNamara concluded the meeting noting that the situation was "worsening by the hour." Any commitment must come "sooner rather than later."[26] It might already be too late. At best, as the army and marines pointed out, a thousand men a day could be put on the ground—insufficient to defend the capital and probably themselves. The communists could eventually send in five extra men for every one sent by the United States. Even if there was little combat, the Americans could expect large numbers of casualties from "disease and dysentery." The scenario was drawn of troops arriving in Laos, being unable to progress much beyond the airstrip, and then somehow being rescued by nuclear strikes against China. It was only at this point that Kennedy let it be known through James Reston of the *New York Times* that he was not going to follow "military moves which would transform the fiasco in Cuba into a disaster in Laos."[27]

When the NSC met on 1 May, McNamara set in motion another debate by proposing a move into Laos, "recognizing that if we do we must be prepared to win." Allen Dulles immediately warned that it would then be necessary to risk a Chinese response, leading Bowles to observe that if there was to be war with China, Laos was not the place to start. The risk was raised of nuclear use and also of a "long debilitating war." Once again "no final decisions were taken." The Joint Chiefs were asked to prepare a presentation for another NSC meeting the next afternoon on the military implications of various alternative measures that might be taken in Southeast Asia.[28]

Still the Joint Chiefs could not produce a consensus, arguing among themselves on the competing merits of ground forces and air strikes. Afterward McNamara and Gilpatric attempted to pull all the conflicting advice together. Their case for intervention was hardly enthusiastic. The benefits were negative—avoiding erosion of the American position in Southeast Asia and its reputation as an ally, and denying the communists encouragement. Against this the terrain was unfavorable, the Laotian forces unimpressive, and the dangers of escalation considerable. Nonetheless the two most senior Pentagon officials favored setting a forty-eight-hour deadline for a cease-fire, which, if not honored, could be followed by a move of U.S. forces into Laos to protect key communication and population centers.

The two set out an unappetizing menu for the decisions that might follow should U.S. forces be engaged and the major communist powers come in on the side of the Pathet Lao. At best McNamara and Gilpatric made each move palatable by presenting it as a proportionate response to enemy action, in a mechanical escalatory process. The relationship of each move to ultimate objectives, however, remained unclear.

> We must promptly counter each added element brought against our forces with a more than compensating increment from our side. If the Pathet Lao keep coming, we must take any military action required to meet the threat. If North Viet-Nam attacks, we must strike North Viet-Nam. If Chinese volunteers intervene, we will have to go after South China. . . . To achieve a settlement at lower levels of escalation requires us to be willing to conduct ourselves without flinching from such escalation, or threats thereof, even though we should take every reasonable precaution that the situation not get out of hand.[29]

At the NSC meeting the options were discussed once more. Frustrated, the president directed that military contingency planning continue and that the Pentagon and State come up with a joint position. The more the military advice was reviewed the weaker it seemed. The decision was constantly deferred.

In the end procrastination turned out to be the best policy. Moscow had been unnerved by the evident American preparations for intervention in Laos and anxious lest larger issues, including Berlin, get lost over what Khrushchev considered a minor squabble. Souvanna was joined in Moscow by Prince Souphanouvong of the Pathet Lao in mid-April, and the two called for a cease-fire to be verified a week later by the International Control Commission for Laos and followed by a new international conference. Next they went on a joint mission to Beijing and Hanoi. The cease-fire order was broadcast to the Pathet Lao from Hanoi on 2 May. The timing had been predicted by McGeorge Bundy a month before. He had been paying attention to the monsoon rains that had started early that year. He expected the terrain to become so saturated that "further movements of substantial equipment will become extremely difficult."[30]

The Vienna summit offered an opportunity to consolidate this apparent breakthrough. Harriman had become convinced that only Moscow could prevent continual violations of the cease-fire and urged Kennedy to use the opportunity to pin Khrushchev down. A joint commitment to a neutralist Laos was the summit's only positive outcome. Kennedy and Khrushchev agreed to try to control their clients. After the summit the president told Harriman, "I want a settlement. I don't want to send troops."[31] Though for the moment the immediate crisis, and the pressure for intervention, had eased, the administration could not be sure that it would not build up again. The Pathet Lao and North Vietnamese were constantly straining against the constraints of a cease-fire.

The debates over military options in Laos convinced Kennedy that in this particular case the risks attached to direct intervention were too high to justify any putative benefits. By emphasizing the likelihood of a major confrontation developing out of a comparatively modest intervention, the military succeeded in confirming the president's own fears about escalation. It was assumed that the local military advantages rested sufficiently with the communists, so that until the full weight of American military power could be brought to bear, any insertion of American forces could be trumped immediately. This gloomy prognosis was reinforced by the perceived hopelessness of the local Laotian force under Phoumi's command. No strategy could compensate for the chronic weaknesses of indigenous anticommunists. If this assumption could be generalized throughout Southeast Asia, then the American position had to be recognized as being irredeemably weak. American policy makers had accepted this with Laos; why might they think any different with South Vietnam?

33

Commitment without Combat

IF A STAND HAD TO BE TAKEN, then Vietnam did appear to be more promising than Laos. In geographical and political terms it seemed to be the key to the future of the cold war in Asia. William Sullivan later recalled how Vietnam had "logistical access to the sea and therefore we had military advantages. It was an articulated, functioning nation. Its troops were tigers and real fighters. And therefore the advantages would be all on our side to have the confrontation and showdown in Vietnam, and not get sucked into this Laos operation."[1] Furthermore, having been obliged to compromise with communists in Laos, the United States felt almost obliged to stand up to them in Vietnam. This was the most obvious example of Khrushchev's "wars of national liberation."[2]

After the Second World War the French had tried to hold on to Vietnam but failed in the face of a communist offensive that tapped nationalist, anticolonial sentiment. The United States provided political and material backing to the French, but no more. After French forces were defeated at Dien Bien Phu in early 1954 the Geneva conference divided Vietnam into two along the seventeenth parallel, with a communist government in the North and an anticommunist government in the South. In North Vietnam the communists under Ho Chi Minh were firmly in control; in the South Emperor Bao Dai had chosen Ngo Dinh Diem to be prime minister. Diem came from an old mandarin family. He was a devout Catholic and his nationalist credentials were impeccable. When he took over his strife-torn country it seemed beyond anyone to hold it together, battling against local religious sects, gangsterism, and networks of communist agents. By the end of 1955 he had pushed aside Bao Dai and had himself adopted as president. The next year he refused to implement the requirement in the Geneva accords for elections leading to unification, and he concentrated on using his autocratic powers to develop his country economically.

As early as 1951 Kennedy, on visiting Vietnam, had taken a realistic view of the long-term hopelessness of French colonial rule and the power of local nationalism. In 1956, as a senator, Kennedy had succumbed to the Diem myth, believing that this was a man who could combine nationalism with anticommunism and economic success. By this time, Diem's regime was becoming steadily more unpopular. He was from the Catholic minority (and had encouraged Catholics from the North to flee to the South to boost their numbers) and had come to rely excessively on his family when exerting his power. The more this was criticized, the more South Vietnam became a police state. Discontent among the political and military elite expressed itself in coups and assassination attempts, one of the most substantial of which took place in late 1960. The communists saw their opportunity. In May 1959 from the North's capital of Hanoi came the call for the unification of Vietnam through all "appropriate means." Guerrilla warfare techniques were used to undermine government control in the countryside. In December 1960, as Kennedy was preparing to enter the White House, the communists formed the National Liberation Front of South Vietnam—the Viet Cong.

ROSTOW AND COUNTERINSURGENCY

Although Rostow had done little detailed work on Southeast Asia, he had been assigned this brief as part of the division of responsibility within the National Security Council staff. It appealed to him as a potential test bed of theories of modernization, where strategies of counterinsurgency and of economic development could work hand in hand.

His own theory of counterinsurgency was quite distinctive. Mainstream theory started from the bottom up. As the conditions of everyday life deteriorated, the "insurgents" ingratiated themselves with the rural population and undermined the government. Rostow, however, started from the top down, seeing the insurgents as the carriers of a disease, an epidemic deliberately spread by Moscow and Beijing. This presumption of external instigation encouraged a focus on the means of infiltration, stressing guerrilla warfare as the current stage of a global communist offensive designed to exploit the universal urge to modernize. For this reason Rostow was always drawn to the big picture rather than the local detail. One critic claims that he was so certain of the common threat of an international contagion leaping across countries, or even continents, that "he flatly refused to listen to 'particularistic' briefings on countries like China or Vietnam and would send the briefer away as irrelevant."[3] Another notes how the influence of particular historical factors got played down, while Rostow's approach "reduced ethnic and cultural patterns to irrelevance." For this reason "it was tacitly dismissed by the career services of government as being of little practical value."[4] This may be so, but Rostow retained influence at the higher political level, and his theories led naturally to his active and eloquent support for policies that assumed that success required addressing an insurgency's external support as much as, if not more than, its internal roots.

So for Rostow the situation in South Vietnam appeared altogether more serious than one that could be addressed by better advice and training to the South Vietnamese. Political leverage depended on an evident willingness in the United States to use force. "The situation on the ground was so bad," he later commented, "that I didn't see how diplomacy, by itself, was going to work." As a result of these views there was an element of urgency in Rostow's view of the problem that drove him during 1961 to press hard for substantial action.

> Until 1961 I had never taken home a problem of public policy and worried about it, in the sense that it was on my mind when sleep got light. But I did worry about Vietnam—where it was hard to get people to understand how tough a well-advanced guerrilla war, with an open frontier is. My nightmare was . . . that we wouldn't deal with it early enough. Things would go very bad. Then we would have to deal with it convulsively, in a war. We would let the thing sag away from us into a mess where nothing short of a substantial war with Communist China would redress the balance. I had a sense that unless I could get people to understand it and face it early this might be the outcome. I wasn't afraid that we wouldn't fight to save Southeast Asia. I was sure we would. . . . But I was afraid that we would do so under certain circumstances that were too damned dangerous in a nuclear age and too costly.[5]

Rostow impressed on Kennedy the severity of the situation in Vietnam not long after the inauguration, even though Eisenhower had barely mentioned the problem in their preinauguration meeting.

BACKING DIEM

Contrary to Rostow's view, many of the South Vietnamese government's difficulties were a function more of its weak political base than of communist determination. Political stirrings in the South Vietnamese army led Diem to distrust any successful general. To the frustration of American advisers, the army appeared to be organized for every conceivable political purpose other than defeating the supposed enemy. The most fundamental question of all for the United States in its Vietnam policy was therefore whether it was worth supporting Diem. Answers varied. Some believed him to be a good leader who was following wise policies; others felt that he must be convinced to abandon an unwise course; yet others thought that he was unable to reform himself or his country and simply should be abandoned. Rostow was of the middle view. Though aware of the need for an improved military organization and political program and prepared to think through how to get these with a new leader should Diem be overthrown, he judged that the United States had "no alternative except to support Diem." The outcome of a succession crisis could not be predicted. The priority was to defeat communism rather than preserve a particular regime. But Diem had revealed that even client states were not as malleable as might be hoped. "We still have to find the technique for bringing our great bargaining power to bear on leaders of client states to do things they ought to do but don't want to do."[6]

As we have seen, to engage Kennedy's attention Rostow used the report prepared by Edward Lansdale based on his visit to Vietnam during the last weeks of the Eisenhower administration, just after the unsuccessful coup attempt against Diem. He urged an indifferent president to read it carefully as an excellent introduction to the developing crisis in Southeast Asia. Kennedy was impressed, commenting, "This is the worst one we've got, isn't it?"[7] Lansdale presented a bleak picture of an anticommunist government on the ropes, with the communists close to achieving their objective of taking the country over in 1961. If this disaster was to be avoided, then Diem needed firm material and political backing. He knew of Diem's unpopularity and poor strategy, yet Lansdale remained convinced that there was no alternative and that, with the right methods, Diem could be persuaded to adopt more sensible policies. The wrong method would be to lecture Diem without any sensitivity to Asian sensibilities. Where Lansdale differed with Rostow was in his stress on the insurgency in the South rather than a threat of an invasion from the North.

Lansdale's ideas for countering communism in Vietnam were as valid as any others being canvassed at the time, but they were contradicted by his commitment to Diem, who was never going to be ready to institute the necessary reforms. Lansdale believed, summing up the message of *The Ugly American*, that what Asians needed was the right sort of advice delivered by the right sort of Americans. There should be in Saigon a "hard core of experienced Americans who know and really like Asians, dedicated people who are willing to risk their lives for the ideals of freedom, and who will try and influence and guide the Vietnamese towards U.S. policy objectives with the warm friendship and affection which our close alliance deserves." Few doubted that Lansdale had anyone other than himself in mind.

The ploy almost worked. Kennedy could be easily impressed by tough-minded, charismatic men of action and was now positively disposed toward Lansdale, who was invited to join a meeting with the president and his top officials. Kennedy told Lansdale that he now had a "sense of the danger and urgency of the problem in Vietnam," and even impetuously offered him the Saigon embassy. Lansdale failed to accept at once, and the offer was later dropped as the general's accumulated bureaucratic enemies questioned his judgment.

Finding a home in the Pentagon with Roswell Gilpatric, Lansdale "set out on his own to educate the new team."[8] Though his influence was soon circumscribed, in these early days he was able to set the administration off on a particular course. This reflected less his infectious enthusiasm for taking on guerrillas, or his faith in civic action, than his utter conviction that they were consistent with fulsome support of Diem. Elbridge Durbrow, the U.S. ambassador to Saigon, was struck more by the Diem regime's repression, nepotism, and military incompetence. Durbrow appreciated the high stakes in Vietnam but saw little point in supporting Diem unless a serious effort was made to set in motion political change, and he was prepared to use Vietnam's dependence on American support as a lever to get Diem to do so. Unfortunately he received no support from Washington, and it became easy for Diem to dismiss him as an irritant.

This was at issue at the White House meeting on 28 January. Lansdale's briefing came after a lackluster presentation of a counterinsurgency plan prepared by the Saigon embassy. This involved a two-track combination of military aid with economic and political reform, but the compelling reasons for linking these two was not fully explored. When his turn came, Lansdale praised the American military assistance group in Saigon but damned the "Foreign Service people" as being defeatist and disinterested in the counterinsurgency task. Lansdale agreed that reforms were needed but suggested that Diem was unlikely to move in this direction so long as he was suspicious that the Americans favored those plotting coups against him. The president picked up on his concerns about Diem's morale and wondered whether a gesture of support from the new administration would help. Lansdale—and Rusk—agreed.[9]

After the meeting Lansdale wrote to Diem with a series of suggestions for improving his government and widening his political base.[10] Diem took the hint and announced in early February a series of modest reforms. These were sufficient to wrong-foot Durbrow, who was to retire as ambassador soon anyway. General McGarr, head of the military assistance group, began to implement the counterinsurgency program with no allowance for any pressure on Diem, who in April consolidated his position further with a somewhat dubious election victory won with 90 percent of the vote.

Just after this, on 12 April, Rostow was proposing actions to boost Diem further. Top priority was a "full time first-rate back-stop man in Washington," almost certainly a reference to Lansdale, and a visit to Saigon by the vice president. Only at the end of the list came a reference to the tactics to persuade Diem to broaden the base of his government. Here he suggested Kennedy write to Diem affirming American support but also making clear the urgency attached to "a more effective political and morale setting for his military operation." In the event, Kennedy's letter commended Diem for his "courageous leadership" but offered little advice on how best to govern his country.[11]

Durbrow's replacement as ambassador, Frederick "Fritz" Nolting, saw it as his task to repair relations with the regime, even if this meant not pushing Diem too hard on reform. Out of Saigon now came a tune of dogged optimism, to be sung with barely a change in lyrics or melody for the next two years. Nolting pronounced Diem "a man dedicated to high principles by himself and his people . . . I think the United States should have no hesitation on moral grounds in backing Diem to the hilt." The South Vietnamese president's egoism might have led to an over-concentration of power and authority, but "we can bring about amelio-rations and improvements gradually in proportion to the confidence which he has in us and in his ability to make concessions without slipping."[12]

Rather than worry about how to convince Diem to change, Kennedy accepted in the first months of his presidency that his main priority was to convince Diem that the United States was on his side. The South Vietnam leader questioned, on the basis of the treatment of anticom-munists in Laos, whether, when it came to the crunch, he would be backed by Washington. In May Vice President Lyndon Johnson went on his morale-boosting trip to Saigon. Though disconcerted by Diem and his entourage, Johnson concluded that there was no choice but to work with him, and so decided to dispel any doubts about American backing. LBJ hailed Diem as "the Winston Churchill of today" in the sort of casual endorsement that would have come naturally to a Democratic Party hope-ful in a congressional race but which gathered extra significance when proffered to a controversial Asian autocrat, especially one who saw no hyperbole in such comparisons. Kennedy was now stuck with Diem.

IN SEARCH OF A POLICY

If there was little choice but to work with the current government of South Vietnam, then the policy issues remaining were largely military in nature, concerned with helping Diem defeat the communists. Much of 1961 was taken up with Kennedy's attempt to discover how this should be done. He posed the question but never quite got the answer he wanted—a more efficient and focused counterinsurgency campaign that did not require large-scale intervention by American forces.

A task force was hurriedly established after a cabinet meeting on 20 April. It was led by Gilpatric, for whom Lansdale was the operations officer, and included Rostow. The "Program of Action to Prevent Com-munist Domination of South Vietnam" was presented to the president in draft form on 27 April. It was then redrafted before finally being reviewed by Kennedy on 11 May. Gilpatric considered it an inconclusive exercise, because of the need to put something together before the vice president went to Vietnam. By and large its emphasis was on nonmilitary activities, though it did call for an increase in U.S. advisers. According to Gilpatric, "even that small an increase was greeted by the President with a great deal of impatience."[13] Though small, the number was not insignificant. Under the 1954 Geneva accords the French had been allowed 685 military advisers, and while the Americans were not a party to the accords, they had taken over this allocation from the French and decided to stick to the ceiling. But as the North Vietnamese were believed to be violating the accords, Kennedy no longer felt bound by the treaty and so he ordered, in secret, 500 extra advisers.[14]

In early May Rostow raised the question of the conditions under which it would be wise to put American troops into Vietnam. He pushed hard for their use beyond improving the counterinsurgency effort, providing sufficient force on the ground to provide a "trip-wire," so that any attack upon them would trigger a much more substantial American involvement, and even dealing with an intervention by the Chinese. Then into the deliberations came the first positive proposal from the Joint Chiefs for the dispatch of combat troops to South Vietnam. This recommendation came on 10 May. The objective would be to deter the North Vietnamese and Chinese while impressing Asian nations generally with American resolve. The process would be to ask Diem to ask the United States to fulfil its SEATO obligations. However, despite the Joint Chiefs' predilection for intervening only if there was a readiness to accept the logic of a major war, they were not after a large-scale deployment. Only a nucleus would be required; it could be reinforced later.[15] Lansdale weighed in on the side of the Joint Chiefs in a memo to Gilpatric. These troops offered a symbol of national power. An enemy would be aware that in engaging these troops he would be engaging the whole strength of the United States.[16]

All these recommendations were shaped by the situation in Laos. The same set of people had been spending the first days in May considering a large-scale intervention in Laos, and it was not a great leap to start thinking about intervention in Vietnam, especially if the failure to act in the former had aggravated the problems of the latter. More specifically, the deliberations on Laos had focused attention on the North Vietnamese role, and it was to this that they were responding. In addition, they thought the refusal to act in Laos, combined with the irresolution demonstrated in the Bay of Pigs, required some visible demonstration of American will to reassure Diem. The president, however, had had enough of proposals for military intervention for the moment and was prepared only to allow the issue to be studied further. He wanted the focus kept on the counterinsurgency effort.[17] Yet despite Kennedy's refusal to countenance direct American military involvement, out of the NSC meeting of 11 May came NSAM 52, committing the United States to preventing communist domination in South Vietnam.

In Saigon the vice president asked Diem whether he wanted U.S. combat troops. No, replied Diem, that would be inappropriate, but more American troops in a training role, to help South Vietnam build up its army by another 100,000 men—that would be a different matter. At the time the South Vietnamese Army was 150,000 with support for another 20,000 under discussion with the United States. At Johnson's suggestion, Diem wrote two letters to Kennedy. The first, on 15 May, acknowledged Washington's interest in his country's predicament. The second, to follow, would provide more detail on what was needed.

When Johnson reported back to Kennedy he warned against the assumption that "because conditions have turned bad in Laos they must inevitably turn bad in Viet-Nam." He recognized the danger of a "progressive disintegration of the government's hold over the nation" and saw the risk of American support being used to "put down the Vietnamese people" as well as a Communist rebellion. Yet his principal conclusion was that there was no alternative to Diem. He needed to be persuaded— in a "sensitive" manner—to get closer to his people and to strengthen democratic institutions. As the United States had held back in Laos, the onus was now on it to reassure Saigon rather than the other way round.

But while Johnson saw a need for increased military and economic assistance, this had to be coupled with a clear, if private, understanding that

> barring an unmistakable and massive invasion of South Viet Nam from without we have no intention of employing combat U.S. forces in Viet Nam or using even naval or air-support which is but the first step in that direction.

Recalling the French inability to control the country with several hundred thousand men, he conjured up a specter of the Americans.

> bogged down chasing irregulars and guerrillas over the rice fields and jungles of Southeast Asia while our principal enemies China and the Soviet Union stand outside the fray and husband their strength.[18]

34

Deciding not to Decide

THE INITIAL POLICY DEBATE had served to narrow rather than extend the range of options. The basic dilemma of American policy was encapsulated rather than resolved by NSAM 52. Vietnam must not fall to the communists, but the administration was unprepared to move hard against Diem or introduce American forces in a combat role. For the moment there was little choice but to do more of the same, but how much more was undecided. From the middle of May, the Viet Cong began operating with greater numbers, frequency, and effectiveness. The continuing use of Laos as a communist supply route reduced Diem's chances of ever eliminating the communist threat. In March the Viet Cong had been estimated at around 9,000 fighters. By the end of June the estimate had moved up to 12,000, with as many as 15,000 troops from the North getting themselves in position in Laos.

ROSTOW AND TAYLOR

Rostow was especially concerned. Having been initially prepared to accept the problem in South Vietnam as one of improving counterinsurgency operations and encouraging Diem to broaden the base of his government, he was now convinced that its key lay in the changing regional and international environment. The growing Soviet campaign over Berlin led him to fear that the communists might be tempted to add to the pressure in Southeast Asia.

In March 1961, on his return from his first visit to Fort Bragg, convinced about the need to take on the communists at their own game, Rostow had urged that a way be found to "bring to bear our unexploited counter-guerrilla assets on the Vietnam problem." If capabilities were being developed, they should be used where they were needed. By the time of his next visit to Fort Bragg, in June 1961, his views had developed further. There he gave a speech, approved by Kennedy, designed to provide a rationale for the new thrust being given to special warfare.

He located the demands of guerrilla warfare in terms of the revolutionary process under way and the American objectives of allowing for a diverse and plural world of independent nations. Guerrilla warfare as practiced by communists was a "disease," for its origins lay outside the country in which it occurred. For this reason it was not simply a symptom of dissatisfaction with a particular government. With an external sanctuary it was very easy for a small band of men to impose a "terrible burden" on "any government in a society making its way toward modernization." Thus the sending of men and weapons across international boundaries was an act of aggression and should be treated as such. However, the methods of guerrilla warfare in themselves were not the preserve of communists. The American revolutionary war and the Peninsular campaign during the Napoleonic wars had their own examples. The challenge, Rostow therefore insisted, was to develop ways to deal with this form of warfare:

> [W]ith purposeful efforts most nations which might now be susceptible to guerrilla warfare could handle their border areas in ways which would make them very unattractive to the initiation of this ugly game. We can learn to prevent the emergence of the famous sea in which Mao Tse-Tung taught his men to swim. This requires, of course, not merely a proper military program of deterrence but programs of village development, communications, and indoctrination. The best way to fight a guerrilla war is to prevent it from happening. And this can be done.

This focus on political and economic reform, in addition to military action, was in line with mainstream counterinsurgency theory.

In Laos and South Vietnam what made the difference was the role of Hanoi, guiding guerrilla operations and inserting men and equipment. Without this "there was not the slightest reason to believe that the inherent strength of communism in either Laos or South Vietnam would lead to a communist takeover."[1] So though the general message of his speech stressed the importance of preventing situations reaching the point of a full-blown insurgency, in South Vietnam the requirement was already one of cure rather than prevention.

The Viet Cong had mounted an "unsubtle operation by the book, based more on murder than on political or psychological appeal." Their message was based on threats to those who failed to cooperate rather than on the benefits of communism. As only partial remedies could be found in the country itself, Vietnam required "the assumption of international responsibility for the frontier problem."[2] This was a reference to the negotiations then getting started in Geneva, through which the Americans hoped it would be possible to limit North Vietnam's use of Laos as a supply route to South Vietnam. Rostow later observed: "From beginning to end I regarded the closing of the Laos trails as the primary American interest in the Laos conference." An alternative was direct interference with the supply routes, but given "the nature of the terrain, the length of the frontiers and the low density of the traffic," any measures using ground or air forces would be costly. That left a third option: "direct attack on North Vietnam sufficiently costly to induce Hanoi to end its war against South Vietnam."

In the buildup to June's Vienna summit, Rostow had urged this line on the president, proposing that he warn Khrushchev that his "activities in Laos and South Vietnam, could lead to war."[3] Thereafter Rostow constantly highlighted the infiltration problem in Southeast Asia and urged Kennedy to threaten tough action if the communists did not desist. That June he also raised for the first time with Kennedy the possibility of air strikes against the North.[4] Kennedy showed no interest in such proposals. Nonetheless, Rostow persevered and was fortified that month by the acquisition of an important bureaucratic ally. General Maxwell Taylor, fresh from his Bay of Pigs inquiry, was the newest recruit to the White House inner circle. Following a "chance encounter with the President outside the door of his White House office," Taylor's first task was to review military planning in Vietnam. Kennedy had just received Diem's second letter. Along the lines discussed with Johnson, this referred to the deteriorating situation resulting from Laos and asked for American payment ($175 million) and training for extra Vietnamese troops (from 170,0000 to 270,000). Diem proposed that the training be done by "selected elements of the American armed forces." Kennedy asked Taylor to draft an appropriate response.[5]

TAKING ON HANOI

Taylor was of like mind to Rostow when it came to the conviction that Southeast Asia was of great importance in the overall Soviet scheme. Both were concerned that the current preoccupations with Berlin should not leave this region neglected. Both insisted on the need to think of diplomacy and armed force together rather than on separate tracks. Both saw Laos as the key to Vietnam. So long as the North was able to exploit the infiltration routes through Laos there were limits as to what could be done in South Vietnam. Unfortunately the situation in Laos was unlikely to convince allies (and in particular Britain) that dramatic action need be taken, and anyway SEATO Plan 5 (the most developed option in the event of a collapse in the cease-fire in Laos) would be an inappropriate response. The administration was still inclined to negotiate toward a neutral Laos as the least unpalatable of a bad set of options, but the American bargaining position was weak as military options in the event of the collapse of the negotiations were so unappealing. At the very least, therefore, the development of a more satisfactory military position was essential to strengthening the hand of the negotiating team.

The options appeared to be to find direct means of interdiction, in effect placing a substantial force in Laos to cut off the communist supply routes, or to implement a more coercive strategy directed against the North by means of either air attack or a land incursion into North Vietnam. The first of these options required the United States either to intervene directly or gather indigenous forces to take on the task. This made the second option look more attractive, though it would be a dramatic change of course and the political ground needed to be prepared.

During July Rostow worked with Taylor on these options. He wrote to Dean Rusk on 13 July, asking whether North Vietnam should be accused of aggression at the UN. This would "free our hands and our consciences for whatever we have to do," that is, create the pretext for action to "radically reduce the external component in Diem's guerrilla war." What about a "counter-guerrilla operation" in the North, which might use American air and naval strength "to impose about the same level of damage and inconvenience that the Viet Cong are imposing in the south"? If Northern troops crossed the border in numbers, why not retaliate with a comparable operation in the North, for example, "capture and holding of the port of Haiphong"?

> Behind all this is a view, which I believe Alexis Johnson shares, that we are unlikely to be able to negotiate anything like a satisfactory Laos settlement unless the other side believes that we are prepared, as an alternative to a satisfactory settlement, to fight. My anxiety has been that our present military plan, focussed on the Mekong valley (which I assume the other side knows) might not be an effective and persuasive deterrent. I would assume that a posture aimed more directly against North Viet Nam is more likely to be diplomatically persuasive.[6]

Thus, for the moment, Rostow's ideas were largely framed in terms of a proportionate response and deterrence.

On 18 July Taylor met with Alexis Johnson, whom he had known since they had been together in prewar Japan, and Rostow to develop the "diplomatic foundation" for military action against the North by means of more evidence of actual North Vietnamese aggression. The next day William Bundy, assistant secretary for international security affairs at the Pentagon, asked Lemnitzer to evaluate reprisal measures that might be taken against the North, including maritime measures "up to and including blockade" and "degrees of interdiction-type air and sea patrols." In the event of increased guerrilla activity, these "air and naval operations against North Viet Nam would be, in a sense, our equivalent." Again, the concept was one of proportionate response. Taylor, along with the Joint Chiefs, focused on the infiltration problem and thought less in terms of proportionate response than in orthodox military terms. The outcome was similar: a requirement for air attacks and even the development of guerrilla operations against north Laos and North Vietnam. On 26 July Taylor told the president that his first priority would be a secure base in the south of Laos to cover the South Vietnamese flank and provide a base for direct operations against North Vietnam.[7]

Rostow had sent Kennedy a memorandum on 21 July that had come back with presidential handwriting scrawled on top: "too difficult to read." In the revised version he claimed that "a crucial determinant" of the American bargaining position over Laos will be "Khrushchev's view of our military contingency plan in Southeast Asia." Rostow presented direct attacks on the North as an alternative to more orthodox military operations by raising the possibility of revising military contingency planning so as to put a "lighter weight in the Mekong Valley and a greater direct threat to North Viet-Nam."[8]

KENNEDY DECIDES NOT TO DECIDE

This concerted push to take the war to the North might have been expected to find favor with Kennedy if, as has been suggested, he returned from the Vienna summit persuaded to take a hard line on Vietnam. The best evidence for this is his comment to columnist James Reston just after Vienna: "Now we have a problem in making our power credible, and Vietnam looks the place."[9] Certainly he received arguments that difficulties in Berlin reinforced the case to make a firm stand in Vietnam, and he was well aware of the political consequences of anything that could be presented as a "retreat" in Vietnam.[10]

Yet with the Berlin crisis coming to a boil and a serious prospect of a major European war, Kennedy was unlikely to want to open up yet another front. Indeed, the more hawkish of Kennedy's advisers were concerned that Berlin was distracting attention from Southeast Asia. As a practical matter, Berlin closed off the more ambitious military options, at least until army strength had been built up to cope with a number of simultaneous crises. Kennedy made clear at the end of August that he did not want a Southeast Asian crisis "at the height of the Berlin crisis," and suspected that Khrushchev felt the same way.[11]

Rather than embrace the hawks' campaign for escalation over Vietnam, the president stopped it in its tracks during a policy review on 28 July when he met with senior State Department and White House staff. In preparation for this meeting Taylor and Rostow came together again in a joint memo to press their case for an integrated approach, looking at the region as a whole and bringing the political and military tracks in line with each other. The policy choices they put as graceful disengagement, finding a "convenient political pretext" to attack "the regional source of aggression in Hanoi," or else a buildup of indigenous military, political, and economic strength to contain the thrust from Hanoi while preparing for intervention if the situation got worse or the Chinese intervened. They assumed, correctly, that the administration's policy was the third, but given the proposition that on current policies Laos and South Vietnam could be lost to communism, their preference was clear enough.[12]

A State Department memorandum, influenced by Alexis Johnson and reflecting the Taylor-Rostow line, asserted that the consensus was to ensure the security of the whole area against further communist encroachments, and to resist this if necessary by "appropriate military means." This included covert action to "interdict" North Vietnamese pressure on South Vietnam. If "these contacts do not prove successful," then there would need to be an "overt indication that the continuation of overt DRV aggressive policy against Laos and Viet-Nam may result in direct retaliatory action against her."[13]

As Kennedy interrogated his advisors on these radical options, it became apparent that the "detailed aspects of this military plan had not been developed," nor was it clear "how great an effect action against Haiphong or Hanoi would have on North Vietnam." Kennedy stressed the importance of "realism and accuracy in such military planning" and observed that optimism with regard to military plans in Laos had been "invariably proven false in the event." He emphasized "the reluctance of the American people and of many distinguished military leaders to see any direct involvement of U.S. troops in that part of the world." When told that this time it would be different, with a proper plan and a clear American commitment, he reported President de Gaulle's view (acquired during his visit in early June), based on "painful French experience," of the "difficulty of fighting in this part of the world."

Alexis Johnson pressed Kennedy for a "willingness to decide to intervene if the situation seemed to him to require it." He got no decision. Kennedy repeated his preference for negotiations in Laos. Nothing would be worse, he observed, than "an unsuccessful intervention in this area." He lacked "confidence in the military practicability of the proposal which had been put before him."[14] In addition to de Gaulle, Kennedy had also been influenced by a conversation on 20 July with General Douglas MacArthur, Truman's nemesis in Korea, who now strongly advised the president against sending ground forces to Vietnam, essentially because the communists were expert in guerrilla warfare and the Americans were not.

So for the moment any increased military activity would depend on local forces. The initial response to Diem's request for support to increase his army by 100,000 was to offer a 30,000-man increase, but only once the established target of 170,000 had been reached. All this would take well into 1962. In discussion of these numbers the main issue considered was not the radical step of taking the war to the communists but the more defensive question of whether Diem needed extra forces to cope with the insurgency or else prepare for a direct push from the North. When Kennedy wrote to Diem on 5 August he made the extra support contingent upon an agreement on a strategic plan to deal with Viet Cong subversion and to use the new troops effectively for that purpose.[15]

Rostow summed up for Kennedy what he understood to be the president's position:

> [Y]ou would wish to see every avenue of diplomacy exhausted before we accept the necessity for either positioning U.S. forces on the Southeast Asian mainland or fighting there; you would wish to see the possibilities of economic assistance fully exploited to strengthen the Southeast Asian position; you would wish to see indigenous forces used to the maximum if fighting should occur; and that, should we have to fight, we should use air and sea power to the maximum and engage minimum U.S. forces on the Southeast Asian mainland.[16]

This hardly suggested a president aching for an excuse to prove himself and American resolve by taking the war to the communists in Vietnam.

THE PRESSURE CONTINUES

Despite having indicated his extreme caution, Kennedy had not stifled the pressure for stronger action. He was prepared to have the plans studied and the situation on the ground investigated. Here began a pattern of his presidency. Uncomfortable with the quality of the information he was receiving from the U.S. mission in Saigon, he continued to believe that a visit by senior advisers would enable him to get a more accurate fix on the situation. So in the meeting on 28 July he accepted the case for sending Taylor to South Vietnam to assess the military situation, a proposal made by Rostow in his memo of the two days before.[17] Both advisers "literally jumped at this opportunity," and within two days they had come up with the sort of questions that needed addressing. They also felt that American thinking needed to be developed further. A visit in August would be premature; better to wait until the rainy season was over.[18]

Meanwhile they kept up their clamor to get the president to accept that lines must be drawn somewhere, that there must be a point when communist aggression against Southeast Asia prompted a military response. Given that the president was unlikely to back an abrupt escalation by an immediate strike against Hanoi, Rostow formulated an early version of a graduated strategy:

> This graduated pressure could take the form of air strikes against the land lines of communications and supply centers, and sea interdiction of logistical traffic along the east coast of Viet-Nam. It could also include a naval blockade in the Gulf of Tonkin to isolate the Port of Haiphong. The interdiction operation would be susceptible to flexible control at all times to meet a changing military and political situation.

Beyond this Rostow believed that a naval and air plan would be needed to deal with Chinese intervention. This would require "a definition of the nuclear threshold." He remained convinced that the current main plan—SEATO Plan 5—was too inflexible, especially as a renewed Pathet Lao offensive would probably lead to intervention by the North Vietnamese and even possibly by the Chinese. The best deterrent would be a clear signal, through military deployments, that an enlarged battle would involve North Vietnam directly. If military action was required against the North (for which a spectrum of capabilities would be required), it would "be merely a sanction designed to force a negotiation."[19]

The Joint Chiefs were also keeping up the pressure. On 10 August the president was briefed by General Lemnitzer on SEATO Plan 5. The general also now had an alternative plan that would involve SEATO countries working with Thai and Vietnamese units to conduct a wide range of operations against northern Laos, North Vietnam, and southern China. A third, but still underdeveloped, option would concentrate on pushing communists out of southern Laos, and if possible securing the Mekong Valley as a way of protecting South Vietnam against infiltration. This latter option was supported by the Vietnam Task Force and was backed by Taylor in a memorandum to Kennedy on 11 August. Rostow remained unconvinced, because of the sheer size of the operation required. He was concerned that his own pet project—a "spectrum of measures designed to put increasing pressure on the Vietminh"—had been insufficiently studied, especially in terms of their link to a political framework.[20]

As the pressure mounted again on the president, with the issue coming to a head in Washington, Rostow, to his frustration, was about to leave for a vacation. Urged on by Taylor, and supported by Alexis Johnson, he sent a memorandum to Kennedy. He took care to copy it to the president's brother, who was now clearly growing in influence over foreign affairs and was a great fan of Taylor's.[21] Here again Rostow acknowledged that Kennedy was unwilling to contemplate new military plans that did not place primary reliance on indigenous forces.[22] Unfortunately, he warned, sufficient indigenous forces were probably not available: Diem's forces were already stretched, Phoumi's were inept, and the Thais would not move except with substantial support. The major plan available— SEATO Plan 5—could not work without large-scale American involvement, and would only get the involvement of the other major allies, and in particular the British, in the event of a crude break in the Laos ceasefire. For more ambiguous situations there was little agreed.[23] Again he posed the problem in terms of proportionate response—to get into a position to "mobilize outside forces for whatever level of military activity the other side imposed upon us." By preparing in this way, the seriousness of the American commitment would be communicated to both the communists and the allies (such as the Thais) before it became necessary to dispatch large numbers of American troops to the area.[24]

Rostow was still searching for a flexible option, capable of impressing the communists while respecting the president's determination to avoid large-scale use of American forces. At the same time Taylor was focusing on how best to control disputed and strategically important territory in Laos. His approach involved encouraging the local countries to form a common front against North Vietnam, if necessary preparing for operations against the North—Thais in the air and the South Vietnamese on land. To make all this work, the United States should develop a sense of the "upper and lower limits" of its military involvement.[25]

The weight of senior administration opinion worked against these ambitious plans. On 24 August, when the Southeast Asia Task Force met, Averell Harriman ensured that he continued to get support for his negotiating efforts over Laos. He was dismissive of the basis for any military action in Laos. The tabled plan, reflecting Rostow's ideas, was attacked by Harriman and McNamara and even Rusk (though it emanated from his department). Taylor attempted a defense but failed. The task force was told to emphasize the determination to get a settlement in Laos and only suggest military options to cope with a negotiating failure.[26]

By now the Berlin situation was hot, and on 13 August the city was divided. Some two weeks later, on 29 August, the president did meet with his senior officials to discuss the situation in Southeast Asia, but there was great wariness about stepping up a military commitment while things were so uncertain in Europe. Rusk and McNamara agreed that "the Berlin situation would preclude military action in Laos." Now that the United States was contemplating sending six divisions to Europe, it would be impossible to fight a war in Southeast Asia at the same time without general mobilization. Even the initial deployment of 13,000 American troops required under SEATO Plan 5, should a breakdown in negotiations require a sudden show of American force, would cause strains. McNamara remained worried that the Soviets might even try to up the ante in Asia to drain U.S. naval and air assets away from Europe, where they might be sorely needed. It was difficult to encourage allies to prepare for any expanded effort, for there could be no guarantee that the Americans would be able to provide full support.[27] The options within Laos therefore remained unimpressive. For the moment Southeast Asia was a lower priority than Europe.

35

The Taylor Report

THROUGH THE SUMMER REPORTS issuing from Saigon were generally optimistic. Diem had done nothing to strengthen his political position, but
his forces were apparently holding their own even if they were not exactly
winning. He did not seem keen for the American military presence to
become too prominent, aware that this might offend nationalists and afford extra opportunities to the Americans should they try to displace him.
Then in September the situation began to deteriorate. A series of Viet
Cong actions, some close to Saigon, set the alarm bells ringing in Washington. Diem did not start asking for American troops, but he did ask for
a treaty with the United States as a means of demonstrating confidence
in his regime.

At the start of October Rostow warned the president:

> For us the gut issue as I see it is this: We are deeply committed in Viet-
> Nam: if the situation deteriorates, we will have to go in; the situation is, in
> fact, actively deteriorating; if we go in now, the costs—human and other-
> wise—are likely to be less . . . but whatever you decide next week, I come
> back to my old pitch: it is essential that Generals Taylor and Lansdale take
> a good, hard look at Viet-Nam on the ground, soon.[1]

In July Kennedy had already decided in principle to send Taylor, so he
needed little encouragement to confirm the decision. The trip was announced on 13 October. What Kennedy expected from the trip was revealed in a story that he apparently planted in the *New York Times* the
day after the announcement. This suggested that Taylor was not keen on
the use of U.S. troops and preferred that combat units should be provided
by affected countries. As this leak followed indications from Saigon that
Diem had become interested in having American combat units, it had the

effect of warning him not to push the case too publicly. A cable from Lemnitzer to Admiral Felt (commander in chief, Pacific) indicated Kennedy's concern that there was too much emphasis on the possibility of combat troops, leading to a possible letdown in Vietnamese morale if the United States decided against this.[2]

Rostow was soon attached to Taylor's entourage, but there was no figure of equivalent seniority from the State Department. Though sending two known hawks could be taken to imply that the president wanted and expected a hawkish conclusion, and it certainly precluded a more dovish one, a more prosaic argument is simply that these were the two responsible members of his own staff.[3] If he expected a particular conclusion, it may have had something to do with counterinsurgency, as Rostow had been associated with this issue from the start and it was one of Taylor's main responsibilities. He asked them to "consider what could be accomplished by the introduction of SEATO or United States forces into South Vietnam" but also how the effectiveness of South Vietnamese forces could be rendered more efficient. Rusk accepted that the mission was largely to assess the military rather than political situation and was happy for Taylor to do this.[4] Rostow might have been expected to provide a political evaluation, but he was mainly preoccupied with infiltration routes. Lansdale, who had been kept out of Vietnam policy making since the spring through the combined efforts of the State Department and the Joint Chiefs, was on the team. He had the contacts, not least with Diem, to explore the political scene in Saigon, but he and Taylor had little rapport.[5] Taylor saw Lansdale as an idea man—but the ideas were not very good. "He could turn out ideas faster than you could pick them up off the floor, but I was never impressed with their feasibility."[6]

The group left on 17 October and returned at the end of the month. The full report complete with annexes was passed to the president on 3 November.[7] This was understood by all concerned to be a critical moment in decision making, the point at which policy was to be set. An intense debate within the administration, covering all options, had already begun and was concluded only when decisions were taken on 14 November. Even then some issues continued to be debated.

One of the few matters not in contention was the commitment to South Vietnam. Taylor's report set the tone:

> From all quarters in Southeast Asia the message on Vietnam is the same; vigorous American action is needed to buy time for Vietnam to mobilize and organize its real assets; but the time for such a turn around has nearly run out. And if Vietnam goes, it will be exceedingly difficult if not impossible to hold Southeast Asia. What will be lost is not merely a crucial piece of real estate, but the faith that the U.S. has the will and the capacity to deal with the Communist offensive in that area.

THE PROBLEM

The report's analysis of the threat to South Vietnam was pure Rostow. It spoke of a "communist strategy" rather than a North Vietnamese strategy, implicating the Soviet Union and China in a unified campaign of subversion. (The lack of interest in the possible implications of the Sino-Soviet split was striking.)[8] This strategy was unusually tricky because it relied on sending guerrillas rather than regular armies across borders to avoid being labeled aggressive according to international law and practice. Its origins could be traced to Mao's three-stage offensive, which started with creating the political base before moving on to the second phase of actual guerrilla warfare, in preparation for the third and final phase of overt conventional warfare.[9] It was only, Taylor and Rostow suggested, the prospect of U.S. intervention that was deterring a move to this third phase. This meant that while attacks on South Vietnamese military units and government officials served to create a pervasive sense of ungovernability, insecurity, and frustration, disaffection with Diem was being used to create a political crisis and so discourage the United States from getting involved.

Unlike the Viet Minh war against the French, the report claimed, and contrary to other informed analyses of the time, the communists could no longer carry persuasively the nationalist banner and were overly reliant on terror. Positive support for the communists was said to be barely a couple of percent of the population. Yet at the same time the deficiencies at all levels of the Diem regime were acknowledged. One explanation for the poor attitude in Saigon was uncertainty over American intentions, the idea that a new initiative by Washington could boost morale to the point where it could overcome these other deficiencies became a familiar refrain over the coming years.

To Rostow it was the nature of infiltration that distinguished Vietnam from the successful campaigns in the Philippines (an island) and Malaya (a peninsula with a narrow neck).[10] Though the infiltration problem into South Vietnam through Laos was at the heart of the analysis, the report disclaimed precise knowledge of the forces being infiltrated and even observed that Hanoi's need to conceal its role imposed important limitations on what it could achieve. This was a matter on which Rostow resolutely refused to entertain contrary views. "We delude ourselves," observed the State Department's William Jordan in September, "if we visualize the Viet Cong effort in the South as primarily a movement of large, organized units across the GVN [Government of Vietnam] border." Although sent to gather evidence of infiltration he stressed the importance of local recruitment "both by persuasion and by terror." Nonetheless, Rostow believed that Jordan's report could be used to accuse North Vietnam of aggression in the United Nations. A National Intelligence Estimate of 5 October reported that 80 to 90 percent of the estimated 17,000 Viet Cong had been recruited locally and there was little evidence that they relied on external supplies.[11] McGarr reported to Lemnitzer at this time, and so presumably briefed Taylor and Rostow, that rather than a tiny minority, 25 percent of the South's population actively assisted the Viet Cong, with another 25 percent sitting on the fence.[12]

A 1961 RAND study of Viet Cong tactics addressed this issue head on. It noted that the "so-called Ho Chi Minh Trail" was no more than paths running through the mountains, unsuitable for large arms shipments. The weapons captured from the communists were either home-made or captured, sometimes in operations designed to acquire equipment from the Vietnamese army. The North might provide a limited amount of specialist equipment, but its basic role was in providing guidance, training, and moral support. The basic problem was that the "Communists are arousing the people to fight and work for them." They did not just rely on terror. The conclusion: Until Diem's government "has the active and continuing support of the Vietnamese masses and the troops, all the economic and military aid in the world, though it may delay it, will not halt the Communist advance."[13] The Taylor-Rostow report gave every impression of confirming the established prejudices of its authors rather than drawing on the best available advice to form a fresh opinion.

POLITICAL OPTIONS

The two did not attempt to come up with a remedy to the Diem problem. During the trip they received plenty of evidence of discontent with the regime. Diem added his contribution by declaring a national emergency just before the team arrived. His scant interest in changing the character of his government and his limited grasp of his domestic predicament were evident in formal meetings. Even Lansdale, who had been called in especially by Diem for a consultation and remained loyal to his old friend, noted the corrosive influence of Diem's brother Nhu, to whom increasing power had been given after the 1960 coup attempt.[14]

The team considered but rejected the "removal" of Diem. It would be both dangerous and unnecessary, as the administrative weaknesses could not be overcome. William Jordan agreed that it would be unwise to attempt to engineer a coup ("not something we do well"), though he still felt that the pressures for change were reaching "explosion point." His solution was to identify "with the people of Viet Nam and with their aspirations" rather than with Diem and "to press for measures that are both efficient and more democratic." "We must suggest, not demand; we must advise not dictate; but we must not hesitate to stand for the things that we and the Vietnamese know to be worthwhile and just in the conduct of political affairs."[15]

This in itself would have been an important shift in policy. Up to this point, as Robert Johnson of the NSC staff acknowledged, the policy was to make "at least one more effort to do the job with Diem." This had meant letting up "somewhat on continuous haggling over reforms." He hoped "that we will now condition our military intervention (if it occurs) on real performance on a whole series of reforms designed primarily to make the governmental operations—including military operations— more efficient." As the administration considered Taylor's report Ambassador Nolting was asked for his views on getting Diem to accept as a quid quo pro some delegation of authority to the Americans. "Feeling is strong," he was told, "that major changes will be required if joint effort is to be successful in that U.S. cannot be asked further to engage its prestige and forces while machinery of Diem government remains inadequate." The ambassador soon dampened any hopes that anything would be agreed to willingly by Diem, and certainly not measures that would "be interpreted by him and by most Vietnamese as handing over Govt of SVN to U.S."[16]

The Americans were left dependent upon Diem for their position in Vietnam yet aware that this was a fragile base for their efforts. Taylor described how the Americans should be "a limited partner in the war, avoiding formalized advice on the one hand, trying to run the war, on the other." The language obscured the problem. If the Americans were to be the senior partner, they would in effect have become a colonial power; as the junior partner, they tied their commitment to an unstable autocrat; an equal partnership was a recipe for constant attempts at mutual manipulation. In the event, Diem's refusal to permit the development of an authentic Vietnamese opposition meant that the main noncommunist challenge to Diem's power would come from American advisers and the reporters who would follow them.

MILITARY OPTIONS

In his memo of 5 October Rostow had proposed a 25,000-man SEATO border patrol force in Vietnam. He saw the advantages of this in political as much as military terms. It would bolster Diem while giving the United States more leverage over the South's military efforts, restrain the North Vietnamese, and provide a bargaining chip in any negotiations.[17] The Joint Chiefs were unimpressed. The proposal lacked feasibility. They stuck to the position they had been holding for some time: the implementation of SEATO Plan 5 in a "concentrated effort" in Laos. The plan would be to base forces just within Vietnam so as to be able to respond with force against the North Vietnamese should they intervene in South Vietnam or Laos. An overt North Vietnamese intervention would require 200,000 SEATO troops, to be raised to almost 280,000 if the Chinese got involved. Should this happen, consideration would have to be given to "whether to attack selected targets in North China with conventional weapons and whether to initiate use of nuclear weapons against targets in direct support of Chinese operations in Laos." Recognizing that such a plan was unlikely to be followed, they allowed for an interim plan that would have the Americans relieving units of the South Vietnamese Army to enable them to take offensive actions against the Viet Cong.[18]

On 11 October, prior to the visit to Vietnam, Kennedy met with the team leaders. Alexis Johnson had prepared a paper cobbling together Rostow's concept and the Joint Chiefs' interim proposal. The paper suggested a force of 20,000 troops based at Pleiku, perhaps to be doubled in the event of an effort to "clean up the Viet Cong threat," and even more if the Chinese got involved. Everything depended upon whether the extra American contribution would lead "to much more and better fighting by Diem's forces." The political advantages would be felt in bargaining with Moscow and Hanoi, and a stronger Saigon, but the plan would not actually solve the problem of the guerrillas within South Vietnam and provided no response to smaller-scale communist operations.[19]

Most of the options for a stepped-up American military effort had come from the White House and the Pentagon rather than the responsible commanders close to the South Vietnamese situation. Admiral Felt for example, provided Washington with a carefully argued case against sending combat troops after he had spoken to Taylor, en route to Saigon, in Hawaii. He saw the propaganda advantages it would give the communists, the tempting targets they would be offered, and the likelihood that the Americans would get steadily drawn into the fighting.[20] Yet Taylor later stated that it was the views of the military closest to the situation that persuaded him, against what he knew to be Kennedy's wishes, to recommend getting American forces to Vietnam soon.[21] It is not even clear that Diem wanted an American military presence. The idea that one might be useful appears to have been pressed on him by Taylor.

On the basis of his visit, Taylor proposed a military commitment of some 6,000–8,000 troops, some logistical and some combat, to be sent initially under the guise of assisting with recovery from a serious but not abnormal flood that had covered much of the Mekong Delta that year.[22] This token force was recognized to have only a limited military potential but could be seen as the basis of something bigger—inevitably so, given that stopping infiltration and clearing up the guerrilla war posed potentially limitless demands. Introducing the report, Taylor indicated just how far it might be necessary to go:

[I]t is clear to me that the time may come in our relations to Southeast Asia when we must declare our intention to attack the source of guerrilla ag-

gression in North Vietnam and impose on the Hanoi Government a price
for participating in the current war which is commensurate with the damage
being inflicted on its neighbors to the south.

On Taylor's return to Washington the idea of the flood relief was widely
derided as being half-baked: neither one thing nor the other. If the commitment was to be wholehearted—McNamara drew the parallels with
Berlin—then the United States would have to be prepared for a major
investment, and Taylor's scheme, by linking troops to the immediate
problem of flood damage, would in fact detract from that commitment.
This pretext for going in would provide one for getting out, especially if
the military position got rougher. This would not send the right signals
to the rest of Southeast Asia.

At this stage McNamara was impressed by the argument that if Vietnamese forces were satisfactory, then there was no need for American
forces, but if they were not, it was doubtful whether the United States
could do the job in the face of an apathetic and hostile population. The
State Department also tended in this direction. They wanted to see a
better performance from the South Vietnamese and were concerned
about American forces becoming directly involved in combat. NSC staff
member Robert Komer took a more fatalistic view: "I'm no happier than
anyone about getting involved in a squalid, secondary theater in Asia. But
we'll end up doing so sooner or later anyway because we won't be willing
to accept another defeat. If so, the real question is not whether but how
soon and how much."[23]

Rostow had never shirked from this prospect. En route to Saigon he
suggested to Taylor that a plan for "limited but systematic harassment by
U.S. naval and air power of North Viet-Nam" be prepared. The idea was
that if the communists targeted America's "main weakness," Diem, the
United States would target the communists' main weakness, the "vulnerability of the Hanoi-Haiphong complex," using their main strength of
naval and air power. He was aware of the problems of legitimacy and
escalation, but all measures that might "save" South Vietnam carried such
risks and "this form of graduated air-naval harassment would be a real
puzzler for them."[24] "Rostow argued so forcibly for a contingency policy
of retaliation against the North, graduated to match the intensity of Hanoi's support of the Viet Cong," recalled Schlesinger, "that 'Rostow Plan
6' became jocularly established in the contingency planning somewhere
after SEATO Plan 5."[25] Kennedy referred to him as the "Air Marshal."

Already there was a tension developing between the proposal that air
strikes serve as a means of dealing with the problem of infiltration and
the idea that they should be a means of coercing the North. One reason
Taylor could dismiss the risks of "backing into a major Asian war" by
way of South Vietnam was that the North's vulnerability to "conventional
bombing" could be "exploited diplomatically in convincing Hanoi to lay

off SVN." He claimed that "nothing is more calculated to sober the enemy and to discourage escalation . . . than the knowledge that the United States has prepared itself soundly to deal with aggression at any level."[26] Yet intelligence estimates warned that Americans actions would simply produce counters from the communists. Stepped-up American support for Diem would lead to more supplies for the Viet Cong. This would probably not be stopped by a bombing campaign against the North, but if there was one, it would lead to a strong response from the Soviet Union and China, who could not allow their ally to fall.[27]

36

Decisions

IF THE TAYLOR-ROSTOW REPORT had been intended to galvanize the American government into action, initially it seemed to have succeeded. Momentum was building up behind a step change in the character of the American contribution to the South's war effort. On 8 November McNamara, Gilpatric, and the Joint Chiefs told Kennedy that they were "inclined to recommend that we do commit the U.S. to the clear objective of preventing the fall of South Vietnam to Communism and that we support this commitment by the necessary military actions." These would go beyond the tentative first steps proposed by Taylor. The flood relief force would not convince the enemy that "we mean business."[1]

According to McNamara, almost as soon as he sent the memo he started to worry that "we had been too hasty in our advice to the President." "For the next couple of days, I dug deeper into the Vietnam problem. The more I probed, the more the complexity of the situation and the uncertainties of our ability to deal with it by military means became apparent. I realized that seconding the Taylor-Rostow memo had been a bad idea."[2]

As the State Department was then inclined to postpone any firm decision, McNamara combined with Rusk, but not the Joint Chiefs, to argue for a firm commitment with the possibility of combat forces but an initial focus on bolstering the capacity of the South Vietnamese government to fight its own war. They commented on the hopelessness of Diem's situation if "the flow of men and supplies from North Viet-Nam continues unchecked and the guerrillas enjoy a safe sanctuary in neighboring territory," and so did not preclude U.S. forces striking "at the source of the aggression in North Viet-Nam." At the same time they saw some possibilities in building upon any settlement in Laos to ensure that its territory was not used for the transport of forces from North to South Vietnam. Most important, as a settlement at this point hung in the balance, it was unwise to do anything for the moment that would stimulate "a communist breach of the cease-fire and a resumption of hostilities in Laos." Once an agreement was reached, then U.S. forces might go to Vietnam to register American determination that any agreements be honored, and an approach could be made to Moscow to warn that it was unacceptable for communists to move men and supplies into South Vietnam.[3]

Having been in the discussion of a draft version of this second memo on 9 November, Rostow submitted his own memo to arrive at the same time, challenging the recommendation to stop short of sending combat troops. The coming decision would signal American intentions and could influence future communist decisions on infiltration and the Laos negotiations. He regarded the State Department view that U.S. actions should be inhibited "for fear of enemy escalation" as dangerous. Kennedy pointedly responded by asking Rostow to read again the latest National Intelligence Estimate on "Probable Communist Reactions to Certain U.S. Actions in South Viet-Nam," which had warned of the communist ability to up the ante further at each level of American action. Rostow stuck to his position that the communists did not want to take on American military strength, and that China would be reluctant to go to war with the United States at this time.[4]

Kennedy, by contrast, took the notion of escalation very seriously. This is reflected in reported conversations from this period. On 7 November George Ball, then undersecretary of state for economic affairs, told Kennedy that he opposed sending troops to Vietnam, warning on the basis of the French experience of "three hundred thousand men in the paddies and jungles" in five years. Ball was surprised at the "overtone of asperity" in Kennedy's response: "George, I always thought you were one of the brightest guys in town, but you're just crazier than hell. That just isn't going to happen."[5] Ball himself was uncertain whether the president was making a prediction that events would not follow this line or that he would not let such a situation develop.[6]

The second construction was correct. Kennedy was well aware of the pressures that would follow any initial commitment of troops either to boost the morale of the South or to cut off infiltration routes from the North. On the first, he told Schlesinger as the Taylor report was being discussed:

> They want a force of American troops. They say its necessary to restore confidence and maintain morale. But it will be just like Berlin. The troops will march in; the bands will play; the crowds will cheer; and in four days everyone will have forgotten. Then we will be told we have to send in more troops. It's like taking a drink. The effect wears off, and you have to take another.[7]

On the second, he told Hilsman in early 1962:

> No matter what goes wrong, or whose fault it really is, the argument will
> be that the Communists have stepped up their infiltration and we can't win
> unless we hit the north. Those trails are a built-in excuse for failure, and a
> built-in argument for escalation.[8]

Kennedy was also aware of the need to sell any policy to Congress and
the American people. He was well aware of the limited appetite for a
major commitment to Vietnam in Democratic Party circles, made clear
by such influential figures as Senators Mansfield and Russell. Having
spent much of the year coping with the surge of tension surrounding
Berlin, he was reluctant to add yet another crisis on the other side of the
world. In addition, the Vietnamese problem had some specific features
that would make it difficult to make the case for the dispatch of troops
in a combat role. The most obvious was the poor image of President
Diem and his regime. This was not a cause to stir American hearts. A
lesser problem, but relevant to any attempt to bring allies and neutrals
on board, or at least keep them quiet, was the doubtful legality of inserting
American personnel on a large scale in the light of the 1954 Geneva
accords. The State Department had been gathering evidence of North
Vietnamese breaches of these agreements to present to the International
Control Commission monitoring the accords. Kennedy saw this evidence
(which was less than compelling) and its publication as vital to an effort
to justify any future American breaches.

   The first review of the options, on 11 November 1961, was inconclusive. Kennedy's drift was clear and his staff was getting restless. McGeorge
Bundy pressed for an early statement on his readiness to send limited
combat units as a means of sending a clear signal to the belligerents; "the
odds are almost even that the commitment will not have to be carried
out."

> This conclusion is, I believe, the inner conviction of your Vice President,
> your Secretaries of State and Defense, and the two heads of your special
> mission, and that is why I am troubled by your natural desire to act on
> other items now, without taking the troop decision.

On the morning of 15 November the NSC met to discuss a draft National
Security Action Memorandum. This proposed that the Pentagon develop
plans for the use of American forces to defend South Vietnam and boost
its morale, assist in counterinsurgency operations, and prepare to deal
with a full communist military intervention. It also approved a set of
immediate actions to provide additional logistical and material support to
Vietnamese forces, as well as training, high-level advice, and economic
assistance, with some provision for participation in the government machinery. At the meeting Kennedy made as formidable a case against the

dispatch of American combat troops to Vietnam as can be found in any of the memos and reports circulating at the time.[9]

The problem was not only his fear of becoming involved simultaneously on two fronts on opposite sides of the world but the lack of a clear basis upon which to justify involvement in Vietnam. Compared with Korea—"a clear case of aggression"—the conflict in Vietnam was "more obscure and less flagrant."

> The President then expressed his strong feeling that in such a situation the United States needs even more support from allies in such an endeavor as Vietnam in order to avoid sharp domestic partisan criticism as well as strong objections from other nations of the world. The President said that he could even make a rather strong case against intervening in an area 10,000 miles away against 16,000 guerrillas with a native army of 200,000, where millions have been spent for years without success.

After a short discussion on the improbability of French or British support, Kennedy continued, comparing

> the obscurity of the issues in Viet Nam to the clarity of the position in Berlin, the contrast of which could even make leading Democrats wary of proposed activities in the Far East.

When Rusk suggested that the Berlin example of firmness and resolve might also work in Vietnam "without resort to combat," Kennedy disagreed, saying that

> the issue was clearly defined in Berlin and opposing forces identified whereas in Viet Nam the issue is vague and action is by guerrillas, sometimes in a phantom-like fashion.

McNamara argued that this would change by the very fact of American action, especially if directed against the North as well, but Kennedy worried about the vulnerability of the aircraft carriers required for such an operation. Rusk then indicated his concern with a politically motivated attack on Hanoi rather than one directed against the sources of supply into the South. Lemnitzer asserted that without U.S. action "Communist conquest would deal a severe blow to freedom and extend Communism to a great portion of the world." Kennedy asked how he could justify action in Vietnam when the United States was not acting against Cuba, inviting the obvious riposte that the Joint Chiefs of Staff also wanted the United States to "go into Cuba."

Kennedy's reluctance to approve the measures outlined in the draft memorandum were evident.

> He cautioned that the technique of U.S. action should not have the effect of unilaterally violating Geneva accords. He felt that a technique and timing

must be devised which will place the onus of breaking the accords on the other side and require them to defend their actions.

This led him to conclude that the coming weeks must be given to building up the necessary political support, both domestically and internationally, for American action. When the final National Security Action Memorandum was published a week later, all references to preparing for the introduction of American forces had been removed.[10] Nonetheless, the number of advisers was to be increased and their rules of engagement extended. The first was killed on 22 December 1961.

COUNTERINSURGENCY

Diem had been led by Taylor to anticipate a firm commitment of American troops. That they did not materialize was a source of embarrassment and humiliation. After failing to deliver the goods, the Americans then began to lecture Diem on the need to broaden his government and engage in economic and social reform if he was to get further assistance. The advice was unwelcome and ignored. Diem wanted more military support and less political interference. The whole episode left him even less receptive to American ideas for change. Coupled with the revival of coup talk in Saigon, it reinforced his mistrust of the Americans. The Americans once again had to come to terms with their limited leverage. At the end of 1961 at a conference he had called in Honolulu, McNamara acknowledged that Diem was "the only man we had."[11]

Support for not making a big effort to get Diem to change his ways came from an unlikely, and largely unintentional, quarter. John Kenneth Galbraith had written to Kennedy on 20 November suggesting that the insurgency itself was no big deal and could not prosper at all if the government was acting effectively. But this government was not and never would be effective. "Diem will not reform either administratively or politically in any effective way. . . . It is politically naïve to expect it"—as it was to insist that there was no alternative to Diem. Galbraith's basic recommendation was to wait until there was a political crisis in Saigon and then stand back and wait for a new military regime that would at least offer a "new start." His central assumption was prescient but his optimistic account of the consequences of a coup was not, and he underestimated the Viet Cong.[12] In terms of practical policy the memo was of scant comfort to Kennedy, but it might at least have provided him with grounds for rueful reflection that no matter what he did, the United States was not going to find the irresistible force to shift this immovable object in Saigon.

Diem was sufficiently savvy to realize that he dare not constantly contradict his American friends, so he played them along, listening politely and doing little on the political front. He even found that he could get around Kennedy by appearing to go along with American proposals for counterinsurgency operations, which developed after Kennedy had decided against sending troops.

The American army's approach to counterinsurgency was to clear away the Viet Cong from particular areas using regular forces and then hand over the cleared territory to the Civil Guard. Economic reform could be implemented once these areas were secure. The plan called for initial action in the provinces around Saigon, and then operations would move southward to the Mekong Delta, where the communists were strongest. Counterinsurgency theory suggested something more political than just killing communist guerrillas. It relied on winning the "hearts and minds" of the people to the point where they would be willing and able to help themselves. General Wheeler, director, joint chiefs of staff, derided this "fashionable idea," saying that the "essence of the problem in Vietnam is military."[13] The army considered the situation far too serious for such experimentation. Lemnitzer wrote to Taylor on 18 October conveying the view of the Joint Chiefs that "in recent months the insurgency in Vietnam has developed far beyond the capacity of police controls."[14]

At this point Roger Hilsman, of the State Department's Bureau of Intelligence and Research, entered the policy arena. Like Rostow, he had come to government from academia with a known interest in guerrilla warfare. Unlike Rostow, he had actual experience in Burma during the Second World War. In August 1961 he published an article in the *Marine Corps Gazette* entitled "Internal War: The New Communist Doctrine." In this he urged that guerrilla operations be recognized as quite distinct from regular operations. They required smaller units of lighter forces, not bound by terrain. He warned that "rigid adherence to the principle of concentration keeps units at unwieldy battalion or even regimental levels, usually with erroneous stress on holding land rather than destroying enemy forces." As important was the attention he gave to the problem of political support. This was a function not simply of modernization but of obtaining popular appreciation through spreading the benefits of economic growth. He paid attention to issues of local administrative competence and the role of mass parties in broadening a government's political base.[15]

As the debate on the Taylor report was reaching its uncertain conclusion, Hilsman reported the conclusion of an extensive study undertaken by INR of the policy implications of the "new Communist tactics of guerrilla warfare and subversion." The most effective way of countering Viet Cong tactics, this argued, was not with regular troops, but with "a sophisticated combination of civic action, intelligence, police work, and constabulary-like counter-guerrilla forces that use a tactical doctrine quite different from the traditional doctrine of regular forces." The analysis indicated a basic problem with the current campaign. The army's reliance upon firepower had become a means of recruiting converts to the communists, as it could never be sufficiently discriminate to avoid harming civilians. At first glance, Hilsman recognized, the use of troops to seek out the Viet Cong appeared possible, even on the Taylor report's presumption that fifteen governmental soldiers were needed for every one guerrilla. As the Viet Cong force was estimated at 16,000, a South Vietnamese force notionally put at over 280,000 ought to be able to manage. But this latter number included the Civil Guard and self-defense forces plus many other ineffectual personnel. Nor could the South Vietnamese organize themselves properly to get maximum value from their numbers. Ideally such a campaign should be fought by small, mobile, self-reliant formations of some 50 men, but such units required the sort of leadership skills in short supply in Vietnam.[16] As an alternative, Hilsman's group had come up with the idea of starting with protecting the population in order to secure government control while the regular South Vietnamese army challenged for areas under communist control.

At the same time as Taylor's visit a British counterinsurgency expert, Robert Thompson, was making something of a stir in Saigon. Part of a British mission invited by Diem for advice, Thompson had developed the concept of "strategic hamlets," based on his successful experience with "new villages" in Malaya. The idea was that the guerrillas must be separated from the people, and that required the government to gain administrative control of the countryside and then prove themselves in charge and able to provide security. The advice was controversial, not least to the Americans because it was provided by a British officer insinuating himself into the decision-making loop. There were also doubts about the validity of the Malayan experience, which was based on a geographically isolated country with a clear sense of identity facing a lackluster enemy.

Kennedy remained bothered by the lack of attention and effort being given by the Pentagon, and in particular the army, to deal with communist-sponsored subversion and guerrilla warfare.[17] Attracted by Hilsman's approach, he asked him to go to McNamara's Honolulu conference in December and then on to South Vietnam. Hilsman's views were reinforced when he observed an operation close to Saigon. Aircraft and South Vietnamese infantry attacked suspected Viet Cong troops, only to find that the communists had left and the casualties were all civilians. There he met up with Thompson, whose ideas meshed with his own. While the American army still held an unshakable conviction in "main force war," Thompson framed the issue in more constabulary terms.[18] On his return to Washington, Hilsman explained his ideas to Kennedy, who then asked him to write them up. This was done under the heading "A Strategic Concept for Vietnam." His report stayed close to Thompson's ideas, stressing the need to focus on the battle for control of the villages, using civic action as much as purely military operations.

The great advantage of this scheme was that Diem liked it. It suited him to have in Thompson an independent source of advice to the Americans and to have a strategy that did not inflate the importance of the Vietnamese army, the main threat to his regime. He and his brother saw the opportunity to use the political aspects of the strategic hamlets plan to strengthen their power in the country while at the same time impressing the Americans by taking up one of their "big ideas." Nolting, who was relieved to see Diem taking any initiative, especially one that apparently appreciated the economic and political dimensions to the conflict, was also a supporter. In March 1962 it was agreed that the concept should be followed. Even from the start there were indications that Diem and his brother would distort the concept; nonetheless, for want of anything better the Americans persisted, and for a while they were able to convince themselves that it was working.

STRONG MEN

It was perhaps typical of Kennedy that he was more influenced by two figures at the margins of policy making, in this case a middle-ranking official and a British officer, than he was by those at its core. His readiness to back unorthodox people and ideas was an attractive trait, but it was also one that could have unfortunate consequences when policy implementation still depended on a system dominated by the orthodox. The sudden adoption of Hilsman as a key player on Vietnam was a symptom of Kennedy's own frustration with his inability to establish a policy-making process that generated the policy he wanted.

This frustration appears to have been the main emotion left over after the NSC meeting on 15 November. This began the process that led to the major personnel changes over the Thanksgiving weekend. The most notorious casualty was Chester Bowles, widely deemed ineffectual and long-winded; he had only just survived an attempt to marginalize him the previous July. Bowles was a natural dove on Vietnam, but so was his replacement, George Ball, and neither made Indochina a personal priority during the Kennedy years. More significant in terms of Vietnam was Kennedy's determination to replace the unsatisfactory Walter McConaughy, assistant secretary for Far Eastern affairs, with Averell Harriman. Far Eastern affairs had never quite recovered from the attacks on its integrity during the McCarthy period, when it had been blamed for almost willfully "losing" China. Rusk had suggested Alexis Johnson, an active accomplice of Taylor and Rostow, for this role. Bundy considered Johnson not "that dispassionate" and saw Harriman as a "strong man," someone "wholly responsive to your policy."[19] Given what we know about Harriman's own preferences at the time, seeing a role for a negotiating effort while remaining wary of Diem, this judgment is highly significant.

The most strident of the hawkish voices in the White House, Walt Rostow, was moved to the Policy Planning Staff of the State Department.

This was a job he had coveted as suited to his talents, although the lengthy long-term planning papers had scant influence on administration thinking. According to one of Kennedy's assistants, the president was pleased to have Rostow out of the White House, as he had become "a bloody bore—he talked too much; he'd get in there and he'd beat Kennedy's ear."[20] In February 1962 Kennedy described him as "one of the more vociferous members of the hard-boiled school on Vietnam." Rostow did not play a major role in Vietnam policy again until after Kennedy's death. In the National Security Council, Michael Forrestal, adopted by Harriman when age seventeen after his father's suicide, and a good friend of the Kennedys, took over the Indochina desk. He saw himself as "Kennedy's Ambassador to the sovereign state of Averell Harriman." Harriman, Hilsman, and Forrestal now exercised an increasing influence on Kennedy's Vietnam policy, to the point where the president started to feel that it was on the right track.[21]

Yet the actual implementation of policy still depended on the military, and this was to limit what could be achieved in terms of new initiatives in counterinsurgency. A whole series of developments had been pushing the military into a central role in Vietnam policy making. The CIA was still in disgrace over the Bay of Pigs and was not to be handed another major operation. Although the resident military officer in the White House, Taylor was slated for Lemnitzer's job as chairman of the Joint Chiefs of Staff. He had revealed himself to be a largely conventional military officer, marked more by his ability to talk in terms the Kennedy White House understood than for great originality in content.

Up to this point McNamara had acted as a forceful advocate of the military position, saving his critical faculties for the management of the Pentagon. Now, as the number of U.S. advisers rose, he found himself taking over responsibility at the Washington end for the management of a conflict in a distant country.[22] The tension already evident in his relations with the Joint Chiefs was to spread over into operational matters. On 13 January the chiefs passed him a memo describing in lurid terms the risks being run in Southeast Asia. They took issue with the decision not to engage in combat in Vietnam. If the current effort failed to produce results, they warned, then forces would eventually have to be deployed, by which time the delay would have rendered their task much more difficult. As requested, McNamara passed the memo on to Kennedy, adding that he did not endorse it.[23]

Meanwhile the military mission in Saigon, sensitive to lines of command, was constantly resisting intruders and looking for ways to maintain its position vis-à-vis the foreign service officers at the embassy. One critical recommendation by Taylor was to downgrade the role of Lieutenant General Lionel McGarr as head of the Military Assistance Advisory Group. McGarr's relationship with Diem was poor. He had become progressively frustrated at the inefficiencies of the South Vietnamese forces and the lack of a serious counterinsurgency program. He had, at least, understood that the difficulties were political, and so he could not share Nolting's enthusiasm for Diem.

A new Military Assistance Command, Vietnam (MACV), was established, headed by General Paul Harkins. Harkins had some credentials for the job, but his main advantages appeared to lie in his ability to get along with people and his personal relationship with Taylor, with whom he had been close through much of his army career. Harkins effectively became Taylor's agent in Saigon.[24] Only Bundy registered any anxiety about such a critical appointment being pushed through without consideration of whether the man was up to the job. After McGarr had been told of the new arrangement he sent a disappointed letter back to Lemnitzer in which he recorded his frustration with policy makers who demanded a solution based on large-scale military victories without "comparable strong demands for political-economic-psychological advances."

Nolting, who had struck up some sort of relationship with Diem, was to stay, although his position was being undercut by the strengthened military command. His own inclinations were not going to lead him to be forceful with the Vietnamese. Rostow had continued to push for Lansdale to go to Saigon to provide an activist presence and stir up Diem. Lansdale had by this time irritated almost everybody concerned with Vietnam except the Kennedys. He had now become suspicious even of those who wanted to send him to Saigon. He saw Rostow's plan to send him as a personal adviser to Diem as requiring that he "clobber him from up close." Lansdale saw this as "duty without honor and I'd be damned if I'd do that."[25] As we have seen, Robert Kennedy instead recruited him to help devise covert operations against Cuba.

Kennedy had been searching for a course of action that would allow him to sustain the American commitment to Vietnam without getting into a war. The logical answer to this conundrum had been an improved counterinsurgency effort, but this had faltered on ingrained military orthodoxy and the refusal of Diem to provide the appropriate political context. The North Vietnamese were making the situation worse through infiltration, but as Kennedy did not want to insert troops into Laos or bomb Hanoi, he had to hope that this problem could be handled through some sort of deal with Moscow. He had raised America's military profile, but with advisers rather than combat units. He had gained time but lost leverage over Diem, who was left supported by a divided and second-rate U.S. mission. Yet by early 1962 he believed that he was starting to make progress. This was an illusion, but for eighteen months Kennedy could put the Vietnam problem to one side, as he assumed that the strategic hamlets program was being implemented with energy and efficiency.

37

The Influence of Laos

IT HAS BEEN CLAIMED that when confronting the various options for Vietnam presented to him in November 1961 Kennedy "turned his back on the route toward a negotiated settlement."[1] Given what we know about Kennedy's readiness to enter into negotiations on Berlin, Laos, and even Cuba, such a posture in this case would have been surprising. In fact Kennedy demonstrated the same interest in a negotiated outcome over Vietnam. It is important, however, to clarify what he saw to be the role of negotiations in such conflicts.

His starting point was the cold war. His large project was to consolidate what Khrushchev called peaceful coexistence in such a way that it would be acceptable to the American people and his allies. He did not expect to be able to roll back communism, but neither did he intend to preside over its expansion. It was one thing to envisage two great alliances–cum–ideological blocs coexisting, but agreements at the top had to work their way down to every spot where a serious ideological confrontation had developed. Ideological civil wars, fought in the name of the cold war, often drew upon a range of social, economic, and religious cleavages as well as personal rivalries. This meant that not only did the superpowers have to show restraint themselves but they also might well have to impose restraint on their local clients.

The lesson that might be drawn from the experience of Germany, China, and Korea was that the most stable solution to these civil wars was partition. In Germany his readiness to accept the de facto existence of two separate states, as well as a divided Berlin, was the starting point for his diplomacy, even though this went against the aspirations of his German allies. With China as well he understood that it was politically impossible to recognize the legitimacy of the communist regime in Beijing, but he could deny the Nationalists support for realizing their dream of a return to the mainland. This could be done so long as the Nationalists depended on the United States to defend them against the communists' determination to complete the unification of China on their terms. In Korea neither side accepted the division as natural, but in practice two separate countries had developed; the war had shown that communist aggression could be resisted but also that liberation from communism was no easy matter. A stability of sorts had taken hold, reinforced by a substantial American force and the lack of any serious communist political presence in the South. With Vietnam it was natural to apply the same model. In this case too there was opposition to the country's division across the political spectrum, but it could still be supposed that the point of a negotiated settlement would be to consolidate this division.

There were two complicating factors in the case of Vietnam. First, unlike Germany, China, and Korea, there was a civil war raging within the noncommunist part. Diem had failed to impose his will on South Vietnam and was opposed by a range of political and religious groups in addition to the Viet Cong. If there was to be a lasting peace, there had to be some deal within the South as well as one with the North. The second complicating factor was Laos. In one sense this was a positive influence, in that negotiations were under way on a long-term settlement. Their success was in some ways crucial to Vietnam because of the use of Laos for communist infiltration from North to South Vietnam. But these negotiations were proceeding on a different basis to partition. The objective was unity under a neutral government, made possible by the existence of a credible neutral leadership. It was natural for proponents of an active diplomacy on Vietnam to attempt to read across from Laos, and that is what Kennedy tried to do, but the Laotian model did not necessarily apply. Furthermore, even in Laos ensuring a tolerable composition to the government required threats to use force in support of clients but also pressure on clients to agree to a reasonable settlement. At some point American pressure on clients risked reducing their capability to resist communist pressure, at another point the inherent weakness of clients limited the American capacity to reinforce them. Thus military and diplomatic instruments were in no sense alternatives in either Laos or Vietnam. The art of managing, and if possible resolving, these conflicts lay in using them in a complementary fashion.

BUILDING ON LAOS

The Taylor-Rostow report did not seriously consider a diplomatic initiative. During the debate within the administration prompted by the report, Abram Chayes and Chester Bowles pushed for such an initiative. In this they were backed by John Kenneth Galbraith, the distinguished, iconoclastic economist and now ambassador to India, visiting Washington in November with Indian prime minister Pandit Nehru. He found the

Taylor report to be "curious" in recommending "vigorous action" even though the "appendices say it cannot possibly succeed given the present government in Saigon." Convinced that Diem could not succeed, this group proposed long-term neutralization for Vietnam along Laotian lines. One reason they failed to get very far was the limited political clout of the advocates. Bowles had little credibility left within the administration, Kennedy found Nehru irritating, and Galbraith's position was somewhat predictable. After Bundy charged his old Harvard colleague with never being prepared to urge the use of force, Galbraith conceded that his enthusiasm for it was always rather low.[2] Chayes later observed, "We had all the non-power in the [State] Department, and so it just never flew . . . [I]t was simply regarded as not within the realm of possibility."[3] Neutralization represented too much of a dramatic change in American policy, and it was an overt rejection of the Diem regime. That did not preclude other diplomatic steps. Averell Harriman had already set one in motion, and his political star was rising.

Harriman became virtually a co-conspirator with Kennedy in pushing forward on a Laos settlement against considerable bureaucratic resistance, and with little help from the communists. He had managed to get authority to accept Souvanna as prime minister, bypass Phoumi if need be, and accept that a neutralist government might contain a number of disagreeable elements. He had been exploring the possibility of a Vietnam settlement based on Laos since 12 September 1961, when he had met privately with Ambassador Pushkin, his Soviet opposite number in the Geneva talks on Laos. The discussion was fruitful, with Pushkin offering assurances—even guarantees—on future Pathet Lao and North Vietnamese behavior.[4] It was an important conversation, news of which persuaded seasoned Kremlin watchers such as Thompson and Kennan that Khrushchev was able to negotiate sensibly and bring the Chinese along with him. At the end Harriman "felt him out on why not settle hostilities between two Viet-Nams, accepting divisions with peaceful relations between them." Pushkin thought this might be desirable but felt it was beyond his authority to discuss it. A couple of weeks later he again expressed some cautious interest.[5] Unfortunately, Pushkin lacked the discretion allowed Harriman. This was reflected in the actual negotiations on Laos, where progress did not match up to Pushkin's private promises.

Senior administration officials saw few prospects for useful Vietnam negotiations. When a number met on 5 October for an informal lunch to discuss "the suggestion that talking direct to the Soviets might have some use," this "was pretty unanimously rejected."[6] Yet that same day Kennedy met Harriman and took a more positive view. They saw an effective Laos agreement as a means of easing the situation in Vietnam but also as a starting point for a Vietnam deal. The first requirement was agreement on Laos, and Kennedy took the opportunity of a meeting with Gromyko the next day to urge that the Geneva negotiations must not be allowed to falter when they were so close to success, and that any agreements should be enforced. This would require Laos not being used as a base for activities against South Vietnam. These concerns were reflected in Harriman's new instructions—he was to seek more than just an agreement in principle from Moscow that there should be no infiltration from Laos into Vietnam, including proposals on how this might be enforced and "what responsibility Soviets would assume." In addition, "within your discretion and at time you consider suitable," Harriman could inform Pushkin that he was authorized to explore with him "ways and means whereby relations between North and South Viet-Nam could be stabilized."[7]

During discussions on the Taylor-Rostow report, Harriman had warned that any U.S. deployment in Vietnam could "blow open" the Laos talks, which he claimed to be moving to a successful conclusion. He succeeded in getting this danger recognized, as well as the possibility of some diplomatic initiative on Vietnam. When Kennedy wrote to Ambassador Nolting about the decisions just taken in response to the Taylor-Rostow report, he gave as one reason why combat troops were not to be sent to Vietnam the argument that "the introduction of U.S. or SEATO forces into SVN before Laotian settlement might wreck chances for agreement, lead to break up of Geneva conference, break Laos cease fire by communists with resumption of hostilities."[8] He also told the veteran journalist Arthur Krock that he was under such pressure from the Pentagon to send troops to Vietnam, even though it was difficult to "interfere in civil disturbances created by guerrillas," that he was thinking of writing to Khrushchev to hold back the North Vietnamese.[9] This is in fact what he did, following up Harriman's move with one of his pen pal letters to Khrushchev. He pointed to the value of a final agreement on Laos as a means of improving the atmosphere for the Berlin negotiations, stressing the importance of a balanced government under Souvanna Phouma in Laos and of the withdrawal of foreign (i.e., North Vietnamese) troops. He added:

> In addition to so instructing your spokesmen at Geneva, I hope you will increasingly exercise your influence in this direction on all of your "corresponding quarters" in this area: for the acceleration of attacks on South Viet-Nam, many of them from within Laotian territory, are a very grave threat to peace in that area and to the entire kind of world-wide accommodation you and I recognize to be necessary. If a new round of measures and counter-measures, force and counter-force occurs in that corner of the globe, there is no foretelling how widely it may spread.[10]

As a diplomatic initiative, this was very much at the highest level. It contained no proposals for Vietnam, only a call for mutual restraint, as extra communist forces would prompt an American response. From Kennedy's perspective this was no small matter. He assumed Khrushchev knew of the pressure he faced to send troops to Vietnam, and that the Russian understood that it would not be possible to resist this much longer in the face of continued provocation from the North.

Harriman set down his ideas on what this might mean in terms of negotiating about Vietnam. A possible settlement would involve the cessation of hostilities; acceptance for the time being of the division of Vietnam; reunification only through peaceful means, including elections; mutually advantageous trade and economic relations; and strengthened mechanisms for observation and enforcement. At the same time he warned against staking American prestige on a "repressive, dictatorial and unpopular regime." The point about this proposal was that it was not for the neutralization of Vietnam. It was essentially to establish normal relations between the two as separate countries. Yet Harriman's memo also indicated the fundamental problem with this approach. Why should the communists agree to a deal that would enhance the security of an unpopular regime? Rostow argued that unless steps were first taken to "stabilize and strengthen the military, political, and psychological position on the ground," the readiness to talk would in itself signify a loss of nerve.[11]

Harriman had first shown his draft to Rusk, who had replied that it was a "matter of timing," bearing in mind "other communications." This was a reference to a letter from Khrushchev, dated 10 November, that discussed the problems of coalition formation in Laos and ignored the infiltration issue. He focused on the weak point in the Harriman plan by blaming the problems in Vietnam on the "bankrupt policy" of the Diem regime rather than "some kind of interference or incitement from outside," and warned of the dangers of sending troops to suppress national liberation movements.[12] This was hardly encouraging, yet Kennedy still wrote to Rusk and McNamara requesting them to consider Harriman's proposal and the possibility that he might return early to Geneva to discuss the matter further with Pushkin. He also raised the question of a further communication with Khrushchev on the dangers of the situation.[13] There is no evidence of any discussion at the next NSC meeting of a diplomatic initiative. Nonetheless, the day after this Kennedy did write to Khrushchev.

The letter began with Laos and suggestions on how the negotiations might be taken forward. On Vietnam Kennedy was careful not to argue for the government and policies of Diem, but he did take issue on the role of external interference. He cited the evidence and stated the firm opinion of the United States that the government of South Vietnam was

> undergoing a determined attempt from without to overthrow the existing government using for this purpose infiltration, supply of arms, propaganda, terrorization, and all the customary instrumentalities of communist activities in such circumstances, all mounted and developed from North Vietnam.

He insisted that these actions were at variance with the Geneva accords and that American support for Diem's government was a "serious obligation." The United States would "undertake such measures as the circumstances appear to warrant." If the Soviet Union could persuade Hanoi to honor its obligations,

> there would be no need for the United States to consider, as we must at the present, how best to support the Government of Vietnam in its struggle for independence and national integrity.

Kennedy concluded by observing that he had written about Laos and Vietnam because both "are at a distance from our own countries and can be considered areas in which we ought to be able to get agreement."[14]

What did Kennedy expect from this communication? It could be that he was preparing the ground for more drastic action later on by setting out his complaint against Hanoi in the hope that this might influence the strategic calculations of the other side. There was no specific proposal, only a request for restrained North Vietnamese behavior. However, when placed in the context of the ongoing negotiations, it suggests that all he really needed was that proposals currently on the table with regard to Laos be considered seriously. As for Vietnam itself, for the moment there was little scope for movement. Harriman and Pushkin talked that November and again in January. A year later Harriman complained to Dobrynin that he had not been given "any indication that the Soviet Union was prepared to arrive at a practical solution." The stumbling block was inevitably Diem. Pushkin had proposed his removal, leading Harriman to counter that he thought that Ulbricht, the East German leader, should also be replaced. This ended the conversation.[15] The South Vietnamese had been kept in ignorance of these approaches.

COERCING ALLIES

The hopes invested in the Geneva negotiations as a means of not only sorting out Laos but also creating new options for Vietnam and demonstrating the possibility of superpower cooperation on issues of peripheral interest appeared, during the first months of 1962, to have been overstated. Harriman's policy had been to transfer American affections from Phoumi to Souvanna Phouma on the presumption that Moscow and Beijing would do likewise—back Souvanna while controlling the local communists sufficiently to ensure that an agreement worked. Though Phoumi had nothing like Diem's power, the problems of getting him to agree to a deal illustrated those that would be faced if Diem had to be brought to negotiations.

Phoumi supposed that the Americans would not—dared not—abandon him. He had little interest in serving under Souvanna in a coalition government. His lack of political support and the unimpressive quality of the forces under his command meant that his bargaining position depended upon direct American military backing. He had his supporters in

Washington, but starting in late 1961 they lost ground as Harriman took charge of Far Eastern affairs. Roger Hilsman entitles the part of his memoir dealing with this period as "Phoumi versus Harriman."[16]

When Phoumi refused to accept Souvanna as head of the government (a proposition that Harriman had got the State Department to accept, but with difficulty), there was a debate in Washington over the advisability of "graduated" sanctions, starting with stopping military deliveries. The main risk of this form of pressure on Phoumi was that it might lead him to take yet more "desperate and foolish actions." This was why the Americans wanted the Soviet Union to keep the Pathet Lao under control while they went about taming Phoumi. There was even discussion with the president at the White House of financial support, effectively to bribe Phoumi to accept a settlement.[17]

On 23 February a telegram was sent from the White House to the embassy in Vientiane requiring that the ambassador speak to Phoumi at the earliest possible opportunity (which did not come until 6 March):

[M]ake clear to him that your government really will not allow itself to be driven into a war in Laos by Phoumi's intransigence. You should emphasize further that Souvanna is increasingly at odds with Pathet Lao and that we now have a real opportunity to unite non-Communists with strong international support. Phoumi can play a major role in increasing the prospect for such success but he cannot expect U.S. support if he blocks it.

As there was no evidence that the Pathet Lao was being restrained— indeed, communist military strength was growing—putting pressure on Phoumi via his military supplies did not seem prudent. Instead Harriman stopped cash payments to Phoumi (for his troops' wages). He also got Thailand, which had been supporting Phoumi, to join in the pressure. In mid-April Hilsman lamented that the "mild sanctions" taken thus far had not succeeded. That Kennedy shared this frustration is indicated by his own proposal to withdraw Special Forces from Laos. He was persuaded to reduce this to a threat to remove some of the less important teams and then not to make this too public lest an announcement unbalance the delicate policy of putting pressure on Phoumi while avoiding encouraging the Pathet Lao to launch an offensive. By 2 May the message appeared to have got through to Phoumi and he was shifting his position. After this Kennedy became anxious that Harriman ease up on Phoumi to get his future cooperation.[18]

PRESSURE ON ENEMIES

Because of the lack of restraint on the communist side, the pressure on Phoumi became bound up with a renewed confrontation with the Pathet Lao. At the start of 1962 the CIA had concluded that neither side had the upper hand, although the communists had an advantage in guerrilla warfare while Phoumi's forces should do better in more conventional operations. By the end of January, however, it had become painfully evident that there were few circumstances in which the Royal Laotian Army could prevail, especially if taking on Pathet Lao forces backed by North Vietnamese regulars. With reason, the communists believed that time was on their side. Even if they were ready to discuss a political settlement, the objective was to strengthen their own position.[19] In their own internal discussions at the time the North Vietnamese and their Pathet Lao proteges viewed Geneva in entirely instrumental terms. Whatever arrangements they were prepared to support in the short term, they did not believe in coalition government over the long term.

Starting in February concern grew over communist movements around the town of Nam Tha. The communists there were facing pressure from some 9,000 Hmong (Meo) tribesmen who had been armed by the CIA in an effort to undercut communist support. The Meos had been unusually effective as a guerrilla movement, and support to them had been sustained, even after the May cease-fire, as a check on the communists. Kennedy had been persuaded that as cease-fire violations were likely in the first instance to be prompted by an attempt to deal with the Meo, the stronger the Meo the more careful that Pathet Lao would have to be.[20] In practice the communists were provided with a pretext to justify their own cease-fire violations. As was often the case under Kennedy, there was very little serious discussion of the implications of supposedly covert moves that often seemed easier to approve than overt military moves whose value was extensively debated.

Soon Pathet Lao probes against the Meo were used by Phoumi as reason to send 5,000 troops and artillery units to the airstrip at Nam Tha.[21] As this was close to their bases, the communists could not tolerate this force. The Americans feared a repeat performance of Dien Bien Phu. They warned Phoumi of the vulnerability of what was then some 10 percent of his total strength. As the Americans assumed that communist strategy would be to expose their opponents' political and military weaknesses through a series of actions rather than an all-out offensive throughout Laos, they feared that Phoumi was walking into what was increasingly seen as a trap awaiting his forces at Nam Tha.[22]

On 2 May 1962 came the first fire against the Royal Laotian Army defense perimeter from Pathet Lao and North Vietnamese troops. On 6 May it took four Vietnamese battalions barely six hours to overrun Nam Tha. As Phoumi's men fled, the communists started moving to the Thai border. So complete was the rout of the army that when Rusk telegraphed to the U.S. embassy in Laos the conclusions of the major deliberations of 12 May he observed that "we have reports which raise suspicion that [Phoumi] might have deliberately invited a major engagement at Nam Tha and designed the subsequent planned retreat into Thailand to embarrass U.S. and call our hand on issue of military support for FAR [Royal Laotian Armed Forces]." Ball had already wondered to Kennedy whether "the whole retreat was contrived, as though Phoumi was willing to see it take place, scaring us and getting us involved."[23]

If so, the tactic nearly worked. The intelligence community's assessment was that this was less the start of a general communist offensive than an opportunity to demonstrate local strength. It would improve the communist position in future negotiations while indicating impatience with the American failure to deliver Phoumi to a coalition. They would wait to see the American response before proceeding further. Hilsman and Harriman warned the White House that the deterrent effect of potential U.S. intervention, which had held the Pathet Lao back in the past, had now been downgraded. In order to prevent a communist takeover (and also a situation that could require large numbers of American troops) the deterrent needed to be "reinvigorated." This could be achieved by fleet movements and the dispatch of marines to the Thai border.[24]

Hilsman was braced for a battle with the "never again" view—that the use of force in Vietnam should be either all out or not at all—when the president met his advisers on 10 May. He proposed that "any move we make be tailored in such a fashion as not to provoke the Viet Minh or the Chinese into large-scale counter-action, but rather to suggest to them that we were prepared to resist encroachments beyond the cease-fire line." In a private record of the events of those days, dictated on 11 May, Hilsman reported that Forrestal had already discovered through Maxwell Taylor that the military were "going soft on us again . . . every time they beat their chests until it comes down to do some fighting and then they start backing down." At the meeting army chief of staff General Decker, acting chairman of the Joint Chiefs, came in with what Hilsman described as "the damnedest collection of mush and softness I have seen in a long time." The Joint Chiefs argued for naval movements but no dispatch of troops for the moment, and proper backing for Phoumi, though he was by then in retreat. The old contingencies for full-scale intervention were held in readiness.[25] Kennedy, with Rusk and McNamara, as well as Lemnitzer, then out of the country, was reluctant to take any quick decisions, and the issue was deferred to 12 May.

By the time of this meeting the *New York Times* had reported, obviously on the basis of a Pentagon leak, that Kennedy had given up on Phoumi and was moving the fleet only as a token "show of force." This created exactly the impression that the State Department had been desperate to avoid; it undermined deterrence and led to a fear that the communists would push further. The president was worried by the domestic political consequences—from both left and right—of the accusation of bluffing, and this may have led him to take the more visible step of sending troops. He was especially bothered by the prospect of Eisenhower—who had assigned such a high priority to Laos in January 1961—urging intervention. The former president had already criticized the attempt to establish a neutralist government as reminding him of the way that China had been lost. As Eisenhower now warned that he might make a public statement, Kennedy sent McCone and Forrestal to see him. They secured Eisenhower's agreement to the plan to send a limited number of troops into Thailand, thereby strengthening Kennedy's hand in any argument with the military.[26]

McNamara had already been through the issue with the senior military officers who had been gathered in Saigon to discuss the situation in South Vietnam. When the secretary of defense had raised the crisis in Laos and a communist push to the Mekong River, the officers were unprepared. Flustered, Lemnitzer advocated SEATO Plan 5, an intervention to seize key points along the Mekong, while Admiral Felt suggested air strikes. McNamara dismissed their ideas; it was by no means clear what would be achieved by SEATO Plan 5, while an air strike raised the risk of a North Vietnamese response and a wider conflict. As Newman observes, McNamara now "knew several proposals he would not be making to the president when he returned."[27]

By 12 May the top men were back in Washington to meet the president. Harriman was arguing that it was possible to wait to see how the situation was developing before ordering a battle group to Thailand, and also that the United States could use Phoumi's current discomfort to cause his "withdrawal from the Lao political scene into a purely military capacity."[28] Hilsman was offering his own ideas for a "graduated" plan of action for Laos.[29] Phase one would seek to warn communists that the United States would prevent a military takeover of Laos while reassuring them that communist territory was not to be threatened. The military moves would be designed "to give the communists pause in their pursuit of military gains and at the same time to give them no reason for the kind of fear that would lead them to escalation." Meanwhile the ground would be prepared for a government of national union. One aspect of this would be a campaign to denigrate Phoumi—a series of moves to reduce his "influence and prominence" and demonstrate an American concern for the people of Laos.

If that failed to produce a new cease-fire and a more pliable Phoumi, the next phase would involve strengthening the American military position in order to intervene if necessary to defend the Laotian government. "The plan," added Hilsman pointedly, "calls for cool nerves and both austerity and restraint on the part of the military." No actual moves would be made into Laotian territory. Absent a radical change in Phoumi's attitude, it would be necessary to "proceed with his replacement." Hilsman hoped that the Thais, who were also expected to take an active part in the military preparations, would "handle the elimination problem . . . with appropriate oriental finesse."

Phase three would follow if the communists did not stop their advances. There would be a "limited" intervention to secure government territory, with the interest in a coalition government still proclaimed. Thai forces would move across the Mekong, backed up by American units. The U.S. battle group would move into the Laotian capital, Vientiane. This phase carried great risks—additional North Vietnamese troops and possibly some communist "volunteers"—but Hilsman assumed that there would be no communist interest in escalation either. In general he was optimistic that phase one would suffice.

Rusk and McNamara took the moderate line that the basic policy should not be changed. Phoumi should not be misled into believing that the United States was rushing in to rescue him from his own mistakes, but the Seventh Fleet should be moved into position and airborne units alerted in case action was required. The president emphasized, however, "that he was authorizing only precautionary dispositions of military forces, and that no landings or other military action in Thailand should be taken with respect to the situation until more information was available on the actual situation in Laos."

Rusk wrote to the embassy in Laos requiring that they make it known in Vientiane that the United States considered Phoumi personally responsible for the defeat at Nam Tha, and that he should cease to be a central political figure and revert to being a military commander. Supplies to help with his military tasks would follow compliance. The next day, Sunday, the president set in motion the movement of the U.S. battle group to Thailand, still anxious to retain an element of "reversibility in all military actions."[30] On 15 May it was announced that troops were being sent to Thailand.

The move had the desired effect. The next day the Pathet Lao announced that it would resume negotiations. As they had no intention of taking over all of Laos, it is hard to say that the communists had really been deterred. They certainly had no desire to see the Americans in a position to play a more assertive role. Within the State Department, this was another small victory for graduated response and against an all-or-nothing approach. On 11 June agreement was reached on the new government. Souvanna would lead it, with Phoumi and Prince Souphanouvong as his deputies. Khrushchev wrote cheerfully to Kennedy, who responded in kind, agreeing that this settlement could be "most helpful in leading towards the resolution of other international difficulties." As a sweetener for Khrushchev, agreed by Robert through the Bolshakov channel, the press was told that U.S. forces would be leaving Thailand.[31] A cease-fire was proclaimed on 23 June, and on 6 July a declaration of neutrality was presented to the Geneva conference. This was approved two weeks later by the foreign ministers of countries represented at the conference. All foreign troops were to leave and all military assistance was to be terminated.

BACK TO VIETNAM

With one agreement in place to reduce conflict in Southeast Asia, why not another? There is evidence that there was interest in Hanoi in the idea of a new Geneva conference to apply the Laotian model to South Vietnam. The thinking behind this was that Kennedy had shown himself reluctant to intervene in Laos and was prepared to accept a settlement that in the long term probably spelled defeat for his clients. This was one reason why the Pathet Lao had been told not to exploit fully their victory in Nam Tha. Hanoi did not want the Americans to feel obliged to intervene in Laos and was under some pressure from Moscow to show restraint.

With this in mind, in July the North Vietnamese told their comrades in the South to prepare for political negotiations, and this included the development of a much broader political front, with noncommunist elements (including some communists who had maintained a neutral status) opposed to Diem. The idea would be to get a government in the South tolerated by the Americans but eventually able to call for unification with the North.[32] This strategy depended on the Americans being prepared to turn against Diem as they had turned against Phoumi—except more so.

After his disappointing encounter with Pushkin in January, Harriman was unsure whether much could be done for Vietnam by diplomatic means. In April Galbraith had managed to interest Kennedy again in his ideas for a negotiated settlement.[33] Although Harriman agreed that Diem was a "losing horse," he was unsure that the time was ripe for a big Vietnam initiative. Kennedy still thought it worth exploring the issue in order to be "prepared to seize upon any favorable moment to reduce our involvement, recognizing that the moment might yet be some time away," so he asked Harriman to discuss Galbraith's ideas with McNamara and the Joint Chiefs. At the same time Galbraith was told to approach the Indian government to see if it would act as an intermediary with Hanoi.

The Pentagon and the State Department, including Hilsman and Harriman, were opposed to an initiative. Galbraith noted with dismay Ambassador Nolting's belief that they dare not discuss a negotiated outcome lest it undermine Diem's confidence in the United States. The idea was rejected formally at a White House meeting on 1 May, at a time when the Laos situation was itself extremely tense.[34] Even so, Kennedy had suggested to Galbraith that he might set up a channel of his own with Hanoi if an opportunity presented itself. One possibility was an Indian member of the International Control Commission who had spoken encouragingly to Galbraith about a recent trip to Hanoi. Galbraith proposed that he be used as a channel of communication, and Kennedy agreed. Nothing, however, appears to have come out of this contact.[35]

It was Galbraith's advocacy of a neutral South Vietnam as much as negotiations as such that generated opposition. This was a difficult notion to operationalize. Unsurprisingly, Diem disliked the idea, and this is one reason why Diem took some persuading to sign up to the Laos accords in the summer. Even if he could agree to the principle of neutralization, he had no faith in any Northern promises of compliance. The effort to get him to sign led to another argument with Harriman, with whom personal relations were already poor, and in the end required that Kennedy assure Diem that he understood the difference between Laos and South Vietnam.

Even so, the president instructed Harriman to broach the idea of a separate peace conference with the North Vietnamese if he got a chance at Geneva. On 22 July Harriman did talk to the North Vietnamese foreign minister. The report of the talks confirms that the two sides had little basis on which to proceed: Hanoi blamed Washington for shoring up Diem, and Washington blamed Hanoi for promoting the insurgency. About the same time, Forrestal and Harriman had lunch with Pushkin; the result was a "propaganda blast." This led Forrestal to conclude that the Russians had no interest in being helpful on Vietnam and would continue to support the North's action against the South so long as there was a chance of success. He picked up the communist support for a broadly based National Front, which did demonstrate flexibility over the possibility of a noncommunist regime, but Forrestal saw this as basically a means of getting at Diem. He drew the conclusion that the communist strategy would be to generate a political crisis in Saigon, and that therefore Diem needed to be persuaded to strengthen his own political position. With the state of the war uncertain, and no definite military trend having yet emerged, Forrestal judged that the time was not ripe for a major initiative such as an international conference.[36] Kennedy thus did not reject a negotiated route out of Vietnam. The problem was that the sort of negotiation that interested him was not available. Though the Korean problem could be contained through a substantial military deployment on the border, the Vietnamese problem could not because the communists were already a force in the South's domestic politics. Nor was there a political figure as acceptable as Souvanna who might lead a neutralist South Vietnam, and Diem was no Phoumi. Kennedy was not (yet) prepared to dump Diem, but any diplomatic strategy that failed to address the character of his regime could not provide a long-term solution.

IMPLEMENTING THE GENEVA ACCORDS

During the course of 1963 Kennedy became increasingly disenchanted with Diem, but this did not result in a readiness to sacrifice him for the sake of a negotiated settlement. The reason was that he became just as disenchanted with the ability of Khrushchev to honor an agreement. The

North Vietnamese appeared to have signed up in 1962 only on sufferance to Moscow, with little intention of implementing the accords. As Hanoi moved closer to Beijing in 1963 their interest dwindled further.

From the start few had great expectations for the Geneva agreement. The American recognized that it would be difficult to control movement of North Vietnamese troops through Laos, and in fact some 2,000 personnel would infiltrate by this route in 1962. They would have to be dealt with in South Vietnam. Also the agreement contained the seeds of partition on ideological lines. Nonetheless, Harriman believed it to be important for the United States to follow the accords so that the onus for any transgression would fall on the communists. Kennedy concurred. Six hundred sixty-six American personnel were withdrawn under the supervision of the ICC before the October 1962 deadline, though at the same time, special arrangements were made to keep the Royal Laotian Army supplied and to assist Meo tribesmen. Kennedy went out of his way to boost Souvanna as an independent leader, despite his recent status as the communists' favorite, and even welcomed him to Washington. Word was passed to the communists that any coup against him would rekindle the debate over U.S. intervention.

The Russians also complied with the terms of the accords, removing 500 military technicians and cutting back on overt support to the Pathet Lao (assuming that Hanoi would pick up the slack). At this time it would seem that the Soviet objective was to use Laos as a positive example to the Americans of how agreements could work, an example that might usefully be applied to European affairs. Foreign Minister Kuznetsov wrote to the Chinese: "[H]ow would socialist proposals to guarantee a free city status for West Berlin look if socialist countries began to violate the only recently signed Geneva agreement?"[37]

It soon became apparent that Hanoi had no intention of relinquishing its use of and control over the infiltration routes into South Vietnam. Only 40 North Vietnamese technicians withdrew through ICC checkpoints. U.S. intelligence concluded that a mere 1,500 of its 9,000 ground troops were withdrawn by the October deadline. The ICC was not allowed access to certain zones by the Pathet Lao. In November when meeting Mikoyan (following the missile crisis) Kennedy complained about a monthly tally of 500 infiltrators reaching South Vietnam through Laos. Mikoyan said that his country was fulfilling its obligations, and quickly changed the subject.[38] According to one source, Khrushchev had already ordered an end to airlifts of military assistance to the Pathet Lao, in effect washing has hands of his Southeast Asian allies: "If they want a war, it will be their own affair."[39] While this was an earnest of his good intentions to Washington, it had the effect of reducing his leverage over the Pathet Lao.

In consequence, relations between communists and neutralists in Laos deteriorated. Souvanna's leadership had been indecisive and his forces lost ground to the Pathet Lao. This led to a complete break by April 1963 with Souvanna explicitly blaming the communists for aggression. The United States began to give covert support to all noncommunist factions but the risk now was that the lack of a firm response would make it appear as if the country was being abandoned to the Pathet Lao. The president was once again being asked to consider a graduated form of military response, starting with covert operations and moving on to air strikes against Pathet Lao positions and ultimately to attacks against North Vietnam. Again Kennedy authorized the first stage and left the later moves for further review, preferring to seek out a political solution. Accepting that the source of the problem lay in Hanoi, Kennedy ordered visible preparations for operations against North Vietnam, including a carrier task force being moved into the waters off South Vietnam, with orders broadcast in uncoded text so that there could be no mistaking the intent. Again Phoumi's independent actions served to complicate the situation.[40]

The fact that Souvanna was now blaming the communists for a collapse in the cease-fire and that Britain was demanding action from the Soviet Union as cochairman of the Geneva agreement because of these violations was a considerable embarrassment to Moscow. It claimed to be trying to bring the North Vietnamese and Pathet Lao along, but in practical terms it only seemed to be obstructionist, preventing the ICC from exploring violations. In truth, Moscow was losing control of the situation. This was the other side of the coin to the benefits the Sino-Soviet dispute had brought in emboldening Khrushchev to move toward a test ban treaty. At the same time it meant that he was suffering a net loss of influence over the communist parties of Southeast Asia. The North Vietnamese had become increasingly worried that the Russians had lost interest in their problems and were indeed as revisionist as the Chinese were claiming. In March Hanoi openly tilted in China's direction.

Even in the middle of April, Kennedy still felt that somehow Moscow was responsible for what was going on in Laos. This was why he was looking to retaliate by upping the ante in Cuba at this time, although his aides were clearly unsure about what one crisis had to do with the other. On this basis he decided that a direct approach be made to Khrushchev to salvage his only negotiating achievement with the Soviet Union, which now appeared on the verge of collapse. He rang Harriman: "[A]m I talking to the architect of the Geneva accords?" Harriman, not appreciating the irony, insisted that if all went down, he would take the blame. Kennedy said, "I have a piece of it." They decided that Harriman should go to Moscow with Forrestal to demand action from Khrushchev. Harriman was not sure that he would achieve anything, "but he guaranteed he wouldn't do any harm."[41] He delivered a letter from Kennedy for Khrushchev stressing how the agreement reached in Vienna between them on Laos was "an important milestone in Soviet/American relations" and that if they could work together to make Laos neutral, they could "make progress in resolving other matters which are at issue between us."[42]

Khrushchev answered the president's point frankly to Harriman: "We are still true to the word we gave him in Vienna, but the situation is very delicate. Our word is in regard to a third party and this makes for a real problem." The problem was that without an airlift or other assistance program to call off, and with China and Hanoi collaborating now on a more militant line, Khrushchev had little leverage. In effect Khrushchev had given up on Laos. He dismissed its significance, appearing not to have "the foggiest notion" of the geography or personalities of the country. He "did not know all those silly Laotian names or the individuals to whom these names belonged." This was a small country of two million people, and "no matter what happens there, there will be no waves created in the river or the ocean." At one point he threw his hands up, exclaiming, "Laos, Vietnam, all Southeast Asia. You and the Chinese can fight over it. I give up. We give up. We don't want any of it." By now the situation had become clear to Washington. The Americans could embarrass Khrushchev by harping about his failure to live up to commitments in Laos, but they could not get a real improvement on the ground. When Rusk met with Khrushchev in August, the Soviet leader essentially washed his hands of the matter.[43]

In his memoirs, Rusk stressed the importance of the flouting of the Geneva accords as a "major disappointment" to Kennedy, the impact of which "has been greatly underestimated." He claimed that neutralism would have been entertained seriously if the Geneva accords had been honored by the North Vietnamese: "In view of Hanoi's wholesale violation of the accords, we didn't believe Hanoi would accept a neutral South Vietnam." For those such as Rostow who believed that the insurgency in South Vietnam was dependent upon nourishment from the North, this failure to respond to the flouting of the Geneva accords appeared as "the greatest single error" in American policy.[44]

38

In the Dark

IN ADDITION TO HIS DISAPPOINTMENT with the Laos accords, another reason for Kennedy not to push for a negotiated settlement after the summer of 1962 was confidence that counterinsurgency policies were working. Until well into 1963 the top figures in the administration had no reason to doubt that this was the correct course. As far as Kennedy was concerned, probably until his death, the problem in Vietnam was not insoluble and counterinsurgency was a valid model. It was put at risk, it seemed, by political ineptitude in Saigon.

A strategic hamlets policy placed enormous demands on those responsible for its implementation, requiring patience, close coordination of political and military activity, and considerable sensitivity to conditions on the ground. For his bowdlerized version of this strategy, Diem relied on his brother, Ngo Dinh Nhu. Against American advice they decided to take on a difficult province, Binh Duong, rather than start with a less challenging task in a more secure area and build upward. Diem made it as hard as possible for American observers to monitor the developing situation on the ground and disregarded their warnings that he was going about the construction of strategic hamlets in such a way as to alienate the population rather than win them over. The theorists of counterinsurgency, including Thompson, saw such programs as a means of bringing security to villagers and allowing them to opt for a noncommunist but also, one hoped, enlightened government. Diem and his brother saw the program as a means of extending their political control, even if it left the population even more disgruntled and fearful than before. The speed with which they sought to achieve control made for impressive headlines early on, in terms of the numbers of hamlets established, and even disoriented the communists, but resources were soon stretched so far that the hamlets neither gained good government nor provided security. The result was an illusion. It took time before it was appreciated, observed Charles Maechling, that "you could have all this visible apparatus of control outside and at the same time be controlling nothing inside."[1]

For their part the communists, having become anxious during 1961 that they might have to cope with a large-scale American intervention, observed the new initiative with some relief and set about destroying the hamlets. As Hanoi took some time to sort out its response, there were initial grounds for optimism in Washington that the situation had been turned around. This view was encouraged by the new Military Assistance Command, Vietnam (MACV), with General Paul Harkins, an unfortunate choice as its first commander. The South Vietnamese told the Americans what they wanted to hear and denied them access to the contested areas where they might have formed a more critical opinion. When asked for information they lacked, rather than admit ignorance their inclination was to make something up.[2] Looking back, McNamara acknowledged that, in the absence of means to assess the war's complex political aspects, he and the U.S. military became overly impressed with "quantitative measurements such as enemy casualties (which became infamous as body counts), weapons seized, prisoners taken, sorties flown, and so on." Indeed, by the summer of 1962 Kennedy was sufficiently impressed by the reports of progress, as well as unfavorable comment on the first American casualties, to encourage McNamara to begin to draw up plans for the start of a gradual scaling down of the American advisory strength, starting in 1963. McNamara, priding himself on his caution, had put back Harkins's estimate of victory to 1965. Harkins was given orders in July 1962, aptly described in *The Pentagon Papers* as "almost Micawberesque," to plan on the basis that the insurrection would be "under control at the end of three years." Harkins, who had no responsibility for strategic hamlets, was relying on conventional operations. To justify his optimism he needed a decisive push against the communists, which was always unlikely to materialize. Regardless, in May 1963 he accepted instruction to finish plans for the replacement of U.S. forces, with the first elements—some 1,000 troops—being withdrawn by the end of 1963.[3] Kennedy was content to assume that the situation in Vietnam was as good as could be expected and that the American contribution had peaked.

SUPPRESSING DOUBTS

This wishful thinking was buoyed by exaggerated reports from the field on setbacks to the Viet Cong. The skeptics found it difficult to get a hearing until late in 1962, when first Senator Mansfield gave Kennedy a damning report on the situation and then, in response, Hilsman was sent with Forrestal to Saigon to make their own evaluation. Contrary to earlier reporting, they now warned that progress was slow and the advantage still lay with the enemy. They remained unhappy with the military preference for large-scale operations and air interdiction. In January 1963 their point was underlined when, following a decision by Hanoi to adopt more aggressive tactics, two Viet Cong companies attacked Ap Bac, a village in the Mekong Delta, and defeated a force of three South Vietnamese regular battalions. The battle revealed numerous defects in command and training. Those close to events knew that South Vietnamese generals had been fearful lest they annoy Diem by becoming too successful (and thus threatening his power) or too costly in terms of casualties. Whenever the army had an advantage they conspicuously failed to press it home.

The Joint Chiefs were told that Ap Bac had been one of the "bloodiest and costliest" battles in the war and a morale builder for the Viet Cong, yet the MACV worked hard to present the battle as a more even affair and of limited long-term significance.[4] Harkins tried to hold to the official line that Ap Bac had been a success because the Viet Cong did not attempt to hold their positions. Pessimistic analyses from advisers working closely with the South Vietnamese were suppressed. The most notorious were those of Colonel John Paul Vann, a charismatic senior adviser with South Vietnamese forces, who had been to the fore at Ap Bac. He was deeply critical of the corruption and ineptitude demonstrated here as elsewhere, and was becoming dismissive of the official statistics.[5]

Kennedy, who was not particularly focused on Vietnam at this time (this being just after the missile crisis), appears to have been prepared to accept the battle as a blip rather than an indicator of a trend. Many of the civilian professionals remained worried. Yet even Hilsman and Forrestal, in town at the time and now conscious of the discrepancy between the previous reporting back to Washington and the reality of the war's progress, still did not claim a revelation of fundamental strategic flaws. They did not challenge the basic strategic concept, for which Hilsman shared some responsibility, and were ready to believe that "we are probably winning," if only slowly. Winning would just take longer than had previously been anticipated. The CIA was more accurate in describing a "slowly escalating stalemate."[6]

Taylor sent army chief of staff General Wheeler to report on the situation. He returned from his trip with a voluminous report and an upbeat message: "[T]he principal agreements for eventual success have been assembled in South Vietnam." If there was a problem, he averred, it was infiltration, thus pointing to the need to take the war to the North at some point.[7] The extent to which such military views were trusted by the White House staff is indicated by Forrestal's apology to the president for arranging a meeting with Wheeler; it was a "complete waste of time," he said, because of "rosy euphoria" generated by Wheeler's report.[8]

Without a shared appraisal of the situation there was no basis for an honest debate on alternatives. Kennedy was always happy to defer a problem that was currently far from a crisis point, so a message that all was well, even if he suspected it was untrue, was still welcome. The best hope for such an appraisal came from the intelligence community. The Office of National Estimates had been pressing to take on "Prospects in South Vietnam" since September 1962, when their analysts first began to sense that the trends were not as good as claimed. The first draft of the estimate, submitted to the Board of National Estimates on 25 February 1963, warned that the struggle in the South would be "protracted and costly." It listed "very great weaknesses" that would be "difficult to surmount." These included a "lack of aggressive and firm leadership at all levels of command, poor morale among the troops, lack of trust between peasant and soldier, poor tactical use of available force, a very inadequate intelligence system and obvious Communist penetration of the South Vietnamese military organization."[9]

The director of central intelligence, John McCone, took issue with the draft from the start. One reason was own hawkish views, which inclined him to stress China and North Vietnam as the source of the South's troubles, and his good relations with General Victor Krulak, the Pentagon's chief counterinsurgency officer and a fully signed up optimist. McCone's confidence in his estimators had also been shaken following the flawed estimate of September 1962 on the likelihood of the Soviet Union deploying missiles in Cuba. Now he professed himself shocked by the divergence between its gloomy conclusions and "the people who know Vietnam best."

These people were not analysts but senior policy makers, and their views were now canvassed before a new draft could be written. The consensus from all concerned, including Hilsman and Forrestal, was that the assessment was just too pessimistic. Harkins wanted the draft to acknowledge the "steady and notable progress" with the strategic hamlets program, while the Joint Chiefs followed Wheeler's line that "the principal ingredients for eventual success" were in place. The military was particularly critical of the lack of confidence in the army of South Vietnam, the most critical ingredient of all if the planned American withdrawal was ever to take place. The estimators defended their judgments but were overruled. When the NIE was released in April 1963, and despite the occasional note of caution, it reflected the confident official lines: "Communist progress has been blunted . . . the situation is improving."

AT ODDS WITH THE PRESS

Less easy to control was the press. For much of 1962 and 1963 Kennedy appears to have assumed that one of the greatest threats to his Vietnam strategy came from the American press corps in Saigon. It was the bloodshed associated with the failed 1960 coup that led the *New York Times* to send Homer Bigart to Saigon, His caustic reporting became the inspiration for David Halberstam of the *New York Times*, Neil Sheehan of UPI, and Peter Arnett of AP. They persisted in relating that all was not well in the war against communism. The role played by these and other young reporters was important in the events that were to follow. They were not hostile to the war effort but rather deemed this a very serious matter and took it upon themselves to challenge an inadequate American military command and an undeserving American ally. Kennedy did not look upon them favorably. His antipathy can be traced back to early 1962, when journalists had exposed the fact that, contrary to the Geneva accords and to many presidential statements, U.S. personnel with the South Vietnamese army were going beyond advice and were actually engaging in combat. The Republican National Committee had embarrassed him when it picked up these reports and accused him of being "less than candid" on American involvement in the war. These were not "combat troops in the generally accepted sense of the word" was the president's response.[10] As Kennedy agreed to various measures to intensify the campaign against the Viet Cong, including the use of defoliants, he constantly sought to impose limits or obscure the full implications of what was going on. When, for example, it was agreed in late March 1962 that U.S. aircraft could intercept communist aircraft over South Vietnam, he was anxious that no publicity be given to the U.S. role when and if a communist plane crashed.[11]

The embarrassment the press caused Kennedy led to a February 1962 cable setting out clear, and restrictive, guidelines to the U.S. mission in Saigon on dealings with the press. This required close cooperation with the reporters so that appeals could then be made to their "good faith." At the same time they were also to be kept away from operations that could lead to "undesirable dispatches"—that is, those indicating that Americans were "leading and directing combat missions" or which might lead to sensational stories about children or civilians becoming the "unfortunate victims" of these operations. The reporters also had to understand the risks inherent in "frivolous, thoughtless criticism" of Diem. It was hoped that "if newsmen feel we are cooperating they will be more receptive to explanation that we are in a vicious struggle where support of South Vietnamese is crucial and that articles that tear down Diem only make our task more difficult."[12]

Appeals to good faith harked back to the Second World War, when the press had been supportive of—indeed part of—the war effort. Many based in Saigon still saw their role in those terms, trusting what they were told by senior officers. They had no great expectations about the character of the regimes that the United States supported. The younger generation of reporters were more inclined to report what they saw, not what they were told to see, and they were loath to pull their punches when it came to the excesses of the Diem regime. The South Vietnamese government denounced them so regularly (on occasion seeking to expel them), that they became a form of institutionalized opposition to the official American line, especially so long as the U.S. mission was dominated by cheerleaders such as Ambassador Nolting and General Harkins. "The closer one gets to the actual contact level of this war," Halberstam wrote in October 1962, "the further one gets from official optimism."

Both Nolting and Harkins saw no alternative to Diem and they constantly urged more understanding of Diem's predicament and patience in the search for reform. Nolting was by this time considered so close to Nhu that he was not getting honest assessments from his Vietnamese associates because they assumed that any criticisms would get back to the regime.[13] This set them on a collision course with those whose reports constantly created an air of crisis surrounding both Diem and the whole American project in Vietnam. John Mecklin, public affairs officer with the U.S. mission, later observed that it was really the mission that was "operating in a world of illusion." In this context the "feud with the newsmen was an angry symptom of bureaucratic sickness."[14] Its capacity to believe its own propaganda added to its confidence in its own reports and contempt for the newsmen as "bad" reporters rather than just critics, a view they communicated to Kennedy.

Kennedy accepted that this group was unprofessional because the stories filed were so at variance with the official advice he was receiving. At issue was domestic support for his Vietnam policy. He was not anxious for the American people to believe that the United States was at war in Vietnam, let alone that current policies were misconceived or failing. Kennedy's press strategy from May 1961 to September 1963 had largely been to refuse to talk about it on television or in the press, or even to give backgrounders. This was despite recommendations from his advisers that he explain the policy. He even complained about the number of high-level visitors to Saigon, which appeared to add to the American commitment to Vietnam.[15] In general he was giving it a very low priority, compared, for example, with the time being spent on Cuba and Laos.

In late 1962 Senator Mike Mansfield, a close friend of Kennedy's and a Far Eastern specialist, visited Saigon. He spent time with the journalists and also with the U.S. mission and was inclined to believe the former's critical, pessimistic assessment—to the point that he refused to read the obligatory optimistic parting statement prepared for him by the mission, substituting something more discouraging of his own. Returning to Washington, Mansfield prepared a report for Kennedy. He warned of the immense problems facing the strategic hamlets program, the dangerous power of Nhu, and the risk that if the current policies could not be made to work, the United States would be dragged into a massive military commitment along French lines. He encouraged the president to look for ways to lighten the American load rather than increase it. Kennedy read the report after Christmas, while sailing off Florida, and O'Donnell records him commenting that he was angry with Mansfield "for disagreeing with our policy so completely and . . . with myself because I found myself agreeing with it."[16] At a news conference just after talking to Mansfield Kennedy was notably cautious: "[W]e don't see the end of the tunnel, but I must say I don't think it is darker than it was a year ago, and in some ways lighter." A few weeks later official optimism reappeared in the State of the Union message: "The spear point of aggression has been blunted in Viet-Nam."[17]

Even those in government most wary about the claims made by the U.S. mission, such as Hilsman and Forrestal, saw the newsmen as biased and irresponsible. Having been specifically asked by Kennedy to attend to the press role during their trip to Vietnam in early 1963, they described the newsmen as being "bitter" with regard to Diem, ready to "seize on anything that goes wrong and blow it up as much as possible." They wanted a systematic campaign to get the facts out to counter the "pessimistic (and factually incorrect) picture conveyed in the press."[18] This was, of course, the time when these two still felt that the CIA analysts were too pessimistic. Yet Ap Bac had provided the press with more evidence that the official line diverged seriously from reality, and they were soon working hard to undermine it.[19] The initial result of their efforts was anguished communications throughout the policy-making community over how to get better press. This was unlikely to be achieved by the knee-jerk response from the U.S. civilian and military officials in Saigon, which was to accuse the press of peddling rumors and playing into the communists' hands. The response of the Diem government was even harsher.

In March Diem tried to expel Bigart and François Sully of *Newsweek*, only to be restrained by Nolting. In late April, Mecklin became one of Kennedy's few Vietnam-related visitors, indicating just how much he saw the problem in terms of news management. Mecklin warned the president off simply blaming the reporters and explained that the American mission had to be much more frank. The advice was accepted, but Kennedy also saw now the inherent conflict of interest between a democratic if unruly press corps and an authoritarian regime.[20] The young reporters had become essential to the anti-Diem campaign, and Diem's actions fed their credibility.

DIEM IN TROUBLE

At the start of 1963 American officials were still wary about changing the "present policy of total public and private support of [Diem's] person and family." Mansfield's observations were published in February in the form of a Senate Foreign Relations Committee report, which alarmed the Saigon elite as preparing the political ground for an American pullout. At the same time Diem began to warn the embassy that South Vietnam should not be seen as an American "protectorate."[21] With some reason, he felt that he was losing control of the situation. American military advisers were attaching themselves everywhere to his troops, while aid was being delivered directly through American channels, circumventing his own provincial administrators.[22] The more Diem expressed his disquiet, the more that influential American and Vietnamese figures, many of whom had previously supported him, saw him as being an even greater liability. The more they made their views known, the more wary Diem became, and so relations between the client and the protector began to deteriorate.

Ngo Dinh Nhu, Diem's controversial brother, gave an interview to Warren Una of the *Washington Post* that appeared on 12 May. In this he complained that there were too many American advisers and they were making it appear as if this was an American war. At least half could be safely withdrawn, he suggested, while the rest should show more patience with their South Vietnamese partners. The time was not yet ripe for an offensive. They should certainly avoid exposing themselves to enemy fire; that was why they were starting to get killed. In addition, they should stop plotting coups. This interview went down badly in Washington and almost became self-fulfilling. In addition to prompting official protests and a hurt note from Harkins, whose claims that conditions for a big offensive were almost ripe had been undercut, it led Hilsman to start searching for ways of punishing Diem without harming the war effort.[23] This incident came just after Kennedy had actually asked for a plan for troop withdrawals. Although Nolting was asked to tell Diem that it was in America's "interest to reduce our military commitment in SVN as fast as VC threat effectively reduced," and some reductions might later be possible, the threat was still too high for this to be safe. Kennedy's public response when asked about the interview was to promise to withdraw troops anytime the government of South Vietnam suggested it. By this time Kennedy appears to have concluded that the U.S. had to get out of Vietnam. He told Mansfield that he had come round to the Senator's way of thinking when they met with other congressional leaders that spring. He could see no political support for a deeper involvement in Vietnam and, on the basis of complacent official reports, had set in motion troop withdrawals. There was also an effort to stress Vietnamese-led strategic hamlets more than American-backed regular army sweeps, which tended to do more damage to rural life than to the Viet Cong.[24] He could not suggest that the Americans would stay beyond their welcome.

To get out of Vietnam was not a definite decision, as later claimed, so much as a working assumption. In dealing with the press Kennedy stuck to the line that the U.S. was in Vietnam for the long term. Any suggestion that Vietnam was to be abandoned and he could soon lose control of events. The model was not abrupt departure but gradual disengagement, which then seemed possible. The schedule certainly suited the presidential election time-table but it was most dependent upon a degree of military and political stability in Vietnam. Unfortunately whatever stability there was at that moment was only surface deep.

In May a crisis suddenly flared, reflecting long-standing Buddhist hostility to a government that was openly biased in favor of Catholics even though the latter group represented, at least nominally, no more than 10 percent of the population, while more than 70 percent were nominal Buddhists. During the 1950s Diem had encouraged his fellow Catholics to flee from the North to help him shore up his base in the South. The American press corps helped publicize the Buddhists' grievances, in part hoping that this might help bring Diem down. The reporters were later criticized for mistaking a highly politicized urban group for a mass movement, and failing to understand the complexity of religion and culture in Vietnam.[25] The Buddhists themselves had a keener sense of public relations than the regime, using self-immolation as a shocking protest gesture certain to attract international attention. The effect was reinforced by provocative statements by Nhu and his wife, who acquired notoriety by her offer to provide gasoline after an elderly monk burned himself to death. Having traveled the country trying to make sense of the war against the communists, the reporters now stayed in Saigon waiting for the next dramatic event in the Diem presidency. The nature of the regime being defended now became the top issue in the American public's understanding of the war's conduct. From politicians, academics, clerics, and editorials came a surge of demands for political change in South Vietnam.

So if Kennedy could be persuaded that the military situation in South Vietnam was under control, it was hard to convince him that the same could be said about the political situation. The news management issue had moved well beyond unfavorable reporting, and the main problem was now the highly public acts of the Vietnamese leadership. Diem was warned that the Kennedy administration would soon have little choice but to dissociate itself from the regime. Diem's attempts at compromise were halfhearted and came to naught. He saw the Americans as stirring the pot and became even more defiant in consequence. A rebuke by Nolting's deputy on 13 June became public knowledge the next day. Gradually American diplomats and reporters were making common cause. On 3 July Halberstam reported that "some American officials" wanted a new government in Saigon and that "some young military officers" were ready to oblige. The impression had been gained, however, that "they would like the Americans to make a public statement calling for a change. It is widely believed here that any statement from Washington critical of Ngo Dinh Diem for his handling of the Buddhist crisis would touch off an internal military strike at the government."[26] This was a political act as much a report, semiauthoritative given the range of Halberstam's contacts and not calculated to ease Diem's suspicions of his American friends. The story also contained an essential truth: that Diem had become so isolated, and the Americans so prominent, that he was vulnerable to a word of criticism. Washington did not really need to conspire to overthrow him.

Potential plotters sensed American power, but also that they could be its victims. As the attempted coup just before Kennedy had come to office had been in effect thwarted by American officials, in that their attempts to broker a deal allowed Diem and his brother some breathing space during which they mobilized loyal troops, dissident generals were chary about confiding in Americans. They would certainly want a green light from Washington before having another go. The question for the summer of 1963 was whether the moment for the green light had come.

Counterinsurgency theory suggested that the government had to win over "hearts and minds." Generating a widespread popular appeal was hardly Diem's forte. An alternative view, to which the military inclined, was that these situations called for tough leadership. The communists were more likely to take advantage of signs of softness than a hard line. Added to this was the view that Diem was "the only bastard we have." It was unwise to upset him unless one was sure that there was an alternative who would not only be more liberal and reformist, if that was what was wanted, but have the clout to see these policies through. The most likely alternative would be a general, who might offer a more focused effort in the field but would be an unlikely instrument of liberal democracy. A final factor was the extent to which Diem might play the nationalist card against the United States. American warnings—if anything, gently put—concerning the malign influence of Ngo Dinh Nhu on the counterinsurgency program resulted in Diem expressing his irritation with attempts to direct the course of his government. He still had the authority to do a deal with the communists that would cut the Americans out altogether, and he was not unhappy for that to be appreciated in Washington.

The situation was not unusual for the cold war. The Americans were backing a regime that was anticommunist but also nondemocratic. This made declarations about the "free world" seem hollow and required ignoring gross abuses of human rights. At another level it also suggested a certain lack of confidence in the precepts of liberal democracy, accepting that desperate circumstances made the effort to develop legitimacy based on a form of representative government less rather than more necessary. The tough social scientists of the nation-building, modernization school put a great deal of effort into trying to get their minds around this problem, for they did not wish to deny that liberal democracy was the highest stage of political development. Perhaps, though, they reasoned, for economically underdeveloped and insecure countries tough leaders made more sense, and legitimacy might be found through nonwestern means. There was always the fallback argument that however bad the regime, a communist replacement was likely to be much worse.

At a more mundane level it was awkward to deal with any government other than the one in place. If the Americans started meeting with dissidents, rebels, and insurrectionists, let alone conspiring with them, and the regime still hung on, then relations would plummet and the struggle against communism would suffer. On the other hand, if the Americans overtly supported a regime and it was overthrown, then they would be condemned by the new government for their association with the old. This was what had happened in Cuba.

The basic problem was identified by Hans Morgenthau in an influential article of May 1962. He warned of the danger of supporting regimes such as that of Diem, "whose political weakness compels us in the end to commit ourselves militarily beyond what our national interest would require." He saw the logic of the current Vietnam strategy leading to a Korean-type war fought in even less favorable circumstances and with all the attendant domestic stresses. He argued that the American objective should be to establish a "viable political order, which constitutes the only effective defense against Communist subversion."[27] Morgenthau believed that "a general" could be found upon which to base such an order. In the past, though, generals had never been the basis of a viable Vietnamese political order. Only a general might have the strength to topple Diem, but that did not mean that he would have the political capacity to build a popular government. The Americans had tolerated for many years a situation in which Diem had done his best to ensure that there was no obvious alternative to him.

Even more influential, because of the direct influence it had on Henry Cabot Lodge as he prepared for his new job as ambassador to South Vietnam, was an article by Charles Mohr of *Time* magazine. Mohr was one of the more skeptical members of the American press corps in Saigon but saw no alternative to Diem. The problem, he claimed, was that Ambassador Nolting had been too weak in pressing Diem to address the problems of nepotism, corruption, and tyranny that were eroding the legitimacy of his government and the American capacity to provide support. Mohr described the two governments as being like "two teenagers playing head-on collision chicken in souped-up hot rods . . . The trouble is, the U.S. chickens out before Diem does." Lodge was struck by this metaphor of a game of chicken as he contemplated his own dealings with Diem.[28]

The metaphor already had wide currency, but largely as part of the attempt by civilian nuclear strategists, such as Schelling and Kahn, to conceptualize the problems of crisis management in the nuclear era. How did one convey to the opponent that one would not, perhaps could not, swerve first when the consequences of a collision would be so disastrous? The metaphor worked for these purposes by highlighting the common interest in avoiding a catastrophic outcome even while the starting point was complete antagonism. The problem with the metaphor in Vietnam was that the two protagonists supposedly were starting with a common interest, which a game of chicken would disrupt to the point where either might prefer a collision.

39

Coercion and Clients

EARLY IN JULY the possibilities of a coup against Diem were actively discussed in Washington. Given the political turmoil in Saigon, a coup would become more likely if the Americans spoke out against Diem. Whether this would help or hinder the war effort was a matter of debate, and on the resolution of that debate hinged the attitude the American government might take should evidence emerge of a plot. The next month matters came to a head. On 22 August Lodge arrived in Saigon as American ambassador.

The necessity of replacing Nolting was to Hilsman and Forrestal the natural corollary of their growing sense that something would have to be done about Diem. At the very least they saw a need to start pressing him about how he should improve his military and political strategy. They could not allow themselves to be associated with his more objectionable practices.[1] For this purpose Lodge was an intriguing choice. He had been displaced from the Senate by Kennedy in 1952 and in 1960 he had been on the Republican ticket for the vice presidency. Despite this, he was not that far ideologically from Kennedy's New Frontier. In addition, he came from a patrician background with a strong sense of public duty; he had long experience as U.S. ambassador to the United Nations; he was a linguist; and he even had a Buddhist for an uncle.[2] Kennedy had been attracted by the idea of a local strongman of his own, able to pull the competing parts of the American effort in Saigon together, improve the terrible relations that had developed there with the American press, and put real pressure in Diem. Apparently at Lodge's own instigation, his name was put forward by Rusk as a bipartisan figure, useful when it came to getting wider congressional support for policy. It no doubt occurred to Kennedy that if the policy got into trouble, the association of a leading Republican would be helpful. The choice certainly reflects Kennedy's tendency to phrase the problem at this time in political terms—Washington's more than Saigon's.

Lodge's arrival coincided with a sharp deterioration in Vietnam. Before Nolting left he had told Diem that if he attacked pagodas, the United States would have to condemn his action. News that they had indeed been attacked came as Nolting, Lodge, and Hilsman met in Hawaii. On 21 August, with Buddhists urging open revolt against the Diem regime, martial law had been declared and Nhu had ordered a move against Buddhist pagodas, leading to many injuries and some 1,400 monks arrested. Nhu had his special forces disguise themselves as regular army units, who were then blamed. Initially, as Nhu had cut their telephone lines, American diplomats accepted this version. Disgruntled senior South Vietnamese officers approached the U.S. embassy asking that Diem be told to remove his brother from power if he was to receive continued American support.

Lodge saw the attacks on the pagodas as timed for his benefit. Almost at once he was possessed with an unshakable conviction that the United States could not support the status quo in Saigon. Something had to give. This he signaled by his first act as ambassador—visiting Buddhist monks who had taken refuge in a U.S. building. He also moved to build close relations with Halberstam, Sheehan, and other dissident reporters, inviting them to his residence. Kennedy had given him an analysis by Robert Manning, a former *Time* correspondent now in the State Department, of the press corps in Saigon, which reported their "unanimous bitterness toward, and contempt for the Diem government." Their criticisms stemmed from the damage being done to a worthwhile policy rather than, as the South Vietnamese implied, procommunist sympathies.[3] Having been the recipients of leaked information from low-ranking officials and officers, exasperated with the refusal of Harkins and Nolting to accept negative material, the reporters now had access to the top American source in Vietnam, and for his part Lodge came to view these men as having a better grasp of the situation in Vietnam than many of the officials he had inherited. In Washington as well, for a vital moment Halberstam's dramatic and urgent analysis created a deep sense of crisis.

THE SATURDAY NIGHT CABLE

After two days in Saigon, Lodge received a telegram from Washington with incendiary advice. The disaffected generals were to be told that Nhu's presence in power would not be tolerated.

> U.S. Government cannot tolerate situation in which power lies in Nhu's hands. Diem must be given chance to rid himself of Nhu and his coterie and replace them with best military and political personalities available.
>
> If, in spite of all your efforts, Diem remains obdurate and refuses, then we must face the possibility that Diem himself cannot be preserved.

After discussing how military leaders should be warned of the limits to American support unless Nhu was removed from the scene, the telegram advised that the ambassador and his team "should urgently examine all possible alternative leadership and make detailed plans as to how we might bring about Diem's replacement if this should become necessary."[4] This did not find an unwilling or shocked recipient. Lodge was prepared to take an even more decisive line: He cabled back to Washington his own preference for a direct approach to the plotters rather than alerting Diem to their existence. Despite having barely been in Saigon long enough to start developing his own network of contacts, Lodge was signaling his own preference for a coup.

Kennedy met with his most senior advisers on 26 August to find them in uproar. They were furious that such a dramatic policy decision had been made by middle-ranking officials over a weekend when, it so happened, almost all of the top echelon of government was out of town. What Taylor later called the "end-run" had been led by Roger Hilsman, recently promoted to assistant secretary for Far Eastern affairs, backed by his predecessor in the post, Harriman, who had recently moved on to become undersecretary of state for political affairs, and Forrestal of the NSC staff. This group had long despaired of Diem, and with Lodge in Saigon they now had a powerful ally. They were also the most in tune with Kennedy's own views and were the ones to whom Kennedy often turned directly for advice. Seized of the urgency and potential of the moment after Nhu's move against the pagodas, they had sought to get approval from the Pentagon and the CIA by sidestepping their likely opponents.

Kennedy's style of government led to him working with a group of officials he liked and trusted, even though this might mean keeping others with clear responsibilities for a policy area in the dark about his thinking or initiatives. In this instance he was caught by this rather haphazard approach to the policy-making process. Consequently he was furious with the group because their tactics had aggravated the divisions within his government, and all three now had to work hard to regain Kennedy's respect.

Taylor was livid at being unable to advise against a coup. McCone lacked confidence that a coup would improve matters and was wary of the role his own operatives would have to play in bringing one to a successful conclusion. Rusk and McNamara were unhappy with the very idea of the United States attempting to engineer the fall of a government with which it had close relations. At most McNamara was ready to employ the advisers, equipment, and money being provided to Diem to extract concessions.[5] Any coup should be left to the South Vietnamese. Moreover, before Americans got tied up with any coups they should at least be able to form some view on the prospects for success and the consequences of success.

This was a critical moment in the development of American policy, though not because the telegram itself was immediately consequential. Read strictly, it was not actually calling for a coup and, anyway, no coup materialized. This was partly Hilsman's fault. Aware that the South Vietnamese army generals were cross that the Americans had blamed them instead of Nhu's secret police for the pagoda raids, he gave UPI a story that exonerated the army and then arranged for the Voice of America to broadcast it. The actual broadcast went a little further. American officials were said to have indicated that "the U.S. may sharply reduce its aid to Vietnam unless President Diem gets rid of secret police officials responsible for the attacks."[6] This was of greater significance than the cable. It was so blatant that Diem was alerted to the danger he faced, and the coup evaporated.

Kennedy later took the view that the importance of the cable was that it had set Lodge on a course that he was to follow until the coup did eventually come, just over two months later. Yet the course had already begun to form in the ambassador's mind. In addition, if there was one thing that Washington agreed upon, it was that Diem's current policies, and the free hand he gave to his sinister brother and sister-in-law, were intolerable. The collision course had already been set. The only question was the form the collision might take and its outcome.

The moment was critical, because the squabbling among his advisers revealed to Kennedy a policy-making process in disarray. This was not a good time for him. Personally he was still grieving for the loss of his stillborn son at the start of the month. Politically he was pleased to have the test ban treaty, but he could not know for sure that it would be ratified. On the domestic front the civil rights issue was heating up, and this was always likely to eat into his political support, especially in the South. His ratings had slipped from 60 percent to below 50 percent. The great March on Washington, where Martin Luther King Jr. was to proclaim his dream, was scheduled for that week. He was having trouble with Congress on most issues. He had assumed that at least he did not have to worry too much about Vietnam, believing that his basic strategy was correct. This was not the product of much thought on the president's part. He had been content to accept assurances that all was going well. On these assurances he could look forward to a gradual withdrawal of U.S. advisers, to be completed just after the 1964 election.

The weekend events revealed that nothing could be taken for granted. This crisis was more intense and more difficult than he had realized, and there was no consensus among his advisers on how to handle it. Indeed, they were at each other's throats. He was therefore annoyed at those in the bureaucracy with whom he was normally most in sympathy for acting in such a way as to exaggerate this confusion; he was left with no choice but to try to get a grip on policy. A sure sign of his concern was that for the first time Robert Kennedy, though deeply preoccupied with the developing black revolution in America's South, was also brought into Vietnam deliberations.[7]

Robert Kennedy's first observation, having discussed matters with McNamara and Taylor, was that "our policy had not been discussed as every other major decision since the Bay of Pigs had been discussed."[8] This was largely the president's own fault. He had scheduled few meetings on the subject. Over the next weeks there was no shortage of meetings, but still no definitive policy emerged. The divisions in the government reflected real disagreements, combined with distinctive institutional interests and clashing personalities.

A distraught Nolting was back in Washington. He had been on vacation as the crisis deepened. His deputy, William Truehart, had then engaged in what Nolting believed to be rank insubordination by sending back from Saigon cables that were far less supportive of Diem. Then he had discovered that he was to be replaced by Lodge; finally, a desperate attempt to persuade Diem to behave more sensibly had turned into an exercise in futility. He recognized that the most likely alternative to Diem would be a military government that would call on the United States for military forces as the Vietnamese preferred to have the Americans fight for them.[9]

Kennedy allowed Nolting to be heard to ensure that the pro-Diem case got an airing, but that made for furious arguments with Harriman. McNamara and Taylor at the Pentagon resented the influence of Hilsman and Lodge as well as their airy dismissal of military judgments, while McCone believed that amateurs were dabbling in the black art of coup making, which they did not begin to understand. Lodge did succeed in establishing in Saigon, as Kennedy had wished, a unified position, but only because he systematically excluded or ignored those in the U.S. mission, and in particular Harkins and the CIA station chief, John Richardson, with whom he disagreed. He took advice when it coincided with his own opinion and argued back or simply took no notice when it did not. Time and again he received instructions to meet Diem to express American concerns, but he ignored them, preferring to keep Diem guessing. Within and between Saigon and Washington lines of communication became blocked and distorted. To Kennedy's even greater irritation the press became a natural means of ventilating concerns and exposing the foolishness of bureaucratic opponents.

The basic problem was that no good policy was available. Getting the optimum outcome—an independent and free South Vietnam—depended on the quality of the South Vietnamese military and political effort. The basic question was what should be done if that effort failed. The administration found this too awkward to confront directly at this time. They still assumed that the war could be won. Posing the question of what would happen if it could not be won pointed to the two extreme answers—either precipitate withdrawal and the probable "loss" of South

Vietnam, or undertaking a much more substantial military commitment. Before these extreme positions were reached, other possibilities might be an attempt at a negotiated settlement on the basis of neutralization, on one hand, or a new military strategy with a different sort of American backing, on the other. These possibilities were all raised during the course of the month, but none was followed seriously. At no point did Kennedy act as if the problem was anything other than one of getting a government in South Vietnam deserving of American support and capable of prosecuting the war against communism.

In one of the many meetings held at this time, on 31 August, when Kennedy was not present, Paul Kattenburg, in charge of the Interdepartmental Working Group on Vietnam and recently returned from the country, raised the question of withdrawal. He had concluded during his visit that Diem's position was desperate and that the masses wanted not just change but also an end to the war. Most important, he felt that the army was unlikely to achieve either objective. This developed into a growing feeling that Washington simply did not understand the struggle going on in Vietnam, and in particular the extent to which communism and nationalism had become identified with each other. The Washington argument was between proponents of an orthodox military strategy with the existing government and of a more radical counterinsurgency strategy with an alternative government. Kattenburg understood that neither would work, a thought that crystallized for him as he listened to the vice president, the secretaries of state and defense, and the chairman of the Joint Chiefs of Staff discuss the problem. None of them really knew what he was talking about, and none had a real grasp of Vietnamese history and politics. Having briefly explained why current policies could not succeed, "I finally and imprudently for such meetings blurted out that I thought we should now consider 'withdrawal with honor.'" He got hostile questioning from Taylor, flat disagreement from Nolting, and then a dusty response from Rusk: "[W]e will not pull out of Vietnam until the war is won." McNamara agreed, and then the vice president weighed in. From a practical and political viewpoint, he insisted, "it would be a disaster to pull out."[10]

Kattenburg's experience provided a clear warning that a certain subject was taboo, although with the Kennedys and Harriman absent and all the hard-liners present, this was an unpromising setting in which to propose such a radical departure. The first sentence in a note reporting a conversation between Hilsman and Bundy straight after this meeting was "The important thing is to win the war."[11] Robert Kennedy at least posed the question of withdrawal a few days later (and received a similar response from Rusk), but the general tenor of the discussions almost took for granted the necessity for, and plausibility of, the eventual defeat of the communists. At the same time there was an equal disbelief in the possibility of large-scale American military involvement. In September Rusk identified the "outer limits to policy," saying that "we do not get out and turn South Viet-Nam over to the Viet-Cong . . . we do not use large-scale forces to occupy the country and run it ourselves."

Perhaps more striking than the inability to contemplate the complete failure of policy was the fact that while the consensus was generally anti-coup, nobody was arguing that some pressure should not be put on Diem. It is unclear whether those opposing a coup (other than McCone) actually grasped the processes involved or understood the destabilizing effect on Diem's regime of any visible manifestation of American disquiet. In terms of American actions, the distinction between the coercion of Diem and ensuring his overthrow was blurred, especially as American contacts with the plotters at all times had to be circumspect.

The idea that Americans could work with disaffected members of the local elite to engineer the resignation of an anticommunist dictator who had become an embarrassment was not new. It had worked with Syngh-man Rhee in Korea in 1960. The most recent experience with this sort of escapade had been with Phoumi in Laos, who had been successfully coerced. Harriman did, in fact, urge Rusk that "we should tell Diem what we were going to do and stick to it. We had gone through the same thing with Phoumi!"

Whether or not they consciously adopted the model, Harriman and Hilsman followed a similar approach. As with Phoumi, they were convinced that Diem had become the main obstacle to a policy outcome consistent with American interests, and the example of Phoumi suggested that these local strongmen could be outmaneuvered. Rusk, by contrast, tended to hark back not to Phoumi but to the earlier strongmen of Asian politics—Chiang Kai-shek and Synghman Rhee—and he was haunted by the memory of China being lost to communism because the United States withdrew support from Chiang in response to his oppressive policies.[12]

In Laos, Souvanna was waiting to lead an alternative government and offered some prospect of serving as a unifying force. Neutralism had been accepted, as Phoumi's forces proved themselves to be totally incapable of taking on the Pathet Lao, and American pressure had been geared toward obliging him to accept the political logic of his military weakness. In Vietnam the military situation seemed to be much more hopeful, so Diem's failure was becoming a liability by creating conditions that could threaten gains and push the counterinsurgency program into reverse gear. Remarkably, the policy makers made few attempts to determine whether the war was actually still relatively unaffected by the political turmoil in Saigon. Even the anti-Diem faction warned of future decline rather than imminent disaster. Hilsman sketched a "graph of the future" with the current regime showing "a slow but steady deterioration downwards in which apathy in the army, a drifting off of junior officers and noncommissioned officers, possibly student and labor strikes would slowly but surely degrade the war effort."[13]

Diem's main crime was to be found in his conspicuous repression. Lodge observed that the "United States can get along with corrupt dictators who manage to stay out of the newspapers. But an inefficient Hitlerism, the leaders of which make fantastic statements to the press, is the hardest thing on earth for the U.S. Government to support."[14] For Kennedy this was a severe public relations problem. He was bothered that, as a Catholic, he was accused of supporting a Catholic regime in its persecution of another religious group, and that, as a leader of a democratic country, he could be charged with complicity in brutality and repression. He wanted the persecution to stop, and with this, he hoped, would stop domestic criticism of current policy. His discussions of demands started with Diem removing his brother Nhu from office, largely because of his association in the public mind with the worst excesses of the regime, and finding a way to stop Madame Nhu from making outrageous statements. His requirement was a government that would not embarrass Washington. The American people needed to be reassured "that we are not asking Americans to be killed to support Madame Nhu's desire to barbecue bonzes."[15] There was a much hazier notion about the sort of government would best serve Vietnamese interests.

PRESSURE ON DIEM

Kennedy's first step on 26 August had been to confirm the policy embodied in the weekend telegram. All present were asked if the president should rescind the instructions he had already approved to Lodge. None stepped forward. As he had begun to work with a group of generals, to abandon them now would close off even more options for the future. Lodge was given discretion to suspend aid to South Vietnam if necessary and to keep in touch with the plotters. With the bit between his teeth, the new ambassador cabled Washington that the United States was now embarked "on a course from which there is no *respectable* turning back: the overthrow of the Diem government."[16]

When this set of plotters backed off, Kennedy then urged caution on Lodge. He saw the danger of the United States becoming committed to a course of action that could end in humiliation. He reserved the right to alter his previous instructions. Recalling the Bay of Pigs, he wrote to Lodge: "I know from experience that failure is more destructive than an appearance of indecision."[17] Yet while Kennedy was wary about instigating the overthrow of Diem, he did accept that there was no turning back from the criticism of Diem's policies. Having attempted to maintain silence on Vietnam, Kennedy had been unable to take a lead. Now, even if he had wanted to make the case for Diem, he would have found it difficult to change American opinion. During August, for example, when the president had said not a public word, David Halberstam had fifteen page-one stories and nine inside-page stories published on Vietnam under his byline in the *New York Times,* and the paper had developed a firm anti-Diem editorial line.[18]

Kennedy's first public initiative was an interview with the respected television presenter Walter Cronkite, of CBS News, on 2 September. Bundy prepared guidance for the interview. It started by stressing the areas of agreement with the government of South Vietnam, in particular the defeat of the communist campaign. It endorsed the strategic hamlets program and paid due note to the "outstanding leadership" provided in the past by Diem. Important differences had developed, however, "over certain acts of arbitrary power."

> Our difficulties over such acts is double: First, as a democratic people, we cannot approve of this kind of repression in a situation in which we are closely engaged and where our resources provide much of the government's strength. Second, we believe that such acts undermine the unity of the people of the country, weaken confidence in the government, and so play into the hands of the Communists.

This concern was being communicated to the government "continuously." The American effort in Vietnam was large but would be put into question "if the essential conditions for success were no longer present." However, this point had not yet been reached. American "support for the people of South Vietnam will continue as long as it is wanted and can be effective." Note that the support was for the people rather than the government.[19]

For Kennedy the problem with the Cronkite interview was that thirty minutes of discussion was cut down to twelve minutes of broadcast, and this resulted in a far more anti-Diem piece than the president had intended.[20] The televised interview had Kennedy getting straight to the point, replying to Cronkite's first question by stating that:

> I don't think that unless a greater effort is made by the Government to win popular support that the war can be won out there. In the final analysis, it is their war. They are the ones who have to win or lose it. We can help them, we can give them equipment, we can send our men out there as advisers, but they have to win it, the people of Viet-Nam, against the Communists.

On air Kennedy criticized the government for getting "out of touch with the people," but expressed confidence that with "changes in policy and perhaps with personnel" the government could regain popular support. He did not demur when Cronkite observed that Diem had shown no intention of "changing his pattern." "If he does not change it," remarked Kennedy, "that is his decision. . . . Our best judgment is that he can't be successful on this basis." Only then did he add, "I don't agree with those who say we should withdraw. That would be a big mistake."[21] In his public utterances thereafter he tried to redress the balance, and never deviated from the view that victory in Vietnam did matter. In mid-September he told an interviewer that he did accept the "domino theory," and that if "South Vietnam went," this would "give the impression that the wave of the future in Southeast Asia was China and the Communists."[22]

On 3 September Kennedy met with all his senior advisers on Vietnam and set out his thinking. First, he had cooled toward the idea of a coup. If the Vietnamese generals wanted to act, they could contact the United States—"meanwhile, we assume that they are not acting and that we are going down a diplomatic route." Second, the military situation was not a factor at this time. The meeting participants agreed that "no action need be taken in connection with current restrictions to our military forces." Maxwell Taylor had with him an upbeat assessment of operations in Vietnam indicating "favorable trends in all military activities, despite Saigon's preoccupation with the unstable political situation."[23] Third, there was no interest in a negotiated outcome. On 29 August President de Gaulle of France had offered to help negotiate a deal between the two Vietnams to turn them into a unified state. This was against the backdrop of contacts between Hanoi and Saigon in which Nhu was believed to be involved. Given the arguments with de Gaulle over European policy and the lack of any serious French financial or military contribution to the travails in its former colonies, there was little reason to take de Gaulle's offer seriously. Kennedy did not suppose that neutralization was really an option—it "was not working in Laos."

Lodge's instructions after this meeting confirmed the administration's preference for persuasion rather than a coup. For example, though the draft version told Lodge to emphasize to Diem that the president had "carefully understated degree of his concern" in the Cronkite interview, the final version toned this down. The embassy was to reestablish working relations with the Vietnamese government and military, and press Diem directly for a positive response to the president's concerns. The United States would continue to express its discontent with repression, Diem must be told, but the objective would be to improve the situation and not to overthrow the government.[24] Lodge was skeptical. He did not expect much from the South Vietnamese president. At the very least something had to be done about the United States' lack of "leverage" over Diem, which was necessary if this diplomatic route was to be pursued. All the ambassador could think of was possible congressional action against aid to South Vietnam or withholding more explicit American backing for Diem's policies. Kennedy was in fact thinking along similar lines, asking Hilsman to explore "things we could do that would not have a material effect immediately but would send them the word." Hilsman had already taken steps to identify measures that would not affect the war effort. He had also found a clear sentiment in Congress for putting pressure on Diem.[25]

The development of ideas for putting pressure on Diem was taken further on 6 September, when top policy makers met again. There was now momentum in the United Nations for a resolution condemning the Diem regime, while U.S. public opinion was becoming more hostile to the South Vietnamese leader. Rusk warned that if the situation continued to deteriorate, the United States would be faced with "no alternative short of a massive U.S. military effort." He wanted Lodge to tell Diem that without prompt action "there will be a drastic effect in the U.S. involving both reduction in economic and military assistance and strong pressure to withdraw U.S. political support of South Vietnam." Yet he also clearly felt that it was difficult to calibrate policy without far better information on the military situation. In the absence of his brother (who arrived late), Robert Kennedy asked the hard questions. Could the war be won with Diem and Nhu? Was there any chance that they would change? Why not "grasp the nettle now," threatening Diem with a cut in the U.S. effort?

At the apparent suggestion from the attorney general that full withdrawal should be considered, Rusk warned against threatening such a serious step. He wanted a more cautious start, although he subsequently made clear that he did not exclude pulling out. Bundy agreed that the decisive moment had yet to arrive when it had to be said that "we can't win with Diem." Taylor reminded the company of the Joint Chiefs' assessment that the war could be won with Diem. Robert asked again what should be done if the war could not be won with Diem. This time McNamara responded that the question could not be answered because Washington lacked sufficient information (in itself a striking admission). Out of this came a recommendation that General Krulak, the Pentagon's counterinsurgency chief, be sent out to make a report. While this was being done Lodge was told to initiate talks with Diem to ascertain his attitudes and to bring home to him the urgent need to repair the image of his government. He was not to make any direct threats until Krulak's assessment was complete. Lodge did as he was asked. His report of the meeting with Diem was not encouraging: "Although I stated what I intended to state many times, I did not feel he was really deeply interested. He seemed totally absorbed with his own problems here and was justifying himself and attacking his enemies."[26]

On 10 September, after a whirlwind visit, Krulak, reflecting the standard military line, submitted his report: "The shooting war is still going ahead at an impressive pace. It has been affected adversely by the political crisis, but the impact is not great. . . . [T]he Viet Cong war will be won if the current U.S. military and sociological programs are pursued, irrespective of the grave defects in the ruling regime."[27] After these conclusions had been reported, Joseph Mendenhall of the State Department's

Far East Planning Office, who had accompanied Krulak, gave his impressions. He pointed to a virtual breakdown of government in Saigon and an atmosphere of fear and hate, warning that the war would be lost with Diem. After hearing the two reports, Kennedy queried: "The two of you did visit the same country, didn't you?"

Krulak explained the difference by suggesting that Mendenhall had visited the metropolitan areas, while he had obtained a more national view. Nolting added that Mendenhall was known to be anti-Diem and had assumed, incorrectly, in 1961 that the communists were winning.[28] However, Mendenhall's pessimism was backed up by Rufus Phillips, formerly of the CIA and now of the Agency for International Development, who was well connected in Saigon, and John Mecklin, of the United States Information Agency (USIA), who argued that the whole government in Saigon had to be removed and that in the ensuing chaos it might be necessary to send in U.S. combat troops.[29] With these divergent opinions expressed before him, the president could only ask that they not be expressed in the press, and suggested a further meeting the next day.

That evening the principals met again, without the president, to try to give some shape to American policy; the occasion simply prompted an argument between Harriman and McNamara. Harriman saw little purpose in attempting to work with Diem; McNamara believed that the United States had to work with him, and so the main effort had to be put into forcing a change in his policies. At its conclusion Edward R. Murrow, the head of USIA, asked to be relieved of writing press guidance, as "the guidance could not be written until our policy was clear."[30]

Into this confusion Lodge intervened with a powerful telegram. He argued bluntly for supporting a coup. The situation in Vietnam, he warned, was "worsening rapidly," and the United States had to use "whatever sanctions it has to bring about the fall of the existing government and the installation of another." The best method he saw of doing this involved the suspension of aid. He gave powerful reasons to doubt the confident military judgment that operational performance need not be drastically affected by political discontent, and expressed his view that the discontent was becoming more intense—to the point where "the ship of state here is slowly sinking." A wait-and-see policy would leave the educated classes disillusioned with the United States and result in the systematic elimination of alternative leaders. He posed a series of questions on the modalities of orchestrating a change in government—the use of leaks and formal statements to create the right impression, offering inducements to the right leader (the United States did "not want to substitute a Castro for a Batista"), evacuating dependents, taking remedial action to protect the poor from the withdrawal of aid, and supplying the Vietnamese army directly.[31]

This was one politician writing to another, and it impressed Kennedy, who thought it the most "powerful" assessment he had seen.[32] It had a big impact on Bundy, who sensed his master's moods, and so strengthened Harriman while weakening the position of McNamara and Taylor in the internal arguments. Yet with Rusk worried that Diem had still not been given a chance, Kennedy could not easily ignore the misgivings of all his most senior foreign policy advisers. The deadlock persisted. Somehow a course of action had to be identified upon which all could agree. Once again graduated response offered a way out. This was not an administration that liked to close off options earlier than was absolutely necessary, as Michael Forrestal observed when examining, at the request of Bundy, the merits of a minimalist approach (involving little more than private and public requests for changes).

> If our objectives are not achieved after a reasonable point of time, or if the situation deteriorates to a point where hard evidence indicates that an eventual collapse of the war effort is uncertain, we should still be able to move up the scale and adopt more aggressive tactics.

On the other hand, once a program of graduated sanctions had been adopted, it would not be so easy to turn back. The problem with a minimalist approach was the time it might take to bring results, allowing negative tendencies toward apathy or neutralism to take hold. However, as no coups were apparently imminent, and with the lack of consensus on measures to pressure Diem, never mind move beyond pressure, policy had shifted, in Bundy's words, from "one of urgent action to sequential steps."[33]

Hilsman drafted two alternative cables with an accompanying memorandum, reflecting ideas that had begun to develop during the discussion on the Lodge memorandum on 11 September. The approach represented by the first cable was based on pressure, and threatened the aid program unless Nhu's authority was curtailed; the second cable aimed for reconciliation with Diem.[34] Hilsman sought to sharpen the debate and force a conclusion with these two alternatives. Reconciliation would require public acquiescence in Diem's current policies, plus a friendly dialogue with Diem seeking to persuade him that positive changes were needed (perhaps using Lansdale as a trusted intermediary). Hilsman did not have high hopes of such a strategy succeeding. He was more confident about graduated pressure, a scheme of escalating actions by the United States, with tactical suggestions on their implementation and manner of public disclosure, linked to particular demands. The campaign of graduated pressure would begin with phase one, in which there were continued conversations with Diem to urge reform, with a stress on the growing demands from Congress; action would be confined to the "limited, voluntary evacuation of American dependants." In phase two, Diem would be informed reluctantly that it had "become politically necessary take certain actions convince U.S. public supporting only those GVN efforts with which we agree." These actions would involve certain aid programs, the withdrawal of support from South Vietnamese government organs supporting repression, measures to prevent equipment provided by the United States being used for repression, cuts in some financial payments, and the evacuation of all dependents. Phases three and four would effectively involve an explicit move to a coup. The ultimate sanction would involve complete disassociation from the Diem regime and a public statement of preference for an alternative.

Hilsman recognized the reluctance in the government to move to phases three and four, as they would create a situation over which the United States had little control. On the other hand, he had little confidence in the reconciliation track. His recommendation was therefore to try phases one and two of the pressure track and then, if these failed to produce the desired result, to move over to the reconciliation track. Forrestal, getting more frustrated, assumed that phase one might be a basis for a break in the impasse. That this might be possible was indicated by Krulak's observation that sticking to phase one would "make the idea of reconciliation compatible with the idea of escalating pressure." This left phase two the main area for debate.

Instructions to Lodge drafted by Bundy started from the presumption that there would be no good opportunity to get rid of the present government in the immediate future, so the expectations of progress were modest, though the measures to be proposed to Diem required a fundamental change of political direction on his part. Lodge, who had been reluctant to talk with Diem when his hand was so weak, was told to get the dialogue going.[35]

In his considered response to his new instructions Lodge took care not to rule out turning against Diem in the future, describing the proposed policy as an "interim measure" and making clear the unlikelihood of Diem and Nhu agreeing to dismantle the political structure upon which they rested. "They have scant comprehension as to what it is to appeal to public opinion as they have really no interest in any other opinion than their own." He was looking for means to signal displeasure to Diem without undermining the economy or the war effort. If an answer was found to this conundrum, Lodge observed, it would "be one of the greatest discoveries since the enactment of the Marshall Plan in 1947." "[T]he U.S. has never yet been able to control any of the very unsatisfactory governments through which we have had to work in our many very successful attempts to make these countries strong enough to stand alone."

Weeks of intense and bitter debate within Washington had failed to develop a coherent plan for dealing with Diem. It had no reliable means of persuading Diem to reform or organizing a satisfactory succession. This was because its prime concern was not the governance of South Vietnam but victory in the war against communism. If these priorities could have been reversed, then the problem would have been much easier.

The threat to withdraw American support would have been credible. As it was, the erosion of public sympathy for Diem's regime, then threatening to take American policy out of the administration's control, was the most important bargaining chip available to Washington. Far less impressive was the effort to develop sanctions serious enough to impress Diem without hurting the war effort. Such an effort led inevitably to the symbolic and the marginal. Even then the divisions within the American government impeded the development of options. Thus Harkins objected to any sanctions related directly to the war effort or even actions that could suggest, as would the evacuation of American families, that the war was anything other than being won.[36] The many U.S. agencies operating out of Saigon were wary about identifying any areas in their programs that could be cut, lest the budgetary provision never be restored.[37]

Hilsman had developed a complex package of measures with the sort of calibration of objectives and measures (and detailed linkages between the two) that impressed policy-making circles, though supposing a totally unrealistic degree of American control. It is doubtful if he took this package very seriously. As he admitted in a direct letter to Lodge, the only point of selective cuts in aid packages was to signal to the Vietnamese officer class how much the United States disapproved of the current regime, so that they might create the pressure on their generals for a coup. Lodge, who had doubted from the start that Diem and Nhu could be persuaded to bend to the United States' will, concurred. He had arrived in Saigon prepared to talk tough to Diem but had seen no evidence that he was going to be offered tough actions with which to accompany his talk. As even selective aid cuts were proving difficult to design, he had concluded that the best way of indicating disapproval was to stay silent and avoid Diem. This was despite regular entreaties from Washington urging him to put American concerns to Diem directly. He wrote back to Hilsman that "I have never realized before in my life how much attention silence could attract," adding that Madame Nhu was attacking him in her newspaper for his silence.[38] In the event, it was the inability of the American government to engage in any serious sense at all with the South Vietnamese government that sealed the latter's fate.

40

Diem's Assassination

IT HAS BEEN ARGUED that the basic reason the Americans turned against Diem was that he was pursuing a negotiated settlement with Hanoi. As an explanation of Kennedy's motives, this is clearly inadequate. There is no evidence that he opposed the idea in principle. Kennedy just did not see how the politics could work out, especially given the Laos experience. As he explained to Souvanna Phouma, who was also backing the idea, the "necessary ingredients" were lacking, including a "personality who could lead a united people"—that is, a Vietnamese equivalent to Souvanna.[1] Diem was clearly not such a man. Moreover, the president's exasperation with the dictator set in long before a possible deal became an issue.

The idea that Hanoi might be interested in a deal was not wholly preposterous. This was the view of most Westerners who knew the North well. Its economy was in a poor state, Sino-Soviet acrimony was a burden, and there was little to relish in the prospect of a deeper American involvement, especially if that meant an even greater dependence upon China. The French were encouraging the Northern leadership to think through the possibilities of some sort of settlement with Saigon, which would see the Americans off without a fight. This was the foundation for de Gaulle's call for the reunification and neutralization of Vietnam.[2] Hints emanated from Hanoi of respect for Diem's nationalism, a role for him in a unified Vietnam, and the possibility of a period of grace before unification, allowing sufficient time for the Americans to disengage without appearing to have been pushed out. Nhu made little secret of his Northern contacts and appeared quite enthusiastic about how a deal with the communists might be used to prevent the Americanization of his country. He could see articulate and well-informed Americans developing their own local connections, forming their own judgments, dispensing their own largesse and effectively subverting his family's rule. Having suppressed noncommunist opponents, the only alternative to relying on American power for survival was to move to the communists.

While China, in a militant mood, might have been lukewarm the Soviet Union, as cochairman of the Geneva Conference, could see only benefits. For this reason it probably encouraged Mieczyslaw Maneli, the Polish representative on the ICC, to work closely with the French in promoting one. Britain, the other cochairman, could see the merits in the proposals. Macmillan had been a keen advocate of the Laos accords and would have happily backed any initiative supported by the Americans.

Many influential Americans also argued for a negotiated withdrawal as preferable to sustaining an unsavory regime against a determined opponent. This was the view taken publicly by columnists Reston and Lippmann and in private by Mansfield. Kennedy appreciated that if the U.S. was to leave Vietnam this would be through agreement with the government of South Vietnam. As it was not hard to imagine circumstances when such an agreement would be hard to extract, it seems strange that he did not jump at the opportunity to accept an invitation to depart. Kennedy's reticence has been explained by a fixation with the need to beat off the communist challenge come what may to the exclusion of all diplomacy. This seems barely credible given his awareness of the scale of this task, his even greater reticence about having American troops fight the war for the Vietnamese, and his past interest in negotiations.

Neither Kennedy nor his aides dismissed the idea of a peace settlement, but they had in mind peaceful coexistence rather than unification, at least in the first instance, and so assumed that anything satisfactory required a stronger South. In the light of the official line on the state of the war that was not a forlorn hope. So for Kennedy diplomatic initiatives lacked urgency and therefore priority. Soundings and preliminary conversations had been going on for some months before de Gaulle made his public statement on 29 August, and his formulation remained vague. Diem himself had said nothing on the matter. There was no peace plan on the table. For Kennedy at this time Vietnam was largely a political problem which could only be complicated rather than resolved by talk of a peace settlement.

The dramatic events of late August demanded that he refocus on Vietnam after months of neglect. As he did so he had no reason to believe that any of the proponents of a settlement were serious about a lasting peace. The motives of the North in wishing to create the political conditions for American disengagement were obvious. Once that had been achieved they could go back to winning the war. The experience of Laos gave Kennedy and his advisers absolutely no confidence that an agreement would be honored. It was accepted, including by those supporting the idea, that a peace process set in motion at this time would probably end with unification under communist leadership. The best outcome would be that Hanoi would stay independent of Moscow and Beijing. This would still be seen as a defeat for the "free world." As for de Gaulle everything he did in 1963, in Europe even more so than in Asia, was assumed to be motivated by a visceral anti-Americanism and was discounted accordingly. The French were assumed to be dabbling in Indochina out of colonialist nostalgia, without applying any real resources to the problem. Some display of interest in French ideas was made, but the basic message to Paris was to back off.

What then of Nhu and Diem? Harriman's tentative explorations of diplomatic solutions in 1962 foundered on the North's insistence that Diem was the main obstacle to peace. Now, apparently, Hanoi deemed him a "patriot." Could a man whose career had been based on fervent anticommunism take this seriously, and if he was prepared to reverse course abruptly what would be the consequences of meeting Hanoi's minimum demand of American withdrawal? If Diem suddenly gave notice to the Americans to quit he could expect uproar, and probably a coup by those who saw their future best guaranteed by the current alignments. No single event was likely to destabilize the regime more, and Diem would have needed reliable communist guarantees that they would not simply use the opportunity to push his regime aside and take over the country. In practice serious peace-making required American connivance, but the coalition behind this effort and the presentation of their views was almost calculated to turn the Americans off. If it was meant to be taken seriously, the effort was counterproductive, encouraging the administration to distance themselves from a suspect enterprise rather than embrace a chance for peace.

The Americans interpreted the furtive contacts with Hanoi, and Nhu's open boasting, as largely designed for their benefit. It was connected to a campaign of threats and harassment already under way against many Americans in Saigon. CIA Director John McCone explained the reported contacts with Hanoi as an attempt by the Ngo family to gain leverage over the U.S. If Ho Chi Minh really was prepared to deal with Diem that indicated that American policy was probably working. Nonetheless, there was no evidence that Hanoi was interested in rapprochement on anything other than its own terms. He added, "During recent weeks, ARVN generals have indicated that any approach to the North on Nhu's part would provide them with the necessary excuse to 'save Vietnam' by mounting a coup."[3]

Nhu had given more ammunition to his opponents, providing evidence of unreliability and instability, injecting urgency into demands that he be removed from the scene. Lodge warned that Nhu's only trump card was to ask the U.S., in the course of a negotiation with North Vietnam, "to leave South Vietnam or to make a major reduction in forces."[4] On 14 September, the day after sending this cable, Lodge attempted to use this readiness to talk to the communists by persuading Joe Alsop, who was in

Saigon, to publish a column attacking Diem's brother for preparing to do a deal.[5]

Alsop had been impressed by Lodge's briefing but more so by his interview with Nhu, whom he concluded was "stark, raving mad." Nhu made claims about his personal following and his deal-making capacity with the communists, as well as deriding Diem as being an "old fool and no good." This persuaded Alsop that the status quo was "not viable," a conclusion he passed on to Kennedy on his return to Washington. Politically this was of great significance: If Alsop thought this way, then Diem's Washington constituency was going to be very small.[6]

Diem's reputation in Washington was almost beyond repair. Few had confidence in his readiness to reform himself. The administration could not agree whether the war could or could not be won with an unreconstructed Diem. Kennedy decided to buy more time. As he gave consideration to the elaborate plans for pressure and reconciliation drawn up by Hilsman he decided to send another high-level mission to Saigon, this time to be led by Robert McNamara and Maxwell Taylor.[7]

MCNAMARA-TAYLOR MISSION

The stated purpose of the visit was to provide yet another evaluation of the military effort against the Viet Cong. At this level it was hard to see what could be achieved. McNamara and Taylor had accepted Harkins's optimistic line. At most McNamara supposed, on the eve of his departure, that the issue was between a view that the situation was satisfactory and durable and one that argued that it was satisfactory but likely to deteriorate if adverse political trends continued. There was no reason to suppose that more briefings by the same American officers in Vietnam who had recently briefed Krulak would inspire a different picture.

The real importance of the trip was political. Kennedy wanted McNamara to meet Diem. The anti-Diem group viewed this aspect of the trip negatively. Sending two figures close to MACV thinking to Saigon would be taken by Diem as a positive sign that the United States had decided to "forgive and forget." Lodge saw this as a direct challenge to his strategy of keeping his distance from Diem, which he felt was having some success. Kennedy's calculation was different. Sending the two most senior members of his government most hostile to the Harriman-Hilsman line to Vietnam would keep the military on board. They also had the best chance of persuading Diem that he had to reform. Most important, if they failed, others in Washington would have to accept the view that U.S. policy could no longer be based on Diem.

Forrestal contrasted McNamara's view with that of Harriman. The latter saw "a world in which the only successful way to resist the Communist menace is to provide the people concerned with an alternative worth fighting for." The secretary of defense was convinced that "if enough of the enemy can be identified and killed by methods his department has been so successful in developing, there will be time to concentrate on the political and social welfare of the people in those countries where insurgency exists."[8] The question was whether McNamara now believed that political change could wait, and the answer was inevitably going to be found in the impact on the war effort. Kennedy posed the problem in these terms to McNamara and Taylor before they left, against the views of George Ball. Policy should be based on the "harm which Diem's political actions are causing to the effort against the Viet Cong rather than on our moral opposition to the kind of government Diem is running." This was reflected in the eventual report, which described the "overriding objective" of the United States as "denying this country to Communism." Deep concern was expressed about "repressive practices," but still, the determining factor in U.S. relations with the regime would be "effective performance in the conduct of the war." Sullivan, in Harriman's office, expressed frustration with this line. While the Americans might want Vietnam to develop as a free state, the objective of Diem and Nhu was to defeat subversion "so that Viet Nam can develop as a totalitarian state." This, in Nhu's words, would "challenge the communists on their own grounds using their own methods."[9] Vietnam was about defeating communism rather than promoting democracy.

Given the experience of Krulak and Mendenhall, it would have been no surprise to the visitors from Washington to find the U.S. missions at odds, offering completely different assessments. After upbeat Harkins, insisting that the war was being won with Diem, came downbeat Lodge, warning of the Vietnamese army being unable to cope and the theoretical possibility of a communist takeover.[10] Harkins's job, however, was becoming more difficult, as senior Vietnamese figures had been saying since mid-September that the war was starting to go badly. Duong Van Minh, the most senior general in the army, told Lodge that the Viet Cong were "steadily gaining in strength" and had "more of the population on their side than has the GVN." Secretary of Defense Nguyen Ngoc Thuan confirmed that the war was going badly (and that he wanted to leave the country).[11] Harkins moved immediately to deny the report of Thuan's views and discredit Minh (as contributing nothing to the war effort).[12] There was a suspicion that proponents of a coup were talking down the course of the war to jolt the Americans into action.

Nonetheless, doubts were growing among the American team, especially the civilians. Sullivan put this down to the civilians being more concerned with the "psychological" and less with the "physical" aspects of the problem, with what made the people "receptive and susceptible to the subversive and propaganda activities of the Viet Cong" rather than the activities associated with counterinsurgency. Yet he did not suggest that the military were actually wrong in their assessments of the physical aspects of the problem.[13]

McNamara, with his insatiable appetite for facts and figures, was given a heavy diet from Harkins-trained officers who were determined to put a positive gloss on the war's progress. His crisscrossing Vietnam in search of facts did not get him any closer to the military truth during his trip. Yet Lodge also worked on him, and his discussions with people notionally in Diem's government as well as Patrick Honey, a resident British scholar, started to bring home to him the depth of anger and fear among the South Vietnamese elite, never mind the masses. In one striking meeting he met Vice President Tho with Taylor and Lodge. Tho chided the Americans for failing to do anything about police state methods. Most alarming for Taylor was Tho's dismissal of the strategic hamlets program and his explanation for the popularity of the Viet Cong—extreme discontent with the government.[14]

Even more of an eye-opener might have been the meeting with the president himself. For two hours Diem held forth on how well everything was going (described in the American report as "The Monologue") before McNamara managed to get a word in edgewise. Diem dismissed the American suggestion that there was a serious political crisis, took no note of warnings about the effect of public opinion on the American ability to support his government, and, after a moment's hesitation, rallied to the defense of Madame Nhu as a much misunderstood woman. He acknowledged that there might be a Buddhist problem only in that he had been too kind to them in the past and allowed them to become irresponsible and communist-led. Diem's manner, noted the American account, was one of "at least outward serenity and of a man who had patiently explained a great deal and who hoped he had thus corrected a number of misapprehensions."[15]

In their joint report Taylor and McNamara asserted, "The military campaign has made great progress and continues to progress." Though the favorable military trends could be reinforced if the repressive tendencies were reversed and jeopardized if they were not, there was no need to change the military program, which was "sound in principle." Still sanguine on the military situation and opposed to actively encouraging a coup, they expressed anxiety over the political scene and examined the pressures, in addition to displays of disapproval, to convey this. They concluded that the most promising course of action, as against reconciliation or a coup, was "an application of selective, short-term pressures, principally economic, and the conditioning of long-term aid on the satisfactory performance by the Diem government in meeting military and political objectives which in the aggregate equate to the requirements of final victory."[16]

The major instrument here was the Commodity Import Program,

where action had already been suspended. The potential political impact of reductions in military and economic aid was undoubted, but so was their military impact; it was seen as too double-edged an approach to be adopted.

All this indicated that McNamara and Taylor had at least faced up to the seriousness of the political situation. But their own discussions with Diem and others should have made them realize that this form of pressure was unlikely to succeed. Diem had refused point blank to acknowledge that there was a problem, and he knew that the Americans were so committed to the war that they were unlikely to press ahead with action that would harm its effective prosecution. It was more likely, as the report half acknowledged, that adoption of this step would merely delay consideration of the more drastic options. It would, if anything, serve to encourage a coup as a strong indication of American displeasure. For this sort of pressure to work it needed to be kept as a private matter between the two governments. That was always a forlorn hope.

The problem for Taylor and McNamara was further compounded by the established proposals for withdrawal of American troops. This became one of the most controversial aspects of their report while it was being drafted. The existing plan was to take out 1,000 troops by the end of the year, moving on to a virtually complete withdrawal by 1965, when either the war would be won or the South Vietnamese forces would be sufficiently well trained to fight it themselves. The relentless military optimism left little room to abandon the plan, except that it was now impossible for even Taylor and McNamara to avoid the prospect of the situation deteriorating. Maintaining the withdrawal plan in the report struck many of those on the team as not only phony but dangerous in its specificity. Many in the State Department, including the pro-coup lobby, were becoming reconciled to the idea of an increase in the American military effort. They could not see how this could be avoided if the situation on the ground was as serious as they suspected, and likely to be made worse in the aftermath of a coup.

On their return Kennedy met with McNamara and Taylor. He began as usual, asking about the press in Saigon, describing them as "impossible." Through this period Kennedy appeared constantly exasperated by the press. He would ring up Hilsman and ask about the provenance of particular news stories, and demand analyses from the officials about the veracity of others. Halberstam was a special source of irritation; he asked McNamara and even the CIA for detailed analyses (the agency found his facts generally accurate but the emphasis in his reports questionable). As Kennedy's exasperation was nothing compared to Diem's, whose preferred solutions were also more extreme, the administration had found itself defending the reporters, thereby further aggravating relations with the regime. Kennedy warned McNamara and Taylor on the eve of their trip that they would receive many complaints about the press, some justified. He sympathized with an Alsop column entitled "The Crusaders," accusing the newsmen of an excess of zealotry. At the same time his best advice was to get on with the job at hand. "The way to confound the press is to win the war."[17] Back from Saigon, McNamara deemed Halberstam's writings to be colored by an "idealistic philosophy." Bundy, who knew him from Harvard, considered him "a gifted boy who gets all steamed up." Later that month Kennedy suggested—unsuccessfully—to the publisher of the *New York Times* that Halberstam be moved from Vietnam.[18]

The meeting paid less attention to the state of the war than of the press. Kennedy appeared impressed that the Viet Cong were taking "quite a licking," though McNamara expressed concern that they still replaced their losses. Taylor, more optimistic, concentrated on the body counts, later revealed to be highly exaggerated, describing them as the "only firm datum we have." When Kennedy asked why the North Vietnamese could not simply continue to resupply the Viet Cong, he was told this was now being prevented. As a result, remarked Taylor, the Viet Cong must be "awfully tired." On this basis McNamara remained convinced that the military campaign could be completed by 1965 and that, even if this was optimistic, the Vietnamese could be trained to take over American functions.[19]

Nonetheless, Kennedy was wary about committing himself in the presidential statement to accompany the release of the report to removing 1,000 military personnel by the end of the year in case this turned out to be overly optimistic. McNamara argued in favor. It indicated that the United States had a withdrawal plan, put more stress on the training of the Vietnamese, and would be of great value in meeting the views of Senator Fulbright and others "that we are bogged forever down in Vietnam" and will be there for decades. As McNamara seemed content with the prediction, it was decided to keep it out of the presidential announcement but have it in the McNamara-Taylor report, from where it had been excised by other members of the team for precisely the same reasons as the president's. They were appalled by its inclusion and saw how this message of unwarranted optimism would obscure any political signals. Their fears were confirmed by the next day's *New York Times* headline: "Vietnam Victory by End of '65 Envisaged by U.S."[20]

Because McNamara and Taylor were not perturbed about the military situation, they believed that the proposed withdrawals could be justified on their own terms. This does not support Taylor's later claim that Kennedy was using the threat of withdrawal as a means of putting pressure on Diem. This would require that the move could be reversed, and that was not Kennedy's intention. He was—as ever—keeping his options open. Getting the thousand-man cut out of the way immediately would allow him to claim continuity in policy if questions arose in Congress, yet it also cleared the decks for what might be turbulent times ahead. For the same reason he excised the words "overriding objective," proposed by McNamara and Taylor with regard to denying Vietnam to communism, leaving in language about supporting "the efforts of the people of that country to defeat aggression." He was not going to up the American stake at that moment.[21] Long-term strategy was in a state of suspended animation. When all was in flux in Saigon, too much could be read into any departure from past positions in Washington.

THE COUP

That turbulent times were likely was evident from the fact that even as the McNamara-Taylor report was being discussed in Washington, another coup was being set in motion. The plotters made contact on 2 October, and three days later Lucien Conein, of the U.S. mission, was in touch with General Duong Van Minh ("Big Minh"), who was seeking reassurance that American support would still be forthcoming in the event of a coup. This is normally considered the day when Kennedy, in effect, acquiesced in a coup.

Kennedy's discussions with McNamara and Taylor on 2 October on their return from Saigon do not, however, suggest that he was set on Diem's overthrow. The basic question had not changed: "Do we get more out of him [Diem] by being conciliatory or by putting pinpricks into him?" McNamara thought the pressure went beyond pinpricks and would force concessions. The objective was to get a more creditable government, though not necessarily one that was more democratic. The Americans were offended by the crudeness of the authoritarianism as much as the fact of it. McNamara observed that "any other regime that replaces Diem would have to follow much the same program of oppression but they could do it . . . without Madame Nhu or Brother Nhu and the others." Bundy chipped in. With a "totalitarian regime the question is whether they're gonna make asses of themselves." When drafting his statement, Kennedy acknowledged Ball's argument that it was important in the UN and elsewhere to suggest that the Americans had a general opposition to repressive measures, and not just because of their military consequences. He still believed that for domestic purposes it was better to argue "on a hard-boiled basis that is this going to hurt the war?"[22]

A few days later, on 5 October, the senior group met again to discuss instructions for Lodge. Kennedy was hoping at this point that Diem would get the message from American actions, without this having to be spelled out in public, to seek out Lodge and come to an understanding. Similarly, he argued that the withdrawal of troops should not be given a great fanfare but should follow the normal practice of bringing home personnel no longer required. When considering the instruction to be given to Lodge with regard to a coup, Kennedy was content with the idea that while avoiding a direct involvement in the plots, American actions at that time might encourage those anxious for change. This still avoided direct responsibility. There was still an issue as to whether covert contacts should be maintained with potential plotters. Once again the problem lay in the gap between covert intent and a much more open reality. McNamara had apparently been shocked by how much had already reached the press. Referring to the CIA man in contact with the conspiracy, McNamara observed that "it's taken as gospel now that this government tried to overthrow Diem's government and used Conein for that purpose." When Kennedy asked who he was, McNamara described him as "a colorful figure . . . well known to all the reporters in Vietnam. He's well known to the Vietnamese government." Any continuing role for Conein would signal continuing support for a coup. As he was still contacting dissidents, "it's open as though we were announcing it over the radio. Continuing this kind of activity strikes me as absurd." Taylor and McNamara were also dismissive of Conein's main contact—General Duong Van Minh, then military adviser to the president (a job description that caused some amusement, as this was Taylor's former title). While it was considered desirable to have another, less obvious, point of contact to the generals, it was by no means clear that any alternative would enjoy Conein's access.[23]

That day Lodge received three cables from Washington. The longest gave him the results of the deliberations on the McNamara-Taylor report. It set out actions "designed to indicate to Diem Government our displeasure at its political activities and to create significant uncertainty in that government and in key Vietnamese groups as to future intentions of the United States." As these measures—such as continued suspension of the Commodity Import Program—would eventually harm the counter-insurgency effort, they would have to be kept under review. The objectives listed were designed to ease the political crisis, but Lodge was told that this was no package of demands tightly geared to a package of sanctions, and certainly should not be presented as such in public. The United States had not made up its mind on what Diem needed to do to get the resumption of full cooperation with the United States, but he would need to do something. The idea was to maintain "flexibility" in the light of Diem's actions. Crucially, Lodge's tactic of keeping his distance from the Vietnamese president was endorsed. Diem would have to come to him.

A second cable emphasized the importance of not conducting a campaign of pressure in the press (despite the desire of some officials and reporters to do so). "Nothing could be more dangerous than an impression now that a set of major actions is being kicked off and a set of requirements imposed on GVN by U.S." The third, from Bundy, specifically discussed a coup. It ordered that "no initiative should now be taken to give any active encouragement to a coup." However, Lodge was authorized to build contacts with a possible alternative leadership.[24] Again, all this suggests a reluctance to commit to any course of action; the belief was that by standing back from the regime the United States could abjure responsibility for its fate. "Wait and see" had become a policy in itself.

The well-publicized departure of CIA bureau chief John Richardson, considered to be close to Nhu and opposed to a coup, had already been widely read as a clue to the administration's position.[25] As October progressed, the main response by the Diem regime was to step up its public attacks on the United States and threats against American personnel. The position remained that the United States was not actively seeking a coup but would not thwart one. Harkins, in whom Lodge showed no confidence, tended to discourage coup planning, while the ambassador tended in the other direction. This sent confusing signals to would-be plotters, and in particular General Tran Van Don, acting chief of the Joint General Staff, who was Conein's main contact. On the night of 23 October Conein met with Don and assured him that the U.S. government would not oppose a coup but wished to know more about its prospects. He was told that a coup was imminent but the degree of support available was unclear. The lack of corroboration caused anxiety in Washington, as did the danger that Conein might implicate the United States in the conspiracy.[26] That night Don met Conein again, reported that the coup would take place on 2 November, and promised that the new government would be open, democratic, and pro-Western without being a vassal of the United States. No plans, however, were available for American scrutiny.

This was the context for an intense discussion in the Oval Office on 25 October. The administration had understood that dissociating itself from Diem might lead to pressure for a change. This was not quite the same as actively seeking Diem's overthrow, but now that the mission was in touch with an alternative government, that fine line might be crossed. If, as some in the CIA feared, Don was in fact being managed by Nhu, then it would soon be apparent that senior American personnel were agitating for a coup. The CIA's other concern was that a coup led by Don would not be decisive. They looked "forward to a period of confusion with possibly a second coup to follow."

While that prospect was unappealing, it was not possible, as McNamara acknowledged, to walk away from the previous policy of putting pressure on Diem to mend his ways, because no obvious mending had yet taken place. This had by itself made a coup more likely. McNamara indicated that he was expecting one anyway on the basis of his conversation with Patrick Honey in Saigon, who had told him that if he and Taylor left the city without endorsing the government, within four weeks there would be a change. His impression was that "forces were buoying up to the point that all they wanted to see was a sign that the U.S. would not prevent them overturning the government." Kennedy observed: "Well we've certainly given them that." To which McNamara responded: "We've given them that sign. And my personal feeling is that that's all we could do, keep in touch. Not to encourage through our contact, but just to keep informed."

But the subtle form of dialogue that seemed appropriate from Washington's perspective was likely to be thwarted by Lodge's enthusiasm for a coup, and the chaotic state of the mission, with its lack of cohesion and discipline. Lodge was proud that he was in effect micromanaging Conein, discussing his every contact with him. McNamara expressed his dismay at the amateurishness of the U.S. operation, conducted by "a press-minded ambassador and an unstable Frenchman, five times divorced. It's the damnedest arrangement I've ever seen." He knew that the contacts with the plotters could not be masterminded from Washington, but he would prefer to be "dealing through some experienced men of sound judgment." It was, as McCone indicated, too late to reorganize matters in this way, and as Bundy ruefully noted, "[E]veryone will say we did it even though we didn't. We'd still look guilty . . . whether they're really going to do it on November 2."

The problem was now not just how to manage Diem but also how to manage Lodge. There was a lack of confidence in Washington about what administration officials were being told, but at the same time no way of getting better information without an American of some standing spending time with plotters. McCone took the view that Lodge's refusal to deal directly with the South Vietnamese government was reducing the substantive intelligence on Diem's thinking. Kennedy observed that "he's there and we can't fire him so we're going to have to give him directions." This would include an expression of concern about the coup planned for 2 November. He wanted to have a reliable assessment of its chances and some idea of the local correlation of forces. The president still wanted Lodge to put specific demands to Diem to see if he could get him to reform.[27] Lodge was due in Washington at the start of November. Then he could be given new instructions, though the coup was scheduled for before he returned.

Toward the end of the month Diem eventually took the initiative to talk to Lodge, but he had nothing to offer.[28] Soon Washington was awash with stories of plots and plotters, and another meeting was called with the president. Intelligence on the balance between pro-coup and anti-coup forces in Saigon made the outcome hard to predict, though the advantage was marginally shifting to the former. As the Americans knew this, it had to be assumed that so did Diem and that he had time to make his own arrangements. Few assumed that he would go down without a fight. In this transparent situation, what was the meaning of American silence? If they spoke, was it to ask both sides to avoid a prolonged civil war, which was the most definite interest they had? Was it to support the plotters, knowing that the American position would be untenable with Diem if they failed? Or was it to support Diem, knowing the effect this would have on morale among both senior officers and civilians?

Intriguingly, it was Robert Kennedy, who had come down hard on Diem in September, who expressed his reservations about becoming too strongly associated with an attempt at his overthrow. He worried about "putting the whole future of the country and really Southeast Asia in the hands of somebody we don't know very well." If it failed, "Diem is going to tell us to get the hell out of the country." The evidence that there was a chance of success was flimsy. He wanted the generals to be stopped, believing that it was possible to put pressure on someone in Diem's position without prompting a move against him. This reflected Washington's continued failure to grasp the dynamics of the situation, desperately searching for a middle way that would bring a change of policy without a change of government.

Robert soon found support. Taylor warned that even a successful coup would slow down the war effort. McCone, who had been anxious about the direction of policy for some time, weighed in behind these two. Rusk was uncertain, as was Harriman, on whether a coup would happen, but still sure that Diem could not carry his country to victory. Given the uncertainties, Kennedy's inclination was to discourage a coup.[29] There was still no conviction behind American policy. At best clarity might come with more information, preferably about the plotters and their plans.

Reflecting Kennedy's position, Lodge was told "the burden of proof must be on the coup group to show a substantial possibility of quick success, otherwise, we should discourage them from proceeding."[30] As Bundy realized, it was absurd for the Americans to want to review plans without accepting responsibility for their implementation. The considerations of whether it would be better or worse for the war effort if Diem was replaced had given way to a fear that there was to be a civil war. The split within the Saigon elite was a reality. The question was whether it could be resolved quickly, either way, or would be fought out on the streets.

"[D]o not think we have the power to delay or discourage a coup," replied Lodge. The plotters, understandably, were reluctant to disclose the details of their plot. This was a Vietnamese affair over which the Americans had little influence, unless they were prepared to turn over the generals to Diem.[31] On receipt of this Kennedy professed admiration for Lodge's "nerve, if not his prudence." Harkins, who had been kept in the dark by Lodge, by now had been drawn into the debate and came back with a strong argument against a coup, on the grounds that there was no other leader with Diem's strength of character when it came to fighting communists. Still nervous and without compelling evidence that all would be well, Washington refused to accept Lodge's provocation that the United States had "no power to delay or discourage a coup."[32]

Washington still felt that it could orchestrate events. It was, as Lodge's deputy, William Truehart, complained, typical of the wish to manage events from afar. "They wanted to give an order and then lean over your shoulder as you carried it out and never give up the right to stop you at any point."[33] The later tendency to blame Lodge for pushing the coup beyond the desire of Washington policy makers is warranted in terms of the ambassador's own aloof, uncommunicative, and supremely confident style, but it assumes that another personality, working with the same policy, could have produced a more satisfactory outcome.[34]

On 1 November 1963 Diem asked to see Lodge. He was now rattled, perhaps aware that a coup was close to fruition. Still defending himself, he asked Lodge to tell the president that he was a "good and frank ally." He wanted to "settle questions now than talk about them after we have lost everything . . . I take all his suggestions very seriously and wish to carry them out but it is a question of timing." Lodge recognized that this might be the start of a serious discussion of a package deal, but he did not give his report of the meeting any priority. There was no point. The coup was already under way. Within hours Diem was back in touch asking to know about the American attitude to the rebellion then in motion. Lodge expressed concern about Diem's safety.[35] Despite American attempts to organize safe passage out of the country, Diem was murdered along with his brother. The fact that the Americans could not be direct participants in the coup meant that they could not control its development and grisly conclusion.

Kennedy was shocked. He thought Diem had deserved better and recognized the moral implications of American complicity in the overthrow of a supposedly friendly government. In a memo dictated for his own records he recorded his respect for Diem's achievement in holding his country together under adverse conditions for ten years, and described the way he was killed as "abhorrent." He left open the question of whether the generals could turn things around politically in Saigon, but displayed no confidence. To Kennedy the fault went back to the Saturday night cable, to which he should not have consented. It had "encouraged Lodge along the course to which he was in any case inclined."[36]

AFTERMATH

The murder of Diem and his brother was shocking, and the pretense that the two had committed suicide simply incredible. On the other hand, the speed of the coup was a relief. The greatest fear had been of a civil war. Initial reports were euphoric: smiling people offering a welcome to the Americans. It was not long, however, before the coup leaders began to live up to the worst expectations.

Lodge considered the American approach vindicated by the coup, hoping that a way had now been found for "not being everywhere saddled with responsibility for autocratic governments simply because they are anti-communist," and commending the "ingenuity which was shown in working out a way to put pressure on Diem and Nhu without endangering the war effort, and without lowering the basic living standards of the people."[37] In the event, as he had surmised, the delay in formulating a policy worked as well as any specific measures to unnerve Diem and Nhu.

The key equation involved the local political forces within Saigon, and some clash was inevitable given the refusal of Diem to revamp his government and revive its popular appeal. Once the Americans had demonstrated their lack of commitment to Diem himself and had confirmed this privately, the drama followed its own national logic. While the Americans found themselves with yet another gradualist strategy, it could not work in a gradualist manner. Either there would be no real change in Saigon or else it would be abrupt and dramatic.

The end of Diem's reign was momentous. He had dominated South Vietnamese politics effectively since the country had been formed after the 1954 accords. He had been feted as an anticommunist modernizer, embraced first by Eisenhower's administration and then by Kennedy's. He was a substantial figure on the Asian scene. He had also spent much of his career guarding against internal challenges to his power, especially after the coup attempt of 1960. The war had obliged him to place more reliance than he would have liked on the only force in Vietnam able to challenge him, the army, so his military strategy had always been designed with one eye on the domestic political implications. This was undoubtedly harming the military effort, as the disposition of units and instructions to generals were geared to the president's personal security, just as the strategic hamlets program and the distribution of American aid had been geared to enhancing his power and that of his family. Those who argued that the war was being lost with Diem were right, and their judgment that he lacked the capacity to reform in the ways required by Washington was also correct.

Unfortunately, the arguments of those opposed to a coup that there was no obvious successor to Diem and that there had been a stunning lack of political analysis on the consequences of a coup were also correct. Many of those accepting of a coup acknowledged that the logic of the situation would be to draw the United States even more deeply into responsibility for the government of the country and the prosecution of the war. It was by and large on this side of the argument that could be found some recognition that the events being set in motion could end with U.S. troops in combat. The Americans did have ideas about who suitable civilian leaders might be, but power had been seized by generals, and there had not been much planning about how to advise the Vietnamese to organize civil-military relations post-coup.

What had been Kennedy's objectives through this period? At one level he was attempting to find a basis for unity within his own government. The arguments surrounding Vietnam had polarized his administration with an intensity and acrimony that he found shocking. He was as dissatisfied as ever with the performance of the military. Their inability to provide convincing analyses to civilian officials whom he normally trusted, never mind the press corps, left him without an adequate feel for the true state of affairs. He appears to have been genuinely perplexed as to why he was receiving such conflicting reports. Given McNamara's famed capacity for digging deep and hard, catching out the unprepared briefer, and being ready to challenge the conventional military wisdom head on, this was the last person Kennedy would have expected to be the victim of systematic deception. The president would have been surprised, as was McNamara himself, to learn how his secretary of defense had been caught out by the military playing his game, giving him the hard data he craved at the expense of the truth he needed.

The disarray within his administration, the inability to agree on the actual state of the war, and the refusal of Diem to grasp the sort of political problems he was causing for his ally left the president struggling to get a grip on the situation. These problems were magnified through the media. Kennedy was highly sensitive to their role in the formation of opinion and the shaping of public moods, and though he was aware that, despite his constant entreaties, divisions within his government kept the Washington and Saigon press corps busy, he did not appreciate that press reporting was generally more accurate than that of the military.

At the start of October he had not decided on any particular course of action. He was not determined to get rid of Diem because he was not sure that he could, and he was aware of the dangerous consequences of failure. Ever since the Bay of Pigs he had been wary of situations in which he had been asked to align himself with the adventures of others. The reason that he was finding it so hard to distance himself from the Vietnamese government in a graceful and nondisruptive fashion is that he had allowed himself to become so close to Diem in the past. The new policy was two years too late. Here lay the folly, because it left the United States with only unpalatable choices as the regime began to fail. The problem had become one of limiting the public relations damage. In the end, Kennedy did not really choose to overthrow Diem, although his indecision had the same effect as an anti-Diem choice.

41

Kennedy to Johnson

THE ASSASSINATION OF PRESIDENT KENNEDY on 22 November 1963 came less than three weeks after that of Diem. Which was the turning point in the American involvement in Vietnam? The argument that it was Diem's death presumes that the relationship between the two countries had undergone a fundamental change. So long as Diem was in power, the United States could claim to be operating in the country at the invitation of an independent regime. The degree of American responsibility for the overthrow of the regime created an obligation to deal with the consequences. Furthermore, the rapid deterioration of the political and military position in the country demanded action: It was impossible for Washington to walk away. Having stressed the character of Diem's regime—and his reluctance to take advice—as the biggest obstacle to the successful prosecution of the war, there was now an obligation of sorts to extract the best from the new political situation and support the new leadership.

This judgment needs to be handled with care. The American commitment to South Vietnam transcended its commitment to Diem, illustrated by the extent to which it had been taken for granted, rather than seriously addressed, during the debate over Diem. Second, coincident with the death of Diem was the stripping away of the veils that had obscured the true position on the ground from the eyes of official Washington. The continuing misrepresentation of the counterinsurgency program by the Diem regime and the U.S. military was no longer tenable. Even if Diem had lived, the evidence of communist progress could not have been ignored. For Washington up to this point the crisis had largely been political in character; it was about to become military.

The argument that Kennedy's death was the most critical presumes that he would have followed substantially different policies than his successor and would have avoided the calamity of direct military intervention.

The anecdotal evidence that Kennedy wanted to get out is considerable.[1] But no account suggests that he expected to be able to extract the United States from Vietnam until after the 1964 election. As argued earlier, to get out of a Vietnam was less of a definite decision than a working assumption, based on a hope for stability rather than an expectation of chaos. Kennedy died not knowing whether political stability could be restored after Diem and with perceptions of the state of the war on the edge of a qualitative change. It requires something of a leap of faith to assume that Kennedy would have stuck to a predetermined policy come what may. This was, after all, a man who prized flexibility and keeping open all his options. There is certainly no reason to doubt his dismissal of the suggestions that he might end up fighting a major land war in Vietnam, but then Johnson, too, professed himself resistant to the idea. In 1964 Robert was asked what his brother would have done if the South Vietnamese had been on the brink of defeat: "We'd face that when we came to it."[2]

The search for the answer to the question of what Kennedy would have done had he lived requires some speculation on how he would have responded to the situation confronted by his successor.[3] To complicate matters further, this is a different issue from whether matters would have followed the same course under Kennedy as they did with Johnson. Leaving aside issues of personality and predispositions, Johnson's circumstances were quite different precisely because of Kennedy's death. Kennedy may not have been impressed with the performance of his own administration over Vietnam, but he understood the strengths and weaknesses of his top officials and he was growing in confidence in his own political capacity. Johnson inherited an administration that was not of his construction, without a mandate of his own, but with his own distinctive perspectives on the wider issues of foreign policy.

CHANGES IN PERSONNEL

Johnson retained Kennedy's foreign policy team, although the superficial continuity hid important changes. McGeorge Bundy stayed on as adviser on national security affairs, Dean Rusk as secretary of state, Robert McNamara as secretary of defense, and John McCone as director of central intelligence. While Rusk was probably taken more seriously by Kennedy than his detractors realized, the secretary of state was undoubtedly closer to Johnson. Both were from similar poor southern backgrounds, and Johnson allowed Rusk to offer advice in the form that he preferred.[4] The new president appeared to be somewhat in awe of McNamara, probably more so than his predecessor. Meanwhile Robert Kennedy, who had been steadily carving out a role for himself as a foreign policy adviser, could not easily serve a man whom he had never particularly liked and who now governed in place of his dead brother. The in-house liberals—Arthur Schlesinger Jr. and Theodore Sorensen—left to write their biographies.

The most important changes were in the area of Vietnam policy. Johnson had been opposed to the coup against Diem. Those who had promoted it—Harriman, Hilsman, Forrestal, Lodge—suffered a diminution of influence. Johnson was wary of Lodge lest he find an excuse to launch a campaign for the Republican nomination from the Saigon embassy.[5] Hilsman decided to leave government almost immediately. Michael Forrestal left the National Security Council staff in the summer of 1964. More junior figures, such as Kattenburg, were soon banished from Vietnam policy making. William Bundy, McGeorge's brother, moved from the Pentagon to take Hilsman's job as assistant secretary for Far Eastern affairs. Walt Rostow also returned to the fray. As director of the State Department's Policy Planning Staff, he had hardly been involved in Vietnam policy during 1963. In much of the period since 1961 he had been taken up with writing and rewriting a Basic National Security Policy document, a process that he had not finished by the time of Kennedy's death and which had done little for his credibility in government. Bundy had concluded that he could not stop Rostow from producing papers, but he did not have to read them.[6] With Johnson's return he began to exercise growing influence, and eventually, in 1966, succeeded Bundy as Johnson's national security adviser. Though it took time for the differences in personnel and presidential style to make themselves felt, their cumulative impact was to strengthen the hand of those who were confident in the role that military instruments might play in Vietnam, and to marginalize skeptics and dissenters.

COMMITMENTS

The real difficulty in speculating on whether Kennedy would have followed a course different from Johnson's is that he had not yet been fully confronted with just how bad the situation was in Vietnam as a result of the persistence of weak government in Saigon and a strong communist insurgency. During the second half of 1963 most strategic questions had been put on hold as Washington debated whether matters could be improved by a change of personnel or policy in Saigon. There was little comprehension of the dreadful state of the country. In response to a query from Rusk, Lodge had observed in mid-October, "We appear to me to be doing little more than holding our own. This looks like a long, smoldering struggle, with political and military aspects intertwined, each of which is stubborn in its own way." This was not the gloomiest possible prognosis, although it still led Harkins to complain to Taylor that his views on the military situation were being disregarded despite their positive consistency. "On balance we are gaining in the contest with the VC" (16 October); "the general trend continues to be favorable" (23 October); "[o]n balance trend continues to be favorable" (30 October).[7]

In late October alarms began to be sounded when Tom Hughes, director of the State Department's Bureau of Intelligence and Research, sent Rusk an analysis suggesting that the positive trends of earlier in the year had gone into reverse almost as soon as the political turmoil had begun to grip South Vietnam. The significance of this report was that it used statistics supplied by the Pentagon based on reports from MACV. It reported "an unfavorable shift in the military balance. Since July 1963, the trend in Viet Cong casualties, weapons losses, and defections has been downward while the number of Viet Cong armed attacks and other incidents has been upward."[8]

Even though the CIA was moving to the same conclusion, the first instinct of the military, and of McNamara personally, was to challenge the right of the State Department to circulate such assessments, as well as deny the validity of its conclusions.

An opportunity to assess the situation came on 20 November, when senior policy makers from Washington met with the team from Saigon. Lodge offered a hopeful assessment, suggesting that the generals understood the need for political, economic, and social measures, although he was also wary about pushing them too hard on democratization. Harkins gave no indication that he was overly worried about the military situation. McCone then came in with a far more sobering forecast. He suggested that the Viet Cong had decided to step up their efforts since the coup and that the Vietnamese military was not yet in a situation to cope.[9]

Over the following weeks the U.S. military began to concur. It was apparent that the communists were virtually in control of the whole delta region, while the inertia of the new government caused anxiety. In mid-December the Defense Intelligence Agency came up with an estimate that warned that "the Communist capability to extend or escalate the insurgency has not been significantly negated."[10] According to Hughes, this estimate "virtually plagiarized" his own.[11]

Meanwhile hopes of political improvement post-coup soon evaporated. Lodge's first advice to the generals was to create the right impression through judicious press statements, but he spent little time advising them on such matters as the composition of the government. He concentrated on image.[12] The Americans were looking for prompt restoration of a constitutional government and an end to repression, plus a demonstration that the coup had reflected a national demand rather than a foreign trick. The generals were to provide a political program to enthuse the people as well as a determination to fight the communists, though the best way to enthuse the people was probably to work toward the end of the war. The ambassador still took the view that as a result of the coup, the war could be shortened and Americans could get home.

The coup leaders said all the right things to Lodge about their preference for a civilian government and their eagerness to stay united in the fight against the Viet Cong. Soon problems began to emerge, though. The generals began to argue over patronage (who would control promotions) and cabinet positions; they also began suspecting counter-coups, necessitating their own brand of repression. Kennedy wrote to Lodge of his concern that "the new Government can limit confusion and intrigue among its members, and concentrate its energies upon the real problems of winning the contest against the Communists and holding the confidence of its own people." These were the areas where Diem had failed in the eyes of the Kennedy people; it was now a "severe test" for the new leaders.[13]

In January 1964 there was yet another coup within the military junta when General Nguyen Khanh became premier. Regular changes of government narrowed the base of officials available for administrative duty, as officials who had worked with the previous regime were presumed to be disloyal. With each successive coup, the limited Vietnamese administrative capacity, required to put American-sponsored reform programs into effect, declined further.[14]

The worsening situation would have been as irritating in an election year for Kennedy, as it was for Johnson. Johnson took further Kennedy's commitment to civil rights, accepting the risks this posed for the Democratic Party's position in the South. In this, of course, he was helped by the country's postassassination mood. Kennedy, like Johnson, would have been heartened by the prospect of Senator Barry Goldwater as the Republican nominee for president, as Goldwater was a right-wing and eminently beatable opponent, and Kennedy would have been content to play the man of peace in contrast to Goldwater's demands for tough action against communism.

Reluctant to take any drastic action before November 1964 but with the situation in Vietnam getting steadily worse, what might Kennedy have done? There were indications immediately after the coup that the communists might have been prepared to explore a possible political settlement, but that was not what the Americans wanted at that time. Columnist James Reston was not alone in criticizing the "let's get back to the war" spirit and arguing for consideration of a negotiated settlement and neutralization.[15] But even many critics were not prepared yet to negotiate over what would come down to essentially the timing of a communist takeover. David Halberstam, as skeptical and informed as any American observer of the time, was still not questioning the basic American commitment. Vietnam was a vital interest. Withdrawal would be dishonorable and send the wrong message to allies and adversaries elsewhere. It would also mean a "drab, lifeless and controlled society for a people who deserved better."[16]

Although the option of South Vietnam being neutralized was regularly proposed by President de Gaulle of France and picked up by liberal commentators at home, this position had no high-level advocates. Kennedy had earlier resisted proposals that confined neutralization to the South. After the coup Forrestal proposed sticking to the public line that South Vietnam would not need support were it not for the North's war of subversive aggression; as soon as the South could cope on its own then the Americans would be out. Off the record he explained that South Vietnam was simply not strong enough to approach the bargaining table with the North.[17] The Americans were also nervous of the effect on the generals if it was thought that the Americans were already looking for a way out. Bundy observed to Johnson in February that the key difference from Laos was the lack of a local balance of forces. Take out the United States and South Vietnam "would collapse like a pack of cards." Until there was a noncommunist group capable of looking after itself, any moves to neutralization undermined the efforts under way to build up South Vietnam.

Complete chaos might have provided a compelling reason to attempt withdrawal from Vietnam before 1965. The case would have been stronger if a sufficiently broadly based government had been available to provide cover. Kennedy had indicated that he would organize a withdrawal through a request from the South Vietnamese government. Those ready for such a step in 1964, such as Senator Russell, Johnson's confidant, also saw this as the obvious escape route should one be desired, but Johnson had no interest in such a move.[18]

One difference is that under Johnson the withdrawal option was completely ruled out almost at once. After Diem's death, Kennedy told Forrestal that he wanted a complete review of how the United States had got into Vietnam, "what we thought we were doing and what we now think we can do . . . I even want to think about whether or not we should be there."[19] Such thoughts were not for Johnson. He had no trouble accepting the "domino theory," the idea that once Vietnam went to communism the rest of Southeast Asia would soon succumb. Indeed, as one who actually enjoyed a game of dominoes, the metaphor might have appealed to him more than to his predecessors. Nor did he doubt that his country's reputation was on the line. Other allies would be alarmed if the United States walked away from its commitments. The sudden change of president required reassurance on this score, and so Johnson immediately reaffirmed the policy of his predecessors by signing National Security Action Memorandum 273. This stated: "It remains the central objective of the United States in Vietnam to assist the people and Government of that country to win their contest against the externally directed and supported Communist conspiracy."[20]

With this agreed, Rusk, who had been the first to dismiss any talk of abandoning Vietnam in September, now moved to take the issue off the agenda. In February 1964 he forbade a new Vietnam Task Force to plan for an American withdrawal from Vietnam. This replaced the group that had been led by Kattenburg, who had imprudently made his doubts known and was now excluded from Vietnam policy making. Almost every friendly government tried to warn the administration that by ruling out negotiations with the North it was heading for a fall. When Johnson decided to communicate with Hanoi, via the Canadians, in June 1964, the message was "fuzzy," satisfying neither Lodge, who wanted military sticks with which to beat the North, nor Harriman, who wanted political carrots to entice them. By now conciliation had become synonymous with weakness while the mischievous French were presumed to be behind all pressure for negotiations.[21]

OPTIONS

Johnson had generally been more hawkish on Vietnam than Kennedy, opposed to the move against Diem and wary of the commitment to withdraw 1,000 troops. Nonetheless, his basic political instincts were the same as Kennedy's—to avoid withdrawal or escalation. The lines of policy were also the same—to provide military training and political guidance to the South Vietnamese to enable them to get their own grip on the war effort. At the start of 1965 Johnson accepted that this required an air campaign against the North, known as Rolling Thunder, and by the summer of that year he had further accepted that this should lead naturally to the introduction of substantial ground forces.[22] As this was clearly an outcome that he had been anxious to avoid, is it the case that it was the logical and inescapable consequence of the commitment to an independent, noncommunist South Vietnam? If so, as Kennedy had embraced the same commitment, can we assume that he would have avoided the same logic? As the alternatives polarized between talk or war with the North, with even America's clients in Saigon unsure about their preference, would Kennedy have dismissed all talk of negotiations?

The story of the decision making that led to the deep American intervention in Vietnam is complex. It was moved along by specific events as much as policy analysis, from the Tonkin Gulf incident of August 1964 to the bombing in Pleiku in February 1965. Each American move was contested internally, and one might wonder whether a different political configuration within the administration might have produced different options. Would Kennedy have ordered retaliation for an apparent attack on a U.S. destroyer in the Tonkin Gulf while the evidence was still uncertain? Would Ball's famous dissent of October 1964 been so easy to ignore if Harriman and Hilsman had been available to back it up and ensure that the president took note? Would Kennedy have made known his own misgivings about intervention with sufficient clarity that Bundy would not have been tempted to toy with desperate political rationales for halfhearted bombing campaigns?

It is dangerous to assert answers to these questions with confidence.

There is some validity, however, in looking at the development of Vietnam options during the first months of 1964. The major policy departure of 1965 was the launch of a bombing campaign against the North. This was not a new option. Kennedy had considered it and rejected it in the past. If he had lived and been obliged to review the surprisingly grim position as it was presented to his successor at the end of 1963, might he have done so again?

From 1961 the debate within the administration had been between the counterinsurgency theorists, who believed that the Viet Cong had to be denied their popular base, and the traditional military view that wars were won by eliminating the armed forces of the enemy and frustrating their operations. The counterinsurgency theorists complained that the military's preference for shelling or bombing areas where the enemy was believed to be hiding, but from where they had usually moved on, led to the killing of innocent civilians. Being on the receiving end of American firepower was not calculated to turn people against communism. On this basis, after Diem's death, Hilsman was still arguing "that there was one more chance to carry out an effective counter-guerrilla operation." The basic problem had not changed. Until the Viet Cong's ability to gain recruits and supplies from South Vietnamese villages was broken, there could be no success.[23]

The sudden reemergence of a military crisis at the end of 1963 highlighted the differences between the two approaches but also left both appearing wanting. Whatever the U.S. military had been doing alongside the South Vietnamese army over the previous two years had not been a great success, and Hilsman's brainchild for counterinsurgency had been the strategic hamlets program. Reporting back on the Honolulu meeting on 22 November, hours before Kennedy's assassination, Bundy observed that "everyone recognized that the strategic hamlets, even though associated with Nhu, had to remain the center of the war effort." Only later did it become apparent that this had been both inapt and inept, geared more to maintaining Diem's political control than fighting communism. More seriously, Johnson was less inclined to the political theory behind counterinsurgency strategy. McCone observed after his first meeting with the new president how his tone was different from Kennedy's: "Johnson definitely feels that we place too much emphasis on social reforms; he has very little tolerance with our spending so much time being 'do-gooders.' "[24]

The time was therefore ripe for the advocacy of alternative approaches, involving taking the war to the North. Kennedy had not been opposed in principle to attacks against the North. Given his fascination with guerrilla warfare, it would have been surprising if he had shown no interest in covert operations against North Vietnam. These had been approved as early as May 1961, in NSAM 52, leading to groups of men being periodically air-dropped into the North, where they were invariably and speedily captured. By 1963 the CIA had concluded that this effort was pointless, given the firm control exercised by the communists over their own territory. At the same time, and despite this experience, the American military decided that they should work with the South Vietnamese army to try something similar. They believed that their operations would benefit from being on a larger scale.

In May 1963 plans were requested at a Pentagon conference for South Vietnamese hit-and-run operations against the North.[25] The planning was not pushed with any urgency, as Diem had little interest in such operations. Kennedy was never asked for a view. At the Honolulu conference on 20 November, with Diem now dead and an awareness of the developing military problems, the Pentagon pushed for much more substantial actions. The MACV and CIA were ordered "to prepare a twelve-month, three-phase plan for actions against North Vietnam in a campaign of graduated intensity."[26] There is no reason to suppose that Kennedy would have done other than encourage South Vietnamese operations against the North, but he had always resisted American involvement in operations of this sort.

Reviewing options for Johnson in December, Forrestal noted that tight police control had prevented any progress in clandestine operations against the North.

> It would be worthwhile exploring the possibility of larger-scale operations against selected targets in the North *provided* we carried them out in connection with a political program designed to get a practical reaction out of Hanoi. So far such a program has not been worked out and—even more importantly—the capacity for carrying out larger-scale operations does not now exist.

As far as Forrestal was concerned, the first priority was to bring "the government effectively to the villages in such a way as to win the peasants' confidence and support."[27]

On leaving government, Hilsman sent Bundy a memo that accepted the case for small-scale covert operations to give Hanoi a sense of its vulnerability, but argued against anything more than that until it could be shown that the Viet Cong was losing out in the South. Otherwise it would be seen "as an act of desperation, and will, therefore, not be effective in persuading the North Vietnamese to cease and desist."[28] This memo came at a time when the military was proposing reconnaissance over Laos to prepare for a bombing campaign against infiltration routes, now being emphasized as the best explanation for the dismal state of the war. Hilsman, Harriman, and Forrestal concluded that bombing would lose what was left of the Laos accords, put the Americans in apparent charge of the war, and lead to retaliation by the North.

The other reason for bombing would be political. In December McNamara requested that the Saigon mission prepare plans that would include varying levels of pressure all designed to make clear to the North Vietnamese that the U.S. will not accept a Communist victory in South Vietnam and that we will escalate the conflict to whatever level is required to insure their defeat.[29]

The resulting report, which McNamara received when he visited Saigon on 18–20 December, identified measures of "escalating intensity" ranging from minor propaganda moves to destruction of major resources by raids or bombing. According to Krulak, the study was

> based on the premise that by covert means the North Vietnamese would be warned that their support of the Viet Cong insurgents was about to bring down direct punishment and, after an interval, to proceed with selected elements of the escalative program making clear always that it would stop when the assistance to the Viet Cong stopped.

The Pentagon's counterinsurgency chief claimed that "the great bulk of resources for such a program are already in country, and selected steps could be undertaken promptly."[30] The plan was to be studied by an interdepartmental group.

Though McNamara received these plans, he did not propose radical new steps to Johnson. He was largely concerned with the political situation that had awaited him in Saigon. The generals supposedly running the country were "indecisive and drifting," with no talent for political administration. The local U.S. team was in disarray, with Lodge ("a loner") and Harkins working on separate tracks and barely consulting with each other. McNamara blamed distorted Vietnamese reporting (rather than the Pentagon's gullibility) for ignorance of how bad the situation had been since July.

He paid more attention to the North's infiltration through Cambodia and Laos, yet he still judged plans for cross-border operations into Laos neither politically acceptable nor militarily effective. He described to the president only plans for covert action—sabotage and psychological operations. Though warned of their inherent triviality, McNamara believed that some might allow for "maximum pressure with minimum risk." Out of this came OPLAN [Operations Plan] 34A, designed to inflict "increasing punishment upon North Vietnam and to create pressures, which may convince the North Vietnamese leadership, to desist from its aggressive policies."[31] Hanoi was to learn that a communist victory would not be accepted in the South and the United States was prepared to "escalate the conflict to whatever level is necessary to insure their defeat." This was, as Moïse has observed, "to put it bluntly, silly." No covert operations could send those messages.[32] They could not be readily combined with political demands, nor could the level of pain inflicted be regulated according to the responsiveness of Hanoi.

THE NORTHERN STRATEGY

Nonetheless OPLAN 34A was approved by Johnson on 16 January, albeit in a modest form, and operations began in February. There is no reason to suppose that Kennedy would not have approved measures that were both limited and covert. Not surprisingly, the results were disappointing, and though the program continued after a poor performance in its first phase, the second phase was even less ambitious, although the tempo was increased. It is by no means clear that senior policy makers paid the program much attention or endowed it with high expectations. If anything, its pathetic quality was used to argue for taking the war to the North by more determined means. There remained confusion over whether operations could interfere directly with communist infiltration or simply hurt Hanoi through sabotage. In the event, the main importance of OPLAN 34A was to help trigger the Tonkin Gulf episode.

The idea of taking the war to the North in a decisive fashion was first put to President Johnson by Lodge in a form he had intended to use to present it to President Kennedy. In meetings in Washington on 24 November, Lodge observed that there had been some indications that the North was interested in a deal, largely to get the Americans out. As, officially, the Americans were already planning to leave, he argued that the United States should extract some "quid quo pro." He therefore proposed getting word to Hanoi of American impatience and readiness to attack the North if the Viet Cong was not called off. If, on the other hand, the insurgency did end, the Americans would leave. The idea was not so much to secure the neutralization of South but of North Vietnam.[33] This, of course, was still on the basis that things could only improve now that Diem was out of the way. It also assumed that Hanoi would not wish to be rendered more dependent upon the Chinese, and that the Sino-Soviet split was creating opportunities for isolating Hanoi. The idea, which fitted in with Kennedy's beliefs, was therefore to sustain two separate countries rather than move to unification.[34] This line of argument was somewhat undermined almost immediately by McCone's warning that all was not well in South Vietnam.

In January Maxwell Taylor proposed that U.S. forces should join those of South Vietnam in a range of actions, including a bombing campaign. In February President Johnson instructed his advisors to produce contingency planning with the aim of "shaping such pressures so as to produce the maximum credible deterrent effect on Hanoi."[35] By March the Joint Chiefs were pressing hard for overt military action against the North. McNamara was skeptical but, for want of anything better, he let the preparatory work for an eventual campaign start.

By now Walt Rostow was reasserting his view, held from 1961 but resisted by Kennedy, that it was vital to threaten the North directly. During 1962 and 1963 there had been the occasional standard memo demanding tough action against the North.[36] Now Rostow reentered the Vietnam policy arena by requesting in early February an interdepartmental committee on "Alternatives for Imposition of Measured Pressures Against North Vietnam." This provided the first sustained examination of the strategic case for taking the war to the North. The primary objective of the proposed strategy was "a reduction in the level of Communist activity in Laos and South Vietnam to the point where our counterinsurgency strategy could succeed." The method would be to exploit

> (a) Communist fears that military action might escalate to levels highly dangerous for them, (b) DRV concern lest the rudimentary but cherished industrialization in the North be wiped out, and (c) DRV apprehensions that increasing Chinese involvement would cost them the control they have struggled so long to gain over the territory and the people of North Vietnam.

At the same time the strategy would seek to exclude Chinese or Soviet involvement and rejuvenate the counterinsurgency effort in the South.

The available options were to carry on with the current covert and nonattributable activity, to move to more overt activities, such as a higher-profile U.S. military presence in the area, and to include direct attacks, probably by air, upon the North's territory. Underlying each alternative was "the broad concept that military actions, whether combatant or not, would be taken for the political purpose of channeling the decisions of DRV leadership." The objective was strategic coercion.

The most important feature of this study was that it pinpointed basic flaws with the Northern strategy. The primary objective was unlikely to be attained without action on the ground by the United States and greater "dynamism" by the South Vietnamese forces. If Hanoi claimed to be complying with U.S. demands, it would be extremely difficult to measure this convincingly, in which case how could a cessation of pressures by the United States be justified? If, on the other hand, Hanoi was clearly not complying, how could the United States withdraw without escalating further? Although considered unlikely, unless the very survival of North Vietnam was threatened, escalation could "raise questions of introduction of U.S. ground troops, possible war with Communist China and nuclear weapon use."[37]

The conclusion was stark:

> It is not likely that North Vietnam would (if it could) call off the war in the South even though U.S. actions would in time have serious economic and political impact. Overt action against North Vietnam would be unlikely to produce reduction in Viet Cong activity sufficiently to make victory on the ground possible in South Vietnam unless accompanied by new U.S. bolstering actions in South Vietnam and considerable improvement in the government there. The most to be expected would be reduction of North

Vietnamese support of the Viet Cong for a while and, thus, the gaining of some time and opportunity by the government of South Vietnam to improve itself.[38]

The paper also warned that such a policy would be so blatant that the damage to the United States' reputation if it failed would be even greater than the failure of a counterinsurgency policy.

This was a compelling analysis and in an efficient policy-making process would have all but killed off the Northern strategy. There is no way of knowing whether it would have percolated to Kennedy or to his senior advisers if he had been still been president. It is known that it never reached the top levels of the Johnson administration. Rostow did not accept its conclusions and effectively suppressed the report. He assured Rusk that sanctions against the North would have desirable effects.

In March 1964, the month of its completion, he even began briefing journalists on his ideas, taking as his cue a line in President Johnson's State of the Union address that had referred to the "problem of infiltration . . . practiced by those in Hanoi and Havana who ship arms and men across international borders to foment insurrection." He explained that this raised the problem of frontiers. *Newsweek* published a "Rostow Plan" that called for a blockade of Haiphong Harbor, followed by raids against the North Vietnamese coast and then bombing, by either American or South Vietnamese aircraft, of strategic targets in the North.[39]

Johnson was less than pleased. He complained on 2 March about Rostow's "propaganda move on to really invade North Vietnam." He spoke to him two days later about "speaking up for the administration and raising hell about having a little war up in North Vietnam." As Rostow tried to explain, Johnson exploded: "The President doesn't know the position of the administration, so *you* can't know it." Johnson was objecting not so much to Rostow's ideas as to briefings to the press that then had to be denied, thereby adding to the sense of public confusion surrounding Vietnam policy.[40]

The Northern strategy was analyzed further in April 1964 when the Joint Chiefs of Staff held a war game (SIGMA-I-64) to explore the possibility that air strikes against the North would force them to buckle under. The response of the Red Team, playing Hanoi, was to pour troops into the South, posing to the Blue Team the choice of further expansion of the war, thereby risking Chinese intervention, or backing down. Later CIA participants warned McCone that those pushing for strikes against the North did not appreciate the extent to which the communist campaign in South Vietnam was largely indigenous nor the damage to the international reputation of the United States if it engaged in an attack against the North to save a society in the South that did not want to save itself. Once again the analysis came back to the need to ensure that there was already real strength in the South before anything was attempted against the North.[41] The Joint Chiefs were in no hurry to broadcast this conclusion, while McCone's own predilections and uneasy relationship with Johnson may have counseled him against drawing it to the NSC's attention. Only George Ball appeared aware of the war game and its negative conclusion.

At this point Johnson showed no interest in taking the war to the North and was sticking to a policy of training the South Vietnamese to fight their own war. By the late spring, however, policy makers began to show some signs of desperation. In May McNamara canceled the plan to withdraw U.S. personnel. The Joint Chiefs' proposals for an air campaign against the North started to be taken up by the South Vietnamese. Bundy was also showing an interest in a Northern strategy if all else failed. For some time he had been convinced, mistakenly, that the problem was largely one of morale. If the South Vietnamese could just get themselves into the right frame of mind, they could begin to take on the communists effectively. As early as March Bundy had wondered to Johnson whether McNamara should look at sending some more troops as "a stiffener." They were not needed to win the war but "to show that we think this damned thing can be done." This was "essentially a state-of-mind problem."[42] Changing their client's mental state became a military objective in itself. If the South Vietnamese began to take tough action against the enemy (or even felt able to support the United States in doing so), then that would be a victory of sorts, irrespective of any tangible effects on the enemy effort.[43] An air campaign fitted in with this, though as a last resort and only if preceded by the "appropriate diplomatic and political warning and preparations" to produce a response by the North that, it was hoped, would make its actual implementation unnecessary. Hanoi would be told that no challenge was being mounted to communist rule over the North and that if it left the South alone, there could be major improvements in relations.

Lodge also argued along these lines, claiming in June, "Not only would screams from the North have a tonic effect and strengthen morale here; it is also vital to frighten Ho." There was no guarantee, however, that the North, as it was bombed, would suddenly appeal for a settlement. More likely, as the analysis had demonstrated, the communists would respond with intense pressure against the South, and Khanh was unsure whether his forces could cope. The consequences could be even more dire. Bundy, in forwarding the recommendation to Johnson for "selected and carefully graduated military force against North Vietnam" at the end of May, expressed the "hope and best estimate of most of your advisers" that the use of force would not result in a "major military reply from Red China, and still less from the Soviet Union." Nor was it inevitable that it would "trigger acts of terror and military operations by the Viet Cong which could engulf the Khanh regime." Nonetheless, two risks were identified: "escalation toward major land war or the use of nuclear weapons," and "a reply in South Vietnam itself which would lose that country to neutralism and so eventually to communism."[44]

While the case for air strikes against the North was being promoted from the first months of 1964, this was matched by a striking absence of any argument in favor of ground troops. In part this was because the problem in South Vietnam had never been a lack of manpower but rather its lack of motivation and effective mobilization. The Americans provided logistical support, training, and advice to help the South Vietnamese army and looked to wider reforms to raise morale.

There were already 5,000 Americans in Vietnam as advisers with the South Vietnamese Army and 18,000 in operational support. In the summer of 1964 General Westmoreland, who had replaced Harkins, asked first for 900 more advisers and then a further 4,200 personnel. This was agreed to, but he had to wait until after the election. It was not until September that Bundy, in reporting McNamara's opposition to an increased U.S. military presence, wondered whether the available contingencies for "limited escalation" were enough. "A still more drastic possibility which no one is discussing," he observed, "is the use of substantial U.S. armed forces in operations against the Viet Cong." He took on the Korean analogy.

> I myself believe that before we let this country go we should have a hard look at this grim alternative, and I do not think it is a repetition of Korea. It seems to me at least possible that a couple of brigade-sized units put in to do specific jobs about six weeks from now might be good medicine everywhere.[45]

This did not appear to be the president's own inclination. He was campaigning as the "peace" candidate in the presidential election against Senator Barry Goldwater. He promised that he would not send American "boys" to do "what Asian boys ought to be doing for themselves." The large-scale introduction of ground forces was seen, along with withdrawal, as one of the "extreme" options. By and large, those arguing for an air campaign saw it as an alternative to a land war. It was only as Rolling Thunder began in March 1965 that they were obliged to acknowledge that they were not alternatives but came together. As had been predicted, the communists responded to an air campaign against the North with a vigorous ground campaign in the South.

The trend in opinion favored the Northern strategy. Eventually Bundy's arguments on an air campaign against the North to boost morale in the South carried the day, but this was a poor argument, born of desperation. It failed to anticipate the likely response of the North. Moreover, those who had studied the Northern strategy most carefully knew it to be flawed and could make a compelling case that this was so, but this view was not one that reached the senior levels of government. Only

George Ball recognized its force, and his advocacy suffered not only because he was up against all the senior figures on the NSC, but also because his own preferred course of action, which was to find a diplomatic escape route, appeared so feeble.

Had he lived, Kennedy, like Johnson, would have faced a growing mismatch between his commitment to South Vietnam and the means available to sustain this commitment. Kennedy, like Johnson, would have faced increasing pressure to follow a Northern strategy, though he had resisted this in the past. It is probably fair to say that, unlike Johnson, he would have looked hard at methods by which he might have escaped from this commitment including negotiations with the North. We cannot be sure that he would have continued to reject the Northern strategy, as he had done before, but to assume otherwise is to accept that any president at the start of 1965 was almost doomed to take a decision that not only turned out to be calamitous and counterproductive but was recognized as such by knowledgeable people at the time.

Conclusion

———

DEATH CAME WITHOUT WARNING. The schedule for 22 November 1963 combined presidential and political duties in Texas, with speeches for a conservative state showing more of the president's conservative side. The year coming to an end had been one of real achievement, during which Kennedy had seized the opportunity to improve relations with Moscow and accepted, with some trepidation, the challenge of civil rights at home. His first term was turning out to be more courageous, at least in domestic policy, than he had intended, and among the many strategic decisions awaiting him was how far he dare base his 1964 campaign on this liberal turn or whether he had to find ways of qualifying his message to make it more acceptable to more conservative opinion. Much would depend on whether the Republicans ceded the center ground of American politics, as they did for Lyndon Johnson by nominating Barry Goldwater for president.

The management of domestic politics—civil rights and the economy— would probably decide the 1964 election, but foreign affairs always provide those moments of crisis that can make or break an administration. Cuba had already led to his most striking moments of triumph and humiliation, and still long-term policy was unsettled, with the administration simultaneously exploring means of overthrowing Castro and coming to some deal. Kennedy had yet to find ways of building on the test ban treaty to relax cold war tensions further. This modest success had itself been a function of the deepening Sino-Soviet split, and by late 1963 Khrushchev was getting worried that the Americans might believe that his freedom of maneuver was now so severely constrained they could take advantage. A letter he had sent to Kennedy in October proposing a wide range of initiatives on arms control as well as Berlin had not been answered, although a positive reply had been drafted, approved for dispatch but, because of a "clerical error," not actually sent.[1] A more belligerent tone was starting to return in November, with warnings about Cuba and even incidents in Berlin, with traffic on the autobahn being harassed. Having got hold of some Live Oak contingency plans, the Russians were trying out American reactions. They demanded that the tailgates of trucks be lowered so that they could count troops inside. Kennedy was not disposed to go to war on this matter, but the Berlin specialists saw more tests if this apparently trivial demand was conceded. While the argument raged in Washington the Russians backed off. Then an academic Sovietologist from Yale, Frederick Barghoorn, was arrested as a spy and was released only after Kennedy's personal, and public, intervention.

In addition, just as the Sino-Soviet split had created possibilities for a U.S.-Soviet détente, it had also made Southeast Asia more dangerous, with Moscow's moderating influence on the wane. Kennedy had managed to prevent Laos from turning into a flash point for a major confrontation, but this had aggravated his problems in South Vietnam. Vietnam had never been one of Kennedy's priorities, and when the crisis came in the summer of 1963 he was strikingly unprepared to deal with it. He wanted Vietnam to be a test bed for ill-developed theories of counterinsurgency, but the appropriate political prerequisites were never met, while the American military preferred to stick to forms of warfare that were far better developed, though wholly inappropriate. Kennedy wanted South Vietnam to be a country that could demonstrably deserve support, with a decent government capable of putting up a good fight. In the event, his efforts only compounded the folly of the Eisenhower administration. Diem had been presented as an anticommunist stalwart, but his very dependence on the United States undermined his nationalist claims, and then his narrow political base increased the dependence. Once it became apparent that Diem could never be other than authoritarian and ineffectual his fate was sealed, because American support was the only thing he had going for him.

The loss of Diem made it harder for the Americans to withdraw, if only because policy was so clearly geared to creating a government better able to prosecute the war. It would have been marginally easier to abandon Diem than his successors, though it would not have been that easy and the political fallout in the United States if Saigon had succumbed quickly to effective communist rule could have been severe. Hanoi was after the unification of Vietnam, and while its position on the composition of a future government might have been more flexible than appreciated at the time, this would have been a bitter pill to swallow. Kennedy, as Johnson, would have been engaged in a desperate attempt to sustain a commitment to a noncommunist South Vietnam without large-scale military involvement.

Without Kennedy the balance within the administration during 1964 shifted in favor of the hawks, and the case for air strikes against the North gained in credibility. Kennedy may not have been disposed to give de Gaulle the satisfaction of acceding to calls for an international conference, but he might well have been tempted to allow Harriman the chance to deal directly with Hanoi. One reason for this would have been the poverty of the case for air strikes, exaggerating as it did the positive effects on the South Vietnamese and discounting (against expert advice) the likely forms of communist retaliation. It is possible to imagine Kennedy facing the same pressures that led to Rolling Thunder—and by extension to the introduction of ground forces in a combat role—but his approach to this and similar crises suggests that he would have resisted this pressure. This is not to say that he was determined to withdraw. This may have been his preference, but as likely he would have persevered with established policy, possibly providing more military and economic support just so long as he could claim that this was still a Vietnamese war.

This would have fitted in with the pattern of crisis management established up to November 1963. Military measures were sought that were sufficient to satisfy conservatives without risking major war, while negotiated outcomes were pursued to the extent that any conservative revolt could be contained. To this end Kennedy's policy initiatives were designed to provide him with maximum latitude; he preferred to add options rather than remove them, even if this meant that contradictory courses were sustained at the same time, and he disliked definitive, irreversible decisions. To check that the calibration was correct he preferred to take one step at a time and then assess the situation before moving on to the next step. This fitted in both with his natural political caution and the hazardous circumstances of the cold war. The strategy for doing this was described as graduated, measured, flexible, or selective response.

For Kennedy it seemed to work. His experience of successive crises encouraged this approach, to the point where it moved from a predisposition to something of a dogma. There it remained in the U.S. government, and even in NATO, where its influence could be felt long after John Kennedy's death. As one looks at the events covered in this book, it is by no means evident that graduated response worked except as a means of demonstrating commitment from the start of the crisis while leaving the way open to diplomacy. In practice the governing factor was the clarity of political objectives and their attainability rather than the quality of successive military moves. A lot of escalation was considered but, under Kennedy at least, not much was practiced. The first military steps normally produced results, and Khrushchev, the usual target, might have feared that Kennedy could lose control of his government to the militarists. This perception helped defuse the Berlin and Cuban crises.

The premium put on activism rather then reflection meant that by default there was a tendency to work within and accept, rather than subvert and change, the fundamentals of the established policy consensus. Yet the image of Kennedy as being all tactics and no strategy is unfair. He did come to office with a strategy for the conduct of the cold war that he then tried to implement. At its core was a respect for the Soviet Union as a competitor for international influence, and a belief that deals could be struck with Moscow to render this competition less dangerous.

Kennedy feared nuclear war. It was the one option he would have liked to renounce but could not because of alliance commitments. He was after a test ban treaty from the start of his administration and was reluctant to start testing again even after the moratorium was ended unilaterally by Khrushchev. He was convinced, along with many of his generation, that deals with aggressive and authoritarian regimes could only be achieved from a position of strength. The proposition had some validity—Khrushchev certainly believed that he could get more out of the West if it was assumed that the Soviet Union enjoyed a military edge—but it also led naturally to arms racing.

The acquisition of military strength supported a belief in a wide range of options. The actual use of armed force was a different matter, and Kennedy understood that he could only sustain the support of the American people with good cause. He went to great lengths to clarify what he thought was and was not worth fighting for. He was prepared to commit American forces to fight for West Berlin but not East Berlin; to get missiles out of Cuba but not remove Castro; to defend Taiwan but not liberate China. In these cases this clarity helped in the resolution of the crises. One reason for his reluctance to send troops to South Vietnam was his belief that the unappealing nature of Diem's regime and the nature of the conflict had the makings of an unpopular war. Whenever his willingness to seek a diplomatic settlement was in doubt he demonstrated a readiness to communicate with his adversaries and search for acceptable compromises. In the cases of Berlin, the Cuban missile crisis, and Laos he was prepared to circumvent the concerns of allies in order to defuse a developing crisis. He authorized informal talks with Cuba and North Vietnam. It was not his style to close off opportunities for negotiation.

His desire to keep his options open had a less attractive side in his tendency to approve undercover activities, both military and diplomatic, in the belief that the political costs associated with more overt actions could thereby be avoided. The most egregious examples of this were with Cuba, but to this can be added the support of Meo tribesmen in Laos and South Vietnamese operations against the North, and for that matter the readiness to allow U.S. advisers in Vietnam to get involved in combat so long as this was deniable. In none of these cases did the putative gains begin to match the costs, and it often seemed as if the government was more successful in deceiving itself than others. Back door diplomacy was more justifiable, especially if the front door was closed, and it could often be kept really secret, but even then relatively uncontrolled forms of communication could send confused signals.

Where Kennedy's strategic vision really let him down was in the development of an approach to the conduct of the cold war in the third world. The basic problem, which he had tried to avoid while a senator, was in exaggerating the importance of the cold war to the upheavals that accompanied the decline of the old empires. As Hugh Brogan has observed, "essentially conservative statesmen (even if they are liberals) exhibit a certain frivolity" when claiming allegiance to the idea of revolution.[2] Americans found it difficult to understand why they were seen by so many third world leaders to be more part of the problem than the solution, let alone the comparative appeals of notions of state socialism. Kennedy's effort to establish a new strategy for the third world could chalk up some success in its more positive aspects (for example, the Peace Corps) but not in its military aspects. There were quieter successes away from Cuba and Vietnam, but there was no escaping the noisy failures in these two countries.

Part of the problem lay in an exaggerated view of the extent to which communist insurgencies were controlled from Moscow. From the start he was trying to find a way of consolidating peaceful coexistence—he had no plan for winning the cold war. In the end he did make a breakthrough at this level, but the corollary of this approach was that he had no basis for understanding and dealing with other independent centers of communist power. Castro was always defined as the problem, and this led to an inability to begin to think about how he might be allowed to run a country on socialist lines so close to the United States. By 1963 the limits to Khrushchev's influence in Hanoi became apparent. Kennedy started to appreciate that these conflicts could be dealt with not by means of great power bargaining but on their own terms. By then he had a lot of ground to make up.

This was not the only way in which Kennedy exaggerated the Soviet position. He entered office still believing that Soviet military strength was growing and that its economy could sustain this growth for the indefinite future. On this basis he initially took Khrushchev's bluster seriously. It took until 1963 for him to get the measure of Khrushchev and start to appreciate the severity of his opponent's problems—in agriculture, economics, and alliance management. The fact that he presided over what is now generally recognized to be a turning point in the cold war can be put down to this being the time when the Soviet challenge simply ran out of steam.[3] Nonetheless, it is to Kennedy's credit that he created the conditions for the European détente that took root at the end of the decade and for demonstrating in words and deeds that the superpowers must cooperate to prevent a nuclear catastrophe. The wars he feared, and which often seemed so close during his few years in office, were not fought, at least not by Americans. For all his mistakes and misadventures, Kennedy's achievement was that he could be remembered for crises rather than hot wars, and that he left the cold war in a far less dangerous state than he found it.

Acknowledgments

I wish to acknowledge the support of a British Academy Readership, which allowed me to take extended study leave to complete this manuscript. This work has been gestating for some ten years, and I have had a number of opportunities to discuss the issues it addresses with numerous professional colleagues as well as some veterans of the Kennedy years. I hope they will forgive me if I do not mention all by name, but I would like to acknowledge those who took the trouble to read and comment on the manuscript in an earlier draft, especially Arthur Schlesinger Jr., Carl Kaysen, Arne Westad, and Beatrice Heuser as well as the anonymous reviewers for Oxford University Press whose comments made a significant difference to the final shape of this book. I am grateful for my editors at Oxford University Press, Thomas LeBien and Susan Ferber, for their advice and support. I am grateful to Andy Weir, who first introduced me to the new Kennedy tapes. At the University of Virginia, work on transcribing new Kennedy tapes is proceeding under the guidance of Philip Zelikow. When this work is complete it will stimulate even more revisions to Kennedy scholarship. Jill Kastner also let me see her transcripts of Kennedy's discussions on Berlin and the test ban. I am especially grateful to George Eliades, who allowed me to share the fruits of his considerable labors on the Kennedy tapes connected with Vietnam prior to their full publication; there are few greater sacrifices a scholar can make. John Gearson and Kori Schake both provided me with helpful materials on Berlin, as did Sharon Ghamari on the work going on at RAND at this time. Jon Persoff's and Fran Burwell's last minute assistance was invaluable.

Like many others, I have been a beneficiary of the oral histories, especially of the Cuban missile crisis, for which Jim Blight has acted as an impresario, and the marvelous work undertaken by the National Security Archive and the Cold War International History Project. Jim Hershberg, Christian Ostermann, Tom Blanton, and Bill Burr in particular deserve thanks for the enthusiasm and dedication with which they have opened up the darker recesses of recent history. An opportunity to work with

Jeremy Isaacs and his team as a consultant on their cold war series was a great help, not least because of the contact it required with John Gaddis and Vlad Zubock. I have also been helped by materials produced under the aegis of the nuclear history program, in which Ernest May, Uwe Nerlich, Wolfgang Krieger, Bob O'Neill, and Catherine Kelleher played such leading roles. Bob and Catherine, with Michael Howard, deserve special mention for all the valuable advice and encouragement they have given me throughout my career. In different ways Steve Smith and Colin Gray have been invaluable in helping me sort out my ideas. I have also been fortunate in being able to work with a remarkable set of colleagues in the War Studies Group at King's College.

Projects such as this cannot but be shared by my whole family, and they have, as always, provided me with support and welcome distractions as required. This book, however, is particularly dedicated to my son Sam. When I began to work on this topic he had barely started school. As it is published he is at university studying history for himself. One of the great satisfactions of this book lies in the many improvements that have resulted from his suggestions on both detail and structure.

Notes

Sources are listed in the notes in abbreviated form. Full details may be found in the bibliography.

Preface

1. Schlesinger, *A Thousand Days;* Sorensen, *Kennedy.*
2. Paterson, "Introduction," 23.
3. Reeves, *A Question of Character.*
4. Hersh, *The Dark Side of Camelot.*
5. There are a number of excellent biographies available: Parmet, *JFK;* Giglio, *The Presidency of John F. Kennedy;* Reeves, *President Kennedy;* Brogan, *Kennedy.* For a robust defense of Kennedy against the revisionist critiques, see Schlesinger, "JFK Revisited."
6. Beschloss, *KvK;* Reeves, *President Kennedy.*

Introduction

1. For a balanced assessment, see White, "Behind Closed Doors: The Private Life of a Public Man," 256–76.
2. Kennedy, *Profiles in Courage;* Kennedy, *Why England Slept.*
3. As with other politicians of his generation, Chamberlain's appeasement of Hitler at Munich remained a potent source of symbolism. Cuervo, "John F. Kennedy and the Munich Myth."
4. This intense relationship with the media comes over vividly in Bradlee, *Conversations with Kennedy.*
5. Wofford, *Of Kennedys and Kings,* 426; Paterson, *Meeting the Communist Threat,* 200–203.
6. Liddell Hart, *Deterrent or Defense,* 247–48. Kennedy's review of Liddell Hart appeared in *Saturday Evening Post,* 3 September 1960. Quoted in Schlesinger, *Thousand Days,* 110.

Chapter 1

1. Schlesinger, *The Vital Center*, xxiii.

2. For more background on the formation of the ADA, see Gillon, *Politics and Vision*.

3. Title of a book edited by leading British socialist in 1949 containing articles by prominent intellectuals, including a number of former communists. Crossman, ed., *The God That Failed*.

4. Gleason, *Totalitarianism*, 4.

5. For a full discussion of Niebuhr and his influence on American foreign policy, see Brands, *What America Owes the World*, ch. 7. The essentials of his position were first set out in Niebuhr, *Moral Man and Immoral Society*. A particularly influential essay from this time was Niebuhr, "The Illusion of World Government." See also Pells, *The Liberal Mind in a Conservative Age*, 136–37.

6. Morgenthau, *Politics Among Nations*.

7. Schlesinger, *The Vital Center*, 222, 226–27.

8. In the summer of 1947 an article appeared under the authorship of "X" in *Foreign Affairs*, making public the somber analysis developed by Kennan from the Moscow embassy in a telegram to the State Department. Lippmann's critique, developed in fourteen successive columns, was later published under the title *The Cold War*. Credit for coining the term was disputed, and Lippmann himself claimed to have first heard it in Europe to describe Germany's war of nerves against France in the 1930s. Lippmann undoubtedly popularized it. Steel, *Walter Lippmann and the American Century*, 444–45.

9. Acheson, *Present at the Creation*.

10. Kennan, *Russia, the Atom and the West*.

11. Isaacson and Thomas, *The Wise Men*, 323.

12. Acheson, *Present at the Creation*, 108, 15, 30, 33.

13. Brinkley, *Dean Acheson*, 105.

14. From a 1961 essay on John Foster Dulles, in Morgenthau, *Truth and Power*, 91.

Chapter 2

1. Address by Secretary John Foster Dulles, "The Evolution of Foreign Policy," speech to the Council on Foreign Relations, New York, January 1954, reprinted in Bobbit, Freedman, and Treverton, eds., *U.S. Nuclear Strategy*.

2. Brinkley, *Dean Acheson*, 20–22.

3. Taylor, *The Uncertain Trumpet*, 6.

4. Morgenthau, "Atomic Force and Foreign Policy," 505. Quoted in Acheson, *Power and Diplomacy*, 52.

5. Kissinger, *Nuclear Weapons and Foreign Policy*. On Kissinger as a strategist, see Freedman, "Henry Kissinger." One of the first books on this theme was Osgood, *Limited War*. For a survey of the work of this school, see Halperin,

Limited War in the Nuclear Age. See also Kaufman, ed., *Military Policy and National Security*.

6. Kissinger, *Nuclear Weapons and Foreign Policy*, 144.

7. Acheson, who approved of the rest of the book, challenged Kissinger's theory using Nitze, "Limited Wars or Massive Retaliation." On the army's efforts, see Bacevich, *The Pentomic Era*.

8. Acheson, *Power and Diplomacy*, 85.

9. RAND came from "*r*esearch *and* development." For histories, see Smith, *The RAND Corporation*, and Kaplan, *The Wizards of Armageddon*.

10. Kahn, *On Thermonuclear War*. See also Garnett, "Herman Kahn."

11. Hitch and McKean, *The Economics of Defense in the Nuclear Age*.

12. Von Neumann and Morgenstern, *Theory of Games and Economic Behavior*.

13. For a full presentation of this approach, see Quade, ed., *Analysis for Military Decisions*.

14. Wohlstetter et al., "Selection and Use of Strategic Air Bases." On Wohlstetter, see Rosencrance, "Albert Wohlstetter," 57.

15. Schelling, *The Strategy of Conflict*, 233. The intellectual origins of Schelling's thought, from such diverse areas as oligopoly theory and gestalt psychology, are explored in Ayson, *Thomas Schelling and the Concept of Stability*. See also Williams, "Tom Schelling."

16. This movement is described in Wittner, *Resisting the Bomb*.

17. Divine, *Blowing on the Wind*.

18. Riesman and Macoby, "The American Crisis," 22, 27. One of the editors was Marcus Raskin, who was working for McGeorge Bundy on the National Security Council staff (at Riesman's suggestion) by the time the book was published. As the book was under attack by the Republican right, Raskin was told to take his name off the cover. Nonetheless, Raskin suffered from guilt by association and eventually left the NSC staff. Bird, *The Color of Truth*, 218–19.

19. Waskow, "The Theory and Practice of Deterrence," 146–47.

20. These ideas were developed by Schelling with Morton Halperin, a young colleague at Harvard, in *Strategy and Arms Control*.

21. The proceedings of this conference first appeared in *Daedalus* 89, 4 (1960), and then in Brennan, ed., *Arms Control, Disarmament and National Security*.

22. Schelling, *The Strategy of Conflict*, 193–94, 208.

23. Kissinger, *The Necessity for Choice*.

24. Kahn, *On Thermonuclear War*, 226.

25. Ibid., 139.

26. It was known as the Gaither Report after its chairman, H. Rowen Gaither, and had originally been established to consider the case for civil defense. Nitze, *From Hiroshima to Glasnost*, 166–69. Wohlstetter's influential briefing to the panel was published as Wohlstetter, "The Delicate Balance of Terror."

27. As the main beneficiary of massive retaliation, the USAF had little sympathy for the complaints of the army and navy. The best guide to the interservice rivalries of this period remains Huntington, *The Common Defense*.

28. I deal with this in Freedman, *U.S. Intelligence and the Soviet Strategic Threat*.

Chapter 3

1. Bowles, *The Conscience of a Liberal*, 59. See also Schaffer, *Chester Bowles*.
2. Ball, *The Past Has Another Pattern*, 208.
3. Rostow, *The Diffusion of Power*, 164.
4. Rostow, *The Stages of Economic Growth*.
5. Rostow, *An American Policy in Asia*, 42, cited in Rostow, *The Diffusion of Power*, 283–84.
6. Rostow, *The Diffusion of Power*, 119. One of the most influential was Lucien Pye. See his *Guerrilla Communism in Malaya*.
7. Pye, *Politics, Personality and Nation-Building*, 13. Cited in Shafer, *Deadly Paradigms*, 62.
8. Rostow, *The United States in the World Arena*, 478–80.

Chapter 4

1. Schlesinger, *Thousand Days*, 181.
2. In *Libre Belgique*, 14 October 1960, cited in Weissman, *American Foreign Policy in the Congo, 1960–1964*, 116.
3. See Nash, "Bear Any Burden?" 121–22.
4. Schlesinger, *Thousand Days*, 311.
5. Merry, *Taking on the World*, 342. See also Yoder, *Joe Alsop's Cold War*.
6. Nash, "Bear Any Burden?" 123–24.
7. Sorensen, *Kennedy*, 513.
8. Speech of 14 June 1960, U.S. Senate, reprinted in second edition of Nevins, ed., *John F. Kennedy*.
9. Sorensen, *Kennedy*, 240. The full text of the speech is found on 245–48 and in Sorensen, ed., "*Let the Word Go Forth*," 12–15.
10. Brinkley, *Dean Acheson*, 47.
11. Ibid., 116; Isaacson and Thomas, *The Wise Men*.
12. Bundy, ed., *The Patterns of Responsibility*.
13. His father worked in the War Department during the Second World War, and McGeorge helped Henry Stimson, former secretary for war, write his memoirs.
14. The 1960 acceptance speech had a number of authors, including Kennedy himself. The phrase "New Frontier" appears to have come from Canadian journalist Max Freedman. Bird, *The Color of Truth*, 183.
15. See the portrait in Halberstam, *The Best and the Brightest*, 193–200.
16. Paul Kattenburg describes him as "a powerful intellectual" and, in retrospect, "the single most influential thinker in both the Kennedy and Johnson administrations." Kattenburg, *The Vietnam Trauma in American Foreign Policy, 1945–75*, 88.
17. On the development of Harriman's views on the cold war, see Twing, *Myths, Models, and U.S. Foreign Policy*, ch. 5.

18. Cited in Reeves, *A Question of Character*, 288.

19. Neustadt, *Presidential Power*.

20. Reeves, *President Kennedy*, 113–14.

Chapter 5

1. Shapley, *Promise and Power*, 102–3.

2. Hitch and McKean, *The Economics of Defense in the Nuclear Age*.

3. White, "Strategy and the Defense Intellectuals"; NHP/Berlin, 202; Jardini, "Out of the Blue Yonder," 5–6. For a critique of the role of systems analysis, see Rosen, "Systems Analysis and the Quest for Rational Defense."

4. Bundy to Kennedy, 30 January 1961, FRUS, VIII, 18–19. He refers to the "view of nearly all your civilian advisers." Ball, *Politics and Force Levels*, 34–38; Kaplan, *The Wizards of Armageddon*, 260.

5. McNamara to Kennedy, Memorandum on Review of FY 1961 and FY 1962 Military Programs and Budgets, 20 February 1961, FRUS, VIII, 35.

6. Kaplan, *The Wizards of Armageddon*, 260.

7. Herken, *Counsels of War*, 139.

8. Taylor, *The Uncertain Trumpet*, 131. For a similar 1960 view, see Kissinger, *The Necessity for Choice*, 15.

9. See Freedman, *U.S. Intelligence*, 69–71.

10. As reported in the *New York Times* on 7 February 1961. McNamara recalls saying that the gap was in the United States' favor, and also that he offered to resign. McNamara and VanDeMark, *In Retrospect*, 20–21; Shapley, *Promise and Power*, 98–99.

11. McNamara to Kennedy, Memorandum on Review of FY 1961 and FY 1962 Military Programs and Budgets, 20 February 1961, Annex B, FRUS, VIII, 46–47.

12. Rusk to McNamara, 4 February 1961; McNamara to Kennedy, Memorandum on Review of FY 1961 and FY 1962 Military Programs and Budgets, 20 February 1961; Bundy to Sorensen, 13 March 1961, FRUS, VIII, 25–27, 35, 66.

13. Finletter to Kennedy, 29 May 1961, NSA/Berlin, 3045.

14. President's conversation with De Gaulle, 2 June 1963, NSA/nuclear, 958.

15. Heuser, *NATO, Britain, France and the FRG*, 44

Chapter 6

1. On this, see Beschloss, *Mayday*.

2. Nevins, *Strategy of Peace*, 19–25.

3. McCloy to Kennedy, 8 March 1961; National Intelligence Estimate 4–61, Probable Short-Term Reactions to U.S. Resumption of Nuclear Tests, FRUS, VII, 14–17, 1–7.

4. Moscow to State, 28 January 1961; Notes on Discussion, 11 February 1961; FRUS, V, 48, 65.

5. Seaborg, *Kennedy, Khrushchev and the Test Ban*, 29–53.

6. Record of Meeting, 4 May 1961, FRUS, VII, 59.

7. Thompson to Bohlen, 25 January 1961; Memorandum, 30 January 1962, FRUS, V, 359–60.

8. Kennedy, *Robert Kennedy in His Own Words*, 258.

9. Fursenko and Naftali, *Secret History*, 110–12.

10. Ibid., 112–13, 116–19, 122. One puzzle is that in 1964 Robert was adamant that Bolshakov had told him "quite clearly" that there could be an agreement on a test ban. *Robert Kennedy in His Own Words*, 263. It may be that Bolshakov was given more leeway than indicated by the Soviet archives, or he may have tried to put a positive spin on the message he was transmitting, or else Robert may have misread the message. The concession reported by Robert was a move from the Soviet position of fifteen unmanned detection stations on Soviet soil to the American position of nineteen. However, this was from memory, and as he remarked in 1964, "[S]tupidly, I didn't write many of the things down. I just delivered the messages verbally to my brother" (260).

11. Moscow to State, 24 May 1961, FRUS, XIV, 66–69.

12. Fursenko and Naftali, *Secret History*, 123–24.

13. A useful summation of this material is found in Beschloss, *KvK*, 167–69.

14. Beschloss, *KvK*, 177; Fursenko and Naftali, *Secret History*, 125–27.

15. See variety of State Department papers: 23 May 1961; 25 May 1961; 1 June 1961; Kennan to Rusk, 2 June 1963, FRUS, V, 139–48, 153–61, 164–68, 169. Moscow to State, 24 May 1961; Lightner to State, 25 May 1961; Thompson to State, 27 May 1961, FRUS, XIV, 66–69, 74–78. Thompson to State, 27 May 1961, FRUS, V, 163–64.

16. O'Donnell and Powers, *"Johnny, We Hardly Knew Ye,"* 341. Full transcripts of the Vienna summit can be found in FRUS, V, 172–230.

17. FRUS, V, 238, 260. The proposal had come from a study group chaired by Tom Schelling.

18. Circular Telegram from State, 8 June 1961, FRUS, V, 239.

19. The line he had been given in a number of briefing papers was that "[t]he situation in all of Berlin—not West Berlin alone—is abnormal because the situation in all of Germany is abnormal." Department of State. Position Paper, 25 May 1961, FRUS, XIV, 72.

20. Zubok and Harrison, "The Nuclear Education of Nikita Khrushchev," 156.

Chapter 7

1. On Soviet-GDR relations during the crisis see Harrison, "Ulbricht and the Concrete 'Rose.' " For a good discussion of Soviet decision making, see Adomeit, *Soviet Risk-Taking and Crisis Behavior*.

2. Tusa, *The Last Division: Berlin and the Wall*, 232.

3. Gearson, *Harold Macmillan and the Berlin Wall Crisis, 1958–1962*.

4. Mayer, *Adenauer and Kennedy*, 7–9. See Kennedy, "A Democrat Looks at Foreign Policy," for his early criticism of Adenauer's role.

5. Memorandum of Conversation, 13 March 1961, FRUS, XIV, 29; Mayer, *Adenauer and Kennedy*, 20–21.

6. Cited in Brinkley, *Dean Acheson*, 96–97.

7. Ibid., 117–18.

8. Bundy, Memorandum, 4 April 1961, NSA/Berlin, 2023.

9. The President's Meeting with Prime Minister Macmillan, 5 April 1961, FRUS, XIV, 36–40.

10. Schlesinger, *Thousand Days*, 344; Brinkley, *Dean Acheson*, 125–26.

11. See Mayer, *Adenauer and Kennedy*, 22; Brinkley, *Dean Acheson*, 128–29.

12. Remarks at Foreign Service lunch of mid-June 1961. Cited in Brinkley, *Dean Acheson*, 127. Such remarks did not endear Acheson to Kennedy when they got back to him.

13. Catudal, *Kennedy and the Berlin Wall Crisis*, 122.

14. Schlesinger, *Thousand Days*, 35; Sorensen, *Kennedy*, 586.

15. Rusk, *As I Saw It*, 294; Remarks by Martin Hillenbrand on Berlin Crisis Working Group, 11 October 1988, in NSA/Berlin, 2945; O'Donnell and Powers, *"Johnny, We Hardly Knew Ye,"* 344.

16. Rusk, *As I Saw It*, 222; Schlesinger, *Thousand Days*, 347; Sorensen, *Kennedy*, 587; Catudal, *Kennedy and the Berlin Wall Crisis*, 153.

Chapter 8

1. Record of Meeting, 16 June 1961, FRUS, XIV, 119–24.

2. Memorandum, 14 June 1961, FRUS, XIV, 117–24.

3. The Acheson Report, FRUS, XIV, 138–59; National Security Action Memorandum No. 58, FRUS, XIV, 162–65.

4. *Washington Post*, 21 June 1961, cited in Kern, Levering, and Levering, *The Kennedy Crises*, 76.

5. Kern, Levering, and Levering, *The Kennedy Crises*, 252.

6. Slusser suggests this was a deliberate probe of Kennedy's intentions by Khrushchev. He notes that the Soviet leader used a phrase similar to that of Kornienko in a speech to military cadets a few days later. Slusser, *The Berlin Crisis of 1961*, 45, 53. However, Kornienko later denied this, suggesting that he had acted to counter the impact of Ambassador Menshikov's public comment that the West would not fight for Berlin. Harrison, "Ulbricht and the Concrete 'Rose.' "

7. Schlesinger, *Thousand Days*, 386.

8. Oral history interview with Abram Chayes, 9 July 1964, NSA/Berlin, 2926.

9. Isaacson, *Kissinger*, 111, 113. Schlesinger was one of his few friends at court. Schlesinger, *Thousand Days*, 389.

10. Schlesinger to Kennedy, 7 July 1961, FRUS, XIV, 173–75; Schlesinger, *Thousand Days*, 387–88.

11. They were old associates. Harriman had been born in November 1891, Acheson some sixteen months later. Both attended the same high-class prep school, Groton (where Harriman taught Acheson how to row), and both went to Yale.

12. FRUS, XIV, 176–77.

13. Catudal, *Kennedy and Berlin*, 150.

14. Memorandum, 12 July 1961; Memorandum of Discussion in National Security Council, 13 July 1961, FRUS, XIV, 187–91, 192–94; Schlesinger, *Thousand Days*, 352. Kennedy convened a small meeting for his senior officials (excluding Acheson) for after the full NSC discussion to consider the issues. Military Choices in Berlin Planning, 13 July 1961, FRUS, XIV-VI, Supplement, Document 90.

15. Memorandum, 17 July 1961, FRUS, XIV, 209–12. See also President's Meeting with Joint Chiefs of Staff, 18 July 1961, FRUS, XIV, 18–19. This indicates that he was less than persuaded at this point of the nonnuclear option. The next day Bundy reported that "there is general agreement in the steering group that the national emergency is not now necessary, but a hard wing of the Kohler group, led by Acheson and Nitze, disagrees." Bundy to Kennedy, 19 July 1961, FRUS, XIV, 217; Catudal, *Kennedy and Berlin*, 178–79.

16. Memorandum of Minutes of the NSC Meeting, 19 July 1961 FRUS, XIV, 219–22.

17. Report by Dean Acheson, "Berlin: A Political Program," transmitted 31 July, FRUS, XIV, 99, 245–59. See also Paper Prepared by the Four-Power Working Group on Germany and Berlin, 8 August 1961, FRUS, XIV, 316–18.

18. For text, see Theodore Sorensen, ed., *"Let the Word Go Forth,"* 257–63. Unfortunately Sorensen has edited the speech to exclude the reference to civil defense, on the grounds that this was later regretted by Kennedy.

19. Schlesinger, *Thousand Days*, 392. On the efforts to convince the leading liberal columnist Marquis Childs that it could have been worse and that the buildup was really quite mild, see Kern, Levering, and Levering, *The Kennedy Crises*, 86–87.

20. Reeves, *President Kennedy*, 202.

21. Bundy, *Danger and Survival*, 368–69.

22. Meeting with European Ambassadors, Paris, 9 August 1961, FRUS, XIV, 318–19.

Chapter 9

1. Catudal, *Kennedy and Berlin*, 125; Harrison, "Ulbricht and the Concrete 'Rose,' " reports Kvitsinsky's belief that Ulbricht might just have been trying to ensure that his public utterances conformed with private communications from Khrushchev.

2. In particular, an article in *Newsweek* (3 July 1961) had described the Pentagon's proposals for the defense of Berlin, including nuclear options. Catudal, *Kennedy and Berlin*, 155–57.

3. For accounts of Soviet-GDR decision making, see Zubok and Pleshakov, *Inside the Kremlin's Cold War*, 251–53; Zubok, "Khrushchev and the Berlin Crisis (1958–62)"; Harrison, "Ulbricht and the Concrete 'Rose' "; Wyden, *The Wall*.

4. Schechter and Deriabin, *The Spy Who Saved the World*, 262.

5. Catudal, *Kennedy and Berlin*, 229–33; Schild, "The Berlin Crisis," 112; interviews with Martha Mautner and John Mapother in "Cold War."

6. Bonn to State, 12 July 1961, FRUS, XIV, 191–92; Ausland, Discontent in East Germany, 18 July 1961, NSA/Berlin, 2189.

7. State to Berlin, 22 July 1961, reprinted in Ausland, *Kennedy, Khrushchev, and the Berlin-Cuba Crisis, 1961–1964*, 116–17; Catudal, *Kennedy and Berlin*, 189; Bonn to State, 24 July 1961, NSA/Berlin, 2220.

8. Rostow, *The Diffusion of Power*, 231.

9. Catudal, *Kennedy and Berlin*, 201–3. Kennedy did not disavow Fulbright's remarks.

10. Nitze, *Hiroshima to Glasnost*, 199–200; interview with John Mapother in "Cold War."

11. Bundy to Kennedy, 14 August 1961; Kennedy to Rusk, 14 August 1961; Meeting of the Berlin Steering Group, 15 August 1961, FRUS, XIV, 330–34.

12. Kennedy to McNamara, 14 August 1961, NSA/Berlin, 2300.

13. Kastner, "Kennedy, Adenauer and the Berlin Crisis" (unpublished paper).

14. Brandt to Kennedy, 16 August 1961, FRUS, XIV, 345–46.

15. Berlin Mission to State, 16 August 1961, FRUS, XIV, 343.

Chapter 10

1. Zubok and Pleshakov, *Inside the Kremlin's Cold War*, 256.

2. Berlin Steering Group, 17 August 1961, FRUS, XIV, 347–49.

3. Kennedy to Brandt, 18 August 1961, FRUS, XIV, 352.

4. Kern, Levering, and Levering, *The Kennedy Crises*, 92–93; interview with Martha Mautner, "Cold War." Morrow of USIA, visiting Berlin at the time, helped persuade Kennedy that he had to do something.

5. For a lucid account of events after 13 August, see Tusa, *The Last Division*, 301–17.

6. FRUS, VII, 110–12, 114–15, 116–24.

7. Sorensen, *Kennedy*, 619; Reeves, *President Kennedy*, 222. (A witness suggested to me yet another profanity.)

8. Schlesinger, *Robert Kennedy*, 429–30.

9. Stevenson memo, Murrow to Kennedy, 31 August 1961; Kennedy to Macmillan, 5 September 1961, FRUS, VII, 149–52, 164; Beschloss, *KvK*, 307; Reeves, *President Kennedy*, 227; interview with Herbert York, "Cold War."

10. SNIE 11-11-61: Implications of the Soviet Resumption of Nuclear Testing, 8 September 1961, FRUS, VII, 167.

11. This pattern in Khrushchev's behavior was picked up at the time by Horelick and Rush, *Strategic Power and Soviet Foreign Policy*. Initially this was a classified study. See also Fursenko and Naftali, *Secret History*, 138.

12. Taylor to President, 4 September 1961, FRUS, XIV, 392.

13. Meeting of Berlin Steering Group, 7 September 1961, FRUS, XIV, 395–38; Acheson to Truman, 21 September 1961, NSA/Berlin, 2495.

14. Burr, "Soviet Cold War Military Strategy: Using Declassified History," 13; Scott, "Espionage and the Cold War," 31

15. Ball, *Politics and Force Levels*, 95; Sagan, "SIOP-62: The Nuclear War Plan Briefing to President Kennedy," 26.

16. NIE 11-8/1-61, Strength and Deployment of Soviet Long Range Ballistic Missile Forces, 21 September 1961, FRUS, VIII, 131–38. On this matter Penkovsky appears as "reliable clandestine reports."

17. *Washington Post*, 25 September 1961. See Ball, *Politics and Force Levels*, 96.

18. Slusser, *Berlin Crisis*, 309–12.

19. Adamsky and Smirnov, "Moscow's Biggest Bomb."

20. Zubok and Harrison, "The Nuclear Education of Nikita Khrushchev," 152.

21. Hilsman suggests Gilpatric, McNamara's deputy, was chosen to avoid the appearance of a high-level threat, although he was still a figure senior enough to be noticed. Hilsman, *The Cuban Missile Crisis*, 7–8; Beschloss, *KvK*, 329–30. Another purpose of the speech was to encourage the West Europeans to build up their conventional forces. Bundy recalled the stress on American nuclear superiority as being important in reassuring the allies. Bundy, *Danger and Survival*, 382. In July Komer had criticized Gilpatric for being "feeble" in suggesting that NATO would only respond to a Berlin crisis with conventional means when Khrushchev needed to be reminded of the nuclear dangers. Komer to Bundy, Nuclear Weapons and Berlin, 20 July 1961, FRUS, XIV–VI, Supplement, Document 97. Another benefit of the speech was that it informed those parts of the bureaucracy without privileged intelligence access on American strength.

22. Slusser, *Berlin Crisis*, 382–84.

23. NSAM 116, 1 December 1961, FRUS, VII, 252–53.

24. Schlesinger to Kennedy, Bundy to Kennedy, 29, 30 December 1961, FRUS, VII, 282–87, 291–95, 297–303, 306–7.

25. Kaysen, Memorandum, 11 October 1961, NSA/nuclear, 433. See also Kaysen to Kennedy, 22 November 1961, FRUS, VIII, 210–11. This is of some interest in that in 1967 McNamara justified the U.S. buildup of this time as an almost mechanical reaction to worst-case estimates of Soviet plans. See McNamara, "The Dynamics of Nuclear Strategy," 18 September 1967, reprinted in Bobbit, Freedman, and Treverton, *U.S. Nuclear Strategy*, 274.

26. Beschloss, *KvK*, 344. Kennedy eventually approved a force of 1,840 nuclear missiles, a 68 percent increase over the 1,096 envisaged by Eisenhower's last defense budget. In April 1961 the U.S. strategic nuclear arsenal consisted of 3,012 weapons; by July 1964 it was 5,007. Nash, "Bear Any Burden?" 124–25.

27. The interview was in *Newsweek*, 13 November 1961, cited in Ball, *Politics and Force Levels*, 98.

28. Beschloss, *KvK*, 344–45.

29. Bundy to Kennedy, 11 August 1961, NSA/Berlin, 228; Bundy to Kennedy, 14 August 1961; Berlin Steering Group, 17 August 1961, FRUS, XIV, 330–31, 347–49, 387. Kennan asserted to Bowles that "unless the West shows some disposition to negotiate in the sense of coming forward with some ideas and proposals of its own, the hard line is going to be pursued in Moscow not only to the

very brink but to the full point of a world catastrophe. We could not form a judgment on their willingness to negotiate unless we tried." Kennan to Bowles, 22 September 1961, FRUS, XIV, 435–37.

30. Kennedy to Rusk, 21 August 1961, FRUS, XIV, 359–60.

31. Mayer, *Adenauer and Kennedy*, 47. Harriman was prepared to argue for a denuclearized control zone in East and West Germany, along the lines proposed by Poland in the late 1950s, in a memo passed on to Kennedy by Schlesinger, 1 September 1961, NSA/Berlin, 2430.

32. This is the core thesis of Trachtenberg, *A Constructed Peace*.

33. Kennedy to Adenauer, 4 September 1961, FRUS, XIV, 389–91.

34. Kennan to Rusk, 5 September 1961, FRUS, XIV–VI, Supplement, Document 158.

35. Paris to State, 10 September 1961, FRUS, XIV–VI, Supplement, Document 167. Rusk had worked for the Rockefeller Foundation. Khrushchev was convinced that Rockefeller must play a large role in a capitalist society. He had suggested as much to Lippmann in an interview earlier in the year.

36. Rusk, *As I Saw It*, 225; Bundy to Kennedy, 28 August 1961, FRUS, XIV–VI, Supplement, Document 148; President to Rusk, 12 September 1961, FRUS, XIV, 402–3.

37. Bundy, Memorandum, 20 September 1961, FRUS, XIV, 429–31.

38. Beschloss, *KvK*, 315–16. The day before the speech his brother told *Meet the Press* that Khrushchev must realize that the president would be prepared to use nuclear weapons, so that any Soviet miscalculation could put the world at risk.

39. Ibid., 312–16; Salinger, *With Kennedy*, 193–99.

40. Khrushchev to Kennedy, 29 September 1961, FRUS, XIV, 444–55.

41. Kennedy to Khrushchev, 16 October 1961, FRUS, XIV, 502–8.

42. Slusser, *Berlin Crisis*, 309–12.

43. Clay to Rusk, 26 September 1961, FRUS, XIV, 437–38.

44. The most detailed account of the episode is Garthoff, "Berlin 1961."

45. Tusa, *The Last Division*, 336.

46. Garthoff, "Berlin 1961," 152; Beschloss, *KvK*, 334. Robert's own account, as recorded by Schlesinger, implausibly contains no reciprocal offer in exchange for Soviet tanks "out of there in twenty-four hours." Schlesinger, *Robert Kennedy*, 500.

47. Interview with John Mapother in "Cold War"; Tusa, *The Last Division*, 337.

48. Ausland, *Kennedy, Khrushchev, and the Berlin-Cuba Crisis*, 41.

Chapter 11

1. NSC 5803, 7 February 1958, FRUS, IX, 631–44.

2. McNamara to Kennedy, 5 May 1961, FRUS, XIV, 61–65.

3. Ibid.

4. Memorandum, 9 August 1961, FRUS, XIV, 321.

5. Rusk to McNamara, 21 July 1961, FRUS, XIV–VI, Supplement, Document

100. The British were told on 24 July that "the immediate emphasis in any discussion of NATO should now be on Berlin rather than on the longer term problems." Cited in Pedlow, "Flexible Response Before MC 14/3," 250. NHP/Berlin, 108–9.

6. McNamara to Kennedy, 25 August 1961, FRUS, XIV–VI, Supplement, Document 142.

7. Nitze, *Hiroshima to Glasnost*, 203–4.

8. Kennedy to Rusk, 28 August 1961, FRUS, XIV, 379. Of these it was civil air traffic that was most in his mind. Here the first response would be to use military transport, covered by fighter escorts if necessary. The fighters would be allowed to respond by force to an air attack and drive off buzzing aircraft. The line would be drawn at deep pursuit or attacks on airfields. Kennedy overruled a recommendation that there should be a standing instruction to reply to antiaircraft attack by counterattack. Bundy, Memorandum, 31 August 1961, FRUS, XIV, 384–85.

9. Shapley, *Promise and Power*, 119.

10. Nash, "Bear Any Burden?" 121.

11. Note from Carly Kaysen, 17 May 1999.

12. FRUS, V, 249.

13. Kaplan argues that he was encouraged by Robert; *The Wizards of Armageddon*, 310–11. Schlesinger, however, has Robert saying that he was "in a minority-of-one" against. Schlesinger, *Robert Kennedy and His Times*, 428. Initially Robert was an enthusiast, as he was for all his brother's projects, but this dimmed over time.

14. Kaysen to Bundy, 7 July 1961, NSA/Berlin, 2143.

15. Reeves, *President Kennedy*, 271–72.

16. FRUS, VIII, 378; Kaplan, *The Wizards of Armageddon*, 311–14.

17. Notes on NSC Meeting, 20 July 1961, NSA/nuclear, 386.

18. Meeting, 27 July 1961, FRUS, VIII, 123.

19. Memorandum of Conference with President Kennedy, 6 February 1961, FRUS, VIII, 27–30.

20. Sagan, "SIOP–62: The Nuclear War Plan Briefing to President Kennedy."

21. Schoenbaum, *Waging Peace and War*, 330; Reeves, *President Kennedy*, 230; Gilpatric, oral history.

22. Meeting, 20 September 1961, FRUS, VIII, 130.

23. Pedlow and Welzenbach, *The CIA and the U–2 Program, 1954–1974*, 195–97.

24. Lemnitzer to Kennedy, 27 September 1961, FRUS, VIII, 152–53.

25. Taylor to Kennedy, 19 September 1961, FRUS, VIII, 126–29.

26. Draft Memorandum from McNamara to Kennedy, 30 September 1961, FRUS, VIII, 154–55.

27. Smith to Taylor, Strategic Air Planning and Berlin, 7 September 1961, NSA/nuclear, 331; Kaplan, *The Wizards of Armageddon*, 209–30; Herken, *Counsels of War*, 160; Bird, *The Color of Truth*, 206–7. NHP/Berlin, 190.

28. Trachtenberg, *History and Strategy*, 217, reports that the paper was in Ach-

eson's files. Hillenbrand suggests that Acheson's approach—of threatening the Russians with an arms race—was "consistent with Herman Kahn's pamphlets and briefings going back to 1957–58." Martin Hillenbrand on Berlin Crisis Working Group, 11 October 1988, in NSA/Berlin, 2945.

29. Schelling, Nuclear Strategy in the Berlin Crisis, FRUS, XIV, 170–72. Trachtenberg, *History and Strategy*, 224.

30. In selling the idea at RAND, he stressed his interest in "the 'political' use of military force in an acute crisis . . . to influence the enemy, and to influence the enemy's expectations about what confronts him, what to expect of us, what risks he runs, what threats he must take into account and what we would accept, and so forth." See Schelling, "Berlin Decision Exercise" (19 July 1961), RAND Archive. I am grateful to Robert Ayson for drawing this memorandum to my attention. Schelling and Ferguson provided an account of the exercise at Harvard in 1988; NSA/Berlin, 2946. See also the discussion in NHP/Berlin. On the influence of war-gaming, see the forthcoming work by Sharon Ghamari, "Simulating the Unthinkable," in *The Intuitive Science of the Unthinkable: Herman Kahn, RAND, and Thermonuclear War*.

31. NSA/Berlin, 2946. Kaufman stresses that nationality did not make a difference, and this convinced him of the need for nonnuclear options. Interview with William Kaufman, "Cold War." NHP/Berlin, 112.

32. Kaplan, *The Wizards of Armageddon*, 302; Memo for Taylor, 8–11 September, NSA/Berlin, 02499.

33. Kaysen to Kennedy, 22 September 1961, FRUS, XIV-VI, Supplement, Document 182.

34. Herken, *Counsels of War*, 158–59. Schelling later denied that he was proposing anything other than "serious military targets." NHP/Berlin, 297–7.

35. Minutes of Meeting, 10 October 1961, FRUS, XIV, 487–89; Nitze, *Hiroshima to Glasnost*, 204. Trachtenberg tends to discount Nitze's interest in nuclear strikes and suggests that he and McNamara would have opted instead for a naval blockade as the least unappealing of all the options. Trachtenberg, *History and Strategy*, 226. Adenauer favored a blockade as a way of keeping the fighting away from Germany, and also because of his belief that the Soviet Union was vulnerable economically. Kastner, "Kennedy, Adenauer and the Berlin Crisis," 18.

36. Assistant Secretary of Defense, ISA (Nitze), Memorandum for JCS, 6 November 1961, NSA/nuclear, 962. Nitze had developed the distinction between action policy and declaratory policy in the 1950s. See Nitze, "Atoms, Strategy and Policy."

37. Nitze, *Hiroshima to Glasnost*, 205.

38. McNamara to Kennedy, 18 September 1961 (with annex from Norstad), 26 June 1961, FRUS, XIV-VI, Supplement, Document 177.

39. JCS to McNamara, Berlin Contingency Planning, 26 June 1961, FRUS, XIV-VI, Supplement, Document 75.

40. Lemnitzer to Norstad, 16 August 1961, FRUS, XIV-VI, Supplement, Document 118.

41. At least that was what he told the British. Report of conversation, 1

November 1961 (PREM 11/159659). I am grateful to John Gearson for bringing this document to my attention.

42. Beatrice Heuser has drawn attention to the extent that the British were promoting their own ideas on the employment of nuclear weapons, and their proximity to those of Norstad. Heuser, *NATO, Britain, France and the FRG*, 48–52.

43. Norstad to McNamara, 16 September 1961, NSA/Berlin, 2482; Memorandum, 4 October 1961, FRUS, XIV–VI, Supplement, Document 191. He said he wished that he had not introduced concepts such as "pause" and "threshold" into the discussion. Legere and Smith to Taylor, 28 September 1961, NSA/Berlin, 02511. I am grateful to Kori Schoke for drawing my attention to the importance of the exchanges with Norstad.

44. Bundy to Kennedy, 3 October 1961, FRUS, XIV–VI, Supplement, Document 190.

45. Kennedy to Norstad, 10 October 1961, NSA/Berlin, 2541.

46. Kennedy to Clay, 8 October 1961, FRUS, XIV, 484–86.

47. Kennedy to Norstad, 20 October 1961, FRUS, XIV, 521.

48. Memorandum of Meeting, 9 November 1961, FRUS, XIV, 557.

49. Norstad to Kennedy, 16 November 1961, NSA/Berlin 2630. On the background to the paper, see Pedlow, "Flexible Response before MC 14/3," 257–58.

50. Rusk and McNamara Memo to President, 5 December 1961; Taylor to Kennedy, 4 December 1961, NSA/Berlin, 240; Kennedy to Norstad, 5 December 1961, NSA/Berlin, 242; Pedlow, "Flexible Response before MC 14/3," 259.

51. Kaufman, *The McNamara Strategy*, 65–66.

52. Enthoven and Smith, *How Much Is Enough?* 132–36; Nitze, *Hiroshima to Glasnost*, 210; Stromseth, *The Origins of Flexible Response*, 46–47.

53. Transcript of 1982 interview cited in Stromseth. McNamara repeated the same claim a number of times. See McNamara, "The Military Role of Nuclear Weapons," 76; Shapley, *Promise and Power*, 123–25. Bundy believes that this came well after the most tense months of the crisis. Bundy, *Danger and Survival*, 376. One Pentagon planner described Mountbatten's view at this meeting. In the event of a conflict planned moves should be carried out to well short of nuclear use and then, if these did not work, "quit." NHP/Berlin, 190.

54. The speech is reprinted in Bobbit, Freedman, and Treverton, *U.S. Nuclear Strategy*. Kaufman suggests that Kennedy approved it against the objections of Bundy. Interview with William Kaufman, "Cold War," 1997.

55. McNamara's analysts in the Pentagon accepted that TNWs had a role in complicating Soviet planning and providing a possible intermediate option. More pragmatically, they were aware of the extensive deployments of TNWs and their role as an earnest of the U.S. guarantee. They could not be removed without enormous political fuss. Enthoven and Smith, *How Much Is Enough?* 128. TNW numbers were actually raised during the 1960s (especially 1963–66) from 3,500 to 7,000 warheads.

56. Alsop, "Kennedy's Grand Strategy."

57. Beschloss, *KvK*, 371.

58. Ausland, *Kennedy, Khrushchev, and the Berlin-Cuba Crisis*, 67.

59. Memorandum, 6 May 1962, NSA/nuclear, 972. The British and French appear to have responded more along the lines of what they anticipated than what they heard. For a more enthusiastic report, see FRUS, XIII, 392–93.

60. Pedlow, "Flexible Response before MC 14/3," 265.

61. FRUS, XIII, 442.

62. Address by McNamara, NATO Ministerial Meeting, 14 December 1962, FRUS, VIII, 443.

63. Legere, Memorandum, 19 July 1962, FRUS, XV, 230–32.

64. See Bundy's attempt to clarify matters. Bundy to President, 20 July 1961, FRUS, XV, 232–34.

65. Smith to Taylor, 9 August 1962, FRUS, XV, 266–69. Ausland's briefing is reproduced in Ausland, *Kennedy, Khrushchev, and the Berlin-Cuba Crisis*, 156–69. Also, see Kastner transcript of meeting tape.

66. Bundy to Kennedy, FRUS, XV, 313–15.

Chapter 12

1. Ausland, *Kennedy, Khrushchev, and the Berlin-Cuba Crisis*, 44–45.

2. As early as 23 August 1961, when tension was high after the barriers had gone up, Khrushchev complained about the misuse of the air corridors. The complaint was followed immediately by allied statements warning Khrushchev to stay clear.

3. Pedlow, "Flexible Response before MC 14/3," 263.

4. Trachtenberg, *A Constructed Peace*, 340–41.

5. Regular reference is made to discussions with Robert in the letters exchanged between the two leaders in March.

6. For text, see FRUS, XV, 69–71.

7. Mayer, *Adenauer and Kennedy*, 70–73.

8. Adenauer to Kennedy, 14 April 1961; Rusk to Schroeder, 14 April 1961, FRUS, XV, 112–13.

9. Trachtenberg, *A Constructed Peace*, 345–48. Trachtenberg finds the Soviet inability to accept the American demands on Berlin "hard to understand," but it is hard only if one accepts his argument that German nuclear weapons mattered more than anything else to Khrushchev.

10. Ausland, *Kennedy, Khrushchev, and the Berlin-Cuba Crisis*, 54.

11. Kennedy to Khrushchev, 5 June 1962; Khrushchev to Kennedy, letter received in White House on 5 July; Kennedy to Khrushchev, 17 July 1962. FRUS, VI, 133–34, 137–41, 142–47.

12. Selvage, "The End of the Berlin Crisis, 1961–62." A boycott was by no means certain. In quadripartite discussions the French and Germans had reached a tentative agreement to take selective economic countermeasures if there was persistent harassment on access routes to Berlin. The British had reserved their position until the event.

13. This was a special planning group for Berlin, established by Norstad in

1959. Any plans arising out of Live Oak had to be ratified by the participating governments (United States, United Kingdom, and France). Under Kennedy it became quadripartite with the addition of a German officer. An indication that the Americans knew that Khrushchev was aware of contingency planning is in Thompson to Rusk, 28 July 1962, FRUS, V, 470.

14. Fursenko and Naftali, *Secret History*, 185–86.

15. A tough message was sent back via Bolshakov. Schlesinger, *Robert Kennedy*, 512.

16. McNamara to Kennedy, 21 June 1961, FRUS, XV, 192–95.

17. Memorandum, 31 August 1962, FRUS, XV, 290–95.

18. Bundy to Sorensen, 23 August 1962; Kennedy to Mansfield, 28 August 1961, FRUS, XV, 284–85, 290.

19. Thompson to State, 25 July 1962, 28 July 1962, FRUS, XV, 253, 255.

20. FRUS, XV, 285; Sorensen, *Kennedy*, 667–68.

21. Memorandum of conversation between Udall and Khrushchev, 6 September 1962, FRUS, XV, 308–10.

22. SNIE 11-15-62, Current Soviet Tactics on Berlin, 13 September 1962, FRUS, V, 495–97.

23. FRUS, XV, 324; Kohler to State, 16 October 1962, FRUS, XV, 360.

24. Khrushchev to Kennedy, 28 September 1962, FRUS, VI, 152–61.

Chapter 13

1. Fursenko and Naftali, *Secret History*, 65.

2. The ideological inspiration behind the Alliance for Progress is well captured by Schlesinger's account in ch. 8 of Schlesinger, *Thousand Days*. For a full accounts of the origins and implementation of the alliance, see Martin, *Kennedy and Latin America*; Rabe, *The Most Dangerous Area in the World*.

3. McClintock, *Instruments of Statecraft*, 148–49.

4. Immerman, *The CIA in Guatemala*; Gleijeses, *Shattered Hope*. The implications of Guatemala for the Bay of Pigs episode provides a major theme of Higgins, *The Perfect Failure*.

5. Bissell with Lewis and Pudlo, *Reflections of a Cold Warrior*, 87–88; Thomas, *The Very Best Men*, 120.

6. Thomas, *The Very Best Men*, 237–39.

7. Aguilar, ed., *Operation Zapata*, 5. The Taylor Report can be found in FRUS, X, 576–606.

8. Blight and Kornbluh, eds., *Politics of Illusion*, 52–53.

9. For example, "U.S. Helps Train an Anti-Castro Force at Secret Guatemalan Air-Ground Base," *New York Times*, 10 January 1961.

10. Vandenbroucke, *Perilous Options*, 16; memorandum by Clark Clifford, cited in Schlesinger, *Robert Kennedy*, 444.

11. Thomas, *The Very Best Men*, 245.

12. Testimony of Rusk, 4 May 1961, FRUS, X, 451. Rusk observed that the

critics also exaggerated, in that the response in the OAS and UN was not as bad as it could have been.

13. On doubts within the CIA, see Powers, *The Man Who Kept Secrets*, 133–40.

14. Schlesinger, *Thousand Days*, 239–40.

15. Nixon, *The Memoirs of Richard Nixon*, 220. See also White, *The Cuban Missile Crisis*, 11–12.

16. This is the conclusion of the most thorough investigation of the topic. See Helgerson, *CIA Briefings of Presidential Candidates, 1952–1992*, ch. 3.

17. John Patterson, who had a loose connection with preparations under Eisenhower, describes how he warned Kennedy that there might be an invasion a few weeks before the election. See Strober and Strober, *Let Us Begin Anew*, 325–26; Hersh, *The Dark Side of Camelot*, 176–78.

18. Beschloss, *KvK*, 103–4.

19. Luncheon with Kennedy, 16 May 1961, FRUS, X, 526.

20. Kirkpatrick, "Inspector General's Survey of the Cuban Operation," para. 45. This has been reprinted in Kornbluh, ed., *Bay of Pigs Declassified*. For interesting background to the report, see Warner, "Lessons Unlearned."

21. Fursenko and Naftali, *Secret History*, 92; Bissell, *Reflections*, 163; CIA Briefing Paper, Cuba, 17 February 1961, Annex B to Kirkpatrick, "Inspector General's Survey."

Chapter 14

1. Staff Study, Pentagon, 16 January 1961, FRUS, X, 36–40.

2. Barnes to Esterline, 18 January 1961, FRUS, X, 42–43.

3. Vandenbroucke, "The 'Confessions' of Allen Dulles," 373.

4. Memorandum of Conversation, 22 January 1961; Kennedy Meeting with Joint Chiefs, 25 January 1961; Memo Prepared by CIA, 26 January 1961; Memorandum from JCS to McNamara, 27 January 1961, FRUS, X, 46–52, 54–55, 56, 57–58, 65.

5. Sorensen, *Kennedy*, 297.

6. Memorandum of Discussion on Cuba, 28 January 1961, FRUS, X, 61–64. See also Higgins, *The Perfect Failure*, 81–82; Schlesinger, *Thousand Days*, 216.

7. Memorandum for McNamara from JCS, *Military Evaluation of the Cuban Plan*, 3 February 1961, FRUS, X, 67–78; Bissell, *Reflections*, 164; Schoenbaum, *Waging Peace and War*, 293.

8. Mann to Rusk, 15 February 1961; CIA Paper, 17 February 1961; Bundy to Kennedy, 18 February 1961; CIA Memorandum, 25 April 1961, FRUS, X, 95–99, 99–107, 358. Bissell may not have read Mann's paper.

9. Higgins, *The Perfect Failure*, 116.

10. Woods, *J. William Fulbright, Vietnam, and the Search for a Cold War Foreign Policy*, 26–27.

11. Schlesinger, *Thousand Days*, 229. He warned on 15 March of another "U–2 imbroglio" and poor preparations for media questions, and on 5 April that the

United States would be held accountable for whatever happened. The new image of the United States under Kennedy's leadership, outlined in glowing terms, could be damaged. He also doubted that Castro could be toppled so easily and was as unimpressed as Fulbright with the competence of exile leaders. Schlesinger to Kennedy, 15 March, 5 April, 10 April 1961, FRUS, X, 156–57, 186–89, 196–203.

12. Rusk, *As I Saw It*, 210.

13. Kirkpatrick, "Inspector General's Survey," 61.

14. Aguilar, ed., *Operation Zapata*, 12. The paper, "Proposed Operation Against Cuba," appears as Annex C to Kirkpatrick, "Inspector General's Survey." In all these papers there are references to "large scale guerrilla action"—an ambiguous phrase.

15. Aguilar, ed., *Operation Zapata*, 76.

16. Ibid., 9.; Schlesinger, *Thousand Days*, 219; McClintock, *Instruments of State-craft*, 145. Memorandum of Meeting with Kennedy, 8 February 1961; Meeting on 6 April, FRUS, X, 90–91, 159, 185, 191–92.

17. Vandenbroucke, "The 'Confessions' of Allen Dulles," 368.

18. CIA Briefing Paper, Cuba, 17 February 1961, Annex B to Kirkpatrick, "Inspector General's Survey." Also in FRUS, X, 99–107.

19. Beschloss, *KvK*, 105.

20. Testimony of Lt. Col. Egan, operations officer for the project, 1 May 1961, FRUS, X, 416; Taylor, *Swords and Plowshares*, 187.

21. Testimony of Shoup, 8 May 1961, FRUS, X, 496.

22. On 4 January a CIA official had warned that unless the Cuban air force and naval vessels capable of opposing the landing were knocked out or neutralized before the final run into the beach, "we will be courting disaster." Aguilar, ed., *Operation Zapata*, 15.

23. Schlesinger, *Thousand Days*, 245. Its total strength was put at 15 B–26s and 10 Sea Furies. This neglected T–33 trainers, which had a combat capability and, in the event, played an important role.

24. See comments by Douglas Dillon (in charge of conceptual planning for the operation in the State Department during the Eisenhower administration) in Blight and Welch, *On the Brink*, 30.

25. Higgins, *The Perfect Failure*, 73–74.

26. Aguilar, ed., *Operation Zapata*, 326, 346.

27. McClintock, *Instruments of Statescraft*, 148.

28. Wyden, *Bay of Pigs*, 101; National Security Action Memorandum No. 31, 11 March 1961, FRUS, X, 144.

29. CIA, Revised Cuban Operation, 17 March 1961, para. 2, Annex D to Kirkpatrick, "Inspector General's Survey." The area had not actually seen any guerrilla warfare that century.

30. Meeting of Study Group, 24 April 1961, FRUS, X, 354; Bissell, "Response to Lucien S. Vandenbroucke," 379.

31. Aguilar, ed., *Operation Zapata*, 178. However, at a meeting on 29 March Kennedy asked whether the force could fade into the brush and not look like a

failure; Bissell indicated that if it failed, it would have to be withdrawn. FRUS, X, 177.

32. Bundy to Kennedy, 15 March 1961, FRUS, X, 158. See also Bissell, *Reflections*, 170.

33. Higgins, *The Perfect Failure*, 96–97. Testimony of McNamara, 3 May 1961, FRUS, X, 439–40. McNamara did not miss the implausibility of guerrilla warfare in the Zapata area because of the swamps.

34. Aguilar, ed., *Operation Zapata*, 191.

35. Schlesinger, *Thousand Days*, 216; Aguilar, ed., *Operation Zapata*, 9, 13; Higgins, *The Perfect Failure*, 83; Lemnitzer to Cuba Study Group, cited in Schlesinger, *Robert Kennedy*, 452.

36. Dulles, *The Craft of Intelligence*. See also Taylor, *Swords and Plowshares*, 190; Vandenbroucke, "The 'Confessions' of Allen Dulles," 367; Bissell, "Response to Lucien S. Vandenbroucke," 380; Kirkpatrick, "Inspector General's Survey," 54.

37. CIA Special National Intelligence Estimate, 8 December 1960. Cited in Schlesinger, *Robert Kennedy*, 453.

38. Cited in Wyden, *Bay of Pigs*, 99.

39. Thomas, *The Very Best Men*, 247.

40. Vandenbroucke, "The 'Confessions' of Allen Dulles," 369. This is also the position taken in Gleijeses, "Ships in the Night."

Chapter 15

1. Sorensen, *Kennedy*, 295. When asked his opinion of the scheme by Kennedy in early April, Dean Acheson is said to have hoped that it was not being taken seriously, as "it was not necessary to call in Price Waterhouse [the accountants] to discover that 1,500 Cubans weren't as good as 250,000 Cubans." Brinkley, *Dean Acheson*, 127.

2. Reeves, *President Kennedy*, 82–84.

3. Beschloss, *KvK*, 114.

4. Sorensen, *Kennedy*, 298; Editorial Note, FRUS, X, 177.

5. Lemnitzer to Dennison, 13 April 1961, FRUS, X, 219. When Dennison asked the president in February whether he would "be engaged in any possible bail-out operations" the reply was "definitely no, that if anything went wrong the force would fade into the hinterland." Testimony of Dennison, 28 April 1961, FRUS, X, 402.

6. Aguilar, ed., *Operation Zapata*, 21, 31.

7. In the event, when the mission faltered, four pilots were sent into action and killed. The first man to fire shots was an American CIA paramilitary operative. Vandenbroucke, *Perilous Options*, 192.

8. Beschloss, *KvK*, 115; Schlesinger, *Thousand Days*, 193.

9. Stevenson to Rusk and Dulles, 16 April 1961, FRUS, X, 230. Confusion was compounded by a genuine defection the previous day. Vandenbroucke, *Perilous Options*, 40, 194.

10. Schoenbaum, *Waging Peace and War*, 247–48.

11. Aguilar, ed., *Operation Zapata*, 13, 222–23; Rusk, *As I Saw It*, 211–12; Cabell to Taylor, 9 May 1961, FRUS, X, 235–37.

12. Luncheon with Kennedy, 16 May 1961, FRUS, X, 528.

13. Taylor, *Swords and Plowshares*, 186.

14. This explanation was first revealed in Charles Murphy, "Cuba: The Record Set Straight." The story was probably leaked by Arleigh Burke, though Kennedy blamed Cabell. Brugioni, *Eyeball to Eyeball*, 61; Vandenbroucke, *Perilous Options*, 103.

15. Schoenbaum, *Waging Peace and War*, 299.

16. Bundy to President, 18 April 1961, FRUS, X, 272.

17. He also made a similar point to Nixon. Beschloss, *KvK*, 144–45.

18. Vandenbroucke, "The 'Confessions' of Allen Dulles," 371.

19. Memorandum of Conversation, 18 April 1961, FRUS, X, 274–75.

20. Blight and Kornbluh, *Politics of Illusion*, 98.

21. Burke to Dennison, 18 April 1861, FRUS, X, 277, 3:23 PM

22. Gray to Dennison, 18 April 1961, FRUS, X, 276.

23. Vandenbroucke, *Perilous Options*, 46.

24. JCS to Dennison, 19 April 1861, FRUS, X, 290; Schlesinger, *Thousand Days*, 252; Wyden, *Bay of Pigs*, 270–71; Beschloss, *KvK*, 122–23; O'Donnell and Powers, "*Johnny, We Hardly Knew Ye*," 316–17.

25. Dennison to Burke, 18 April 1861; Burke to Dennison, 19 April 1861, FRUS, X, 288–91.

26. Cited in Higgins, *The Perfect Failure*, 103. Higgins described this as "in a nutshell . . . the gist of Kennedy's military failure at the Bay of Pigs."

27. Wyden, *Bay of Pigs*, 272 (observation attributed to Schlesinger).

28. Reeves has traced the phrase to the wartime diaries of Mussolini's son-in-law and foreign minister, Galeazzo Ciano. Reeves, *President Kennedy*, 678.

29. Aguilar, ed., *Operation Zapata*, 40.

30. Schlesinger, *Thousand Days*, 292.

Chapter 16

1. Cited in Blaufarb, *The Counter-Insurgency Era*, 54–55. Kennedy had said something similar to newspaper editors on 20 April, immediately after the debacle. Sorensen, *Kennedy*, 630.

2. Letter from Kennedy to Taylor, cited in Taylor, *Swords and Plowshares*, 184.

3. Bird reports a claim from Cuban sources that one of the decoy ships that was part of the Zapata operation contained a force of some 164 men dressed as Cuban soldiers who were to stage an attack on Guantánamo in order to provoke an American intervention. The plan was aborted when a Cuban patrol was encountered. Bird, *The Color of Truth*, 198–99. This sounds, however, like the diversionary landing planned for Oriente province, which was a known part of the plan. Rusk had at one point suggested that the invasion take place close to the base, but the military wanted the base kept as clear as possible from the operation.

4. Robert to John Kennedy, 19 April 1991, FRUS, X, 302–4. At the same time he was ready to allow the OAS to guarantee the territorial integrity of Cuba.

5. His objections were laid out in Bowles to Rusk, 31 March 1961, FRUS, X, 178–81.

6. Bowles, Notes, 20 and 22 April 1961, FRUS, X, 304–6, 313–14.

7. Rostow to Kennedy, 21 April 1961, FRUS, X, 311. His description of the original conversation with Robert is in Strober and Strober, *Let Us Begin Anew*, 349–50.

8. The request, McNamara added, "should not be interpreted as an indication that U.S. military action is probable." Their analysis, in the light of the poor international reaction to the latest escapade, was that any military operation "should be swift, sharp and overwhelming and should present the world with a fait accompli." The plan envisaged 16 percent casualties. On the assumption of 60,000 troops, excluding air and sea units, this suggests just under 10,000 casualties. The operation would take twenty-five days to prepare and eight days to get control of the island. McNamara to Lemnitzer, 20 April 1961; Joint Chiefs of Staff to McNamara, 26 April 1961; McNamara to Joint Chiefs, 1 May 1961, FRUS, X, 306–7, 371–83, 405.

9. Record of Actions at the 478th Meeting of the National Security Council, FRUS, X, 315–17. The White House kept on pushing the brigade against Pentagon resistance when it came to enlisting foreign nationals. The basic problem was recruitment of suitable Cubans.

10. State Department, Plan for Cuba, 27 April 1961, FRUS, X, 391–95.

11. Bowles, Notes, 27 April 1961; Combined INR/ONE Estimate on Cuba, 2 May 1961; Interagency Task Force, Paper for NSC, 4 May 1961; Notes on 483rd Meeting of NSC, 5 May 1961; Recommendations of the Cuban Study Group, 13 June 1961, FRUS, X, 397, 417–22, 459–75, 476–77, 606; FRUS, X, Document 204.

12. CIA, Program of Covert Action Aimed at Weakening the Castro Regime, 19 May 1961, FRUS, X, 544–60.

13. CIA, *CIA Targets Fidel*, 25, 108.

14. The Church Report, 71.

15. Ibid., 82; Vandenbroucke, *Perilous Options*, 30. A memorandum for the record prepared on 14 May 1962 reports that only six people knew of the scheme and it was never part of the invasion plan. FRUS, X, 808.

16. CIA, *CIA Targets Fidel*, 48–50; The Church Report, 157. Hersh, *The Dark Side of Camelot*, 187–92, makes much of this, largely because Bundy rather urgently refreshed his memory during the course of the Church Committee's investigations. He argues that this is "overwhelming" evidence linking Bundy and Kennedy to murder plots. However, the three assassination plots alleged to be underway at the time—against Lumumba in the Congo and Trujillo in the Dominican Republic as well as Castro—had all been set in motion some time before. Lumumba was assassinated before the administration took office. It is possible that Bissell was trying to get a general sort of authorization for continuing activities from an old friend who had barely had time to get his feet under the table.

17. FRUS, X, 659–60.

18. Inter-Agency Staff Study, Plan for Cuba, undated, FRUS, X, 677–84.

19. Kent to McCone, 3 November 1961, FRUS, X, 672. This was prepared for a meeting with Kennedy that day.

20. The Church Report, 138–39.

Chapter 17

1. Editorial Note, FRUS, X, 666. The debate is described by Schlesinger, *Robert Kennedy*, 474–76.

2. Memorandum from President, 30 November 1961, FRUS, X, 688–89.

3. Hilty, *Robert Kennedy*, 422–24.

4. For an evaluation of the impact of Lansdale's team in South Vietnam, see McClintock, *Instruments of Statecraft*, 126–31.

5. Greene, *The Quiet American*, 61. Greene later observed that he would never have chosen Lansdale "to represent the danger of innocence." Currey, *Edward Lansdale*, 198.

6. The phenomenon of this book is discussed in Iversen, "The Ugly American: A Bestseller Reexamined."

7. Lederer and Burdick, *The Ugly American*, 233. Hillendale was not the "ugly American" of the title.

8. Schlesinger, *Robert Kennedy*, 462.

9. Lansdale, "Program Review," 18 February 1962, in Chang and Kornbluh, *The Cuban Missile Crisis*, 23. Also FRUS, X, 745–47.

10. Helms to McCone, 19 January 1962, FRUS, X, 720.

11. Memorandum for Record, 14 December 1961; Memorandum, 20 January 1961; Memorandum, 25 January 1962; Hilsman to Alexis Johnson, 20 February 1962, FRUS, X, 698, 722, 728–30, 747–48.

12. Thomas, *The Very Best Men*, 289.

13. For an unflattering portrait of Harvey, see Schlesinger, *Robert Kennedy*, 478–79.

14. U. Alexis Johnson, cited in Desch, " 'That Deep Mud in Cuba,' " 331.

15. Blight and Kornbluh, *Politics of Illusion*, 114; Schlesinger, *Robert Kennedy*, 480.

16. NIE 85-2, The Situation and Prospects in Cuba, 21 March 1962; Kent to McCone, 6 April 1962; Harvey to McCone, 10 April 1962, FRUS, X, 773–74, 781–82, 786–90.

17. Guidelines for Operation Mongoose, 14 March 1962; Meeting between Cardona and Bundy, 29 March 1962; Memorandum, McCone, 12 April 1961, FRUS, X, 771, 778, 791–92. Allison and Zelikow, *Essence of Decision*, 84, 132.

18. The Church Report, 102–3.

19. Harvey provided an oral briefing on his "field trip" to the Special Group Augmented but did not report on his meeting with Rosselli. Memorandum by McCone, 4 May 1961, FRUS, X, 804; The Church Report, 104.

20. Memorandum for the Record, 14 May 1962, FRUS, X, 807–9.

21. The Church Report, 133. Hersh takes this literally as a request to be kept informed about future plans. Hersh, *The Dark Side of Camelot*, 290–92. He does not cite Houston's evidence that Kennedy had been upset by the CIA's role and the potential effect on criminal prosecutions. "If you have seen Mr. Kennedy's eyes get steely and his jaw set and his voice get low and precise, you get a definite feeling of unhappiness."

22. Currey, *Edward Lansdale*, 247. FRUS, X, 923–24. Lansdale's memo of 13 August 1961, minus the offending passage, is in FRUS, X, 925. It is perhaps of note that Goodwin has reported McNamara suggesting something similar just after the Bay of Pigs. Reeves, *President Kennedy*, 113.

23. The Church Report, 165.

24. NIE 85-2-62, The Situation and Prospects in Cuba, 1 August 1962; Memorandum of Conversation with Robert Kennedy, 18 July 1962; Hurwitch to Martin, 18 and 26 July 1962, FRUS, X, 850, 893–94, 846–50, 885.

25. Taylor to Kennedy, 17 August 1962, FRUS, X, 944–45.

26. McCone, Memorandum, 4 October 1962, FRUS, XI, 11–13.

27. Helms, Memorandum for the Record, 16 October 1962, in McAuliffe, ed., *CIA Documents on the Cuban Missile Crisis*, 154.

Chapter 18

1. Kern, Levering, and Levering, *The Kennedy Crises*, 100, 256.

2. Memorandum of Conversation, 5 October 1962, in McAuliffe, ed., *CIA Documents on the Cuban Missile Crisis*, 116.

3. FRUS, V, 357.

4. Gribkov and Smith, *Operation ANADYR*; Beschloss, *KvK*, 332.

5. Interview, 19 March 1998; "Cold War."

6. Khrushchev, *Khrushchev Remembers*, 494–95. The best account of Khrushchev's reasoning and decision-making process is in Fursenko and Naftali, *Secret History*. They amplify their material on the lack of thought about possible American reactions in Fursenko and Naftali, "Soviet Intelligence and the Cuban Missile Crisis." May and Zelikow, *The Kennedy Tapes*, 673–78, provides a concise review of available evidence. Also Beschloss, *KvK*, chs. 14 and 15.

7. Office of Current Intelligence, CIA, Cuban Situation, 3 July 1962; NIE 85-2-62, The Situation and Prospects in Cuba, 1 August 1962, FRUS, X, 840, 893–94.

8. McCone's continual concern on the issue is fully reflected in the material in McAuliffe, ed., *CIA Documents on the Cuban Missile Crisis*. See in particular a memo for the record by McCone of 31 October 1962 in which he reviewed his warnings (13–17). As McCone's analysis started from the assumption that the SAMs were being sent to protect missiles (rather than to protect Cuba from air attack, as was the case), he had the right answer for the wrong reasons.

9. Editorial Note, FRUS, X, 923–24. McCone's view (though not attributed) was reported in the 1 October issue of *Aviation Week and Space Technology*. Reeves, *President Kennedy*, 365.

10. Substance of Board of National Estimates, memo of 15 August 1962, FRUS, X, 941–43.

11. Memorandum for the File, John McCone, Discussion in Secretary Rusk's Office, 21 August 1962, in McAuliffe, ed., *CIA Documents on the Cuban Missile Crisis*, 21–23. See also FRUS, X, 947–49.

12. Memorandum of Meeting with the President, John McCone, 23 August 1962, in McAuliffe, ed., *CIA Documents on the Cuban Missile Crisis*, 27–29. Also FRUS, X, 947–49.

13. Schlesinger to Bundy, 22 August 1961; Hilsman to Ball, 25 August 1963, FRUS, X, 950–53, 963–66.

14. Rostow to Bundy and Bundy to Kennedy, 31 August 1961, FRUS, X, 1001–3.

15. Beschloss, *KvK*, 421, 423. He told Bowles as late as 14 October that "the U.S.S.R was not shipping offensive weapons and well understood the dangers of doing so." FRUS, V, 517.

16. *New York Times*, 5 September 1962.

17. Statement by President Kennedy on Cuba, 13 September 1962. In Larson, ed., *The "Cuban Crisis" of 1962*, 18.

18. Reeves, *President Kennedy*, 347, 366.

19. In Fursenko and Naftali, "The Pitsunda Decision," it is argued that this involved introducing tactical nuclear weapons into the crisis. However, Garthoff, "New Evidence on the Cuban Missile Crisis," qualifies this account in important respects. See also Garthoff, "U.S. Intelligence in the Cuban Missile Crisis," 29, 58.

20. When these revelations first came out it appeared that the local commander had initially been given some discretion on their use. See Fursenko and Naftali, "Soviet Intelligence and the Cuban Missile Crisis"; Fursenko and Naftali, *Secret History*, 206–12, 216–17.

21. SNIE 85-3-62, The Military Buildup in Cuba, 19 September 1962, FRUS, X.

22. This was the explanation provided by Sherman Kent, then chairman of the Board of National Estimates. Kent, "A Crucial Estimate Relived," 111–19. The episode is discussed fully in Garthoff, "U.S. Intelligence in the Cuban Missile Crisis." On receiving a report on the intelligence performance, "[i]n general the President agreed with Sherman Kent's position that the Soviets made a bad guess to our response." Memorandum, 7 January 1963, FRUS, X, 652.

23. This indicates the nature of the relationship between the two and also the premium Robert placed on appearing tough. Memorandum, 10 September 1962, FRUS, X, 105.

24. Kent, "A Crucial Estimate Relived." According to Hilsman, there was a file five inches thick, containing 3,500 reports relating to missiles, for 1959 alone, before any Soviet arms had reached Cuba. Hilsman, *The Cuban Missile Crisis*, 28.

25. DIA, Briefing Paper, 1 October 1962, FRUS, XI, 1–3.

26. Interview with Sam Halpern, "Cold War"; Hilsman, *The Cuban Missile Crisis*, 37, 60; Garthoff, "U.S. Intelligence in the Cuban Missile Crisis," 23.

27. OPLAN 312 was the air strike; OPLAN 314 was for a subsequent land invasion; OPLAN 316 was a variant of 314 with less time for the invasion force.

28. Hershberg, "Before 'The Missiles of October,' " 254; Nitze, *Hiroshima to Glasnost,* 216. Hershberg's account draws heavily on Dennison, *CINCLANT Historical Account of Cuban Crisis,* 29 April 1963.

29. There is no mention of the suspicions in a memo by Hilsman to Ball on the latest intelligence, 2 October 1962, FRUS, XI, 7–8.

30. The arrival of offensive missiles was only one of the six contingencies outlined by McNamara. The others were a Soviet move against West Berlin, a direct Cuban attack against the U.S. forces based at Guantánamo Bay, a popular uprising against the Castro regime (à la Operation Mongoose), Cuban subversion elsewhere, and a "decision by the President that the affairs in Cuba have reached a point inconsistent with continuing U.S. national security." McNamara to Taylor, 2 October 1962, FRUS, XI, 6–7; Hershberg "More New Evidence on the Cuban Missile Crisis."

31. Nonetheless, one meeting to review the plans at Fort Bragg was postponed because of the immediate demands posed by the need to control racial violence at the University of Mississippi. Desch, " 'That Deep Mud in Cuba,' " 332.

32. *Castro* spelled backward. The exercise was not actually suspended until 20 October.

33. Hilsman, *The Cuban Missile Crisis,* 39–43.

34. Ibid., 37–38. It appears that Robert Kennedy's frustration with slow progress on Mongoose was one reason why McCone felt able to get more approval for more direct overflights of Cuba. McCone, Memorandum, 4 October 1962, FRUS, XI, 12. The transfer of responsibility to the air force caused major irritation within the CIA. The president personally approved the flight. For background, see Pedlow and Welzenbach, *The CIA and the U-2 Program.*

35. Editorial Note, FRUS, XI, 29–30.

36. Bundy, *Danger and Survival,* 684–85; Allison and Zelikow, *Essence of Decision,* 339.

Chapter 19

1. For a vivid description of the workings of the Joint Chiefs at that time, see Brugioni, *Eyeball to Eyeball,* ch. 9.

2. Ball insists that the discussions were conducted "at a high intellectual level, and with the somber intensity that the situation required." He notes that critics such as Beschloss, who complain that Kennedy had failed to impose discipline on the initial discussions, do not understand how a president is best served in such discussions. Too much guidance and he would have stifled debate. Ball, "JFK's Big Moment."

3. CIA, Memo, 16 October 1962; SNIE 18–62, Soviet Reactions to Certain U.S. Courses of Action in Cuba, 19 October 1962; SNIE 19–62, Major Consequences of Certain U.S. Courses of Action in Cuba, 20 October 1962, in McAuliffe, ed., *CIA Documents on the Cuban Missile Crisis,* 141–42, 197–98, 214–

15. For this analysis, see Garthoff, "U.S. Intelligence in the Cuban Missile Crisis," 24–26.

4. McCone, Memorandum, 19 October 1962, in McAuliffe, ed., *CIA Documents on the Cuban Missile Crisis*, 170.

5. See Garthoff, *Reflections on the Cuban Missile Crisis*, 206–7. For an earlier version of Garthoff's views, see Garthoff, " 'The Meaning of Missiles.' "

6. SNIE 11-18-62 and SNIE 11-20-62, in McAuliffe, ed., *CIA Documents on the Cuban Missile Crisis*. Llewellyn Thompson discussed Khrushchev's move from early on in terms of forcing a settlement on Berlin. McCone, Memorandum of Meeting, 17 October, in McAuliffe, ed., *CIA Documents on the Cuban Missile Crisis*, 52. McCone himself described the prime Soviet objective as being to establish a "trading position" which could "force removal of U.S. overseas bases and Berlin." Memorandum, 17 October 1962, in McAuliffe, ed., *CIA Documents on the Cuban Missile Crisis*, 162.

7. Hershberg, "New Evidence on the Cuban Missile Crisis"; though Vasily Kuznetsov, deputy minister of foreign affairs, argued for pressure against Berlin in response to that against Cuba. Khrushchev "replied quite harshly, saying that we did not need that kind of advice." Gromyko denied that there was ever any linkage. Allyn, Blight, and Welch, *Cuba on the Brink*, 73, 147. In his memoirs, Khrushchev did assert, without elaboration, that "[t]he Americans knew that if Russian blood were shed in Cuba, American blood would surely be shed in Germany." *Khrushchev Remembers: The Last Testament*, 500.

8. Bundy, *Danger and Survival*, 421–22.

9. Record of Meeting, 5 October 1961, FRUS, XV, 347.

10. May and Zelikow, *The Kennedy Tapes*, 176.

11. Kern, Levering, and Levering, *The Kennedy Crises*, 117–18, 122.

12. May and Zelikow, *The Kennedy Tapes*, 92, 342. On Castro's preference see Allyn, Blight, and Welch, *Cuba on the Brink*.

13. Sorensen, *Kennedy*, 753.

14. For a full report of the meeting, see FRUS, XI, 110–14.

15. For Gromyko's own account, see Gromyko, *Memories*, 176–77. He describes this as "perhaps the most difficult" conversation of his career.

16. Gromyko to Moscow, 20 October and 19 October 1962, in *Cold War International History Bulletin* 8–9 (1996–97): 279–80, and 5 (1995): 66. Gromyko to Moscow, 20 and 19 October, *Cold War International History Bulletin*, 8–9 (1996–97): 279–82, and 5 (1995): 66. Dobrynin reported back at this time comments purported to have been made by Kennedy at a seminar for leading media figures organized by the State Department on 16 October (that is after he had been informed about the bases). This has the president ruling out action against Cuba "until there are signs of overt Cuban aggression against the countries of the Western hemisphere," playing down the significance of the Soviet military supplies, and saying, intriguingly, that: "There can be no deal struck with the USSR regarding its renunciation of bases in Cuba in exchange for the USA's renunciation of bases in other parts of the world (in Turkey, for example)." Dobrynin to Moscow, 19 October 1962.

17. General Carter, Memorandum, 17 October 1962, in McAuliffe, ed., *CIA Documents on the Cuban Missile Crisis*, 146.

18. Blight and Welch, *On the Brink*, 78.

19. Minutes of the 506th Meeting of the National Security Council, 21 October 1962, FRUS, XI, 146; Garthoff in Allyn, Blight, and Welch, *Cuba on the Brink*, 163. The air strike plan called for 1,190 sorties on the first day. For a full discussion of military planning, see Desch, " 'That Deep Mud in Cuba.' "

20. Brugioni, *Eyeball to Eyeball*, 308–10; Garthoff, "U.S. Intelligence in the Cuban Missile Crisis," 28–29.

21. Allyn, Blight, and Welch, *Cuba on the Brink*, 58–59, 61, 67.

22. Cited in Desch, " 'That Deep Mud in Cuba,' " 339–40.

23. May and Zelikow, *The Kennedy Tapes*, 85–86.

24. Bundy appears to be using the word *surgical* here in the same way that the military does. However, according to Herken, Bundy thought the word appropriate for a different reason, but this was probably a retrospective thought. "Surgery is generally bloody, messy and not final." Cited in Herken, *Counsels of War*, 166. Ball, who opposed the notion of a surgical strike at the time, has made a similar point. Drawing on his experience in the U.S. Strategic Bombing Survey after World War II, he concluded that "if the medical profession should ever adopt the air force definition of 'surgical,' anyone undergoing an operation for appendicitis might lose his kidneys and lungs yet find his appendix intact." Ball, "JFK's Big Moment,"18.

25. May and Zelikow, *The Kennedy Tapes*, 71–2.

26. The Joint Chiefs all generally took a hawkish line. However, General David Shoup, the marine commandant, recorded that he "fought against invasion of Cuba from the start" and warned against taking the Joint Chiefs as a single entity. *New York Times*, 26 October 1968, cited in Allison, *Essence of Decision*, 319. This dissent is by no means evident from the meeting with the Joint Chiefs held by Kennedy on 19 October. May and Zelikow, *The Kennedy Tapes*, 173–88.

27. Historical Division, Joint Secretariat, Joint Chiefs of Staff, Chronology of JCS Decisions Concerning the Cuban Crisis (21 December 1962), NSA/Cuba, 02780, 9–12 (hereafter referred to as "Chronology of JCS Decisions").

28. Robert pleaded at his meeting of the Mongoose team "for new ideas of things that could be done against Cuba" and inquired "about the percentage of Cubans whom we thought would fight for the regime if the country were invaded." He intended to hold a meeting every morning for half an hour. (He almost certainly was not able to do this). Helms, *Memorandum for the Record*, 16 October 1962, in McAuliffe, ed., *CIA Documents on the Cuban Missile Crisis*, 154.

29. May and Zelikow, *The Kennedy Tapes*, 85.

30. Ibid, 94.

31. Ibid, 93.

32. Ibid, 115. The Pearl Harbor analogy was widely accepted by 17 October. See McCone's memorandum for discussion that day in McAuliffe, ed., *CIA Documents on the Cuban Missile Crisis*, 162.

33. Schlesinger, *Robert Kennedy*, 509; Kennedy, *Thirteen Days*, 36. Kennedy incorrectly recollects sending the note to the president.

34. Sorensen, "Summary of Agreed Facts and Premises, Possible Courses of Action and Unanswered Questions, October 17, 1962," in Chang and Kornbluh, *The Cuban Missile Crisis*, 114–15; McCone Memorandum, 17 October 1962, in McAuliffe, ed., *CIA Documents on the Cuban Missile Crisis*, 164.

35. "Brief Discussion with President—9:30 A.M.—17 October 1962," in McAuliffe, ed., *CIA Documents on the Cuban Missile Crisis*.

36. Handwritten Memorandum by Charles Bohlen to Secretary of State, 17 October 1962, NSA/Cuba, 645. Bohlen was about to leave Washington to take up a post as ambassador to Paris. That evening he and the president dined at Joe Alsop's house for a farewell dinner. To maintain the secrecy Kennedy had to extract Bohlen's views through a historical discussion of circumstances in which Russians had withdrawn from a position but without losing face. Merry, *Taking on the World*, 386; Bohlen, *Witness to History*, 488–92.

37. Ball, *The Past Has Another Pattern*, 290–91.

38. McCone Memorandum, Meeting at 8:30 P.M., 17 October 1962, FRUS, XI, 96.

39. May and Zelikow, *The Kennedy Tapes*, 134.

40. Ibid., 149.

41. Lovett shared the hawks' concern that once the issue was in the open the United States would come under great pressure to make concessions to gain a political settlement. John F. Kennedy Library Oral History Interview with Robert Lovett (19 November 1964), NSA/Cuba, 3221. This followed the president's meeting with Soviet Foreign Minister Gromyko.

42. Chronology of JCS Decisions, 16, 19; Sieverts, *The Cuban Crisis, 1962*, 53.

43. A staff study concluded that "the USSR would not resort to general war in direct response to U.S. military action against Cuba, that the most likely Soviet reactions would be at sea, against Iran, or an ICBM 'accident' on the Pacific Test Site (Johnston Island), and that sharp and strong encroaching actions at Berlin, short of direct seizure, could reasonably be expected." Chronology of JCS Decisions, 14. It is difficult to imagine what was presumed likely at Johnston Island!

44. Kennedy, *Thirteen Days*, 39–40.

45. May and Zelikow, *The Kennedy Tapes*, 119.

46. Nitze, *Hiroshima and Glasnost*, 223.

47. Kennedy Library Oral History Interview with Dean Acheson (27 April 1964), NSA/Cuba, 03197. Acheson, "Homage to Plain Dumb Luck," was a caustic review of Kennedy, *Thirteen Days*. Acheson was as scathing about those who favored invasion. It would have been easy to get in, observed Acheson, but "how were you ever going to get out." Bundy later noted: "Between the air strike of Acheson and the air war of the Joint Chiefs there were differences that no one adequately explored." Bundy, *Danger and Survival*, 400.

48. Sorensen, Outline of Options, 18 October 1962, NSA/Cuba, 00671; Sorensen, Draft Air Strike Scenario for 19 October 1962, in Chang and Kornbluh, *The Cuban Missile Crisis*, 128; Minutes of the 505th Meeting of the National Security Council, 20 October 1962, FRUS, XI, 135.

Chapter 20

1. May and Zelikow, *The Kennedy Tapes*, 86.

2. Sieverts, *The Cuban Crisis, 1962*, 52.

3. McCone Memorandum, 17 October 1962, in McAuliffe, ed., *CIA Documents on the Cuban Missile Crisis*, 163, 164. He mentioned "intelligence reports" indicating that a blockade would bring Castro down in four months, but made it clear that this was not his estimate.

4. Sorensen, 17 October 1962, in Chang and Kornbluh, *The Cuban Missile Crisis*, 114–15. (Also NSA/Cuba, 00649.)

5. Norbert Schlei in Strober and Strober, *Let Us Begin Anew*, 373–74, 377.

6. Nitze, *Hiroshima to Glasnost*, 222–23.

7. State Department Paper on a Blockade, 18 October 1962, NSA/Cuba, 00664.

8. Martin, *Kennedy and Latin America*, 409. Unlike other quarantine enthusiasts who wanted to save petroleum products for later, Martin wanted to put an immediate economic squeeze on Castro, in the belief that in these circumstances he might be brought down.

9. May and Zelikow, *The Kennedy Tapes*, 145–47.

10. See, for example, a dialogue between Bundy and Taylor. Ibid., 165.

11. McCone, Memorandum for the File, 19 October 1962 (covers all ExComm meetings on 17 October), in McAuliffe, ed., *CIA Documents on the Cuban Missile Crisis*, 169–73, 183–86. McCone pursued this issue with little support from elsewhere.

12. McCone, "Memorandum for File," 19 October 1962, in McAuliffe, ed., *CIA Documents on the Cuban Missile Crisis*, 185; Kennedy Library Oral History Interview with Roswell L. Gilpatric, 5 May 1970, NSA/Cuba, 03253.

13. Acheson, "Homage to Plain Dumb Luck."

14. Sieverts, *The Cuba Crisis, 1962*, 60.

15. May and Zelikow, *The Kennedy Tapes*, 172; Kennedy, *Thirteen Days*, 46–47.

16. McCone, "Memorandum to USIB Members," 19 October 1962, in McAuliffe, ed., *CIA Documents on the Cuban Missile Crisis*, 193–94.

17. May and Zelikow, *The Kennedy Tapes*, 174–88. See also Historical Division, Joint Secretariat, Joint Chiefs of Staff, Chronology of JCS Decisions, 21 December 1962. NSA/Cuba, 02780, 20.

18. Schlesinger, *Robert Kennedy*, 511.

19. This was not only to keep up appearances; the engagement in Chicago was politically sensitive, as it was intended to disprove the allegation that his good working relationship with Senate minority leader Dirksen of Illinois meant that he was not fully behind the Democratic candidate.

20. Meeting of ExComm, 11:00, 19 October, Notes by Leonard Meeker (NSA/Cuba, 00699), 5.

21. Sieverts, *The Cuba Crisis, 1962*, 65.

22. State Department Internal Paper on Steps Which Would Make Air Strike More Acceptable to Blockade Group, 19 October 1962, NSA/Cuba, 00694.

23. Bundy, *Danger and Survival*, 401.

24. Rusk, *As I Saw It*, 232–33.

25. Nitze describes Acheson explaining that "international law is merely a process based upon past precedent, that it continually evolves as new precedents are created." Nitze, *Hiroshima to Glasnost*, 224. The precedent was apparently President Roosevelt's 1937 "quarantine the aggressor" speech. Beschloss, *KvK*, 458.

26. Minutes of the 506th Meeting of the National Security Council, 21 October 1962, FRUS, XI, 143.

27. Director of Central Intelligence, SNIE 11-18-62, Soviet Reactions to Certain U.S. Courses of Action with Regard to Cuba, 19 October 1962, NSA/Cuba, 696.

28. The impact of these estimates on presidential thinking may be indicated by the fact that on 23 October it occurred to Kennedy to ask for a CIA analysis on the effect on the Cuban economy of a blockade on everything but food and medicine. May and Zelikow, *The Kennedy Tapes*, 293.

29. Director of Central Intelligence, SNIE 11-19-62, Major Consequences of Certain U.S. Courses of Action on Cuba, 20 October 1962, NSA/Cuba, 00721. Brugioni reports that the Pentagon determined that the Soviet Union only had about 15 TU-114 aircraft capable of traveling the 5,100 miles between Cuba and the nearest communist-controlled territory, so that made an airlift highly unlikely. Brugioni, *Eyeball to Eyeball*, 300.

30. The invasion plans are described by Brugioni, *Eyeball to Eyeball*, 294–95.

31. Historical Division, Joint Secretariat, Joint Chiefs of Staff, Chronology of JCS decisions, 21 December 1962 (NSA/Cuba, 02780), 19. Brugioni appears to put this on 18 October. On that day, he writes, McNamara had called Admiral Anderson early in the morning instructing him to work out the plan for a blockade as soon as possible, including an option solely devoted to offensive missiles. By 1:30 P.M. modifications to the old plan were complete. Brugioni, *Eyeball to Eyeball*, 279. The Joint Chiefs designated Admiral Dennison the commander of Blockade Force on 18 October and instructed him to prepare for a limited blockade on the nineteenth. Caldwell, "Department of Defense Operations During the Cuban Missile Crisis," 84.

32. Soviet Statement, 11 September 1962. Reprinted in Larson, *The "Cuban Crisis" of 1962*, 12.

33. Director of Central Intelligence, SNIE 11-18-62, Soviet Reactions to Certain U.S. Courses of Action with Regard to Cuba, 19 October 1962, NSA/Cuba, 00696.

34. Schlesinger, *Robert Kennedy*, 509; McCone Memorandum, Meeting at 8:30 P.M., 17 October 1962, FRUS, XI, 97.

35. Sieverts, *The Cuba Crisis, 1962*, 70–71; May and Zelikow, *The Kennedy Tapes*, 143–44, 172.

36. Minutes of the 505th and 506th Meetings of the National Security Council, 20 and 21 October 1962, FRUS, XI, 134, 148; Nitze, *Paper Agreed by the Berlin-NATO Subcommittee*, 24 October 1962.

37. Brugioni, *Eyeball to Eyeball*, 350. This fear of a threat to Berlin was widely shared, including in Britain.

38. For a report of the group's first meeting, see NSC/ExComm/Ber-NATO, Record of Meeting No. 1, 11 Hours, 24 October 1962, NSA/Cuba, 1190. The agenda covered explaining to allies how U.S. action was not designed to provoke a Berlin crisis but to prevent one from developing later, the implications of potential Soviet inspection of U.S. traffic to Berlin, and the impact of Cuban contingency plans on any necessary military buildup in Europe.

39. Central Intelligence Agency, Office of National Estimates, Survivability of West Berlin, 23 October 1962, FRUS, XV, 394–95 (also NSA/Cuba, 00907).

40. Sorensen, *Kennedy*, 694.

41. Minutes of the 505th Meeting of the National Security Council, 20 October 1962, FRUS, XI, 126–36; Sieverts, *The Cuba Crisis, 1962*, 74–75.

42. Schoenbaum, *Waging Peace and War*, 314.

43. Sieverts, *The Cuba Crisis, 1962*, 75–76.

44. "Pros and Cons of Blockade on POL Shipments, State Department Paper," 21 October 1962, NSA/Cuba, 00732.

45. Minutes of the 505th Meeting of the National Security Council, 20 October 1962, FRUS, XI, 135. Minutes of the 507th Meeting of the National Security Council on Monday, 22 October 1962, 3:00 P.M., Cabinet Room (NSA/Cuba, 0840), 1.

46. Robert McNamara, Notes on 21 October 1962 Meeting with the President, NSA/Cuba, 00738; Bundy, *Danger and Survival*, 401.

47. Taylor, "Reflections on a Grim October"; Nitze, *Hiroshima to Glasnost*, 228; Kennedy, *Thirteen Days*, 51.

48. Memorandum of Meeting with the President, Attorney General, Secretary McNamara, General Taylor, and Mr. McCone, 10:00 A.M., 21 October 1962, in McAuliffe, ed., *CIA Documents on the Cuban Missile Crisis*, 241.

Chapter 21

1. Address by President Kennedy, 22 October 1962, in Larson, ed., *The "Cuban Crisis" of 1962*, 43–45.

2. Another indication that Kennedy was still expecting a long crisis came the next day when, to some resistance, he suggested that Norstad should be retained as SACEUR for the duration of the crisis, that is, perhaps until 1 February 1963. McCone, Memorandum of Meeting of ExComm, 18:00, 23 October 1962, in McAuliffe, ed., *CIA Documents on the Cuban Missile Crisis*, 291.

3. Salinger, *John F. Kennedy: Commander in Chief*, 116.

4. Salinger, *With Kennedy*, 253, 261.

5. Ibid., 266.

6. The concern appeared to be that attacking Cuban territory was a less fateful step than attacking Russian ships.

7. May and Zelikow, *The Kennedy Tapes*, 245–75. His initial impatience with the congressional response was calmed by remembering his own, more militant, first reaction to the news of the Soviet deception. Kennedy, *Thirteen Days*, 57–58.

8. Acheson oral history interview, 27 April 1964. This was Acheson's guess on the next step rather than his own preference, which would have been "more vigorous and incisive." See Brinkley, *Dean Acheson*, 167.

9. Kennedy, *Thirteen Days*, 80, 89.

10. Minutes of the 506th Meeting of the National Security Council, 21 October 1962, FRUS, XI, 149.

11. Statement by the Soviet Government, 23 October 1962, in Larson, ed., *The "Cuban Crisis" of 1962*, 51, 54. The same day Khrushchev sent a letter to Castro rejecting "the shameless demands by the United States government."

12. For Robert's account of the meeting, see Memorandum, 24 October 1962, FRUS, XI, 175–77; May and Zelikow, *The Kennedy Tapes*, 343–45; Allyn, Blight, and Welch, *Back to the Brink*, 80.

13. Sorensen, *Kennedy*, 710. Garthoff suggests that the navy adopted its preferred line, five hundred miles from Cuba, anyway. Garthoff, *Reflections*, 68. For a full analysis of the British role during the crisis see Scott, *Macmillan, Kennedy and the Cuban Missile Crisis*.

14. May and Zelikow, *The Kennedy Tapes*, 296.

15. Ibid., 326.

16. CIA, The Crisis USSR/Cuba, 24 October 1962, in McAuliffe, ed., *CIA Documents on the Cuban Missile Crisis*, 294.

17. May and Zelikow, *The Kennedy Tapes*, 352–57.

18. Kennedy, *Thirteen Days*, 69–71.

19. McCone mentions reports of an attempted intercept at 10:35 with the *Kimovsk*, which had "turned around when confronted by a Navy vessel." McCone, Notes on Leadership Meeting on 24 October 1962, at 5:00 P.M., in McAuliffe, ed., *CIA Documents on the Cuban Missile Crisis*, 297.

20. May and Zelikow, *The Kennedy Tapes*, 353, 357. For Bundy's account, see Executive Committee Record of Action, 24 October 1962, in Chang and Kornbluh, *The Cuban Missile Crisis*, 165.

21. CIA, The Crisis USSR/Cuba, 25 October 1962, in McAuliffe, ed., *CIA Documents on the Cuban Missile Crisis*, 304.

22. Blight and Welch, *On the Brink*. According to Brugioni, carrying offensive weapons or equipment were *Poltava*, *Ugrench*, *Kasimov*, *Dolmatovo*, *Krasnograd*, *Kimovsk*, and *Yuri Gagarin*. Brugioni, *Eyeball to Eyeball*, 387–89.

23. May and Zelikow, *The Kennedy Tapes*, 327; Bundy, *Danger and Survival*, 421. Kennedy remarked on this factor in a press interview just after the crisis as an example of how the United States had underestimated its original power. U.S. National Archives and Records Administration, *Public Papers of the Presidents of the United States, 1962, John F. Kennedy*, 551.

24. Telephone conversation, Kennedy and Ball, 24 October 1962, FRUS, XI, 188–91.

25. CIA, The Crisis USSR/Cuba, 25 October 1962, in McAuliffe, ed., *CIA Documents on the Cuban Missile Crisis*, 304. By the next day, the *Belovodsk*, which had been carrying twelve Hound helicopters, had also turned back. CIA, The

Crisis USSR/Cuba, 26 October 1962, in McAuliffe, ed., *CIA Documents on the Cuban Missile Crisis,* 316.

26. There are many, not wholly consistent, accounts of this episode. Brugioni, *Eyeball to Eyeball,* 415–17; Shapley, *Promise and Power,* 176–78; Abel, *The Missile Crisis,* 154–55; Blight and Welch, *On the Brink,* 64, 154.

27. May and Zelikow, *The Kennedy Tapes,* 395–425; McCone, Executive Committee Meeting 10/25/62—10:00 A.M., in McAuliffe, ed., *CIA Documents on the Cuban Missile Crisis,* 305; White House, Executive Committee Record of Action, 25 October 1962, 10:00 A.M., Meeting No. 4, NSA/Cuba, 01336; Allison and Zelikow, *Essence of Decision,* 125.

28. According to Brugioni, he had initially wanted to stop a British ship to make the point that he was prepared to stop friend and foe alike. The British were furious, and Rusk was told by Ormsby-Gore that it should not be done. Brugioni, *Eyeball to Eyeball,* 418. British public opinion was already very uncertain on the wisdom of American policy.

29. Nitze, *Hiroshima to Glasnost,* 230.

30. Brugioni, *Eyeball to Eyeball,* 472–74.

31. Bromley Smith, Summary Record of NSC Executive Committee Meeting No. 5, 25 October 1962, 5:00 P.M., NSA/Cuba, 01337.

32. May and Zelikow, *The Kennedy Tapes,* 461.

33. Bromley Smith, Summary Record of NSC Executive Committee Meeting No. 5, 25 October 1962, 5:00 P.M., NSA/Cuba, 01337. His deputy, Gilpatric, described his attitude as shaped by the fact that "we had passed a point in arms technology and in history where military force provided solutions except in the strictly deterrent sense. So I started out with the idea of avoiding any military action at all if we could." Oral history, 56.

34. May and Zelikow, *The Kennedy Tapes,* 400.

35. Ibid.,

36. Ibid., 424. A reference on 436–37 is to a memo from Adam Yarmolinsky to McNamara. Rostow's views were developed in a paper: "Escalation of the blockade to POL can credibly be presented to world opinion as a measured increase of pressure to accomplish previously announced and supported objectives." To keep the focus on these objectives, it would be necessary to play down the idea that this was directed at Castro, although it would weaken the Cuban leader internally. State Department, Memorandum from W. W. Rostow, Cuba: Recommendation for POL Blockade, 27 October 1962, NSA/Cuba, 01547.

37. Bromley Smith, Summary Record of NSC Executive Committee Meeting No. 6, 26 October 1962, 10:00 A.M., NSA/Cuba, 01440.

38. Paper prepared by Secretary Dillon's group for ExComm, Scenario for Airstrike Against Offensive Missile Bases and Bombers in Cuba, 25 October 1962, NSA/Cuba, 01334.

39. Chronology of JCS Decisions, 48. Castro reports being told by the head of the Soviet military command on 26 October that all forces were ready, including tactical nuclear weapons units; "Cold War."

40. May and Zelikow, *The Kennedy Tapes*, 474; Allison, *Essence of Decision*, 126, 205.

41. *The Kennedy Tapes*, 477.

42. Blight and Welch, *On the Brink*, 89, 159.

Chapter 22

1. Martin, *Kennedy and Latin America*, 415–21.

2. Kennedy to Khrushchev, 23 October 1962; Khrushchev to Kennedy, 24 October 1962, FRUS, XI, 174–75, 185–87.

3. The Planning Subcommittee's assessment at the time was that the "primary Soviet tactic" was "to draw the U.S. into negotiations, meanwhile getting a standstill." Soviet Tactics in the Short Run, 25 October 1962, FRUS, XI, 216–18.

4. Statement by Acting Secretary General U Thant to UN Security Council, Including Text of Letter to President Kennedy and Chairman Khrushchev, 24 October 1962, in Larson, *The "Cuban Crisis" of 1962*, 10.

5. Ball, *The Past Has Another Pattern*, 301–2. Ball's various conversations with the president and with Stevenson on 24 October are in FRUS, XI, 189–97.

6. Letter from Acting Secretary General U Thant to President Kennedy, 25 October 1962, in Larson, *The "Cuban Crisis" of 1962*, 144–45.

7. May and Zelikow, *The Kennedy Tapes*, 369.

8. Director of Intelligence and Research, Department of State, Soviets Continue to Seek Abandonment of Quarantine While Missiles Stay, 25 October 1962, NSA/Cuba, 01310.

9. Director of Intelligence and Research, Department of State, Soviet Strategy in UN Discussions of Cuba, 25 October 1962, NSA/Cuba, 01311.

10. Walt Rostow to McGeorge Bundy, Soviet Tactics in the Short Run, 25 October 1962, NSA/Cuba, 01339.

11. Joseph Sisco in Strober and Strober, *Let Us Begin Anew*, 390–91; Broadwater, *Adlai Stevenson: The Odyssey of a Cold War Liberal*, 211–12.

12. There was some nervousness about Stevenson's readiness to hold the line in negotiations. Arthur Schlesinger Jr. and John McCloy were sent to keep an eye on him. Schlesinger, *Robert Kennedy*, 516.

13. May and Zelikow, *The Kennedy Tapes*, 463–64.

14. Enough for Kennedy to mention the possibility, tentatively, to Harold Macmillan on the evening of 26 October. May and Zelikow, *The Kennedy Tapes*, 480.

15. The Jupiter issue is explored in Nash, *The Other Missiles of October*. Bernstein, "Reconsidering the Missile Crisis," is an updated version of Bernstein, "The Cuban Missile Crisis."

16. All of this section was underlined, the word *negotiable* doubly so. Stevenson to Kennedy, 17 October 1962, FRUS, XI, 101–2.

17. May and Zelikow, *The Kennedy Tapes*, 142, 156; Minutes of the 505th Meeting of the National Security Council, 20 October 1962, FRUS, XI, 134. When Kennedy suggested, on 18 October, that the missiles in Turkey should be moved

anyway, Bundy "thought this a good idea either under conditions of a strike or during a preliminary talk." McCone, Memorandum for File, 19 October 1962, in McAuliffe, ed., *CIA Documents on the Cuban Missile Crisis*, 184.

18. The work was undertaken by William Bundy in the State Department over the weekend of 20–21 October.

19. Steel, *Walter Lippmann and the American Century*, 535. Brugioni reports the suspicion of some intelligence officers that Kennedy had put Lippmann up to this column. Brugioni, *Eyeball to Eyeball*, 422. Lippmann later told Dobrynin that material from senior officials in the Arms Control and Disarmament Agency pointing to the obsolescence of the missiles had given him the idea—for which he had "caught it hot." Dobrynin to Moscow, 1 November, reprinted in *Cold War International History Bulletin* 8–9 (1996–97): 308.

20. Ball, *The Past Has Another Pattern*, 295 The telegram noted that "Soviet reaction Cuban quarantine likely involve efforts compare missiles in Cuba with Jupiters in Turkey." It pointed out that this could become the basis of a negotiated settlement, although it acknowledged the problems this would create. The telegram requested that contingency preparations be made and an assessment of political consequences provided. State to Turkey, 24 October 1962, FRUS, XI, 180–81.

21. *Washington Post*, 25 October 1962.

22. Nash, *The Other Missiles of October*, 133. It had reported the previous day the possibility that the United States "might be willing to dismantle one of the obsolescent American bases near Soviet territory."

23. May and Zelikow, *The Kennedy Tapes*, 482. Part of Macmillan's idea was to relieve pressure on Turkey.

24. State Department, Memorandum from Raymond Garthoff to Walt Rostow, Concern over the Course and Outcome of the Cuban Crisis, 25 October 1962, NSA/Cuba, 01314. In Garthoff, *Reflections on the Cuban Missile Crisis*, 72, he describes his discomfort, as a known dove, finding himself in a caucus meeting of known State Department hawks, plus Dean Acheson. This contains his other estimates of the period as appendices.

Chapter 23

1. Blight and Welch, *On the Brink*, 119–20.

2. Kennedy, *Thirteen Days*, 65–66, 96–97.

3. Beschloss, *KvK*, 514–16. Hilsman is adamant that Fomin must have been part of a coordinated Soviet probe. Hilsman, *The Cuban Missile Crisis*, 141–42. Fursenko and Naftali, *Secret History*, 264, tends to confirm that this was a private enterprise, prompted by a series of reports picked up from Washington contacts suggesting that the United States was about to invade Cuba. Fomin's real name was Aleksandr Feklisov. His position was known to the United States, which would have given this proposal added credibility. The same idea was circulating elsewhere at the time, and there are some indications that Fomin raised it with U Thant.

4. Although Khrushchev's letter was received by the U.S. embassy in Moscow

during the day, it was well into the evening before it actually reached Washington, and this meant that it was not given as early a reply as later events suggested would have been desirable. Bundy, *Danger and Survival*, 443.

5. Director of Intelligence and Research, Department of State, Implications of the Soviet Initiative on Cuba, 27 October 1962, NSA/Cuba, 01515.

6. Cited in Kennedy, *Thirteen Days*, 199.

7. Kennedy to Khrushchev, 25 October 1962, FRUS, XI, 198; Fursenko and Naftali, *Secret History*, 259–60. This contradicts the suggestion that the first letter was a private initiative and the second reflected power struggles in Moscow. This account also fits in with that from a Soviet source relayed in Garthoff, *Reflections on the Cuban Missile Crisis*, 82.

8. Fursenko and Naftali, *Secret History*, 273–74. Lippmann had been treated as a virtual emissary of the U.S. government when he visited Khrushchev and discussed Berlin in April 1961.

9. Hilsman to Rusk, Trading U.S. Missile Bases in Turkey for Soviet Bases in Cuba; Memorandum by Garthoff, The Khrushchev Proposal for Turkey-Cuba Tradeoff; Bromley Smith, Summary Record of NSC Executive Committee Meeting No. 7, all 27 October 1962, NSA/Cuba, 01518, 01514, 01540. May and Zelikow, *The Kennedy Tapes*, 492–518.

10. Nash, *The Other Missiles of October*, 135. This was still with the understanding that this was for discussion after the Russians had stopped work on the Cuban bases.

11. Allyn, Blight, and Welch, *Cuba on the Brink*, 107, 108, 113–14; see also "Cold War."

12. Hilsman, *To Move a Nation*, 221. On these and other incidents that aggravated the dangers of the situation, see Sagan, *The Limits of Safety*.

13. Burdick and Wheeler, *Fail-Safe*.

14. The White House, Executive Committee Minutes, 23 October 1962, 10:00 A.M., NSA/Cuba, 00966. If "hostile actions should continue after such a single incident and single retaliation," it was expected, but not definitely decided, that action would be taken "to eliminate the effectiveness of surface-to-surface missiles in Cuba."

15. Brugioni, *Eyeball to Eyeball*, 464.

16. Bromley Smith, Summary Record of NSC Executive Committee Meeting No. 8, 27 October 1962, 4:00 P.M., NSA/ Cuba, 01542.

17. In 1989 he put the number at 500 sorties. However, Garthoff has given a figure for the air strike of 1,190 sorties on the first day. Allyn, Blight, and Welch, *Cuba on the Brink*, 97, 163.

18. May and Zelikow, *The Kennedy Tapes*, 581.

19. Vice President Johnson had been inclined to a trade since the morning. Lemnitzer had tried to convince him that these missiles were an important part of the deterrent when they had spoken on the phone earlier that day. Brugioni, citing a letter from Lemnitzer, records Johnson observing, "[S]ince we damn well gave them to the Turks, we can damn well take them back." Brugioni, *Eyeball to Eyeball*, 470.

20. Bromley Smith, Summary Record of NSC Executive Committee Meeting No. 9, 27 October 1962, 9:00 P.M., NSA/Cuba, 01541.

21. Beschloss, *KvK*, 534. The letter can be found in Kennedy, *Thirteen Days*, 100–2, and FRUS, XI, 178–81.

22. Martin, *Kennedy and Latin America*, 435–36; Johnson, oral history interview, 7 November 1964 (NSA/Cuba, 3219), 18.

23. Bundy, *Danger and Survival*, 432–33.

24. Rusk in Blight and Welch, *On the Brink*, 173–74; Rusk, *As I Saw It*, 240–41. For skepticism, see May and Zelikow, *The Kennedy Tapes*, and White, *The Cuban Missile Crisis*, 202–3.

25. Ambassadors in NATO were warned that by Sunday lunchtime a Soviet vessel (the *Groznyy*) would reach quarantine area "and an incident may occur." "In these circumstances the United States government may find it necessary within a very short time in its own interest and that of fellow nations in the Western Hemisphere to take whatever military action may be necessary to remove this growing threat to the Hemisphere." State Department to Ambassadors, 28 October 1962, NSA/Cuba, 01580.

26. His full account is published in May and Zelikow, *The Kennedy Tapes*, 607–9.

27. Dobrynin to Moscow, 27 October 1962, reprinted in *Cold War International History Bulletin* 5 (1995): 79–80.

28. Khrushchev, *Khrushchev Remembers: The Last Testament*, 528.

29. Khrushchev, *Khrushchev Remembers: The Glasnost Tapes*, 170–83; Allyn, Blight, and Welch, *Cuba on the Brink*, 109–11, 116; Garthoff, *Reflections on the Cuban Missile Crisis*, 91–92; "Cold War." Castro's letter is reprinted in Chang and Kornbluh, *The Cuban Missile Crisis*, 189. His concerns had already been communicated by the Soviet ambassador in Havana, Aleksandr Alekseev.

30. *Khrushchev Remembers: The Last Testament*, 498. Of minor importance was another contact between Scali and Fomin. On the morning of 27 October Scali was contacted by Hilsman and sent off to convey Washington's anger about the second letter. He told Fomin this was a "stinking doublecross" and that "[w]e are absolutely determined to get those missiles out of there. An invasion of Cuba is only a matter of hours away." While the first conversation between the two may have influenced Khrushchev; reports of this later one arrived after the key decisions had been taken.

31. Khrushchev to Kennedy, 30 October 1962, FRUS, XI, 311.

32. Reeves, *President Kennedy*, 305.

33. This is based on the account by Oleg Troyanovsky, then Khrushchev's special assistant for international affairs, in Allyn, Blight, and Welch, *Cuba on the Brink*, 73–74.

34. Fursenko and Naftali, *Secret History*, 283–85. Letter reprinted in Kennedy, *Thirteen Days*, 173–80.

35. Gromyko to Dobrynin, Dobrynin to Moscow, 28 October 1962, reprinted in *Cold War International History Bulletin* 5 (1995): 76.

Chapter 24

1. DeWitt Armstrong in NHP/Berlin, 237; Bromley Smith, Summary Record of NSC Executive Committee Meeting, 26 October 1962, 10:00 A.M., in Chang and Kornbluh, *The Cuban Missile Crisis*, 178.

2. Welch and Bright, "An Introduction to the ExComm Transcripts"; Sorensen, *Kennedy*, 716. Not everyone sensed this danger. Maxwell Taylor later observed: "I never heard an expression of fear of nuclear escalation on the part of any of my colleagues. If at any time we were sitting on the edge of Armageddon, as nonparticipants have sometimes alleged, we were too unobservant to notice it." "Reflections on a Grim October."

3. Hilsman, *The Cuban Missile Crisis*, 134.

4. *Khrushchev Remembers*, 497–98. Khrushchev also spent the crisis sleeping in his office.

5. Kennedy, *Thirteen Days*, 80, 89, 182. This vivid language did not impress the Americans. McNamara commented on its rambling nature.

6. "The rapidity of the Soviet messages in the past few days suggests a Soviet awareness that time is running short and that the U.S. may be planning further more drastic moves to secure removal of the Soviet missiles, whatever the consequences." Hilsman, Analysis of Khrushchev's Message, 28 October 1962, NSA/Cuba, 01591.

7. Kennedy, *Thirteen Days*, 80, 89, 182.

8. May and Zelikow, *The Kennedy Tapes*, 635; Kennedy, *Thirteen Days*, 117; Beschloss, *KvK*, 544. Anderson later commented: "I personally believe that if an invasion had been accompanied by diplomatic assurances from the United States that its operations were directed only against Castro, then the Soviet Union would not have resorted to war." Interview, *Washington Quarterly* 4 (1982): 85.

9. Bradlee, *Conversations with Kennedy*, 122.

10. E. W. Kenworthy, Anthony Lewis, Max Frankel, et al., "Cuban Crisis: A Step by Step Review," *New York Times*, 3 November 1962, reprinted in Larson, *The "Cuban Crisis" of 1962*; Walter Lippmann, "The Balance of Nuclear Power," *New York Herald Tribune*, 30 November 1962; Kissinger, "Reflections on Cuba."

11. Stewart Alsop and Charles Bartlett, "In Time of Crisis," *Saturday Evening Post*, 8 December 1962; on the origins of this account and its aftermath, see Merry, *Taking on the World*, 387–95. This was taken, unfairly, to reflect Stevenson's active promotion of the trade for Jupiters in Turkey. On this many others, including the president, were sympathetic. Where he went too far, in the eyes of Kennedy, was in suggesting at the NSC meeting on 20 October that a firm American offer should include an "agreement to limit our use of Guantánamo to a specified limited time." Minutes of the 506th Meeting of the National Security Council, 21 October 1962, FRUS, XI, 145. McCone was so worried about Stevenson's interjection about getting rid of Guantánamo (but not the Jupiters) that he later called Robert Kennedy, who confirmed with the president that there was no in-

tention of doing so. McCone, memorandum, 20 October 1962, FRUS, XI, 137–38.

12. It did not, however, as claimed introduce the distinction into the American political lexicon. One actor is quoted as saying: "At first we divided into hawks and doves, but by the end a rolling consensus had developed, and except for Adlai, we had all ended up as hawks or doves." According to Bird, Ray Cline of the CIA coined the distinction between "warhawks" and "Picasso doves" in conversation with Bundy, who passed it on to Bartlett (an old friend). Bird, *The Color of Truth*, 234. There is jocular reference on 27 October by Lyndon Johnson to "warhawks." However, the association of hawks with war and doves with peace goes back to biblical times. A widely circulated memo dated 28 October 1962 by Albert Wohlstetter and Roberta Wohlstetter, who were not insiders, refers to loose statements made by "our own hawks and doves." Notes on the Cuban Crisis, NSA/Cuba, 01565.

13. Editorial Note, FRUS, XI, 655.

14. Press Statement, 20 November 1962, U.S. National Archives and Records Administration, *Public Papers of the Presidents of the United States, 1962, John F. Kennedy*, 830–38. This story is well told in Fursenko and Naftali, *Secret History*, 298–310. See also Schlesinger, *Robert Kennedy*, 550. When Kennedy said on 20 November that "all nuclear weapons were gone from Cuba," this was not true. The tactical warheads were still on the island, and Castro had his eye on them. Aware of Castro's interest, and also of his impetuous behavior, the Russians moved sharply to get the warheads out.

15. Khrushchev to Kennedy, 28 October 1962, FRUS, VI, 189–90.

16. Rusk, *As I Saw It*, 240.

17. Dobrynin to Moscow, 28 October 1962, reprinted in *Cold War International History Bulletin* 5 (1995): 76.

18. Dobrynin to Moscow, 30 October 1962, reprinted in *Cold War International History Bulletin* 8–9 (1996–97): 304.

19. Kennedy, *Thirteen Days*, 109. Sorensen, who edited this book, admitted later to removing a passage that suggested more explicitly that this was part of a deal. Allyn, Blight, and Welch, *Back to the Brink*, 92–93.

20. Bundy, *Danger and Survival*, 434.

21. Memorandum of Conversation, 29 October 1962; Memorandum of Conversation, 28 October 1962, FRUS, XI, 296, 288.

22. Khrushchev, *Khrushchev Remembers: The Last Testament*, 512.

23. Allyn, Blight, and Welch, *Cuba on the Brink*, 214; Allyn, Blight, and Welch, *Back to the Brink*, 149; "Cold War."

24. May and Zelikow, *The Kennedy Tapes*, 659–60; Memorandum of Conversation, 14 December 1962, NSA/nuclear, 1157; Garthoff in Allyn, Blight, and Welch, *Cuba on the Brink*, 283; Nash, *The Other Missiles of October*, 152–53.

25. FRUS, XI, 259.

26. Summary Record, 19th Meeting, ExComm, 3 November 1962, FRUS, XI, 358.

27. Summary Record, 28th Meeting, ExComm, 20 November 1962, FRUS, XI, 502–3.

28. Kennedy to Khrushchev, 21 November 1962; Khrushchev to Kennedy, 22 November 1962, FRUS, VI, 223–24.

29. Memorandum of Conversation, 29 November 1962, FRUS, XI, 545–62.

30. Kennedy to Khrushchev, 14 December 1962, FRUS, VI, 231.

31. Kennedy to Khrushchev, 6 November 1962, FRUS, XI, 399.

32. Thompson to Rusk, 21 February 1963; Summary Record, 38th Meeting, ExComm, 25 January 1963; Summary Record, 40th Meeting, ExComm, 5 February 1963, FRUS, XI, 707, 681–87, 690.

Chapter 25

1. Gallup Poll, 27 February 1963; 21 and 26 March 1963, NSA/Cuba, 2966, 3011, 3018.

2. Ball to Bundy, 6 December 1962, Memorandum for Record, 4 March 1963, FRUS, XI, 587, 713–18; O'Donnell and Powers, *"Johnny, We Hardly Knew Ye,"* 319.

3. Summary Record, 29th Meeting, ExComm, 21 November 1962, FRUS, XI, 509.

4. *Robert Kennedy in His Own Words*, 376. INR, 18 February 1962; Cottrell to Bundy, 19 February 1963, NSA/Cuba 2942, 2945. Memorandum for Record, 28 February 1963, FRUS, XI, 712.

5. May and Zelikow, *The Kennedy Tapes*, 442, 478; Schlesinger, *Robert Kennedy*, 533.

6. Bundy to Kennedy, 4 January 1961, FRUS, XI, 648–51.

7. May and Zelikow, *The Kennedy Tapes*, 382–85; Kennedy's Remarks, 508th Meeting, NSC, 22 January 1963; Colby to McCone, April 1963, FRUS, XI, 669, 975, 987. Power to Taylor, 5 February 1962, NSA/nuclear, 346.

8. Memorandum from the Coordinator of Cuban Affairs (Cottrell) to Ex-Comm, 24 January 1963, FRUS, XI, 670–75.

9. Chase to Bundy, 14 February 1963, FRUS, XI, 700.

10. Fursenko and Naftali, *Secret History*, 291.

11. SNIE 85-4-62, 9 November 1962; Memorandum, 17 March 1962, FRUS, XII, 234–35, 558–64.

12. Rabe, *The Most Dangerous Area in the World*. See also Rabe, "John F. Kennedy and Latin America."

13. Martin, *Kennedy and Latin America*, 368.

14. Summary Record of 509th NSC Meeting, 13 March 1963, FRUS, XI, 715–18.

15. Schlesinger, *Robert Kennedy*, 538–39.

16. There had been seven hit-and-run raids since August 1962, all improvised and largely ineffectual. NSA/Cuba, 3051.

17. Memorandum for Record, 22 March 1963, FRUS, XI, 728; Rusk to Kennedy, 28 March 1963, FRUS, XI, 738.

18. Rusk to Kennedy, 28 March 1963, FRUS, XI, 738.

19. Summary Record, 42nd Meeting, ExComm, 29 March 1963, FRUS, XI, 739–43; McCone Memorandum, FRUS, XI, 744–46. McCone's own memorandum makes clear that actions taken were tougher than those implied by Bromley Smith's official record and that "AG favored a complete stand down before any attempt was made to guide the groups."

20. Schlesinger, *Robert Kennedy*, 540.

21. Hersh's claim that at this meeting the Kennedys' support for "ad hoc exile raids was telegraphed" depends on selective quotation, neglect of Robert Kennedy's practical suggestions on how to stop the attacks, missing the obvious sarcasm in John Kennedy's explanation of why the groups operated in this way, and the assumption that the story about the Bahamas was made up, though this is exactly what McCone told the president. Hersh, *The Dark Side of Camelot*, 380–81. For confirmation by Halpern that greater control was exercised over the Florida-based groups, see Blight and Kornbluh, *Politics of Illusion*, 128.

22. Kennedy to Khrushchev, 11 April 1963, FRUS, XI, 759–60; Briefing Papers for President's Press Conference, 24 April 1963, NSA/Cuba, 3074, 3075.

23. Chase to Bundy, 3 April 1963; Memorandum, 11 April 1963, FRUS, XI, 748–50, 758.

24. The Church Report, 86–89; Thomas, *The Very Best Men*, 299–304.

25. Memoranda from Goodwin to Kennedy, 22 August 1961 and 1 September 1961, FRUS, X, 640–47; Schlesinger, *Robert Kennedy*, 542.

26. Goodwin to Martin, 24 May 1962, FRUS, X, 821–22.

27. Schlesinger, *Robert Kennedy*, 469–70. On the early effort see Smith, "Bay of Pigs Prisoners and a Lost Opportunity."

28. Bundy to Kennedy, 4 January 1963; McCone to Kennedy, 10 April 1963; Memorandum, 26 January 1963, FRUS, XI, 648–51, 756, 687–88.

29. Peter Kornbuh has posted a number of documents on the secret diplomacy with Castro over 1963–64 on the National Security Archive Web site (http://www.gwu.edu/~nsarchiv/). These are Chase to Bundy, 1 March 1963, and Chase, Memorandum for Record, 4 March 1963.

30. Schlesinger, *Robert Kennedy*, 541–42.

31. McCone Memoranda, 15 April 1963; Bundy to Standing Group, The Cuban Problem, 21 April 1963, FRUS, XI; Summary Record of 2nd Meeting of the NSC Standing Group, 23 April 1963; Kent to McCone, 22 April 1963, FRUS, XI, 762–64, 777–78, 780–81.

32. Helms to McCone, 1 May 1963 (from NSA Web site). This appears to be the source for Schlesinger, *Robert Kennedy*, 542. For text of Howard's interview, see NSA/Cuba, 3100. Martin to Salinger, 2 May 1963, NSA/Cuba, 3101.

33. Carter to Bundy, 2 May 1963; Summary Record of 7th Meeting of the NSC Standing Group, 28 May 1963, FRUS, XI, 778–79, 822.

34. Zubok and Pleshakov, *Inside the Kremlin's Cold War*, 270; Fursenko and Naftali, *Secret History*, 296.

35. Memorandum, 25 April 1963, FRUS, XI, 789; Khrushchev to Kennedy,

undated (received 29 April 1963), FRUS, XI, 792. Khrushchev did give "due credit" to the actions taken to deal with the attacks of Soviet vessels.

36. Bureau of Inter-American Affairs, Future Relations with Castro, 20 June 1963, FRUS, XI, 838–42.

Chapter 26

1. Summary Record of 2nd Meeting of the NSC Standing Group, 23 April 1963, FRUS, XI, 780–81.

2. Memorandum from Johnson and Nitze, 10 May 1963, FRUS, XI, 804–13; Draft Memorandum from Office of National Estimates, 13 May 1963, FRUS, XI, 813–14.

3. Summary Record of 7th Meeting of the NSC Standing Group, 28 May 1963, FRUS, XI, 821–23.

4. Memorandum for the Record, 25 April 1963, FRUS, XI, 780–81.

5. Fursenko and Naftali, *Secret History*, 336. It was reported back to Moscow that he judged that "U.S. intelligence overestimated the possibility of opposition to Castro and underestimated the position of the present Cuban government."

6. National Intelligence Estimate, *Situation and Prospects in Cuba*, 14 June 1963; CIA Paper for NSC Standing Group, Proposed Covert Policy and Integrated Program of Action Towards Cuba, 8 June 1963; Memorandum for Record, 19 June 1963, FRUS, XI, 834–36, 828–34, 837–38.

7. Summary Record of 10th Meeting of the Standing Group of the NSC, 16 July 1963, FRUS, XI, 852–53.

8. *Robert Kennedy In His Own Words*, 376–77. Later, apparently in contradiction, he suggests that the projects often ended in disaster and were not "very helpful." He also states categorically that there were no direct assassination attempts on Castro.

9. The Church Report, 173. On 3 October nine operations were approved, several of which involved sabotage. On 24 October thirteen operations were approved, including the sabotage of an electric power plant, an oil refinery, and a sugar mill.

10. Briefing Paper for President's Press Conference, 12 September 1961, NSA/Cuba, 3162.

11. Memorandum of Conversation, 10 September 1963; Chase to Bundy, 12 September 1963; Memorandum of Conversation, 13 September 1963; Memorandum of Conversation, 10 October 1963, FRUS, XI, 861–62, 864–65, 866–68, 875–77.

12. Summary Record of 10th Meeting of the NSC Standing Group, 16 July 1963, FRUS, XI, 850–53.

13. Helms to McCone, Reported Desire of the Cuban Government for Rapprochement with the United States, 5 June 1963 (NSA Web site).

14. Memoranda for the Record from Fitzgerald and McCone, 22 and 24 June 1963, FRUS, XI, 842–45. See also minutes of special group of 6 June, stressing the desirability of communications but also the need for utmost secrecy.

15. Howard, "Castro's Question," 3–5.

16. Memorandum by Attwood, 18 September 1963, FRUS, XI, 868–70. Attwood provided detailed accounts of his initiative to the U.S. government. These are reprinted in FRUS, XI, as Documents 374, 379, and 388, and provide the basis for the following paragraphs. For a full description of the peace initiative, see Kornbluh, "JFK and Castro." See also Attwood, *The Reds and the Blacks*, 142–46, and Schlesinger, *Robert Kennedy*, 549–58.

17. Chase to Bundy, 21 October 1963, FRUS, XI, 877.

18. The Church Report, 174.

19. Memorandum, 5 November 1963, FRUS, XI, 878–79.

20. Schlesinger, *Robert Kennedy*, 553.

21. Future targets for "destruction operations" were an oil refinery and storage facilities, an electric plant, sugar refineries, railroad bridges, harbor facilities, and docks and ships. Memoranda for the Record, White House meeting of 12 November, FRUS, XI, 883–88.

22. Chase, Some Arguments Against Accommodation—A Rebuttal, 12 November 1963 (NSA Web site).

23. Memorandum for the Record, 12 November 1963, FRUS, XI, 888–89; The Church Report, 174. See also Chase to Bundy, 19 November 1963, and Castro to Johnson (via Lisa Howard), 12 February 1964 (NSA Web site).

24. Schlesinger, *Robert Kennedy*, 554; Memorandum of Meeting with President Johnson, 19 December 1963, FRUS, XI, 908.

25. Schlesinger, *Robert Kennedy*, 555.

26. Chase to Bundy, 25 November and 3 December 1963, FRUS, XI, 891, 898–900; Attwood's evidence to Senate Select Committee to Study Governmental Operations with respect to Intelligence Activities, 10 July 1975, 10 (NSA Web site).

27. Memorandum by Smith, undated, FRUS, XI, 902–3.

28. Chase to Bundy, 25 November 1963, FRUS, XI, 890. Bundy later reassured him on this point.

29. Thomas, *The Very Best Men*, 304.

30. Editorial Note on Meeting of 28 November 1963, FRUS, XI, 896; Beschloss, *Taking Charge*, 87.

31. Rabe, *The Most Dangerous Area in the World*, 107.

32. Memorandum of Meeting with President Johnson, 19 December 1963, FRUS, XI, 908; Schlesinger, *Robert Kennedy*, 536.

33. Castro to Johnson (via Lisa Howard), 12 February 1964. The CIA picked up evidence that the Cubans realized that Johnson was unlikely to pursue Kennedy's initiative. Helms to Bundy, 4 March 1964 (NSA Web site).

34. Kornbluh, "JFK and Castro," 101–2.

35. Chase to Bundy, 25 November 1963, FRUS, XI, 890.

Chapter 27

1. Backgrounder on Cuba, 31 December 1961, NSA/Cuba, 2805.

2. Rusk, *As I Saw It*, 283–84.

3. Komer to Bundy, 1 March 1961, Memorandum of Kennedy/Macmillan

Conversation, 5 April 1961, FRUS, XII, 19–20, 42–43; see also discussion of how to deal with Henry Luce, publisher of *Time* magazine and strong supporter of the Nationalists. Kennedy stressed to officials that he did not want to take a high-profile position on this issue. 24 May 1961, FRUS, XII, 63–65. Foot, *The Practice of Power*, 37.

4. Bundy to the Chief of the Central Intelligence Agency Station in Taipei (Cline), 11 October 1961, FRUS, XII, 154–55. Bundy signed his memo "Yours by candlelight for scholarship and skullduggery." Cline reported back that the Nationalists still wanted a public statement of support for the entry of the communists into the UN and a direct private message from Kennedy to Chiang. Cline to Bundy, 14 October 1961, FRUS, XII, 156–57. The message was sent through normal diplomatic channels.

5. Fetzer, "China," 188–89.

6. Komer to Bundy, 29 January 1962; Taipei to State, 6 March 1962; Bundy to Cline, 6 March 1962; Draft Message from Kennedy to Harriman, 9 March 1962, FRUS, XII, 181–84, 190, 191–92, 192–93.

7. SNIE 13-3-62, Probable Consequences of Chinese Nationalist Military Operations on the China Mainland, 28 March 1962, FRUS, XII, 200–1.

8. Hilsman Notes, 31 March 1962; Memoranda to Cline, 31 March 1962, 29 May 1962, FRUS, XII, 204–5, 206–7, 239–40.

9. Conversation of McCone with Chiang Kai-shek, 5 June 1962; McCone Meeting with President, 18 June 1962, FRUS, XII, 241–44, 246–47.

10. Hilsman to Rusk, 18 June 1962; Hilsman, Record of Meeting, 20 June 1962, FRUS, XII, 247–48, 251–52.

11. This episode is covered in Chang, *Friends and Enemies*, 224–26; Fetzer, "China," 189–90; as well as Hilsman, *To Move a Nation*. Ball to Kennedy, 21 June 1962, SNIE 13-5/1-62, Chinese Communist Short-Range Military Intentions, 5 July 1962, FRUS, XII, 258–59. U.S. National Archives and Records Administration, *Public Papers of the Presidents of the United States, 1962, John F. Kennedy*, 510.

12. President Kennedy to President Chiang, 11 April 1963; Meeting, 11 September 1963, FRUS, XII, 359–60, 386–92.

13. Prozumenshikov, "The Sino-Indian Conflict, the Cuban Missile Crisis, and the Sino-Soviet Split."

14. Zubok, "Deng-Xiaoping and the Sino-Soviet Split, 1956–1963." Appended to this article are relevant documents, including a transcript of some of the July consultations.

15. Chang, *Friends and Enemies*, 220.

16. CIA Sino-Soviet Task Force, "The Sino-Soviet Dispute and its Significance." 1 April 1961, UPA. *John F Kennedy National Security File*. For an example of the quality of analysis developed in the government by 1961, see Zagoria, *The Sino-Soviet Conflict, 1956–1961*. Zagoria had been a member of the Sino-Soviet Studies Group (SSSG), set up in the CIA in 1956 to study the developing dispute. Gelman, "The Sino-Soviet Conflict," is from the same group. For background to the analysis see Ford, "The CIA and Double Demonology."

17. This explains why Chang, who fails to mention the Sino-Indian dispute,

finds the shift in Bowles' position so puzzling, Chang, *Friends and Enemies*, 218–19.

18. Fetzer, "China," 182.

19. Authority and Control in the Communist Movement, NIE 10–61, 8 August 1961, FRUS, XII, 114–18.

20. James C. Thomson Jr. to Harriman, 12 January 1962, FRUS, XII, 176–79; Thomson, "On the Making of U.S. China Policy," 226–27; Hilsman, *To Move a Nation*, 344; Chang, *Friends and Enemies*, 223.

21. FRUS, XXII, 229–31. See Ford, "The CIA and Double Demonology."

22. Cited in Whiting, *The Chinese Columbus of Deterrence*, 168. In 1961 these figures had been substantially the other way around. Gallup Poll of 24 March 1963, NSA/Cuba, 3018.

23. CIA, Soviet Policy in the Aftermath of the Cuban Crisis, 29 November 1962; McCone to Kirkpatrick (Executive Director, CIA), 25 February 1963; CIA, Soviet Policies: The Next Phase, 18 March 1963, FRUS, V, 583, 586–87, 634, 649.

24. Sorensen, *Kennedy*, 726; Chang, *Friends and Enemies*, 229; Krock, *Memoirs*, 370.

25. FRUS, VIII, 274. Cited in Seaborg, *Kennedy, Khrushchev, and the Test Ban*, 182. Editorial Note on Meeting of 8 February 1962, FRUS, VII, 646.

26. Seaborg, *Kennedy, Khrushchev, and the Test Ban*, 181; Oliver, *Kennedy, Macmillan and the Nuclear Test-Ban Debate, 1961–1963*, 171.

Chapter 28

1. Sherman Kent (Chairman, Board of National Estimates) to McCone, 8 November 1962, FRUS, V, 556.

2. Editorial Note, FRUS, V, 587–88. The idea of a hotline had been under discussion since early 1961. Its potential importance had been accentuated by the tortuous process of communication during the Cuban missile crisis. A proposal for a special communications link between Moscow and Washington was raised by the United States at the eighteen-nation disarmament talks in Geneva on 29 March and gained a positive response almost immediately. The agreement was actually signed on 20 June.

3. State to Moscow, 28 November 1962; Meeting, 15 February 1963, FRUS, VI, 447, 486–88.

4. Meeting, 26 April 1963; Meeting, 2 August 1963, FRUS, VI, 510, 545.

5. The story is brilliantly told in Cohen, *Israel and the Bomb*.

6. Editorial Note, FRUS, VII, 599–601.

7. Wiesner to Kennedy, 3 November 1962, FRUS, VII, 594–95.

8. There was no formal record kept of the Dean-Kuznetsov conversation. Seaborg, *Kennedy, Khrushchev, and the Test Ban*, 178–81; Editorial Note, FRUS, VII, 623–25. See also Oliver, *Kennedy, Macmillan and the Nuclear Test-Ban Debate*, 146–47; Khrushchev to Kennedy, 19 December 1962, FRUS, VI, 234–37.

9. Kennedy to Khrushchev, 28 December 1962, FRUS, VI, 238–40; Schlesinger, *Thousand Days*, 896.

10. Kohler to State, 16 March 1862, FRUS, V, 642–44. Kohler himself was an experienced State Department official, a Russian speaker who had been at the heart of Berlin decision making. He had been sent in preference to a more political appointment, unnaturally for the administration, because Kennedy had concluded that the nature of the job meant that it was necessary to have someone who could work with the State Department. Beschloss, *KvK*, 407–8. Kohler, unfortunately, was too much of the Foreign Service officer, too much of an Achesonian, and too uncertain in his relations with Kennedy to truly reflect the administration and serve as an interlocutor. This limitation was understood in Moscow, and so Kennedy was left without a reliable channel to Khrushchev other than their correspondence and conversations with Dobrynin.

11. This assumed an 11 percent growth rate, twice that achieved. On this more modest growth rate Soviet GNP would have been around 60 percent that of the United States in 1970. This economic competition rather than military threats was the basis of Khrushchev's famous "we will bury you" boast. CIA, Soviet Policies: The Next Phase, 18 March 1963; NIE 11–63, Main Trends in Soviet Foreign Policy, 22 May 1963, FRUS, V, 264, 645–50, 685–701.

12. Kennedy to Macmillan, 28 March 1963, FRUS, VII, 659. The line on the dispute was taken from a memo from Thompson to Kennedy, 21 March 1963, FRUS, VII, 657. Macmillan's letter had been gestating for some time but may have been prompted by an approach made to former science advisor George Kistiakowsky by a Soviet academician, both attending a meeting in London, who suggested that Moscow might accept an average of five a year over a number of years with no more than seven in a given year. Oliver, *Kennedy, Macmillan and the Nuclear Test-Ban Debate*, 170. The Americans appear to have taken a far more cautious view of this approach, and it does not appear to have been followed through elsewhere, although Sorensen indicates that it was noted. Sorensen, *Kennedy*, 729.

13. Oliver, *Kennedy, Macmillan and the Nuclear Test-Ban Debate*, 157–58.

14. JCS to McNamara, 20 April 1963, FRUS, VII, 683–85.

15. Oliver, *Kennedy, Macmillan and the Nuclear Test-Ban Debate*, 171.

16. Macmillan to Kennedy, 3 April 1963, FRUS, VII, 663–67.

17. Attorney General to President, 3 April 1963, FRUS, VI, 262–65.

18. Kennedy to Khrushchev, 11 April 1963, FRUS, VI, 265–68.

19. President and Prime Minister to Khrushchev, 15 April 1963, FRUS, VI, 268–70.

20. Kohler to State, 24 April 1963, FRUS, VII, 685–86.

21. Cousins, *The Improbable Triumvirate*, 114–17; Beschloss, *KvK*, 586–88.

22. Beschloss, *KvK*, 592–93.

23. Khrushchev to Kennedy, undated, FRUS, VI, 271–79; Khrushchev to Kennedy, 8 May 1963, FRUS, VII, 693–99.

24. Kennedy/Macmillan to Khrushchev, 30 May 1963; Khrushchev to Ken-

nedy, 8 May 1963, FRUS, VII, 707–10, 714–18; Oliver, *Kennedy, Macmillan and the Nuclear Test-Ban Debate*, 178–83.

25. Schlesinger, *Thousand Days*, 900.

26. Sorensen, *Kennedy*, 730–31.

27. Text from Sorensen, ed., *"Let the Word Go Forth,"* 282–90. This was made easier by fact that no U.S. atmospheric tests were planned until the following year, while some Soviet tests appeared imminent.

28. Interview with Martha Mautner, "Cold War."

29. Kennedy was no linguist, and the sentence was based on Bundy's rusty German. Hence the insertion of *ein*, which turned the strict meaning to "I am a doughnut." There is no indication that Kennedy's intention was lost on his audience.

30. Arbatov, *The System*, 95.

Chapter 29

1. Meeting, 30 July 1962, Kastner transcript.

2. Meeting, 1 August 1962, Kastner transcript.

3. Ibid., 236.

4. Schlesinger, *Thousand Days*, 905–9.

5. Chang, *Friends and Enemies*. It is, for example, hard to imagine a leader less receptive to the idea of preemptive attacks than Macmillan, with whom Kennedy is alleged to have raised the matter.

6. McCone record of conversation with Bundy, 10 January 1963. FRUS, XII, 339; Bundy, *Danger and Survival*, 532.

7. SNIE 12-2-63, Communist China's Advanced Weapons Program, 24 July 1963 (from NSA Web site).

8. Kennedy to Harriman, 15 July 1961, FRUS, VII, 801; Seaborg, *Kennedy, Khrushchev, and the Test Ban*, 239.

9. Kent to Harriman, 8 July 1963, FRUS, VII, 771.

10. Seaborg, *Kennedy, Khrushchev, and the Test Ban*, 228; Kohler to the Department of State, Moscow, 18, 19, and 27 July 1963, FRUS, VII, 808, 814, 858. A memorandum from John J. de Martino of the Department of State Executive Secretariat, 2 October 1964, reported that there was no evidence in the records of the negotiations of "any Harriman proposal for a joint US-USSR effort to slow down Red China's nuclear weapons development," though the question of Chinese nuclear capacities came up in various conversations. FRUS, XII, 370–71.

11. Zubok and Harrison, "The Nuclear Education of Nikita Khrushchev," 164.

12. On being told this, Kennedy expressed his hope that his wife's conversations at social occasions were not circulated in government reports. Memorandum of Conversation, 24 July 1963, FRUS, VII, 845.

13. Kennedy had told Macmillan that the United States would need to test if China tested. Memorandum of Conversation, 29 June 1961, FRUS, VII, 754.

14. Policy Planning Meeting, 15 October 1963, FRUS, XII, 309–402; Komer

to Bundy, 5 November 1963, FRUS, XII, 404–5. Bromley Smith wrote to Bundy about the paper: "This event is so far down the road I doubt JFK should be given this year."

15. "We have become suspicious that you, in shipping missiles to Cuba, were trying to place her under your control." Stenogram, Meeting of the Delegations of the Communist Party of the Soviet Union and the Chinese Communist Party, Moscow, 5–20 July 1963. *Cold War International History Project Bulletin*, no. 10.

16. Chang, *Friends and Enemies*, 252.

17. Sorensen, ed., *"Let the Word Go Forth,"* 291–98.

18. Seaborg, *Kennedy, Khrushchev, and the Test Ban*, 264–65.

19. This comes over clearly in John F. Kennedy, *Presidential Recordings*.

20. Memorandum of Conference, 22 July 1963, FRUS, VII, 830.

21. Memorandum, 13 August 1963, FRUS, VII, 877–80. They appear to have been impressed on the Sino-Soviet split. Chang, *Friends and Enemies*, 248–49.

22. He nonetheless did not push his luck too far when speaking in the most conservative states. His planned speech for Dallas on 22 November was full of cold war rhetoric.

Chapter 30

1. Bell, *The Conventions of Crisis*, 2. Bell does not give any reference, and although this comment has been quoted many times since, she is always the only source. The lack of citation is also noted by Blight in *The Shattered Crystal Ball*, 192. He also notes McNamara's later repudiation of the concept: " 'Managing' crises is the wrong term; you don't 'manage' them because you can't 'manage' them." Blight and Welch, *On the Brink*, 99.

2. FRUS, XIII, 449–50, 455.

3. Freedman and Gearson, "Interdependence and Independence"; Neustadt, *Alliance Politics*. This is based on a report on the Anglo-American misunderstanding that Neustadt conducted for Kennedy. See also Murray, *Kennedy, Macmillan and Nuclear Weapons*.

4. Trachtenberg, *A Constructed Peace*, 366–69.

5. Remarks at NSC meeting, 22 January 1962, FRUS, XIII, 485.

6. Acheson's instinctive reaction was to bring every crisis to a head, and his insistence that the battle for German hearts and minds could only be won by promising reunification by force if necessary was hardly calculated to calm wider European anxieties

7. Costigliola, "The Pursuit of Atlantic Community," 50–53.

8. Heuser, *NATO, Britain, France and the FRG*, 149–51. The Germans never showed any practical interest in a nationally produced nuclear force.

9. Trachtenberg, *A Constructed Peace*, 313.

10. Bundy to Kennedy, 15 June 1963, FRUS, XIII, 594; Winand, *Eisenhower, Kennedy, and the United States of Europe*, 349. The Winand book contains a good account of MLF in its wider political context. See also Steinbruner, *The Cybernetic Theory of Decision*.

11. Berlin meeting, 3 August 1962, Kastner transcript.

12. Kennedy to Adenauer, 15 November 1962, FRUS, VI, 445.

13. Meeting, 27 December 1962, FRUS, VIII, 449–50.

14. His brother suggested a study on the advantages and disadvantages of pulling troops out of Europe. Summary record of ExComm, 25 January 1963; Meeting, 28 February 1963, FRUS, XIII, 487–91, 517.

15. Some Lessons From the First Two Weeks of the Cuban Crisis, 1 November 1962, NSA/Cuba, 01806.

16. Rostow to Ball, Some Lessons from Cuba, 15 November 1962, NSA/Cuba, 02296.

17. Undersecretary George W. Ball Addresses the NATO Parliamentarians Conference on NATO and the Cuban Crisis, *U.S. Department of State Bulletin* 47, 1223 (3 December 1962): 831–35, reprinted in Larson, *The "Cuban Crisis" of 1962*.

18. Robert S. McNamara, Testimony Before the House Armed Services Committee, 30 January 1963, cited in Kaufman, *The McNamara Strategy*, 91.

19. Robert S. McNamara, Remarks at the Annual National Veterans Day Ceremony, Arlington National Cemetery, 11 November 1962, cited in Kaufman, *The McNamara Strategy*, 298. See also *CBS Reports*, 12 September 1963, cited in Kaufman, *The McNamara Strategy*, 294. See also Dan Caldwell, ed., "Department of Defense Operations During the Cuban Missile Crisis: A Report by Adam Yarmolinsky. A Report by Special Assistant to the Secretary of Defense, 13 February 1963," *Naval War College Review* 32, 4 (1979): 98.

20. Kaufman, *The McNamara Strategy*, 274. Not everyone agreed with this assessment. General LeMay expressed his conviction that "superior U.S. strategic power, coupled with the obvious will and ability to apply this power, was the major factor that forced the Soviets to back down." Military Procurement Authorization, Fiscal Year 1964, Senate Committee on Armed Services, 1963, 896.

21. Enthoven, "American Deterrent Policy." This was based on Testimony to U.S. Senate Armed Services Committee, Military Procurement Authorization: Fiscal Year 1964 (10 February 1963). Acheson was still insisting on conventional forces to meet all contingencies. Acheson, "The Practice of Partnership."

22. FRUS, VIII, 463–64.

23. Tape transcript cited by Trachtenberg, *A Constructed Peace*, 319. Trachtenberg takes this to demonstrate that the no-cities policy was never taken very seriously. I would put more emphasis on the evidence of its failings.

24. Record of 517th Meeting of NSC, 12 September 1963, FRUS, VIII, 499–507.

25. Keeny to Bundy, 22 November 1963; McNamara to President Johnson, 6 December 1963, FRUS, VIII, 534, 549–50.

26. Schelling, *Arms and Influence*, 166. Schelling later recalled members of a Harvard-MIT arms control seminar "gloating" after listening to the president's 22 October speech: "[W]e just couldn't imagine how Khrushchev could have done such a dumb, blundering act, and we knew that we had him on this one and the only question was how bad a fall we were going to give him." Blight and Welch,

On the Brink, 105. Later Richard Goodwin, who had seen the Cuban issue from the inside, commented on Schelling's confidence that both sides understood that Cuba was not general war by recalling that those taking the decisions "believed there was a concrete and substantial danger of war, not after a series of steps, but as the next step on the next day." He worried about this sort of strategic theory, "for it can lead us to believe we have an understanding of events and a control over their flow which we do not have." Goodwin, "The Unthinkable and the Unanalyzable," 130, 129.

27. Notes on the Cuban Crisis, 28 October 1962, NSA/Cuba, 01565. The basic purpose of the memorandum appears to have been to ensure that Kennedy's non-invasion pledge on Cuba left open the possibility of supporting the Cuban resistance to Castro, which they expected to grow as a result of the crisis. For their considered view of the crisis, see Wohlstetter and Wohlstetter, *Controlling the Risks in Cuba.*

28. In an essay in Knorr and Read, eds., *Limited Strategic War*, 185. The early influence of this idea can be seen in a reference to the "ladder of nuclear escalation," in Kaufman, *The McNamara Strategy*, 72. Eventually he pushed this idea to center stage with Kahn, *On Escalation: Metaphors and Scenarios.*

29. Brodie, "What Price Conventional Capabilities in Europe?"; Brodie, "The McNamara Phenomenon"; Brodie, *Escalation and the Nuclear Option;* Steiner, *Bernard Brodie and the Foundations of American Nuclear Strategy;* Booth, "Bernard Brodie."

30. George and Simon, eds., *The Limits of Coercive Diplomacy;* Rosen, "Vietnam and the American Theory of Limited War"; Pape, "Coercive Air Power in the Vietnam War"; Thies, *When Governments Collide.*

Chapter 31

1. Hilsman, *To Move a Nation*, 413.

2. Rostow, *The Diffusion of Power*, 118–19, 264.

3. Currey, *Edward Lansdale.*

4. Blaufarb, *The Counter-Insurgency Era*, 55; McClintock, *Instruments of Statecraft*, 163; Schlesinger, *Thousand Days*, 309–10; Sorensen, *Kennedy*, 632.

5. As "The Report the President Wanted Published," by "An American Officer," 20 May 1961. See also the special newspaper supplement "Mao's Primer on Guerrilla War," *New York Times Magazine*, 4 June 1961.

6. For a sample of the literature of this period, see Eckstein, ed., *Internal War;* Garthoff, "Unconventional Warfare in Communist Strategy"; Galula, *Counterinsurgency Warfare;* Heilbrunn, *Partisan Warfare;* Lansdale, "Do We Understand Revolution"; Osanka, ed., *Modern Guerrilla Warfare;* Paret and Shy, *Guerrillas in the 1960s.*

7. Blaufarb, *The Counter-Insurgency Era*, 72, 317; Shafer, *Deadly Paradigms*, 114–15.

8. National Security Action Memorandum No. 124, 18 January 1962, *PP* II, 660–61.

9. McClintock, *Instruments of Statecraft*, 170–71; Shafer, *Deadly Paradigms*, 112–13; Maechling, "Insurgency and Counter-Insurgency," 33.

10. Cable, *Conflict of Myths*, 279–80; Maechling, "Insurgency and Counter-Insurgency," 33.

11. Hilsman, *To Move a Nation*, 129.

12. Schlesinger, *Thousand Days*, 307.

13. Hilsman, *To Move a Nation*.

14. Rostow to Kennedy, 10 March 1961, FRUS, XXIV, 83. Rostow discusses the memo in Rostow, *The Diffusion of Power*, 267.

15. Maechling, "Insurgency and Counter-Insurgency," 34.

16. Shafer, *Deadly Paradigms*, 113.

17. Kattenburg, *The Vietnam Trauma*, 111–12.

18. Johnson, "Internal Defense and the Foreign Service." The article is discussed in Blaufarb, *The Counter-Insurgency Era*, 62–66. For a contemporary academic discussion of the issue of popular support, see Johnson, "Civilian Loyalties and the Guerrilla Conflict."

Chapter 32

1. Notes of Conversation Between President-Elect Kennedy and President Eisenhower, 19 January 1961, FRUS, XXIV, 19–20.

2. Schlesinger, *Thousand Days*, 299.

3. The principal members of the task force were Nitze for Defense, Rostow for the White House, and Bissell for CIA. The group was chaired by Graham Parsons, assistant secretary of state for Far Eastern affairs, an Eisenhower holdover and strongly pro-Phoumi. He was replaced in March 1961.

4. Report prepared by the Inter-Agency Task Force on Laos, 23 January 1961, FRUS, XXIV, 28–40.

5. Newman, *JFK and Vietnam*, 10–11; Rusk, *As I Saw It*, 428; Beschloss, *KvK*, 161; Reeves, *President Kennedy*, 74, 111.

6. Hilsman, *To Move a Nation*, 131.

7. Stevenson, *The End of Nowhere*, 142.

8. Kern, Levering, and Levering, *The Kennedy Crises*, 28–29, 40.

9. Rostow to Kennedy, 13 April 1961, FRUS, XXIV, 126.

10. FRUS, XXIV, 1–2.

11. Memorandum of Conference, 2 January 1961, McNamara to Kennedy, 24 January 1961, FRUS, XXIV, 1–2, 41–42. McNamara and VanDeMark, *In Retrospect*, 36.

12. Report Prepared by the Inter-Agency Task Force on Laos, 23 January 1961, FRUS, XXIV, 28–40.

13. SNIE 58-61, Probable Communist Reactions to Certain U.S. Courses of Action with Respect to Laos, FRUS, XXIV, 59–61.

14. Memorandum of Conference with President Kennedy, 9 March 1961, FRUS, XXIV, 77–78.

15. Reeves, *President Kennedy*, 112, puts this discussion after the Bay of Pigs, but Hilsman, *To Move a Nation*, 128, locates it before.

16. Rostow memo to Kennedy, 17 March 1961. Cited in Newman, *JFK and Vietnam*, 13.

17. Schlesinger, *Thousand Days*, 332–33. He incorrectly describes this as a meeting of the NSC.

18. Bundy to Kennedy, 1 April 1961, FRUS, XXIV, 112–14.

19. Hall, "The Laos Neutralization Agreement, 1962," 443.

20. Sorensen, *Kennedy*, 644. He said something similar to Schlesinger, *Thousand Days*, 308.

21. See Hall, "The Laos Crisis of 1961–62." Also Schlesinger, *Thousand Days*, 257–58.

22. Vientiane to State, 26 April 1961; Memorandum of Meeting with President Kennedy, 26 April 1961, FRUS, XXIV, 139–40, 142–44.

23. Bowles to Rusk, 27 April 1961; Rusk to Bowles, 28 April 1961, FRUS, XXIV, 147–49. Rusk at the time was in Ankara attending a NATO meeting.

24. Newman, *JFK and Vietnam*, 16.

25. Cited in Schlesinger, *Thousand Days*, 306, who appears to have got the day wrong.

26. Memorandum of Conversation, 29 April 1961, FRUS, XXIV, 150–54.

27. Beschloss, *KvK*, 161. Kaiser, *American Tragedy*, 51.

28. Notes on the 481st National Security Council Meeting, 1 May 1961, FRUS, XXIV, 162–64.

29. McNamara and Gilpatric to Kennedy, 2 May 1961; Editorial Note, FRUS, XXIV, 166–70.

30. Hall, "The Laos Neutralization Agreement, 1962," 446; Bundy to Kennedy, 1 April 1961, FRUS, XXIV, 114–15.

31. Gibbons, *The United States Government and the Vietnam War*, 2:49.

Chapter 33

1. William Sullivan oral history interview, 5 August 1970. Cited in Gibbons, *The United States Government and the Vietnam War*, 2:24.

2. See comments by William Bundy in ibid., 2:41.

3. Kattenburg, *The Vietnam Trauma*, 88.

4. Maechling, "Insurgency and Counter-Insurgency."

5. Cannon, "Raising the Stakes," 128–29.

6. Rostow to Kennedy, 10 May 1961, FRUS, I, Document 51.

7. Rostow, *The Diffusion of Power*, 265.

8. McClintock, *Instruments of Statecraft*, 199–200; Currey, *Edward Lansdale*.

9. Meeting, 28 January 1961, FRUS, I, 13–19.

10. Lansdale to Diem, 30 January 1961, FRUS, I, 20–23.

11. Rostow to Kennedy, 12 April 1961; Kennedy to Diem, 26 April 1961, FRUS, I, 68–69, 81. A second letter with a number of specific proposals was sent on 8 May.

12. Nolting, 14 July 1961, FRUS, I, 217–18.

13. Gilpatric oral history interview, cited in Cannon, "Raising the Stakes," 130.

14. Rusk, *As I Saw It*, 431.

15. *PP* II, 48–49.

16. Lansdale to Gilpatric, 10 May 1961, cited in Gaddis, *Strategies of Containment*, 244; Newman, *JFK and Vietnam*, 59.

17. Second Meeting of the Presidential Task Force on Vietnam, 4 May 1961, and Rostow to Kennedy, 10 May 1961, FRUS, I, 115–23, 131–32; *PP* II, 49.

18. Report by the Vice President, 23 (?) May 1961, FRUS, I, 152–57.

Chapter 34

1. Rostow, *The Diffusion of Power*, 284.

2. Rostow, "Guerrilla Warfare in Underdeveloped Areas," 108–16. The speech is discussed by Rostow in *The Diffusion of Power*, 284–86. See also Blaufarb, *The Counter-Insurgency Era*, 57–59.

3. Rostow to Bundy, 26 May 1961. Also Rostow to Kennedy, 11 May 1961, UPA. *John F Kennedy National Security File.*

4. Rostow, *The Diffusion of Power*, 286.

5. Taylor, *Swords and Plowshares*, 221.

6. Rostow to Rusk, 13 July 1961, FRUS, I, 206–7.

7. Memorandum, 18 July 1961; William Bundy to Lemnitzer, 19 July 1961; Taylor, 15 July 1961; Taylor to President, FRUS, I, 232, 233–34, 223–25, 243–44.

8. Rostow to President, FRUS, XXIV, 315–17. Ball, *Vietnam-on-the-Potomac*, 57.

9. Halberstam, *The Best and the Brightest*, 76. See also Gibbons, *The United States Government and the Vietnam War*, 2:48–49, and Buzzanco, *Masters of War*, 100. Kaiser, who properly recognizes this as a myth, notes that Reston later indicated that this was only his inference. *American Tragedy*, 102.

10. See, for example, a memo by Robert Komer of the NSC staff on 20 July, reported by Gibbons, *The United States Government and the Vietnam War*, 2:57–58.

11. Robert Johnson to Rostow, 5 September 1961, FRUS, I, 293–95.

12. Rostow and Taylor to Kennedy, 27 July 1961, FRUS, I, 248–49.

13. Memorandum from Steeves, 28 July 1961, FRUS, I, 250–51. Steeves was acting assistant secretary of state for Far Eastern affairs and chair of the Southeast Asia Task Force.

14. Memorandum, 28 July 1961, FRUS, I, 252–56. The mention of the French experience would have pleased President de Gaulle, who noted in his memoirs how Kennedy had appeared not to take any notice of his warnings. He had told the president, "[Y]ou will find that intervention in this area is an endless entanglement. Once a nation has been aroused no foreign power, however strong, can impose its will on it. . . . You will sink step by step into a bottomless political quagmire." De Gaulle, *Memoirs, Renewal and Endeavor*, 256.

15. Kennedy to Diem, 5 August 1961, FRUS, I, 263–67.

16. Rostow to Kennedy, 4 August 1961, FRUS, XXIV, 341.

17. Memorandum, 28 July 1961, FRUS, XXIV, 326.

18. Cannon, "Raising the Stakes," 135; Rostow to President, 29 July 1961, FRUS, I, 256–57.

19. Rostow to Kennedy, 4 August 1961, FRUS, XXIV, 341.

20. Taylor to Kennedy; Rostow to Kennedy, 11 August 1961, FRUS, XXIV, 358–60, 361.

21. Gibbons, *The United States Government and the Vietnam War*, 2:63.

22. Kennedy to Rusk, 14 August 1961, FRUS, XXIV, 370.

23. Rostow was more optimistic about the regional members of SEATO—Australia, New Zealand, the Philippines, and Pakistan—as being willing to start planning for a wider range of contingencies.

24. Rostow to President, 17 August 1961, FRUS, XXIV, 371–74.

25. Taylor to Johnson, 22 August 1961, FRUS, XXIV, 375–76.

26. Gibbons, *The United States Government and the Vietnam War*, 2:64.

27. Meeting, 29 August 1961, FRUS, XXIV, 390–98.

Chapter 35

1. Rostow to President, 5 October 1961, cited in Cannon, "Raising the Stakes," 137.

2. PP II, 82. Lemnitzer to Felt, 13 October 1961, FRUS, I, 362.

3. Kahin, *Intervention*, 136.

4. Rusk, *As I Saw It*, 431.

5. Hilsman, *To Move a Nation*, 421.

6. Cited in Rust, *Kennedy in Vietnam*, 45.

7. Taylor to President, 3 November 1961, FRUS, I, 477–532.

8. The NSC meeting of 15 November has Allen Dulles, in one of his last meetings as director of central intelligence, cautioned against the assumption that the "ideological rift were such that the Soviets and Chinese would not be able nor willing to engage jointly any nation which threatened communist interests." Notes on NSC Meeting, 15 November 1961, FRUS, I, 607.

9. Rostow had warned the president on 15 September that the conflict was now entering the Chinese leader's "Stage 2," which meant "the end of guerrilla warfare and the beginning of open warfare." Rostow to President, FRUS, I, 299.

10. Interview with Walt Rostow, "Cold War."

11. Kaiser, *American Tragedy*, 93–94; PP II, 75. A later estimate observed that even if Laos was blocked off, the infiltrators could still take the longer route through Cambodia.

12. McGarr to Lemnitzer, 12 October 1961, FRUS, I, 351.

13. Tanham, *Communist Revolutionary Warfare*. These findings were based on a field trip undertaken in the summer of 1961. Tanham was being considered at this time as a possible consultant to MAAG.

14. Currey, *Edward Lansdale*, 237–38.

15. Appendix C to report.

16. Gibbons, *The U.S. Government and the Vietnam War*, 2:76, 79.

17. Ibid., 67.

18. Ibid., 67–68; *PP* II, 74.

19. Johnson, 11 October 1961, *PP* II, 70.

20. *PP* II, 83–84.

21. Charlton and Moncrieff, *Many Reasons Why*, 74.

22. The idea of using military personnel for flood relief appears to have originated with McGarr. McGarr to Felt, 23 October 1961, FRUS, I, 424–25. Taylor insisted that this was not simply cover for the introduction of U.S. troops, as the flood was a real problem. Taylor to State, 27 October 1961, FRUS, I, 442.

23. Komer to Bundy, 31 October 1961, FRUS, I, 81; Gaddis, *Strategies of Containment*, 244–45.

24. Rostow to Taylor, 16 October 1961, FRUS, I, 381–82.

25. Schlesinger, *Thousand Days*, 546–47. Sterling Cottrell described the "Rostow Plan" as "applying graduated punitive measures on the DRV with weapons of our choosing." *PP* II, 946.

26. *PP* II, 92, 97.

27. This Special National Intelligence Estimate of 5 November is paraphrased in *PP* II, 107.

Chapter 36

1. McNamara to President, 8 November 1961, FRUS, I, 599–61; Gibbons, *The United States Government and the Vietnam War*, 2:86–88.

2. McNamara and VanDeMark, *In Retrospect*, 39. This contradicts the view in *PP* II, 110, and Kahin, *Intervention*, 137, that the shift from McNamara's first to his second memo came at the president's urging. There is no evidence that the president engaged in any discussions with McNamara between the two memos.

3. *PP* II, 110–16.

4. Rostow to President, 11 and 12 November 1961, FRUS, I, 573–75, 579.

5. Ball, *The Past Has Another Pattern*, 366–67. There are indications that Ball had been sharing his concerns with other officials at this time.

6. Ball, "JFK's Big Moment," 20. So taken aback was Ball that he was "deterred . . . from expressing opposition to the war until after the Tonkin Gulf incident." This indicates the extent to which Ball was not a member of Kennedy's inner circle.

7. Schlesinger, *Thousand Days*, 547.

8. Hilsman, *To Move a Nation*, 439.

9. Draft National Security Action Memorandum, 13 November 1961; Notes of Meeting at White House, 11 November 1961; Bundy to Kennedy, 15 November 1961; Notes on NSC Meeting, 15 November 1961, FRUS, I, 577–78, 605–7, 591–94, 607–10. Buzzanco's claim that the president's "critical ruminations

amounted to little more than devil's advocacy" (*Masters of War*, 111) ignores all the corroborative evidence on Kennedy's thought processes and is best seen as what happens when an implausible thesis meets an unpalatable fact.

10. National Security Action Memorandum No. 111, 22 November 1961, FRUS, I, 656–57.

11. Martin to Cottrell, 18 December 1961, FRUS, I, 742–44.

12. *PP* II, 122–25.

13. Cited in Hilsman, *To Move a Nation*, 426.

14. Gibbons, *The United States Government and the Vietnam War*, 2:105.

15. Hilsman, *To Move a Nation*, 424–27; Blaufarb, *The Counter-Insurgency Era*, 6–62. The essay was reprinted in Greene, ed., *The Guerrilla and How to Fight Him*. This also included Rostow's June speech at Fort Bragg with a foreword by the president.

16. Hilsman to Rusk, 16 November 1961, FRUS, I, 619–28.

17. See, for example, Kennedy to McNamara, 11 January 1962, FRUS, VIII, 235.

18. In Saigon, the CIA station chief, William Colby, was also a proponent of establishing self-help defensive groups among the population who would not have any military designation. Colby, *Honorable Men*, 169; Beckett, "Robert Thompson and the British Advisory Mission to South Vietnam, 1961–1965." For Thompson's own account, see Thompson, *Defeating Communist Insurgency*. See also Cannon, "Raising the Stakes." An example of the points of contention was the Vietnamese Civil Guard. The Americans had been trying to turn the Guard into an efficient military outfit, but their lack of training had made them easy prey to the Viet Cong, who found them a handy source of weapons. General McGarr, head of MAAG, wanted to persevere with the training, while Thompson thought they should be put under police control and brought closer to the population.

19. Bundy to Kennedy, 15 November 1961, FRUS, I, 612–14.

20. Ralph Dungan, cited in Strober and Strober, *Let Us Begin Anew*, 187.

21. Bradlee, *Conversations with Kennedy*, 53; Winters, *The Year of the Hare*, 21. Forrestal was also a close friend of the Kennedys.

22. Newman, *JFK and Vietnam*, 147; McNamara and VanDeMark, *In Retrospect*, 41.

23. McNamara and VanDeMark, *In Retrospect*, 41.

24. Krepinevich, *The Army and Vietnam*, 64–65.

25. McGarr to Lemnitzer, 27 December 1961; Lansdale to General Samuel Williams, 28 November 1961, FRUS, I, 765, 687–89.

Chapter 37

1. Kahin, *Intervention*, 138. This is also the view of Logevall, *Choosing War*.

2. Galbraith, *Ambassador's Journal*, 224, 233.

3. Gibbons, *The United States Government and the Vietnam War*, 2:82–83.

4. Cooper points out that though a "Harriman-Pushkin" agreement along these lines was not published as part of the record, it was implied in the respon-

sibility assigned to the cochairman to report any violations of the accords. *The Lost Crusade*, 190. Moscow never admitted to this understanding.

5. Harriman to State, 13 September 1961, 29 September 1961, FRUS, XXIV, 411, 437.

6. FRUS, I, 321.

7. State to Harriman, 6 October 1961, FRUS, XXIV, 457. Sullivan, Harriman's deputy, confirms that Kennedy was "constantly looking for opportunities to see if we could expand from the Laos agreement." Gibbons, *The United States Government and the Vietnam War*, 2:121. For a vivid description of the Geneva talks, including their sheer tedium, see Cooper, *The Lost Crusade*, 182–91.

8. Kaiser, *American Tragedy*, 111, 114–15. *PP* II, 119.

9. Krock, *Memoirs*, 323–24.

10. Kennedy to Khrushchev, 16 October 1961, FRUS, VI, 38–44.

11. Harriman to Kennedy, 12 November 1961; Rostow to President, 14 November 1961, FRUS, I, 580–82, 601–3.

12. Khrushchev to Kennedy, FRUS, VI, 58–61.

13. Kennedy to Rusk and McNamara, 14 November 1961, FRUS, I, 603–4.

14. Kennedy to Khrushchev, 16 November 1961. The full text is in FRUS, VI, 61–64.

15. Memorandum of Conversation, 28 December 1962, FRUS, V, 599. Harriman recalled that it was Pushkin who had first raised the possibility of talks on a settlement.

16. Hilsman, *To Move a Nation*, 138–40.

17. Rusk to Kennedy, Memorandum, 6 January 1962, FRUS, XXIV, 568–73.

18. Kennedy to Vientiane, Hilsman to Harriman, Forrestal to Kennedy, 17 April 1962; National Security Action Memorandum No. 149, 19 April 1962; Forrestal to Kennedy, 2 May and 22 May 1962, FRUS, XXIV, 633–34, 688–89, 694–96, 711–12, 783; Hilsman, *To Move a Nation*, 141; Newman, *JFK and Vietnam*, 263.

19. Usowski, "Intelligence Estimates and U.S. Policy Toward Laos, 1960–63," 382–83.

20. Memorandum, 29 August 1961, FRUS, XXIV, 398. On the Meo campaign, see Blaufarb, *The Counter-Insurgency Era*, ch. 5.

21. Stevenson, *The End of Nowhere*, 170. Harriman also detected the hand of the CIA, adding to his distrust of the agency. McCone complained at one point that Harriman's views on the CIA were being circulated within Washington.

22. Hilsman, *To Move a Nation*, 141.

23. State to Vientiane, 12 May 1962; Telephone Conversation between Kennedy and Ball, 11 May 1962, FRUS, XXIV, 755–58, 741. Newman cites an unpublished manuscript by William Bundy with essentially the same suggestion. Newman, *JFK and Vietnam*, 263. See also Hall, "The Laos Neutralization Agreement, 1962," 449.

24. Special National Intelligence Estimate, Implications of the Fall of Nam Tha, 9 May 1962; Forrestal to Kennedy, 10 May 1962, FRUS, XXIV, 726–29, 729–33.

25. Pelz, " 'When Do I Have Time to Think?' "; Memorandum, 10 May 1962, FRUS, XXIV, 734–35. The memorandum contains no report of any military objections. Contrary to Hilsman's recollection (Hilsman, *To Move a Nation*, 144), this was not a full National Security Council meeting.

26. McCone took McNamara and Lemnitzer to give Eisenhower a full briefing on 13 May. Kennedy to Ball, 11 May 1962, FRUS, XXIV, 741–42, 760–61.

27. Newman, *JFK and Vietnam*, 264–66. This account is based on an interview with George Allen, then of DIA, who was present at the meeting. The Joint Chiefs later gave McNamara a memorandum confirming the earlier positions: The incident demonstrated the need to support Phoumi more firmly and disregard Souvanna, whom they saw as being ineffectual and unable to control the Pathet Lao. This firm support could take the form of air support and preparations for a full-scale intervention. Joint Chiefs of Staff to McNamara, 11 May 1962, in FRUS, XXIV, 742–44. McNamara's own annotations noted that the Chiefs had not appraised the "ChiCom and NVN capability."

28. Forrestal to Kennedy, 12 May 1962, FRUS, XXIV, 747; Kaiser, *American Tragedy*, 136.

29. On the origins of the paper, see Pelz, " 'When Do I Have Time to Think?' " 225.

30. Hilsman to Harriman, 12 May 1962; Memorandum, 12 May 1962; State to Vientiane, 12 May 1962; Memorandum, 13 May 1962, FRUS, XXIV, 748–54, 345–46, 755–58, 760.

31. Khrushchev to Kennedy, 12 June 1962; Kennedy to Khrushchev, 12 June 1962, FRUS, VI, 134–36. This was a public exchange of letters. *Robert Kennedy: in His Own Words*, 260.

32. Duiker, *U.S. Containment Policy and the Conflict in Indochina*, 205–6.

33. Bowles, reporting on a recent Asian trip, also argued for consideration of a negotiated settlement. Galbraith to Kennedy, Bowles to President, 4 April 1962, FRUS, II, 297–98, 301.

34. Memorandum, 6 April 1962; Williams to McNamara, 14 April 1962; Wood to Harriman, 11 May 1962; Galbraith to Harriman, 19 April 1962; Memorandum, 1 May 1962, FRUS, II, 309–10, 324–27, 387–89, 336, 367.

35. Galbraith to Harriman, 5 May 1962, 10 May 1962; Harriman to Galbraith, 16 May 1962, FRUS, II, 375–76, 379, 399.

36. Kennedy to Diem, 9 July 1962; Memorandum of Conversation, Harriman and North Vietnamese Foreign Minister, Geneva, 22 July 1962; Forrestal to Bundy, 31 July 1962, FRUS, II, 511–13, 867–70, 882; Kaiser, *American Tragedy*, 143.

37. Hall, "The Laos Neutralization Agreement, 1962," 454, 457.

38. Memorandum, 29 November 1962, FRUS, XXIV, 924.

39. Fursenko and Naftali, *Secret History*, 323.

40. Rust, *Kennedy in Vietnam*, 88; Usowski, "Intelligence Estimates and U.S. Policy Toward Laos," 338–340.

41. Summary Record of the 512th National Security Council Meeting, 20 April 1963; Telcom, Kennedy and Harriman, 21 April 1963, FRUS, XXIV, 979, 990.

42. Kennedy to Khrushchev, 23 April 1963, FRUS, VI, 271.

43. Memorandum, 30 April 1963; Memorandum, 26 April 1963; Memorandum, 9 August 1963, FRUS, XXIV, 1004–6; Forrestal interview with Hall, in "The Laos Neutralization Agreement, 1962," 458.

44. Rusk, *As I Saw It*, 429, 434; Rostow, *The Diffusion of Power*, 290.

Chapter 38

1. Quoted in Rust, *Kennedy in Vietnam*, 69.
2. Charlton and Moncrieff, *Many Reasons Why*, 73.
3. *PP* II, 12, 175; McNamara and VanDeMark, *In Retrospect*, 48–49.
4. FRUS, III, 1.
5. For Vann's story, see Sheehan, *A Bright Shining Lie*. See also Newman, *JFK and Vietnam*, 316–19.
6. Hilsman and Forrestal to Kennedy, 25 January 1963 FRUS, III, 49–62; Current Intelligence Memorandum, CIA, 11 January 1963, 19–22. Hilsman noted that optimism in Saigon was based on the vigor with which Nhu had promoted the strategic hamlets program, which had persuaded even Robert Thompson that his earlier pessimism—that too much was being attempted too quickly—was wrong. Hilsman memo, January 1963, 5.
7. Report of an Investigative Team Headed by the Chief of Staff, United States Army (Wheeler), to the Joint Chiefs of Staff, January 1963, FRUS, III, 73–94.
8. Forrestal to Kennedy, 4 February 1963, FRUS, III, 97.
9. All of these had been confirmed at Ap Bac. The source for this section is Harold Ford's invaluable in-house CIA study, *Three Episodes on Vietnam*, episode 1. The final estimate appears as NIE 53–63, Prospects in South Vietnam, 17 April 1963, FRUS, III, 232–35. See also Newman, *JFK and Vietnam*, 313–14.
10. Cooper, *The Lost Crusade*, 193; Kaiser, *American Tragedy*, 128.
11. FRUS, II, 276.
12. Gibbons, *The United States Government and the Vietnam War*, 2:108–11.
13. Hammond, *Reporting Vietnam*, 4. Cooper, *The Lost Crusade*, 175.
14. Mecklin, *Mission in Torment*, 100.
15. This led to National Security Action Memorandum 217, 25 January 1963, FRUS, III, 63; Kern, Levering, and Levering, *The Kennedy Crises*, 144.
16. O'Donnell and Powers, "*Johnny, We Hardly Knew Ye*," 15; Gibbons, *The United States Government and the Vietnam War*, 2:131–34.
17. Cooper, *The Lost Crusade*, 198, 201.
18. Gibbons, *The United States Government and the Vietnam War*, 2:135.
19. Arnett, *Live from the Battlefield*, 97.
20. Cooper, *The Lost Crusade*, 196–97; Mecklin, *Mission in Torment*, 129–151.
21. Forrestal to Harriman, 8 February 1963, Saigon to State, 5 April 1963, FRUS, III, 105–6, 207–13.
22. Hammer, *A Death in November*, 121–22.

23. State to Saigon, 13 May 1963; Harkins to Diem 15 May 1963, Heavner to Hilsman, 15 May 1963, FRUS, III, 294–96, 300, 303–6.

24. Hammer, *Death in November*, 124. Gibbons, *The U.S. Government and the Vietnam War*, 2:137–8.

25. Halberstam, *The Making of a Quagmire*, 194. This criticism is particularly intense in Winters, *The Year of the Hare*. For a more favorable assessment see Prochnau, *Once Upon a Distant War*.

26. Cited in Hammer, *Death in November*, 156. Hammond, *Reporting Vietnam*, 11.

27. Morgenthau, "Vietnam—Another Korea." The importance of this essay is noted by Gibbons, *The United States Government and the Vietnam War*, 2:139–40.

28. Charles Mohr, "Vietnam—Where We Stand and Why." On its importance for Lodge, see Blair, *Lodge in Vietnam: A Patriot Abroad*, 21.

Chapter 39

1. Gibbons, *The United States Government and the Vietnam War*, 2:139.

2. Kennedy may not have been aware of this. Lodge was proud of the fact. Cooper, *The Lost Crusade*, 211.

3. Report to President, undated, FRUS, III, 531–43.

4. Telegram from the Department of State to the Embassy in Vietnam, 24 August 1961, FRUS, III, 628–29. Hilsman's account, which has been challenged in a number of respects, is found in Hilsman, *To Move a Nation*, 488; Newman, *JFK and Vietnam*, 346–51.

5. McNamara and VanDeMark, *In Retrospect*, 54.

6. Hammer, *Death in November*, 180, 182.

7. Schlesinger, *Robert Kennedy*, 713–14.

8. Ibid., 713.

9. Charlton and Moncrieff, *Many Reasons Why*, 86.

10. Kattenburg, *The Vietnam Trauma*, 119–20. For Krulak's minutes, see *PP* II, 741–43, and for Hilsman's see FRUS, IV, 75–76. An editorial note indicates that Lodge had asked Kattenburg to warn that if the United States acquiesced in half measures, "we will be butted out of the country within six months to a year." Hilsman does not mention the incident in his own account of the meeting (Hilsman, *To Move a Nation*, 496–97) but concentrates on the novelty of Johnson being given the chance to present his views.

11. FRUS, IV, 75.

12. State to Saigon, 12 September 1963; Telephone Conversation Between Rusk and Harriman, 31 August 1963, FRUS, IV, 197, 69, 186.

13. Memorandum of a Conversation, Department of State, 30 August 1963, FRUS, IV, 53–57.

14. Blair, *Lodge in Vietnam*, 37.

15. Telegram from the Department of State to the Embassy in Vietnam, FRUS, IV, 79. The pressures were summed up by a *New York Times* story of 31 August juxtaposing U.S. disapproval of the repression of the Buddhists with a story of

two more American advisers killed. Memorandum of Conversation Between Hilsman and Bundy, 31 August 1963, FRUS, IV, 75.

16. *PP* II, 738–39.

17. Cited in Blair, *Lodge in Vietnam*, 46.

18. Kern, Levering, and Levering, *The Kennedy Crises*, 149.

19. Bundy to President, 1 September 1963, FRUS, IV, 82.

20. Salinger, *With Kennedy*, 114.

21. Interview with President, 2 September 1963, FRUS, IV, 93–95.

22. Gibbons, *The United States Government and the Vietnam War*, 2:163.

23. Memorandum of Conference with President, 3 September 1963, Taylor to President, undated, FRUS, IV, 98–99, 103.

24. State to Saigon, 3 September, FRUS, IV, 104–6. For the first draft, see 96–97.

25. Lodge's views are in Telegrams of 4 and 5 September, FRUS, IV, 107–8, 109–10. Kennedy to Hilsman, 5 September; Report on Hilsman and Congress, 5 September, FRUS, IV, 111–12, 113.

26. Conference with the President, 6 September 1963; State to Lodge, 6 September 1963; Lodge to State, 9 September 1963, FRUS, IV, 117–20, 128–29, 140–43.

27. Report by the Joint Chiefs of Staff's Special Assistant for Counterinsurgency and Special Activities (Krulak), 10 September 1963; Memorandum, 10 September 1963, FRUS, IV, 153–60, 161–67.

28. The previous year Mendenhall had written: "[W]e cannot win the war with the Diem-Nhu methods, and we cannot change those methods no matter how much pressure we put on them. Recommendation: get rid of Diem, Mr. and Mrs. Nhu and the rest of the Ngo family." Mendenhall, Vietnam—Assessments and Recommendations, 16 August 1962, FRUS, II, 598.

29. According to Hilsman, there was an "awkward silence" at this point as the specter of a land war in Asia was raised. It "raised Robert Kennedy's question in everyone's minds—was this the time to withdraw entirely?" Hilsman, *To Move a Nation*, 504.

30. Memoranda, 10 September 1963, FRUS, IV, 161–67, 169–71.

31. Lodge to Rusk, 11 September 1963, FRUS, IV, 171–74.

32. He wrote directly to Lodge congratulating him on this "major cable." Blair, *Lodge in Vietnam*, 58.

33. Memorandum by Forrestal, 11 September 1963; Memorandum of Meeting, 12 September 1963, FRUS, IV, 181–83, 199–201. Bundy was following the minimalist line described by Forrestal and described himself to be in favor of waiting, even though Forrestal's memo can be read as a warning against minimalism. The instinctive recourse to the model of graduated pressure can be seen in a CIA memo of the same day which referred to "a program of graduated pressures on Diem which carefully signal to him the likelihood of more compelling U.S. actions, forced upon us by pressures of U.S. public and international opinion." FRUS, IV, 202.

34. The two are found in Memorandum from Hilsman to Rusk, 16 September 1963, FRUS, IV, 221–30.

35. Hilsman to Rusk, 16 September 1963; Forrestal to Bundy, Krulak to Taylor, 17 September 1962; White House to Lodge, 17 September 1963, FRUS, IV, 221–30, 235–36, 242–43, 254.

36. Saigon to State, 19 September 1963; Harkins to Krulak, FRUS, IV, 260–62, 194–95.

37. Blair, *Lodge in Vietnam*, 55.

38. Hilsman to Lodge, 23 September 1963, FRUS, IV, 282–83 (with editorial note on Lodge's reply). Hilsman assumed that generals might be reluctant to undertake a coup because such events tend to allow colonels and majors to displace them.

Chapter 40

1. FRUS, xxiv, 488–89; Kaiser, *American Tragedy*, 257–58. Although I do not fully share his depiction of Kennedy's policies and motives, Logevall's *Choosing War* provides a substantial and authoritative analysis of the diplomatic activity at this time, and the options that might have been available.

2. Hammer, *A Death in November*, 222–30.

3. This analysis was prompted by the Alsop column on 18 September (see note 5 below). CIA Station in Saigon to Agency, 2 September 1963; Memorandum for McCone, 26 September, 1963, FRUS, IV, 89–90, 295–98. There is no evidence Nhu had contact with the North; see McNamara et al, *Argument without End*, 111. This book contains careful analysis, informed by North Vietnamese input, of the diplomatic activity of this time.

4. Saigon to State, Harriman and McCone, 13 September 1963; Call Between Harriman and McCone, 13 September, 1963, FRUS, IV, 203–4.

5. On 18 September 1963 Alsop published "Very Ugly Stuff" in the *Washington Post*, which highlighted the contacts. Blair, *Lodge in Vietnam*, 52–53.

6. Kern, Levering, and Levering, *The Kennedy Crises*, 174–75.

7. White House to Lodge, 17 September 1963, FRUS, IV, 252–54.

8. Meeting in White House, 23 September 1963; Lodge to State, Forrestal to Bundy, 16 September 1963, FRUS, IV, 280–82, 255, 235.

9. Summary record of the 519th Meeting of the National Security Council, 2 October 1963; Memorandum from Taylor and McNamara to the President, 2 October 1963; Sullivan to Hilsman, 3 October 1963, FRUS, IV, 350–52, 336–46, 357–58.

10. Blair, *Lodge in Vietnam*, 61.

11. Saigon to State, 19 September 1963, FRUS, IV, 260–63. See also 272–73 and 291–92.

12. Harkins to Felt (commander in chief, Pacific), 20 September 1963, FRUS, IV; 274–75. The previous day Taylor had also been visited by ex-ambassador Tran Van Chuong "to warn me against the optimistic reports on the military situation coming from military officials in South Vietnam. He is convinced that the basic facts are quite different." Memorandum by Taylor, 19 September 1963, FRUS, IV, 274–75, 268.

13. Memorandum by Sullivan, approx. 5 October 1963, FRUS, IV, 380–83.

14. Saigon to State, 30 September 1963, FRUS, IV, 321–23.

15. Memorandum, 29 September 1963, FRUS, IV, 310–21.

16. Taylor and McNamara to Kennedy, 2 October 1963, FRUS, IV, 339, 345–46.

17. Memorandum of Meeting, 23 September 1963, FRUS, IV, Documents 141, 143.

18. Halberstam, *The Making of a Quagmire*, 268.

19. Meeting, 2 October 1963, Eliades transcript; McNamara and VanDeMark, *In Retrospect*, 80.

20. Summary Record of 519th NSC Meeting, 2 October 1963, FRUS, IV, 350–52; Cooper, *The Lost Crusade*, 216.

21. Schlesinger, *Robert Kennedy*, 716–17.

22. Meeting, 2 October 1963, Eliades transcript.

23. Report of meeting, 5 October 1963, FRUS, IV, 368–70. The discussion of coup planning is not in the official record. It comes from the tape recording (Weir transcript).

24. Rusk to Lodge, Bundy to Lodge, 5 October 1963, FRUS, IV, 371–79.

25. Somewhat bizarrely, Lodge wanted Lansdale to be sent to take his place. It is not clear whether Lodge appreciated the depth of Lansdale's pro-Diem sentiment. At any rate, the request was quickly refused.

26. Bundy to Lodge and Harkins, 24 October 1963, FRUS, IV, 429.

27. Meeting, 25 October 1963, Eliades transcript.

28. Lodge to State, 28 October 1963, FRUS, IV, 442–46.

29. Memorandum of Conversations with President, 29 October 1963, 468–71, 472–73; Eliades transcript.

30. Bundy to Lodge, 29 October 1963, FRUS, IV, 473–75.

31. Lodge to State, 30 October 1963, FRUS, IV, 484–88. This was a strong statement in favor of a coup with which Harkins, who was strongly opposed to the idea, refused to concur. Harkins to Taylor, 30 October 1963, FRUS, IV, 479–82.

32. Meeting on 30 October 1963, Eliades transcript; Bundy to Lodge, 30 October 1963, FRUS, IV, 500–2.

33. Interview in Rust, *Kennedy in Vietnam*, 158.

34. Compare Schlesinger, *Robert Kennedy*, 714, which mentions discussions of the possibility of firing Lodge, and Schlesinger, *Thousand Days*, 990 ("The White House doubters had been mistaken about Lodge"). McNamara is particularly critical of Lodge; see McNamara and VanDeMark, *In Retrospect*.

35. Lodge to State, 1 November 1963, FRUS, IV, 513, 519–20.

36. Tape, 4 November 1963, Eliades transcript.

37. Saigon to State, 6 November 1963, FRUS, IV, 577–78.

Chapter 41

1. For a collection, see Schlesinger, *Robert Kennedy*, 710–12.

2. *Robert Kennedy in His Own Words*. On the lack of a definite plan, see Rusk, *As I Saw It*, 441–42.

3. Lawrence Bassett and Stephen Pelz argue that Kennedy would have found it difficult to admit his failure or abandon a commitment he had made and just deepened; "The Failed Search for Victory: Vietnam and the Politics of War." See also Chomsky, *Rethinking Camelot*. A good discussion of the range of views on this issue is found in Logevall, "Vietnam and the Question of What Might Have Been." Dallek finds it difficult to imagine Kennedy and his advisers following any course other than escalation in 1964–65 but judges that he would have acted differently in 1966–67 when it became clear that the communists were not going to succumb to American power. Kennedy was a politician who resisted compounding errors and taking risks that could lead to a wider war or divisions at home. Dallek, "Lyndon Johnson and Vietnam."

4. After his hectic first year Kennedy had learned to appreciate some of the quiet virtues of the State Department (and Rusk). They may have been largely reactive and not full of clever initiatives, but for the same reason they did not create new problems. Schlesinger was not a fan of Rusk, nor was Robert Kennedy, and their views have affected later historiography. Rusk's role was never conspicuous, and he prided himself on giving his advice privately and then loyally implementing the president's wishes. My impression is that Kennedy grew to appreciate these qualities and took Rusk's advice regularly.

5. Beginning in early March cable traffic with Saigon reflected Johnson's desire to deny him any grounds for complaint. A series of compliments would "build a record" of support. To every proposal, Johnson instructed, the reply should be "Three Cheers! I think your suggestion is a good one." Beschloss, *Taking Charge*, 261.

6. The history of this document can be followed all the way through FRUS, VIII. For Bundy's final view, see 538.

7. Saigon to State, 16 October 1963; Harkins to Taylor, 30 October 1963, FRUS, IV, 401–3, 496–98.

8. Research Memorandum, RFE–90, 22 October 1963, Statistics on the War Effort in South Vietnam Show Unfavorable Trends, *PP* II, 770–80. The background to the document and the furor it generated is described in Hughes, "Experiencing McNamara," 9. Hughes to Rusk, FRUS, IV, 582–84, 635–36.

10. DIA, "The Viet Cong Improved Combat Effectiveness and Insurgency Posture," 13 December 1963, FRUS, IV, 707–10.

11. Hughes, "Experiencing McNamara," 163.

12. Blair, *Lodge in Vietnam*, 75–79.

13. Lodge to State, 4 November 1963, Kennedy to Lodge, 6 November 1963, FRUS, IV, 562–63, 635–37.

14. Rusk, *As I Saw It*, 441.

15. Reston, "Why a Truce in Korea and Not in Vietnam?" *New York Times*, 6 November 1963.

16. Halberstam, *The Making of a Quagmire*, 315–19.

17. Forrestal to Bundy, 7 November 1963, 13 November 1963, FRUS, IV, 581–82, 594–95.

18. Beschloss, *Taking Charge*, 6 and 27 May 1964, 226–27, 363–70.

19. Schlesinger, *Robert Kennedy*, 722.
20. Cited in Gibbons, *The U.S. Government and the Vietnam War*, 3:3.
21. Ford, *Three Episodes*; Logevall, *Choosing War*, 156–63.
22. The literature on Johnson's decision making is immense. My views are found in Freedman, "Vietnam and the Disillusioned Strategist." See, among others, and in addition to works already cited, Berman, *Planning a Tragedy*; Clodfelter, *The Limits of Air Power*; Gallucci, *Neither Peace nor Honor*; Gelb and Betts, *The Irony of Vietnam*; Gibbons, *The United States Government and the Vietnam War*, vol. 3; Smith, *An International History of the Vietnam War*, vol. 2, *The Struggle for South-East Asia, 1961–65*; Thies, *When Governments Collide*; VanDeMark, *Into the Quagmire*.
23. Hilsman, *To Move a Nation*, 525–26.
24. White House meeting, 22 November 1963; Memorandum of Meeting, 24 November 1963, FRUS, IV, 625–26, 637.
25. *PP* III, 150.
26. Newman, *JFK and Vietnam*, 375–76, 435.
27. Forrestal to President, 11 December 1963, FRUS, IV, 699.
28. Hilsman, *To Move a Nation*, 536.
29. Gibbons, *The United States Government and the Vietnam War*, 3:3.
30. Report by Krulak on McNamara's Visit, 21 December, FRUS, IV, 702–3.
31. McNamara to President, 21 December 1963, FRUS, IV, Document 374; Colby, *Honorable Men*, 219–20; *PP* III, 151.
32. Moise, *Tonkin Gulf*, 5.
33. FRUS, IV, 633–37.
34. Lodge, "Toward the Neutralization of North Vietnam," 3 December 1963. Note, however, that the document is dated 30 October. FRUS, IV, 656–59.
35. *PP* III, 154.
36. For example, he had argued in May 1962 for a campaign to inflict selective damage on North Vietnam. Rostow to Rusk, 31 May 1962, FRUS, II, 432–33.
37. Department of State, Policy Planning Council, Alternatives for the Imposition of Measured Pressures Against North Vietnam, 1 March 1964. See Johnson, "Escalation Then and Now." Johnson was the director of the study. Also see Halberstam, *The Best and the Brightest*, 434–39.
38. *PP* III, 156.
39. *Newsweek*, 9 March 1964. The magazine would have hit the newsstands earlier that week.
40. Beschloss, *Taking Charge*, 2 March 1964, 258, 265–66; Moise, *Tonkin Gulf*, 25, incorrectly suggests that the story had little to do with Rostow.
41. Ford, *Three Episodes*.
42. Beschloss, *Taking Charge*, 2 March 1964, 263.
43. Moise, *Tonkin Gulf*, 29.
44. Gibbons, *The United States Government and the Vietnam War*, 3:257.
45. Bundy to President, 31 August 1964. Cited in ibid., 349–50

Conclusion

1. Beschloss, *KvK*, 662–63.
2. Brogan, *Kennedy*, 123.
3. See, for example, Gaddis, *We Now Know*.

Bibliography

PRIMARY SOURCES

U.S. National Archives and Records Administration. *Public Papers of the Presidents of the United States, John F Kennedy*. Volumes for 1961, 1962, and 1963 published in Washington, D.C.: U.S. GPO, in 1962, 1963, and 1964, respectively.

Foreign Relations of the United States. Volumes from this series are referred to as FRUS in the manuscript. Unless otherwise stated, they are all from the 1961–63 collection and the volume numbers relate to the following titles and dates of publication.

I	Vietnam, 1961
II	Vietnam, 1962
III	Vietnam, January–August 1963
IV	Vietnam, August–December 1963
V	Soviet Union
VI	Kennedy-Khrushchev Exchanges
VII	Arms Control and Disarmament
VIII	National Security Policy
X	Cuba, January 1961–September 1962
XI	Cuba, October 1962–December 1963
XII	American Republics, 1961–1963
XIII	Western Europe and Canada
XIV	Berlin Crisis, 1961–1962
XV	Berlin Crisis, 1962–1963
XXII	Northeast Asia
XXIV	Laos Crisis

The National Security Archive has produced a number of valuable microfiche collections. I have made extensive use of the following:

NSA. *The Berlin Crisis: 1958–1962.* London: Chadwyck-Healy, 1993. (Referred to as NSA/Berlin)

NSA. *The Cuban Missile Crisis: The Making of U.S. Policy.* London: Chadwyck-Healy, 1990. (Referred to as NSA/Cuba)

NSA. *U.S. Nuclear History, 1955–1968* London: Chadwyck-Healy, 1997. (Referred to as NSA/nuclear).

I have also made use of *The John F Kennedy National Security File: U.S.SR and Eastern Europe, 1961–1963* (Bethesda, MD: University Publishers of America, 1987). These microfiche collections are available for use at the Liddell Hart Centre for Military Archives at King's College.

All oral histories referred to are in the JFK Library. Relevant excerpts appears in the NSA collections on Berlin and Cuba.

U.S. Congress, Senate. "Alleged Assassination Plots Involving Foreign Leaders." Washington, D.C.: Senate Select Committee to Study Governmental Operations with Respect to Intelligence Activities, 94th Congress, 1st session, 1975, is referred to as the Church Report.

I have used volumes 2 and 3 of the Senator Mike Gravel edition of *The Pentagon Papers: History of the United States Decision Making on Vietnam* (Boston: Beacon Press, 1971). They are referred to as PP II and PP III, respectively.

Ernest R. May's and Philip Zelikow's *The Kennedy Tapes: Inside the White House During the Cuban Missile Crisis* (Cambridge, Mass.: Harvard University Press, 1997) provides an invaluable source on the Cuban missile crisis and is referred to as *The Kennedy Tapes.*

For other transcripts I have used John F. Kennedy, *Presidential Recordings: Winning Senate Support for the Nuclear Test Ban Treaty, 1963* (Cambridge, Mass.: JFK Library, 1988), and also unfinished drafts of transcripts from George Eliades, Jill Kastner, and Andrew Weir. I also used a number of interviews conducted for the television series *The Cold War*, produced by Jeremy Isaacs, referred to as "The Cold War."

A volume of transcripts of discussions with participants in the Berlin crisis was produced under the auspices of the Nuclear History Program, as *Nuclear History Program: Berlin Crisis Oral History Project*, Transcripts (Center for International Security Studies at Maryland, School of Public Affairs, University of Maryland, 1994). These are referred to as NHP/Berlin.

Of the many secondary sources used, two deserve special mention, in addition to the classic works by Schlesinger and Sorensen. The first of these is Aleksandr Fursenko and Timothy Naftali, *"One Hell of a Gamble": The Secret History of the Cuban Missile Crisis* (New York: W. W. Norton, 1997). This book draws on remarkable documentary material from Moscow. It is referred to as *Secret History.* Some years ago Michael Beschloss covered much of this book's ground in his *Kennedy v. Khrushchev* (London: Faber, 1991). I have referred to this as Beschloss, *KvK.*

A number of Web sites now provide invaluable materials for historians. Four used regularly are:

National Security Archive: http://www.gwu.edu/~nsarchiv/index. html

Cold War International History Project: http://cwihp.si.edu

CIA Center for the Study of Intelligence: http://www.cia.gov/csi/index.html

State Department histories: http://www.state.gov/www/about_state/history/frus.html

SECONDARY SOURCES

Elie Abel. *The Missile Crisis.* Philadelphia: J. B. Lippincott, 1966.

Dean Acheson. *Power and Diplomacy.* Cambridge, Mass.: Harvard University Press, 1958.

Dean Acheson. "The Practice of Partnership." *Foreign Affairs* 41 (January 1963): 247–60.

Dean Acheson. *Present at the Creation.* New York: Norton, 1969.

Viktor Adamsky and Yuri Smirnov. "Moscow's Biggest Bomb. The 50-Megaton Test of October 1961." *Cold War International History Project Bulletin* 4 (1994).

Hannes Adomeit. *Soviet Risk-Taking and Crisis Behavior: A Theoretical and Empirical Analysis.* London: George Allen and Unwin, 1982.

Luis Aguilar, ed. *Operation Zapata: The "Ultrasensitive" Report and Testimony of the Board of Inquiry on the Bay of Pigs.* Frederick, Md: Aletheia Books, 1981.

Graham T. Allison. *Essence of Decision. Explaining the Cuban Missile Crisis.* Boston Little, Brown, 1971.

Graham T. Allison and Philip Zelikow, *Essence of Decision: Explaining the Cuban Missile Crisis,* 2nd ed., New York: Addison Wesley, 1999.

Bruce J. Allyn, James G. Blight, and David A. Welch. *Back to the Brink. Proceedings of the Moscow Conference on the Cuban Missile Crisis, January 27–28, 1989.* Cambridge: Harvard University, Center for Science and International Affairs, 1989.

Bruce J. Allyn, James G. Blight, and David A. Welch. *Cuba on the Brink. Castro, the Missile Collapse and the Soviet Collapse.* New York: Pantheon, 1993.

Stewart Alsop and Charles Bartlett. "In Time of Crisis," *Saturday Evening Post.* 8 December 1962.

Georgi Arbatov. *The System. An Insider's Life in Soviet Politics.* New York: Random House, 1992.

Peter Arnett. *Live from the Battlefield.* New York: Simon and Schuster, 1994.

William Attwood. *The Reds and the Blacks.* New York, 1967.

John C. Ausland. *Kennedy, Khrushchev, and the Berlin-Cuba Crisis, 1961–1964.* Oslo: Scandinavian University Press, 1996.

A. C. Bacevich. *The Pentomic Era: The U.S. Army Between Korea and Vietnam.* Washington, D.C.: National Defense University Press, 1986.

Desmond Ball. *Politics and Force Levels: The Strategic Missile Program of the Kennedy Administration*. Berkeley: University of California Press, 1980.

George Ball. "JFK's Big Moment." *New York Review of Books*, 13 February 1992.

George Ball. *The Past Has Another Pattern*. New York: Norton, 1992.

Moya Ann Ball. *Vietnam-on-the-Potomac*. New York: Praeger, 1992.

Lawrence J. Bassett and Stephen E. Pelz. "The Failed Search for Victory. Vietnam and the Politics of War." In *Kennedy's Quest for Victory, American Foreign Policy, 1961–1963*. Ed. Thomas G. Paterson. New York: Oxford University Press, 1989.

Ian Beckett. "Robert Thompson and the British Advisory Mission to South Vietnam, 1961–1965." *Small Wars and Insurgencies* 8, 3 (1997): 41–63.

Coral Bell. *The Conventions of Crisis. A Study in Diplomatic Management*. TK: Oxford University Press, 1971.

Larry Berman. *Planning a Tragedy: The Americanization of the War in Vietnam*. New York: Norton, 1982.

Barton Bernstein. "The Cuban Missile Crisis: Trading the Jupiters in Turkey?" *Political Science Quarterly* 95 (spring 1980).

Barton Bernstein. "Reconsidering the Missile Crisis. Dealing with the Problems of the American Jupiters in Turkey." In *The Cuban Missile Crisis Revisited*. Ed James Nathan. New York: St Martin's Press, 1992.

Michael Beschloss. *Kennedy v. Khrushchev*. London: Faber, 1991.

Michael Beschloss. *Mayday: Eisenhower, Khrushchev and the U-2 Affair*. New York: Harper, 1986.

Michael Beschloss. *Taking Charge. The Johnson White House Tapes, 1963–1964*. New York: Simon and Schuster, 1997.

Kai Bird. *The Color of Truth: McGeorge Bundy and William Bundy: Brothers in Arms*. New York: Simon and Schuster, 1998.

Richard M. Bissell, with Jonathan Lewis and Frances Pudlo. *Reflections of a Cold Warrior: From Yalta to the Bay of Pigs*. New Haven, Conn.: Yale University Press, 1996.

Richard M. Bissell. "Response to Lucien S. Vandenbroucke. 'The "Confessions" of Allen Dulles: New Evidence on the Bay of Pigs.'" *Diplomatic History* 8, 4 (autumn 1984).

Anne Blair. *Lodge in Vietnam: A Patriot Abroad* New Haven: Yale University Press, 1995.

Douglas Blaufarb. *The Counter-Insurgency Era. U.S. Doctrine and Performance* New York: The Free Press, 1977.

James G. Blight. *The Shattered Crystal Ball. Fear and Learning in the Cuban Missile Crisis*. Lanham, Md.: Rowman and Littlefield, 1992.

James G. Blight and Peter Kornbluh, eds. *Politics of Illusion. The Bay of Pigs Reexamined*. Boulder, Colo.: Lynne Rienner, 1998.

James G. Blight and David A. Welch. *On the Brink: Americans and Soviets Reexamine the Cuban Missile Crisis*. New York: Hill and Wang, 1989.

Philip Bobbit, Lawrence Freedman, and Greg Treverton, eds. *U.S. Nuclear Strategy: A Reader*. London: Macmillan, 1989.

Charles E. Bohlen. *Witness to History, 1929–1969.* New York: W. W. Norton, 1973.

Ken Booth. "Bernard Brodie." In *Makers of Nuclear Strategy.* Eds. John Baylis and John Garnett. London: Pinter, 1991.

Chester Bowles. *The Conscience of a Liberal. Selected Writings and Speeches.* New York, 1962.

Benjamin C. Bradlee. *Conversations with Kennedy.* New York: Norton, 1975.

H. W. Brands. *What American Owes the World. The Struggle for the Soul of Foreign Policy.* New York: Cambridge University Press, 1998.

Don Brennan, ed. *Arms Control, Disarmament and National Security.* New York: George Braziller, 1961.

Douglas Brinkley. *Dean Acheson. The Cold War Years, 1953–71.* New Haven: Yale University Press, 1992.

Jeff Broadwater. *Adlai Stevenson. The Odyssey of a Cold War Liberal.* New York: Twayne Publishers, 1994.

Bernard Brodie. *Escalation and the Nuclear Option.* Princeton, N.J.: Princeton University Press, 1966.

Bernard Brodie. "The McNamara Phenomenon." *World Politics* 17, 4 (July 1965).

Bernard Brodie. *War and Politics.* London: Cassell, 1973.

Bernard Brodie. "What Price Conventional Capabilities in Europe?" *The Reporter* 28 (May 1963).

Hugh Brogan. *Kennedy.* London: Longman, 1996.

Dino Brugioni. *Eyeball to Eyeball. The Inside Story of the Cuban Missile Crisis.* New York: Random House, 1991.

McGeorge Bundy. *Danger and Survival. Choices About the Bomb in the First Fifty Years.* New York: Random House, 1988.

McGeorge Bundy, ed. *The Patterns of Responsibility. Speeches and Statements of Dean Acheson.* Cambridge, Mass.: Riverside Press, 1951.

William Burr. "Soviet Cold War Military Strategy Using Declassified History." *Cold War International History Project Bulletin* 4 (1994).

Robert Buzzanco. *Masters of War: Military Dissent and Politics in the Vietnam Era.* Cambridge: Cambridge University Press, 1996.

Larry Cable. *Conflict of Myths: The Development of American Counterinsurgency Doctrine and the Vietnam War.* New York: New York University Press, 1986.

Dan Caldwell, ed., "Department of Defense Operations During the Cuban Missile Crisis: A Report by Adam Yarmolinsky, Special Assistant to the Secretary of Defense, 13 February 1963." *Naval War College Review* 32, 4 (June–July 1979).

Michael W. Cannon. "Raising the Stakes The Taylor-Rostow Mission." *The Journal of Strategic Studies* 12, 2 (June 1989): 125–65.

Honoré Marc Catudal. *Kennedy and the Berlin Wall Crisis.* Berlin: Verlag, 1980.

Gordon Chang. *Friends and Enemies. The United States, China, and the Soviet Union, 1948–1972.* Stanford, Calif.: Stanford University Press, 1990.

Laurence Chang and Peter Kornbluh. *The Cuban Missile Crisis, 1962.* New York: The New Press, 1992.

Michael Charlton and Anthony Moncrieff. *Many Reasons Why*. New York: Hill and Wang, 1978.

Noam Chomsky. *Rethinking Camelot: JFK, the Vietnam War, and U.S. Political Culture*. Boston, Mass.: South End Press, 1993.

Central Intelligence Agency. *CIA Targets Fidel: Secret 1967 CIA Inspector General's Report on Plots to Assassinate Fidel Castro*. Melbourne: Ocean Press, 1996.

Mark Clodfelter. *The Limits of Air Power. The American Bombing of North Vietnam* New York: Free Press, 1989.

Avner Cohen. *Israel and the Bomb*. New York: Columbia University Press, 1998.

William Colby. *Honorable Men*. New York: Simon and Schuster, 1989.

Chester Cooper. *The Lost Crusade: American in Vietnam*. New York: Dodd, Mead and Co., 1970.

Frank Costigliola. "The Pursuit of Atlantic Community." In *Kennedy's Quest for Victory: American Foreign Policy, 1961–1963*. Ed. Thomas G. Paterson. New York: Oxford University Press, 1989.

Norman Cousins. *The Improbable Triumvirate: John F. Kennedy, Pope John, Nikita Khrushchev*. New York: W. W. Norton, 1972.

Richard Crossman, ed. *The God that Failed*. New York: Harper, 1949.

Robert F. Cuervo. "John F. Kennedy and the Munich Myth." In *John F. Kennedy: The Promise Revisited*. Eds. Paul Harper and Joan Iversen. New York: Greenwood Press, 1988.

Cecil B. Currey. *Edward Lansdale. The Unquiet American*. Boston: Houghton Mifflin, 1988.

Robert Dallek. "Lyndon Johnson and Vietnam: The Making of a Tragedy." *Diplomatic History* 20, 2 (1996).

Charles de Gaulle. *Memoirs, Renewal and Endeavor*. New York: Simon and Schuster, 1971.

Michael Desch. " 'That Deep Mud in Cuba': The Strategic Threat and U.S. Planning for a Conventional Response During the Missile Crisis." *Security Studies* 1, 2 (winter 1991).

Robert A. Divine. *Blowing on the Wind. The Nuclear Test Ban Debate, 1954–1960*. New York: Oxford University Press, 1978.

William J. Duiken. *U.S. Containment Policy and the Conflict in Indochina*. Stanford, Calif.: Stanford University Press, 1994.

Allen Dulles. *The Craft of Intelligence*. London: Weiderfeld & Nicholson, 1963.

Harry Eckstein, ed. *Internal War*. New York: Free Press, 1964.

Alain Enthoven "American Deterrent Policy." In *Problems of National Strategy*. Ed. Henry Kissinger. New York: Praeger, 1965.

Alain Enthoven and Wayne Smith. *How Much Is Enough? Shaping the Defense Program, 1961–69*. New York: Harper and Row, 1971.

James Fetzer. "China." In *Kennedy's Quest for Victory: American Foreign Policy, 1961–1963*. Ed. Thomas G. Paterson. New York: Oxford University Press, 1989.

Rosemary Foot. *The Practice of Power: U.S. Relations with China Since 1949*. Oxford: Clarendon Press, 1995.

Harold P. Ford. "The CIA and Double Demonology: Calling the Sino-Soviet Split." *Studies in Intelligence* (winter 1998–99).

Harold P. Ford. *Three Episodes on Vietnam*. Langley, Va.: Center for the Study of Intelligence, CIA, 1998.

Lawrence Freedman. *The Evolution of Nuclear Strategy*. London: Macmillan, 1989.

Lawrence Freedman. "Henry Kissinger." In *Makers of Nuclear Strategy*. Eds. John Baylis and John Garnett. London: Pinter, 1991.

Lawrence Freedman. *U.S. Intelligence and the Soviet Strategic Threat*. Boulder, Colo.: Westview Press, 1977.

Lawrence Freedman. "Vietnam and the Disillusioned Strategist." *International Affairs* 72, 1 (1996).

Lawrence Freedman and John Gearson. "Interdependence and Independence: Nassau and the British Nuclear Deterrent." In *The United States and the European Alliance Since 1945*. Eds. Kathleen Burk and Melvyn Stokes. Oxford: Berg, 1999.

Aleksandr Fursenko and Timothy Naftali. *"One Hell of a Gamble": The Secret History of the Cuban Missile Crisis*. New York: W. W. Norton, 1997.

Aleksandr Fursenko and Timothy Naftali. "The Pitsunda Decision." *Cold War International History Bulletin* 10 (1998).

Aleksandr Fursenko and Timothy Naftali. "Soviet Intelligence and the Cuban Missile Crisis." In *Intelligence and the Cuban Missile Crisis*. Eds. James G. Blight and David A. Welch. London: Frank Cass, 1998.

John Gaddis. *Strategies of Containment. A Critical Appraisal of Postwar American National Security Policy*. Oxford: Oxford University Press, 1982.

John Lewis Gaddis. *We Now Know. Rethinking Cold War History*. Oxford: Clarendon Press, 1997.

John Kenneth Galbraith. *Ambassador's Journal. A Personal Account of the Kennedy Years*. New York: Houghton Mifflin, 1969.

Robert Gallucci. *Neither Peace nor Honor: The Politics of American Military Policy in Viet-Nam*. Baltimore: Johns Hopkins University Press, 1975.

David Galula. *Counterinsurgency Warfare: Theory and Practice*. New York: Praeger, 1964.

John Garnett. "Herman Kahn." In *Makers of Nuclear Strategy*. Eds. John Baylis and John Garnett. London: Pinter, 1991.

Raymond Garthoff. "Berlin 1961. The Record Corrected." *Foreign Policy* 84 (fall 1991): 142–56.

Raymond Garthoff. "The Meaning of Missiles." *Washington Quarterly* (autumn 1982).

Raymond Garthoff. "New Evidence on the Cuban Missile Crisis. Khrushchev, Nuclear Weapons and the Cuban Missile Crisis." *Cold War International History Bulletin* 11 (1998).

Raymond Garthoff. *Reflections on the Cuban Missile Crisis*. 2nd ed. Washington, D.C.: Brookings Institution, 1989.

Raymond Garthoff. "Unconventional Warfare in Communist Strategy." *Foreign Affairs* (July 1962).

Raymond Garthoff. "U.S. Intelligence in the Cuban Missile Crisis." In *Intelligence and the Cuban Missile Crisis*. Eds. James G. Blight and David A. Welch. London: Frank Cass, 1998.

John Gearson. *Harold Macmillan and the Berlin Wall Crisis, 1958–1962*. London: Macmillan, 1998.

Leslie H. Gelb and Richard K. Betts. *The Irony of Vietnam. The System Worked*. Washington, D.C.: Brookings Institution, 1979.

Harry Gelman. "The Sino-Soviet Conflict: A Survey." *Problems of Communism* 13 (March–April 1963).

Alexander George and William Simon, eds. *The Limits of Coercive Diplomacy*. Boston: Little, Brown, 1971.

William Conrad Gibbons. *The United States Government and the Vietnam War: Executive and Legislative Relationships, Vol. II, 1961–1964*. Princeton, N.J.: Princeton University Press, 1986.

William Conrad Gibbons. *The United States Government and the Vietnam War. Executive and Legislative Roles and Relationships, Vol. III, January–July 1965*. Princeton, N.J.: Princeton University Press, 1989.

James N. Giglio. *The Presidency of John F. Kennedy*. Lawrence: University Press of Kansas, 1991.

Steven Gillon. *Politics and Vision*. New York: Oxford University Press, 1987.

Abbott Gleason. *Totalitarianism. The Inner History of the Cold War*. New York: Oxford University Press, 1995.

Piero Gleijeses. *Shattered Hope. The Guatemalan Revolution and the United States, 1944–1954*. Princeton, N.J.: Princeton University Press, 1991.

Piero Gleijeses. "Ships in the Night: The CIA, the White House and the Bay of Pigs." *Journal of Latin American Studies* 27 (February 1995).

Richard N. Goodwin. "The Unthinkable and the Unanalyzable." *New Yorker*, 17 February 1968.

Graham Greene. *The Quiet American*. London: Penguin, 1969.

T. N. Greene, ed. *The Guerrilla and How to Fight Him*. New York: Praeger, 1962.

Anatoli I. Gribkov and William Y. Smith. *Operation ANADYR: The U.S. and Soviet Generals Recount the Cuban Missile Crisis*. Chicago: Edition Q, 1994.

Andrei Gromyko. *Memories*. Trans. Harold Shukman. London: Hutchinson, 1989.

David Halberstam. *The Best and the Brightest*. New York: Random House, 1972.

David Halberstam. *The Making of a Quagmire*. New York: Knopf, 1964.

David K. Hall. "The Laos Crisis of 1961–62." In *The Limits of Coercive Diplomacy*. Eds. Alexander George and William Simon. 2nd ed. Boulder, Colo.: Westview Press, 1994.

David K. Hall. "The Laos Neutralization Agreement, 1962." In *U.S.-Soviet Security: Cooperation, Achievements, Failures, Lessons*. Eds. Alexander L. George, Philip J. Farley, and Alexander Dallin. New York: Oxford University Press, 1988.

William M. Hammond. *Reporting Vietnam: Media & Military at War*. Lawrence: University Press of Kansas, 1998.

Hope Harrison. "Ulbricht and the Concrete 'Rose': New Archival Evidence on the Dynamics of Soviet–East German Relations and the Berlin Crisis, 1958–61." Washington, D.C.: Cold War International History Project, 1993.

B. H. Liddell Hart. *Deterrent or Defense*. New York: Praeger, 1960.

Otto Heilbrunn. *Partisan Warfare*. New York: Praeger, 1962.

John Helgerson. *CIA Briefings of Presidential Candidates, 1952–1992*. Langley, Va.: Center for the Study of Intelligence, CIA, 1996.

Greg Herken. *Counsels of War*. New York: Oxford University Press, 1985.

Seymour Hersh. *The Dark Side of Camelot*. New York: Little, Brown, 1997.

James Hershberg. "Before 'The Missiles of October': Did Kennedy Plan a Military Strike Against Cuba?" In *The Cuban Missile Crisis Revisited*. Ed. James Nathan. New York: St. Martin's Press, 1992.

James Hershberg. "More New Evidence on the Cuban Missile Crisis: More Documents from the Russian Archives." *Cold War International History Project Bulletin* 8–9 (winter 1996–97): 270–73.

Beatrice Heuser. *NATO, Britain, France and the FRG. Nuclear Strategies and Forces for Europe, 1949–2000*. London: Macmillan, 1997.

Trumball Higgins. *The Perfect Failure. Kennedy, Eisenhower and the CIA at the Bay of Pigs*. New York: Norton, 1987.

Roger Hilsman. *The Cuban Missile Crisis: The Struggle over Policy*. Westport, Conn.: Praeger, 1996.

Roger Hilsman. *To Move a Nation: The Politics of Foreign Policy in the Administration of John F. Kennedy*. New York: Doubleday, 1967.

James W. Hilty. *Robert Kennedy, Brother, Protector*. Philadelphia: Temple University Press, 1997.

Charles Hitch and Roland N. McKean. *The Economics of Defense in the Nuclear Age*. Cambridge, Mass.: Harvard University Press, 1960.

Arnold Horelick and Myron Rush. *Strategic Power and Soviet Foreign Policy*. Chicago: University of Chicago Press, 1965.

Lisa Howard. "Castro's Question." *War/Peace Report* (September 1963): 3–5.

Tom Hughes. "Experiencing McNamara." *Foreign Policy* 100 (fall 1995): 155–71.

Samuel Huntington. *The Common Defense. Strategic Programs in National Politics*. New York: Columbia University Press, 1961.

Richard Immerman. *The CIA in Guatemala: The Foreign Policy of Intervention*. Austin: University of Texas, 1982.

Walter Isaacson. *Kissinger. A Biography*. New York: Touchstone, 1992.

Walter Isaacson and Evan Thomas. *The Wise Men: Six Friends and the World They Made*. London: Faber, 1986.

Joan Iversen. *"The Ugly American*. A Bestseller Reexamined." In *John F. Kennedy: The Promise Revisited*. Eds. Paul Harper and Joan P. Krieg. New York: Greenwood Press, 1988.

David Jardini. "Out of the Blue Yonder: How RAND Diversified into Social Welfare Research." *RAND Review* 22, 1 (fall 1998).

Chalmers A. Johnson. "Civilian Loyalties and the Guerrilla Conflict." *World Politics* 14, 4 (July 1962): 646–61.

Haynes Johnson. *The Bay of Pigs*. New York: W.W. Norton, 1964.

Robert Johnson. "Escalation Then and Now." *Foreign Policy* (fall 1985).

U. Alexis Johnson. "Internal Defense and the Foreign Service." *The Foreign Service Journal* (July 1962).

George McT Kahin. *Intervention: How America Became Involved in Vietnam*. Garden City, N.Y.: Anchor Doubleday, 1987.

Herman Kahn. *On Escalation: Metaphors and Scenarios*. London: Pall Mall, 1965.

Herman Kahn. *On Thermonuclear War*. Princeton, N.J.: Princeton University Press, 1960.

David Kaiser. *American Tragedy: Kennedy, Johnson, and the Origins of the Vietnam War*. Cambridge, Mass.: Harvard University Press, 2000.

Fred Kaplan. *The Wizards of Armageddon*. New York: Simon and Schuster, 1983.

Paul Kattenburg. *The Vietnam Trauma in American Foreign Policy, 1945–75*. New Brunswick: Transaction Books, 1980.

William Kaufmann. *The McNamara Strategy*. New York: Harper and Row, 1964.

William Kaufmann, ed. *Military Policy and National Security*. Princeton, N.J.: Princeton University Press, 1956.

Catherine McArdle Kelleher. *Germany and the Politics of Nuclear Weapons*. New York: Columbia University Press, 1975.

George Kennan. *Russia, the Atom and the West*. New York: Harper and Brothers, 1958.

John F. Kennedy. "A Democrat Looks at Foreign Policy." *Foreign Affairs* 36, 1 (1957).

John F. Kennedy. *Profiles in Courage*. New York: Harper, 1956.

John F. Kennedy. *Why England Slept*. London: Hutchinson, 1940.

Robert Kennedy. *Robert Kennedy in His Own Words: The Unpublished Recollections of the Kennedy Years*. New York: Bantam Books, 1988.

Robert Kennedy. *Thirteen Days: A Memoir of the Cuban Missile Crisis*. New York: Norton, 1969.

Sherman Kent. "A Crucial Estimate Relived." *Studies in Intelligence* 8, 2 (spring 1964): 111–19 [declassified 1992].

Montague Kern, Patricia W. Levering, and Ralph B. Levering. *The Kennedy Crises: The Press, the Presidency, and Foreign Policy*. Chapel Hill: University of North Carolina Press, 1983.

Nikita S. Khrushchev. *Khruschev Remembers: The Glasnost Tapes*. Trans. Jerrold Schechter and Vyacheslav Luchkov. Boston: Little, Brown, 1990.

Nikita S. Khrushchev. *Khrushchev Remembers: The Last Testament*. Trans. Strobe Talbott. Boston: Little, Brown, 1974.

Henry A. Kissinger. *The Necessity for Choice*. New York: Harper and Row, 1961.

Henry A. Kissinger. *Nuclear Weapons and Foreign Policy*. New York: Harper and Row, 1957.

Henry A. Kissinger. "Reflections on Cuba." *The Reporter*, 22 Nov. 1962.

Klaus Knorr and Thornton Read, eds. *Limited Strategic War*. New York: Frederick Praeger, 1962.

Peter Kornbluh, ed. *Bay of Pigs Declassified: The Secret CIA Report on the Invasion of Cuba*. New York: The New Press, 1998.

Peter Kornbluh. "JFK and Castro: The Secret Quest for Accommodation." *Cigar Afficianado* (October 1999).

Mark Kramer. " 'Lessons' of the Cuban Missile Crisis for Warsaw Pact Nuclear Operations." *Cold War International History Bulletin* 8–9 (1996): 348–54.

Andrew Krepinevich. *The Army and Vietnam*. Baltimore, Md.: Johns Hopkins University Press, 1986.

Arthur Krock. *Memoirs: Sixty Years on the Firing Line*. New York: Funk and Wagnalls, 1968.

Edward G. Landsdale. "Do We Understand Revolution." *Foreign Affairs* (October 1964).

David L. Larson, ed. *The "Cuban Crisis" of 1962: Selected Documents, Chronology and Bibliography*. Lanham, Md.: University Press of America, 1986.

William J. Lederer and Eugene Burdick. *The Ugly American*. New York: Fawcett House, 1958.

Fredrerik Logevall. "Vietnam and the Question of What Might Have Been." In *Kennedy: The New Frontier Revisited*. Ed. Mark White. London: Macmillan, 1998.

Frederik Logevall. *Choosing War: The Lost Chance for Peace and the Escalation of War in Vietnam*. Berkeley: University of California Press, 1999.

Charles Maechling. "Insurgency and Counter-Insurgency: The Role of Strategic Theory." *Parameters* 14, 3 (autumn 1984).

Edwin McCammon Martin. *Kennedy and Latin America*. Lanham, Md.: University Press of America, 1994.

Ernest R. May and Philip D. Zelikow. *The Kennedy Tapes: Inside the White House During the Cuban Missile Crisis*. Cambridge, Mass.: Harvard University Press, 1997.

Frank A Mayer. *Adenauer and Kennedy: A Study in German-American Relations, 1961–1963*. London: Macmillan, 1996.

Mary S. McAuliffe, ed. *CIA Documents on the Cuban Missile Crisis, 1962*. Washington, D.C.: CIA, 1962.

Robert S. McNamara. "The Military Role of Nuclear Weapons." *Foreign Affairs* 62, 1 (October 1983): 59–80.

Robert S. McNamara and Brian VanDeMark. *In Retrospect: The Tragedy and Lessons of Vietnam*. New York: Random House, 1995.

Robert S. McNamara, James Blight, Robert Brigham, with Thomas Biersteker and Col. Herbert Schandler, *Argument without End: In Search of Answers to the Vietnam Tragedy*. New York: Public Affairs, 1999.

John Mecklin. *Mission in Torment*. Garden City, N.Y.: Doubleday, 1965.

Robert W. Merry. *Taking on the World: Joseph and Stewart Alsop, Guardians of the American Century*. New York. Penguin Books, 1996.

Edwin Moise. *Tonkin Gulf and the Escalation of the Vietnam War*. Chapel Hill: University of North Carolina Press, 1996.

Hans J. Morgenthau. "Atomic Force and Foreign Policy." *Commentary*, June 1957.

Hans J. Morgenthau. *Politics Among Nations: The Struggle for Power and Peace*. New York, 1948.

Hans J. Morgenthau. *Truth and Power: Essays of a Decade, 1960–70.* New York: Praeger, 1970.

Hans J. Morgenthau. "Vietnam—Another Korea." *Commentary,* May 1962.

Norman Moss. *Men Who Play God: The Story of the Hydrogen Bomb.* London: Penguin, 1970.

Charles Murphy. "Cuba: The Record Set Straight." *Fortune,* September 1961.

Donette Murray. *Kennedy, Macmillan and Nuclear Weapons.* London: Macmillan, 1999.

Philip Nash. "Bear *Any* Burden? John F. Kennedy and Nuclear Weapons." In *Cold War Statesmen Confront the Bomb: Nuclear Diplomacy Since 1945.* Eds. John Lewis Gaddis et al. Oxford: Oxford University Press, 1999.

Philip Nash. *The Other Missiles of October: Eisenhower, Kennedy and the Jupiters, 1957–1963.* Chapel Hill: University of North Carolina Press, 1997.

John von Neumann and Oskar Morgenstern. *Theory of Games and Economic Behavior.* Princeton, N.J.: Princeton University Press, 1944.

Richard Neustadt. *Alliance Politics.* New York: Columbia University Press, 1970.

Richard Neustadt. *Presidential Power.* New York: Wiley, 1960.

Allan Nevis, ed. *John F. Kennedy: The Strategy of Peace.* 2nd ed. New York: Harper and Row, 1960.

John Newhouse. *War and Peace in the Nuclear Age.* New York: Alfred A. Knopf, 1989.

John M. Newman. *JFK and Vietnam: Deception, Intrigue and the Struggle for Power.* New York: Warner Books, 1992.

Reinhold Niebuhr. "The Illusion of World Government." *Foreign Affairs* 28, 2 (April 1949).

Reinhold Niebuhr. *Moral Man and Immoral Society: A Study in Ethics and Politics.* New York: Scribner, 1932.

Paul Nitze. "Atoms, Strategy and Policy." *Foreign Affairs,* 34, 2 (1956).

Paul Nitze. *From Hiroshima to Glasnost. At the Centre of Decision.* London: Weidenfeld and Nicholson, 1989.

Paul Nitze. "Limited Wars or Massive Retaliation." *The Reporter,* 5 September 1957.

Richard Nixon. *The Memoirs of Richard Nixon.* New York: Grosset and Dunlap, 1978.

Kenneth P. O'Donnell and David F. Powers. *"Johnny, We Hardly Knew Ye": Memories of John Fitzgerald Kennedy.* Boston: Little, Brown, 1972.

Kendrick Oliver. *Kennedy, Macmillan and the Nuclear Test-Ban Debate, 1961–1963.* London: Macmillan, 1998.

Franklin Mark Osanka, ed. *Modern Guerrilla Warfare. Fighting Communist Guerrilla Movements, 1941–1961.* New York: Free Press, 1961.

Robert Endicott Osgood. *Limited War. The Challenge to American Strategy.* Chicago: University of Chicago Press, 1957.

Peter Paret and John Shy. *Guerrillas in the 1960s.* New York: Praeger, 1962.

Herbert S. Parmet. *JFK: The Presidency of John F. Kennedy.* New York: Dial Press, 1983.

Thomas G. Paterson. "Introduction." In *Kennedy's Quest for Victory: American Foreign Policy, 1961–1963*. Ed. Thomas G. Paterson. New York: Oxford University Press, 1989.

Thomas G. Paterson. *Meeting the Communist Threat: Truman to Reagan*. New York: Oxford University Press, 1988.

Gregory W. Pedlow. "Flexible Response before MC 14/3: General Lauris Norstad and the Second Berlin Crisis 1958–1962." *Storia Delle Relazione Internazionali* 13, 1 (1998).

Gregory W. Pedlow and Donald F. Welzenbach. *The CIA and the U-2 Program, 1954–1974*. Langley, Va.: Central Intelligence Agency, 1998.

Richard Pells. *The Liberal Mind in a Conservative Age*. Middletown, Conn.: Wesleyan University Press, 1989.

Stephen Pelz. " 'When Do I Have Time to Think?' John F. Kennedy, Roger Hilsman, and the Laotian Crisis of 1962." *Diplomatic History* 3, 3 (summer 1979).

Thomas Powers. *The Man Who Kept Secrets: Richard Helms and the CIA*. New York: Knopf, 1979.

William Prochnau. *Once Upon a Distant War: Young War Correspondents and the Early Vietnam Battles*. New York: Time Books, 1995.

M. Y. Prozumenshikov. "The Sino-Indian Conflict, the Cuban Missile Crisis, and the Sino-Soviet Split, October 1962. New Evidence from the Russian Archives." *Cold War International History Project Bulletin* 8–9 (winter 1996–97).

Lucien Pye. *Guerrilla Communism in Malaya: Its Social and Political Meaning*. Princeton, N.J.: Princeton University Press, 1956.

Lucien Pye. *Politics, Personality and Nation-Building*. New Haven, Conn.: Yale University Press, 1962.

E. S. Quade, ed. *Analysis for Military Decisions*. Chicago: Rand McNally, 1964.

Stephen Rabe. "John F. Kennedy and Latin America: The 'Thorough, Accurate, and Reliable Record' (Almost)." *Diplomatic History* 23, 3 (summer 1999): 539–52.

Stephen Rabe. *The Most Dangerous Area in the World: John F. Kennedy Confronts Communist Revolution in Latin America*. Chapel Hill: University of North Carolina Press, 1999.

Richard Reeves. *President Kennedy: Profile of Power*. New York: Simon and Schuster, 1993.

Thomas Reeves. *A Question of Character*. New York: Free Press, 1991.

David Riesman and Michael Macoby. "The American Crisis." In *The Liberal Papers*. Ed. James Roosevelt. New York: Doubleday, 1962.

Stephen Rosen. "Systems Analysis and the Quest for Rational Defense." *The Public Interest* 76 (summer 1984): 121–59.

Stephen Rosen. "Vietnam and the American Theory of Limited War." *International Security* (fall 1982).

Richard Rosencrance. "Albert Wohlstetter." In *Makers of Nuclear Strategy*. Eds. John Baylis and John Garnett. London: Pinter, 1991.

W. W. Rostow. *The Diffusion of Power: An Essay in Recent History*. New York: Macmillan, 1972.

W. W. Rostow. "Guerrilla Warfare in Underdeveloped Areas." In *The Vietnam Reader*. Eds. Marcus Raskin and Bernard Fall. New York: Random House, 1965.

W. W. Rostow. *The Stages of Economic Growth: A Non-Communist Manifesto*. New York: Cambridge University Press, 1960.

W. W. Rostow. *The United States in the World Arena: An Essay in Recent History*. New York: Harper and Row, 1960.

Dean Rusk. *As I Saw It*. New York: Norton, 1990.

William J. Rust. *Kennedy in Vietnam*. New York: De Capo Press, 1985.

Scott Sagan. *The Limits of Safety: Organizations, Accidents, and Nuclear Weapons*. Princeton, N.J.: Princeton University Press, 1993.

Scott Sagan. "SIOP-62: The Nuclear War Plan Briefing to President Kennedy." *International Security* 12, 1 (summer 1987): 22–51.

Pierre Salinger. *John F. Kennedy: Commander in Chief*. New York: Penguin, 1997.

Pierre Salinger. *With Kennedy*. Garden City, N.Y.: Doubleday, 1966.

Howard B. Schaffer. *Chester Bowles: New Dealer in the Cold War*. Cambridge, Mass.: Harvard University Press, 1993.

Jerrold I. Schechter and Peter S. Deriabin. *The Spy Who Saved the World: How a Soviet Colonel Changed the Course of the Cold War*. New York: Charles Scribner and Sons, 1992.

Thomas C. Schelling. *Arms and Influence*. New Haven, Conn.: Yale University Press, 1966.

Thomas C. Schelling. *The Strategy of Conflict*. New York: Oxford University Press, 1963.

Thomas C. Schelling and Morton Halperin. *Strategy and Arms Control*. New York: Twentieth Century Fund, 1961.

Georg Schild. "The Berlin Crisis." In *Kennedy: The New Frontier Revisited*. Ed. Mark White. London: Macmillan, 1998.

Arthur Schlesinger. "JFK Revisited." *Cigar Aficionado*, December 1998.

Arthur Schlesinger. *Robert Kennedy and His Times*. London: Andre Deutsch, 1978.

Arthur Schlesinger. *A Thousand Days*. New York: Fawcett, 1965.

Arthur Schlesinger. *The Vital Center: The Politics of Freedom*. 2nd ed. London: Andre Deutsch, 1970.

Thomas J. Schoenbaum. *Waging Peace and War: Dean Rusk in the Truman, Kennedy and Johnson Years*. New York: Simon and Schuster, 1988.

Len Scott. *Macmillan, Kennedy and the Cuban Missile Crisis: Political, Military and Intelligence Aspects*. London: Macmillan, 1999.

Len Scott. "Espionage and the Cold War: Oleg Penkovsky and the Cuban Missile Crisis." *Intelligence and National Security* 14:3 (autumn 1999): 24–47.

Glenn T. Seaborg. *Kennedy, Khrushchev and the Test Ban*. Berkeley: University of California Press, 1981.

Douglas Selvage. "The End of the Berlin Crisis, 1961–62: New Evidence from the Polish and East German Archives." *Cold War International History Bulletin* 11 (winter 1998): 218–29.

D. Michael Shafer. *Deadly Paradigms: The Failure of U.S. Counterinsurgency Policy.* Princeton N.J.: Princeton University Press, 1988.

Deborah Shapley. *Promise and Power: The Life and Times of Robert McNamara.* Boston: Little, Brown, 1993.

Neil Sheehan. *A Bright Shining Lie.* New York: Random House, 1986.

Franklin Sieverts. *The Cuba Crisis 1962.* Official Internal History of the Missile Crisis, Department of State, 22 August 1963 (NSA/Cuba 03154).

Robert M. Slusser. *The Berlin Crisis of 1961: Soviet-American Relations and the Struggle for Power in the Kremlin.* Baltimore: Johns Hopkins University Press, 1973.

Bruce L. R. Smith. *The RAND Corporation: Case Study of a Non-profit Advisory Corporation.* Cambridge, Mass.: Harvard University Press, 1966.

R. B. Smith. *An International History of the Vietnam War*, vol. 2: *The Struggle for South-East Asia, 1961–65.* London: Macmillan, 1985.

Thomas G. Smith, "Bay of Pigs Prisoners and a Lost Opportunity." *Diplomatic History* 19:1 (winter 1995): 59–86.

Theodore Sorensen. *Kennedy.* New York: Harper and Row, 1965.

Theodore Sorensen, ed. *"Let the Word Go Forth": The Speeches, Statements and Writings of John F. Kennedy.* New York: Dell, 1988.

Ronald Steel. *Walter Lippmann and the American Century.* New York: Vintage Books, 1980.

John Steinbruner. *The Cybernetic Theory of Decision.* Princeton, N.J.: Princeton University Press, 1974.

Barry H. Steiner. *Bernard Brodie and the Foundations of American Nuclear Strategy.* Lawrence: University Press of Kansas, 1991.

Charles Stevenson. *The End of Nowhere: American Policy Toward Laos Since 1954.* Boston: Beacon Press, 1972.

Gerald S. Strober and Deborah H. Strober. *Let Us Begin Anew: An Oral History of the Kennedy Presidency.* New York: Harper and Row, 1993.

Jane Stromseth. *The Origins of Flexible Response: NATO's Debate over Strategy in the 1960s.* London: Macmillan, 1988.

George K. Tanham. *Communist Revolutionary Warfare: The Vietminh in Indochina.* New York: Praeger, 1961.

Maxwell Taylor. *Swords and Plowshares.* New York: Norton, 1972.

Maxwell Taylor. *The Uncertain Trumpet.* New York: Harper, 1959.

Wallace J. Thies. *When Governments Collide: Coercion and Diplomacy in the Vietnam Conflict, 1964–1968.* Berkeley: University of California Press, 1980.

Ewan Thomas. *The Very Best Men: Four Who Dared: The Early Years of the CIA.* New York: Simon and Schuster, 1995.

James C. Thomson Jr. "On the Making of U.S. China Policy, 1961–69: A Study in Bureaucratic Politics." *The China Quarterly* 50 (April–June 1972).

Robert Thompson. *Defeating Communist Insurgency: Experience from Malaya and Vietnam.* London: Chatto, 1966.

Marc Trachtenberg. *A Constructed Peace: The Making of a European Settlement, 1945–1963.* Princeton, N.J.: Princeton University Press, 1999.

Marc Trachtenberg. *History and Strategy*. Princeton, N.J.: Princeton University Press, 1991.

Marc Trachetenberg. "White House Tapes and Minutes of the Cuban Missile Crisis." *International Security* 10, 1 (summer 1985): 171–94.

Ann Tusa. *The Last Division: Berlin and the Wall*. London: Hodder and Stoughton, 1996.

Stephen W. Twing. *Myths, Models, and U.S. Foreign Policy: The Cultural Shaping of Three Cold Warriors*. Boulder, Colo.: Lynne Reiner, 1998.

Peter Usowski. "Intelligence Estimates and U.S. Policy Toward Laos, 1960–63." *Intelligence and National Security* 6, 2 (April 1991): 367–94.

Brian VanDeMark. *Into the Quagmire: Lyndon Johnson and the Escalation of the Vietnam War*. Oxford: Oxford University Press, 1991.

Lucien S. Vanderbroucke. "The Confessions of Allen Dulles: New Evidence on the Bay of Pigs." *Diplomatic History* 8, 4 (fall 1984).

Lucien S. Vandenbroucke. "The Decision to Land at the Bay of Pigs." *Political Science Quarterly* 99, 3 (autumn 1984).

Lucien S. Vandenbroucke. *Perilous Options: Special Operations as an Instrument of U.S. Foreign Policy*. New York: Oxford University Press, 1993.

Michael Warner. "Lessons Unlearned: The CIA's Internal Probe of the Bay of Pigs Affair." *Studies in Intelligence* (winter 1998–99).

Arthur Waskow. "The Theory and Practice of Deterrence." In *The Liberal Papers*. Ed. James Roosevelt. New York: Doubleday, 1962.

Stephen R. Weissman. *American Foreign Policy in the Congo, 1960–1964*. Ithaca, N.Y.: Cornell University Press, 1974.

David Welch and James Bight. "An Introduction to the ExComm Transcripts." *International Security* 12, 3 (winter 1987–88).

Mark White. "Behind Closed Doors: The Private Life of a Public Man." In *Kennedy: The New Frontier Revisited*. Ed. Mark White. London: Macmillan, 1998.

Mark White. *The Cuban Missile Crisis*. London: Macmillan, 1996.

Allen Whiting. *The Chinese Columbus of Deterrence: India and Indochina*. Ann Arbor: University of Michigan Press, 1975.

Phil Williams. "Tom Schelling." In *Makers of Nuclear Strategy*. Eds. John Baylis and John Garnett. London: Pinter, 1991.

Pascaline Winand. *Eisenhower, Kennedy, and the United States of Europe*. London: Macmillan, 1993.

Francis X. Winters. *The Year of the Hare: America in Vietnam, January 25, 1963–February 15, 1964*. Athens, Georgia: The University of Georgia Press, 1997.

Lawrence S. Wittner. *Resisting the Bomb: A History of the World Nuclear Disarmament Movement, 1954–1970*. Stanford, Calif.: Stanford University Press, 1997.

Harris Wofford. *Of Kennedys and Kings*. Pittsburgh: University of Pittsburgh Press, 1980.

Albert Wohlstetter. "The Delicate Balance of Terror." *Foreign Affairs* 37, 2 (January 1959).

Albert Wohlstetter and Roberta Wohlstetter. *Controlling the Risks in Cuba—Adelphi Paper No. 17*. London: ISS, 1965.

Albert Wohlstetter et al. "Selection and Use of Strategic Air Bases." Santa Monica, Calif.: RAND Corporation, 1954.

Randall Bennett Woods. *J. William Fulbright, Vietnam, and the Search for a Cold War Foreign Policy*. Cambridge: Cambridge University Press, 1998.

Peter Wyden. *Bay of Pigs*. New York: Simon and Schuster, 1979.

Peter Wyden. *Wall: The Inside Story of Divided Berlin*. New York: Simon and Schuster, 1989.

Adam Yarmolinsky. "Report by Special Assistant to the Secretary of Defense, 13 February 1963." *Naval War College Review* 32, 4 (June–July 1979).

Edwin M. Yoder. *Joe Alsop's Cold War*. Chapel Hill: University of North Carolina Press, 1995.

Donald Zagoria. *The Sino-Soviet Conflict, 1956–1961*. Princeton, N.J.: Princeton University Press, 1962.

Thomas W. Zeiler. *Dean Rusk: Defending the American Mission Abroad*. Wilmington, Delaware: Scholarly Resources Books, 2000.

Vladislav M. Zubok. "Deng-Xiaoping and the Sino-Soviet Split 1956–1963." *Cold War International History Project Bulletin* 10 (1998).

Vladislav M. Zubok. "Khrushchev and the Berlin Crisis (1958–62)." Washington, D.C.: Cold War International History Project, 1993.

Vladislav M. Zubok and Hope M. Harrison. "The Nuclear Education of Nikita Khruschchev." In *Cold War Statesmen Confront the Bomb: Nuclear Diplomacy Since 1945*. Eds. John Lewis Gaddis et al. Oxford: Oxford University Press, 1999.

Vladislav M. Zubok and Constantine Pleshakov. *Inside the Kremin's Cold War: From Stalin to Khrushchev*. Cambridge, Mass.: Harvard University Press, 1996.

UNPUBLISHED PAPERS

Sharon Ghamari. *The Intuitive Science of the Unthinkable: Herman Kahn, RAND, and Thermonuclear War*. (forthcoming)

Jill Kastner. "Kennedy, Adenauer and the Berlin Crisis: An Assessment of American Diplomacy." 1998.

Index